Lecture Notes in Computer Science 3485

Ralf Steinmetz   Klaus Wehrle (Eds.)

Peer-to-Peer Systems and Applications

Volume Editors

Ralf Steinmetz
TU Darmstadt
KOM - Multimedia Communications Lab
Merckstr. 25, 64283 Darmstadt, Germany
E-mail: Ralf.Steinmetz@kom.tu-darmstadt.de

Klaus Wehrle
Universität Tübingen
Protocol-Engineering and Distributed Systems Group
Morgenstelle 10 c, 72076 Tübingen, Germany
E-mail: Klaus.Wehrle@uni-tuebingen.de

Library of Congress Control Number: 2005932758

CR Subject Classification (1998): C.2, H.3, H.4, C.2.4, D.4, F.2.2, E.1, D.2

ISSN 0302-9743
ISBN-10 3-540-29192-X Springer Berlin Heidelberg New York
ISBN-13 978-3-540-29192-3 Springer Berlin Heidelberg New York

Springer is a part of Springer Science+Business Media

springeronline.com

Printed in Germany

Typesetting: Camera-ready by author, data conversion by Boller Mediendesign
Printed on acid-free paper SPIN: 11530657 06/3142 5 4 3 2 1 0

This book is dedicated to our children:

Jan, Alexander,
Felix, Lena, Samuel & Julius

Foreword

Ion Stoica (University of California at Berkeley)

Starting with Napster and Gnutella, Peer-to-Peer systems became an integrated part of the Internet fabric attracting millions of users. According to recent measurements of several large ISPs, Peer-to-Peer traffic exceeds Web traffic, once the dominant traffic on the Internet. While the most popular Peer-to-Peer applications continue to remain file sharing and content distribution, new applications such as Internet telephony are starting to emerge.

Not surprisingly, the popularity of Peer-to-Peer systems has fueled academic research. In a very short time, Peer-to-Peer has evolved into an exciting research field which brings together researchers from systems, networking, and theory. During the past five years, Peer-to-Peer work has appeared in the proceedings of virtually all top system and networking conferences.

However, while the huge popularity of the Peer-to-Peer systems and the explosion of Peer-to-Peer research have created a large body of knowledge, there is little structure to this body. Surveys on Peer-to-Peer systems and books providing comprehensive coverage on the Peer-to-Peer technologies are few and far apart. The fact that Peer-to-Peer is still a rapidly evolving field makes the relative lack of such materials even more critical.

This book fills this void by including a collection of representative articles, which gives an up-to-date and comprehensive snapshot of the Peer-to-Peer field. One of the main challenges that faces any book covering such a vast and relatively new territory is how to structure the material. This book resolves this conundrum by dividing the material into roughly three parts.

The first part of the book covers the basics of Peer-to-Peer designs, unstructured and structured systems, and presents a variety of applications including e-mail, multicast, Grid computing, and Web services. The book then goes beyond describing traditional systems, by discussing general aspects of the Peer-to-Peer systems, namely the self-organization nature of the Peer-to-Peer systems, and the all-important topic of evaluating these systems. In addition, the book illustrates the broad applicability of Peer-to-Peer by discussing the impact of the Peer-to-Peer technologies in two computer-science areas, namely searching and information retrieval, and mobile computing. No Peer-to-Peer book would be complete without discussing the business model, accounting, and security. This book touches on these topics in the last part.

With this book, Steinmetz and Wehrle have made a successful attempt to present the vast amount of knowledge in the Peer-to-Peer field, which was accumulated over the last few years, in a coherent and structured fashion. The book includes articles on most recent developments in the field. This makes the book equally useful for readers who want to get an up-to-date perspective on the field, as well as for researchers who want to enter the field. The combination of the traditional Peer-to-Peer designs and applications and the discussion of their self-organizing properties and their impact on other areas of computer science make this book a worthy addition to the Peer-to-Peer field.

Berkeley, July 20th, 2005 Ion Stoica

Table of Contents

Part II. Unstructured Peer-to-Peer Systems

Part III. Structured Peer-to-Peer Systems

Part V. Self-Organization

Part VI. Search and Retrieval

Part VII. Peer-to-Peer Traffic and Performance Evaluation

Part VIII. Peer-to-Peer in Mobile and Ubiquitous Environments

Part IX. Business Applications and Markets

Part X. Advanced Issues

List of Authors

List of authors in order of appearance:

Ion Stoica
645 Soda Hall
Computer Science Division
University of California, Berkeley
Berkeley, CA 94720-1776
USA

Ralf Steinmetz
TU Darmstadt
KOM – Multimedia Communications
Merckstraße 25
64283 Darmstadt
Germany

Rüdiger Schollmeier
TU München
Institute of Communication Networks
Arcisstraße 21
80290 München
Germany

Kai Fischbach
Universität zu Köln
Seminar für Wirtschaftsinformatik,
insb. Informationsmanagement
Pohligstr. 1
50969 Köln
Germany

Vasilios Darlagiannis
TU Darmstadt
KOM – Multimedia Communications
Merckstraße 25
64283 Darmstadt
Germany

Klaus Wehrle
Universität Tübingen
Protocol-Engineering &
Distributed Systems Group
Morgenstelle 10c
72076 Tübingen
Germany

Jörg Eberspächer
TU München
Institute of Communication Networks
Arcisstraße 21
80290 München
Germany

Detlef Schoder
Universität zu Köln
Seminar für Wirtschaftsinformatik,
insb. Informationsmanagement
Pohligstr. 1
50969 Köln
Germany

Christian Schmitt
Universität zu Köln
Seminar für Wirtschaftsinformatik,
insb. Informationsmanagement
Pohligstr. 1
50969 Köln
Germany

Katharina Anna Lehmann
Universität Tübingen
Arbeitsbereich für Paralleles Rechnen
WSI – Am Sand 13
72076 Tübingen
Germany

Michael Kaufmann
Universität Tübingen
Arbeitsbereich für Paralleles Rechnen
WSI – Am Sand 13
72076 Tübingen
Germany

Stefan Götz
Universität Tübingen
Protocol-Engineering &
Distributed Systems Group
Morgenstelle 10c
72076 Tübingen
Germany

Karl Aberer
School of Computer and
Communication Sciences
Ecole Polytechnique Fédérale
de Lausanne (EPFL)
1015 Lausanne
Switzerland

Manfred Hauswirth
School of Computer and
Communication Sciences
Ecole Polytechnique Fédérale
de Lausanne (EPFL)
1015 Lausanne
Switzerland

Kostas Katrinis
ETH Zürich, TIK
Gloriastrasse 35
8092 Zürich
Switzerland

Andreas Haeberlen
Rice University & MPI-SWS
Distributed Systems Group
3007 Duncan Hall, 6100 Main St.
Houston TX 77005
USA

Peter Druschel
Rice University & MPI-SWS
Distributed Systems Group
3007 Duncan Hall, 6100 Main St.
Houston TX 77005
USA

Simon Rieche
Universität Tübingen
Protocol-Engineering &
Distributed Systems Group
Morgenstelle 10c
72076 Tübingen
Germany

Heiko Niedermayer
Universität Tübingen
Computer Networks & Internet
Morgenstelle 10c
72076 Tübingen
Germany

Anwitaman Datta
School of Computer and
Communication Sciences
Ecole Polytechnique Fédérale
de Lausanne (EPFL)
1015 Lausanne
Switzerland

Martin May
ETH Zürich, TIK
Gloriastrasse 35
8092 Zürich
Switzerland

Alan Mislove
Rice University & MPI-SWS
Distributed Systems Group
3007 Duncan Hall, 6100 Main St.
Houston TX 77005
USA

Ansley Post
Rice University & MPI-SWS
Distributed Systems Group
3007 Duncan Hall, 6100 Main St.
Houston TX 77005
USA

Andreas Mauthe
Lancaster University
Computing Department
Lancaster, LA1 4YR
UK

Oliver Heckmann
TU Darmstadt
KOM – Multimedia Communications
Merckstraße 25
64283 Darmstadt
Germany

Paul Müller
TU Kaiserslautern
AG ICSY
Gottlieb-Daimler-Straße
67663 Kaiserslautern
Germany

Christian Koppen
Universität Passau
Computer Networks & Computer
Communications Group
Innstraße 33
94032 Passau
Germany

Jan Mischke
McKinsey Company & Inc.
Switzerland

Wolfgang Nejdl
Universität Hannover, KBS
Appelstraße 4
30167 Hannover
Germany

Wolf-Tilo Balke
L3S Research Center
Expo Plaza 1
30539 Hannover
Germany

Kurt Tutschku
Universität Würzburg
Institut für Informatik, Lehrstuhl III
Am Hubland
97074 Würzburg
Germany

Wolfgang Kellerer
DoCoMo Communications
Laboratories Europe GmbH
Landsberger Straße 312
80687 München
Germany

Markus Hillenbrand
TU Kaiserslautern
AG ICSY
Gottlieb-Daimler-Straße
67663 Kaiserslautern
Germany

Hermann de Meer
Universität Passau
Computer Networks & Computer
Communications Group
Innstraße 33
94032 Passau
Germany

Burkhard Stiller
Universität Zürich, IFI
Communication Systems Group
Winterthurerstraße 190
8057 Zürich
Switzerland

Danny Raz
Technion IIT
Department of Computer Science
Haifa 32000
Israel

Wolf Siberski
Universität Hannover, KBS
Appelstraße 4
30167 Hannover
Germany

Gerhard Hasslinger
T-Systems Technologiezentrum
Deutsche-Telekom-Allee 7
64307 Darmstadt
Germany

Phuoc Tran-Gia
Universität Würzburg
Institut für Informatik, Lehrstuhl III
Am Hubland
97074 Würzburg
Germany

Andreas Heinemann
TU Darmstadt
FG Telekooperation
Hochschulstraße 10
64289 Darmstadt
Germany

Max Mühlhäuser
TU Darmstadt
FG Telekooperation
Hochschulstraße 10
64289 Darmstadt
Germany

Christoph Lindemann
Universität Dortmund
Rechnersysteme und
Leistungsbewertung
August-Schmidt-Straße 12
44227 Dortmund
Germany

Thomas Hummel
Accenture European
Technology Park
449, Route des Crêtes
06902 Sophia Antipolis
France

Jan Gerke
ETH Zürich, TIK
Gloriastrasse 35
8092 Zürich
Switzerland

Michael Conrad
Universität Karlsruhe
Institute of Telematics
Zirkel 2
76128 Karlsruhe
Germany

Hannes Hartenstein
Universität Karlsruhe
Institute of Telematics
Zirkel 2
76128 Karlsruhe
Germany

Martina Zitterbart
Universität Karlsruhe
Institute of Telematics
Zirkel 2
76128 Karlsruhe
Germany

Oliver P. Waldhorst
Universität Dortmund
Rechnersysteme und
Leistungsbewertung
August-Schmidt-Straße 12
44227 Dortmund
Germany

Jussi Kangasharju
TU Darmstadt
FG Telekooperation
Hochschulstraße 10
64289 Darmstadt
Germany

Steffen Muhle
Universität zu Köln
Seminar für Wirtschaftsinformatik,
insb. Informationsmanagement
Pohligstr. 1
50969 Köln
Germany

David Hausheer
ETH Zürich, TIK
Gloriastrasse 35
8092 Zürich
Switzerland

Jochen Dinger
Universität Karlsruhe
Institute of Telematics
Zirkel 2
76128 Karlsruhe
Germany

Marcus Schöller
Universität Karlsruhe
Institute of Telematics
Zirkel 2
76128 Karlsruhe
Germany

Daniel Rolli
Universität Karlsruhe
Lehrstuhl für
Informationsbetriebswirtschaftslehre
Englerstr. 14
76128 Karlsruhe
Germany

Ralf Ackermann
TU Darmstadt
KOM – Multimedia Communications
Merckstraße 25
64283 Darmstadt
Germany

Nicolas C. Liebau
TU Darmstadt
KOM – Multimedia Communications
Merckstraße 25
64283 Darmstadt
Germany

Luka Divic-Krnic
TU Darmstadt
KOM – Multimedia Communications
Merckstraße 25
64283 Darmstadt
Germany

Timothy Roscoe
Intel Research Berkeley
2150 Shattuck Avenue
Berkeley, CA 94704
USA

1. Introduction

Klaus Wehrle (Universität Tübingen)
Ralf Steinmetz (Technische Universität Darmstadt)

The term "Peer-to-Peer" has drawn much attention in the last few years; particularly for applications providing file-sharing, but distributed computing and Internet-based telephony have also been successfully implemented. Within these applications the Peer-to-Peer concept is mainly used to share files, i.e., the exchange of diverse media data, like music, films, and programs. The growth in the usage of these applications is enormous and even more rapid than that of the World Wide Web. Also, much of the attention focused on early Peer-to-Peer systems concerned copyright issues of shared content.

But, the concept of Peer-to-Peer architectures offers many other interesting and significant research avenues as the research community has repeatedly pointed out. Due to its main design principle of being completely decentralized and self-organizing - as opposed to the Internet's traditional Client-Server paradigm - the Peer-to-Peer concept emerges as a major design pattern for future applications, system components, and infrastructural services, particularly with regard to scalability and resilience.

The perspective of the Peer-to-Peer concept offers new challenges, e.g., building scalable and resilient distributed systems and a fast deployment of new services. Based on the decentralized Peer-to-Peer approach, new Internet services can be deployed on demand and without spending time-consuming efforts in the process of product placement for the appropriate market, community, or company.

1.1 Why We Wrote This Book

In recent years, the scientific community developed different approaches for Peer-to-Peer-based applications, identified new application scenarios, and improved the scientific advancements of the Peer-to-Peer paradigm. Many researchers have already revealed interesting possibilities and opportunities for the Peer-to-Peer idea.

But, from our point of view, something important is missing: *A fundamental overview of all facets of research in the area of Peer-to-Peer systems and applications.* Also, adequate teaching material for classes and lectures on Peer-to-Peer systems and applications, covering the whole field, is not currently available.

R. Steinmetz and K. Wehrle (Eds.): P2P Systems and Applications, LNCS 3485, pp. 1-5, 2005.

Thus, the editors of this book have followed certain objectives with the writing and editing of this book:

- *Overview of the Peer-to-Peer Research Area:*
  Although research on Peer-to-Peer systems and applications is very young, the Peer-to-Peer concept has already proven to be applicable and useful in many cases. With this book, we want to give a broad overview of the broad range of applications of the Peer-to-Peer paradigm. In addition to a definition of the term "Peer-to-Peer" and a discussion of fundamental mechanisms we want to show all the different facets of Peer-to-Peer research and its applications. These manifold facets are also nicely reflected by the structure of the book and its ten parts.
- *Common Understanding of the Peer-to-Peer Paradigm:*
  After providing a good overview of the research field, our second objective is to define our notion of the "Peer-to-Peer paradigm". In the past, many things were called "Peer-to-Peer" – yet were often not even slightly related to it – and most people only associated "Peer-to-Peer" with popular file-sharing applications and not with the promising advantages and possibilities the paradigm can offer in a variety of other scenarios.
- *Compendium and Continuing Knowledge Base for Teaching:*
  There does not yet exist in the literature a good overview of Peer-to-Peer systems which is also useful for teaching purposes. Thus, the third intention of this book is to provide a common basis for teaching, with material for lectures, seminars, and labs. The knowledge of many experts has been assembled for this book, each in their own specific research area. Thus, teachers can choose from a wide range of chapters on all aspects of Peer-to-Peer systems and applications, and therefore, can design the syllabus for their classes with individual accents. In addition to this text book, electronic slides are available on the companion website.

The idea to write and edit this book arose from a sequence of international and German activities and events that fostered the idea (1) to coordinate and to support research in the area of Peer-to-Peer systems and applications and (2) to establish a highly webbed research community. Among these events have been the KuVS Hot Topics Meeting (GI/ITG KuVS Fachgespräch) "Quality in Peer-to-Peer-Systems" (TU Darmstadt, September 2003) [197], the Dagstuhl Seminar "Peer-to-Peer Systems" (March 2004) [149] and the GI/ITG Workshop "Peer-to-Peer Systems and Applications" (Kaiserslautern, March 2005) [244]. In the course of these events, a scientific community of researchers, mostly from German-speaking countries, but also from elsewhere, in particular the U.S., formed in the area of Peer-to-Peer systems and applications.

1.2 Structure and Contents

This book consists of thirty-two chapters on aspects of Peer-to-Peer systems and applications, grouped into ten parts, each dealing with a major sub-topic. These parts will now be introduced to give a brief overview of each thematic aspect.

Part I: Peer-to-Peer: Notion, Areas, History and Future
Chapter 2 elaborates on our definition of the Peer-to-Peer paradigm and gives a brief overview of the basic Peer-to-Peer concepts. Chapter 3 follows with a journey through the evolution of early Peer-to-Peer systems and Chapter 4 concludes Part I with an overview of Peer-to-Peer application areas.

Part II: Unstructured Peer-to-Peer Systems
Part II deals with all aspects of unstructured Peer-to-Peer systems. Chapter 5 gives an overview of the first and second generations of file-sharing applications. The interesting aspects of small-worlds, random graphs and scale-free networks are addressed in Chapter 6.

Part III: Structured Peer-to-Peer Systems
Part III focuses on the realm of structured Peer-to-Peer systems. First, Chapter 7 introduces the fundamental concepts of Distributed Hash Tables (DHTs) and their potential. Chapter 8 follows with an introduction to selected approaches for DHT algorithms and a discussion of their specific details. Chapter 9 provides an overview of load-balancing and reliability in DHTs. Chapter 10 concludes Part III by looking at the dynamics of self-organizing processes in structured Peer-to-Peer systems, using the example of the P-Grid system.

Part IV: Peer-to-Peer-Based Applications
Part IV presents a selection of Peer-to-Peer-based applications. Starting with end-system-based multicast in Chapter 11, the benefits of realizing services on the application-layer are shown. Chapter 12 presents the completely decentralized e-mail system ePOST running on a structured Peer-to-Peer overlay. Then, Chapters 13 and 14 discuss Peer-to-Peer issues in Grid and Web-Services applications.

Part V: Self-Organization
Part V deals with the fascinating topic of self-organization. General aspects and a characterization of self-organization is given in Chapter 15. Chapter 16 follows with a discussion of self-organization in Peer-to-Peer-based systems.

Part VI: Search and Retrieval
Part VI discusses techniques for search and (information) retrieval in widely distributed systems and addresses scalability aspects. Chapter 17 compares different search strategies and discusses scalability issues. Chapter 18 studies

basic algorithmic tasks on overlay networks. It explores both the communication and the computation needed to perform such tasks. Chapter 19 introduces schema-based Peer-to-Peer systems and relations to Semantic Web and database research. Chapter 20 continues with an survey of information retrieval techniques in Peer-to-Peer infrastructures. Chapter 21 concludes this Part by discussing the challenges of hybrid Peer-to-Peer systems.

Part VII: Peer-to-Peer Traffic and Performance Evaluation
Part VII deals with traffic and load issues of Peer-to-Peer systems and applications. Chapter 22 presents facts about the amount and effects of Peer-to-Peer traffic measured in an ISP's backbone. Chapter 23 deals with traffic characterization and performance evaluation of unstructured systems.

Part VIII: Peer-to-Peer in Mobile and Ubiquitous Environments
Part VIII discusses the emerging topics of using Peer-to-Peer techniques in mobile and ubiquitous environments. Chapter 24 evaluates the use of unstructured and structured Peer-to-Peer techniques in mobile environments. Chapter 25 presents techniques for spontaneous collaboration in mobile ad hoc networks using the Peer-to-Peer paradigm. Chapter 26 deals with epidemic data dissemination for Peer-to-Peer-based lookup services in mobile ad hoc networks. Chapter 27 concludes Part VIII by discussing the communication needs of ubiquitous computing architectures, showing that many similarities with Peer-to-Peer based systems exist, and explaining how they may be explored.

Part IX: Business Applications and Markets
Part IX addresses distributed, self-organizing markets and business applications based on Peer-to-Peer techniques. Chapter 28 discusses revenue models for Peer-to-Peer-based business applications. Chapter 29 focuses on market-managed P2P systems and discusses their requirements. Chapter 30 addresses electronic markets and discusses their Peer-to-Peer nature.

Part X: Advanced Issues
Part X deals with advanced issues concerning Peer-to-Peer-based systems and applications. Chapter 31 addresses security aspects of decentralized self-organized systems on the network and application layers. Chapter 32 addresses accounting aspects in Peer-to-Peer systems and proposes an suitable architecture for this purpose. Chapter 33 concludes with a description of the PlanetLab testbed. PlanetLab is a widely used, global platform for researchers to develop, deploy, and evaluate widely-distributed applications such as Peer-to-Peer systems.

1.3 Teaching Materials and Book Website

The authors of each chapter were asked to supply related teaching materials, in particular slides in the current PowerPoint format. All this e-learning content can be retrieved by instructors from `www.peer-to-peer.info` – the website of this book. The slides can be used without charge and adapted individually by teachers provided that this book and the origin of the material is appropriately acknowledged.

Teachers may also want to publish their modifications at the book website so that they are accessible to a wide audience. Our hope is that contributions from the community will allow the companion website to grow into a large knowledge base.

More information on accessing and using the website can be found at `www.peer-to-peer.info`. Please provide us with your comments on improvements, errors, or any other issues to be addressed in the next edition through this website. Thank you!

1.4 Acknowledgements

The efforts of many people were indispensable in the editing, writing, and reviewing of this book. First and foremost, the editors would like to thank all the authors for their written contribution and for offering appropriate teaching materials. Without the contributions of these experts from the area of "Peer-to-Peer Systems and Applications", this compendium would not have achieved such a success. We also want to thank all reviewers for their comments and remarks on the chapters, which was an important factor in the quality of this book.

Special thanks go to all the people who helped, with great diligence, in the background, especially Stefan Götz, Jens Gogolek, Marc Bégin, and Oliver Heckmann. A special thank-you goes to Simon Rieche, who spent countless hours solving LaTeX riddles, coordinating the review process, and dealing with most of the communication between editors and authors. All of them supported this project with untiring efforts and helped to make it a reality in a smooth in a distributed fashion. We also want to thank our lector, Alfred Hofmann from Springer Publishing, for his spontaneous enthusiasm for this book project and his great support during the entire editing and production process.

Last but not least, we gratefully acknowledge the support, encouragement, and patience of our families and friends.

Tübingen, Darmstadt, August 2005 Klaus Wehrle & Ralf Steinmetz

Part I

Peer-to-Peer: Notion, Areas, History and Future

2. What Is This *"Peer-to-Peer"* About?

Ralf Steinmetz (Technische Universität Darmstadt)
Klaus Wehrle (Universität Tübingen)

Currently, a new and highly interesting paradigm for communication on the Internet, known as *Peer-to-Peer* (*P2P*), is emerging. Although originally designed exclusively for pragmatic (and legally controversial) file swapping applications, Peer-to-Peer mechanisms can be used to access any kind of distributed resources and may offer new possibilities for Internet-based applications.

According to several Internet service providers, more than 50% of Internet traffic is due to Peer-to-Peer applications, sometimes even more than 75% (see also Chapter 22). The continuous growth of the Internet in terms of users and bandwidth is accompanied by increasing requirements of a diversified wealth of applications. Today, the traditional client-server approaches require a tremendous amount of effort and resources to meet these challenges. Thus, three main requirements of future Internet-based applications can be identified:

- *Scalability* is a fundamental prerequisite necessary to satisfy the vast demand for resources such as bandwidth, storage capacity, or processing power of certain applications caused by large numbers of users. Therefore, bottlenecks must be identified and avoided at an early stage of system design so the system can be scaled by several orders of magnitude without loss of efficiency.
- *Security* and *reliability* form core criteria for the availability of strategically important and security-sensitive services in the face of distributed denial-of-service attacks on centralized systems. Furthermore, anonymity and resistance to censorship are of growing importance in today's world.
- *Flexibility* and *Quality of Service* for quickly and easily integrating new services are crucial to the success of emerging Internet technologies. For example, a lack of such features prevents the wide spread deployment of highly desirable services such as group communication and mobility.

It is becoming increasingly obvious that client-server-based applications, which have become popular since the early 1980s, can no longer fully meet the evolving requirements of the Internet. In particular, their centralized nature is prone to resource bottlenecks. Consequently, they can be easily attacked and are difficult and expensive to modify due to their strategic placement within the network infrastructure. The concepts of Peer-to-Peer networking

R. Steinmetz and K. Wehrle (Eds.): P2P Systems and Applications, LNCS 3485, pp. 9-16, 2005.

and Peer-to-Peer computing[1] promise to provide simpler solutions to the problems mentioned above through a fundamental shift of paradigms.

2.1 Definitions

Oram et al. [462] gives a basic definition of the term "Peer-to-Peer" which is further refined in [573]:

[a Peer-to-Peer system is] *a self-organizing system of equal, autonomous entities (peers)* [which] *aims for the shared usage of distributed resources in a networked environment avoiding central services.*

In short, it is *a system with completely decentralized self-organization and resource usage.* Apart from these basic principles, Peer-to-Peer systems can be characterized as follows (though a single system rarely exhibits all of these properties):

Decentralized Resource Usage:

1. Resources of interest (bandwidth, storage, processing power) are used in a manner as equally distributed as possible and are located at the *edges* of the network, close to the peers. Thus with regard to network topology, Peer-to-Peer systems follow the end-to-end argument [531] which is one of the main reasons for the success of the Internet.
2. Within a set of peers, each utilizes the resources provided by other peers. The most prominent examples for such resources are storage (e.g. for audio and video data or applications) and processing capacity. Other possible resources are connectivity, human presence, or geographic proximity (with instant messaging and group communication as application examples).
3. Peers are interconnected through a network and in most cases distributed globally.
4. A peer's Internet address typically changes so the peer is not constantly reachable at the same address (transient connectivity). Typically, peers are dynamically assigned new Internet addresses every time they connect to the network. Often, they may be disconnected or shut down over longer periods of time. Among other reasons, this encourages Peer-to-Peer systems to introduce new address and name spaces above of the traditional Internet address level. Hence, content is usually addressed through unstructured identifiers derived from the content with a hash

[1] We do not distinguish between Peer-to-Peer computing and Peer-to-Peer networking but focus on *Peer-to-Peer (P2P)* as a property, characteristic, method, or mechanism.

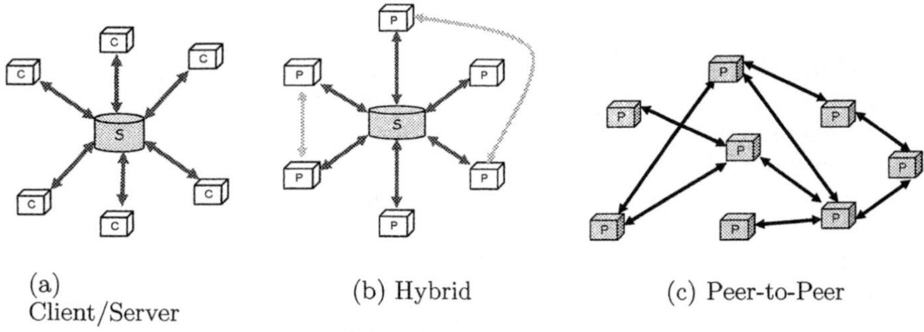

(a) Client/Server (b) Hybrid (c) Peer-to-Peer

Fig. 2.1: Classification of Peer-to-Peer Systems

function. Consequently, data is no longer addressed by location (the address of the server) but by the data itself. With multiple copies of a data item, queries may locate any one of those copies. Thus, Peer-to-Peer systems locate data based on content in contrast to location-based routing in the Internet.

Decentralized Self-Organization:

5. In order to utilize shared resources, peers interact directly with each other. In general, this interaction is achieved without any central control or coordination. This represents one of the main properties of Peer-to-Peer systems which is markedly different from client-server systems: while the the latter rely on centralized coordination through a server as a structural paradigm, Peer-to-Peer systems establish a cooperation between equal partners. This departure from a centralized infrastructure most importantly avoids bottlenecks but is concomitant with the reduced availability of end-systems compared to client-server solutions.
6. Peers directly access and exchange the shared resources they utilize without a centralized service. Thus, Peer-to-Peer systems represent a fundamental decentralization of control mechanisms. However, performance considerations may lead to centralized elements being part of a complete Peer-to-Peer system, e.g. for efficiently locating resources. Such systems are commonly called *hybrid* Peer-to-Peer systems (cf. Fig. 2.1b).
7. In a Peer-to-Peer system, peers can act both as clients and servers (cf. Fig. 2.1c). This is radically different from traditional systems with asymmetric functionality (cf. Fig. 2.1a). It leads to additional flexibility with regard to available functionality and to new requirements for the design of Peer-to-Peer systems.
8. Peers are equal partners with symmetric functionality. Each peer is fully autonomous regarding its respective resources.

9. Ideally, resources can be located without any central entity or service (in Figures 2.1a and 2.1b, centralized services are necessary in contrast to Figure 2.1c). Similarly, the system is controlled in a self-organizing or ad hoc manner. As mentioned above, this guide line may be violated for reasons of performance. However, the decentralized nature should not be violated. The result of such a mix is a Peer-to-Peer system with a hybrid structure (cf. Fig. 2.1b).

2.1.1 Shift of Paradigm in Internet Communication

The Peer-to-Peer approach is by no means just a technology for file sharing. Rather, it forms a fundamental design principle for distributed systems. It clearly reflects the paradigm shift from *coordination to cooperation*, from *centralization to decentralization*, and from *control to incentives*. Incentive-based systems raise a large number of important research issues. Finding a fair balance between give and take among peers may be crucial to the success of this technology.

2.2 Research Challenges in Peer-to-Peer Systems and Applications

One important research aspect is the detailed analysis of the suitability of the Peer-to-Peer paradigm to various types of applications, in particular those beyond the domain of file sharing. During the Workshop *,,Quality in Peer-to-Peer Networks"*[2] a number of types of Peer-to-Peer applications were identified and put on a time scale as illustrated by Figure 2.2. Figure 2.3 lists several possible obstacle to research in the Peer-to-Peer area and its day-to-day use. Figures 2.5 and 2.4 show certain future research challenges as found during the GI-Meetings. The main question was: When do these topics become important?

One of the main challenges of Peer-to-Peer systems lies in the decentralized self-organization of a distributed system and in achieving a high level of quality of service without the need for centralized services. Central to a solution to this problem is to efficiently look up and locate data items and to manage them accordingly. Many aspects of Peer-to-Peer systems base on this functionality. In contrast to centralized server applications, for which the location of data items is inherently known, decentralized systems store content in multiple, possibly distant, locations within the system. There are two main approaches which have been developed to solve this problem: *unstructured* and *structured Peer-to-Peer systems*.

[2] TU Darmstadt, Sept. 2003, http://www.kom.tu-darmstadt.de/ws-p2p/

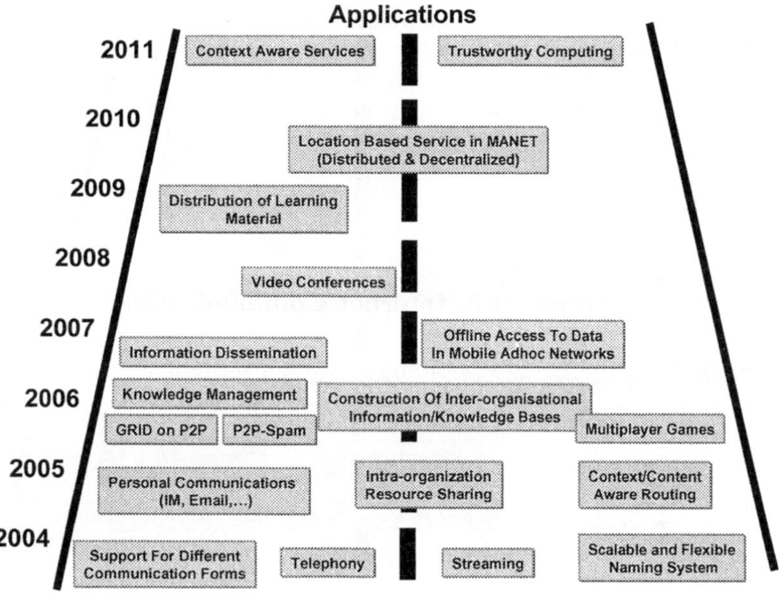

Fig. 2.2: Applications beyond File-Sharing

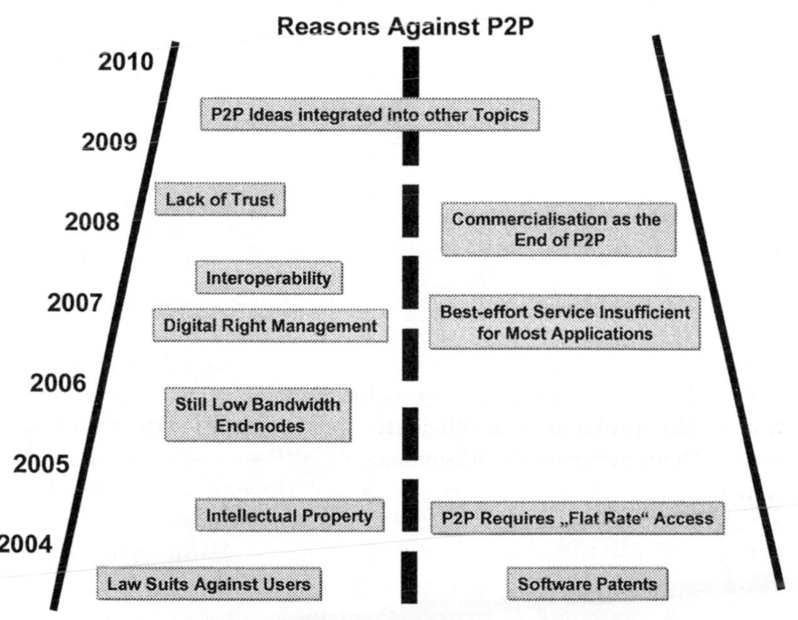

Fig. 2.3: Developments hindering the Development and Dissemination of Peer-to-Peer-Technologie.

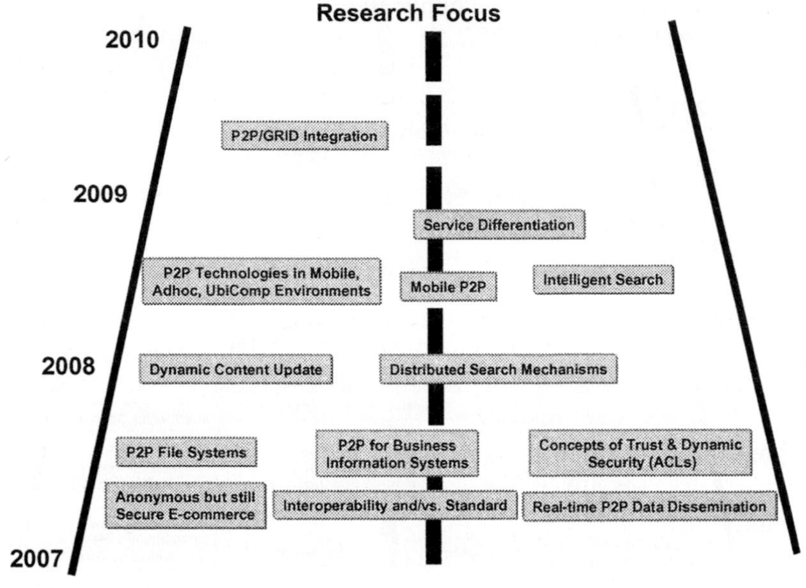

Fig. 2.4: Challenges in Peer-to-Peer Research II (2007 - 2010)

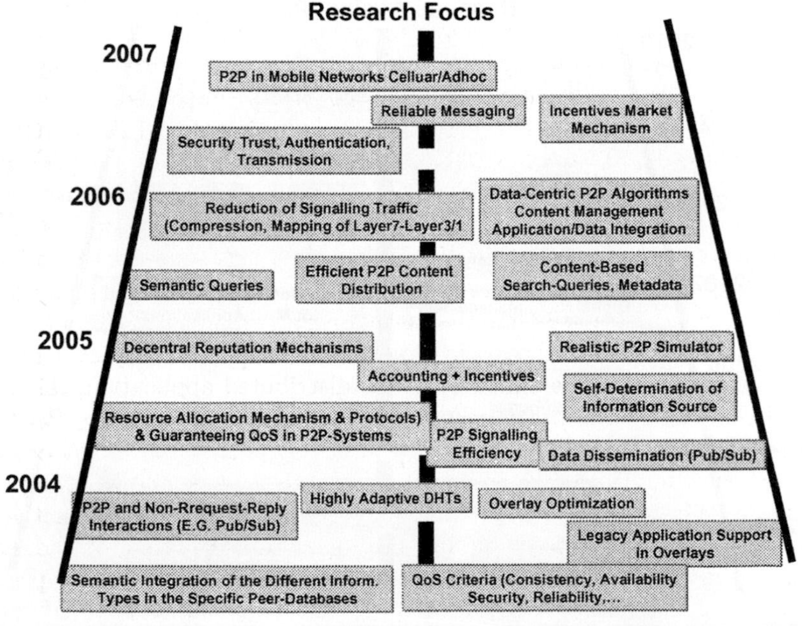

Fig. 2.5: Challenges in Peer-to-Peer Research I (2003 - 2007)

2.2.1 Unstructured Peer-to-Peer Systems

First-generation Peer-to-Peer-based file sharing applications employed so-called unstructured approaches. For example, these systems relied on lookups via a central server which stored the locations of all data items. Only after looking up the location of a data item via the server was the data transferred directly between peers (hybrid approach, cf. Fig. 2.1b). Other approaches, e.g. Gnutella, use a flooding technique, i.e. look-up queries are sent to all peers participating in the system until the corresponding data item or peer is found (cf. Chapter 5).

It is apparent that neither approach scales well. The server-based system suffers from exhibiting a single point of attack as well as being a bottleneck with regard to resources such as memory, processing power, and bandwidth while the flooding-based approaches show tremendous bandwidth consumption on the network. Generally, these unstructured systems were developed in response to user demands (mainly file sharing and instant messaging) and consequently suffer from ad hoc designs and implementations.

Part II of this book discusses unstructured Peer-to-Peer systems in more detail.

2.2.2 Structured Peer-to-Peer Systems

The challenge to develop scalable unstructured Peer-to-Peer applications has attracted the research community. Inspired by the significant advantages and possibilities of decentralized self-organizing systems, researchers focused on approaches for distributed, content-addressable data storage (distributed indexing structures). These so called Distributed Hash Tables (DHTs) were developed to provide such distributed indexing as well as scalability, reliability, and fault tolerance. DHTs outperform unstructured approaches in the above listed properties and efficiency. Commonly, a data item can be retrieved from the network with a complexity of $O(\log N)$ - equal to the complexity of well-known non-distributed search and indexing techniques. The underlying network and the number of peers in structured approaches can grow arbitrarily without impacting the efficiency of the distributed application; this is in marked contrast to the previously described unstructured Peer-to-Peer applications which usually exhibit linear search complexity at best. Necessary management operations, like adding new content or peers and handling failures, commonly have a complexity of $O(\log N)$ and $O(\log^2 N)$, respectively.

Typically, DHTs are based on similar designs, while their search and management strategies differ. Ring-based approaches such as Pastry, Tapestry, and Chord all use similar search algorithms such as binary ordered B*-trees. Geometric designs, such as *Content Addressable Networks* (CAN) or Viceroy also exist. Each peer is assigned a section of the search space $[0, 2^n - 1]$. To provide redundancy, replicas may be stored on neighboring peers. Using a routing tree, e.g. Pastry, or finger tables, e.g. Chord, a request is routed towards the desired data item. For such requests a logarithmic complexity is guaranteed. Often, the amount of routing information is in the order of $O(\log N)$ entries per peer (see also Chapter 8).

Next to the already discussed similarities to known database indexing techniques, DHTs employ additional techniques to manage data structures, to add redundancy, and to locate the nearest instances of a requested data item.

Part III in this book deals with all details on structured Peer-to-Peer systems with a special focus on Distributed Hash Tables.

2.3 Conclusion

To guarantee a wide deployment in the Internet, future distributed systems and applications must cope with several challenges. Apart from scalability, efficiency, and high flexibility, reliability and protection against attacks will form key features of future systems. Their development and successful deployment will have a strong impact on the future of Peer-to-Peer-based applications and systems.

3. Past and Future

Jörg Eberspächer, Rüdiger Schollmeier
(Munich University of Technology)

3.1 Status Quo: Networks (Over)Filled with Peer-to-Peer Traffic

Within the last few years, starting with the introduction of Napster in May 1999, the disruptive technology of Peer-to-Peer networking has encountered an enormous growth. Today the traffic caused by Peer-to-Peer networks represents a significant portion in the Internet. For example in the German Research Network (Deutsches Forschungsnetz DFN) Peer-to-Peer causes up to 60 percent of the traffic [210]. Similar trends can be observed in other networks e.g. in the Abilene backbone [42]. As we can observe in Figure 3.1, at the beginning of 2002 the traffic caused only by the signaling traffic of Peer-to-Peer applications (no user-data-transfers included) already amounts to 50 percent of the total traffic volume (see Figure 3.1).

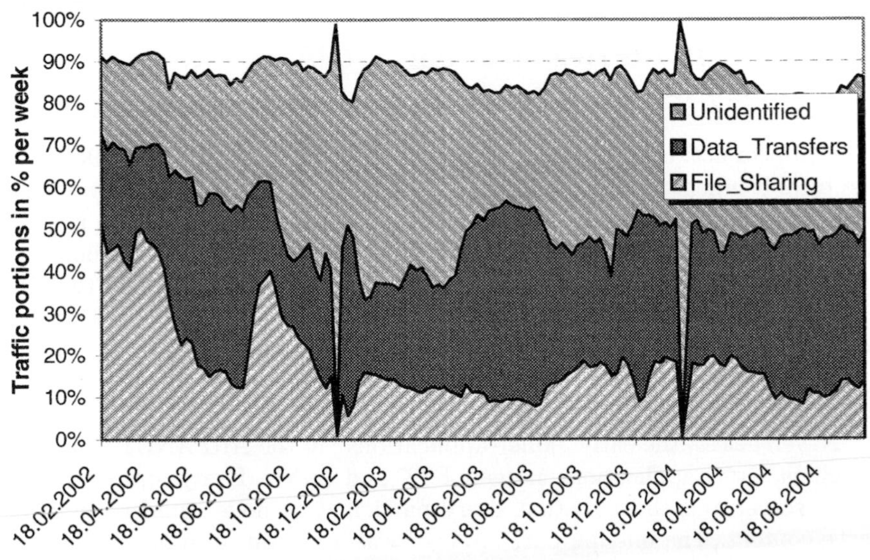

Fig. 3.1: Portions of traffic measured per week in the Abilene Backbone from 18.02.2002 until 18.07.2004 (peaks at 18.12.2002 and 18.02.2004 result from measurement errors. source:[42])

R. Steinmetz and K. Wehrle (Eds.): P2P Systems and Applications, LNCS 3485, pp. 17-23, 2005.

Until the end of 2004 the amount of Peer-to-Peer traffic decreased down to a value of approximately 15 percent. This might point to an increasing efficiency of the Peer-to-Peer protocols, since the signaling traffic is reduced or to a decreasing usage of Peer-to-Peer applications. However if we also have a look at the unidentified traffic and the traffic identified as data-transfers, we can observe that these volumes are increasing and that the total amount of traffic stemming from these three sources stays at a constant level of nearly 90 percent. Analyzing the networking techniques of different Peer-to-Peer applications in more detail this could also indicate that Peer-to-Peer applications are "going underground", i.e. they use TCP port 80, so that they can, on the port level, not be distinguished from common data transfers. Further on more and more Peer-to-Peer applications use so called port hopping, meaning that they change frequently their communication port during run time and can thus not be identified as file sharing applications on the port level. Thus the amount of unidentified traffic and data transfers increases and the amount of identified Peer-to-Peer traffic decreases, while the total amount stays at a constant level of approximately 90 percent.

Hence, Peer-to-Peer communication plays a dominant role in todays networks and is also proliferating into many new application areas. In this chapter, we will have a look at the development of Peer-to-Peer applications in the last few years, analyze the development of the capabilities of the user terminals and finally consider possible directions that development of Peer-to-Peer technology might take in the future.

3.2 How It All Began: From ARPANET to Peer-to-Peer

Peer-to-peer networking is not new. Basically, it started in the late 1960s with the establishment of the ARPANET. The goal of this physical network was to share computing resources and documents between different US research facilities. In this original system there was nothing like a typical client or a typical server. Every host was being treated equally and one could therefore call this network a first Peer-to-Peer network, although this network was not self organizing and no overlay network was established. Everything matched still to a large extent the physical connection and not virtual connections as we can observe them in today's Peer-to-Peer networks.

Nevertheless, the early "killer-applications" in the ARPANET were typical client server applications, namely FTP and TelNet. Every computer could run a server and client so that every participating node could request and serve content. The missing part however was an instance to inform the participating nodes where which content is provided.

Therefore in 1979 the UseNet protocol was developed. It is a newsgroup application, helping to organize the content and offering a self-organizing approach to add and remove newsgroup servers by the participating users via a rigorous "democratic" process. However the application itself is still a typical client server application, with "simple" requesting nodes, the clients, and more powerful content providing nodes, the servers.

Approximately 10 years later, around 1990, there was a rush of the general public to join the Internet community. A number of applications were developed, like WWW, email and streaming. Modem connections via the SLIP and the PPP protocol became increasingly popular, with the result that millions of commercial users and customers joined. The basic communication model was the client/server model, with a simple application on the user side (e.g. the Web Browser) which initiates a temporary connection to a well known server, from which the client downloads the requested content and then disconnects again. It is a simple and straightforward model, which provides also the content provider with an easy model to administrate and to control the distribution of content. Further on new security concerns in the Internet had to be taken into account resulting in an Internet partitioned by firewalls.

3.3 The NAPSTER-Story

This was about to change in May 1999. Home users started to use their connected computers for more than just temporarily requesting content from web or email servers. With the introduction of the music- and file-sharing application Napster by Shawn Fenning [437], the users opened their computers not only to consume and download content, but also to offer and provide content to other participating users over the Internet. This phenomenon is best described by the artificial term SERVENT for one node, which is a combination of the first syllable of the term SERVer and the second syllable of the term cliENT.

Comparing the Peer-to-Peer networks, which started with Napster, to the architecture established by the ARPANET we can observe that in contrast to today's Peer-to-Peer realizations, the ARPANET was not self organizing. It was administrated by a centralized steering committee, and did not provide any means for context or content based routing beyond "simple" address based routing. In current Peer-to-Peer networks, the participating users establish a virtual network, entirely independent from the physical network, without having to obey any administrative authorities or restrictions. These networks are based on UDP or TCP connections, are completely self-organizing and are frequently changing their topology, as users join and leave the network in a random fashion, nearly without any loss of network functionality.

Another decentralized and application-layer oriented communications paradigm is Grid computing which became famous with the project SETI-home [557] . It is often compared to Peer-to-Peer as being a more structured approach with the dedicated aim to especially share computing power and storage space for distributed computations and simulations [217]. Yet, the basic principles in Peer-to-Peer and Grid are similar. However concerning the number of participating users and thus also the traffic volumes Grid computing is taking currently a minor role. Nevertheless it has a high growth potential.

Because of the mostly illegal content shared in the Napster network (content was mostly copyright protected, mp3 compressed music), the Recording Industry Association of America (RIAA) filed in December 1999 a lawsuit against Napster Inc. This was possible, because the Napster network relies heavily on a centralized lookup/index server operated by Napster Inc. This server, which represents a single point of failure in the Napster network could therefore be targeted by the RIAA.

3.4 Gnutella and Its Relatives: Fully Decentralized Architectures

Under the impression of the lawsuit against Napster the company Nullsoft released in March 2000 the Gnutella application as an open source project. In Gnutella the participating peers do not only act as a servent. They additionally take over routing functionalities initially performed in Napster by the Napster server. Thus not only the file exchange and provisioning are completely distributed, but also the content lookup/routing functionality. Thus any central entity and also any single point of failure is avoided. The Gnutella application was taken over by a fast growing development and research community and shortly after its release a variety of similar Peer-to-Peer protocols followed, e.g. Audiogalaxy, FastTrack/KaZaA, iMesh and Freenet [38, 123, 232, 317, 343]. Kazaa is not an open source project and encrypts the signaling traffic between the peers and also to possible centralized elements. Thus the RIAA can not track the peer behavior and as a result can hardly prove any illegal activities on the part of the inventors and operators of the FastTrack network. Other approaches tried to decentralize the Napster server, by distributing the lookup server on several more powerful participating peers [625].

Although the legal pressure on Napster increased further, as some copyright holders, like the hard-rock band Metallica additionally sued Napster, the number of exchanged files in Napster was still growing and reached a total of 2.79 billion files exchanged only within February 2001. However in July 2001 Napster Inc. was convicted and finally had to stop the operation of the Napster server and therefore the service was no longer available.

As we can observe from Figure 3.1 and Figure 3.2, the users of Napster adapted very fast to this situation and switched to other protocols, like Gnutella or FastTrack/Kazaa. In August 2001 for example already 3.05 billion files were exchanged per month via the Gnutella network. The attractiveness of Gnutella did not only result from its distributed structure, but also from the enhanced protocol, which consists of two hierarchical routing layers [359]. The foundation for this development of Gnutella has already been laid in October 2000 by the presentation of the Reflector/SuperPeer concept. These Peer-to-Peer networks with a second dynamic routing hierarchy are called the second generation Peer-to-Peer networks. As shown by Figure 3.2, even today second generation Peer-to-Peer protocols are widely used. Edonkey2000 and FastTrack are based on such an overlay routing concept [184, 358, 410, 423].

However in May 2003 things began to change again. Applications based on the FastTrack protocol caused significantly less traffic, whereas on the other hand the traffic amounts of e.g. Gnutella or Edonkey increased. In addition, we can observe from Figure 3.2, that the traffic caused by the BitTorrent network increased significantly and caused at the end of 2004 the majority of the traffic [127, 320].

Two main reasons explain this phenomenon. First of all in KaZaA the amount of hardly identifiable corrupted content increased significantly due to the weakness of the used hashing algorithm (UUHASH). Thus users switched

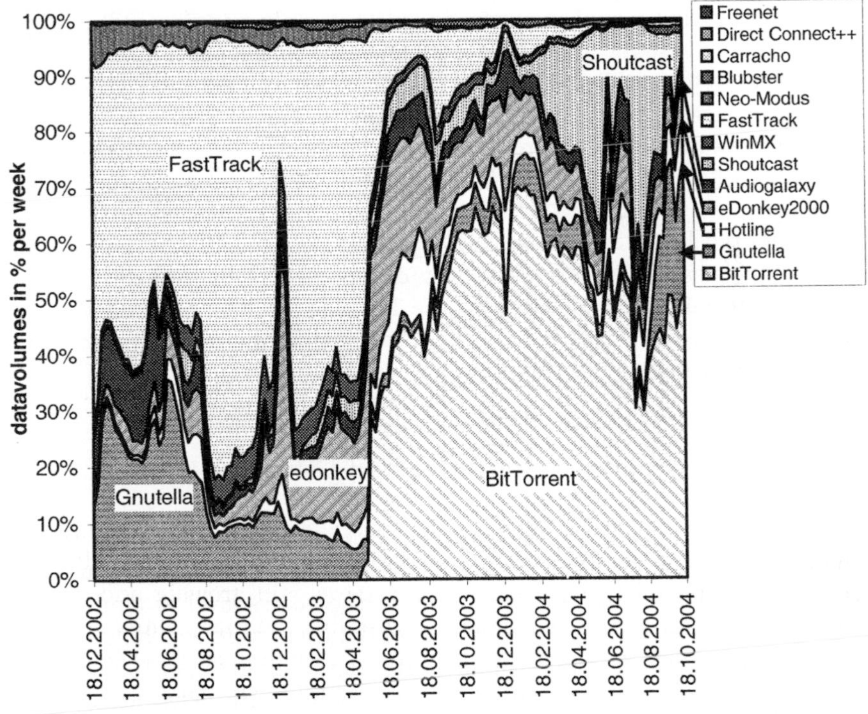

Fig. 3.2: Traffic proportions of the different Peer-to-Peer applications and protocols from the traffic measured per week in the Abilene Backbone from 18.02.2002 until 18.07.2004 (source:[42])

to applications like Gnutella or Edonkey, where the number of corrupted files was significantly smaller. Secondly, upon having a closer look at the traffic caused by the BitTorrent protocol we have to take into account that in contrast to other Peer-to-Peer protocols, in BitTorrent also the traffic caused by the file transfers is part of the measured amount of data given by Figure 3.2.

Today one of the major drivers for Peer-to-Peer is certainly the exchange of all kinds of content (mp3 encoded music, videos, DVDs, pornographic content, software, ...), free of charge and administration. However there do already exist attempts to use this new and successful networking paradigm for other applications and to develop a business case out of it. One first promising approach is to use the Peer-to-Peer overlay network as a kind of distributed phone book to provide means to establish IP based voice communication channels between participants without any centralized instances. One approach, Skype, allows calls free of charge within the Internet any and charges users only at gateways to other fixed telephony systems [567].

To increase the reliability of such a system it is necessary to adapt the overlay routing schemes to reflect the characteristics of a significantly decreased replication rate. Every user is available only once instead of several times as is the case for a common mp3 encoded music file. Further on, it is also necessary to establish a call fast and to receive a dedicated answer from the overlay network, whether a certain user is currently available or not. Therefore research on the third generation of Peer-to-Peer networks started around 2001 [526, 575]. The third generation Peer-to-Peer networks and protocols are mainly characterized by using a proactive routing algorithm based on Distributed Hash Tables (DHTs).

Yet the question why Peer-to-Peer came up in 1999 and developed so rapidly to the major application in the Internet at 2002 has still not been answered completely, though one reason is certainly the possibility to receive copyright protected content for free.

3.5 Driving Forces Behind Peer-to-Peer

In the following we want to have a look at the development of the physical and technical capabilities of the used physical networks and the participating terminals. Regarding the data rates at the access level around 1997/98 the first broadband connections for residential users were available via cable modems which allow data rates of up to 10 Mbps. Beginning in 1999 DSL and ADSL connections became available for the public with data rates of up to 8.5 Mbps. Compared to 56 kbps modem connections the available data rate for the private user was plentiful at the beginning of 2000. Further on the deregulation of the telecommunication markets showed already first effects, as the ISPs and telecommunication network providers reduced their tariffs significantly due to increased competition. Thus not only a significantly increased access data rate became available but additionally at comparably low prices, e.g. flat rates.

In a similar manner the storage space and the processing power of common end user computers evolved. In 1992 the average size of hard disks was around 0.3 Gbyte and developed within 10 years to sizes of several 100 Gbyte. Regarding the processing power personal computers in 1992 were available with clock frequencies of 100 MHz, whereas in 2004 computers with more than 3 GHz are commonly available. Thus the computers available since the beginning of 2000 have capabilities comparable to those of servers a few years earlier. Resulting the technical prerequisites to operate a personal computer as a high performance server and a client at the same time for reasonable prices were available, when the first Peer-to-Peer networks appeared. Additionally we could observe since the end of the 1990s a general trend towards self organizing networks also in the mobile area (mobile ad hoc networks, MANET) [483, 548].

This also resulted in more and more intelligence distributed over a whole network and pushed to the place where it is demanded, i.e. at the edge of the networks. Currently it appears that this trend is still unbroken, as e.g. the application of Peer-to-Peer networks to telephony application or the traffic amounts caused by Peer-to-Peer applications show. A number of other future application areas of Peer-to-Peer networking certainly also include self organizing collaborative environments, context and location based services in conjunction with mobile networks, especially MANETs, Peer-to-Peer media streaming networks or the self organization of active network environments. Therefore certainly a number of open research issues, e.g. how to provide security, trust and authentication or accounting and access control in such a distributed environment to provide the basis for business in the area of Peer-to-Peer have to be solved. Further open problems which have to be addressed also include reliability, availability, load-balancing, QoS and network organization, as well as cross layer communication especially in mobile environments.

There is no doubt about it: Peer-to-Peer technology is yet in its infancy, and will play a key role in next generation networks!

The Peer-to-Peer paradigm provides an alternative way of managing resources

formation availability (ubiquitous computing). Applications can independently recognize which peers are available to them within a computer grid

4. Application Areas

Detlef Schoder, Kai Fischbach, Christian Schmitt
(University of Cologne)

The Peer-to-Peer paradigm provides an alternative way of managing resources in various application domains. The primary emphasis of this chapter is placed on presenting an overview of possible approaches for managing the various types of resources, i.e., information, files, bandwidth, storage, and processor cycles, with Peer-to-Peer networks.

4.1 Information

The following sections explain the deployment of Peer-to-Peer networks using examples of the exchange and shared use of presence information, of document management and collaboration.

- *Presence information:* Presence information plays a very important role in respect of Peer-to-Peer applications. It is decisive in the self-organization of Peer-to-Peer networks because it provides information about which peers and which resources are available in the network. It enables peers to establish direct contact to other peers and inquire about resources. A widely distributed example of a Peer-to-Peer application which essentially uses presence information is instant messaging systems. These systems offer peers the opportunity to pass on information via the network, such as whether or not they are available for communication processes. A more detailed description of the underlying architecture of instant messaging systems can be found in [311].
  The use of presence information is interesting for the shared use of processor cycles and in scenarios related to omnipresent computers and information availability (ubiquitous computing). Applications can independently recognize which peers are available to them within a computer grid and determine how intensive computing tasks can be distributed among idle processor cycles of the respective peers. Consequently, in ubiquitous computing environments it is helpful if a mobile device can independently recognize those peers which are available in its environment, for example in order to request Web Services, information, storage or processor cycles. The technological principles of this type of communication are discussed in [627].

R. Steinmetz and K. Wehrle (Eds.): P2P Systems and Applications, LNCS 3485, pp. 25-32, 2005.

- *Document management:* Customarily Document Management Systems (DMS), which are usually centrally organized, permit shared storage, management and use of data. However, it is only possible to access data which has been placed in the central repository of the DMS. As a result, additional effort is required to create a centralized index of relevant documents. Experience shows that a large portion of the documents created in a company are distributed among desktop PCs, without a central repository having any knowledge of their existence. In this case, the use of Peer-to-Peer networks can be of assistance. For example, by using the NextPage-NXT 4 platform, it is possible to set up networks which create a connected repository from the local data on the individual peers [447]. Indexing and categorization of data is accomplished by each peer on the basis of individually selected criteria.
  In addition to linking distributed data sources, Peer-to-Peer applications can offer services for the aggregation of information and the formation of self-organized Peer-to-Peer knowledge networks. Opencola [380] was one of the first Peer-to-Peer applications to offer their users the opportunity to gather distributed information in the network from the areas of knowledge which interest them. For this purpose, users create folders on their desktop which are assigned keywords which correspond to their area of interest. Opencola then searches the knowledge network independently and continuously for available peers which have corresponding or similar areas of knowledge without being dependent on centrally administered information. Documents from relevant peers are analyzed, suggested to the user as appropriate and automatically duplicated in the user's folder. If the user rejects respective suggestions, the search criteria are corrected. The use of Opencola results in a spontaneous networking of users with similar interests without need for a central control.
- *Collaboration:* Peer-to-Peer groupware permits document management at the level of closed working groups. As a result, team members can communicate synchronously, conduct joint online meetings and edit shared documents. In client/server based groupware a corresponding working area for the management of central data has to be set up and administered on the server for each working group. To avoid this additional administrative task, Peer-to-Peer networks can be used for collaborative work. Currently, the best-known application for collaborative work based on the principles of Peer-to-Peer networks is Groove Virtual Office [261]. This system offers functions (instant messaging, file sharing, notification, co-browsing, whiteboards, voice conferences and data bases with real time synchronization) similar to those of the widely used client/server based Lotus products, Notes, Quickplace and Sametime, but does not require central data management. All of the data created is stored on each peer and is synchronized automatically. If peers cannot reach each other directly, there is the option of asynchronous synchronization via a directory and relay server. Groove

Virtual Office offers users the opportunity to set up so-called shared spaces, which provide a shared working environment for virtual teams formed on an ad-hoc basis, as well as to invite other users to work in these teams. Groove Virtual Office can be expanded by system developers. A development environment, the Groove Development Kit, is available for this purpose [187].

4.2 Files

File sharing is probably the most widespread Peer-to-Peer application. It is estimated that as much as 70% of network traffic in the Internet can be attributed to the exchange of files, in particular music files [579]. (More than one billion downloads of music files can be listed each week [457].) Characteristic of file sharing is that peers which have downloaded the files in the role of a client subsequently make them available to other peers in the role of a server. A central problem for Peer-to-Peer networks in general, and for file sharing in particular, is locating resources (lookup problem) [52]. In the context of file sharing systems, three different models have developed: the flooded request model, the centralized directory model and the document routing model [416]. These can be illustrated best by using their prominent implementations - Gnutella, Napster and Freenet.

Peer-to-Peer networks which are based on the Gnutella protocol function without a central coordination authority. All peers have equal rights within the network. Search requests are routed through the network according to the flooded request model, which means that a search request is passed on to a predetermined number of peers. If they cannot answer the request, they pass it on to various other nodes until a predetermined search depth (ttl=time-to-live) has been reached or the requested file has been located. Positive search results are sent to the requesting entity which can then download the desired file directly from the entity which is offering it. A detailed description of searches in Gnutella networks, as well as an analysis of the protocol, can be found in [517] and [515]. Because the effort for the search, measured in messages, increases exponentially with the depth of the search, the inefficiency of simple implementations of this search principle is obvious [328]. In addition, there is no guarantee that a resource will actually be located. Operating subject to certain prerequisites (such as non-randomly structured networks), numerous prototypical implementations (e.g. [146, 182, 469, 505, 138, 397, 3, 446, 642]) demonstrate how searches can be effected more 'intelligently' (see, in particular, [181], but also [8] for a brief overview). The FastTrack protocol enjoys widespread use in this respect. It optimizes search requests by means of a combination of central supernodes which form a decentralized network similar to Gnutella.

In respect of its underlying centralized directory model, the early Napster [437] can be viewed as a nearly perfect example of a hybrid Peer-to-Peer system in which a part of the infrastructure functionality, in this case the index service, is provided centrally by a coordinating entity. The moment a peer logs into the Napster network, the files which the peer has available are registered by the Napster-server. When a search request is issued, the Napster-server delivers a list of peers which have the desired files available for download. The user can obtain the respective files directly from the peer offering them.

Searching for and storing files within the Freenet network [123, 122] takes place via the so-called document routing model [416]. A significant difference to the models which have been introduced so far, is that files are not stored on the hard disk of the peers providing them, but are intentionally stored at other locations in the network. The reason behind this is that Freenet was developed with the aim of creating a network in which information can be stored and accessed anonymously. Among other things, this requires that the owner of a network node does not know what documents are stored on his local hard disk. For this reason, files and peers are allocated unique identification numbers. When a file is created, it is transmitted, via neighboring peers, to the peer with the identification number which is numerically closest to the identification number of the file and is stored there. The peers which participate in forwarding the file save the identification number of the file and also note the neighboring peer to which they have transferred it in a routing table to be used for subsequent search requests. The search for files takes place along the lines of the forwarding of search queries on the basis of the information in the routing tables of the individual peers. In contrast to searching networks which operate according to the flooded request model, when a requested file is located, it is transmitted back to the peer requesting it via the same path. In some applications each node on this route stores a replicate of the file to be able to process future search queries more quickly. In this process, the peers only store files up to a maximum capacity. When their storage is exhausted, files are deleted according to the least-recently-used principle. This results in a correspondingly large number of replicates of popular files being created in the network, whereas, over time, files which are requested less often are removed. In various studies [416], the document routing model has been proven suitable for use in large communities. The search process, however, is more complex than, for example, in the flooded request model. In addition, it can result in the formation of islands - i.e., a partitioning of the network in which the individual communities no longer have a connection to the entire network [376, 123].

4.3 Bandwidth

Because the demands on the transmission capacities of networks are continuously rising, in particular on account of the increase in large volume multimedia data, effective use of bandwidth is becoming increasingly important. Currently, centralized approaches, in which files are held on the server of an information provider and transferred from there to the requesting client, are primarily used. In this case, a problem arises when spontaneous increases in demand exert a negative influence on the availability of the files since bottlenecks and queues develop. Without incurring any significant additional administration, Peer-to-Peer-based approaches achieve increased load-balancing by taking advantage of transmission routes which are not being fully exploited. They also facilitate the shared use of the bandwidth provided by the information providers.

- *Increased load-balancing:* In contrast to client/server architectures, hybrid Peer-to-Peer networks can achieve a better load-balancing. Only initial requests for files have to be served by a central server. Further requests can be automatically forwarded to peers within the network, which have already received and replicated these files. This concept is most frequently applied in the areas of streaming (e.g., PeerCast [480], Peer-to-Peer-Radio [466], SCVI.net [554]) and video on demand. The Peer-to-Peer-based Kontiki network [361] is pursuing an additional design which will enable improved load-balancing. Users can subscribe to information channels or software providers from which they wish to obtain information or software updates. When new information is available the respective information providers forward it to the peers which have subscribed. After receiving the information, each peer instantaneously acts as a provider and forwards the information to other peers. Application areas in which such designs can be implemented are the distribution of eLearning courseware in an intranet [151], the distribution of anti-virus and firewall configuration updates (e.g. Rumor [406]), and also updating computer games on peer computers (e.g., Descent [489] and Cybiko [416]).
- *Shared use of bandwidth:*In contrast to client/server approaches, the use of Peer-to-Peer designs can accelerate the downloading and transport of big files which are simultaneously requested by different entities. Generally, these files are split into smaller blocks. Single blocks are then downloaded by the requesting peers. In the first instance, each peer only receives a part of the entire file. Subsequently, the single file parts are exchanged by the peers without a need for further requests to the original source. Eventually the peers reconstruct the single parts to form an exact copy of the original file. An implementation utilizing this principle can be found in BitTorrent [127].

4.4 Storage Space

Nowadays, Direct Attached Storage (DAS), Network Attached Storage (NAS) or Storage Area Networks (SAN) are the main design concepts used to store data in a company. These solutions have disadvantages, such as inefficient use of the available storage, additional load on the company network or the necessity for specially trained personnel and additional backup solutions.

However, increased connectivity and increased availability of bandwidth permit alternative forms of managing storage which resolve these problems and require less administrative effort. With Peer-to-Peer storage networks, it is generally assumed that only a portion of the disk space available on a desktop PC will be used. A Peer-to-Peer storage network is a cluster of computers, formed on the basis of existing networks, which share all storage available in the network. Well-known approaches to this type of system are PAST [528], Pasta [430], OceanStore [368], CFS [147], Farsite [13], and Intermemory [254]. Systems which are particularly suitable for explaining the way in which Peer-to-Peer storage networks operate are PAST, Pasta and OceanStore. They have basic similarities in the way they are constructed and organized. To participate in a Peer-to-Peer storage network, each peer receives a public/private key pair. With the aid of a hash function, the public key is used to create an unambiguous identification number for each peer. To gain access to storage on another computer, the peer must either make available some of its own storage, or pay a fee. Corresponding to its contribution, each peer is assigned a maximum volume of data which it can add to the network. When a file is to be stored in the network, it is assigned an unambiguous identification number, created with a hash function from the name or the content of the respective file, as well as the public key of the owner. Storing the file and searching for it in the network take place in the manner described for the document routing model before. In addition, a freely determined number of file replicates are also stored. Each peer retrieves its own current version of the routing table which is used for storage and searches. They check the availability of their neighbors at set intervals to establish which peers have left the network. In this way, new peers which have joined the network are also included in the table.

To coordinate Peer-to-Peer storage networks, key pairs must be generated and distributed to the respective peers and the use of storage has to be monitored. OceanStore expands the administrative tasks to include version and transaction management. As a rule, these tasks are handled by a certain number of particularly high performance peers which are also distinguished by a high degree of availability in the network. To ensure that a lack of availability on the part of one of these selected peers does not affect the functional efficiency of the entire network, the peers are coordinated via a Byzantine agreement protocol [105]. Requests are handled by all available selected peers. Each sends a result to the party which has issued the request.

This party waits until a certain number of identical results are received from these peers before accepting the result as correct.

By means of file replication and random distribution of identification numbers to peers using a hash function, the Peer-to-Peer storage network automatically ensures that various copies of the same file are stored at different geographical locations. No additional administration or additional backup solution is required to achieve protection against a local incident or loss of data. This procedure also reduces the significance of a problem which is characteristic of Peer-to-Peer networks: in Peer-to-Peer networks there is no guarantee that a particular peer will be available in the network at a particular point in time (availability problem). In the case of Peer-to-Peer storage networks, this could result in settings where no peer is available in the network which stores the file being requested. Increasing the number of replicates stored at various geographical locations can, however, enhance the probability that at least one such peer will be available in the network.

The low administration costs, which result from the self-organized character of Peer-to-Peer storage networks, and the fact that additional backup solutions are seldom required are among the advantages these new systems offer for providing and efficiently managing storage.

4.5 Processor Cycles

Recognition that the available computing power of the networked entities was often unused was an early incentive for using Peer-to-Peer applications to bundle computing power. At the same time, the requirement for high performance computing, i.e., computing operations in the field of bio-informatics, logistics or the financial sector, has been increasing. By using Peer-to-Peer applications to bundle processor cycles, it is possible to achieve computing power which even the most expensive super-computers can scarcely provide. This is effected by forming a cluster of independent, networked computers in which a single computer is transparent and all networked nodes are combined into a single logical computer. The respective approaches to the coordinated release and shared use of distributed computing resources in dynamic, virtual organizations which extend beyond any single institution currently fall under the term 'grid computing' [220, 48, 247, 213, 224]. The term grid computing is an analogy to customary power grids. The greatest possible amount of resources, particularly computing power, should be available to the user, ideally unrestricted and not bound to any location - similar to the way in which power is drawn from an electricity socket. The Proceedings [51] provide an overview of diverse aspects of grid computing.

One of the most widely cited projects in the context of Peer-to-Peer which is, however, only an initial approximation of the goal of grid computing, is SETI@home (Search for Extraterrestrial Intelligence) [28]. SETI@home is a scientific initiative launched by the University of California, Berkeley, with the goal of discovering radio signals from extraterrestrial intelligence. For this purpose, a radio telescope in Puerto Rico records a portion of the electromagnetic spectrum from outer space. This data is sent to the central SETI@home server in California. There, they take advantage of the fact that the greater part of processor cycles on private and business computers remains idle. Rather than analyzing the data in a costly supercomputer, the SETI-Server divides the data into smaller units and sends these units to the several million computers made available by the volunteers who have registered to participate in this project. The SETI-Client carries out the calculations during the idle processor cycles of the participants' computers and then sends the results back. In the related literature, SETI@home is consistently referred to as a perfect example of a Peer-to-Peer application in general, and, more specifically, a perfect example of grid computing [414]. This evaluation, however, is not completely accurate, as the core of SETI@home is a classical client/server application, due to the fact that a central server co-ordinates the tasks of the nodes and sends them task packets. The peers process the tasks they have been assigned and return the results. In this system there is no communication between the individual nodes. SETI@home does, however, have Peer-to-Peer characteristics [416]. The nodes form a virtual community and make resources available in the form of idle processor cycles. The peers are, to a large extent, autonomous, since they determine if and when the SETI@home-Software is allowed to conduct computing tasks [28, 29]. The shared accomplishment of these types of distributed computing tasks, however, is only possible if the analytic steps can be separated and divided into individual data packets.

The vision of grid computing described earlier, however, extends far beyond projects such as SETI@home. At an advanced stage of development, it should not only be possible for each network node to offer its own resources, but it should also be possible for it to take advantage of the resources available in the Peer-to-Peer network. A currently influential initiative, the Globus Project [590], which is working on a standardized middleware for grid application, has been greeted with wide acceptance throughout the grid community. The project is being supported by important market players, such as IBM, Microsoft, Sun, HP and NEC.

Part II

Unstructured Peer-to-Peer Systems

5. First and Second Generation of Peer-to-Peer Systems

Jörg Eberspächer, Rüdiger Schollmeier
(Munich University of Technology)

5.1 General Characteristics of Early Peer-to-Peer Systems

Peer-to-Peer (P2P) networks appeared roughly around the year 2000 when a broadband Internet infrastructure (even at the network edge) became widely available. Other than traditional networks Peer-to-Peer networks do not rely on a specific infrastructure offering transport services. Instead they form "overlay structures" focusing on content allocation and distribution based on TCP or HTTP connections. Whereas in a standard Client-Server configuration content is stored and provided only via some central server(s), Peer-to-Peer networks are highly decentralized and locate a desired content at some participating peer and provide the corresponding IP address of that peer to the searching peer. The download of that content is then initiated using a separate connection, often using HTTP. Thus, the high load usually resulting for a central server and its surrounding network is avoided leading to a more even distribution of load on the underlying physical network. On the other hand, such networks are typically subject to frequent changes because peers join and leave the network without any central control.

While some legal aspects of Peer-to-Peer networks are still heavily contended between the entertainment industry and some user groups, we focus on the technical aspects of this approach. In the last years, several Peer-to-Peer technologies were developed. Figure 5.1 provides an overview of current Peer-to-Peer technologies and compares them to the conventional Client-Server model.

As shown in Figure 5.1, in a Client-Server system the server is the only provider of service or content, e.g. a web server or a calendar server. The peers (clients) in this context only request content or service from the server, the IP address of which is assumed to be available to the peers. Content in this context may be an MP3-compressed audio file, the profile of a person a user wants to establish a call to or context information, e.g. where the next taxi can be found. The clients do not provide any service or content to run this system. Thus generally the clients are lower performance systems and the server is a high performance system. This does not exclude that a server may be set up as a server farm with one specified entry point for the clients, which redirects the clients to different computers to share the load.

R. Steinmetz and K. Wehrle (Eds.): P2P Systems and Applications, LNCS 3485, pp. 35-56, 2005.

Client-Server	Peer-to-Peer			
	1. Resources are shared between the peers 2. Resources can be accessed directly from other peers 3. Peer is provider and requestor (Servent concept)			
	Unstructured P2P			Structured P2P
	1st Generation		2nd Generation	
	Centralized P2P	Pure P2P	Hybrid P2P	DHT-Based
1. Server is the central entity and only provider of service and content. → Network managed by the Server 2. Server as the higher performance system. 3. Clients as the lower performance system Example: WWW	1. All features of Peer-to-Peer included 2. Central entity is necessary to provide the service 3. Central entity is some kind of index/group database Example: Napster	1. All features of Peer-to-Peer included 2. Any terminal entity can be removed without loss of functionality 3. → No central entities Examples: Gnutella 0.4, Freenet	1. All features of Peer-to-Peer included 2. Any terminal entity can be removed without loss of functionality 3. → dynamic central entities Example: Gnutella 0.6, JXTA	1. All features of Peer-to-Peer included 2. Any terminal entity can be removed without loss of functionality 3. → No central entities 4. Connections in the overlay are "fixed" Examples: Chord, CAN

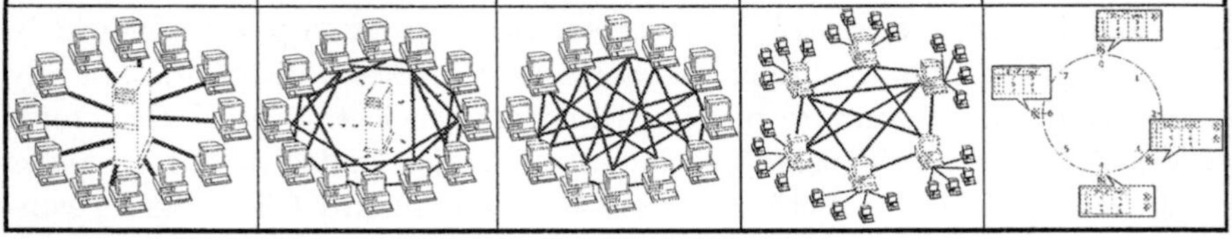

Fig. 5.1: Summary of the characteristic features of Client-Server and Peer-to-Peer networks

In contrast, in Peer-to-Peer systems all resources, i.e. the shared content and services, are provided by the peers. Some central facility may still exist, e.g. to locate a given content. A peer in this context is simply an application running on a machine, which may be a personal computer, a handheld or a mobile phone. In contrast to a Client-Server network, we can generally not distinguish between a content requestor (client) and a content provider, as one application participating in the overlay in general offers content to other peers and requests content from other participants. This is often expressed by the term "Servent", composed of the first syllable of the term Server and the second syllable of the term Client.

Using this basic concept Figure 5.1 outlines various possibilities currently used. Peer-to-Peer networking started with the first generation centralized concept. In this case some central server is still available. However, contrary to the Client-Server approach this server only stores the IP addresses of peers where some content is available, thus greatly reducing the load of that server. However, the address of that server must be known to the peers in advance. This concept was widely used and became especially well known due to Napster, offering free music downloads by providing the addresses of peers sharing the desired content. This approach subsequently lost much of its importance due to legal issues.

As a replacement for that scheme decentrally organized schemes such as Gnutella 0.4 and Freenet became widely used. These schemes do not rely on any central facility (except possibly for some bootstrap server to ease joining such a network), but rely on flooding the desired content identifier over the network, thus reaching a large number of peers. Peers which share that content will then respond to the requesting peer which will subsequently initiate a separate download session.

It is an important drawback of these schemes that they generate a potentially huge amount of signaling traffic by flooding the requests. In fact, that signaling traffic dominates the Internet traffic in some cases even today. To avoid that, schemes like Gnutella 0.6 or JXTA introduce a hierarchy by defining Superpeers, which store the content available at the connected peers together with their IP address. Thus the Superpeers are often able to answer incoming requests by immediately providing the respective IP address, so that on average less hops are required in the search process, thus reducing the signaling traffic.

The above schemes are generally termed "Unstructured Peer-to-Peer", because the content stored on a given node and its IP address are unrelated and do not follow any specific structure. Contrary to that also Peer-to-Peer approaches have been proposed which establish a link between the stored content and the IP address of a node. In the rightmost column of Figure 5.1 such networks are termed "Structured Peer-to-Peer". The link between a content identifier and the IP address is usually based on Distributed Hash Tables (DHT) (cf. Chapter 7). However, in a frequently changing network such an approach requires frequent redistribution of content. We therefore do not address this approach in more detail.

5.2 Centralized Peer-to-Peer Networks

5.2.1 Basic Characteristics

As described above, centralized Peer-to-Peer networks are characterized by the fact that they rely on one central lookup server. The overlay topology of a centralized Peer-to-Peer network can therefore be described as a star network. Every peer is connected to the centralized lookup server, to which it can issue requests for content matching the keywords stated in the request. If the request can be resolved by the centralized lookup server, it returns the access coordinates of the peers (mostly IP-addresses and ports) offering content which is described with the same keywords as stated in the request. The content itself is then transmitted out of band, i.e. not via the signaling (overlay) network, but via an additional, mostly HTTP-based, connection.

The most prominent example application, which is based on a centralized Peer-to-Peer network, is Napster `http://www.napster.com/what_is_napster.html`. Napster is used for (free) file sharing between Internet users and is considered as the starting point of Peer-to-Peer networks. Due to legal issues and the centralized responsibility Napster had to change its service to a legal file sharing service. The basic concept and architecture of the Napster file sharing system is still used by other applications, e.g. Audiogalaxy [38] or WinMX [625]. BitTorrent [127, 320] is a similar file sharing system, the major objective of which is to quickly replicate a single large file to a set of clients.

As depicted in Figure 5.1 the Napster network can be characterized by its centralized topology. The file searching protocol uses a Client-Server model with a central index server. However the file transfer is done in a true Peer-to-Peer way. The file exchange occurs directly between the Napster hosts without passing the server.

With Napster, no file can be found, if the central lookup table is not available. Only the file retrieval and the storage are decentralized. Thus the server represents a bottleneck and a single point of failure. The computing power and storage capabilities of the central lookup facility must grow proportional to the number of users, which also affects the scalability of this approach.

As every node wanting to log into the Napster network has to register at the central server, no keep alive signal or any electronic heart beat must be exchanged between the Napster server and the peer. The server acts comparable to a DNS server to guide each requesting peer to those peers, which host the demanded content. No additional application layer routing is necessary, as the server has a complete network view.

Further on, if the content is shared by at least one participant, the content can be found instantly with one lookup. Thus the content availability in a Napster network can only take the values zero or one. Zero, if the content is not shared by any node, one if the content is shared by at least one node, assuming that the server and the peers work correctly. If the content is available more than once, only the replication rate, and thus in this case the download performance increases, but not the availability of content.

5.2.2 Signaling Characteristics

The messages employed in Napster are fairly simple and easy to track, as they are transmitted as plain text messages. We describe in the following the basic messages used in Napster to announce and to search for content.

Each message to/from the Napster server has the basic structure given in Figure 5.2. The first four bytes provide the <Length> parameter, which specifies the length of the payload of this message. The <Function> parameter stated in the following four bytes, defines the message type, e.g. login or search, which are described in the following. The payload finally carries parameters necessary for the different messages, e.g. the keywords of a search message.

Fig. 5.2: Basic Napster message structure

The blocks/parameters in the payload are separated by spaces. This makes the separation of the information provided in each incoming message possible, as most blocks have no fixed length. We divide the messages in two phases, the initialization and the file request. The <Function> parameter of each message is given in brackets, e.g. SEARCH (0xC8).

Initialization

A registered Napster host, acting as a client, sends to the Napster server a LOGIN (0x02) message to become a member of the overlay network. For user verification this message includes the nickname (<nick>) and <password> of the user who started the application. Further on this message also includes the port number (<port>) on which the peer listens for incoming data requests and information about the clients access data-rate (<Link Type>). The <Client-Info> parameter contains information about the version of the used software. On average a LOGIN-message is about 40 bytes long.

<Nick>	<Password>	<Port>	<Client-Info>	<Link Type>

Fig. 5.3: LOGIN (0x02) message

After a successful login, the server sends a LOGIN ACK (0x03) (size: 20 bytes) to the client. If the <nick> is registered, the email address given at registration time is returned.

If the <nick> is not registered, a dummy value is returned. As soon as the peer is logged in, it sends one "CLIENT NOTIFICATION OF SHARED FILE" (0x64) message for every file it wants to share (see Figure 5.4). Thus routing is possible, as every client announces its shared objects to the Napster server. This message contains the filename (<Filename>) of the file, the MD5-hash value of the file <MD5> [519] and the size in byte of the file (<Size>). The MD5 (Message Digest 5) algorithm produces a 128-bit "fingerprint" of any file. It is extremely unlikely that two messages contain the same hash value.

The MD5 algorithm is therefore intended to provide any user with the possibility to secure the origin of the shared file, even if parts of the file are provided by different Napster users. As specific parameters of the music file, this message additionally provides the bitrate (<Bitrate>), the sampling rate of the MP3 (<frequency>), and the playout time of a music file (<time>). The bit rate represents the quality of the used coding and compression algorithm. The average size of this message is 74 bytes.

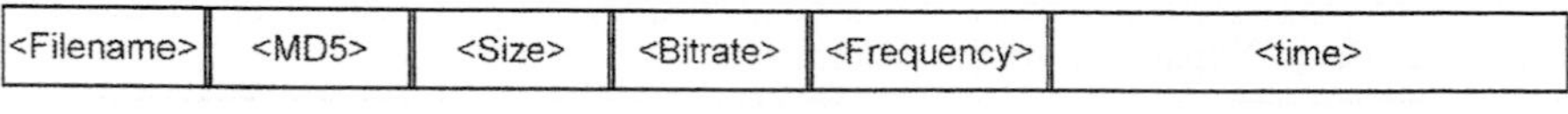

Fig. 5.4: CLIENT NOTIFICATION OF SHARED FILE message (0x64)

File Request

To be able to download a file from the Napster network, peers which share the requested file have to be found. The format of a request is shown in Figure 5.5. Therefore the requesting peer sends a SEARCH (0xC8) message to the Napster server. To specify the search this message contains several parameters stating keywords describing the requested object (artistname and parts of the songname). Further on this message also specifies a filter, e.g. to state a certain quality of the requested file, like the bitrate and the sampling frequency of the requested file. The parameter <compare> can have the values "at least", "at best" or "equal to". Thus the requesting peer can choose the quality of the file and also the file size, which together with the link type (parameter <Link Type> e.g. a T1 connection) of the providing peer can strongly influence the download speed. The parameter <MAX_RESULTS> finally states the maximum number of results the requesting peer wants the Napster server to return. The average size of such a message is 130 bytes.

<Filename contains "Artist Name">	<MAX_RESULTS>	<Filename contains "Song Name">	<Compare> <Link-Type>	<Compare> <BitRate>	<Compare> <Freq>

Fig. 5.5: SEARCH message (0xC8)

Upon receiving a SEARCH message, the Napster server tries to match the parameters stated in the SEARCH message with the entries of its database, consisting of data previously received from other peers upon initialization (CLIENT NOTIFICATION OF SHARED FILE (0x64) messages). If the server can resolve the query, it answers with at least one RESPONSE (0xC9) containing information about shared files matching the previously stated criteria (see Figure 5.6). To provide the requesting peer with information about the available data and where it can be downloaded from, this message contains the full filename (<File-Name>) and the IP-address (<IP>) of the providing peer, so that the requesting peer can download the requested file directly via its HTTP-instance [365]. Further on the file size (<Size>), the playout time (<length>), the sample and the bitrate of the file are stated (<Freq>, <Bitrate>). To check the integrity of the file and to be able to download the file from multiple sources the MD5 hash value of the shared file is also stated (<MD5>). The average size of such a message is 200 bytes.

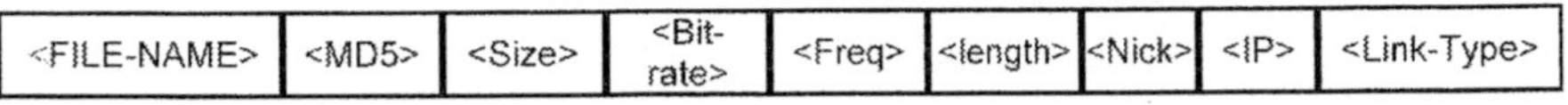

Fig. 5.6: RESPONSE message (0xC9)

5.2.3 Discussion

To summarize the details of the Napster protocol we provide as an example the message sequence chart for the communication between two Napster peers and the Napster server in Figure 5.7. Here the requesting peer (Req) first initializes at the Napster server. As mentioned above the requesting peer (Req) therefore sends a LOGIN message to the Napster server with a payload of 36 bytes, which equals to 0x24 bytes in hexadecimal notation. Upon receiving the acknowledgement it announces its three shared objects to the Napster server. In this example we assume the same message lengths, given by the average message length stated above.

Now the new peer is fully registered with the Napster network and can start a search. Therefore it sends a SEARCH message to the Napster server, including the search keywords describing the requested object. As the Napster server in our example knows two possible peers which share the requested object, it answers with two RESPONSE messages. Thus the peer can now request a download of the requested object from one of the providing peers with a HTTP-Get-request. In case of success, as assumed in this example, the providing peer responds to this request with an OK message, which includes the requested file. In this figure we can clearly see, that besides the initialization traffic only few traffic is caused by this Peer-to-Peer network. The reason is that only one central lookup table is available and therefore no flooding is necessary to find the requested object. The Napster server thus works similar to a DNS-lookup server.

If we assume a user, which shares 10 files and requests one comparatively popular file, which thus would result in 20 responses, we can compute the generated bytes to:

$$\begin{aligned} 1 \cdot (login + login\_ack) + 10 \cdot notif + 1 \cdot search + 10 \cdot response = \\ = 40 + 4 + 10 \cdot 74 + 130 + 10 \cdot 200 = 2914 bytes \end{aligned} \tag{5.1}$$

If we further on assume an average session length of 10 minutes, we can compute the average necessary signaling data rate to 38.85 bits/s, which is very reasonable.

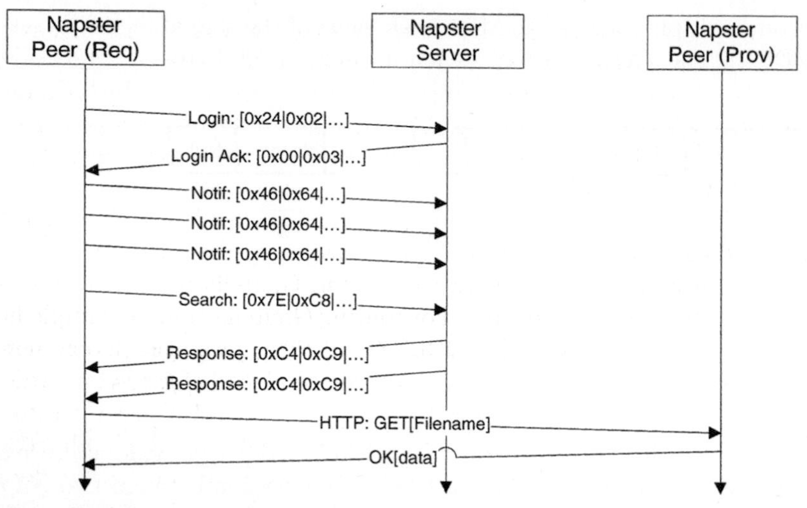

Fig. 5.7: Sample message sequence chart for one Napster server with one requesting and one providing peer

5.3 Pure Peer-to-Peer-Networks

5.3.1 Basic Characteristics

Pure Peer-to-Peer networks/protocols came up shortly after the introduction of Napster. Examples of these protocols are the Freenet protocol and the Gnutella 0.4 protocol [123, 126, 232] . To analyze the properties, possibilities and limitations of pure Peer-to-Peer networks, we describe the Gnutella 0.4 protocol in this section. The Gnutella 0.4 network [126] consists of a large number of nodes which may be distributed throughout the world, without any central element. The overlay topology can be characterized by a node degree distribution as given by equation 5.2 [328]. With this truncated powerlaw distribution, ranging from degree (d) one to a maximum degree of seven, we can describe the topology of a Gnutella 0.4 network and can generate networks graphs as given by Figure 5.8. Here we can observe that separated subcomponents may occur due to the random connection establishment. This is also expected to happen in real networks, although in this case the subcomponents are magnitudes larger, as also the total number of considered nodes is magnitudes larger.

$$p\left(d\right)=\begin{cases} c\cdot d^{-1.4}, \ 0<d\leq 7 \\ 0, \ in\ any\ other\ case \end{cases} , \ with\ c=\left(\sum_{d}\frac{p(d)}{c}\right)^{-1} \tag{5.2}$$

$$\begin{aligned} &average: \ \bar{d}=2.2 \\ &\mathrm{var}\left(d\right)=1.63 \end{aligned}$$

A node becomes part of the Gnutella network by establishing an average of 3 TCP-connections to other active Gnutella nodes, whose IP addresses it may receive from a bootstrap server [549]. New nodes, to which the node can connect if an active connection breaks, are explored by broadcasting PING messages in the virtual overlay network. These PING messages are also used as keep alive pattern and are broadcasted in regular time intervals.

All messages are coded in plain text. This results in large message sizes of QUERY and especially QUERY-HIT messages, as they contain meta data about the queried objects. Similar to Napster, Gnutella uses MD5 hash keys [519] to identify objects explicitly. For routing Gnutella employs simple flooding of the request messages, i.e. QUERY and PING messages. Every new incoming PING or QUERY, which has not been received before, is forwarded to all neighbors except the one it received the message from, if the Time-to-Live (TTL) value (default set to seven hops) is at least one. If a node receives the same message more than once, these messages are not further flooded. Response messages, like PONG or QUERY-HIT messages, are routed back on the same path the request message used, which is called backward routing.

In Gnutella 0.4 the virtual Peer-to-Peer layer is not matched to the physical layer, which leads to zigzag routes, as described in [550]. Only enhancements, as described by the approach of geo-sensitive Gnutella [550], provide means to adapt the virtual network to the physical network.

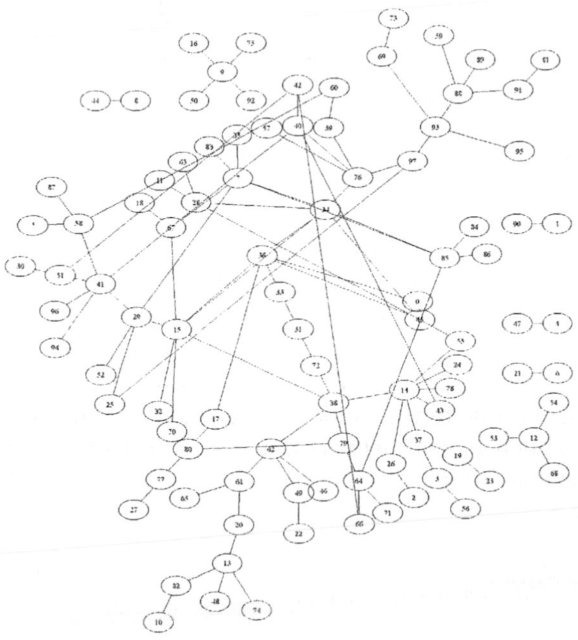

Fig. 5.8: Sample graph of a simulated Gnutella 0.4 network (100 nodes)

5.3.2 Signaling Characteristics

The nodes communicate directly with each other without any central instance . However at the beginning, i.e. in a bootstrap phase, a central entity like a beacon server, from which IP addresses of active nodes can be retrieved, is necessary. If a node already participated in the network, it may also be able to enter the network by trying to connect to nodes, whose addresses it cached in a previous session. As soon as a new node knows the IP address and port of one active Gnutella node it first establishes a TCP connection to this node and then connects to this node by sending the ASCII encoded request string "GNUTELLA CONNECT/<protocol version string>\n\n" to it. If the participating peer accepts this connection request it must respond with a "GNUTELLA OK\n\n".

Gnutella mainly uses four messages as stated above. The messages are setup in a similar manner as in Napster. They consist of a general message header and the additional payload (see Figure 5.9). However since in Gnutella the messages are flooded through the overlay network, some additional parameters are necessary beyond those used for Napster. The <Descriptor ID> is a 16-byte string uniquely identifying the message on the network. Thus circles can be detected, i.e. every message which is received twice by a node is not forwarded any further. Simultaneously and backward routing of possible response messages is possible.

Every node therefore has to store this ID and the IP address from which it received the message for a certain time. The <TTL> (Time-to-Live) value determines the number of hops a message is forwarded in the overlay network. This value is decreased by every node which received the message before the message is forwarded. When the TTL value reaches zero, the message is not forwarded any further, to avoid infinitely circulating messages. Generally a TTL value of seven is considered to be sufficient to reach a large fraction of the nodes participating in the overlay network. The <Hops>-value states the number of hops a message has already been forwarded and is therefore increased by one by every forwarding peer. It can be used to guarantee, that initially no larger value than seven has been used by a requesting peer, as

$$TTL(0) = TTL(i) + Hops(i) \leq 7 \tag{5.3}$$

The <Payload length> parameter states the size of the message so that the next message in the incoming stream can clearly be identified.

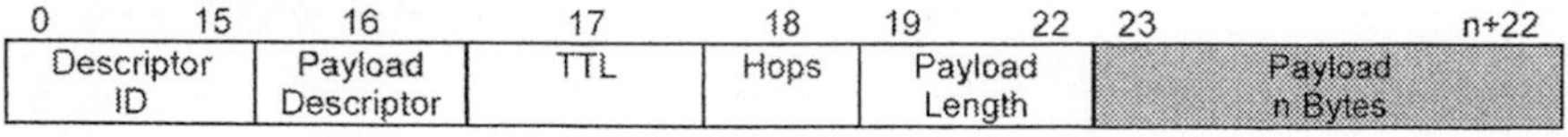

0 – 15	16	17	18	19 – 22	23 – n+22
Descriptor ID	Payload Descriptor	TTL	Hops	Payload Length	Payload n Bytes

Fig. 5.9: Basic Gnutella message structure

However the most important field, which determines the payload is the <Payload-Descriptor> field. The messages we distinguish here are 0x00 for a PING, 0x01 for a PONG, 0x80 for a QUERY and 0x81 for a QUERYHIT message [126]. The network exploration message PING does not contain any payload, whereas in the payload of the PONG message in addition to the contact information (IP address+port) information about the amount of shared files is stated. To search for data, the QUERY message contains, besides the

0 1	2 5	6 9	10 13
Port	IP address	Number of shared files	Number of kilobytes shared

Fig. 5.10: PONG (0x01) payload structure

parameter which states the requested minimum download speed, a null terminated search string containing the keywords separated by blanks, describing the requested object. The average size of this message is 78.4 bytes. If we now assume, that an average word has a length of eight characters plus one character for the blank, we can also compute the average number of words a user states as search criteria, as every character is described with one byte. For Gnutella this results in an average of 7.35 words per QUERY. Similar to the PING messages, the QUERY messages are flooded through the overlay. As soon as one node receives a QUERY-message, it compares the search

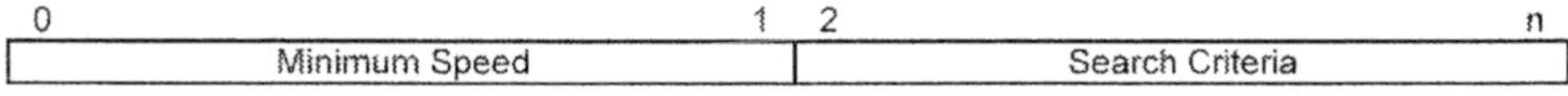

Fig. 5.11: QUERY (0x80) payload structure

keywords to the keywords describing the locally shared content. In case of at least one hit, it sends back a QUERYHIT message which is routed back on the same way the QUERY message was distributed through the network (backward routing). A QUERYHIT message contains the information, as shown in Figure 5.12 and Figure 5.13. However in contrast to Napster one QUERYHIT message can contain in its result set more than only one file. The average size of one QUERYHIT message is 748.8 bytes, which is comparatively large.

0	1 2	3 6	7 10	11 ... n	n+16
Number of hits	Port	IP Address	Speed	Result Set	Node ID

Fig. 5.12: QUERYHIT (0x81) payload structure

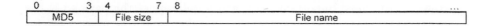

0 3	4 7	8 ...
MD5	File size	File name

Fig. 5.13: Result set structure

5.3.3 Discussion

To summarize the basic signaling behavior of a Gnutella network we assume a sample Gnutella network, where node 1 just joined (see Figure 5.14). Therefore node 1 first sends a CONNECT message to the nodes 5, 2 and 3 (see Figure 5.15). To explore its surrounding further on, node 1 also sends a PING message to its neighbors, which forward this message further and thus this message and its corresponding PONG messages propagate through the network, as shown in Figure 5.15.

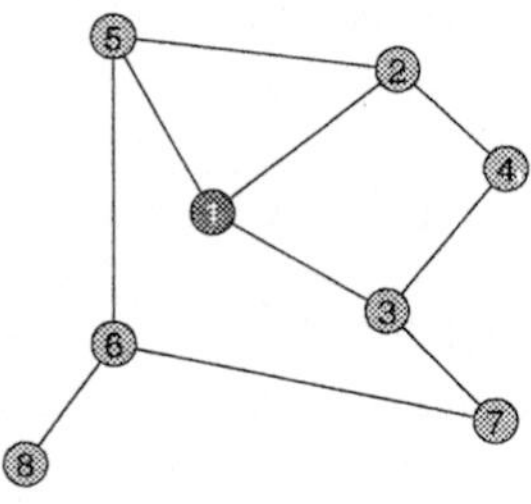

Fig. 5.14: Sample Gnutella 0.4 network

In our example the flooding of the request messages results, as we can see from Figure 5.15, in 12 PING and 12 PONG messages, and 6 messages for the initial connection establishment. Taking the message sizes from above into account (PING: 23 byte, PONG: 37 byte) and assuming for a each connection (GnuCon+OK) message pair 34 byte, this results in a total of 462 bytes. This traffic is necessary to merely explore the network. We can also observe in Figure 5.15, that several messages are not forwarded any further, because they are received for a second time.

If we further on assume that the node would start a search in this small network, this would result in 12 QUERY messages. Assuming that three nodes answer this QUERY, and this results in eight additional QUERYHIT messages, we can calculate a total traffic this node caused in this small network to 6.928 bytes. Together with the initialization traffic we can compute a total of 7.390 transmitted bytes. This is significantly more than the traffic caused by the Napster peer. For a larger network we can assume that the amount of traffic grows even further as the messages are flooded via more hops. The main reason is the distributed nature of the Gnutella network. This causes on the one hand a lot of traffic as no central lookup is available, but on the other hand also makes this network hard to attack, as no central single point of failure exists.

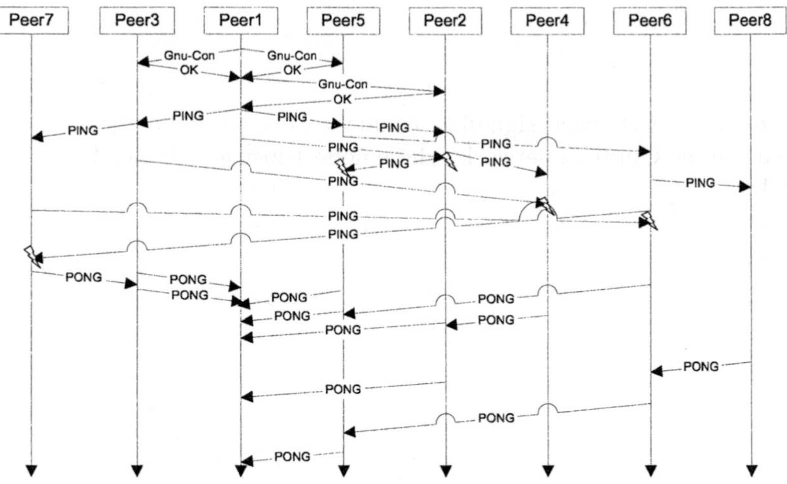

Fig. 5.15: Sample message sequence chart to illustrate the basic signaling behavior of Gnutella 04

Thus the amount of traffic caused by this application is high, although we only considered the traffic on the application layer . If we have a look at the topology of the Gnutella network on a geographical level, it turns out that the overlay topology differs significantly from the physical network, which results in zigzag routes, as depicted by Figure 5.16, Figure 5.17 and Figure 5.18. The route starts in New Mexico/USA. A PING or a QUERY message is sent in the first hop to other nodes located in the USA but also to a node located in Poland, i.e. the request is transmitted for the first time across the Atlantic (see Figure 5.16). Most of the connections of the node located in Poland lead directly back to the USA again. Thus in the second hop this message is transmitted e.g. to a node in California/USA and therefore crosses the Atlantic a second time (see Figure 5.17). In the third hop the message is then transmitted to a node located in Sweden (see Figure 5.18), resulting in a third transmission of the message across the Atlantic. Thus within three hops the message has been transmitted three times across the Atlantic, which results in the zigzag structure shown in Figure 5.18.

Every message routed/flooded in this overlay via the node in New Mexico has to be transmitted at least three times across the Atlantic, before it reaches its destination. The behavior depicted by Figure 5.16 to Figure 5.18 is only one example of a common behavior of the Gnutella topology.

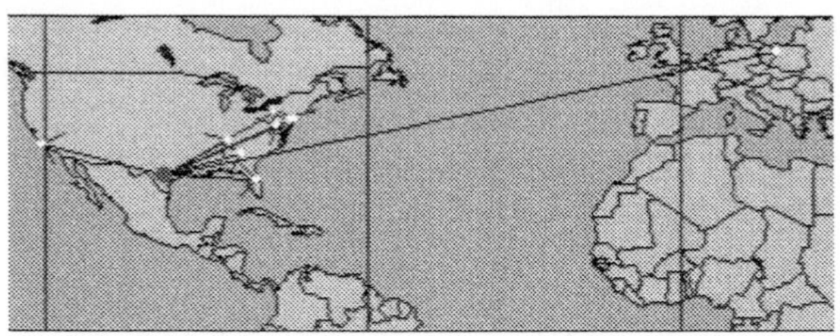

Fig. 5.16: Map of Gnutella Network measured on 12.08.2002 up to 1st hop level

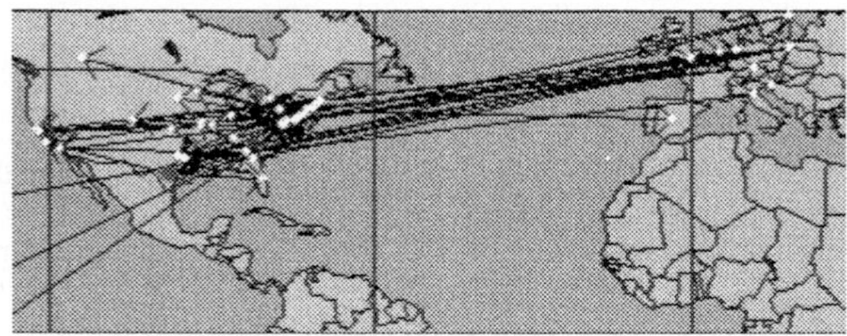

Fig. 5.17: Map of Gnutella Network measured on 12.08.2002 up to 2nd hop level

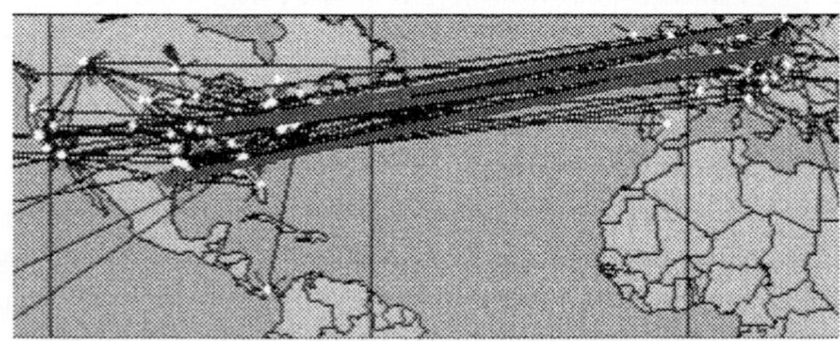

Fig. 5.18: Map of Gnutella Network measured on 12.08.2002 up to the 3rd hop level, including the zigzag PING-PONG route (bold line)

In addition to the unnecessary consumption of bandwidth between the USA and Europe, the zigzag routes cause high delays, which can be perceived by any user logged onto the overlay network. At least every third message crosses several times the Atlantic. The performance of the overlay network could certainly be improved, by directing the message first to nodes in the local proximity of the querying node and then only once across the Atlantic and similar long distances to then distribute the query in the respective local area.

A solution of this problem would be to adapt the virtual overlay to the physical network via cross-layer communication as e.g. proposed in [550]. Further on the large message sizes are also a concern. Here further compression of the signaling traffic can reduce the traffic significantly [424, 530, 585]. However another solution which is discussed in more detail in the next section is the introduction of a dynamic hierarchy, so that not every message has to be flooded through the whole network.

5.4 Hybrid Peer-to-Peer Networks

5.4.1 Basic Characteristics

As outlined above, hybrid Peer-to-Peer networks are characterized by the introduction of another dynamic hierarchical layer. As an example of such a hybrid Peer-to-Peer network we consider in this section the Gnutella 0.6 network.

A major goal of the Gnutella 0.6 architecture is to reduce the high message load, which can be observed in a Gnutella 0.4 network. Therefore several protocol enhancements have been proposed in [522], [523] resulting in the creation of a hierarchy in the network to establish a hub based network. These extensions are subsumed in the Gnutella protocol 0.6 [359]. The messages used in Gnutella 0.4 stay the same to guarantee downward compatibility. However, they are handled differently as explained below.

An efficient way to reduce the consumption of bandwidth is the introduction of hierarchies, as e.g. in Napster the Napster Server. To keep the advantages of Gnutella, i.e. the complete self organization and decentralization, Superpeers and Leafnodes are introduced in [563].

By introducing such enhancements, the load on the network can be reduced without introducing preconfigured, centralized servers. The network is still scalable, but one Superpeer should not have more than 50 to 100 Leafnodes, depending on the processing power and the connection of the Superpeer. Thus it is necessary, that the number of Superpeers increases according to the total number of leafnodes (peers) in the network.

A hybrid Peer-to-Peer network can not be modeled any further with a simple truncated powerlaw distribution. This can not reflect the Superpeers, which are characterized by a high degree and a significantly smaller number than simple peers. However the powerlaw degree distribution for the leafnodes is still expected to hold. Therefore we can assume a node degree distribution as given by equation 5.4.

$$p\left(d\right)=\begin{cases} c\cdot d^{-1.4},\ 1<d\leq 7 \\ c\cdot 1^{-1.4}-0.05,\ d=1 \\ c\cdot 0.05,\ d=20 \\ 0,\ \textit{in any other case} \end{cases},\ \textit{with}\ c=\left(\sum_{d}\frac{p(d)}{c}\right)^{-1} \tag{5.4}$$

$$\textit{average}:\ \bar{d}=2.8$$
$$\operatorname{var}\left(d\right)=3.55$$

Figure 5.19 depicts a sample network which is based on the Superpeer distribution stated above. Due to the nodes with degree 20 it has a hub-like structure, similar to the measured structure of a Gnutella 0.6 network (see Figure 5.20). These hubs dominate the structure of this overlay network. Because of their high degree these nodes establish with a higher probability connections between each other (marked by dashed lines in Figure 5.19). This results in a kind of second hierarchical layer which occurs in the Gnutella 0.6 network. The nodes with a small degree are mainly located at the edge of the network.

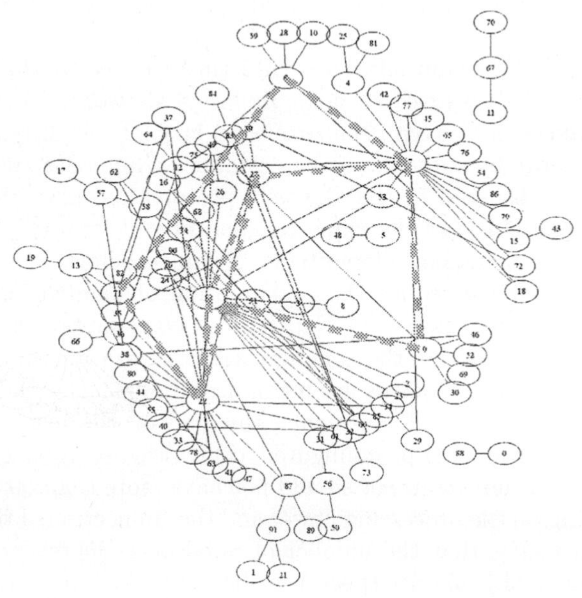

Fig. 5.19: Sample graph of a simulated Gnutella 0.6 network (100 nodes)

Although the number of nodes with degree one is high (47%) in this distribution, the number of separate sub-components is small, which can be observed by inspection. This results in a comparably high number of reachable nodes, within a few hops. This behavior can be explained by the fact, that the average degree of the Superpeer distribution with $\overline{d} = 2.80$ is higher than in the powerlaw distribution for a Gnutella 0.4 network used earlier.

If we transform the abstract network structure depicted by Figure 5.20 into the geographical view, depicted by Figure 5.21, we can make the network visible and can determine e.g. the popularity of the Gnutella network in different countries (see Figure 5.21). Further on we can observe the hub like structure of the Gnutella 0.6 network, which can not be retrieved from the geographical view. However, comparing both figures we can again observe the problem of the random structure, resulting in zigzag routes.

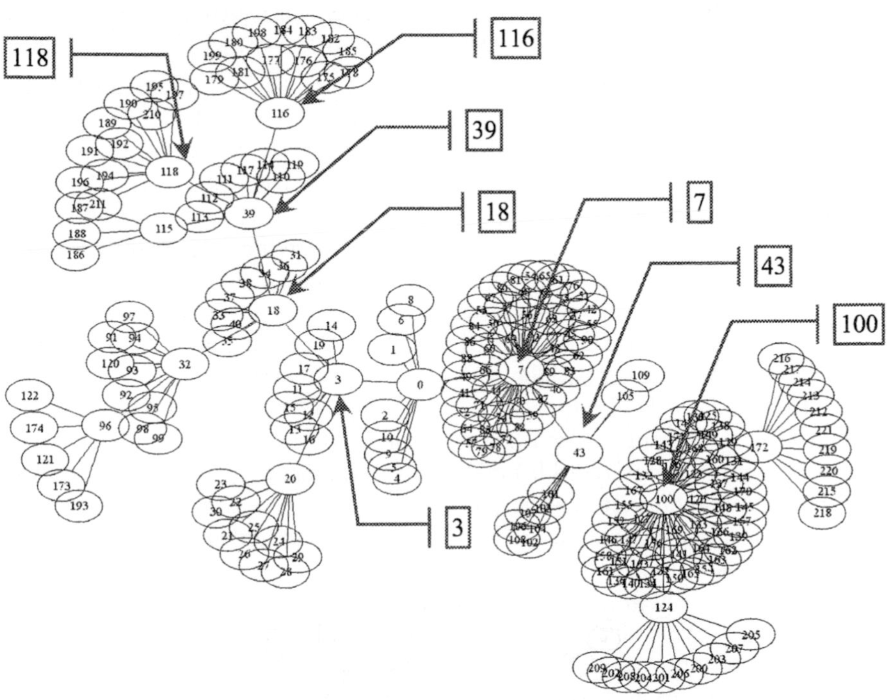

Fig. 5.20: Abstract network structure of a part of the Gnutella network (222 nodes Geographical view given by Figure 5.21, measured on 01.08.2002)

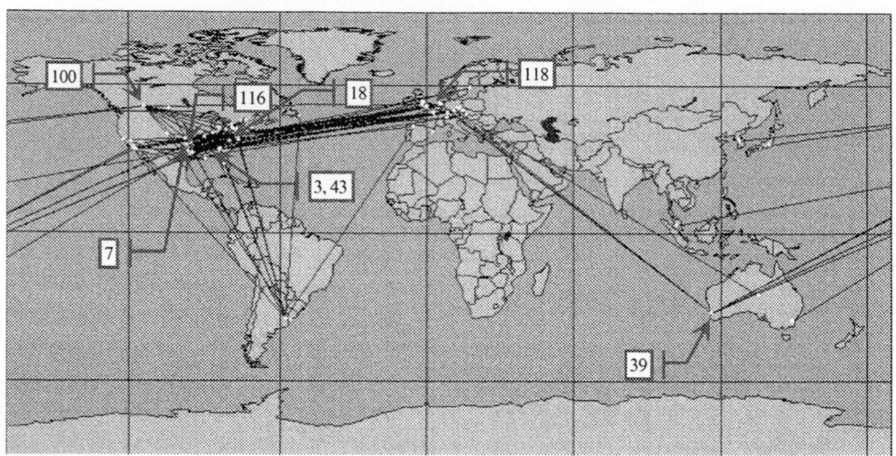

Fig. 5.21: Geographical view of a part of the Gnutella network (222 nodes); the numbers depict the node numbers from the abstract view (measured on 01.08.2002)

5.4.2 Signaling Characteristics

All messages, i.e. PING, PONG, QUERY and QUERYHIT, defined in Gnutella 0.4, are also used in Gnutella 0.6 . However, to reduce the traffic imposed on the Leafnodes and to use the Superpeer layer efficiently, the Leafnodes have to announce their shared content to the Superpeers they are connected to. Therefore the ROUTE_TABLE_UPDATE message (0x30) is used (see Figure 5.22 and Figure 5.23). The <Variant> parameter is used to identify a ROUTE_TABLE_UPDATE message either as Reset or as an Update.

The Reset variant is used to clear the route-table on the receiver, i.e. the Superpeer. Therefore additionally the table length (<Table_Length>) to be cleared must be stated. The parameter <Infinity> is not used currently and was intended to clear the route-table on several nodes, if the route-table would be broadcasted in the overlay.

The variant Patch is used to upload and set a new route-table at the Superpeer. To avoid one large table to be transferred at once, which might block the communication channel of a Gnutella node, it is possible to break one route table into a maximum of 255 chunks, which are numbered with the parameter <Seq_No>, where the maximum number of used chunks is stated with the parameter <Seq_Size>. To reduce the message size further on, the parameter <Compression> can be used to state a compression scheme which is used to compress the route table (0x0 for no algorithm, 0x1 for the ZLIB algorithm). For details of the decompression the parameter <Entry_Bits> is used, which is not explained in detail here. The parameter <DATA> contains 32 bit long hash-values of the keywords describing all objects shared by the

Leafnode. These values are concatenated to each other and transmitted as one data-string, or if necessary broken into smaller chunks, as mentioned above. The average message size of a ROUTE_TABLE_UPDATE is 269 byte.

The Superpeer uses the route tables, to decide which QUERY to forward to which Leafnode. Only in case that at least one keyword stated in the QUERY matches at least one entry in the route table of a Leafnode, the QUERY is forwarded to this Leafnode by the Superpeer.

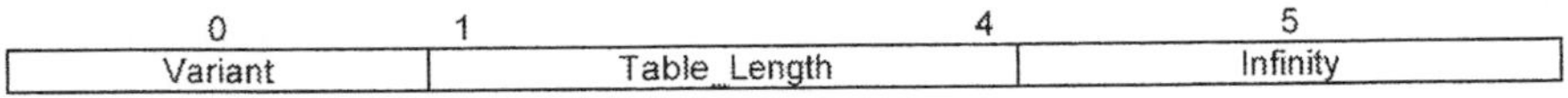

Fig. 5.22: ROUTE_TABLE_UPDATE (0x30) payload structure (Reset, Variant =0x0)

0	1	2	3	4	5 … n+4
Variant	Seq_No	Seq_Size	Compressor	Entry_Bits	DATA

Fig. 5.23: ROUTE_TABLE_UPDATE (0x30) payload structure (Patch, Variant=0x1)

As mentioned above, Superpeers establish a higher hierarchy level, in which they form a pure Peer-to-Peer network, i.e. are connected to each other directly via TCP connections. To one Superpeer several Leafnodes are connected. The Superpeer shields its Leafnodes from the PING and PONG traffic. The Superpeer does not forward incoming PING messages to its Leafnodes. If a Superpeer receives a PING from one of its Leafnodes it answers with a series of previously received PONG messages from other Superpeers, so that the Leafnodes know which other Superpeers are currently available. Therefore the Superpeer also has to initialize PING messages in regular intervals in the Superpeer layer.

Further on Superpeers provide better QUERY routing functionalities by indexing the shared objects of all of their Leafnodes (with the ROUTE_TABLE_UPDATE). Thus the Superpeer forwards QUERY messages to all Superpeers, but only to those Leafnodes which announced to host content described with the same keywords, as given in the QUERY (except the one it received it from and if the TTL is not exceeded and it has not received the same message before). Additionally the Superpeer broadcasts the request in the Superpeer layer, to receive more results.

5.4.3 Discussion

To summarize the properties of a hybrid Peer-to-Peer network, we consider the example Gnutella 0.6 overlay network depicted by Figure 5.24. This figure shows three Superpeers S1 to S3 and seven Leafnodes L1 to L7, whereas node L1 just joined. We assume that the rest of the network is stable, i.e. all ROUTE_TABLE_UPDATE messages have been exchanged successfully between the Leafnodes and their corresponding Superpeers.

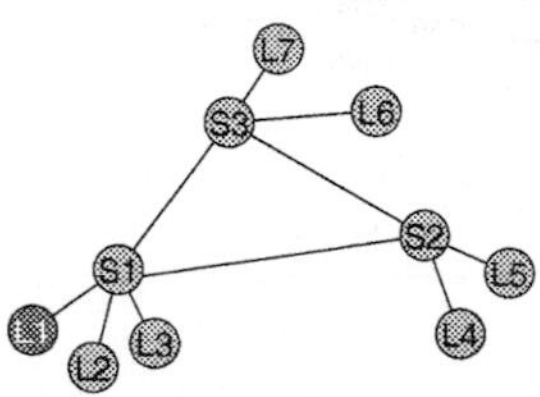

Fig. 5.24: Sample Gnutella 0.6 network

To join the network, node L1 first has to establish a TCP connection to node S1, whose IP address is assumed to be known by L1 (either from a previous session or from a bootstrap server). After it successfully established its TCP connection, node L1 performs the regular handshake with the Superpeer (see Figure 5.25). To announce its shared content to its Superpeer, node L1 sends a ROUTE_TABLE_UPDATE message (RTU) to S1, containing all keywords which describe the content shared by L1. Thus the content of L1 is available in the Gnutella 0.6 network. To be on the safe side, L1 additionally sends a PING message to S1, from which it receives in response three PONG messages announcing the presence of S1, S2 and S3. Thus L1 can still stay connected to the Gnutella 0.6 network, even when S1 fails. For illustration Figure 5.25, also shows how a PING message initiated by S1 is flooded in the Superpeer layer. This is completely in accordance with the Gnutella 0.4 protocol, except that the PING messages are not forwarded to the Leafnodes.

To illustrate further on the search behavior in a Gnutella 0.6 network we assume, that L1 searches an object, whose description matches objects shared by L3, L5 and L7. To initiate the search L1 sends a QUERY message containing the description of the requested object to S1. As only L2 announced to share an object matching the request, S1 forwards this QUERY only to L3. Additionally S1 floods the QUERY in the Superpeer layer, i.e. forwards it to S2 and S3. S2 and S3 also flood it further on in the Superpeer layer, i.e. S2 sends it to S3 and vice versa (assumption: S2 did not receive the QUERY before from S3 and S3 neither from S2). These two QUERY-messages are taken from the network and not flooded any further. However, as the routing table of L5 on S2 and the routing table of L7 on S3 result in a match upon a comparison with received request, S2 forwards the QUERY to L5 and S3 forwards it to L7. Upon receiving the QUERY, L3, L5 and L7 initiate each a QUERYHIT (QUHIT) message, which is then routed back on the shortest path through the overlay to node L1. Now L1 is able to establish a HTTP connection to L3, L5 or L7 to download the requested object.

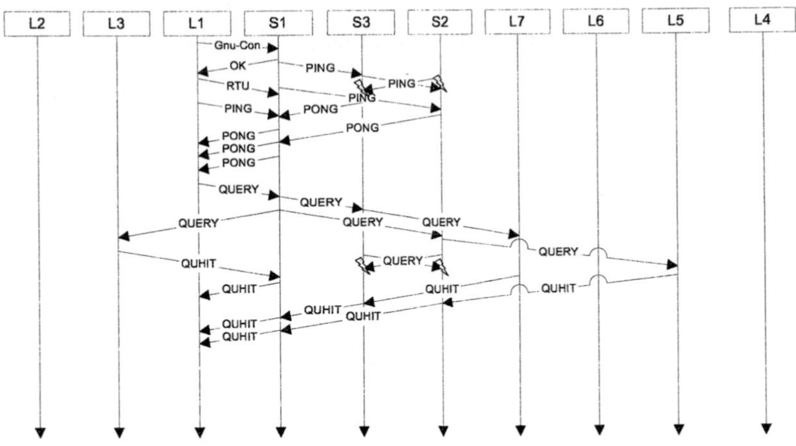

Fig. 5.25: Sample message sequence chart to illustrate the basic signaling behavior of Gnutella 0.6

If we calculate the traffic caused by one node, we again assume 34 byte for the connection message pair (GnuCon+OK). Further on we have to take into account the ROUTE_TABLE_UPDATE (RTU) message with 269 byte. Further on we have to take one seventh (as seven peers participate) of the PING/PONG traffic between the Superpeers into account, which results in our example in 4 PING messages and two PONG messages for every Superpeer, i.e. in total in 12 PING and 6 PONG messages. In addition for S1 we have to take into account three additional PONG messages and one PING message. This results in a total of approximately 508 byte. For the search traffic we also have to take into account one seventh of the previously exchanged RTU-messages, which results in 269 messages, i.e. one RTU message, which we took into account already above. Further on we have to take into account in this example eight QUERY messages (each with 78.4 byte) and eight QUERYHIT messages (each with 748.4 byte). This would result in a total of 6614 bytes for the search traffic. In total the traffic caused by this node can thus be computed to 7122 bytes. This is already less than the traffic caused by the Gnutella 0.4 network. However especially in large, i.e. more realistic, networks the advantage of hybrid Peer-to-Peer networks becomes more evident, as the amount of flooded messages is reduced significantly by the introduction of Superpeers.

Other protocols which establish a similar hierarchical overlay routing structure are edonkey2000 [410] and FastTrack. Applications like Kazaa [343] or Skype [567] and emule [191] or mldonkey [423] are based on these. In FastTrack the peers in the higher hierarchical level are called Superpeers and in edonkey2000 they are simply called servers. Both protocols are proprietary and therefore they are not officially and publicly documented. However a number of details of the two protocols have been re-engineered by users and creators of open source alternative applications [184, 188, 243, 358]. Already some basic measurements, mostly on IP-level, are available, concerning packet and data rates [43, 336, 600].

6. Random Graphs, Small-Worlds and Scale-Free Networks

Katharina Anna Lehmann, Michael Kaufmann
(University of Tübingen)

6.1 Introduction

In this chapter we will introduce two famous network models that arose much interest in recent years: The small-world model of Duncan Watts and Steven Strogatz [615] and scale-free or power-law networks, first presented by the Faloutsos brethren [201] and filled with life by a model of Albert-László Barabási and Réka Alberts [60]. These models describe some structural aspects of most real-world networks. The most prevalent network structure of small-world networks is a local mesh-like part combined with some random edges that make the network small.

The preceding chapters sketched the field of Peer-to-Peer concepts and applications. The field and its history are deeply intertwined with the area of distributed computing and sometimes overlaps with concepts from client-server systems and ad hoc networks. To set a clear foundation we base this chapter on the following, quite general definition of Peer-to-Peer systems:

Definition 6.1.1. *Peer-to-Peer Systems*
A Peer-to-Peer system consists of computing elements that are:

(1) connected by a network,
(2) addressable in a unique way, and
(3) share a common communication protocol.

All computing elements, synonymously called nodes or peers, have comparable roles and share responsibility and costs for resources.

The functions of Peer-to-Peer systems are manifold. They may be coarsely subsumed under **communication of information, sharing services, and sharing resources**. To implement these functions, the system has to provide some infrastructure. What are the requirements to make a Peer-to-Peer infrastructure useful? Here, we will concentrate on the following four conditions:

Condition 1 Decentrality
One inherent claim of the Peer-to-Peer idea is that there is no central point in which all information about the system, data and users is stored. If there is no central organizing element

R. Steinmetz and K. Wehrle (Eds.): P2P Systems and Applications, LNCS 3485, pp. 57-76, 2005.

in a system, each node needs some built-in rules with which it can, e.g., join the system, route information to others, or make queries.

Condition 2 Structure
To share data and other resources efficiently it is helpful if the system is structured in a way that improves searching and facilitates routing.

Condition 3 Reliability despite Dynamic Changes
Nearly all Peer-to-Peer systems are under constant changes: nodes join the system, others leave it, and some are just temporarily unavailable. This necessitates elaborate mechanisms to stabilize important system properties like the diameter and connectivity of the system.

Condition 4 Scalability
One effect of decentralization is that the number of nodes may be arbitrarily large. Nonetheless, the system should be able to service the needs of all nodes in an efficient and fast way.

These four conditions are especially interesting and resemble features of social networks: A social network is inherently self-organized but nonetheless structured. Despite the fact that people are born and die, many global structural properties of social networks are stable. Further, there seems to be no limit to the number of humans that can take part in our global social network - only with respect to the network's structure, of course.
Other 'real' networks that have evolved over time show similar properties, like the Internet, metabolic networks, or the WWW [201, 60, 324]. What makes evolving, decentralized networks structured and stable despite their dynamics? Recent research has revealed that there are two important properties of evolving networks that help to satisfy the above conditions: The first property is termed the *small-world effect*, the second property is a *scale-free degree distribution*. Networks with a small-world effect are called **small-worlds** and networks with a scale-free degree distribution are called **Scale-Free Networks**. Peer-to-peer systems that create overlay networks with these features are likely to satisfy the conditions without further concern. This chapter presents both properties, presents families of networks that display these features and the corresponding decentralized models to create them. To do so, we first define some notions in graph theory in Sec. 6.2. In Sec. 6.3 we will briefly describe how the analysis of social networks was challenged by a series of elegant experiments in the 1960's. Sec. 6.4 presents the most common models that answer the questions raised by those experiments. Specifically, these are models that create families of Small Worlds and Scale-Free networks. In Sec. 6.5 we describe approaches that build small-worlds or Scale-Free overlay networks in Peer-to-Peer systems. In this section we will present the most important properties of each of the network families which influence the per-

formance of Peer-to-Peer systems. In Sec. 6.6 we will summarize the results and discuss possible improvements.

6.2 Definitions

Let $V = \{1, 2, 3, \ldots, n\}$ be the set of all n *nodes*, or *peers*, in the system. Each node is identified and addressable by its number. The underlying network makes it possible to route a message from each node to any other node. Because of the decentralized nature of a Peer-to-Peer system, not every node v is required to store routing information to each and every other node. The set of nodes over which node v will route outgoing messages is denoted by $N(v)$ and called the *neighbors of* v. Every Peer-to-Peer network can be associated with a graph $G = (V, E)$. E is the set of edges $e = (i, j)$ where j is a neighbor of i, i.e., there is at least one entry in the routing table of i that uses j as the next node. For edge $e = (i, j)$, i is the *source node* and j is the *target node*. The number of edges is denoted by m. G is sometimes called the *overlay network* of a Peer-to-Peer system. The edges might be weighted, e.g., with the number of entries that use j as the next node or the cost for the traverse of this edge. All edges are *directed*.

The set of edges can also be represented in the *adjacency matrix* $A(G)$ with dimension $n \times n$. a_{ij} is 1 if and only if the edge $e = (i, j) \in E$. If edges are weighted with a weight function $\omega : E \rightarrow \mathbb{R}$ then a_{ij} is commonly given by $\omega(e = (i, j))$ if $e = (i, j)$ and zero otherwise. The set of *eigenvectors* and *eigenvalues* of a matrix is defined as the set of all vectors x and real numbers λ such that:

$$Ax = \lambda x \tag{6.1}$$

The *outdegree* $k_o(v)$ of a node v is defined as the number of neighbors it has: $k_o(v) = |N(v)|$. The *indegree* $k_i(v)$ is defined as the number of neighbor sets in which v is an element: $k_i(v) = \sum_{w \in V} [v \in N(w)]$. The Boolean expression in brackets is given in Iverson-notation (see [257]) and evaluates to 1 if the expression is true and to zero otherwise. The *degree* $k(v)$ of a node v is defined as the sum of indegree and outdegree. A *path* $P(i, j)$ from node i to node j is defined as a subset $P \subseteq E$ of edges $\{e_1, e_2, \ldots, e_k\}$ where $e_1 = (i, v_1)$, $e_k = (v_{k-1}, j)$ and $\forall\ 1 < l < k$: $e_l = (v_{l-1}, l)$. The *path length* of a path P is defined as the number of edges in it. If the edge set is weighted with a weight function $\omega : E \rightarrow \mathbb{R}$, then the path length $L(P(i, j)$ of a path $P(i, j)$ of two nodes i and j is defined as:

$$L(P(i, j)) = \sum_{e \in P_s(i,j)} \omega(e) \tag{6.2}$$

In the following, we will use the first definition to reduce complexity. All further definitions can be easily transformed for weighted graphs.

Any path with minimal length between two nodes is a *shortest path* between these nodes. The *distance* $d(i,j)$ between two nodes is the length of any shortest path between them. The *diameter* $D(G)$ of a graph G is defined as the maximal distance between any two nodes in the graph:

$$D(G) = \max_{(i,j)\in V\times V} d(i,j) \tag{6.3}$$

The *average path length* $D_{\oslash}(G)$ of a graph G is defined as the sum of the distances over all pairs of nodes divided by the number of all pairs of nodes:

$$D_{\oslash}(G) = \frac{\sum_{(i,j)\in V\times V} d(i,j)}{n\cdot(n-1)} \tag{6.4}$$

A graph is *connected* if there is at least one path between every two nodes. A graph is k-connected if the removal of any set with $k-1$ nodes leaves the graph connected. Let $V_C \subseteq V$ be a subset of nodes. The *induced graph* $G(V_C) = (V_C, E_C)$ is defined as the graph with the following edge set E_C: $E_C = \{e = (i,j)|i,j \in V_C\}$. An induced graph is a *(simple) component* if it is connected.

The set of edges in a graph is formally a relation $\mathcal{R} \subseteq V \times V$ on the set of possible edges. A *network family* is an (infinite) set of graphs with the same relation. Normally, this relation is given as an algorithm that decides which edges are added to the graph and which are not.

6.3 The Riddle – Analysis of Real Networks

In the 1960's Stanley Milgram conducted a series of interesting experiments [413, 596] that posed new questions about how humans are organized into social networks: He prepared letters to a friend of his and sent them to people chosen randomly in Kansas and Nebraska (cf. Fig. 6.1). They were asked to deliver the letter but they got no more information than the name of the recipient, his profession (stock broker) and the town he lived in (Boston). Furthermore, they were asked to deliver the letter in a special way: Instead of using the address, the letter should be given to someone they knew on a first-name basis and which they thought to be 'closer' to the recipient in any way. Eventually, some of the letters reached the broker and, surprisingly, these letters did not need many steps to find him. On average, it were not more than six steps [1]. This result was very surprising because social networks are dominated by relationships to people that live and work near to us. This was especially true in a time when there was no Internet, and where cars and airplanes were too expensive to be an everyday means of transportation for

[1] Most interestingly, the concept of **six degrees of separation** was already mentioned in a short story entitled 'Chains' by the Hungarian writer Karinthy in 1929 [339]

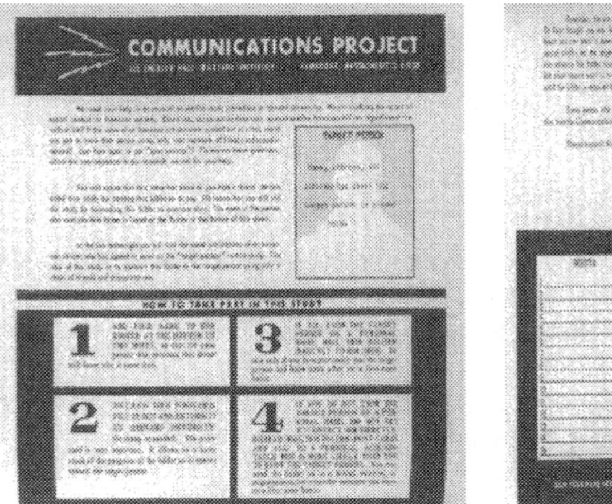

COMMUNICATIONS PROJECT

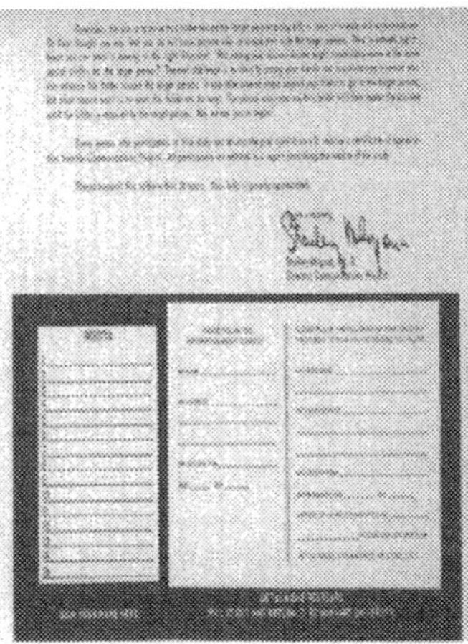

Fig. 6.1: Letter sent in the Milgram Experiment

most people. In terms of graph theory the result signifies that the diameter of social networks is quite small despite their dense local structure. What kind of network model can reproduce this special combination of properties? This is the riddle that was not to be solved until the 1990s. In the following sections we will describe the most important approaches with which social and other evolving networks are modeled today. We will show that some of the features of these networks are interesting for Peer-to-Peer applications and present ideas about how their favored properties can be transferred to Peer-to-Peer overlay networks.

6.4 Families and Models for Random Graphs, Small-Worlds and Scale-Free Networks

Historically, random graphs form the first family of networks that were intensely studied. Since many Peer-to-Peer applications choose neighbors more or less randomly, like Gnutella, this model is also valuable for the analysis of Peer-to-Peer systems.

6.4.1 Random Graphs

The analysis of social relationships as graphs can be traced back to the 1950s [614]. At the same time, the first graph models, concerning random graphs, were introduced. They were so successful that they were used as simulation models for very different networks over the following 30 years. Random graphs were introduced independently by Gilbert [245] and Erdős and Renyi [464]. We will first present the model of Erdős and Renyi, following [84].

Erdős and Renyi's Notation

$\mathcal{G}_{n,m}$ denotes the space of all $\binom{N}{m}$ graphs with n nodes and m edges where $N = \binom{n}{2}$ is the number of possible edges between n nodes. This set can be transformed into a probability space by taking the elements of $\mathcal{G}_{n,m}$ with the same probability. An instance of $\mathcal{G}_{n,m}$, drawn uniformly at random, is denoted by $G_{n,m}$. Since the whole model is based on stochastic processes, we can only give probabilistic statements about **expected properties**, i.e., we say that $G_{n,m}$ shows property P with a high probability if:

$$Pr(G_{n,m} \text{ has } P) \rightarrow 1 \text{ for } n. \rightarrow \infty \tag{6.5}$$

It is important to note here that this is only interesting if m is a function of n. If it is constant for all n, the graph will be disconnected for large n and most interesting properties like the average degree or the connectivity of the graph will vanish with $n \rightarrow \infty$. This leads to a question regarding the first important property of random graphs: When will a random graph be connected with high probability? The following theorem gives the important relationship between m and the connectedness of the resulting graph ([464]):

Theorem 6.4.1. *Connectedness of random graphs*
Let $m_\omega = \frac{n}{2}(\log n + \gamma)$ *where* $\gamma = \gamma(n)$ *is a function of* n. *If* $\gamma \rightarrow -\infty$, *then a typical* G_{n,m_γ} *is disconnected, whereas if* $\gamma \rightarrow \infty$, *a typical* G_{n,m_γ} *is connected.*

This theorem can often be found in the following form: If we ensure that the average degree of nodes is $\Omega(\log n)$, then the random graph will be connected with high probability. In the analysis of most network models it is shown that the average degree grows with $O(\log n)$ which also fulfills the above given theorem, if we set γ to $\log n$.

Gilberts Model

A totally different approach was given by Gilbert in [245]. A graph $G_{n,p}$ is defined as a graph in which the probability that an edge $e = (v, w)$ exists is p. This definition simultaneously gives a construction algorithm: For each possible edge, a random number between 0 and 1 is drawn. Whenever this number is smaller than p, the edge is added to the graph. Again, p can be a function of n, though in this case, families with constant p are also interesting to study.

Connection Between Both Random Graph Models

For $M \sim pN$ the two models $\mathcal{G}_{n,M}$ and $G_{n,p}$ are almost interchangeable [84].

Basic Results for Classical Random Graphs

Here, we will just review some of the important results for Random Graphs that are interesting in comparison with small-worlds and Scale-Free Networks, cited from [80]. We use the Gilbert notation.

For the first theorem cited, the random graph is built up sequentially, by adding random edges one at a time. Analyzing the connectivity of the evolving graph, we can make an interesting observation: After having added approximately $n/2$ edges, we get a giant connected component with a size of $\Theta(n)$ as stated in the following theorem.

Theorem 6.4.2. *Giant Connected Component*
Let $c > 0$ be a constant and $p = c/n$. If $c < 1$ every component of $G_{n,p}$ has order $O(\log n)$ with high probability. If $c > 1$ then there will be one component with high probability that has a size of $(f(c) + O(1)) \cdot n$, where $f(c) > 0$. All other components have size $O(\log n)$ [84].

This theorem is easy to remember and nonetheless surprising: The giant connected component emerges with high probability when the average degree is about **one**.

The next property concerns the degree distribution: If one node is drawn randomly from V, how high is the probability $P(k)$ that it has degree k? In random graphs the degree distribution is described as a Poisson-distribution $P(k) = \frac{c^k e^{-c}}{k!}$ as stated in the following theorem:

Theorem 6.4.3. *Degree distribution*
Let X_k be the number of nodes with degree k in $G_{n,p}$. Let c be a constant with $c > 0$ and $p = c/n$. Then, for $k = 0, 1, 2 \ldots$

$$Pr\left((1-\epsilon)\frac{c^k e^{-c}}{k!} \leq \frac{X_k}{n} \leq (1+\epsilon)\frac{c^k e^{-c}}{k!}\right) \tag{6.6}$$

as $n \to \infty$ [84].

This can easily be seen by the following argument: First, we can construct $G_{n,p}$ in a Bernoulli experiment with $\binom{n}{2}$ variables $X_{ij}, i \neq j, i, j \in V$ that are 1 with probability p. The degree of node i is the sum of all variables X_{ij} and for reasonably small p and $n \to \infty$, the degree can be described by a Poisson distribution.

The next question to be answered is the diameter of $G_{n,p}$. It is given by the following theorem:

Theorem 6.4.4. *Diameter of $G_{n,p}$*
If $pn/\log n \rightarrow \infty$ and $\log n/\log(pn) \rightarrow \infty$ then the diameter of $G_{n,p}$ is asymptotic to $\log n/\log(pn)$ with high probability.

The last property presented here is the expected *clustering coefficient* for random graphs. The clustering coefficient measures how many edges are between neighbors of node i divided by the maximum possible number of edges between them. Thus, it measures how 'clique-like' the neighborhood of node i is where a clique denotes a subgraph in which all nodes are connected to all other nodes. Let $E(N(i))$ denote the number of edges between neighbors of node i. Then, the clustering coefficient $C(i)$ is defined as:

$$C(i) = \frac{E(N(i))}{d(i)(d(i)-1)} \tag{6.7}$$

The clustering coefficient can also be interpreted as the probability that two randomly drawn neighbors of i are themselves neighbors. Seen under this perspective the following theorem is easily proven:

Theorem 6.4.5. *Clustering Coefficient of random graphs*
The clustering coefficient of a random graph is asymptotically equal to p with high probability.

Random graphs were very famous for a long time for two reasons: Many of their properties are exactly solvable in a rigorous analysis. They can be exactly defined and varied in many different ways. Second, they provide a much richer field of application than the other network model that was popular at the time, i.e., regular graphs in which every node has the same degree, such as a lattice. No one doubted that social networks cannot be exactly random, but as long as some of their properties were well described by it, it seemed that random graphs were an easy and useful way to model all kind of different networks.

6.4.2 Small-Worlds – The Riddle's First Solution

Despite the excitement that followed the Milgram experiment there was no convincing network model generating a network that is locally highly clustered and at the same time has a small diameter until 1998. Then, Watts and Strogatz [615] analyzed three different kinds of real networks: A film collaboration network in which two actors are connected by an undirected edge whenever they have acted together in at least one film, the neural network of the worm *C. elegans*, and the power grid of the United States. For each of these networks they measured the average path length in the graph and compared it with a random graph with the same number of nodes and edges. The average path length was in each case slightly higher but clearly within the same order of magnitude. On the other hand one could see that the real networks were much more densely connected on a local level than the random ones. To measure this density, the authors introduced a new measure, the *clustering coefficient* which we have already defined in Equation 6.7. Watts and Strogatz compared the average clustering coefficient of these real networks with the corresponding random networks: The clustering coefficients were at least ten times higher in real networks and for the film collaboration network the factor is more than 1000. With this analysis the surprising result of Milgram's work could be made more intelligible: Real networks have nearly the same diameter as Random Graphs and at the same time show a high, local clustering.

	$D_\oslash$(real)	$D_\oslash$(random)	C(real)	C(random)
Film collaboration	3.65	2.99	0.79	0.00027
Power grid	18.7	12.4	0.08	0.005
C. elegans	2.65	2.25	0.28	0.05

Table 6.1: Average path length $D_\oslash$ and average clustering coefficient C for three real networks, compared with random graphs that have the same number of nodes and the same average degree. The first network represents actors that are connected by an edge if they have contributed to at least one film together, the second is defined as the set of all generators, transformers and substations that are connected by high voltage transmission lines. The neural network of *C. elegans* displays all neurons and considers them as connected if they share a synapse or gap junction. All three networks show the small-world phenomenon, with an average path length comparable to that of the corresponding random graph and a clustering coefficient that is considerably larger than in the random graphs ([615]).

With this, small-worlds are defined as networks with a dense, local structure, evaluated by the clustering coefficient, and a small diameter that is comparable to that of a random graph with the same number of nodes and edges. Watts and Strogatz introduced a very simple network model that is able to reproduce this behavior. It starts with a chordal ring: Nodes are numbered from 1 to n and placed on a circle. Then, every node is connected with its k clockwise next neighbors (Fig. 6.2)

This ring is traversed and for every encountered edge a random number between zero and one is drawn. If it is smaller than a given constant $0 \leq p \leq 1$ the edge will be rewired. The rewiring is done by drawing uniformly at random a new target node from the set of all nodes V, deleting the old edge and inserting the new edge between the old source and the new target node. It is important to preclude duplicate edges in this process. If p is small,

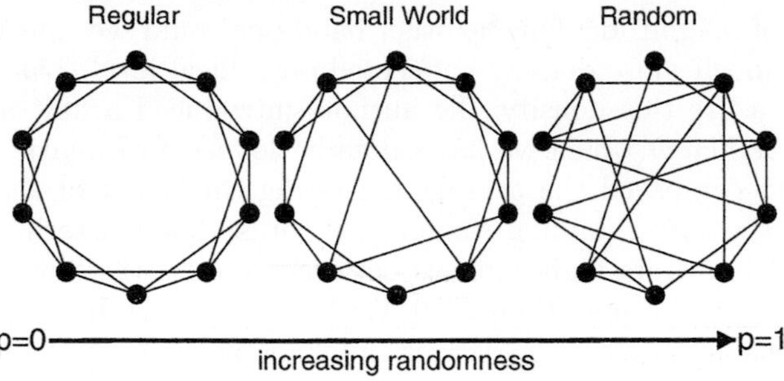

Fig. 6.2: The small-world model introduced by Watts and Strogatz [615] starts with a chordal ring in which n nodes are placed on a circle and connected with their k clockwise next neighbors (here, $k = 2$). With probability p every edge can be rewired once. The rewiring is done by choosing uniformly at random a new target node, such that the old edge is removed and the new one connects the old source node with the new target node. The figure shows that as p grows the model can be tuned between total regularity and total randomness. With sufficiently small p it is possible to maintain the local structure and yet provide an overall small diameter. This state thus displays the properties of small-worlds as they can be found in reality.

almost no edges will be rewired and the local structure is nearly completely preserved. If p is near to 1 the graph produced is claimed to be a random graph with a small average path length. Interesting are the states in between these two extremes. Fig. 6.3 shows the dependency of the clustering coefficient and average path length on p for a graph with 5000 nodes. Clearly, even a quite small p of about 0.005 is sufficient to reduce the diameter so much that it resembles the diameter in the corresponding random graph without losing the local structure that is measured with the clustering coefficient.

Viewed from another perspective, the findings of Watts and Strogatz indicate that a small number of random edges decreases the average path length significantly since they can be viewed as 'short-cuts' spanning the regular graph. With this model a part of the riddle regarding real networks was solved.

In Sect. 6.5 we will present some more properties of small-worlds that are especially interesting for Peer-to-Peer applications. In Subsect. 6.5.1 we will present a more generalized model of Small World Networks in multi-dimensional spaces, introduced by Kleinberg in [353, 354]. But despite the immediate success of the small-world model of Watts and Strogatz the riddle was only partly solved, as would soon become clear.

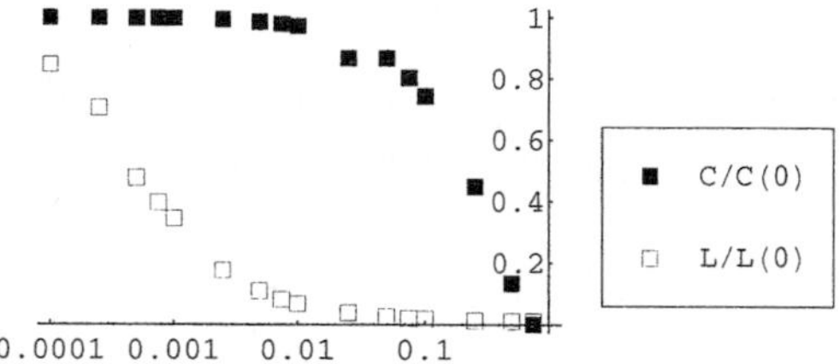

Fig. 6.3: The diagram shows the dependency of the clustering coefficient C and the average path length L on the rewiring probability p. For each probability ten different small-worlds with 5000 nodes have been simulated. The clustering coefficient of the small-world after the rewiring phase was divided by the clustering coefficient of the chordal ring before rewiring. Analogously, the average path length is given in relation to the average path length before the rewiring. It can be clearly seen that a small rewiring probability of approximately 0.005 is sufficient to reduce the average path length to 1/10 without decreasing the clustering coefficient by more than 1.5%.

6.4.3 Scale-Free Networks: How the Rich Get Richer

Although the small-world model explains how two seemingly contradictory properties can be merged into one model, it is clear that it cannot explain *how* these properties emerge in real, evolving networks. Practically no real network can be represented by a ring topology where some edges exist between two randomly chosen nodes. This is a drawback of the model.

But there is another, more significant property missing in the model: In the small-world model nearly every node has the same degree and it is very improbable that a node with a very high degree will emerge. In real random graphs the probability of drawing a node with degree k is proportional to $c^k/k!$. How probable is it to find nodes with a very high degree in real networks?

In 1999, three brothers, Michael, Petros and Christos Faloutsos, made a very extensive analysis of the Internet backbone [201]. They were interested in the following questions: "What does the Internet look like? Are there any topological properties that don't change in time? How will it look like a year from now? How can I generate Internet-like graphs for my simulations?". They examined the inter-domain topology of the Internet from the end of 1997 to the end of 1998. In this phase the Internet grew about 45% in size (number of routers). They found four properties of these networks that follow a power law:

E 1) First, a list of all existing outdegrees was made and sorted. The 'rank' r_i of a node i is defined as its place in the list according to its outdegree $k_o(i)$. The outdegree $k_o(i)$ of a node i is proportional to its rank, to the power of a constant $\mathcal{R}$:

$$k_o(i) \propto r_i^{\mathcal{R}} \tag{6.8}$$

E 2) The number of nodes f_k with the same outdegree k_o is proportional to the outdegree to the power of a constant $\mathcal{O}$:

$$f_{k_o} \propto k_o^{\mathcal{O}} \tag{6.9}$$

E 3) The eigenvalues, λ_j, of a graph are proportional to the order, j, to the power of a constant, $\mathcal{E}$:

$$\lambda_j \propto j^{\mathcal{E}} \tag{6.10}$$

E 4) The total number $P(d)$ of pairs of nodes (i, j) within a distance $d(i, j) \leq d$ is proportional to the degree d to the power of a constant $\mathcal{H}$:

$$P(d) \propto d^{\mathcal{H}} \tag{6.11}$$

This last property is more approximative than the other properties but is nonetheless useful as the authors show in their paper [201].

After the authors had found this self-organizing structure, they asked in their discussion "Why would such an unruly entity like the Internet follow any statistical regularities?". The answer to this question was given by an elegant model of Barabási and Albert in the same year[60]. They examined a part of the World Wide Web (WWW) [60] (see also [20]) and displayed the result as a graph. In this graph, all visited pages were represented as nodes, and two pages were connected by a directed edge (i, j) if page i had a link pointing to page j. In this graph the number of nodes with a given degree was calculated. By dividing it by the number of nodes in the graph, the probability $P(k)$ of drawing uniformly at random a node with degree k is computed. The authors observed that the probability $P(k)$ is proportional to k to the power of a constant γ (similar to E3 above):

$$P(k) \propto k^{-\gamma} \tag{6.12}$$

Networks with this property are called *Scale-Free Networks*, or sometimes *Power-Law Networks*. Barabási and Albert also examined the film collaboration network and power-grid of the USA and found the same property there. To model this property they introduced the following new model that differs in two important aspects from the small-world model and random graph model:

The Barabási-Albert-Model

1. The network grows in time.
2. A new node joining the network will have preferences to whom it wants to be connected. This *preferential attachment* is modeled in the following way: Each new node i wants to connect to m_0 other nodes that are

already in the network. The probability $\Pi_t(j)$ that some old node j gets one of the m edges is proportional to its current degree $k_t(j)$ at time t:

$$\Pi(j) = \frac{k_t(j)}{\sum_{v \in V} k_t(v)} \tag{6.13}$$

$$= \frac{k_t(j)}{2 \cdot m_t} \tag{6.14}$$

with m_t being the number of edges in the graph at time t.

Thus, the network model works as follows:

1. Begin with a small network of at least m_0 nodes and some edges.
2. In each simulation step add one node. For each of its m_0 edges draw one of the nodes j that are already in the graph, each with probability $\Pi(j)$.

It should be clear that this algorithm is not a model in the mathematical sense [80] but rather defines a family of possible implementations. Later, Albert and Barabási could show in [22, 19] that the only requirement for the emergence of a scale-free behavior is that the probability of gaining a new edge is proportional to the degree of a node in each timestep. Thus, it is sufficient that any network model show this preferential attachment in order to generate scale-free networks. This property can be easily remembered as a behavior in which 'the rich get richer'.
To date, many different variants of network models that generate scale-free networks have been published: A mathematical model more precisely defined than the Barabási-Albert-model is the *linearized chord diagram*, introduced in [79]. Here, two groups provide each node with an initial attractiveness that increases the probability of being chosen by a constant value [180, 175]. A quite complicated but powerful model with many parameters was given in [132].

A model that is simple to adapt to Peer-to-Peer systems was first introduced by Kumar et al. [369] for web graphs, and independently by Vazquez et al. [605] and Pastor-Satorras et al. [477] for modeling protein interaction networks: In each timestep of this model, one of the existing nodes is cloned with all the links to other nodes and the clones are connected to each other. Then, both clones lose some edges at random with a very small probability and gain as many new edges to new, randomly drawn target nodes. It can be easily shown that the probability of node j getting a new node in timestep t is proportional to its degree at that time: The more edges it has, the more probable it is that one of its neighbors is chosen to be cloned. If one of the neighbors is cloned, the edge to j is copied and thus the degree of j is increased by 1. Thus, this model shows preferential attachment and the resulting networks are scale-free with respect to the degree distribution.

In the following we want to discuss some of the properties of Small Worlds and Scale-Free Networks that are interesting for Peer-to-Peer systems.

6.5 Applications to Peer-to-Peer Systems

6.5.1 Navigating in Small-Worlds

Jon Kleinberg was also intrigued by the experiments conducted by Milgram and the simple small-world model given by Watts and Strogatz. This latter model explained why there exist short paths in a social network where only a small fraction of edges are actually random. But Kleinberg saw that there was more to it: he asked himself why people can *find* these short paths: "Why should arbitrary pairs of strangers be able to *find* short chains of acquaintances that link them together?" [354]
This question is totally different from the question of why short paths *exist* in a network. It is easy to invent a network with low average path length but where it is impossibility to find those short paths: The difficulty arises if every node just has local information. This is certainly the case in social networks: here, every person just knows a very small number of people on a first-name basis. Of these, one may also know some more data, like the profession, address, hobbies, and so on. When challenged with the task of sending a letter to a stranger via acquaintances, people choose the one friend that they think to be 'next' to the recipient. Milgram's results showed experimentally that the first steps of the letter were the largest (geographically) while later they became shorter as they were closing in on the target area [413].

The aim of Kleinberg was thus to find a family of simple networks with small average path length in which decentralized algorithms are able to find short paths. We will first begin with the underlying network model. It is applicable to multi-dimensional spaces, but here it will be represented in a twodimensional space for simplicity.

The Kleinberg Small-World Model

The model starts with a set of grid points in an $n \times n$ square. Each node i is identified by the two coordinates x_i, y_i that define its position $P(i)$ in the grid. The distance $d'(i,j)$ is here defined as the number of 'lattice steps' separating them:

$$d'(i,j) = |x_i - x_j| + |y_i - y_j| \tag{6.15}$$

The set of (directed) edges is constructed in two parts:

1. First, every node i is connected with all nodes j that are within distance $d'(i,j) \leq q$ for some given integer q.
2. Second, for each node i q additional edges are built. The probability that the ith directed edge has endpoint j is proportional to $d'(i,j)^{-r}$, with r a given real constant. To generate a proper probability distribution, the normalizing constant is given by $\sum_{v \in V} d'(i,v)^{-r}$. This probability distribution is called the *inverse* r^{th}*-power distribution.*

If p and q are given as fixed constants, this network family is described only by parameter r.

Now, a message is to be sent within this network. The transmission model is as follows: We start with two arbitrary nodes in the network, source node s and target node t. The goal is to transmit the message from s to t with as few steps as possible. An algorithm is defined as *decentralized* if at any time-step the current message holder u has knowledge of only:

DA 1) the set of local contacts among all nodes (i.e. the underlying grid structure),
DA 2) the position, $P(t)$, of target node t on the grid, and
DA 3) the locations and long-range contacts of all nodes that have come in contact with the message.

Here, we just want to state the results of this approach. The proofs can be found in [354]. The first result is that there is only one possible parameter for r in a twodimensional grid where a decentralized algorithm is able to perform the transmission task in expected $O(\log n)$ steps. This efficiency is measured as the *expected delivery time*, i.e., the number of steps before the message reaches its target:

Theorem 6.5.1. *Navigability in Kleinberg Small-Worlds*
There is a decentralized algorithm $\mathcal{A}$ *and a constant* α, *independent of* n, *so that when* $r = 2$ *and* $p = q = 1$, *the expected delivery time is at most* $\alpha \cdot (\log n)^2$.

The next theorem shows that $r = 2$ is the only parameter for which the expected delivery time is polynomial in $O(\log n)$:

Theorem 6.5.2. *(a) Let* $0 \leq r < 2$. *There is a constant* α_r, *depending on* p, q, r, *but independent of* n *so that the expected delivery time of any decentralized algorithm is at least* $\alpha_r n^{(2-r)/3}$.
(b) Let $r > 2$. *There is a constant* α_r, *depending on* p, q, r, *but independent of* n, *so that the expected delivery time of any decentralized algorithm is at least* $\alpha_r n^{(r-2)/(r-1)}$.

These results can be generalized for multi-dimensional spaces. For any k-dimensional space, a decentralized algorithm can construct paths of length polynomial in $O(\log n)$ if and only if $r = k$.

What does this decentralized algorithm look like? In each step, the current message-holder u chooses a contact that is as close to the target as possible, in terms of lattice distance. And that is all. Note, that this very simple algorithm does not make use of DA 3). Accordingly, we do not need any memorization of the route a message has taken to get to node i.

Summarizing, Kleinberg-small-worlds provide a way of building an overlay network for Peer-to-Peer applications, in which a very simple, greedy and local routing protocol is applicable. On the other hand, it requires some information that is not naturally given in a Peer-to-Peer system, namely a distinct mapping for nodes and files to a k-dimensional position. In principle, this can be provided by a *distributed hash table* (DHT) approach but this is not always possible. For more information on DHTs see Chapter 7.

Second, we need a metric that allows us to measure the distance between two positions in the system. Third, and somewhat counter-intuitive to the decentralized approach, we need some global information, especially a list of **all** neighbors within a given distance and a list of all other nodes in the system and their distance to a given node, to choose the q longe range contacts. The next subsections give some approaches that try to achieve this. Protocols discussed in these subsections are explained in more detail in Chapter 8.

6.5.2 Small-World Overlay Networks in Peer-to-Peer Systems

Some papers indicate that Peer-to-Peer systems sometimes voluntarily evolve into a small-world [16, 302, 639]. For Freenet it could be shown that a low to medium load, in terms of the number of files in the system, leads to a small-world network. This is achieved by the following routing table update: Every file is correlated with a key, e.g., by a hash function. The file is originally stored at some node with a similar key. Each request is at every time forwarded to the one node in the routing table that has the closest key to the requested key. The request has a *time to live (TTL)*, i.e., there is a counter in the request that is incremented with every forwarding, and the request is removed when the counter reaches TTL. If a node has no more neighbors to route a request to, it will send a backtracking 'request failed' message. If the request is successful, the file will be sent over the routing nodes back to the requesting node. Every routing node will thereby save the file and add the sending node's key to its routing table. If either the file space or the routing table space is full, the *least recently used (LRU)* entry is replaced by the new entry. With this simple LRU-replacement algorithm, the system copies frequently requested files and most files in the file space are requested many times before they are replaced. But with a high load, i.e., a high number of different files and requests, the set of files at each node is rapidly changing and the number of successful requests for any of the stored files decreases. This unexpected behavior motivated Zhang, Goel, and Govindan to use a small-world overlay network to improve Freenet's performance [639]. The authors try to build a network in which most files on one node were 'close neighbors', and only some of the stored files are 'distant' files. The notion of distance $d(i, x)$ used here is given by the hashkey of each file i to a given random seed x from the key space S. The algorithm works as follows:

1. Each node i chooses a seed $s(x)$ randomly from the key space S when it joins the system.

2. When the datastore at a node is full and a new file f with key $key(f)$ arrives (from either a new insertion of a file or a successful request), the node finds out from the current datastore the file with key v farthest from the seed in terms of the distance in the key space S:

$$d_{\max}(datastore) = \max_{\text{file } g \text{ in datastore}} d(key(g), x) \tag{6.16}$$

(a) If $d(key(f), s(x)) < d_{\max}$ cache f and evict v. Create an entry for f in the routing table. This has the effect of clustering the keys in the routing table around the seed of the node.
(b) Otherwise, cache f, evict v, and create an entry for f in the routing table only with a probability p (randomness). This has the effect of creating a few random shortcuts.

The authors fixed p to 0.03 because this value worked best in the experiments conducted. The procedure is called the *Enhanced-clustering Cache Replacement Scheme* and produces routing table entries that resemble small-worlds in the sense that each node preferentially stores those files that are near to its own key. The authors show that this small, local improvement is able to increase the hit ratio significantly, where the *hit ratio* is defined as the ratio of the number of successful requests to the total number of requests made. The approach of Zhang, Goel and Govindan follows quite closely the original small-world concept of Watts and Strogatz.

Another approach that is more closely related to the Kleinberg small-worlds is given by a protocol named *Symphony* [400]. This approach is similar to the first in that it also relies on a hash-function that assigns each file a unique key with which it is addressable. The idea is that all nodes are placed on a circle with unit perimeter and every node is responsible for (stores) all files with a key equal to or greater than its own key and smaller than the key of the next node. This part of the circle is its *segment of responsibility.* The joining node draws its position on the circle uniformly at random from the interval $[0, 1[$ and connects to its next neighbor on each side. In this property it resembles the *Chord* protocol, introduced in [575]. Additionally, every node tries to connect to k randomly drawn nodes. The probability that a connection with a node responsible for x is established is given by the following probability distribution:

$$P(X == x) = \frac{1}{x \log n} \tag{6.17}$$

This approach has the problem that the total number of nodes n has to be known in advance. The authors estimate this value from the length of the circle each node is responsible for: If all nodes draw their position uniformly at random, the expected mean length of the segment of responsibility is $1/n$. Averaging these lengths over a set of known nodes, the number of nodes in the system can be approximated. The probability distribution belongs to the family of harmonic distributions (a fact which inspired the name for the protocol). As in the Kleinberg paper, the actual routing protocol is greedy: Every message holder sends it to the one node known to have a key next to the requested file key.

The authors ensure that no node has more than a fixed number k of (incoming) long range contacts. If, by chance, one node asks to establish a long-range link to a node that has already reached this number, the latter will refuse the new connection. The most interesting property of this protocol is that it shows a trade-off between the number of links a node has and the expected path length within the network to find a file:

Theorem 6.5.3. *Symphony*
The expected path length in an n-node network with $k = O(1)$ edges, built by the Symphony protocol, is inversely proportional to k and proportional to $(\log n)^2$.

This is true whether long-range links are used in one direction only (from the one building it to the one randomly chosen) or in both directions.

The Symphony approach is elegant and smoothly transforms the idea of Kleinberg small-worlds to the world of Peer-to-Peer systems. An even more sophisticated approach was given by Hui, Lui and Yau in [309]. In their *Small-World Overlay Protocol (SWOP)*, clusters emerge in a self-organized way. The basic idea is again based on a hash-function and nodes that are placed on a unit-perimeter circle. Additionally, every node tries to connect to one random node with the probability distribution in Equation 6.17. Here, n is the number of clusters in the system.

A new node joining the circle will be the basis for a new cluster if both of its neighbors are members of a cluster with a maximum size. Otherwise, it will join the cluster with smaller size and create some *intra-cluster connections*. The maximal cluster size is given as a variable of the system and might be changed dynamically. Each cluster has one designated *head node* that is chosen by some periodically repeated voting mechanism. This head node is responsible for maintaining some 'long-range' inter-cluster connections. The routing protocol is the same greedy protocol used in the other approach: Each message holder will send the message to the one node known to have a key next to the requested file key.

The article is mainly concerned with the proper behavior of a protocol in a *flash crowd scenario*: These are situations, in which some static or dynamic object is heavily requested. The example provided by the authors is the crush on the CNN web server for news documents that was initiated by the 9/11 incident. Here, the news consists not only of static documents but might also be changing within minutes. A careful distribution within the net can prevent server crashes.

The idea proposed by the authors is that heavily requested documents should be copied via the *inter*-cluster links so that nearly every cluster has its own copy. This is sufficient in static scenarios, but an additional version number has to be maintained if the document is changing. The source node can then send update messages over the long-range connections to other nodes holding the copy. The nodes within a cluster can be informed by using local links. Because of the small-world character of the protocol, the clustering coefficient of such a system is high and, depending on the cluster size and the actual value of the clustering coefficient, the update message soon reaches all members of the cluster.

6.5.3 Scale-Free Overlay Networks in Peer-to-Peer Systems

The most prominent feature of Scale-Free Networks is its fault tolerance [21, 129]. Since the degree is very heterogeneously distributed in the system, a random failure will very likely strike one of the nodes with low degree. These are most often not crucial for the connectivity of the network. It has been shown [21] that the diameter of the Internet at the autonomous system level in July, 2000 would not be changed considerably if up to 2.5% of the routers were removed randomly. This is an order of magnitude larger than the failure rate.

The authors further compared the fragmentation of random graphs and Scale-Free Networks. By randomly removing nodes from a random graph the network will soon fragment. For a failure rate of 5% in networks with 10,000 nodes the biggest connected component holds approximately 9,000 nodes. For a failure rate of 18% there is no biggest connected component any more, but only components with a size between 1 and 100. For a failure rate of 45% all components have only one or two nodes. For Scale-Free Networks the story is different: For a failure rate of 5% only some one- or two-node components break off the network. For a failure rate of 18%, the biggest connected component still holds 8,000 nodes with isolated clusters of size 1 to 5. Even for an unrealistically high failure rate of 45% the large cluster persists and the size of the broken-off fragments is below 12.

This behavior is desired for most Peer-to-Peer systems because it stabilizes the network structures in these highly dynamic systems. Fortunately, some of the protocols in Peer-to-Peer systems generate this favoured network topology for free: The idea of Gnutella is that every new node joining the system first connects to a handful of known servers. Later, it remembers some of the nodes involved in queries it is interested in. It could be shown that this behavior leads to pure scale-free or scale-free-like networks [516, 534].

On the other hand, the same scale-free architecture makes a network extremely vulnerable to attacks [21, 129, 532]: If it is possible to detect the hubs of the system and to attack them, e.g., with a Denial-of-Service-Attack, the network is more rapidly fragmented than the corresponding random graph. This led Keyani, Larson and Senthil to the idea of changing the network architecture as soon as an attack is detected. With a local protocol, each node is enabled to decide whether the loss of a neighbor node is probably the result of an attack. To do so, the node periodically tries to connect to its immediate and second degree neighbors (neighbors of neighbors). If, in time period T, the percentage of lost second degree neighbors is greater than the percentage of lost direct neighbors and a given threshold P, an attack is assumed. For this eventuality, every node holds a list of random contacts to other nodes. This list is collected during normal work, e.g., while receiving a query or other messages. In case of a detected attack all detecting nodes establish connections to these nodes, and a random graph is generated. Of course, for 'friendly' times the more robust scale-free network is still favoured and will be restored after the attack is over.

6.6 Summary

This chapter has presented three prominent network models that are able to model different aspects of many complex and dynamic networks. First was the random graph model. It is easy to simulate and many properties can be analyzed with stochastic methods. It can be a good model for some Peer-to-Peer systems. Other Peer-to-Peer systems exhibit the so-called small-world effect: High clustering of nodes that share similar interests and just a few links between nodes with very different interests. These few 'long-range' or 'short-cut' links decrease the diameter such that the average path length in these networks is almost as short as in a random graph with the same number of nodes and links. Finally, we presented a model that generates scale-free networks. In these networks the presence of highly connected nodes ('hubs') is much more probable than in random graphs, i.e., the probability of finding a node $P(k)$ is proportional to $k^{-\gamma}$, where γ is a constant.

Small-world networks are interesting for Peer-to-Peer systems because they provide a good way to structure nodes with similar interests into groups without losing the small diameter of random graphs. Scale-free networks exhibit a good fault tolerance, but on the other hand, the are extremely vulnerable to attacks.

As shown, some authors have already tackled the problem of how desired properties of these three network models can be transmitted to overlay networks in Peer-to-Peer systems using simple and local protocols. Future research will have to show which kind of network model is best for building structured, yet self-organizing overlay networks for Peer-to-Peer systems that are stable despite dynamic changes and scale nicely under the constantly increasing number of peers.

Part III

Structured Peer-to-Peer Systems

7. Distributed Hash Tables

Klaus Wehrle, Stefan Götz, Simon Rieche (University of Tübingen)

In the last few years, an increasing number of massively distributed systems with millions of participants has emerged within very short time frames. Applications, such as instant messaging, file-sharing, and content distribution have attracted countless numbers of users. For example, Skype gained more than 2.5 millions of users within twelve months, and more than 50% of Internet traffic is originated by BitTorrent. These very large and still rapidly growing systems attest to a new era for the design and deployment of distributed systems [52]. In particular, they reflect what the major challenges are today for designing and implementing distributed systems: *scalability*, *flexibility*, and *instant deployment*.

As already defined in Chapter 2, the Peer-to-Peer paradigm relies on the design and implementation of distributed systems where each system has (nearly) the same functionality and responsibility. By definition, these systems have to coordinate themselves in a distributed manner without centralized control and without the use of centralized services. Thus, scalability should be an inherent property of Peer-to-Peer systems. Unfortunately, not all of them have shown this to be true so far. In this chapter, we will demonstrate this by discussing the *lookup problem* – a fundamental challenge for all kinds of massively distributed and Peer-to-Peer systems.

First, we introduce the problem of managing and retrieving data in distributed systems, compare three basic approaches for this, and show that some of them do not scale well, even though they are Peer-to-Peer approaches. As a result, we introduce the promising concept of the Distributed Hash Table (DHT) for designing and deploying highly scalable distributed systems. In this chapter, we focus only on the basic properties and mechanisms of Distributed Hash Tables; specifics of certain DHT approaches are presented in the next chapter.

The remainder of this chapter is organized as follows. After discussing in Section 7.1 general concepts for distributed management and retrieval of data in Peer-to-Peer systems, the subsequent sections introduce Distributed Hash Tables, in particular their fundamentals (Section 7.2), the concept of content-based routing (Section 7.3), and DHT interfaces (Section 7.4). The next chapter presents specific algorithms of popular DHT approaches, e.g., how to organize the address space, and how routing in a Distributed Hash Table is performed. In Chapter 9, we discuss aspects of reliability and load-balancing in Distributed Hash Tables.

R. Steinmetz and K. Wehrle (Eds.): P2P Systems and Applications, LNCS 3485, pp. 79-93, 2005.

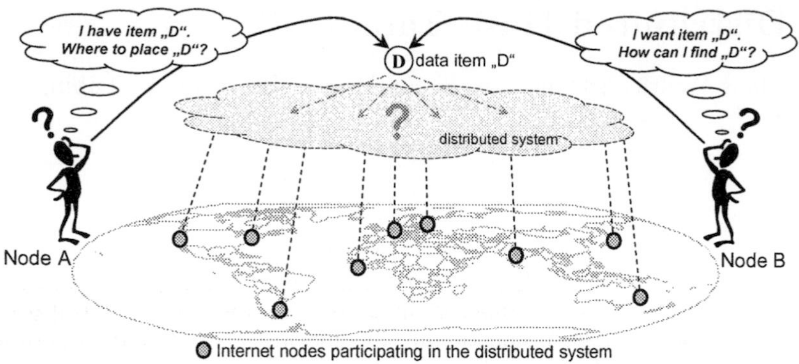

Fig. 7.1: The lookup problem: Node A wants to store a data item D in the distributed system. Node B wants to retrieve D without having prior knowledge of D's current location. How should the distributed system, especially data placement and retrieval, be organized (in particular, with regard to scalability and efficiency)?

7.1 Distributed Management and Retrieval of Data

Peer-to-Peer systems and applications raise many interesting research questions. Because of the completely decentralized character of Peer-to-Peer systems, the distributed coordination of resources, such as storage, computational power, human presence, and connectivity becomes a major challenge (Section 2.1). In most cases, these challenges can be reduced to a single problem: *Where to store, and how to find a certain data item in a distributed system without any centralized control or coordination?* (Figure 7.1) [52]

The lookup problem can be defined as follows: Some node A wants to store a data item D in the distributed system. D may be some (small) data item, the location of some bigger content, or coordination data, e.g., the current status of A, or its current IP address, etc. Then, we assume some node B wants to retrieve data item D later. The interesting questions are now:

- Where should node A store data item D?
- How do other nodes, e.g., node B, discover the location of D?
- How can the distributed system[1] be organized to assure scalability and efficiency?

The remainder of this section presents three approaches to answer these questions and discusses the advantages of drawbacks for each.

[1] In the context of Peer-to-Peer systems, the distributed system – the collection of participating nodes pursuing the same purpose – is often called the *overlay network* or *overlay system*.

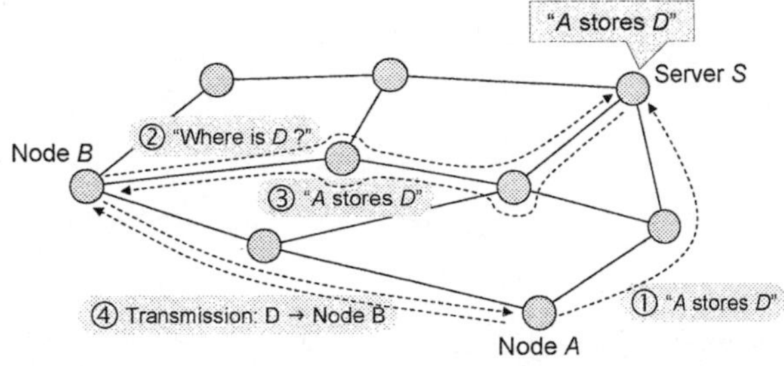

Fig. 7.2: Central Server: (1) Node A publishes its content on the central server S. (2) Some node B requests the actual location of a data item D from the central server S. (3) If existing, S replies with the actual location of D. (4) The requesting node B transmits the content directly from node A.

7.1.1 Comparison of Strategies for Data Retrieval

This section advocates the use of Distributed Hash Tables by comparing three basic strategies to store and retrieve data in distributed systems: *centralized servers*, *flooding search*, and *distributed indexing*.

7.1.2 Central Server

The approach of first generation Peer-to-Peer systems, such as Napster [436], is to maintain the current locations of data items in a central server. After joining the Peer-to-Peer system, a participating node submits to the central server information about the content it stores and/or the services it offers. Thus, requests are simply directed to the central server that responds to the requesting node with the current location of the data (Figure 7.2). Thereupon, the transmission of the located content is organized in a Peer-to-Peer fashion between the requesting node B and the node storing D.

The server-based approach is common in many application scenarios and was the major design principle for distributed applications in the past decades. It has the advantage of retrieving the location of the desired information with a search complexity of $O(1)$ – the requester just has to know the central server. Also, fuzzy and complex queries are possible, since the server has a global overview of all available content. However, the central server approach has major drawbacks, which have been become increasingly evident in recent years. The central server is a critical element within the whole system concerning scalability and availability. Since all location information is stored on a single machine, the complexity in terms of memory consumption is $O(N)$, with N representing the number of items available in the distributed system. The server also represents a single point of failure

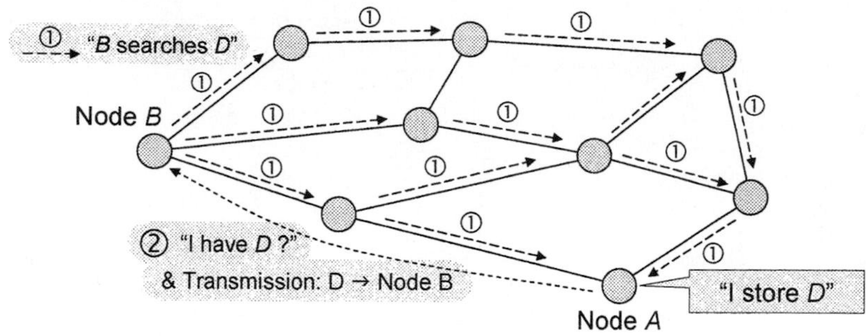

Fig. 7.3: Flooding Search: No routing information is maintained in intermediate nodes. (1) Node A sends a request for item D to its "neighbors" in the distributed system. They forward the request to further nodes in a recursive manner (flooding/breadth-first search). (2) Node(s) storing D send an answer to A, and A transmits D directly from the answering node(s).

and attack. If it fails or becomes unavailable for either of these reasons, the distributed system – as a whole – is no longer useable.

Overall, the central server approach is best for simple and small applications or systems with a limited number of participants, since the costs for data retrieval are in the order of $O(1)$ and the amount of network load (in proximity of the server) and the necessary storage capacity increase by $O(N)$. But, scalability and availability are vital properties, especially when systems grow by some orders of magnitude or when system availability is crucial. Therefore, more scalable and reliable solutions need to be investigated.

7.1.3 Flooding Search

Distributed systems with a central server are very vulnerable since all requests rely on the server's availability and consistency. An opposite approach is pursued by the so-called second generation of Peer-to-Peer systems (cf. Chapter 5.3). They keep no explicit information about the location of data items in other nodes, other than the nodes actually storing the content. This means that there is no additional information concerning where to find a specific item in the distributed system. Thus, to retrieve an item D the only chance is to ask as much participating nodes as necessary, whether or not they presently have item D, or not. Second generation Peer-to-Peer systems rely on this principle and broadcast a request for an item D among the nodes of the distributed system. If a node receives a query, it floods this message to other nodes until a certain hop count (Time to Live – TTL) is exceeded. Often, the general assumption is that content is replicated multiple times in the network, so a query may be answered in a small number of hops.

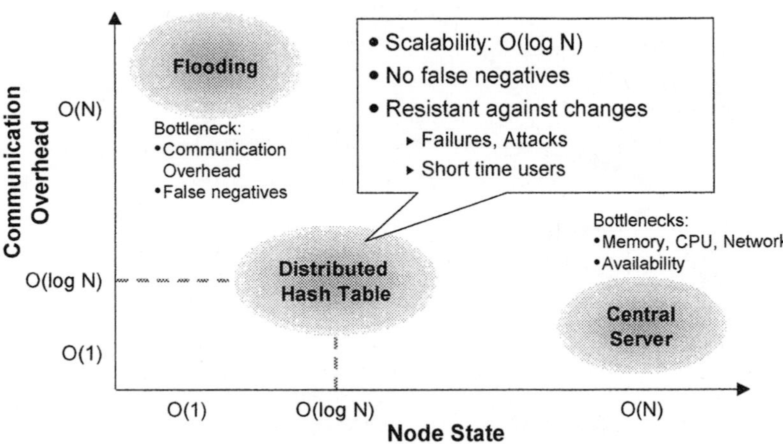

Fig. 7.4: Comparison of complexity in terms of search effort (y-axis) and storage cost per node (x-axis). Bottlenecks and special characteristics of each approach are named.

A well-known example of such an application is Gnutella [249], which is described in more detail in Section 3.4. Gnutella includes several mechanisms to avoid request loops, but it is obvious that such a broadcast mechanism does not scale well. The number of messages and the bandwidth consumed is extremely high and increases more than linearly with increasing numbers of participants. In fact, after the central server of Napster was shut down in July 2001 due to a court decision [438], an enormous number of Napster users migrated to the Gnutella network within a few days, and under this heavy network load the system collapsed (Section 3.4).

The advantage of flooding-based systems, such as Gnutella, is that there is no need for proactive efforts to maintain the network. Also, unsharp queries can be placed, and the nodes implicitly use proximity due to the expanding search mechanism. Furthermore, there is are efforts to be made when nodes join or leave the network.

But still, the complexity of looking up and retrieving a data item is $O(N^2)$, or even higher, and search results are not guaranteed, since the lifetime of request messages is restricted to a limited number of hops. On the other hand, storage cost is in the order of $O(1)$ because data is only stored in the nodes actually providing the data – whereby multiple sources are possible – and no information for a faster retrieval of data items is kept in intermediate nodes.

Overall, flooding search is an adequate technique for file-sharing-like purposes and complex queries.

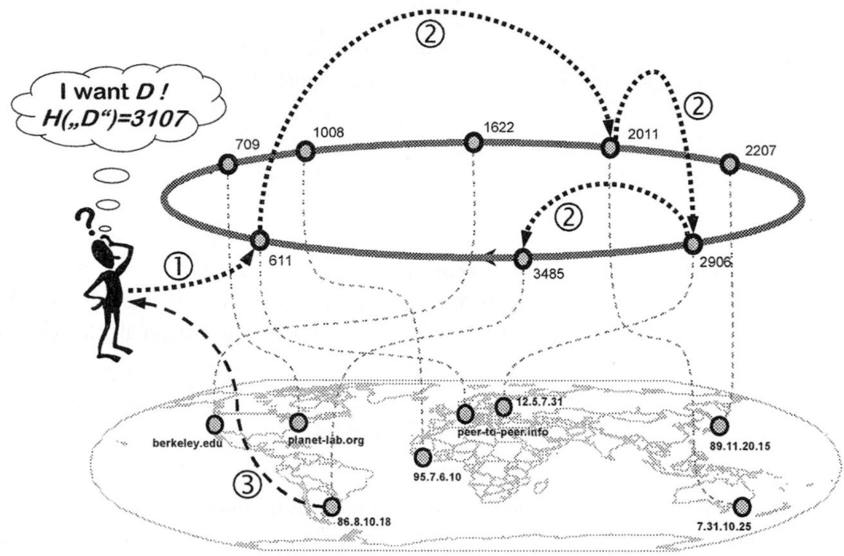

Fig. 7.5: Distributed Hash Table: The nodes in the distributed system organize themselves in a structured overlay and establish a small amount of routing information for quick and efficient routing to other overlay nodes. (1) Node A sends a request for item D to an arbitrary node of the DHT. (2) The request is forwarded according to DHT routing with $O(\log N)$ hops to the target node. (3) The target node sends D to node A.

7.1.4 Distributed Indexing – Distributed Hash Tables

Both central servers and flooding-based searching exibit crucial bottlenecks that contradict the targeted scalability and efficiency of Peer-to-Peer systems. Indeed, central servers disqualify themselves with a linear complexity for storage because they concentrate all references to data and nodes in one single system. Flooding-based approaches avoid the management of references on other nodes and, therefore, they require a costly breadth-first search which leads to scalability problems in terms of the communication overhead.

A better solution for the lookup problem should avoid these drawbacks and should enable scalability by finding the golden path between both approaches (Figure 7.4). In this case, scalability is defined as follows: the search and storage complexity per node should not increase significantly – by means not more than $O(\log N)$, even if the system grows by some orders of magnitude.

Distributed Indexing, most often in the form of Distributed Hash Tables, promises to be a suitable method for this purpose. In the realm of Peer-to-Peer systems, these approaches are also often called *structured Peer-to-Peer systems* because of their structured and proactive procedures. Distributed

Hash Tables provide a global view of data distributed among many nodes, independent of the actual location. Thereby, location of data depends on the current DHT state and not intrinsically on the data.

Overall, Distributed Hash Tables posses the following characteristics:

- In contrast to unstructured Peer-to-Peer systems, each DHT node manages a small number of references to other nodes. By means these are $O(\log N)$ references, where N depicts the number of nodes in the system.
- By mapping nodes and data items into a common address space, routing to a node leads to the data items for which a certain node is responsible.
- Queries are routed via a small number of nodes to the target node. Because of the small set of references each node manages, a data item can be located by routing via $O(\log N)$ hops. The initial node of a lookup request may be any node of the DHT.
- By distributing the identifiers of nodes and data items nearly equally throughout the system, the load for retrieving items should be balanced equally among all nodes.
- Because no node plays a distinct role within the system, the formation of hot spots or bottlenecks can be avoided. Also, the departure or dedicated elimination of a node should have no considerable effects on the functionality of a DHT. Therefore, Distributed Hash Tables are considered to be very robust against random failures and attacks.
- A distributed index provides a definitive answer about results. If a data item is stored in the system, the DHT guarantees that the data is found.

7.1.5 Comparison of Lookup Concepts

The following table compares again the main characteristics of the presented approaches in terms of complexity, vulnerability and query ability. According to their complexity in terms of communication overhead, per node state maintenance, and their resilience, Distributed Hash Tables show the best performance unless complex queries are not vital. For fuzzy or complex query patterns, unstructured Peer-to-Peer systems are still the best option.

System	Per Node State	Communication Overhead	Fuzzy Queries	Robustness
Central Server	$O(N)$	$O(1)$	✓	×
Flooding Search	$O(1)$	$\geq O(N^2)$	✓	✓
Distributed Hash Table	$O(\log N)$	$O(\log N)$	×	✓

Table 7.1: Comparison of central server, flooding search, and distributed indexing.

7.2 Fundamentals of Distributed Hash Tables

This section introduces the fundamentals of Distributed Hash Tables, such as data management, principles of routing, and maintenance mechanisms. Chapter 8 provides a detailed explanation of several selected Distributed Hash Table approaches.

7.2.1 Distributed Management of Data

A Distributed Hash Table manages data by distributing it across a number of nodes and implementing a routing scheme which allows one to efficiently look up the node on which a specific data item is located. In contrast to flooding-based searches in unstructured systems, each node in a DHT becomes responsible for a particular range of data items. Also, each node stores a partial view of the whole distributed system which effectively distributes the routing information. Based on this information, the routing procedure typically traverses several nodes, getting closer to the destination with each hop, until the destination node is reached.

Thus, Distributed Hash Tables follow a proactive strategy for data retrieval by structuring the search space and providing a deterministic routing scheme. In comparison, the routing information in unstructured systems is not related to the location of specific data items but only reflects connections between nodes. This reactive strategy results in queries being flooded on demand throughout the network because routing cannot be directed towards the lookup target. With a centralized system, the lookup strategy is implicit: routing a query (above the IP level) is unnecessary since the lookup procedure itself is confined to a single system.

7.2.2 Addressing in Distributed Hash Tables

Distributed Hash Tables introduce new address spaces into which data is mapped. Address spaces typically consist of large integer values, e.g., the range from 0 to $2^{160}-1$. Distributed Hash Tables achieve distributed indexing by assigning a contiguous portion of the address space to each participating node (Figure 7.6). Given a value from the address space, the main operation provided by a DHT system is the lookup function, i.e., to determine the node responsible for this value.

Distributed Hash Table approaches differ mainly in how they internally manage and partition their address space. In most cases, these schemes lend themselves to geometric interpretations of address spaces. As a simple example, all mathematical operations on the address space could be performed modulo its number of elements, yielding a ring-like topology.

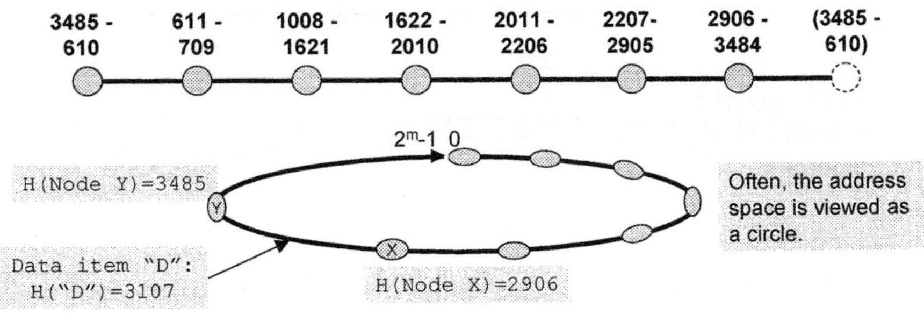

Fig. 7.6: A linear address space with integer values ranging from 0 to 65,535. The address space is partitioned among eight peers.

In a DHT system, each data item is assigned an identifier *ID*, a unique value from the address space. This value can be chosen freely by the application, but it is often derived from the data itself via a collision-resistant hash function, such as SHA-1 [207]. For example, the ID of a file could be the result of hashing the file name or the complete binary file. Thus, the DHT would store the file at the node responsible for the portion of the address space which contains the identifier.

The application interfaces of Distributed Hash Tables abstract from these details and provide simple but generic operations. Based on the lookup function, most DHTs also implement a storage interface similar to a hash table. Thus, the put function accepts an identifier and arbitrary data (e.g., the hash value of a file and the file contents) to store the data (on the node responsible for the ID). This identifier and the data is often referred to as *(key,value)*-tuple. Symmetrically, the get function retrieves the data associated with a specified identifier.

With this generic interface and the simple addressing scheme, Distributed Hash Tables can be used for a wide variety of applications. Applications are free to associate arbitrary semantics with identifiers, e.g., hashes of search keywords, database indexes, geographic coordinates, hierarchical directory-like binary names, etc. Thus, such diverse applications as distributed file systems, distributed databases, and routing systems have been developed on top of DHTs (see Chapters 11 and 12) [526, 367, 574, 373].

Most DHT systems attempt to spread the load of routing messages and of storing data on the participating nodes evenly (Chapter 9) [513, 450]. However, there are at least three reasons why some nodes in the system may experience higher loads than others: a node manages a very large portion of the address space, a node is responsible for a portion of the address space with a very large number of data items, or a node manages data items which are particularly popular. Under these circumstances, additional load-balancing mechanisms can help to spread the load more evenly over all nodes. For

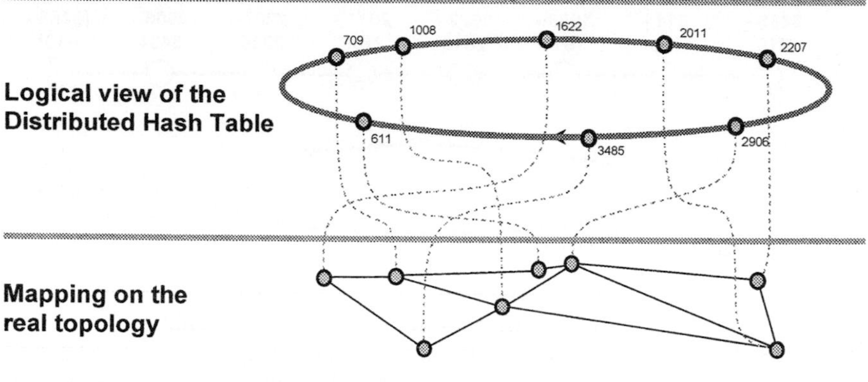

Fig. 7.7: Overall and underlay view of a Distributed Hash Table.

example, a node may transfer responsibility for a part of its address space to other nodes, or several nodes may manage the same portion of address space. Chapter 9 discusses load-balancing schemes in more detail.

7.2.3 Routing

Routing is a core functionality of Distributed Hash Tables. Based on a routing procedure, messages with their destination IDs are delivered to the DHT node which manages the destination ID. Thus, it is the routing algorithms of DHTs which solve the lookup problem.

Existing DHT systems implement a large variety of approaches to routing. However, the fundamental principle is to provide each node with a limited view of the whole system by storing on it a bounded number of links to other nodes. When a node receives a message for a destination ID it is not responsible for itself, it forwards the message to one of these other nodes. This process is repeated recursively until the destination node is found.

The choice of the next-hop node is determined by the routing algorithm and the routing metric. A typical metric is that of numeric closeness: messages are always forwarded to the node managing the identifiers numerically closest to the destination ID of the message. Ideally, such a scheme reliably routes a message to its destination in a small number of hops. Obviously, it is challenging to design routing algorithms and metrics such that node failures and incorrect routing information have limited or little impact on routing correctness and system stability.

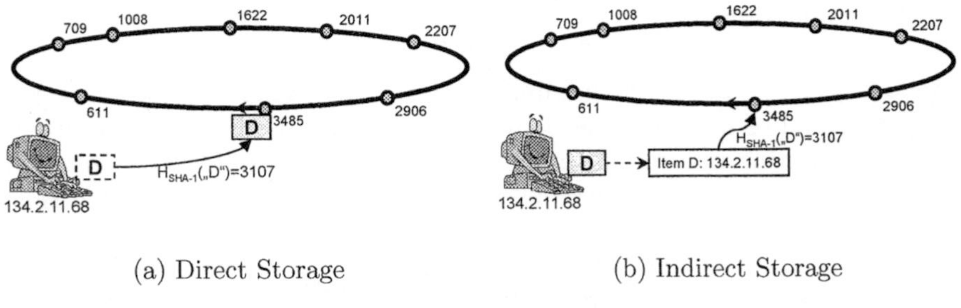

(a) Direct Storage (b) Indirect Storage

Fig. 7.8: Two methods of storing data in Distributed Hash Tables.

7.2.4 Data Storage

There are two possibilities for storing data in a Distributed Hash Table. In a Distributed Hash Table which uses direct storage, the data is copied upon insertion to the node responsible for it (Figure 7.8(a)). The advantage is that the data is located directly in the Peer-to-Peer system and the node which inserted it can subsequently leave the DHT without the data becoming unavailable. The disadvantage is the overhead in terms of storage and network bandwidth. Since nodes may fail, the data must be replicated to several nodes to increase its availability. Additionally, for large data, a huge amount of storage is necessary on every node.

The other possibility is to store references to the data. The inserting node only places a pointer to the data into the Distributed Hash Table. The data itself remains on this node, leading to reduced load in the DHT (Figure 7.8(a)). However, the data is only available as long as the node is available.

In both cases, the node using the Distributed Hash Table for lookup purposes does not have to be part of the Distributed Hash Table in order to use its services. This allows to realize a DHT service as third-party infrastructure service, such as the OpenDHT Project [511].

7.3 DHT Mechanisms

Storage and retrieval of distributed data is the main purpose of Distributed Hash Tables. In this section, common mechanisms for the management of data and nodes in Distributed Hash Tables are discussed. These tasks address the insertion and retrieval of data and the arrival, departure, and failure of nodes.

7.3.1 Overview

To store or access data in a Distributed Hash Table, a node first needs to join it. The arrival of new nodes leads to changes in the DHT infrastructure, to which the routing information and distribution of data needs to be adapted. At this stage, the new node can insert data items into the Distributed Hash Table and retrieve data from it. In case a node fails or leaves the system, the DHT needs to detect and adapt to this situation.

7.3.2 Node Arrival

It takes four steps for a node to join a Distributed Hash Table. First, the new node has to get in contact with the Distributed Hash Table. Hence, with some bootstrap method it gets to know some arbitrary node of the DHT. This node is used as an entry point to the DHT until the new node is an equivalent member of the DHT. Then, the new node needs to be assigned a partition in the logical address space. Depending on the DHT implementation, a node may choose arbitrary or specific partitions on its own or it determines one based on the current state of the system. Third, the routing information in the system needs to be updated to reflect the presence of the new node. Fourth, the new node retrieves all $(key, value)$ pairs under its responsibility from the node that stored them previously.

7.3.3 Node Failure

Node failures must be assumed to occur frequently in distributed systems consisting of many unreliable and often poorly connected desktop machines. Thus, all non-local operations in a Distributed Hash Table need to resist failures of other nodes. This reflects the self-organizing design of DHT algorithms. They have to be designed to always fulfill their purpose and deal with all likely events and disruptions that may happen.

For example, routing and lookup procedures are typically designed to use alternative routes towards the destination when a failed node is encountered on the default route. This is an example of reactive recovery, i.e., a fault is handled during a regular DHT operation. Many Distributed Hash Tables also feature proactive recovery mechanisms, e.g., to maintain their routing information. Consequently, they periodically probe other nodes to check whether these nodes are still operational. If they are not, the corresponding routing entry is replaced with a working node.

Furthermore, node failures lead to a re-partitioning of the DHT's address space. This may in turn require *(key, value)*-pairs to be moved between nodes and additional maintenance operations such as adaptation to

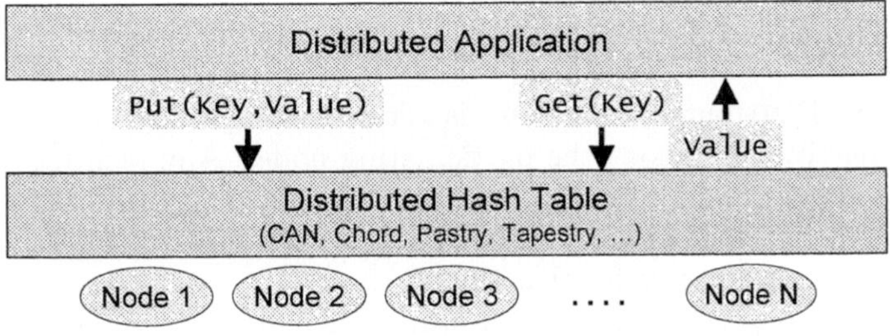

Fig. 7.9: Interface of a Distributed Hash Table. With a simple put-/textsfget-interface, the DHT simply abstracts from the distribution of data among nodes.

new load-balancing requirements. When a node fails, the application data that it stored is lost unless the Distributed Hash Table uses replication to keep multiple copies on different nodes. Some Distributed Hash Tables follow the simpler soft-state approach which does not guarantee persistence of data. Data items are pruned from the Distributed Hash Table unless the application refreshes them periodically. Therefore, a node failure leads to a temporary loss of application data until the data is refreshed.

7.3.4 Node Departure

In principle, nodes which voluntarily leave a Distributed Hash Table could be treated the same as failed nodes. However, DHT implementations often require departing nodes to notify the system before leaving. This allows other nodes to copy application data from the leaving node and to immediately update their routing information leading to improved routing efficiency. When triggered explicitly, replication and load-balancing mechanisms can also work more efficiently and reliably.

7.4 DHT Interfaces

There are two angles from which the functionality of Distributed Hash Tables can be viewed: they can be interpreted as routing systems or as storage systems. The first interpretation focuses on the delivery of packets to nodes in a DHT based on a destination ID. In the second, a Distributed Hash Table appears as a storage system similar to a hash table. These notions are reflected in the interface that a Distributed Hash Table provides to applications.

7.4.1 Routing Interface

Routing in a Distributed Hash Table is performed in the logical address space which is partitioned among the participating nodes. Any identifier from the address space can serve as a destination address for a message. Thus, the functionality provided by the DHT is to forward a message for an ID to the node which is responsible for this identifier.

An interface with two primitives suffices to build distributed applications on this foundation. The send primitive accepts a destination ID and a message and delivers the message from an arbitrary node in the system to the node which manages the destination ID. The receive primitive passes incoming messages and their destination identifiers to the application on the receiving node.

All other details of DHT management, such as node arrival and departure or repair mechanisms, are implemented by the Distributed Hash Table itself and are not exposed to the application. This generic, stateless interface implements little functionality but leaves a lot of flexibility to the application design. In particular, the storage and retrieval of data including load-balancing strategies can be implemented on top of the routing interface.

7.4.2 Storage Interface

As a storage system, a Distributed Hash Table implements an interface for persistently storing and reliably retrieving data in a distributed manner. On each node, the application interface provides the two main primitives of a hash table. The put primitive takes a $(key, value)$ pair and stores it on the node responsible for the identifier key. Similarly, the get primitive accepts an identifier and returns the value associated with the specified identifier.

The implementation of this interface adds to a Distributed Hash Table another level of complexity beyond correct and efficient routing. The storage layer needs to deal with routing failures, prevent data loss from node failure through replication, achieve load-balancing, provide accounting and admission control, etc. DHT implementations use different solutions to address these problems as described in Chapter 8.

7.4.3 Client Interface

Given the above interfaces, a node can only utilize its primitives after joining a Distributed Hash Table. However, a distributed system can also be structured such that the nodes participating in the DHT make available the DHT services to other, non-participating hosts. In such an environment, these hosts act as clients of the DHT nodes. This setup can be desirable where, for example, the Distributed Hash Table is run as an infrastructure service on a dedicated set of nodes for increased reliability. The interface between clients and DHT nodes is also well-suited to realize access control and accounting for services available on the Distributed Hash Table. Note that this interface can itself be implemented as an application on top of the DHT routing or storage layer.

7.5 Conclusions

Distributed Hash Tables provide an efficient layer of abstraction for routing and managing data in distributed systems. By spreading routing information and data across multiple nodes, the scalability issues of centralized systems are avoided while data retrieval is significantly more efficient than in unstructured Peer-to-Peer networks. Also, the generic interface of Distributed Hash Tables supports a wide spectrum of applications and uses.

DHT implementations, such as those discussed in Chapter 8, focus on different conceptual and functional aspects. This is reflected in their different properties, such as scalability, routing latency, fault tolerance, and adaptability. Since the design of a Distributed Hash Table has to meet several, often conflicting, goals, each system exhibits its own strengths and weaknesses in different application scenarios.

Among these design challenges are:

- *Routing efficiency:* The latency of routing and lookup operations is influenced by the topology of the address space, the routing algorithm, the number of references to other nodes, the awareness of the IP-level topology, etc.
- *Management overhead:* The costs of maintaining the Distributed Hash Table under no load depend on such factors as the number of entries in routing tables, the number of links to other nodes, and the protocols for detecting failures.
- *Dynamics:* A large number of nodes joining and leaving a Distributed Hash Table – often referred to as *"churn"* – concurrently puts particular stress on the overall stability of the system, reducing routing efficiency, incurring additional management traffic, or even resulting in partitioned or defective systems.

Distributed Hash Tables also face fundamental challenges related to the principle of distributed indexing. For example, it is not clear how Distributed Hash Tables can operate reliably in an untrusted environment with Byzantine faults, i.e., when participating nodes are non-cooperative or malicious and damage the system. Furthermore, data retrieval in Distributed Hash Tables is based on numeric identifiers. Thus, query metrics based on tokens of strings or any other arbitrary data as well as fuzzy searches are very difficult to achieve efficiently. Among others, it is these challenges that will drive research in the area of Distributed Hash Tables in the future.

8. Selected DHT Algorithms

Stefan Götz, Simon Rieche, Klaus Wehrle (University of Tübingen)

Several different approaches to realizing the basic principles of DHTs have emerged over the last few years. Although they rely on the same fundamental idea, there is a large diversity of methods for both organizing the identifier space and performing routing. The particular properties of each approach can thus be exploited by specific application scenarios and requirements.

This overview focuses on the three DHT systems that have received the most attention in the research community: Chord, Pastry, and Content Addressable Networks (CAN). Furthermore, the systems Symphony, Viceroy, and Kademlia are discussed because they exhibit interesting mechanisms and properties beyond those of the first three systems.

8.1 Chord

The elegance of the Chord algorithm, published by Stoica et al. [575] in 2001, derives from its simplicity. The keys of the DHT are l-bit identifiers, i.e., integers in the range $[0, 2^l - 1]$. They form a one-dimensional identifier circle modulo 2^l wrapping around from $2^l - 1$ to 0.

8.1.1 Identifier Space

Each data item and node is associated with an identifier. An identifier of a data item is referred to as a *key*, that of a node as an *ID*. Formally, the $(key, value)$ pair (k, v) is hosted by the node whose ID is greater than or equal to k. Such a node is called the *successor* of key k. Consequently, a node in a Chord circle with clockwise increasing IDs is responsible for all keys that precede it counter-clockwise.

Figure 8.1 illustrates an initialized identifier circle with $l = 6$, i.e., $2^6 = 64$ identifiers, ten nodes and seven data items. The successor of key $K5$, i.e., the node next to it clockwise, is node $N8$ where $K5$ is thus located. $K43$'s successor is $N43$ as their identifiers are equal. The circular structure modulo $2^6 = 64$ results in $K61$ being located on $N8$.

R. Steinmetz and K. Wehrle (Eds.): P2P Systems and Applications, LNCS 3485, pp. 95-117, 2005.

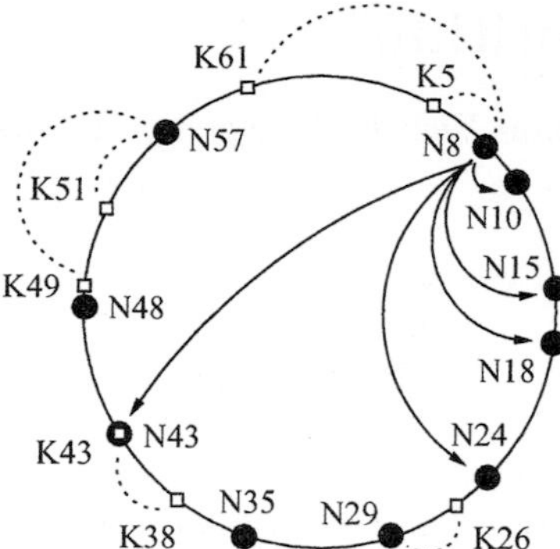

Finger Table of N8		
Idx	Target ID	Successor
0	N8 + 1	N10
1	N8 + 2	N10
2	N8 + 4	N15
3	N8 + 8	N18
4	N8 + 16	N24
5	N8 + 32	N43

Fig. 8.1: A 6-bit Chord identifier space. Dotted lines indicate which nodes host which keys. Black lines represent the fingers of node $N8$.

8.1.2 Routing

Given a Chord identifier circle, all identifiers are well-ordered and keys and nodes are uniquely associated. Thus, each $(key, value)$ pair is located and managed on a single, well-defined node. The DHT is formed by the set of all $(key, value)$ pairs on all nodes of an identifier circle. The key to efficient lookup and modification operations on this data is to quickly locate the node responsible for a particular key.

For a very simple routing algorithm, only very little per-node state is required. Each node needs to store its successor node on the identifier circle. When a key is being looked up, each node forwards the query to its successor in the identifier circle. One of the nodes will determine that the key lies between itself and its successor. Thus, the key must be hosted by this successor. Consequently, the successor is communicated as the result of the query back to its originator.

This inefficient form of key location involves a number of messages linear to the number of nodes on the identifier circle. Chord utilizes additional per-node state for more scalable key lookups.

Each node maintains a routing table, the *finger table* (cf. Figure 8.1), pointing to other nodes on the identifier circle. Given a circle with l-bit identifiers, a finger table has a maximum of l entries. On node n, the table entry at row i identifies the first node that succeeds n by at least 2^{i-1}, i.e., $successor(n + 2^{i-1})$, where $1 \leq i \leq l$. In Figure 8.1, for example, the second finger of node $N8$ $(8+2^1 = 10)$ is node $N10$ and the third finger $(8+2^2 = 12)$ is node $N15$. The first finger of a node is always its immediate successor on the identifier circle.

As a finger table stores at most l entries, its size is independent of the number of keys or nodes forming the DHT. Each finger entry consists of a node ID, an IP address and port pair, and possibly some book-keeping information. Even for large identifiers, e.g., $l = 256$, this is a relatively small amount of data per node which can be efficiently managed and searched. The routing information from finger tables provides information about nearby nodes and a coarse-grained view of long-distance links at intervals increasing by powers of two.

The Chord routing algorithm exploits the information stored in the finger table of each node. A node forwards queries for a key k to the closest predecessor of k on the identifier circle according to its finger table. When the query reaches a node n such that k lies between n and the successor of n on the identifier circle, node n reports its successor as the answer to the query.

Thus, for distant keys k, queries are routed over large distances on the identifier circle in a single hop. Furthermore, the closer the query gets to k, the more accurate the routing information of the intermediate nodes on the location of k becomes. Given the power-of-two intervals of finger IDs, each hop covers at least half of the remaining distance on the identifier circle between the current node and the target identifier. This results in an average of $O(log(N))$ routing hops for a Chord circle with N participating nodes. For example, a Chord network with 1000 nodes forwards queries, on average, in roughly $O(10)$ steps. In their experiments, Stoica et al. show that the average lookup requires $\frac{1}{2}log(N)$ steps.

8.1.3 Self-Organization

The Chord system described so far also needs to allow for nodes joining and leaving the system as well as to deal with node failures.

Node Arrivals

In order to join a Chord identifier circle, the new node first determines some identifier n. The original Chord protocol does not impose any restrictions on this choice. For example, n could be set at random assuming that the probability for collisions with existing node IDs is low in a identifier space large enough. There have been several proposals to restrict node IDs according to certain criteria, e.g., to exploit network locality or to avoid identity spoofing.

For the new node n, another node o must be known which already participates in the Chord system. By querying o for n's own ID, n retrieves its successor. It notifies its successor s of its presence leading to an update of the predecessor pointer of s to n. Node n then builds its finger by iteratively querying o for the successors of $n + 2^1$, $n + 2^2$, $n + 2^3$, etc. At this stage, n has a valid successor pointer and finger table. However, n does not show up in the routing information of other nodes. In particular, it is not known to its predecessor as its new successor since the lookup algorithm is not apt to determine a node's predecessor.

Stabilization Protocol

Chord introduces a *stabilization* protocol to validate and update successor pointers as nodes join and leave the system. Stabilization requires an additional predecessor pointer and is performed periodically on every node. The `stabilize()` function on a node k requests the successor of k to return its predecessor p. If p equals k, k and its successor agree on being each other's respective predecessor and successor. The fact that p lies between k and its successor indicates that p recently joined the identifier circle as k's successor. Thus, node k updates its successor pointer to p and notifies p of being its predecessor.

With the stabilization protocol, the new node n does not actively determine its predecessor. Instead, the predecessor itself has to detect and fix inconsistencies of successor and predecessor pointers using `stabilize()`. After node n has thus learnt of its predecessor, it copies all keys it is responsible for, i.e., keys between $predecessor(n)$ and n, while the predecessor of n releases them.

At this stage, all successor pointers are up to date and queries can be routed correctly, albeit slowly. Since the new node n is not present in the finger tables of other nodes, they forward queries to the predecessor of n even if n would be more suitable. Node n's predecessor then needs to forward the query to n via its successor pointer. Multiple concurrent node arrivals may lead to several linear forwardings via successor pointers.

The number of nodes whose finger table needs to be updated is in the order of $O(log(N))$ in a system with N nodes. Based on the layout of a finger table, a new node n can identify the nodes with outdated finger tables as $predecessor(n - 2^{i-1})$ for $1 < i \leq l$. However, the impact of outdated finger tables on lookup performance is small, and in the face of multiple node arrivals, the finger table updates would be costly. Therefore, Chord prefers to update finger tables lazily. Similar to the `stabilize()` function, each node n runs the `fix_fingers()` function periodically. It picks a finger randomly from the finger table at index i $(1 < i \leq l)$ and looks it up to find the true current successor of $n + 2^{i-1}$.

Node Failures

Chord addresses node failures on several levels. To detect node failures, all communication with other nodes needs to be checked for timeouts. When a node detects a failure of a finger during a lookup, it chooses the next best preceding node from its finger table. Since a short timeout is sufficient, lookup performance is not significantly affected in such a case. The `fix_fingers()` function ensures that failed nodes are removed from the finger tables. To expedite this process, `fix_fingers()` can be invoked specifically on a failed finger.

It is particularly important to maintain the accuracy of the successor information as the correctness of lookups depends on it. If, for example, the first three nodes in the finger table of node n fail simultaneously, the next live finger f might not be the true live successor s. Thus, node n would assume that a certain key k is located at f although it is located at s and would accordingly send incorrect replies to queries for k. The stabilization protocol can fail in a similar fashion when multiple nodes fail, even if live fingers are used as backups for failed successors.

To maintain a valid successor pointer in the presence of multiple simultaneous node failures, each node holds a successor list of length r. Instead of just a single successor pointer, it contains a node's first r successors. When a node detects the failure of its successor, it reverts to the next live node in its successor list. During `stabilize()`, a successor list with failed nodes is repaired by augmenting it with additional successors from a live node in the list. The Chord ring is affected only if all nodes from a successor list fail simultaneously.

The failure of a node not only means that it becomes unreachable but also that the data it managed is no longer available. Data loss from the failure of individual nodes can be prevented by replicating the data to other nodes. In Chord, the successor of a failed node becomes responsible for the keys and data of the failed node. Thus, an application utilizing Chord ideally replicates data to successor nodes. Chord can use the successor list to communicate this information and possible changes to the application.

Node Departures

Treating nodes that voluntarily leave a Chord network like failed ones does not affect the stability of the network. Yet it is inefficient because the failure needs to be detected and rectified. Therefore, a leaving node should transfer its keys to its successor and notify its successor and predecessor. This ensures that data is not lost and that the routing information remains intact.

8.2 Pastry

The Pastry distributed routing system was proposed in 2001 by Rowstron and Druschel [527]. Similar to Chord, its main goal is to create a completely decentralized, structured Peer-to-Peer system in which objects can be efficiently located and messages efficiently routed. Instead of organizing the identifier space as a Chord-like ring, the routing is based on numeric closeness of identifiers. In their work, Rowstron and Druschel focus not only on the number of routing hops, but also on network locality as factors in routing efficiency.

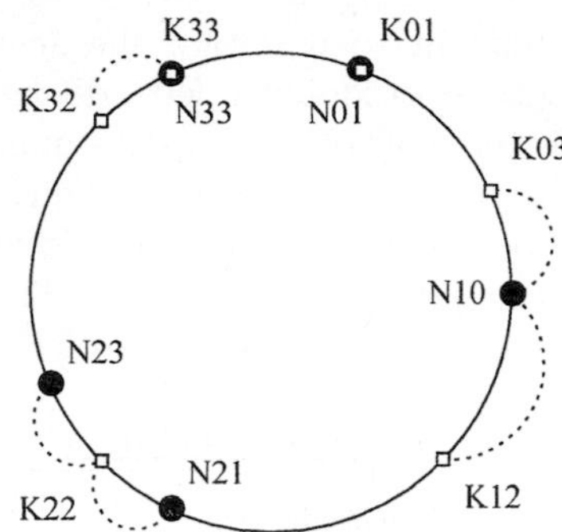

Fig. 8.2: A 4-bit Pastry identifier space with six keys mapped onto five nodes. Numeric closeness is an ambiguous metric for assigning keys to nodes as illustrated for key $K22$.

8.2.1 Identifier Space

In Pastry, nodes and data items uniquely associate with l-bit identifiers, i.e., integers in the range of 0 to $2^l - 1$ (l is typically 128). Under such associations, an identifier is termed a *node ID* or a *key*, respectively. Pastry views identifiers as strings of digits to the base 2^b where b is typically chosen to be 4. A key is located on the node to whose node ID it is numerically closest.

Figure 8.2 illustrates a Pastry identifier space with 4-bit identifiers and $b = 2$, so all numbers are to the base of 4. The closest node to, e.g., key $K01$ is $N01$, whereas $K03$ is located on node $N10$. The distances of key $K22$ to node $N21$ and $N23$ are equal so both nodes host this key to satisfy the requirements.

8.2.2 Routing Information

Pastry's node state is divided into three main elements. The *routing table*, similar to Chord's finger table, stores links into the identifier space. The *leaf set* contains nodes which are close in the identifier space (like Chord's successor list). Nodes that are close together in terms of network locality are listed in the *neighborhood set*.

Pastry measures network locality based on a given scalar network proximity metric. This metric is assumed to be already available from the network infrastructure and might range from IP hops to actual the geographical location of nodes.

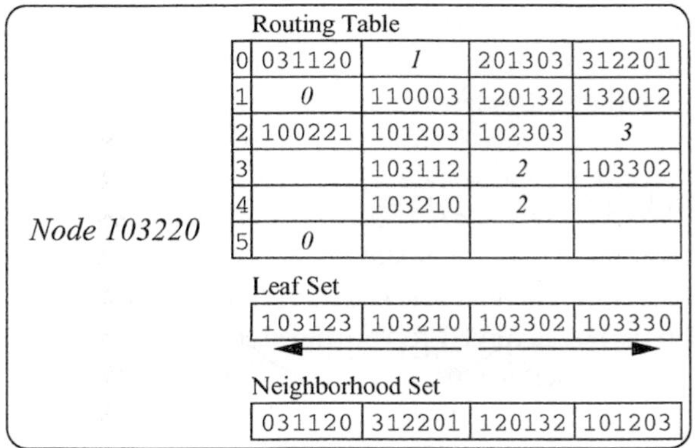

Routing Table
0 031120 1 201303 312201
1 0 110003 120132 132012
2 100221 101203 102303 3
3 103112 2 103302
4 103210 2
5 0
Node 103220
Leaf Set
103123 103210 103302 103330
Neighborhood Set
031120 312201 120132 101203

Fig. 8.3: Pastry node state for the node 103220 in a 12-bit identifier space and a base of 4 ($l = 12$, $b = 2$). The routing table lists nodes with the length of the common node identifier prefix corresponding to the row index.

Routing Table

A Pastry node's routing table R (see Figure 8.3) is made up of $\frac{l}{b}$ rows with $2^b - 1$ entries per row (an additional column in Figure 8.3 also lists the digits of the local node ID for clarity). On node n, the entries in row i hold the identities of Pastry nodes whose node IDs share an i-digit prefix with n but differ in digit n itself. For example, the first row of the routing table is populated with nodes that have no prefix in common with n. When there is no node with an appropriate prefix, the corresponding table entry is left empty.

Routing tables built according to the Pastry scheme achieve an effect similar to Chord finger tables. A node has a coarse-grained knowledge of other nodes which are distant in the identifier space. The detail of the routing information increases with the proximity of other nodes in the identifier space. Without a large number of nearby nodes, the last rows of the routing table are only sparsely populated. Intuitively, the identifier space would need to be fully exhausted with node IDs for complete routing tables on all nodes. In a system with N nodes, only $log_{2^b}(N)$ routing table rows are populated on average.

In populating the routing table, there is a choice from the set of nodes with the appropriate identifier prefix. During the routing process, network locality can be exploited by selecting nodes which are close in terms of a network proximity metric.

Leaf Set

The routing table sorts node IDs by prefix. To increase lookup efficiency, the leaf set L of node n holds the $|L|$ nodes numerically closest to n. The routing table and the leaf set are the two sources of information relevant for routing. The leaf set also plays a role similar to Chord's successor lists in recovering from failures of adjacent nodes.

Neighborhood Set

Instead of numeric closeness, the neighborhood set M is concerned with nodes that are close to the current node with regard to the network proximity metric. Thus, it is not involved in routing itself but in maintaining network locality in the routing information.

8.2.3 Routing Procedure

Routing in Pastry is divided into two main steps. First, a node checks whether the key k is within the range of its leaf set. If this is the case, it implies that k is located on one of the nearby nodes of the leaf set. Thus, the node forwards the query to the leaf set node numerically closest to k. In case this is the node itself, the routing process is finished.

If k does not fall into the range of leaf set nodes, the query needs to be forwarded over a longer distance using the routing table. In this case, a node n tries to pass the query on to a node which shares a longer common prefix with k than n itself. If there is no such entry in the routing table, the query is forwarded to a node which shares a prefix with k of the same length as n but which is numerically closer to k than n.

For example, a node with a routing table as in Figure 8.3 would send a query for key 103200 on to node 103210 as it is the leaf set node closest to the key. Since the leaf set holds the closest nodes, the key is known to be located on that node. A query for key 102022, although numerically closer to node 101203, is forwarded to node 102303 since it shares the prefix 102 with the key (in contrast to 10 as the current node does). For key 103000, there is no routing table entry with a longer common prefix than the current node. Thus the current node routes the query to node 103112 which has the same common prefix 103 but is numerically closer than the current node.

This scheme ensures that routing loops do not occur because the query is routed strictly to a node with a longer common identifier prefix than the current node, or to a numerically closer node with the same prefix.

8.2.4 Self-Organization

In practice, Pastry needs to deal with node arrivals, departures, and failures, while, at the same time, maintaining good routing performance if possible. This section describes how Pastry achieves these goals.

Node Arrival

Before joining a Pastry system, a node chooses a node ID. Pastry itself allows arbitrary node IDs, but applications may have more restrictive requirements. Commonly, a node ID is formed as the hash value of a node's public key or IP address.

For bootstrapping, the new node n is assumed to know a nearby Pastry node k based on the network proximity metric. Now n needs to initialize its node, i.e., its routing table, leaf and neighborhood set. Since k is assumed to be close to n, the nodes in k's neighborhood set are reasonably good choices for n, too. Thus, n copies the neighborhood set from k.

To build its routing table and leaf set, n needs to retrieve information about the Pastry nodes which are close to n in the identifier space. To do this, n routes a special "join" message via k to a key equal to n. According to the standard routing rules, the query is forwarded to node c with the numerically closest node ID. Due to this property, the leaf set of c is suitable for n, so it retrieves c's leaf set for itself.

The join request triggers all nodes, which forwarded the request towards c, to provide n with their routing information. Node n's routing table is constructed from the routing information of these nodes starting at row zero. As this row is independent of the local node ID, n can use the entries at row zero of k's routing table. In particular, it is assumed that n and k are close in terms of the network proximity metric. Since k stores nearby nodes in its routing table, these entries are also close to n. In the general case of n and k not sharing a common prefix, n cannot re-use entries from any other row in k's routing table.

The route of the join message from n to c leads via nodes $v_1 ... v_n$ with increasingly longer common prefixes of n and v_i. Thus, row 1 from the routing table of node v_1 is also a good choice for the same row of the routing table of n. The same is true for row 2 on node v_2 and so on. Based on this information, the routing table can be constructed for node n.

Finally, the new node sends its node state to all nodes in its routing data. These nodes can update their own routing information accordingly. In contrast to the lazy updates in Chord, this mechanism actively updates the state in all affected nodes when a new node joins the system. At this stage, the new node is fully present and reachable in the Pastry network.

The arrival and departure of nodes affects only a relatively small number of nodes in a Pastry system. Consequently, the state updates from multiple such operations rarely overlap and there is little contention. Thus, Pastry uses the following optimistic time-stamp-based approach to avoid major inconsistencies of node state: the state a new node receives is time-stamped. After the new node initializes its own internal state, it announces its state back to the other nodes including the original time-stamps. If the time-stamps do not match on the other nodes, they request the new node to repeat the join procedure.

Node Failure

Node failure is detected when a communication attempt with another node fails. Routing requires contacting nodes from the routing table and leaf set, resulting in lazy detection of failures. Since the neighborhood set is not involved in routing, Pastry nodes periodically test the liveness of the nodes in their neighborhood sets.

During routing, the failure of a single node in the routing table does not significantly delay the routing process. The local node can choose to forward the pending query to a different node from the same row in the routing table. Alternatively, a node could store backup nodes with each entry in the routing table.

Failed nodes need to be evicted from the routing table to preserve routing performance and correctness. To replace a failed node at entry i in row j of its routing table (R_j^i), a node contacts another node referenced in row i. Entries in the same row j of the the remote node are valid for the local node. Hence it can copy entry R_j^i from the remote node to its own routing table after verifying the liveness of the entry. In case it failed as well, the local node can probe the other nodes in row j for entry R_j^i. If no live node with the appropriate node ID prefix can be obtained in this way, the local node expands its horizon by querying nodes from the preceding row R_{j-1}. With very high probability, this procedure eventually finds a valid replacement for the failed routing table entry R_j^i, if one exists.

Repairing a failed entry in the leaf set L of a node is straightforward by utilizing the leaf sets of other nodes referenced in the local leaf set. The node contacts the leaf set entry with the largest index on the side of the failed node in order to retrieve the remote leaf set L'. If this node is unavailable, the local node can revert to leaf set entries with smaller indices. Since the entries in L' and L are close to each other in the identifier space and overlap, the node selects an appropriate replacement node from L' and adds it to its own leaf set. In the event that the replacement entry failed as well, the node again requests the leaf sets of other nodes from its local leaf set. For this procedure to be unsuccessful, $\frac{|L|}{2}$ adjacent nodes need to fail simultaneously. The probability of such a circumstance can be kept low even with modest values of $|L|$.

Nodes recover from node failures in their neighborhood sets in a fashion similar to repairing the leaf set. However, failures cannot be detected lazily since the nodes in the neighborhood set are not contacted regularly for routing purposes. Therefore, each node periodically checks the liveness of nodes in its neighborhood set. When a node failure is detected, a node consults the neighborhood sets of other neighbor nodes to determine an appropriate replacement entry.

Node Departure

Since Pastry can maintain stable routing information in the presence of node failures, deliberate node departures were originally treated as node failures for simplicity. However, a Pastry network would benefit from departure optimizations similar to those proposed for Chord. The primary goals would be to prevent data loss and reduce the amount of network overhead induced by Pastry's failure recovery mechanisms.

Arbitrary Failures

The approaches proposed for dealing with failures assumed that nodes fail by becoming unreachable. However, failures can lead to a random behavior of nodes, including malicious violations of the Pastry protocol. Rowstron and Druschel propose to amend these problems by statistically choosing alternative routes to circumvent failed nodes. Thus, a node chooses randomly, according to the constraints for routing correctness, from a set of nodes to route queries to with a bias towards the default route. A failed node would thus be able to interfere with some traffic but eventually be avoided after a number of retransmissions. How node arrivals and departures can be made more resilient to failed or malicious nodes is not addressed in the original work on Pastry.

8.2.5 Routing Performance

Pastry optimizes two aspects of routing and locating the node responsible for a given key: it attempts both to achieve a small number of hops to reach the destination node, and to exploit network locality to reduce the overhead of each individual hop.

Route Length

The routing scheme in Pastry essentially divides the identifier space into domains of size 2^n where n is a multiple of 2^b. Routes lead from high-order domains to low-order domains, thus reducing the remaining identifier space to be searched in each step. Intuitively, this results in an average number of routing steps related to the logarithm of the size of the system. This intuition is supported by a more detailed analysis.

It is assumed that routing information on all nodes is correct and that there are no node failures. There are three cases in the Pastry routing scheme, the first of which is to forward a query according to the routing table. In this case, the query is forwarded to a node with a longer prefix match than the current node. Thus, the number of nodes with longer prefix matches is reduced by at least a factor of 2^b in each step, so the destination is reached in $log_{2^b}(N)$ steps.

The second case is to route a query via the leaf set. This increases the number of hops by one.

In the third case, the key is neither covered by the leaf set nor does the routing table contain an entry with a longer matching prefix than the current node. Consequently, the query is forwarded to a node with the same prefix length, adding an additional routing hop. For a moderate leaf set of size $|L| = 2 * 2^b$, the probability of this case occurring is less than 0.6% so it is very unlikely that more than one additional hop is incurred.

As a result, the complexity of routing remains at $O(log_{2^b}(N))$ on average. Higher values of b lead to faster routing but also increase the amount of state that needs to be managed at each node. Thus, b is typically 4 but Pastry implementations can choose an appropriate trade-off for the specific application.

Locality

By exploiting network locality, Pastry routing optimizes not only the number of hops but also the costs of each individual hop. The criteria to populate a node's routing table allow a choice among a number of nodes with matching ID prefixes for each routing table entry. By selecting nearby nodes in terms of network locality, the individual routing lengths are minimized. This approach does not necessarily yield the shortest end-to-end route but leads to reasonable total route lengths.

Initially, a Pastry node uses the routing table entries from nodes on a path to itself in the identifier space. The proximity of the new node n and the existing well-known node k implies that the entries in k's first row of the routing table are also close to n. The entries of subsequent rows from nodes on the path from k to n may seem close to k but not necessarily to n. However, the distance from k to these nodes is relatively long compared to the distance between k and n. This is because the entries in later routing table rows have to be chosen from a logarithmically smaller set of nodes in the system. Hence, their distance to k and n increases logarithmically on average. Another implication of this fact is that messages are routed over increasing distances the closer they get to the destination ID.

8.3 Content Addressable Network *CAN*

Ratnasamy et al. presented their work on scalable content-addressable networks [505] in 2001, the same year in which Chord and Pastry were introduced. In CAN, keys and values are mapped onto numerically close nodes. Locating objects and routing messages in CAN is very simple as it requires

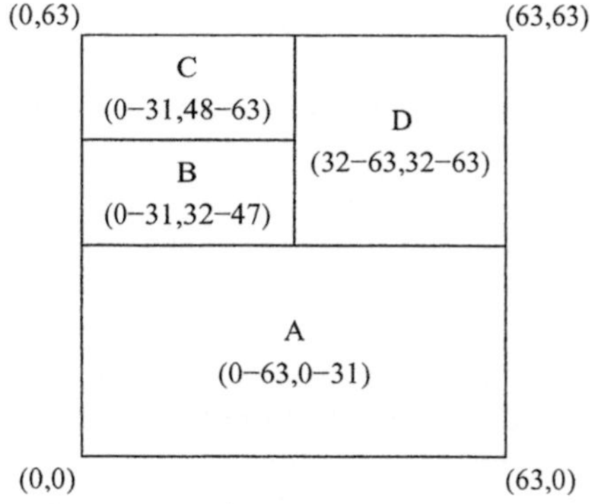

Fig. 8.4: A two-dimensional six-bit CAN identifier space with four nodes. For simplicity, it is depicted as a plane instead of a torus.

knowledge only about a node's immediate neighbors. However, CAN introduces the notion of multi-dimensional identifier spaces by which routing efficiency is greatly improved compared to linear neighbor traversal in a single dimension. CAN generalizes the Chord and Pastry approaches in certain areas and introduces design optimizations also applicable to other DHT systems.

8.3.1 Identifier Space

A CAN identifier space can be thought of as a d-dimensional version of a Chord or Pastry identifier space. Each data item is assigned an identifier, e.g., of the form $< x, y, z >$ for $d = 3$. All arithmetic on identifiers is again performed modulo the largest coordinate in each dimension. The geometrical representation of a CAN identifier space is thus a d-torus. The original work on CAN suggests a space with continuous coordinates between 0.0 and 1.0 but it also applies to discrete coordinate spaces.

The identifier space in CAN is partitioned among the participating nodes as shown in Figure 8.4. Each node is said to *own* a *zone*, i.e., a certain part of the identifier space. CAN ensures that the entire space is divided into non-overlapping zones. In Figure 8.4, a two-dimensional identifier space (represented by a plane instead of a torus for simplicity) is divided into four zones. In contrast to Chord and Pastry, CAN does not assign a particular identifier to a node. Instead, the extent of its zone is used to locate and identify a node.

As typical for $(key, value)$ pairs in DHTs, CAN keys are derived from the value (or a representation of it) by applying a uniform hash function. The easiest way of deriving multi-dimensional identifiers from flat hash values is to apportion a fixed set of bits to the coordinate in each dimension. For example, a 160-bit hash value would be divided into two 80-bit segments

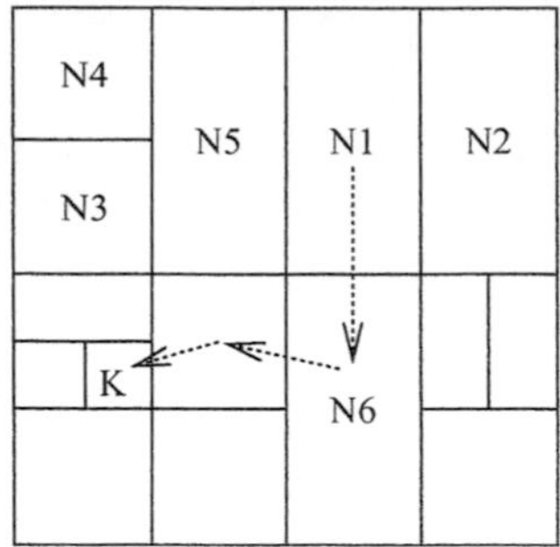

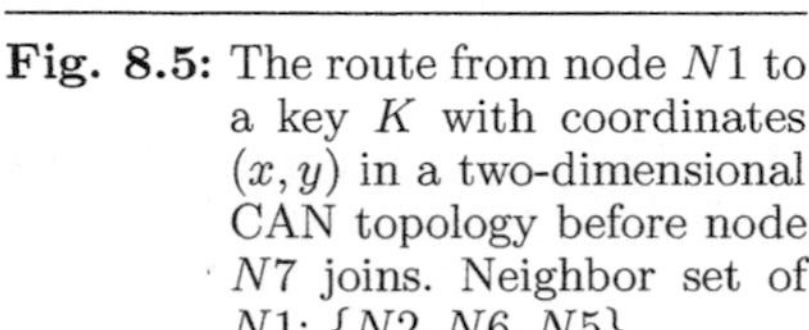

Fig. 8.5: The route from node $N1$ to a key K with coordinates (x, y) in a two-dimensional CAN topology before node $N7$ joins. Neighbor set of $N1$: $\{N2, N6, N5\}$

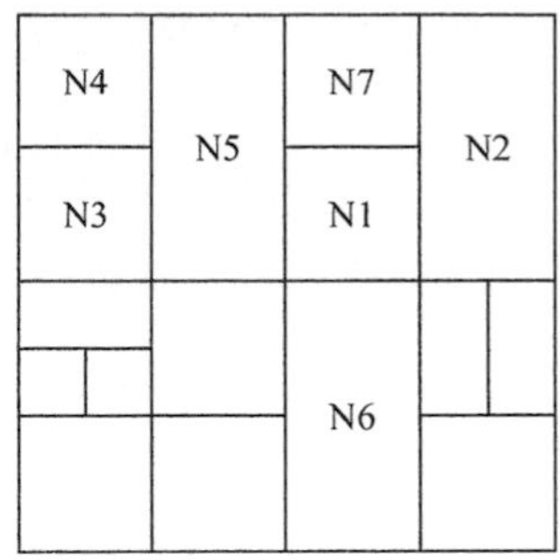

Fig. 8.6: New node $N7$ arrives in the zone of $N1$. $N1$ splits its zone and assigns one half to $N7$. Updated neighbor set of $N1$: $\{N7, N2, N6, N5\}$.

which represent $< x, y >$ coordinates in a two-dimensional identifier space. Because a key represents a point P in the identifier space, $(key, value)$ pairs are stored on the node owning the zone which covers P.

8.3.2 Routing Information

For routing purposes, a CAN node stores information only about its immediate neighbors. Two nodes in a d-dimensional space are considered neighbors if their coordinates overlap in one dimension and are adjacent to each other in $d-1$ dimension. Figure 8.5 illustrates neighbor relationships. For example, node $N1$ and $N6$ are neighbors as they overlap in the y dimension and are next to each other in the x dimension. At the same time, node $N5$ and $N6$ are not neighbors as they do not overlap in any dimension. Similarly, node $N1$ and $N4$ overlap in the x dimension but are not adjacent in the y dimension, so they are not neighbors of each other.

The routing information in CAN is comprised of the IP address, a port, and the zone of every neighbor of a node. This data is necessary to access the CAN service on a neighbor node and to know its location in the identifier space. In a d-dimensional identifier space partitioned into zones of equal size, each node has $2d$ neighbors. Thus, the number of nodes participating in a CAN system can grow very large while the necessary routing information per node remains constant.

8.3.3 Routing Procedure

Conceptually, routing in CAN follows a straight line in the cartesian identifier space from the source to the destination coordinates. Each node contributes to this process utilizing its neighbor information.

Each CAN message contains the destination coordinates. If the local node does not own the zone that includes these coordinates, it forwards the message to the neighbor with the coordinates closest to the destination, as illustrated in Figure 8.5. In a d-dimensional space equally partitioned into n zones, this procedure results in an average of $O((d/4)(n^{\frac{1}{d}}))$ routing steps. This expresses the intuitive consequence that increasing the number of dimensions significantly reduces the average route length.

8.3.4 Self-Organization

CAN dynamically organizes nodes into an overlay network which implements the operations in the identifier space. It assigns zones of the identifier space to individual nodes in such a way that zones do not overlap and there are no gaps in the identifier space. This partitioning needs to be robust when nodes join or leave a CAN system or when they fail.

Node Arrival

A node n joining a CAN system needs to be allocated a zone and the zone neighbors need to learn of the existence of n. The three main steps in this procedure are: to find an existing node of a CAN system; to determine which zone to assign to the new node; and to update the neighbor state.

Like Chord and Pastry, CAN is not tied to a particular mechanism for locating nodes in the overlay network to be joined. However, Ratnasamy et al. suggest using a dynamic DNS name to record one or more nodes belonging to a particular CAN system. The referenced nodes may in turn publish a list of other nodes in the same CAN overlay. This scheme allows for replication and randomized node selection to circumvent node failures.

Given a randomly chosen location in the identifier space, the new node n sends a special *join* message via one of the existing nodes to these coordinates. Join messages are forwarded according to the standard CAN routing procedure. After the join message reaches the destination node d, d splits its zone in half and assigns one half to n (cf. Figure 8.6). In order to ease the merging of zones when nodes leave and to equally partition the identifier space, CAN assumes a certain ordering of the dimensions by which zones are split. For example, zones may be split along the first (x) dimension, then along the second (y) dimension and so on. Finally, d transfers the $(key, value)$ pairs to n for which it has become responsible.

Node n and d exchange neighborhood information such that n learns of its neighbors from d and d adds n to its own set of neighbors. Then node n immediately informs all its neighbors of its presence. Through *update* messages, every node in the system also provides its direct neighbors periodically with its own neighborhood and zone information. Thus, only a small region of the identifier space is affected by node arrival. Its size depends on the number of dimensions but stays constant with the total number of nodes in the system.

Node Failure

The zones of failing or leaving nodes must be taken over by live nodes to maintain a valid partitioning of the CAN identifier space. A CAN node detects the failure of a neighbor when it ceases to send update messages. In such an event, the node starts a timer. When the timer fires, it sends *takeover* messages to the neighbors of the failed node. The timer is set up such that nodes with large zones have long timeouts while small zones result in short timeouts. Consequently, nodes with small zone sizes send their takeover messages first.

When a node receives a takeover message, it cancels its own timer provided its zone is larger than the one advertised in the message. Otherwise, it replies with its own takeover message. This scheme efficiently chooses the neighboring node with the smallest zone volume. The elected node claims ownership of the deserted zone and merges it with its own zone if possible. Alternatively, it temporarily manages both zones.

The hash-table data of a failed node is lost. However, the application utilizing CAN is expected to periodically refresh data items it inserted into the DHT (the same is true for the other systems presented here). Thus, the hash table state is eventually restored.

During routing, a node may find that the neighbor to which a message is to be forwarded has failed and the repair mechanism has not yet set in. In such a case, it forwards the message to the live neighbor next closest to the destination coordinates. If all neighbors failed, which are closer to the destination, the local node floods the message in a controlled manner within the overlay until a closer node is found.

Node Departure

When a node l deliberately leaves a CAN system, it notifies a neighbor n whose zone can be merged with l's zone. If no such neighbor exists, l chooses the neighbor with the smallest zone volume. It then copies the contents of its hash table to the selected node so this data remains available.

As described above, departing and failing nodes can leave a neighbor node managing more than one zone at a time. CAN uses a background process which reassigns zones to nodes to prevent fragmentation of the identifier space.

8.3.5 Routing Performance

CAN comes with a number of design optimizations which focus both on reducing the number of hops in a CAN overlay and on lowering path latencies. In combination, these steps result in a significant overall improvement of routing performance.

Increasing the number of dimensions in the identifier space reduces the number of routing hops and slightly increases the amount of neighbor state to store on each node. The average path length in a system with n nodes and d dimensions scales as $O(d(n^{\frac{1}{d}}))$. Higher dimensionality also improves routing fault tolerance because each node has a larger set of neighbors to choose from as alternatives to a failed node.

CAN also supports multiple instances of a DHT in different coordinate spaces termed *realities*. A node is present in all identifier spaces and owns a different zone in each of them. In each reality, all DHT data is replicated and distributed among the nodes. Thus, a system with r realities implies that each node manages r different zones and neighbor sets, one for each reality.

With multiple realities, data availability is improved through the replication of data in each reality. Also, a node has more options to route around failed neighbors. Furthermore, a node can choose the shortest route from itself to a destination in all realities. Thus, the average length of routes is reduced significantly. The different advantages and per-node state requirements of multiple dimensions and realities need to be traded off against each other based on application requirements.

The nonconformance of a CAN overlay and the underlying IP infrastructure may lead to significantly longer route lengths than direct IP routing. Hence, CAN suggests incorporating routing metrics which are not based on the distance between two nodes in the identifier space. For example, each node could measure the round-trip time (RTT) to neighboring nodes and use this information to forward messages to those neighbors with the best ratio of RTT and ID space distance to the destination. Experiments show an improvement of 24% to 40% in per-hop latency with this approach [505].

Another optimization is to *overload* a zone by allowing multiple nodes to manage the same zone. This effectively reduces the number of nodes in the system and thus results in fewer routing hops. Each node also forwards messages to the neighboring node with the lowest RTT in a neighbor zone, thus reducing per-hop latency. Finally, when the DHT data for a zone is replicated among all nodes of that zone, all these nodes need to fail simultaneously for the data to be lost.

With multiple hash functions, a (*key*, *value*) pair would be associated with a different identifier per hash function. Storing and accessing the (*key*, *value*) at each of the corresponding nodes increases data availability. Furthermore, routing can be performed in parallel towards all the different locations of a data item reducing the average query latency. However, these improvements come at the cost of additional per-node state and routing traffic.

The mechanisms presented above reduce per-hop latency by increasing the number of neighbors known to a node. This allows a node to forward messages to neighbors with a low RTT. However, CAN may also construct the overlay so it resembles more closely the underlying IP network. To place nodes close to each other, both at the IP and the overlay level, CAN assumes the existence of well-known landmark nodes. Before joining a CAN network, a node samples its RTT to the landmarks and chooses a zone close to a landmark with a low RTT. Thus, the network latency en route to its neighbors can be expected to be low resulting in lower per-hop latency.

For a more uniform partition of the identifier space, nodes should not join a CAN system at a random location. Instead, the node which manages the initial random location queries its neighbors for their zone volume. The node with the largest zone volume is then chosen to split its zone and assign half of it to the new node. This mechanism contributes significantly to a uniform partitioning of the coordinate space.

For real load-balancing, however, the zone size is not the only factor to consider. Particularly popular (*key*, *value*) pairs create hot spots in the identifier space and can place substantial load on the nodes hosting them. In a CAN network, overload caused by hot-spots may be reduced through caching and replication. Each node caches a number of recently accessed data items and satisfies queries for these data items from its cache if possible. Overloaded nodes may also actively replicate popular keys to their neighbors. The neighbors in turn reply to a certain fraction of these frequent requests themselves. Thus, load is distributed over a wider area of the identifier space.

8.4 Symphony

The Symphony protocol can be seen as a variation of Chord that exploits the small world phenomenon. As described by Manku et al. in [400], it is of constant degree because each node establishes only a constant number of links to other nodes. In contrast, Chord, Pastry, and CAN require a number of links which depends on the total number of nodes in the system. This basic property of Symphony significantly reduces the amount of per-node state and network traffic when the overlay topology changes. However, with an increasing number of nodes, it does not scale as well as Chord.

Like Chord, the identifier space in Symphony is constructed as a ring structure and each node maintains a pointer to its successor and predecessor on the ring. In Symphony, the Chord finger table is replaced by a constant but configurable number k of long distance links. In contrast to other systems, there is no deterministic construction rule for long distance links. Instead, these links are are chosen randomly according to harmonic distributions (hence the name *Symphony*). Effectively, the harmonic distribution of long-distance links favors large distances in the identifier space for a system with few nodes and decreasingly smaller distances as the system grows.

The basic routing in this setup is trivial: a query is forwarded to the node with the shortest distance to the destination key. By exploiting the bi-directional nature of links to other nodes, routing both clockwise and counter-clockwise leads, on average, to a 25% to 30% reduction of routing hops. Symphony additionally employs a *1-lookahead* approach. The lookahead table of each node records those nodes which are reachable through the successor, predecessor, and long distance links, i.e., the neighbors of a node's neighbors. Instead of routing greedily, a node forwards messages to its direct neighbor (not a neighbor's neighbor) which promises the best progression towards the destination. This reduces the average number of routing hops by 40% at the expense of management overhead when nodes join or leave the system.

In comparison with the systems discussed previously, the main contribution of Symphony is its constant degree topology resulting in very low costs of per-node state and of node arrivals and departures. It also utilizes bi-directional links between nodes and bi-directional routing. Symphony's routing performance ($O(\frac{1}{k}log^2(N))$) is competitive compared with Chord and the other systems ($O(log(N))$) but does not scale as well with exceedingly large numbers of nodes. However, nodes can vary the number of links they maintain to the rest of the system during run-time based on their capabilities, which is not permitted by the original designs of Chord, Pastry, and CAN.

8.5 Viceroy

In 2002, Malkhi et al. proposed Viceroy [399], another variation on Chord. It improves on the original Chord algorithm through a hierarchical structure of the ID space with constant degree which approximates a butterfly topology. This results in less per-node state and less management traffic but slightly lower routing performance than Chord.

Like Symphony, Viceroy borrows from Chord's fundamental ring topology with successor and predecessor links on each node. It also introduces a new node state called a *level*. When joining the system, a node chooses a random level in the range from 1 to $log(N)$. Thus, the Viceroy topology can be thought of as $log(N)$ vertically stacked rings. However, the node ID still serves as the unique identifier for nodes so that no two nodes may occupy the same node ID, regardless of their level.

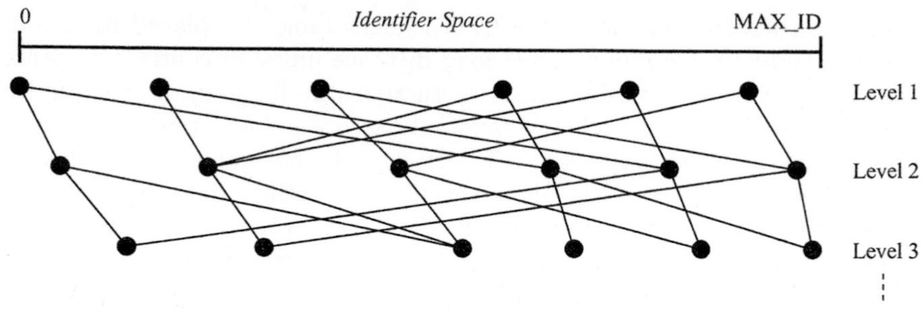

Fig. 8.7: A Viceroy topology with 18 nodes. Lines indicate short- and long-range downlinks; other links and lower levels are omitted for simplicity.

A Viceroy node n maintains a total of seven links to other nodes, independent of the network size. As n's two closest neighbors in the ID space, i.e., its successor and predecessor, might reside on any level, it also establishes a *level-ring link* to each of the closest nodes clockwise and counter-clockwise on its own level l. In order to connect to other levels, n creates an uplink to a nearby node at level $l - 1$ and a short-range and long-range downlink to level $l + 1$. The long-range downlink is chosen such that it connects to a node at a distance of roughly $\frac{1}{2^l}$. Thus, the distance covered by the long-range links is reduced logarithmically with lower levels as depicted in Figure 8.7.

The routing procedure is split into three phases closely related to the available routing information. First, a query is forwarded to level one along the uplinks. Second, a query recursively traverses the downlinks towards the destination. On each level, it chooses the downlink which leads to a node closer to the destination, without overshooting it in the clockwise direction. After reaching a node without downlinks, the query is forwarded along ring-level and successor links until it reaches the target identifier. The authors of Viceroy show that this routing algorithm yields an average number of $O(log(N))$ routing hops.

Like Symphony, Viceroy features a constant degree linkage in its node state. However, every node establishes seven links whereas Symphony keeps this number configurable even at run-time. Furthermore and similar to Chord, the rigid layout of the identifier space requires more link updates than Symphony when nodes join or leave the system. At the same time, the scalability of its routing latency of $O(log(N))$ surpasses that of Symphony, while not approaching that of Chord, Pastry, and CAN.

8.6 Kademlia

In their work on Kademlia [405], Maymounkov and Mazières observe a mismatch in the design of Pastry: its routing metric (identifier prefix length) does

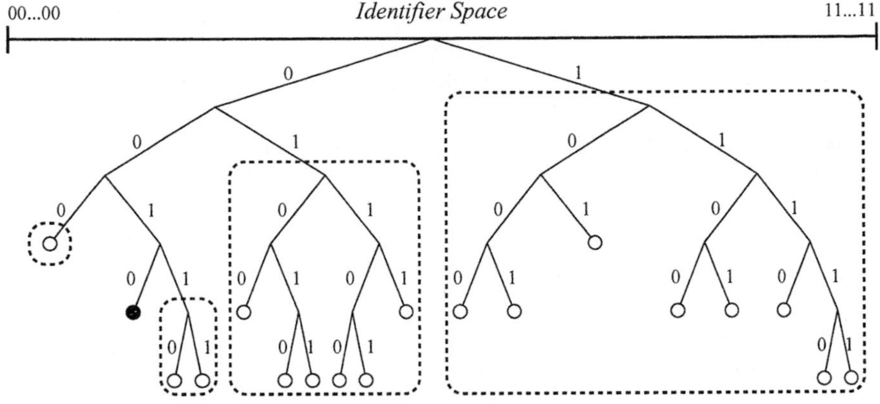

Fig. 8.8: An example of a Kademlia topology. The black node 0010 knows about the subtrees that do not match its identifier as indicated by the dotted squares. Each node successively forwards a query to α nodes in a destination subtree.

not necessarily correspond to the actual numeric closeness of identifiers. As a result, Pastry requires two routing phases which impacts routing performance and complicates formal analysis. Thus, Kademlia uses an XOR routing metric which improves on these problems and optionally offers additional parallelism for lookup operations.

Kademlia's XOR metric measures the distance between two identifiers i and j by interpreting the result of the bit-wise exclusive OR function on i and j as an integer. For example, the distance between the identifiers 3 and 5 is 6. Considering the shortest unique prefix of a node identifier, this metric effectively treats nodes and their identifiers as the leaves of a binary tree. For each node, Kademlia further divides the tree into subtrees not containing the node, as illustrated in Figure 8.8.

Each node knows of at least one node in each of the subtrees. A query for an identifier is forwarded to the subtree with the longest matching prefix until the destination node is reached. Similar to Chord, this halves the remaining identifier space to search in each step and implies a routing latency of $O(log(N))$ routing hops on average.

In many cases, a node knows of more than a single node per subtree. Similar to Pastry, the Kademlia protocols suggests forwarding queries to α nodes per subtree in parallel. By biasing the choice of nodes towards short round-trip times, the latency of the individual hops can be reduced. With this scheme, a failed node does not delay the lookup operation. However, bandwidth usage is increased compared to linear lookups.

When choosing remote nodes in other subtrees, Kademlia favors old links over nodes that only recently joined the network. This design choice is based on the observation that nodes with long uptime have a higher probability of remaining available than fresh nodes. This increases the stability of the routing topology and also prevents good links from being flushed from the routing tables by distributed denial-of-service attacks, as can be the case in other DHT systems.

With its XOR metric, Kademlia's routing has been formally proved consistent and achieves a lookup latency of $O(log(N))$. The required amount of node state grows with the size of a Kademlia network. However, it is configurable and together with the adjustable parallelism factor allows for a trade-off of node state, bandwidth consumption, and lookup latency.

8.7 Summary

The core feature of every DHT system is its self-organizing distributed operation. All presented systems aim to remain fully functional and usable at scales of thousands or even millions of participating nodes. This obviously implies that node failures must be both tolerated and of low impact to the operation and performance of the overall system. Hence, performance considerations are an integral part of the design of each system.

Since the lookup of a key is probably the most frequently executed operation and essential to all DHT systems, a strong focus is put on its performance. The number of routing hops is an important factor for end-to-end latency, but the latency of each hop also plays an important role. Generally, additional routing information on each node also provides a chance for choosing better routes. However, the management of this information and of links to other nodes in a system also incurs overhead in processing time and bandwidth consumption.

System	Routing Hops	Node State	Arrival	Departure
Chord	$O(\frac{1}{2}log_2(N))$	$O(2log_2(N))$	$O(log_2^2(N))$	$O(log_2^2(N))$
Pastry	$O(\frac{1}{b}log_2(N))$	$O(\frac{1}{b}(2^b-1)log_2(N))$	$O(log_{2^b}(N))$	$O(log_b(N))$
CAN	$O(\frac{D}{2}N^{\frac{1}{D}})$	$O(2D)$	$O(\frac{D}{2}N^{\frac{1}{D}})$	$O(2D)$
Symphony	$O(\frac{c}{k}log^2(N))$	$O(2k+2)$	$O(log^2(N))$	$O(log^2(N))$
Viceroy	$O(\frac{c}{k}log^2(N))$	$O(2k+2)$	$O(log_2(N))$	$O(log_2(N))$
Kademlia	$O(log_b(N))$	$O(b \cdot log_b(N))$	$O(log_b(N))$	$O(log_b(N))$

Table 8.1: Performance comparison of DHT systems. The columns show the averages for the number of routing hops during a key lookup, the amount of per-node state, and the number of messages when nodes join or leave the system.

Table 8.1 summarizes the routing latency, per-node state, and the costs of node arrivals and departures in the systems discussed above. It illustrates how design choices, like a constant-degree topology, affect the properties of a system. It should be noted that these results are valid only for the original proposals of each system and that the $O()$ notation leaves ample room for variation. In many cases, design optimizations from one system can also be transferred to another system. Furthermore, the effect of implementation optimizations should not be underestimated. The particular behavior of a DHT network in a certain application scenario needs to be determined individually through simulation or real-world experiments.

9. Reliability and Load Balancing in Distributed Hash Tables

Simon Rieche, Heiko Niedermayer, Stefan Götz, Klaus Wehrle
(University of Tübingen)

After introducing some selected Distributed Hash Table (DHT) systems, this chapter introduces algorithms for DHT-based systems which balance the storage data load (Section 9.1) or care for the reliability of the data (Section 9.2).

9.1 Storage Load Balancing of Data in Distributed Hash Tables

DHTs are used increasingly in widely distributed applications [52, 573]. Their efficient, scalable, and self-organizing algorithms for data retrieval and management offer crucial advantages compared with unstructured approaches. However, the underlying assumption is a roughly equal data distribution among the cooperating peers of a DHT. If there is a significant difference in the load of nodes in terms of data managed by each peer, i.e., data is concentrated on just a few peers, then the system may become less robust.

Alongside their crucial advantages, DHTs still show one major weakness in the distribution of data among the set of cooperating peers. All systems usually rely on the basic assumption that data is nearly equally distributed among the peer nodes. In most DHT approaches this assumption is based on the use of hash functions for mapping data into the DHT's address space. Generally, one assumes that hash functions provide an even distribution of keys and their respective data across the DHT address space. If there is a significant difference in the load of nodes in terms of data managed by each peer, the cost for distributed self-organization of such systems may increase dramatically. Therefore, appropriate mechanisms for load-balancing are required in order to keep the complexity of DHT search algorithms in the intended range of $O(logN)$ or less, where N is the number of nodes in the DHT.

But, as proved in many papers [99, 501, 513], the simple assumption of getting an equally distributed value space simply by using hash functions does not hold. Therefore, several approaches for balancing the data load between DHT peers have been developed.

The following figure [513] shows simulations by simply hashing data into the target address space of a Chord ring. The distribution of documents among the nodes was analyzed. For each scenario, a simulated DHT with 4,096 nodes was subjected to multiple simulation runs. The total number of

R. Steinmetz and K. Wehrle (Eds.): P2P Systems and Applications, LNCS 3485, pp. 119-135, 2005.

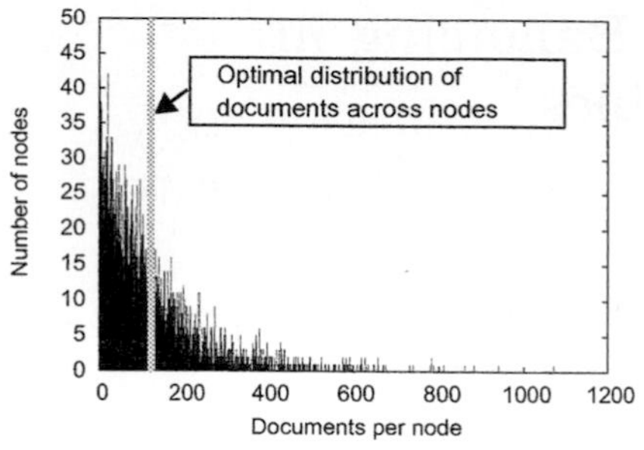

(a) Frequency distribution of DHT nodes storing a certain number of documents

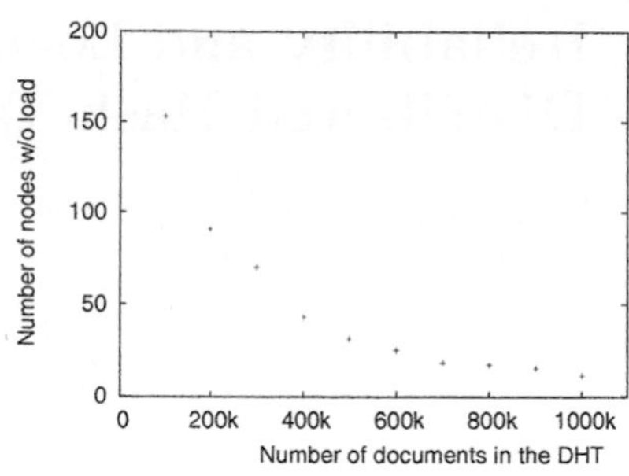

(b) Number of nodes not storing any document

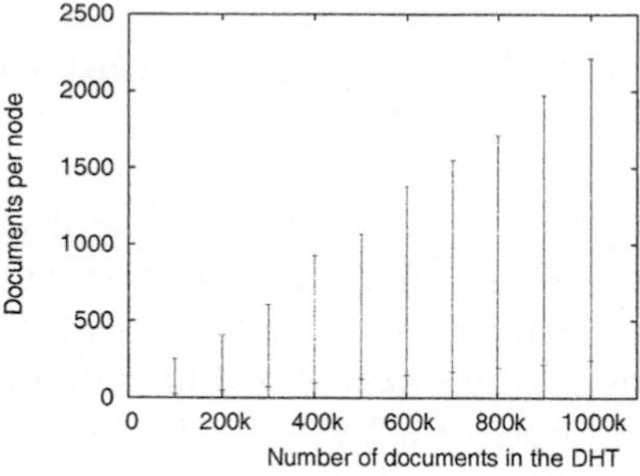

(c) Minimum, average, and maximum number of documents per node

Fig. 9.1: Distribution of data among a Chord DHT without load-balancing mechanisms.

documents to be stored ranged from 100,000 to 1,000,000 and for this purpose the Chord ring's address space had a size of $m = 22$ bits. Consequently, $2^{22} = 4{,}194{,}304$ documents and/or nodes could be stored and managed in the ring. The keys for the data and nodes were generated randomly. The load of a node was defined by the number of documents it stored.

The graphs in Fig. 9.1 clearly show that the assumption of an equal distribution of data among peers by simply using a hash function does not hold. For example, Fig. 9.1(a) shows how many nodes (y-axis) store a certain number of documents (x-axis). It is obvious that there is an unequal distribution of documents among the nodes. For an easier comparison, the grey line indicates the optimal number in the case of equal distribution – approximately 122 documents per node in this example. Additionally, Fig. 9.1(b) plots the number of nodes without a document.

Fig. 9.1(c) shows the distribution of documents in a Chord DHT without load-balancing. Between 100,000 and 1,000,000 documents were distributed across 4,096 nodes. The upper value indicates the maximum number of documents per node,and the lower value (always zero) the minimum number. The optimal number of documents per node is indicated by the marker in the middle. Even with a large total number of documents in the whole DHT, there are some nodes not managing any document and, consequently, are without any load. Some nodes manage a data load of up to ten times the average.

9.1.1 Definitions

Before discussing approaches for load-balancing in DHT systems, a clear definition of the term *load* has to be given [501]. Also, it must be made clear under what conditions a node may be referred to as *overloaded*, and a system as *optimally balanced*.

The data load of a peer node is usually determined by the amount of stored data per node. In the following, the load of a node is the sum of all data stored in this node. The total data load of a Peer-to-Peer (P2P) system is defined as the sum of the loads of all nodes participating in the system. The load of a system with N nodes is optimally balanced, if the data load of each node in the system is around $1/N$ of the total load. A node is referred to as *overloaded* or *heavy* if it has a significantly higher load compared with one in an optimal distribution. A node is *light* if it stores significantly less data than the optimum.

9.1.2 A Statistical Analysis

Before discussing algorithms for load-balancing, this section takes a look at the underlying statistics [450]. At the end of this section, theoretical evidence is provided for the empirical behavior. In the following, N is the number of nodes in the DHT, and m the number of data items.

Distribution of Data Items Among Peers with Equal-Sized Intervals

A simple model for load distribution is to consider all nodes to be responsible for intervals of equal size. Thus, when distributing a data item, each node is hit with a probability of $\frac{1}{N}$. Focusing on one node, the distribution of the data items is a series of independent Bernoulli trials with a success probability of $\frac{1}{N}$. The number of data items on this node (successful Bernoulli trials) is therefore following the binomial distribution.

The binomial distribution p_b and its standard deviation σ_b are defined as follows:

$$p_b(load == i) = \binom{m}{i}\left(\frac{1}{N}\right)^i\left(1-\frac{1}{N}\right)^{(m-i)} \quad (9.1)$$

$$\sigma_b = \sqrt{\frac{m}{N}\left(1-\frac{1}{N}\right)} \quad (9.2)$$

As an example, more than 300,000 collected file names from music and video servers were hashed, and the ID space was divided into intervals according to the first bits of an ID, e.g., 8 bits for 256 intervals. The load of each of these intervals is distributed closely around the average with the empirical standard deviation ($\sigma_{Experiment} = 34.5$) being close to the theoretical one ($\sigma_{Binomial} = 34.2$).

However, the assumptions of this model are not realistic for DHTs because interval sizes for nodes are not equal. The next section will deduce the interval size distribution.

Distribution of Peers in Chord

This section looks at the distribution of nodes on the Chord ring, or any other system randomly assigning node IDs. For the sake of simplicity, we use a continuous model, i.e., we consider the ID space to be real-valued in the interval $[0, 1)$. The number of nodes in a Peer-to-Peer network (at most, say a billion, i.e., roughly 2^{30} nodes) is small compared to the 2^{160} IDs in Chord's ID space.

- n-1 experiments with U(0,1).
- Determine the distribution of the IDs of the peers in the experiments.

The rationale for using this continuous model is that it is easier than a discrete one and the ID space is large compared with the number of nodes in it.

The continuous uniform distribution is defined as:

$$U(x) = \begin{cases} 0 & x < 0 \\ x & 0 \leq x < 1 \\ 1 & x \geq 1 \end{cases}$$

Let L be the distribution of the interval size. It is given as the minimum of $N-1$ experiments[1]:

[1] For our statistical analysis it does not matter if the node responsible for the data is at the beginning or the end of the interval.

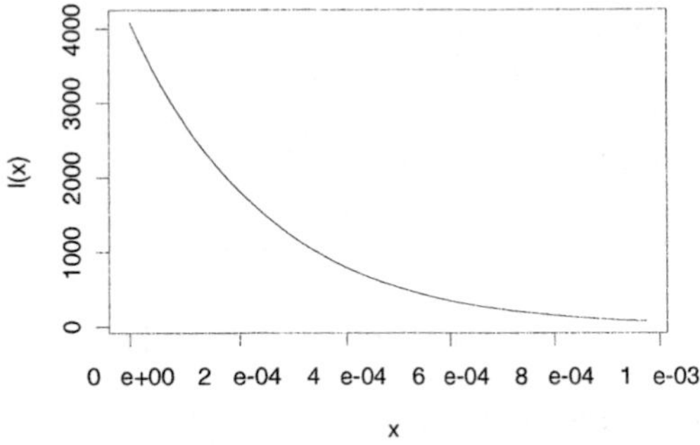

Fig. 9.2: Probability Density Function for Continuous Model with 4,096 nodes.

$$\begin{aligned} L(x) &= 1 - \prod_{i=1}^{N-1} (1 - U(x)) = 1 - (1 - U(x))^{N-1} \\ &= \begin{cases} 0 & x < 0 \\ 1 - (1-x)^{N-1} & 0 \leq x < 1 \\ 1 & x \geq 1 \end{cases} \end{aligned}$$

And the probability density function (pdf) shown in Fig. 9.2:

$$l(x) = \frac{dL}{dx} = \begin{cases} (N-1)(1-x)^{N-2} & 0 \leq x < 1 \\ 0 & else \end{cases}$$

It is interesting that the form of the probability density function and the load distribution are quite similar. This is even better illustrated when this calculation is done for a discrete ID space. To use this formula as an

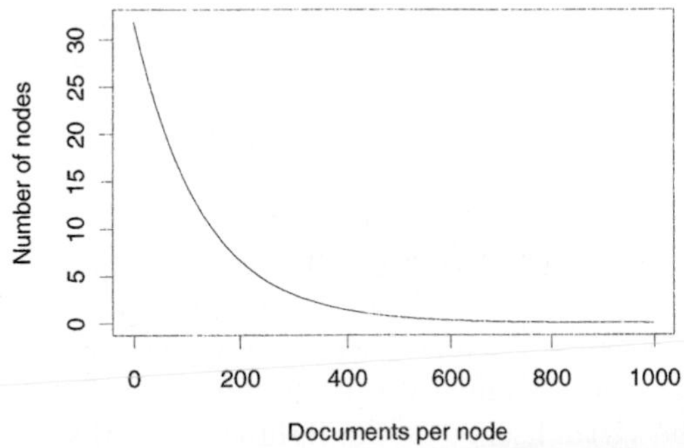

Fig. 9.3: Load Distribution (mean load = 128; 4,096 nodes) approximated with a scaled probability function from the Discrete Model.

approximation for the load, we use the number of data items as the ID space. Consequently, we get an approximation for the probability of a certain load (e.g., probability that a node has load = 10 items). If we multiply these probabilities with the number of nodes, we get the frequency distribution shown in Fig. 9.3.

9.1.3 Algorithms for Load Balancing in DHTs

To solve the problem of load-balancing, several techniques have been developed to ensure an equal data distribution across DHT nodes [512]. This chapter presents *Virtual Servers* [501], *Power of Two Choices* [99], *Heat Dispersion Algorithm* [513], and *a Simple Address-Space and Item Balancing* [338].

For clarity,the algorithms are mainly explained with Chord, but they are suitable for most of the different DHT systems.

The Concept of Virtual Servers

The virtual server approach [501] is based on the idea of managing multiple partitions of a DHT's address space in one node. Thus, one physical node may act as several independent logical nodes. Each virtual server will be considered by the underlying DHT as an independent node. Within a Chord system, one virtual server is responsible for an interval of the address space, whereas the corresponding physical node may be responsible for several different and independent intervals.

The basic advantage of this approach is the simplicity of displacement of virtual servers among arbitrary nodes. This operation is similar to the standard join or leave procedure of a DHT and content will be distributed as ranges of hash values across a the nodes. Every participating node manages virtual servers and has knowledge of all their neighbors from the fingers in the finger-table. For example with Chord, this relates to all fingers within the routing table. Now each node can transfer virtual servers to other nodes.

Transfer. The idea of the algorithm is to move a virtual server from a heavy to a light node. This transfer can be organized using three different schemes, known as: One-to-One, One-to-Many, and Many-to-Many.

In all of these schemes, the best virtual server which gets transferred is the one which satisfies the following three constraints. First, the transfer of a virtual server doesn't make the node which receives the virtual server heavy. Second, the virtual server is the lightest virtual server that makes the releasing node light. And third, if there is no virtual server whose transfer can make a node light, then the heaviest virtual server from this node gets transferred.

The third constraint results in the transfer of the largest virtual server that will not make the receiving node heavy, therefore, the chance of finding another light node in the next round which can receive a virtual server of this heavy node is increased.

One-to-One Scheme. This scheme is the simplest one. Two nodes are picked at random and a virtual server is transferred from a heavy node to a light one. Each light node periodically selects a node and indicates a transfer if that node is heavy, and if the above tree rules hold.

One-to-Many Scheme. This scheme allows a heavy node to consider more than one light node at a time. Each heavy node transfers a virtual server to one node of a known set of light nodes. For each light node of this set, the best virtual server is computed as described above and only the lightest virtual server of these will be transferred.

Many-to-Many Scheme. This scheme matches many heavy nodes to many light nodes. In order to get many heavy nodes and many light nodes to interact, a global pool of virtual servers is created – an intermediate step in moving a virtual server from a heavy node to a light node. The pool is only a local data structure used to compute the final allocation.

In three phases (unload, insert, and dislodge) the virtual servers to be transferred are computed. In the first one (unload) each heavy node puts the information about its virtual servers into a global pool until this node becomes light.

The virtual servers in the pool must then be transferred to nodes in the next step (insert). This phase is executed in rounds, in which the heaviest virtual server from the pool is selected and transferred to a light node, determined using the rules above. This phase continues until the pool becomes empty, or until no more virtual servers can be transferred.

In the final phase (dislodge), the largest virtual server from the pool is exchanged with another virtual server of a light node which is lighter and does not make the node heavy. If such a node is found, the insert step begins again, otherwise the algorithm terminates and the rest of the virtual servers in the pool stay at their current nodes.

Power of Two Choices

The algorithm *Power of Two Choices* [99] relies on the concept of multiple hash functions. These functions are used to map data into the address space of a DHT. For the processes of inserting and retrieving, the results of all hash functions are calculated. In the case of inserting a new document, all respective hash values are computed and the corresponding nodes are retrieved. Finally, the document is stored on the retrieved node with the lowest load in terms of stored data.

In formal terms, every node knows the universal hash function $h_1, h_2, \cdots, h_d$ which maps data onto the ring and so a node can compute

$h_1(x), h_2(x), \cdots, h_d(x)$ to insert the data x. For each of these computed results, the node responsible for this ID in the DHT is located. The data is now placed on the peer with the lowest load.

There are two ways to implement the search. A simple implementation requires that all hash functions be recalculated. After all lookups are made to find the peers associated with each of these values, one node must have successfully stored the data. These searches can be made in parallel and thus enable searching in little more time than their classic counterparts since this approach uses a factor of d more network traffic to perform each search.

The second way of searching is to use redirection pointers. Insertion proceeds exactly as before, but in addition to storing the item at the least loaded peer, all other peers store a redirection pointer to this node. To retrieve document x, it is not necessary to calculate all possible hash functions $h_1, h_2, \ldots, h_d$, because each possible node $h_1(x), h_2(x), \ldots, h_d(x)$ stores a pointer to document x. Thus, each of these nodes can forward the request directly to the node which is actually storing the requested document. Hence, a request for a certain key has to be made only to one of the d possible nodes. If this node does not store the data, the request is forwarded directly to the right node via the pointer. Nevertheless, the owner of a key has to insert the document periodically to prevent its removal after a timeout (soft state). Lookups now take at most only one more step.

Load Balancing Similar to Heat Dispersion

Rieche et. al [513] introduce another load-balancing algorithm for DHTs. Content is moved among peers similar to the process of heat dispersion [521]. Usually, a material warmer than its environment emits heat to its surroundings until a balanced distribution is reached in the entire system. To deploy a similar algorithm for balancing load among peers in a DHT, [513] proposes a very simple approach which needs only three rules. But nodes in a DHT can not simply move documents arbitrarily to other nodes, e.g., their neighbors, because this would result in an inconsistent and inefficient search. This reduces the performance and advantages of a DHT. Therefore, the algorithm moves only complete intervals, or contiguous parts of them, between the nodes in the DHT.

It seems appropriate to summarize the algorithm based on the DHT system Chord [575]. Although the Chord system has been modified, the efficient Chord routing algorithms remain unchanged. First of all, any fixed positive number f is chosen. f indicates the minimum number of nodes assigned to a specific DHT interval. If more than f nodes are assigned to a specific interval, one or more of them may be moved to a different interval. In case of more than $2f$ nodes, the respective interval can be split almost evenly. Now, a node has to manage approximately half of the documents. Each node periodically checks the data loads in its neighborhood – mainly its successors and predecessors – as well as destinations referenced in its DHT routing table. This number f helps to balance the load, but also to make Chord more fault tolerant.

The first node takes a random position in the Chord ring and a new node is assigned to any other existing node in the system. This receiving node announces each joining node to all other nodes responsible for the same interval. Following this, a portion of the documents located within this interval are copied to the new node. Then, the original methods to insert a node in Chord are performed. Now the nodes, located within the same interval, can balance the load with nodes of other intervals according to one of three various methods.

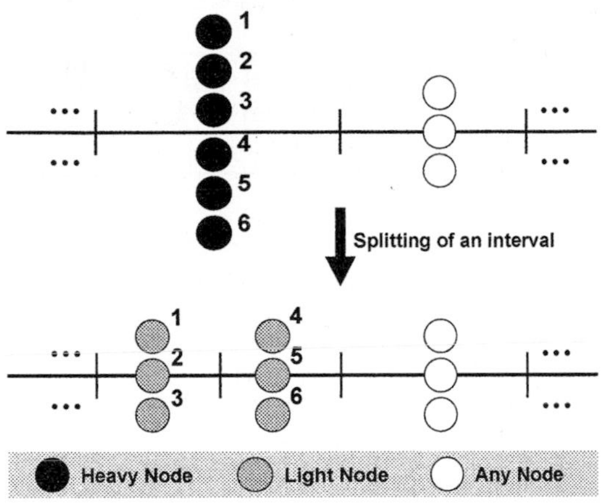

Fig. 9.4: Splitting of an Interval: Nodes 1 to 6 are assigned to the same interval and are overloaded in terms of data load. Since only three nodes are necessary to maintain an interval, this interval can be split.

2f Nodes with Excessive Load. If $2f$ different nodes are assigned to the same interval, and each node stores significantly more documents than average, then this interval gets divided. The point of separation is the center of the interval. It can be easily computed as the half of the interval borders or the half of the hash values representing the stored documents. This implies that no load in terms of data has to be moved anywhere, and the respective nodes lose approximately half of their data load at once. Finally, the predecessors and successors will be adapted accordingly. Figure 9.4 shows an example of such an interval division.

More than f Nodes in an Interval. Intervals with more than f but less than $2f$ nodes can release some nodes to other intervals. If nodes within a particular interval are overloaded, they wait for additional nodes to join them. If

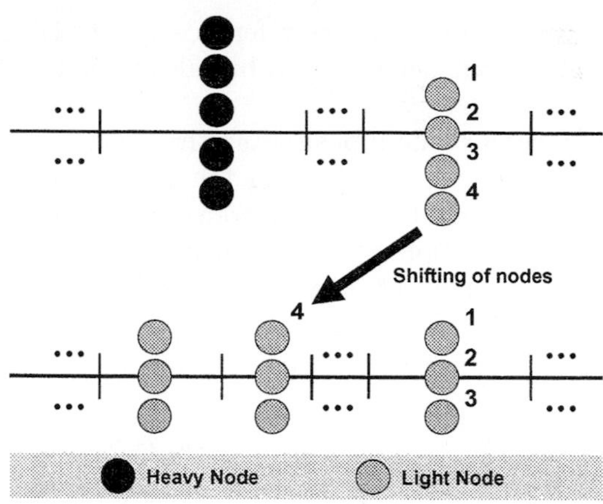

Fig. 9.5: Moving nodes: Nodes 1 to 4 are assigned to an interval. Since only three nodes are necessary to maintain an interval, node 4 can be transferred into another overloaded interval.

some nodes are very light, they periodically send this information to other nodes placed in different intervals. These desired destinations (intervals) can be found using routing entries of appropriate finger tables. Even if an interval with a heavy load exists, nodes can be moved to this interval. Based on the new situation, accumulated nodes within the new interval can try to split it by the rules described above.

Figure 9.5 shows an example of such a shifting of nodes to regions of higher load. Nodes 1 to 4 are very light in terms of data load and are responsible for the same interval. Since only three nodes are required, node 4 can be moved to an overloaded interval that should be divided.

No more than f Nodes within an Interval. As an additional alternative, interval borders may be shifted. Nodes can compare their load with the load of their immediate predecessors and successors. If its own interval shows more load than its neighbor's, part of the load can be released and thus interval borders will be shifted. Figure 9.6 shows an example of such a shifting of interval borders.

A Simple Address Space and Item Balancing

Karger and Ruhl introduce two protocols for load-balancing [338], especially for Chord [575]. The first balances the distribution of the key address space to nodes, the second directly balances the distribution of data among the nodes.

Address-Space Balancing. Each node has a fixed set of $O(\log N)$ possible positions in the Chord ring. These places are called virtual nodes (in com-

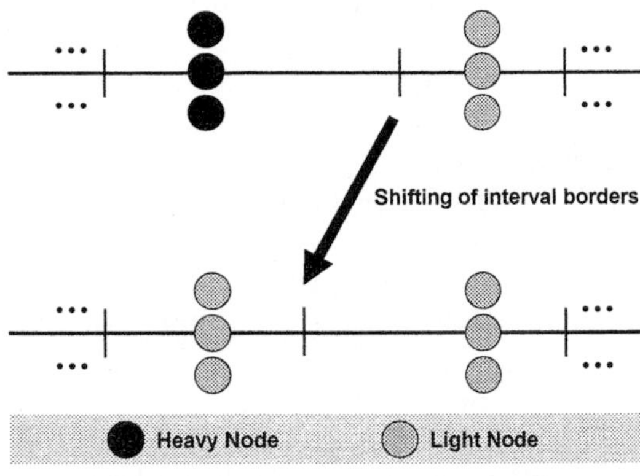

Fig. 9.6: Intervals adjusted between neighbors: The nodes within the right interval act together and are light, but the nodes located within the interval before are overloaded. Interval borders can be changed there.

parison to virtual servers in section 9.1.3) and are computed with different hash functions applied to their own ID. Each node chooses only one virtual node to become active. The address of a node is denoted as $(2b + 1)2^{-a}$ by $\langle a, b\rangle$, where a and b are non-negative integers and $b < 2^{a-1}$. This is an unambiguous notation for all addresses with finite binary representation. These addresses are ordered according to the length of their binary representation, so $\langle a, b\rangle < \langle a', b'\rangle$ if $a < a'$ or ($a = a'$ and $b < b'$).

Each node now chooses its ideal state. Given any set of active virtual nodes, each (possibly inactive) one spans a certain range of addresses between itself and the succeeding active virtual node. Each real node has activated the virtual node that spans the minimal possible (under the ordering just defined) address space. Thus, each node occasionally determines which of its virtual nodes spans the smallest address space and activates that particular virtual node.

Item Balancing. This also shifts interval borders. Nodes can compare their load with the loads of other nodes. If its own interval shows more load than its neighbor's, part of the load can be released and thus interval borders between two intervals will be shifted.

9.1.4 Comparison of Load-Balancing Approaches

To analyze load-balancing in a DHT, a complete Chord ring simulator was developed in [513] to investigate and to compare the load-balancing algorithms *Virtual Servers* [501], *Power of Two Choices* [99], and *Heat Dispersion Al-*

gorithm [513]. The focus was on the distribution of documents among the nodes.

Simulation Scenarios

In each scenario, a Chord DHT with 4,096 nodes was simulated and multiple simulations were run per scenario to confirm the results. The simulation in [513] shows that the results are comparable with the simulations presented in [99]. The total number of documents to be stored ranged from 100,000 to 1,000,000. The keys for the data and nodes were generated randomly. For this purpose, the Chord ring's address space had a size of $m = 22$ bits. Consequently, $2^{22} = 4{,}194{,}304$ documents and/or nodes could be stored and managed in the ring. In the simulation, the load of a node is defined as the number of documents it stores.

Simulation Results

Fig. 9.7(a) shows the distribution of documents in Chord without load-balancing. Between 10^5 and 10^6 documents were distributed across 4,096 nodes. The upper value indicates the maximum number of documents per node, the lower value the minimum number. The optimal number of documents per node is indicated by the marker in the middle.

Even for a large number of documents in the DHT, there are some nodes not managing any documents and, consequently, without any load. Some nodes have a load of up to ten times above the optimum. Fig. 9.7(b) shows that *Power of Two Choices* works much more efficiently than the original Chord without load-balancing. However, there are still obvious differences in the loads of the nodes. Some are still without any document.

Applying the concept of *Virtual Servers* with the One-to-One scheme (cf. Fig. 9.7(c)) results in a more efficient load-balancing. Nevertheless, this is coupled with a much higher workload for each node because it has to manage many virtual servers. Additionally, the data of all virtual servers of one physical node has to be stored in the memory of the managing node.

Fig. 9.7(d) shows that the best results for load-balancing are achieved by using the *heat dispersion algorithm*. Each node manages a certain amount of data and load fluctuations are relatively small. Documents are only moved from neighbor to neighbor. Using virtual severs, however, results in copying the data of a whole virtual server. As a result, the copied load is always balanced. In addition, more node management is necessary.

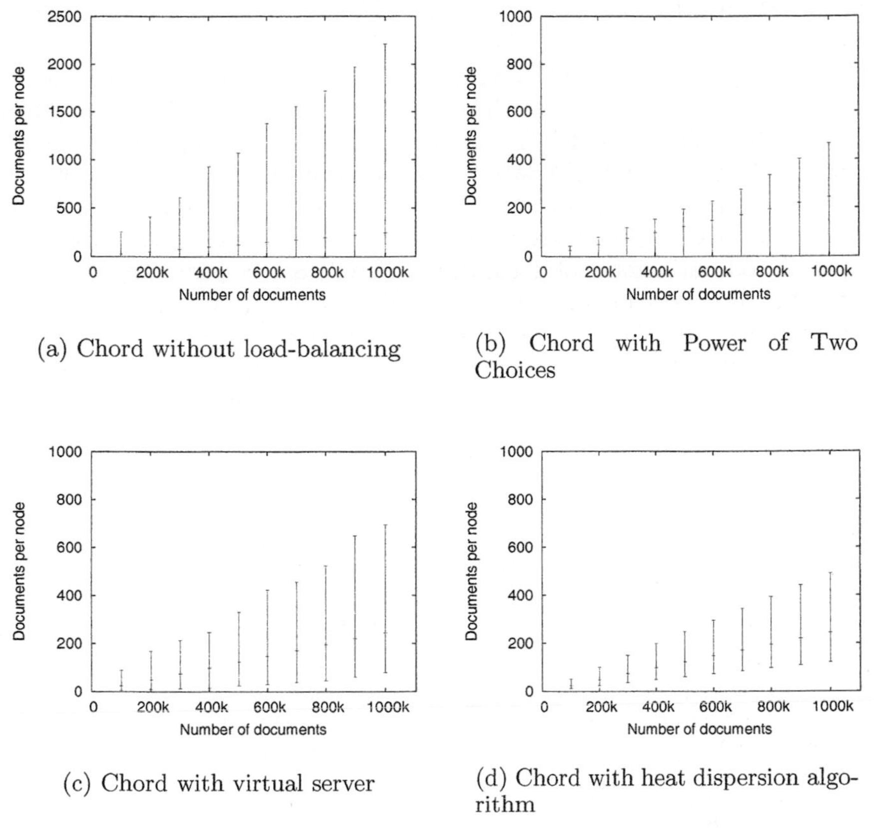

(a) Chord without load-balancing

(b) Chord with Power of Two Choices

(c) Chord with virtual server

(d) Chord with heat dispersion algorithm

Fig. 9.7: Simulation results comparing different approaches for load balancing in Chord.

9.2 Reliability of Data in Distributed Hash Tables

Through much research in the design and stabilization of DHT lookup services, these systems aim to provide a stable global addressing structure on top of a dynamic network of unreliable, constantly failing and arriving nodes. This will allow building fully decentralized services and distributed applications based on DHTs. This section shows algorithms for ensuring that data stored at failing nodes is available after stabilization routines of the Peer-to-Peer-based network have been applied.

There are two ways to store data in the DHT in a fault-tolerant manner. One is to replicate the data to other nodes, another is to split the data and make them more available through redundancy.

9.2.1 Redundancy

The idea to increase availability through redundancy is realized by splitting each data item into N fragments. Then K redundant fragments are computed by means of an erasure code. Thus, any N of the $N + K$ fragments will allow reconstruction of the original data. For each fragment, its place in the ring is computed. The data is split to $K + N$ different keys. Each fragment is stored using the standard Chord assignment rule. A read corresponds to $K + N$ recursive-style lookups and is successful if at least N parts are available. But, every time a node crashes, a piece of the data is destroyed, and after some time, the data may no longer be computable. Therefore, the idea of redundancy also needs replication of the data.

9.2.2 Replication

Another more fault-tolerant way to store the data is to replicate it to other nodes. This section describes two ways to replicate data in Chord.

Successor-List

The authors of Chord show in [575] a possibility to make the data more reliable in their DHT. The idea to make the data in Chord more fault-tolerant is to use a so-called *successor-list*. This list is also used to stabilize the network after nodes leave. The *successor-list* of any node consists of the f nearest successors clockwise on the Chord ring.

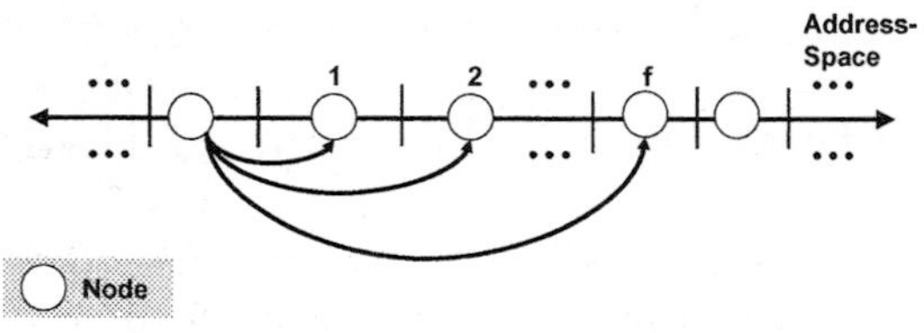

Fig. 9.8: Successor-list of a node with f nearest nodes clockwise on the Chord ring.

Because every node stores a successor-list of f nodes, the whole system has $n * f$ additional links in a network with n nodes. This implies that a lot of extra traffic is used just to keep the links consistent in case of node failures or arrivals.

Figure 9.8 shows an example for a node and its successor-list. A node stores pointers to the f nearest nodes clockwise on the Chord ring.

The reliability of data in Chord is an application task. Therefore, the successor-list mechanism helps a higher layer software to replicate inserted data to the next f nodes. Any application using Chord has to ensure that replicas of the data are stored at the f nodes succeeding the original node. Figure 9.9 shows replication of data by the application using the successive nodes in the ring.

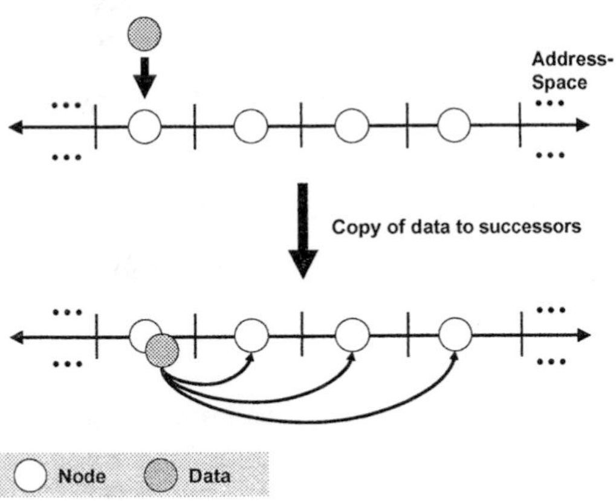

Fig. 9.9: Replication of inserted data in Chord by the application.

The application has to periodically check the number of replications of the inserted data and the stabilization routine has to repair the network successfully. Also, every node now has f intervals to store, hence the load of each node increases dramatically.

Multiple Nodes in One Interval

The approach [514] uses multiple nodes per interval.

Each interval of the DHT may be maintained by several nodes at the same time. In order to ensure correctness of this technique, each node stores additional pointers to nodes maintaining the same interval. In Chord, these additional pointers could be implemented as additional finger entries in another routing table. In CAN, they would be deployed as new neighbors. Let f be the minimum number of nodes assigned to a specific DHT region (or interval).

If a new node joins an existing interval, it announces itself to all other nodes responsible for the same interval. Additionally, all data associated with this interval is copied to the new node.

The first node takes a random position in the Chord ring and a new node is assigned to any existing node in the system. This receiving node announces each joining node to all other nodes responsible for the same interval. Following this, parts of documents located within this interval are copied to this new node. Then, the original methods to insert a node in Chord are performed. To keep the complexity of the routing tables low, each node stores only one reference to the list of nodes for each finger within its own routing table to other intervals.

Figure 9.10 shows an example of the distribution of intervals on different nodes, where each interval has the minimum of two different nodes assigned to it.

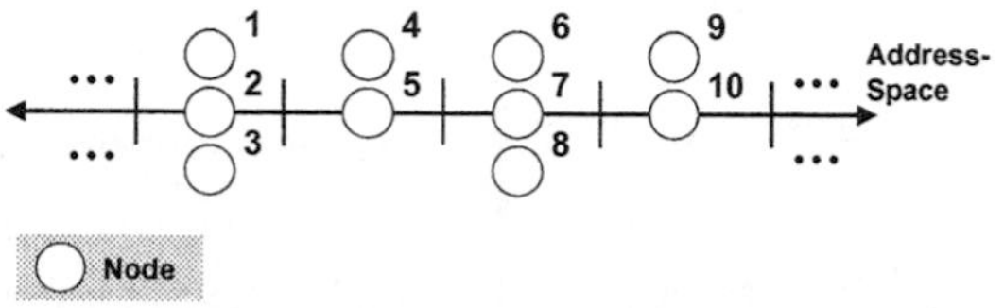

Fig. 9.10: Intervals with minimum of two nodes assigned to them.

According to [575], each node may maintain several virtual servers, but most of them store only one. This allows nodes with higher performance to store several virtual servers. Chord can take advantage of the high computational power of certain nodes. Such a node declares itself responsible for two or more intervals. Thus, it manages several virtual servers, and each virtual server is responsible for separate disjoint intervals. However, all intervals stored at the virtual servers in the same physical node shall not be identical in order to guarantee fault tolerance.

If new data has to be inserted into an interval, it will be distributed by one node to all other nodes responsible for the same interval. But, no copies of the data are replicated clockwise to the next n nodes along the ring, as in the original Chord DHT. Figure 9.11 shows the distribution of replicas of the inserted data to the neighbors responsible for the same interval.

If any node leaves the system and any other node takes notice of this, the standard stabilization routine of Chord is performed. The predecessors and successors are informed, and afterwards, inconsistent finger table entries are identified and updated using the periodic maintenance routine.

Thus DHT systems become more reliable and far more efficient due to the structured management of nodes. Generally, random losses of nodes are not critical because at least f nodes manage one interval cooperatively. The modified DHT system can cope with a loss of (f-1) nodes assigned to the same interval. In case of less than f nodes within one interval, the algorithm immediately merges adjacent intervals.

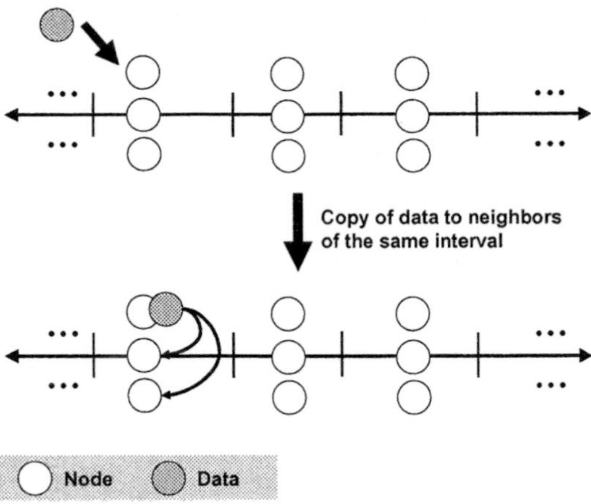

Fig. 9.11: Copy of data to the neighbors responsible for the same interval.

9.3 Summary

This chapter introduces algorithms for DHT-based systems which balance the storage data load or care for the reliability of the data.

All systems usually rely on the basic assumption that data is nearly equally distributed among the peer nodes. But, as shown, the simple assumption of getting an equally distributed value space simply by using hash functions does not hold. To achieve a continuous balance of data and, moreover, to ensure the scalability and efficiency in structured Peer-to-Peer systems, load-balancing mechanisms have to be applied. Therefore, this chapter introduces some algorithms for balancing storage load in DHTs. Although the algorithms are explained based on Chord, most of them can be easily adapted to other DHTs, such as CAN.

The second part of the chapter shows two ways to store data in the DHT in a fault-tolerant manner. One is to replicate the data to other nodes, and another is to split the data, thus making them more available through redundancy.

10. P-Grid: Dynamics of Self-Organizing Processes in Structured Peer-to-Peer Systems

Karl Aberer, Anwitaman Datta, Manfred Hauswirth (EPFL)

10.1 The Concept of Self-Organization

Peer-to-peer systems are often characterized as self-organizing systems. Such characterization is frequently used to informally express properties of Peer-to-Peer systems such as the distribution of control, locality of processing, and the emergence of global structures from local interactions. Self-organizing systems are considered as being particularly scalable and failure resilient.

In this chapter we would like to explore the nature of self-organization in Peer-to-Peer systems in more detail, with a particular emphasis on structured overlay networks. Overlay networks facilitate the organization of application-specific address spaces in Peer-to-Peer systems by constructing a logical network on top of the physical network. They are one of the central concepts that have been introduced in the field of Peer-to-Peer systems. We will investigate the issue of self-organization first for unstructured overlay networks, such as Gnutella [126], where issues of self-organization are more widely studied, and then show how self-organization also plays a role for the design of structured overlay networks. We will study self-organization for the P-Grid structured overlay network [3] which has been designed as a highly self-organizing system.

Self-organizing systems are well-known from many scientific disciplines, in particular from physics and biology, for example, crystallization processes or insect colonies. In computer science self-organization and the resulting phenomena have been studied in particular in the field of artificial intelligence (agent systems, distributed decision making, etc.).

Self-organization is the process of evolution of a complex system with local interaction of system components only, resulting in system states with certain observed or intended global properties. A self-organizing process is driven by randomized local variations—movements of molecules in the case of crystallization, movements of individual insects in insect colonies. These "fluctuations" or "noise", as they are also called, lead to a continuous perturbation of the system and allow the system to explore a global state space until it enters into equilibrium states. These states correspond to the global, emergent structures [294].

R. Steinmetz and K. Wehrle (Eds.): P2P Systems and Applications, LNCS 3485, pp. 137-153, 2005.

More formally, a self-organizing system can be described as a Markovian process. Given a set of possible states S, which usually is very large, the evolution of a complex system can be described deterministically by a function $f_T : S \to S$. In practice, the lack of information about the precise state will make a deterministic description of the system evolution infeasible. Thus a more realistic way to describe the system evolution is by a stochastic process where for each given state s_i we can give the probability that a state s_j is reached, i.e. $P(s_j|s_i) = M_{ij} \in [0,1]$, where M is the transition matrix of a Markovian process. Given the probability distribution of states $P(s_i, t)$ at time t it is thus possible to calculate the time evolution of the system as

$$P(s_j, t+1) = \sum_i M_{ij}\ P(s_i, t).$$

Usually we are interested in emergent properties of such self-organizing systems. Emergent properties are global properties of the state space that result after the system has converged to an equilibrium. In the following we will demonstrate how this view of self-organizing systems can be adopted in the context of Peer-to-Peer systems.

10.2 An Example of Self-Organization in Unstructured Peer-to-Peer Systems

Unstructured Peer-to-Peer systems have generated substantial interest because of their self-organization behavior resulting in interesting global structural properties of their state, in particular the structure of the resulting network graphs. For example, the Gnutella network graph exhibits the following characteristics [516]:

1. The network has a small diameter, which ensures that a message flooding approach for search works with a relatively low time-to-live (approximately 7).
2. The node degrees of the overlay network follow a power-law distribution. Thus few peers have a large number of incoming links, whereas most peers have a very low number of such links.

These properties result from the way Gnutella performs network maintenance: Each peer discovers other peers by constrained flooding. From the discovered peers a fixed number of randomly selected peers are used to construct the Gnutella network. Thus nodes in the network graph have a constant out-degree. During this process peers with a larger number of incoming connections are more likely to be selected. This corresponds to a *preferential attachment* mechanism during network construction. Preferential attachment has been identified as a mechanism that generates a power-law distribution of node degrees for many types of networks, for example, the World Wide

Web, citation networks, and genetic networks. Similarly, for unstructured overlay networks this mechanisms leads to a power-law distribution of nodes' in-degrees.

A non-rigorous argument why preferential attachment generates power-law distributed node degrees is as follows [422]. We model the system state by the distribution of node degrees. Let $P(j,t)$ be the probability that at time t a node has in-degree j and assume that at each time step one peer joins the network and adds one additional connection. Assume that with probability α the node to which the new peer connects is chosen uniformly randomly and with probability $1-\alpha$ proportionally to the current node degree. Then the process of network evolution can be modeled as follows.

$$P(j,t+1) = P(j,t)+\alpha(P(j-1,t)-P(j,t))+(1-\alpha)((j-1)P(j-1,t)-jP(j,t)).$$

Now assume that the degree distribution is in steady state, i.e. $P(j,t) = c_j, t > 0$. We can derive

$$\frac{c_j}{c_{j-1}} = 1 - \frac{2-\alpha}{1+\alpha+j(1-\alpha)} \approx 1 - \frac{2-\alpha}{1-\alpha}\frac{1}{j}$$

where the approximation is valid for large j. This relationships is satisfied approximately for

$$c_j \approx j^{-\frac{2-\alpha}{1-\alpha}}.$$

To see this, note that for this c_j we have

$$\frac{c_j}{c_{j-1}} \approx (1-\frac{1}{j})^{\frac{2-\alpha}{1-\alpha}} \approx 1 - \frac{2-\alpha}{1-\alpha}\frac{1}{j}$$

This is a first example of how a self-organization process results in a global structural feature, namely the power-law degree distribution. The probability that a node has a given in-degree remains invariant while the network grows, thus the system is in a dynamic equilibrium during network construction.

The structure of the resulting overlay network is the basis for performing searches efficiently. In Gnutella, searches are performed by message flooding. A low network diameter, as in the power-law graph, guarantees low search latency. Message flooding however induces a high consumption of network bandwidth. Therefore other strategies for performing searches in Gnutella networks have been investigated. The independence of the network maintenance and search protocols makes it possible to use alternative search strategies which may exploit the emergent overlay network structure more efficiently. Examples of such alternative strategies are the random walker model [397] and the percolation search model [537], which both exploit the specific structure of the network.

To summarize, we can observe two important points for unstructured overlay networks such as Gnutella. First, the structure of the network and its global properties are induced by the (self-organizing) dynamic process used for their construction. Second, the design of efficient search algorithms exploits the structural features of the overlay network that results from the self-organized construction process. In the following we will show that the same principles can be applied analogously for structured overlay networks.

10.3 Self-Organization in Structured Peer-to-Peer Systems

One of the important drawbacks of unstructured overlay networks is the high network bandwidth consumption during searches, apart from the fact that successful searches are not guaranteed unless all peers are contacted. This motivated the development of structured overlay networks where nodes coordinate among themselves by partitioning the key space and maintaining state information on the resources stored at neighboring nodes. This enables the implementation of directed searches and thus to dramatically reduce bandwidth consumption used in search. This approach, however, requires also a higher degree of coordination among the nodes while constructing and maintaining the overlay network.

To achieve this coordination, maintenance algorithms are provided that maintain structural invariants during the lifetime of the overlay network. Typically these structural invariants are ensured through localized operations. This is the approach taken by most structured overlay networks, such as Chord [575]. The structural invariant of Chord is related to the selection of routing table entries. Each node maintains a link to the first node located on predefined partitions of the key space, which are increasing exponentially in size with distance from the node. During network maintenance, for example, during a node join, the routing tables of the joining node and existing nodes in the network are updated immediately such that after the join is completed, the structural constraints on the routing tables are satisfied. This approach is very different from the self-organization mechanism we have analyzed for unstructured networks, where a structural property, i.e., the node in-degree distribution, is ensured not through localized operations but as a property resulting from a self-organization process.

In the following we will show how self-organizing processes can also be used in the context of structured overlay networks. With such an approach structural properties are not guaranteed through localized operations, but emerge as a global property from a self-organization process. We will demonstrate this approach for the P-Grid overlay network [3]. P-Grid uses self-organizing processes for the initial network construction to achieve load-balancing properties as well as for maintenance to retain structural properties of the overlay network intact during changes in the physical network. We will give first an overview of the structural design of P-Grid and then discuss its self-organization mechanisms and the techniques used for their analysis. Our focus is on the exemplification of general self-organization principles which are applicable to many overlay networks to varying extents and with different performance implications as we will briefly discuss at the end of this chapter.

10.3.1 The Structure of P-Grid Overlay Networks

We assume that the data keys are taken from the interval $[0, 1[$. The structure of a P-Grid overlay network is based on two simple principal ideas: (1) the key space is recursively bisected such that the resulting partitions carry approximately the same workload. Peers are associated with those partitions. Using a *bisection approach* greatly simplifies decentralized load-balancing by local decision-making. (2) Bisecting the key space induces a canonical trie structure which is used as the basis for implementing a standard, distributed *prefix routing scheme* for efficient search.

This is illustrated in Fig. 10.1. At the bottom we see a possible skewed key distribution in the interval $[0, 1[$. We bisect the interval such that each resulting partition carries (approximately) the same load. Each partition can be uniquely identified by a bit sequence. We associate one or more peers (in the example exactly two) with each of the partitions. We call the bit sequence of a peer's partition the peer's path. The bit sequences induce a trie structure, which is used to implement prefix routing. Each peer maintains references in its routing table that pertain to its path. More specifically, for each position of its path, it maintains one or more references to a peer that has a path with the opposite bit at this position. Thus the trie structure is represented in a distributed fashion by the routing tables of the peers, such that there is no hierarchy in the actual overlay network. This construction is analogous to other prefix routing schemes that have been devised [491, 527]. Search in such overlay networks is performed by resolving a requested key bit by bit. When bits cannot be resolved locally, peers forward the request to a peer known from their routing tables.

P-Grid uses replication in two ways in order to increase the resilience of the overlay network when nodes or network links fail. Multiple references are kept in the routing tables, thus providing alternative access paths, and multiple peers are associated with the same key space partitions (*structural replication*) in order to provide data redundancy. The self-organization mechanisms we will discuss for P-Grid will relate to these two replication mechanisms.

Contrary to standard prefix routing approaches P-Grid does not assume a maximal key length that limits the tree depth and thus search cost. This assumption would compromise the load-balancing properties achieved by bisection. Thus search efficiency is not guaranteed structurally, since in the worst case search cost is related to the maximal path length of the trie, which for skewed key distributions can be up to linear in the network size.

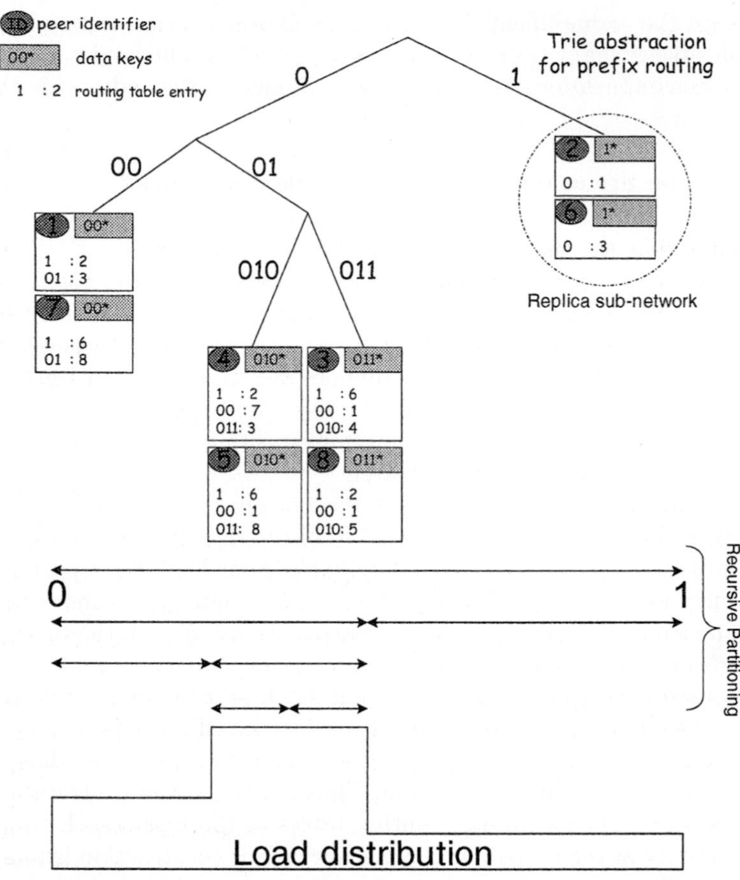

Fig. 10.1: P-Grid structure

To guarantee efficient search, P-Grid constructs its routing tables in a randomized fashion. For example, all peers that adopted 0 as the first bit of their path, can choose at the first level of their routing table any peer with first bit 1. This is in contrast to a deterministic approach where a specific peer would have to be chosen, e.g., the first in the respective interval. It turns out that with such a randomized approach in expectation routing cost is exactly $\log n$, where n is the number of leaves of the trie underlying the routing table construction. Informally, by randomly selecting in the routing tables peers among all peers that can resolve the next bit during routing, in expectation more than one bit will be resolved in a single step. An analysis for the routing cost is found in [2].

There is another motivation for having a trie-structured overlay network instead of a standard distributed hash table: The real advantage of traditionally using a hash table in main memory is the constant time of lookup, insert, and delete operations. But to facilitate this, a hash table sacrifices the order-relationship of the keys. However, over a network, where only parts of the hash table are stored at each location, we need multiple overlay hops anyway. For most conventional DHTs the number of hops is logarithmic in the network size. Thus the main advantage of constant-time access no longer exists. In fact the fundamental issue to address now is, whether we can realize a search tree, which still is similarly efficient as a DHT in terms of fault-tolerance, load-balancing, etc., but also provides properties such as preservation of key ordering and hence supports efficient exact queries but also efficiently enables higher-level search predicates such as substring search, range queries [157], etc. This is a major goal in the design of the P-Grid overlay network.

10.3.2 Dynamics of P-Grid Overlay Networks

From a structural perspective P-Grid is based on a distributed trie structure that preserves key ordering. This naturally enables prefix and range queries [157]. However, a number of algorithmic issues need to be addressed in order to adapt the structure of the overlay to a given key distribution and to maintain it in a dynamic network environment.

Usually maintenance for overlay networks is considered for a *sequential node join and leave model.* Algorithms are provided for inserting new nodes contacting an existing network node. The arrival of a new node requires updates to the routing tables of the new node and of some of the existing nodes in the network. In case of node failures or uncooperative node departure, routing table entries need to be repaired. This is performed by maintenance algorithms which either periodically poll routing table entries or piggy-back repair actions to other operations, e.g., searches.

In addition to these standard techniques P-Grid also supports the efficient construction of an overlay network from scratch. We call this the *bootstrapping problem* and it corresponds to the standard database problem of index construction. For addressing this problem, it is critical that the large number of peers participating in the construction of the overlay network can work *in parallel.*

This problem has been largely ignored in the literature, but has to be solved for a number of practical reasons, in particular for data-oriented applications. The need to bootstrap a new overlay structure can occur for semantic needs of applications, e.g., for indexing new attribute types of resources with structured metadata annotations or due to performance considerations, e.g., for periodically rebuilding an inverted file in a Peer-to-Peer retrieval system rather than continuously maintaining it, or for operational reasons, e.g., for rebuilding an overlay network after catastrophic failure, where the standard maintenance method is no longer capable of reconstructing a stable overlay network.

In the following we will first discuss a self-organizing process that is used to realize efficient bootstrapping of P-Grid networks, and then discuss a routing table maintenance technique used in P-Grid for maintaining consistency of routing tables under network churn which is based on an adaptive, self-organizing process.

10.3.3 Bootstrapping a P-Grid Overlay Network

The process of bootstrapping an overlay network from scratch should be performed with low latency, i.e., highly parallel, and with minimal bandwidth consumption. At the same time, for a P-Grid overlay network it should simultaneously achieve two load-balancing properties:

1. The partitioning of the search space should be such that each partition holds approximately the same load, e.g., measured as the number of keys present in the partition.
2. Each resulting partition should be associated with approximately the same number of peers, such that the availability of the different data keys is approximately the same.

P-Grid achieves these goals by a distributed, self-organizing process. Using a self-organizing process allows to largely decouple the operation of different peers and thus enables the parallelization of the task.

The design of the process takes advantage of the fact that a P-Grid overlay network structure results from the recursive bisection of the key space. The process is based on random encounters of peers. These are initiated by performing random walks on a pre-existing unstructured overlay network. In their encounters the peers decide whether the current partition contains a sufficient number of keys to justify a further split. The problem to solve is that a large number of peers have to split fast into two peer populations of which the ratio matches the ratio of the key set sizes in the two partitions.

We provide the algorithm used for the basic case of performing a bisection into two partitions 0 and 1 with $n+1$ peers, where the workload associated with the two partitions is p and $1-p$. We assume that each peer knows the value of p and that $0 \leq p \leq \frac{1}{2}$. Then the problem can be formulated as follows.

1. *Proportional replication:* Each peer has to decide for one of the two partitions such that (in expectation) a fraction p of the peers decides for 0 and a fraction $1-p$ for 1. Thus the average workload becomes uniformly distributed among the peers.

2. *Referential integrity:* During the process each of the peers has to encounter at least one peer that decided for the other partition. Thus the peers have the necessary information to construct the routing table.

The second condition makes the problem non-trivial, since otherwise peers could simply select partition 0 with probability p and 1 otherwise. P-Grid uses the following distributed algorithm to solve the problem.

1. Each undecided peer initiates interactions with a uniformly randomly selected peer until it has reached a decision.
2. If the contacted peer is undecided the peers perform a balanced split with probability $0 \leq \alpha(p) \leq 1$ and maintain references to each other.
3. If the contacted peer has already decided for 1 then the contacting peer decides for 0 with probability $0 \leq \beta(p) \leq 1$ and with probability $1-\beta(p)$ for 1. In the first case it maintains a reference to the contacted peer. In the second case it obtains a reference to a peer from the other partition from the contacted peer.

We can model this algorithm as a Markovian process. We assume that in each step i one peer without having found its counterpart so far contacts another randomly selected peer. We denote by $P(0,t)$ and $P(1,t)$ the expected number of peers that have decided in step t for 0 and 1 respectively. Initially $P(0,0) = P(1,0) = 0$. At the end of the process at some step t_e we have $P(0,t_e) + P(1,t_e) = n+1$. We analyze the case $\alpha(p) = 1$. Then the model can be given as

$$
\begin{aligned}
P(0,t) &= P(0,t-1) + \frac{1}{n}(n - P(0,t-1) - (1-\beta)P(1,t-1)) \\
P(1,t) &= P(1,t-1) + \frac{1}{n}(n - \beta P(1,t-1))
\end{aligned}
$$

In order to determine the proper value of β for a given value of p, we have to solve the recursive system. By standard solution methods we obtain

$$
\begin{aligned}
P(0,t) &= \frac{n}{\beta}(2\beta - 1 + (1 - \frac{\beta}{n})^t - 2\beta(\frac{n-1}{n})^t) \\
P(1,t) &= \frac{n}{\beta}(1 - (1 - \frac{\beta}{n})^t)
\end{aligned}
$$

We observe that the recursion terminates as soon as no more undecided peers exist, i.e., as soon as $P(0,t_e) + P(1,t_e) = n+1$. By evaluating this termination condition we obtain

$$
t_e(n) = \frac{\log(2)}{\log(\frac{n}{n-1})} + 1 \tag{10.1}
$$

Note that t_e does not depend on p, and thus the partitioning process requires the same number of interactions among peers independent of load distribution. By definition $p = \frac{P(0,t_e)}{n+1}$, thus we obtain a relationship among the network size $n+1$ and the load distribution p with $\beta(p,n)$. For large networks, by letting $n \to \infty$, we obtain the following relationship among p and $\beta(p)$

$$p = 1 - \frac{1}{\beta}(1 - 2^{-\beta}) \tag{10.2}$$

Positive solutions for $\beta(p)$ cannot be obtained for all values of p. From Equation 10.2 we derive that positive solutions exist for $p \geq 1 - \log(2)$. Informally speaking, since balanced splits are always executed unconditionally, the algorithm cannot adapt to arbitrarily skewed distributions. Therefore for $0 \leq p < 1 - \log(2)$ we have to pursue a different strategy, by reducing the probability of balanced splits, i.e. $\alpha(p) < 1$. The analysis of this case is analogous and therefore we omit it here.

Various non-trivial issues still need to be addressed to extend this basic process to a complete method for constructing a P-Grid overlay network with load-balancing characteristics. The value of p is normally not known, thus it needs to be estimated from the key samples the peers have available locally. This introduces errors into the process which require non-trivial corrections. The process needs to be performed recursively, thus errors in proportionally bisecting the key space accumulate. The process needs to be approximately synchronized to leave the assumptions made for the basic process valid. The bisection process should terminate as soon as the number of peers in the same partition falls below a threshold. Since peers cannot know during the bootstrapping all potential replica peers in the same partition, other criteria, based on the locally available keys, need to be evaluated. Solutions for these problems have been developed and it has been shown that in fact it is possible to efficiently construct a P-Grid overlay network satisfying the desired load-balancing properties based on the elementary process introduced in this section [6, 7].

10.3.4 Routing Table Maintenance

Another aspect of overlay network dynamics is related to the dynamics of the underlying physical networks. Entries in routing tables can turn stale due to temporary or permanent failures of peers or network connections. Standard approaches that address this problem use periodic probing or correct entries immediately upon changes (correction-on-change).

These approaches are specifically designed for environments where peer reliability is relatively high. For P-Grid we assume the contrary, i.e., peers are generally unavailable. Therefore P-Grid relies on a high degree of redundancy in the routing tables, such that with high probability routing can be performed successfully. Trying to keep all redundant routing entries continuously consistent would not be appropriate in a highly dynamic network. P-Grid rather uses a lazy approach, where routing entries are only corrected if routing fails. We distinguish two possibilities when to perform a repair: (1) immediate repair of stale routing table entries (among a large number of redundant entries) encountered during routing (correction-on-use) and (2) initiate repairs upon failure of all redundant entries at one level of the routing table of a peer (correction-on-failure) [5].

Using a lazy repair approach one can tolerate a certain fraction of stale routing entries in the routing tables. This has the advantage that routing entries to peers that are only temporarily unavailable and reappear, do not require a repair. Furthermore, peers can maintain their path and thus the keys they store also in case of temporary absence, which further reduces the maintenance cost.

In order to enable repairs, P-Grid uses the overlay network itself as a directory for storing the current binding of logical peer identifiers to their current physical address. Peers joining the network have to provide this data. For repair then the binding can be retrieved from the overlay network. Note that during repairs more failures may occur, such that repairs may recursively trigger other repairs. Recursive triggering queries for repair has an inherent self-healing property. With few stale mappings, there is hardly any deterioration in answering the queries, but as the stale entries accumulate over time, they lead to more frequent recursions. An important question is whether such a system can operate in a stable state. For analyzing this, we will model the overlay network as a dynamical, self-organizing system.

To illustrate the route maintenance mechanism we first provide a simple example below. Note that though in the example P-Grid is used as a self-referential directory service for storing identity-to-address mappings of peers, the approach is generally applicable and provides a generic self-contained directory service, such that any information about the participating peers (e.g., trust, history, resource meta-data, etc.) can be stored within the system itself.

Figure 10.2 shows a typical state of a P-Grid network.

Peer P_i is denoted by i inside an oval. Online peers are indicated by shaded ovals, offline peers by unshaded ovals. Peers under the same branch are replicas. For example, P_1 and P_7 are both responsible for paths starting with 000. Without loss of generality we assume that the identity of a peer p (Id_p) has a length of 4 bits. Thus P_7 holds the public key and latest physical address mapping about P_1 (updated by P_1) because P_7 is responsible for the paths 0000 and 0001. The shaded rectangle in the upper-right corner of each peer shows the peer IDs that a peer is responsible for, i.e., whose public key and physical address mapping it manages. Note that there exists

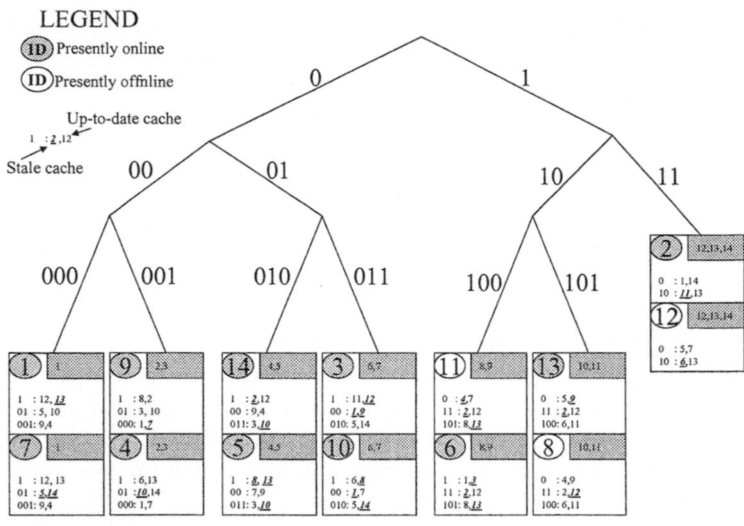

Fig. 10.2: An example P-Grid network

no dependency between the peer identity ($id_{P_7} = 0111$) and the path it is associated with ($\pi(P_7) = 0000$). In its routing table P_7 stores references for paths starting with 1, 01 and 001, so that queries with these prefixes can be forwarded closer to the peers holding the searched information. The cached physical addresses of these references may be up-to-date (for example, P_{13}'s) or be stale (denoted by underlining, for example, $\underline{P_5}$).

A peer P_q decides that it has failed to contact a peer P_s, if one of the following happens: (1) No peer is available at the cached address (trivial case) or (2) the contacted peer has a different identifier. In either of these cases an up-to-date identity-to-address mapping can be obtained by querying the P-Grid. If peer P_s goes offline, and comes online later with a different IP address, it can insert a new identity-to-address mapping into P-Grid.

If a peer fails to contact peers in its routing table, it initiates a new query to discover the latest identity-to-address mapping of any of those peers. If this is successful it forwards the query.

Assuming the initial setup while the P-Grid is in the state shown in Figure 10.2, the query processing will work as follows. Assume that P_7 receives a query $Q(01*)$. P_7 fails to forward the query to either of P_5 or P_{14} since their cache entries are stale. Thus P_7 initiates a recursive query for (P_5), i.e., $Q(0101)$, which needs to be forwarded to either P_5 or P_{14}. This fails again. P_7 then initiates a recursive query for (P_{14}), i.e., $Q(1110)$, which needs to be forwarded to P_{12} and (or) P_{13}. P_{12} is offline, so irrespective of the cache being stale or up-to-date, the query cannot be forwarded to P_{12}. P_{13} is online, and the cached physical address of P_{13} at P_7 is up-to-date, so the query is forwarded to P_{13}. P_{13} needs to forward $Q(P_{14})$ to either P_2 or P_{12}. Forwarding to P_{12} fails and so does the attempt to forward the query to P_2 because P_{13}'s cache entry for P_2 is stale. Thus P_{13} initiates a recursive query for (P_2), i.e., $Q(0010)$. P_{13} sends $Q(P_2)$ to P_5 which forwards it to P_7 and/or P_9. Let us assume P_9 replies. Thus P_{13} learns P_2's address and updates its cache. P_{13} also starts processing and forwards the parent query (P_{14}) to P_2. P_2 provides P_{14}'s up-to-date address, and P_7 updates its cache.

Having learned P_{14}'s current physical address, P_7 now forwards the original query $Q(01*)$ to P_{14}. This does not only satisfy the original query but P_7 also has the opportunity to learn and update physical addresses P_{14} knows and P_7 needs, for example, P_5's latest physical address (we assume that peers synchronize their routing tables during communication since this does not incur any overhead). In the end, the query $Q(01*)$ is answered successfully and additionally P_7 gets to know the up-to-date physical addresses of P_{14} and possibly of P_5. Furthermore, due to child queries, P_{13} updates its cached address for P_2. Figure 10.3 shows the final state of the P-Grid with several caches updated after the the completion of $Q(01*)$ at P_7.

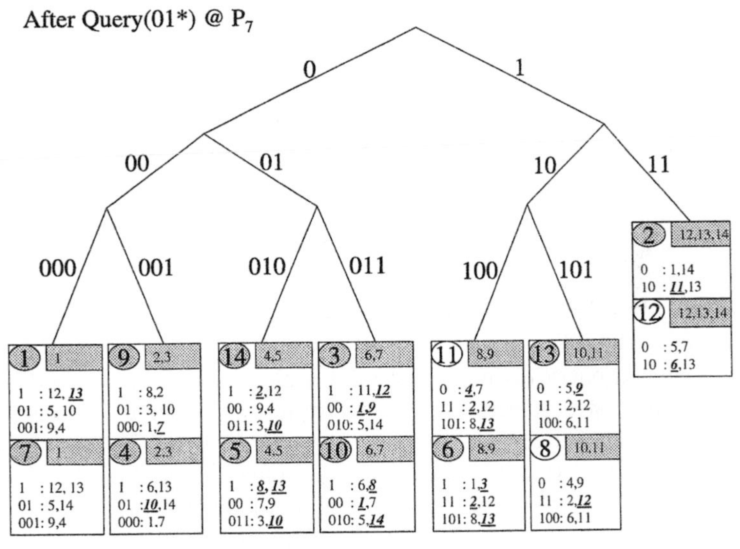

Fig. 10.3: P-Grid after query(01*) at P_7

Peers thus do not discard routing information immediately if it is not usable, since peers may come online at a later time. However, it is also possible that a peer never rejoins the network, and thus a garbage collection mechanism can be used in the background which can be obtained with no or marginal overhead.

10.3.5 Analysis of the Maintenance Mechanism

As the example illustrates, the maintenance mechanism is a highly recursive process. If too many entries become stale the network runs the risk of being no more able to restore correct routing table entries and to catastrophically fail. Thus it is important to understand under which conditions the network remains stable. In order to analyze this we will model the algorithm as a self-organizing process.

We will analyze the dynamics of one of the possible variants of maintenance, eager correction-on-use, in which during routing all routing table entries are probed and get repaired if they are encountered to be stale. We chose this variant here as the analysis is not overly complex. We further simplify the analysis here by considering that only the address changes but the peers always stay online. A complete analysis also considering the probability of peers being online (p_{on}) for both the maintenance mechanisms is much more complicated but uses the same ideas. A detailed analysis taking into account all parameters is given in [5].

We analyze the degree of consistency of routing tables by modeling the time evolution of the probability $P_\mu(t)$ that a entry in a routing table is stale. We assume that at each time step t one query is issued by a peer and a peer changes its address with probability p_c between two queries. The queries issued as a result of the maintenance mechanism will repair a certain fraction of stale routing table entries. The process is in a stable dynamic equilibrium if the expected number of repaired entries matches the expected number of entries becoming stale. The analysis will allow us to determine for which parameters the system is in such an equilibrium state.

In the following n is the number of leaves of the P-Grid tree and r is the number of redundant references kept in a routing table at each depth. We will assume in the following a balanced P-Grid tree.

While cached entries continuously get stale owing to network dynamics, they trigger recursive queries in order to update the stale mappings. In each step of processing a query, an expected number of $rP_\mu(t)$ stale references are encountered and thus trigger a new recursive query. Thus, if we denote by N_{rec} the total number of queries triggered by one original query and consider that in a balanced P-Grid the expected search cost is $\frac{\log_2 n}{2}$ we obtain the recursive relationship $N_{rec} = 1+rP_\mu(t)\frac{\log_2 n}{2}N_{rec}$. The relationship is recursive since each query triggered for repair is expected to recursively trigger more queries.

Not every query (original or recursively triggered) will succeed. Denoting the probability of failure of a query by ϵ, the probability of successfully routing a query is $1-\epsilon = (1-P_\mu(t)^r)^H$ where H is the number of times the query needs to be forwarded to reach the leaf node. Thus, the expected value of the achievable success probability is $1-\epsilon = E_H[(1-P_\mu(t)^r)^H]$. For a balanced

P-Grid, H is a binomial random variable of size $log_2 n$ and parameter 0.5. Hence, $1 - \epsilon \approx (1 - \frac{P_\mu(t)^r}{2})^{\log_2 n}$.

We now can give the Markovian process that determines the time evolution of $P_\mu(t)$.

$$P_\mu(t+1) = P_\mu(t) - p_c(1 - P_\mu(t)) + \frac{1}{r \log_2 n}(N_{rec} - 1)(1 - \epsilon) \tag{10.3}$$

N_{rec} and ϵ can be expressed in terms of $P_\mu(t)$. The negative contribution in the recursion corresponds to the fraction of correct routing table entries of a peer that turns stale between two queries issued by the peer and the positive contribution is the fraction of incorrect routing table entries of a peer that are repaired due to recursively triggered and successfully processed queries.

The system is in a dynamic equilibrium if $P_\mu(t) = \mu$ for some constant μ.

$$p_c(1 - \mu) r \log_2 n = (N_{rec} - 1)(1 - \epsilon)$$

In this state the rate at which changes occur in the system will equal the rate at which self-maintenance is done due to recursions. This allows us to determine the equilibrium state for different network dynamics expressed by p_c.

In Figure 10.4 we provide contour maps corresponding to N_{rec} values, with p_{on} in the x-axis and $r_{up} = p_c/(1+p_c)$ in the y-axis. If we consider that there are two kinds of events that trigger the whole self-maintenance process in the system–queries and changes in peers' address mapping–r_{up} represents the fraction of these events being the changes. The interpretation of the plot is thus that if a system is willing to incur an N_{rec} factor of increase of effort per query with respect to the ideal case ($p_{on} = 1$ and $p_c = 0$), the network will operate for all p_{on}, p_c combinations below the curve, with the success probability being 1. If the system is unwilling to use more than N_{rec} effort and if the system operates in the region above the curves of Figure 10.4, there is a non-zero failure probability, which increases with the distance from the curve. Figure 10.4 thus captures two important trade-offs in the system. The first trade-off is that of efficiency versus probabilistic success guarantee of queries. The second trade-off is the system's resilience against the two "demons" of networks, i.e., the network dynamics p_c versus average availability of peers in the network p_{on}.

10.4 Summary

We have seen three examples of how self-organizing processes induce structural features of Peer-to-Peer overlay networks, one example for unstructured overlay networks and two examples for structured overlay networks. Each of

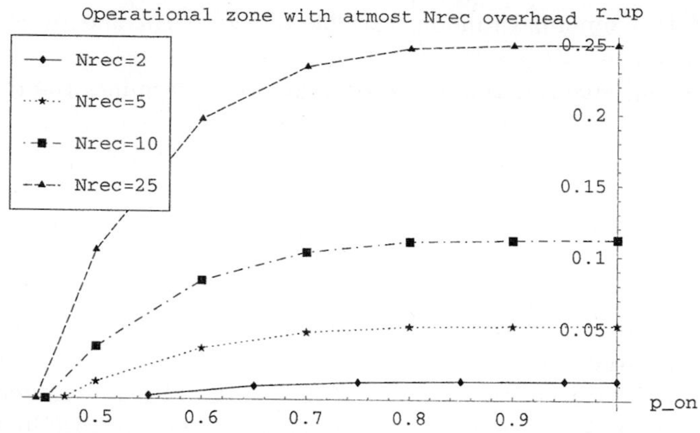

Fig. 10.4: Analytical result: Contour maps for N_{rec}

the examples was slightly different both in the nature of the process studied, in the type of equilibrium obtained as well as in the purpose for which the model of the process was developed.

The ideas presented in this chapter which we explored during the process of designing and implementing the P-Grid system are generally applicable, however. Often dynamic systems will have to be analyzed as Markovian systems, be it for a-posteriori analysis, or to study their evolution over time, given a set of rules for local interactions, or to investigate the equilibrium state in the presence of perturbations.

Also, in the context of Peer-to-Peer systems, reactive route maintenance strategies have been studied by other projects, e.g., in DKS, as well as other systems also try to address the problem of fast and parallel overlay construction mechanisms, for example, [31]. Other systems that focus more on storage load-balancing for arbitrary load distributions and use small-world routing include SkipGraphs [36] and Mercury [72] (among several other recent Peer-to-Peer proposals). Increasingly, there is a confluence of ideas which arrived independently by various research groups dealing with self-organization problems.

More importantly, analysis of network evolution and maintenance are either explicitly or implicitly assuming a Markovian model, an analytical approach which we tried to present here formally by elaborating on three different self-organizing processes. In the case of modeling preferential attachment in unstructured overlay networks the stochastic model has been developed to explain a-posteriori a phenomenon that has been observed in many artificial and natural networks, including Peer-to-Peer overlay networks. Thus it is used to explain empirical evidence. The model itself identifies a dynamic equilibrium state that is maintained throughout network growth. The dynamics of the network results from the network growth.

In contrast, the stochastic model developed for bootstrapping P-Grid overlay networks is used in order to a priori derive certain design parameters for a distributed algorithm, i.e., the probabilities by which peers take local decisions in order to lead the system globally to a desired state. Also the nature of the stochastic process is different as it is a transient process that converges during network growth to a static equilibrium point. The dynamics of the network results from active interactions performed by peers.

The approach taken for maintenance of P-Grid networks again differs in terms of modeling and methodology. Here the stochastic model is used to determine under which network conditions a stable system behavior for a given algorithm can be expected. As in the first example the stochastic model is used to analyze a dynamic equilibrium state. However, in this case as opposed to the previous examples, the network is stable in size. The dynamics of the network results from operations externally triggered by failures in the physical network.

This illustrates that the basic concept of modeling the large-scale behavior of Peer-to-Peer networks as self-organizing, dynamic processes leaves ample room for different modeling and analysis approaches and has various methodological uses. We would also like to point to the fact that the analysis techniques presented in this chapter mostly have involved substantial approximations and do not necessarily conform to a rigorous mathematical treatment for analyzing dynamical systems. In that respect there exists a substantial need and potential for further interdisciplinary research drawing on the substantial body of knowledge from studying self-organizing systems in other domains. Thus the field of modeling and analyzing complex Peer-to-Peer systems as self-organizing systems currently is still in its early stages.

Part IV

Peer-to-Peer-Based Applications

11. Application-Layer Multicast

Kostas Katrinis, Martin May (ETH Zurich)

11.1 Why Multicast on Application Layer

Since the early days of the Internet, extending routing capabilities beyond point-to-point communication has been a desired feature, mostly as a means of resource discovery. The limited size of the Internet at that time permitted the technique of broadcasting a single packet to every possible node. With its growth, Internet-wide broadcasting became increasingly expensive which imposed constraining the scope of broadcast packets to end points that expressed interest in receiving packets of a specific service (Selective Broadcast [612]). This was in fact the first attempt to offer indirectly a group communication service over the Internet. Still, Deering's seminal work [161] is regarded as the groundwork in Internet-wide group communication. In his host-group model, Deering also specified the extensions to unicast routing protocols required to support many-to-many communication. Since the first appearance of the host-group model, a lot of research and standardization effort has been put into ubiquitous *multicast* natively implemented on routers (network-layer service). Despite years of ongoing work, deployment of native IP-multicast still remains poor [170] and this has motivated the search for alternative approaches. However, it has been shown that the design choice of offering multicast at the network layer violated the end-to-end argument [531]. Specifically, the end-to-end argument suggests that it is only worth pushing a service to lower layers of a system if, by doing so, the returned performance/cost improvement outweighs the increased complexity of implementing the service at the network layer. Clearly, network-layer multicast and, in particular, its de facto Any-Source Multicast standard (the Any-Source Multicast model is implemented in the PIM-SM/MBGP/MSDP protocol suite) is violating the end-to-end principle, for many of its deployment problems require the realization of the service at the network layer (e.g., source discovery, inter-domain routing). Alternatively, one of the newly arisen multicast proposals tries to more closely adhere to the end-to-end argument by shifting the service implementation to higher in the protocol stack, namely to the application layer.

Application-Layer Multicast (ALM) does not assume any support from the network, i.e., it assumes just an elementary unicast forwarding service. All specific group communication functionality including group management (integrating new members into an existing group or coping with member departures), multicast tree formation, and packet replication, is moved to the application layer. In particular, ALM systems organize the participating

R. Steinmetz and K. Wehrle (Eds.): P2P Systems and Applications, LNCS 3485, pp. 157-170, 2005.

nodes in the service as an overlay network; the end-to-end IP paths among each node pair constitute the links of the overlay network. Group information and forwarding state, stored in the overlay nodes, are then used for packet replication over the overlay links and to deliver data packets originating from any source to the entire group.

11.2 Design Aspects and Taxonomy

The ultimate goal of an ALM scheme is to build an efficient overlay network and thus to maximize the service quality received by the service consumers (group members). The QoS (Quality of Service) parameters of interest may vary, depending on the requirements of the group communication application utilizing the ALM service. For instance, an interactive teleconferencing application would require an overlay optimized for stringently minimized delivery delays and high bandwidth, whereas a TV streaming service could tolerate larger overlay delays, but demands low loss and high bandwidth.

To date, numerous application-layer systems have been proposed to realize multicast. Most of these schemes are based on the same fundamental design choices and those characteristics are used here to classify the different proposals. A principal characteristic refers to routing organization: many ALM overlays first build a richly connected graph termed *mesh* (therefore, the general approach is referred to as *mesh-first*) and subsequently construct the distribution tree as a subgraph of the mesh (ESM [307] and ALMI [482]). In contrast, other ALM schemes first build a spanning tree on the overlay nodes (*tree-first* approach) and then enrich the tree by adding additional control links (Yoid [228], HMTP [638]).

A second classification characteristic is associated with the type of overlay used. Many ALM schemes implement multicast on top of a structured overlay network like CAN 8.3, Pastry 8.2, or Chord 8.1 by defining a virtual space and positioning the overlay nodes in it. Direct IP routing is abstracted to routing in the virtual space and accordingly, overlay multicast is abstracted to one- or many-to-many communication across the nodes in the virtual space. Representative examples of this class of ALM systems are CAN multicast [506] and Scribe [109]. Note that still the majority of ALM proposals is based on unstructured overlays, using explicit routing mechanisms.

Finally, some of the proposed ALM schemes build overlays solely with end user systems, thereby shielding their operation against abrupt departure or failure of overlay nodes (ESM, ALMI, HMTP). In contrast to those, other systems (like Overcast [322] and RON [26]) assume the existence of fixed nodes (equivalently termed proxies, replicators, or multicast service nodes in the bibliography) that are deployed inside the network and which are essentially responsible for routing in the overlay. In these latter systems, end user nodes do not usually participate in packet replication and group management, and act only as service consumers.

In the next section, we follow one of the possible taxonomies: classifying ALM based on structured or unstructured overlays. For each category, we further distinguish two sub-categories with reference to the peculiarities of each category.

Finally, before delving into the specification details of ALM systems, it is important to identify the performance overhead and service costs introduced by moving multicast functionality to the application layer. Below is a list of metrics that are often used to evaluate any given ALM system, but that also represent a guideline for ALM design in general:

- *Relative Delay Penalty (RDP) or Stretch*: Strictly defined as the ratio of the one-way overlay delay of a node pair over the unicast delay among the same nodes in the identical direction. The goal here is to match routing proximity as closely as possible to underlying IP routing, reducing the resulting delay penalty.
- *Throughput*: Similarly to RDP, this performance metric measures the effective data throughput achieved for a single receiver (over time or on average).
- *Stress*: Stress is defined as the number of times the same packet traverses a specific physical link in either direction. Essentially, it quantifies the cost of moving the replication effort to end systems in terms of data bandwidth.
- *Control Overhead*: Number of control messages exchanged throughout an ALM session. This metric represents the cost in terms of control message exchanges.

11.3 Unstructured Overlays

11.3.1 Centralized Systems

The term "centralized" in the context of ALM design does not refer to data replication handled by a centralized entity; instead, it points out the design principle of a centralized entity handling group management and creation/optimization of the distribution tree. This is the approach taken in the Application Level Multicast Infrastructure (ALMI [482]).

The entire coordination task in ALMI is assigned to the "*session controller*", as shown in the architecture diagram (Figure 11.1). The session controller - residing either on a dedicated server of the service provider or at a group member node - exchanges point-to-point messages (dashed arrows) via unicast with every overlay node (drawn as a circular point). It is worth mentioning that the controller does not lie on the data path, i.e., is not part of the distribution tree (marked with bold, solid arrows), thus avoiding bottlenecks in data distribution.

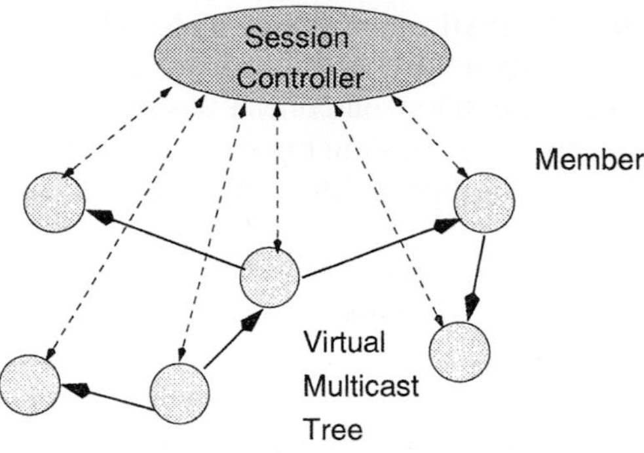

Fig. 11.1: Simplified ALMI architecture

A node that wants to join an ALMI session sends a *JOIN* message to the session controller. Note that the discovery of the session controller's location for a given session ID is beyond the scope of the system specification and realized by third party means, for example via a known URLs or e-mail notification. When the newly arrived node is accepted into the group, it receives a response containing its *member ID* (identifier in the overlay) and the location of a parent node to which it should append itself. Finally, the newly added node sends a *GRAFT* message to its parent and obtains in response the data ports for the two-way communication with its parent. Node departures are realized similarly by signaling the session controller with a *LEAVE* message.

Tree creation and maintenance are also tasks performed by the session controller. Given a performance metric of interest (e.g., delay), the controller computes locally a minimal spanning tree on the group members graph and assigns the upstream and downstream nodes to each overlay node in the distribution tree. Note that, unlike other ALM systems, ALMI builds a single shared tree with bidirectional links that is jointly used by all members for data distribution. Measurement data for the metric to be optimized is provided by each overlay node to the controller on a point-to-point basis. For this purpose, each overlay node actively probes every other node and reports the results to the controller. Obviously, this generates an $O(n^2)$ message overhead. To scale the monitoring service to larger groups, ALMI limits the degree of each node in the monitoring graph. Although this may initially lead to sub-optimal multicast trees, over time each node dynamically prunes bad links and adds new links to the monitoring topology, resulting in more efficient multicast trees.

Recapitulating, the centralization approach adopted by ALMI offers two primary advantages: high control over the overlay topology and ease of implementation. Moreover, as a side-effect of the first advantage, detection of malicious nodes is easier to realize because all control operations pass through the session controller. On the other hand, ALMI is plagued with the scalability and dependability concerns of all centralized systems. While the first deficiency remains unresolved, ALMI tries to alleviate the negative effects of controller failures by introducing *backup controllers*. These synchronize periodically with the main controller's state and, in case of failure detection, one of the backup controllers replaces the session coordinator.

11.3.2 Fully Distributed Systems

Fully distributed application-layer multicast systems do not rely on a single (or a few) coordinating entities for routing organization and group management. Instead, each node maintains information about the overlay topology - either partly or entirely - and self-configures/self-adapts to changes in the overlay topology or the underlying network condition.

End System Multicast (ESM [307]) constitutes a fully distributed ALM scheme - and is one of the elementary studies on application layer multicast. ESM overlay networks utilize exclusively end systems, assuming only basic unicast IP service and thus avoiding any proxy or dedicated server infrastructure deployed within the network. Group management and packet replication among the end systems is managed by a protocol called *Narada*. *Narada* employs the mesh-first approach: overlay nodes first organize themselves in a redundant mesh graph. On top of this mesh, source-specific multicast trees are then created for data distribution. Consequently, service quality is at best as good as the quality of the mesh. Therefore, *Narada* attempts to ensure that the properties of the mesh meet the performance requirements of the application running over ESM. More precisely, a good mesh should comprise overlay links whose quality (e.g., delay, available bandwidth) is comparable to the quality of the IP path connecting the two endpoints of the overlay node pair. Second, it is desirable that each node has a limited fan-out, regulating the replication effort and stress at each overlay node.

Group management in *Narada* is equally distributed on all nodes. For the sake of robustness and efficiency of mesh maintenance, each overlay node keeps track of every group member. As ESM targets at small to medium sized multicast groups, scalability is not considered an important issue. If a node want to join the group it contacts a small number of arbitrary group members (the ID and location of these members is provided by a third party service not provided by the system, e.g., via URL or e-mail notification). The arrival of a new member is announced to all nodes by forcing each overlay member to broadcast periodic *heartbeat* messages ("refresh" messages) on the mesh. This leads ultimately to a situation where every overlay node is aware of the newly arrived node. Similarly, when a node decides to leave the group, the remaining group members detect its departure after they stop receiving heartbeat messages from the leaving node. Note that the latter may also

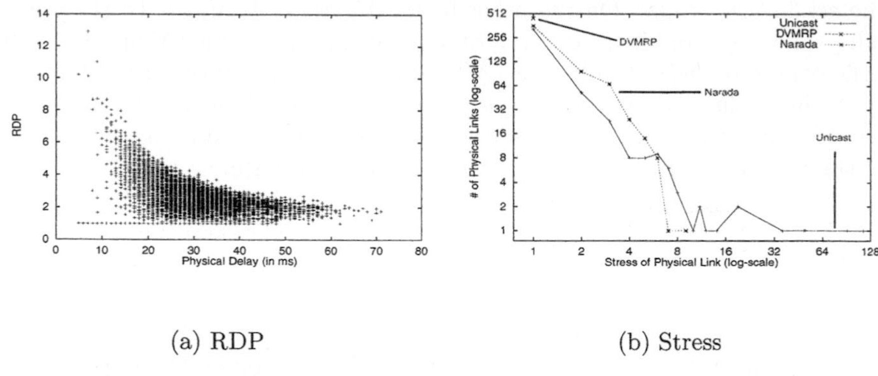

(a) RDP (b) Stress

Fig. 11.2: Delay performance of ESM and induced cost in terms of link stress

occur when the abrupt failure of a node causes the partitioning of the mesh. For this reason, when node A has not received any refresh message from node B for a given time period, it starts actively probing node B. If B responds, A creates an overlay link to B to repair the partition. Otherwise, it presumes the departure of B and ultimately deletes B from its group member list.

The mesh constructed with *Narada* is heavily influenced by randomizing effects, such as link failures after node departures, additions of bad quality "emergency" links during partition repair, or additions of arbitrary links during node arrivals (recall that a newly arrived node creates arbitrary links to a few bootstrap nodes). Also, throughout the session, the varying conditions of the network substrate may render a previously good mesh formation obsolete. Due to the reasons mentioned above, ESM employs periodic re-evaluation of the constructed mesh. This re-constructed mesh is achieved autonomically by each member actively probing its mesh links and adding new, or dropping existing, links. Various heuristics are used for evaluation of the utility of link additions/drops, incorporating the effects of a potential overlay reconfiguration on the entire group [307].

Finally, data delivery in ESM follows the reverse-path forwarding [150] concept: a node n_i that receives a packet from source S via a mesh-neighbor n_j forwards the packet, if and only if n_j is the next hop on the shortest path of n_i to S. If that condition holds, n_i replicates the packet to all of its mesh-neighbors that use n_i as their next hop to reach S. The forwarding algorithm requires each node to maintain an entry to every other node in its routing table, which does not only contain the next overlay hop and the cost associated with the destination, but also the exact path that leads to it. This extra information is also used for loops-avoidance and count-to-infinity problems.

Figure 11.2(a) plots the delay penalty with regard to native unicast delay obtained with an ESM overlay. The data originate from a simulation of the

Narada protocol, incorporating 1024 nodes, 3145 links and a group size of 128, where the out-degree of each node was limited to 3 to 6 neighbors. The plot conveys that *Narada* minimizes the delay penalty experienced by node pairs with high unicast delay, whereas the penalty increases for small unicast delay values. The fairly large RDP values for node pairs with very low unicast delays are justified by the fact that even a small suboptimal configuration of the overlay topology magnifies the tiny delay of nodes residing close by to a large penalty. Still, the effective delay among these node pairs adheres to real-time requirements. In addition, the histogram in Figure 11.2(b) compares the physical link stress in ESM against two common alternatives: naive unicast and IP multicast using DVMRP [161]. Intuitively, native multicast is optimal in terms of stress (stress 1 across all links). It is worth mentioning that ESM manages to limit the maximum link stress to 9. In contrast, native unicast leads to a longer tail, loading few links with stress greater than 9, and worse, transmitting the same packet 128 times over a single link.

Summarizing, End System Multicast builds self-organizing overlays and therefore provides increased robustness with minimal configuration effort. As it does not require any support from network internal application-layer entities, it constitutes a ready-to-deploy solution. Furthermore, beyond the system specification presented herein, *Narada* can be optimized against various QoS metrics, such as throughput or node out-degree [306]. Finally, an asset of the entire ESM endeavor is that the system prototype has already been used for various Internet broadcasts, spanning multiple continents connecting home, academic and commercial network environments [305]. One of the limitations of ESM is its inability to scale to large group sizes, mainly because of the volume of routing information that needs to be exchanged and maintained by each node. A major concern common to all host-based ALM solutions is service interruption due to abrupt node failures. This failure type however, is one of the major open issues in peer-to-peer research in general.

11.4 Structured Overlays

Shortly after the introduction of multicast at the application layer, scaling to large group sizes (i.e., thousands of nodes) became a major concern in ALM research. Scalability is difficult to achieve with unstructured overlays - in the centralized case because of the bottleneck at the central point of control (as in all centralized systems) and in the distributed case owing to the large amount of state and control traffic required to establish a global view of the entire overlay topology (node clustering in those schemes may further increase the scalability of the distributed model). Instead, building a multicast service on top of a structured overlay provides increased scalability. In short, a *structured overlay* is an application-layer network whose nodes form a virtual space. Part III in this book contains a thorough review of structured overlays and provides insight into issues pertaining to their design and performance.

Two approaches have been taken towards extending the routing infrastructure of a structured overlay to support multicast and these differ primarily in the manner they implement packet replication:

1. Directed flooding of each message across the virtual space.
2. Forming a tree, rooted at the group source used to distribute messages from a specific source to the group members (tree leaves).

In the following, we review one representative system from each of the two categories and end with a comparison of the two.

11.4.1 Flooding-Based Replication

A Content-Addressable Network (CAN [505] [504] and Section 8.3) utilizes a d-dimensional Cartesian coordinate space that is dynamically split into distinct coordinate zones (finite coordinate intervals of the space) and each zone is allocated to an overlay node according to a hash function. Two nodes in the space are neighbors if their zones overlap along d-1 dimensions and differ in exactly one dimension. Point-to-point routing is then accomplished by simply looking up the neighbor's set at each node and greedy-forwarding towards the node with coordinates closer to the destination's coordinates. New nodes join the system by contacting one of the well-known (e.g., retrievable via a DNS query) bootstrap nodes, and then the requests are forwarded to the destination node from which they claim a share of its space. Similarly, node departures result in merging the freed coordinate space with the zone of a neighboring node.

Multicast in CANs [506] is achieved by forming a "mini" CAN consisting of the CAN nodes that are members of the multicast group. Given a multicast group identified by G, the identifier is hashed to a coordinate space (x, y). The node responsible for the hashed coordinate space becomes the bootstrap node of the new "mini" CAN. The rest of the group members follow the usual CAN construction process to join the new multicast CAN. It is worth mentioning that as each node in the CAN has maximally $2d$ neighbors (where d stands for the CAN's dimensions), the per node multicast state requirements are independent of the number of multicast sources in the group.

Replication of messages to enable delivery to multiple destinations is realized as follows:

1. The source of the group forwards a message to all neighbors.
2. A node that receives a message from a neighboring node across dimension i forwards the message to all its neighbors across dimensions $1..(i-1)$ and to its neighbors across dimension i, but only in the opposite direction from which it received the message.

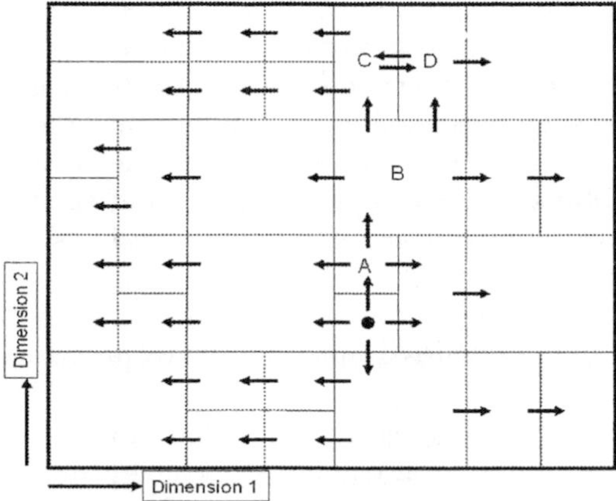

Fig. 11.3: Multicasting in a sample two-dimensional CAN

3. If a message has already traversed at least half of the distance from the source across a particular dimension, then the message is not forwarded by a receiving node.
4. Each node caches the sequence numbers of received messages and discards messages it has already forwarded.

Intuitively, rules 1 and 2 ensure that a message reaches all dimensions of the virtual space and additionally that the message is flooded to all nodes in one single dimension. Rule 3 prevents the flooding process from looping. A sample one-to-many communication in a two-dimensional CAN is depicted in Figure 11.3, where the listed forwarding rules are applied on a hop-by-hop basis to flood a message to all members of the CAN. Note that if the coordinate space is not perfectly partitioned, then a node may receive multiple copies of the same packet. This is particularly true for nodes C and D in the flooding example presented in Figure 11.3. [506] specifies enhancements to the elementary forwarding process for avoiding, but not entirely eliminate, an important fraction of duplicates.

11.4.2 Tree-Based Replication

Pastry [527] is a self-organizing overlay network of nodes, where each node routes requests and interacts with local instances of one or more applications. Each node in the Pastry overlay is assigned a 128-bit identifier, the *nodeId*. The nodeId determines the node's position in a circular nodeId space, ranging from 0 to 2^{128-1}. Message forwarding in Pastry is performed as follows: A node with nodeId id_1 intending to reach a destination node with nodeId id_n, forwards the message to the node with nodeId id_2, where a prefix of id_2 matches in more than b bits the identifier id_n compared with the match of id_1. If no such match exists, the node forwards the message to the node with the numerically closest nodeId. It can be proven that the described routing scheme always converges [527]. Forwarding decisions, as well as mapping of nodeIds to IP addresses, is accomplished using routing state maintained at each node. A more detailed presentation of the Pastry system can be found in section 8.2, which discusses thoroughly the routing table structure (section 8.2.2), node bootstrapping (section 8.2.4), failure handling (section 8.2.4) and proximity matching from the geographical/IP-level proximity to the identifier space (section 8.2.5).

Scribe [109] builds a large-scale, fully decentralized, many-to-many distribution service on top of a Pastry infrastructure. Multicast distribution is essentially core-based, using a Pastry node as the rendezvous point. Group members "join" the tree routed at the well known rendezvous point, while group sources send multicast data directly to the core. Scribe exposes the following simple API calls to group communication applications:

- **Create(credentials,topicId)**: creates a group identified by a unique topicId, which is the result of hashing a textual description of the group's topic concatenated with the nodeId of the creator node. Credentials are used for applying access control to group creation.
- **Subscribe(credentials, topicId, eventHandler)**: commands the local Scribe instance to join the group identified by the topicId, resulting in receiving multicast data of a particular group. Arriving group data are passed to the specified event handler.
- **Unsubscribe(credentials, topicId)**: causes the local node to leave the specified group.
- **Publish(credentials, topicId, event)**: used by group sources to communicate an event (i.e., multicast data) to the specified group.

An application intending to create a group uses Scribe's "create" API call. Then Scribe passes a CREATE message using the topicId and credentials specified by the application to the local Pastry instance. The message is routed to the node with the nodeId numerically closest to the topicId. The receiving node checks the credentials, adds the topicId to the locally maintained groups and becomes the rendezvous point (RP) for the group. Adding a leaf to the tree rooted at the RP is a receiver-initiated process: Scribe asks Pastry to route a SUBSCRIBE message using the relevant topicId as the message destination key. At each node along the route towards the RP, the message is intercepted by Scribe. If the node already holds state of the particular topicId, it adds the preceding node's nodeId to its *children table* and forwards the message to the RP. If state does not exist, it creates a children table entry associated with the topicId and again forwards the message towards the RP. The latter process results in a reverse-path forwarding [150] distribution tree

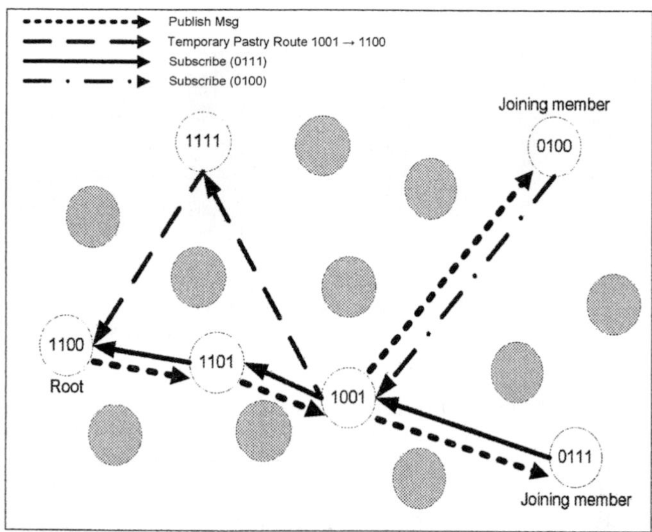

Fig. 11.4: Tree creation and data replication in a sample Scribe overlay.

(assuming path symmetry). Multicast sources address messages to the group by calling Scribe's "publish" primitive. This leads to a PUBLISH message - enclosing the group data - being forwarded towards the RP (using either Pastry or directly by using the IP address of the RP, if already discovered). As soon as the PUBLISH message reaches the RP node and provided that a) state of the specified topicId exists on the RP, and b) the credentials match, the RP "inserts" the message into the distribution tree by replicating it to all nodes in its children table. The same replication in the internal part of the tree assures that the PUBLISH message reaches all subscribed receivers. Finally, departures from the distribution tree are accomplished in a similar manner, using the "unsubscribe" API call provided by Scribe.

Figure 11.4 illustrates a sample Pastry overlay, where for the sake of presentation we only highlight nodes forming the Scribe distribution tree. In this example, we assume that the b parameter of Pastry is configured to $b = 1$, i.e., prefix matching is performed one bit at a time. We further assume that a group with $topicId = 1100$ has already been created. Because the RP node of a group is specified by locating the node with the numerically closest nodeId to the topicId of the group, in this example, node 1100 constitutes the RP. Let us assume that node 0111 is the first receiver that joins the group. For this, it asks Pastry to forward a SUBSCRIBE message to the RP. The message reaches its first "Pastry-hop", in this case node 1001. The SUBSCRIBE is intercepted by Scribe at node 1001, creating a children table entry with the nodeId 0111 as its single child and associating the table with the topicId. Finally, the message is forwarded towards the RP. En route to

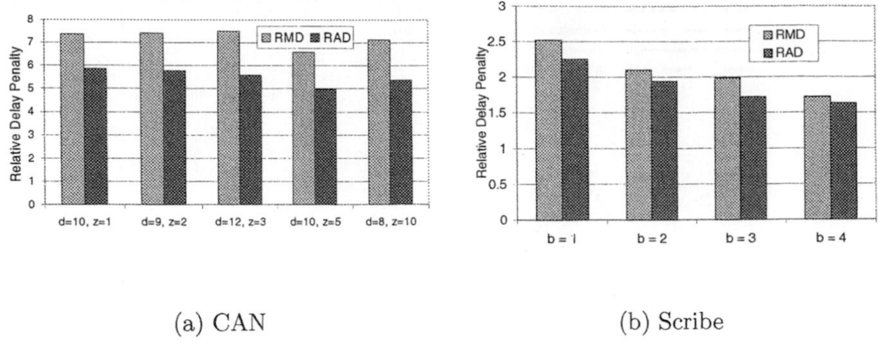

(a) CAN (b) Scribe

Fig. 11.5: Relative delay penalty in various configurations of CAN multicast and Scribe.

the RP, the message accumulates state on the nodes it traverses, including the RP itself. As soon as the SUBSCRIBE message is treated at the RP, multicast data start flowing on the distribution tree (which in this case is a single node chain) towards node 1100. Now, let's look at how the arrival of a receiver in the "vicinity" of node 1100, namely of node 0100, affects the distribution tree. Following the common join process, node 0100 sends a SUBSCRIBE message towards the RP. The message is again delivered first to node 1001. Normally, the message would follow the path 1001-1111-1100 to reach the RP. However, since node 1001 already possesses state of the group 1100, it just adds node 0100 to its respective children table entry and terminates the SUBSCRIBE message.

11.4.3 Performance/Cost Evaluation

Selecting the more appropriate alternative between flooding and tree-based group communication is not trivial. Generally, the latency and bandwidth overhead for constructing per-group dedicated overlays are both greater with flooding mechanisms. On the other hand, flooding exclusively incorporates the members of a group into the group management and replication effort. As a result, they are considered appropriate for small groups. If this is a desired asset for the ALM service provider, flooding should be the mechanism of choice.

A thorough quantitative comparison of the two mechanisms is presented in [110]. The paper does not confine the evaluation to flooding over CAN, and tree-multicast over Pastry (a.k.a. Scribe), but experiments further with other alternative combinations as well (e.g., tree-multicast using CANs). The evaluation is performed using a random topology of 5050 routers and 80000 end system nodes randomly assigned to routers. All end systems are part of a sin-

	Maximum Stress	Average Stress
CAN (d=10, z=1)	1958	3.49
CAN (d=9, z=2)	1595	3.27
CAN (d=12, z=3)	1333	2.93
CAN (d=10, z=5)	985	2.73
CAN (d=8, z=10)	631	2.69
Scribe (RAND)	1910.6	3.87
Scribe (TOP)	23999.4	3.90

Table 11.1: Maximum and average link stress in CAN and Scribe multicast. RAND corresponds to randomly assigning nodeIds to newly arriving Pastry nodes, whereas TOP denotes a topologically aware assignment of nodeIds, taking proximity into consideration.

gle multicast group with the same single source over all runs. Since there are various parameter sets possible for the instantiation of a CAN/Pastry overlay, the authors have experimented with various configurations: a) in CAN, by tuning the dimensions d of the Cartesian space and the maximum number of nodes allowed in each zone, and b) in Pastry, by tuning the parameter b (number of bits matched during per hop prefix matching).

A small excerpt of the results is illustrated in Figure 11.5 and Table 11.1. Figure 11.5 shows that tree-based multicast over Pastry is superior to CAN-flooding in terms of both maximum (RMD) and average (RAD) relative delay penalty, making the former more suitable for delay-sensitive applications (e.g., multi-point teleconferencing). In contrast, certain configurations of CAN-flooding manage to economize link utilization compared with Pastry, as outlined in Table 11.1. Consequently, for a non delay-critical application (e.g., TV broadcasting), CAN-flooding offers a cheaper solution. For more detailed comparisons, including further metrics and evaluation against a larger number of concurrent groups, please refer to [110].

11.5 Hot Topics

In this section we touch on various issues driving the future of application-layer multicast. Some of them are already part of ongoing work; others promise to unleash the full potential of multicast overlays.

Topology-Awareness:
Matching proximity in the overlay sense with the actual proximity of the underlying IP substrate is key in improving the performance (delivery delay, throughput) and cost (stress) of ALM. While this is a pure necessity in structured overlays [502], efforts are being spent on achieving a closer match in unstructured overlays as well [370].

Quality of Service:
Recently, the provision of (probabilistic) QoS guarantees in overlay communication [383] is receiving increasing interest. To name an example, an overlay node can take advantage of redundancy in overlay paths [539] to a given destination and alternate over the several path options according to path conditions. For instance, if node A is able to reach node B using two loss-disjoint paths P1 and P2, A is able to pick the path with the lowest loss rate to increase quality [538]. Similarly, multi-path routing together with redundant coding inside the overlay can be used in k-redundant, directed acyclic graphs to increase data throughput [643].

Multi-source Support:
Many of the existing ALM schemes employ source-specific multicast trees. Still, various multicast applications inherently have multiple sources (such as teleconferencing or online multi-player games). The trivial solution manifests itself by creating one tree per source; still, it is evident that this is not the most efficient solution in all practical cases. Alternatively, the overlay routing algorithm may take application semantics into consideration to provide economical multi-source support [341] (e.g., by creating trees on demand and applying tree caching).

Security:
Malicious node behavior can harm the performance and stability of an application-layer multicast overlay. For example, Mathy et al. showed in [401] the impact of malicious nodes reporting false delay measurement values. Clearly, shielding overlay networks with powerful cheating detection and avoidance mechanisms is an interesting challenge.

11.6 Summary

In the preceding sections, we have introduced a first set of interesting applications of peer-to-peer networks: application-layer multicast. In this field, peer-to-peer technology has helped to overcome the slow adaptation of multicast mechanisms at the network layer. While unstructured and centralized peer-to-peer systems allowed for fast deployment of those networks, the family of unstructured peer-to-peer networks offer *unlimited* scalability. The vast amount of ongoing work will unleash further improvements of the existing multicast systems and introduce new applications of peer-to-peer technology in other networking areas.

12. ePOST

Alan Mislove, Andreas Haeberlen, Ansley Post, Peter Druschel
(Rice University & Max Planck Institute for Software Systems)

ePOST is a Peer-to-Peer email system that provides the same functionality as existing, server-based email systems while providing better availability, scalability, fault tolerance, and security. The ePOST system has been in production use within the Computer Science department at Rice University since early 2004 and is being adopted by an increasing number of outside users.

Traditional email and news services, along with newer collaborative applications like instant messaging, bulletin boards, shared calendars, and whiteboards, are among the most successful and widely used distributed applications. Today, such services are mostly implemented in the client-server model, where messages are stored on and routed through dedicated servers, each hosting a set of user accounts. This partial centralization limits availability, since a failure or attack on a server denies service to all the users it supports. Also, dedicated infrastructure and a substantial maintenance and administration effort are required to provide services to large numbers of users.

A decentralized, cooperative approach, i.e., a Peer-to-Peer (P2P) based solution like ePOST, seems like a natural fit for collaborative applications. Rather than requiring dedicated server infrastructure, ePOST scales organically with the number of participating users, since each participant contributes resources to offset the additional demand he places on the system. Also, ePOST removes all single points of failure by distributing the services across all member nodes, thus providing the potential for a more highly available system. Lastly, the self-organizing properties of ePOST promise to reduce the cost of maintaining email services.

To use ePOST, users download and run a Pastry [527] node on their desktop, which connects to the ePOST overlay network. Folder information and email messages are stored in the network using the PAST [526] distributed hash table, and the Scribe [109] multicast system is used to efficiently communicate among users. To allow for users to view and send mail, each ePOST node acts as a IMAP, POP3, and SMTP server. Thus, each user has their own private mail server on their desktop, which he accesses using any standard mail client program.

ePOST is built upon the POST distributed messaging system. POST offers a resilient, decentralized infrastructure by providing three basic, efficient services to applications: *(i)* secure, durable storage, *(ii)* metadata based on single-writer logs, and *(iii)* event notification. While ePOST is currently the

R. Steinmetz and K. Wehrle (Eds.): P2P Systems and Applications, LNCS 3485, pp. 171-192, 2005.

only deployed application built upon POST, a wide range of collaborative applications, such as instant messaging and shared calendars, can be constructed on top of POST using just these services.

The architecture of ePOST is shown in Figure 12.1. In this chapter, we start by describing scoped overlays, which provide autonomy and locality for organizations using ePOST. Next, we describe the POST system, which provides support for secure, reliable messaging and data storage. We then describe how ePOST is built using POST. Lastly, we detail the Glacier data durability system, which ePOST and POST use to ensure that data is durable even in the event of a large-scale correlated failure.

Layers			*Function*
Email Client			*Interacts with user*
IMAP	POP3	SMTP	*Standard email access protocols*
ePOST			*Uses POST to provide email services*
POST			*Securely and reliablely delivers messages*
Glacier	PAST	Scribe	*Stores data / disseminates messages*
Pastry			*Routes messages in overlay*

Fig. 12.1: ePOST Stack

12.1 Scoped Overlays

In most structured overlays, applications cannot ensure that a key is stored in the inserter's own organization, a property known as *content locality*. Likewise, one cannot ensure that a routing path stays entirely within an organization when possible, a property known as *path locality*. In an open system where participating organizations have conflicting interests, this lack of control can raise concerns about autonomy and accountability [279]. This is particularly problematic when deploying highly reliable services, as organizations may require that internal data and message traffic remain local. For instance, organizations using ePOST will probably want all intra-organizational email data to stay within the organization, even in encrypted form.

Moreover, participants in a conventional overlay must agree on a set of protocols and parameter settings such as the routing base, the size of the neighbor set, failure detection intervals, and the replication strategy. Optimal settings for these parameters depend on factors like the expected churn rate, node failure probabilities, and failure correlation. These factors may not be uniform across different organizations and may be difficult to assess or estimate in an Internet-wide system. The choice of parameters also depends on the required availability and durability of data, which may differ between participating organizations. Yet, conventional overlays require global agreement on protocols and parameter settings among all participants. For example, Company A may use mostly of desktop PCs with a high churn rate, while Company B may use mostly dedicated servers. In a traditional overlay, these two companies are required to use the same replication and fault tolerance parameters, even though they may be inappropriate for both.

The ePOST system is organized as a hierarchy of overlay instances with separate identifier spaces. This hierarchy reflects administrative and organizational domains, and naturally respects connectivity constraints. This technique leaves participating organizations in control over local resources, choice of protocols and parameters, and provides content and path locality. Each organization can run a different overlay protocol and use parameter settings appropriate for the organization's network characteristics and requirements. Scoped overlays generalize existing structured overlay protocols with a single ID space, thus leveraging prior work on all aspects of structured Peer-to-Peer overlays, including secure routing [108].

12.1.1 Design

A *multi-ring* protocol interfaces between organizational rings and implements global routing and lookup. To applications, the entire hierarchy appears as a single instance of a structured overlay network that spans multiple organizations and networks. The rings can use any structured overlay protocol that supports the key-based routing (KBR) API [148].

Figure 12.2 shows how our multi-ring protocol is layered above the KBR API of the overlay protocols that implement the individual rings. Shown at the right is a node that acts as a gateway between the rings; an instance of the gateway node appears in each separate ring. The structured overlays that run in each ring are completely independent. In fact, different protocols can run in the different rings, as long as they support the KBR API. Thus, in the example discussed above, company A and company B can run separate rings with different protocols and parameters while maintaining connectivity between them.

12.1.2 Ring Structure

The system forms a two-level tree of rings, consisting of a *global ring* at the root and several *organizational rings* at the lower level. Each ring has a globally unique *ringId*, which is known to all members of the ring. The global ring has a well-known ringId consisting of all zeroes. It is assumed

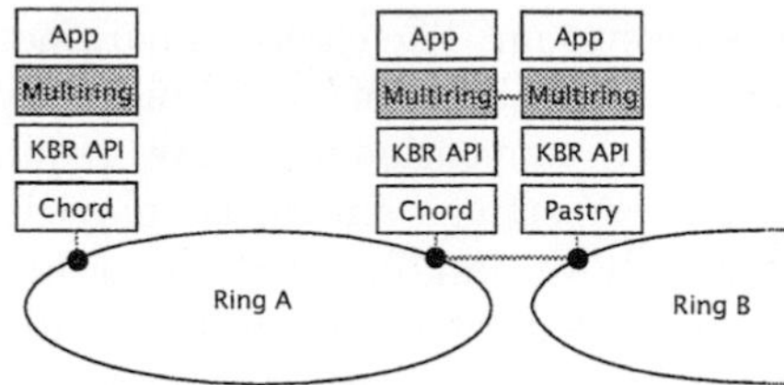

Fig. 12.2: Diagram of application layers. Note that rings may be running different protocols, as in this example.

that all members of a given ring are fully connected in the underlying physical network, i.e., they are not separated by firewalls or NAT boxes.

All nodes in the entire system join the global ring, unless they are connected behind a firewall or a NAT. In addition, each node joins an organizational ring consisting of all the nodes that belong to a given organization. A node is permitted to route messages and perform other operations only in rings of which it is a member.

An example configuration is shown in Figure 12.3. Nodes shown in gray are instances of the same node in multiple rings and nodes in black are only in a single ring because they are behind a firewall. The nodes connected by lines are actually instances of the same node, running in different rings. Ring A7 consists of nodes in an organization that are fully connected to the Internet. Thus, each node is also a member of the global ring. Ring 77 represents a set of nodes mostly behind a firewall.

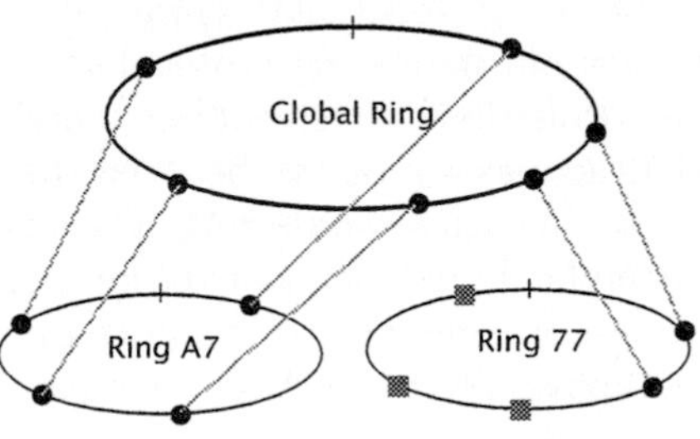

Fig. 12.3: Example of a ring structure.

The global ring is used primarily to route inter-organizational queries and to enable the global lookup of keys, while application objects are stored in the organizational rings. Each organizational ring defines a set of nodes that use a common set of protocols and parameter settings; they enjoy content and path locality for keys that they insert into the overlay. In addition, an organizational ring may also include nodes that are connected to the Internet through a firewall or NAT box.

12.1.3 Gateway Nodes

Recall that a node that is a member of more than one ring is a gateway node. Such a node supports multiple virtual overlay nodes, one in each ring, but uses the same nodeId in each ring. Gateway nodes can forward messages between rings, as described in the next subsection. In Figure 12.3 above, all of the nodes in ring *A7* are gateway nodes between the global ring and ring *A7*. To maximize load balance and fault tolerance, all nodes are expected to serve as gateway nodes, unless connectivity limitations (firewalls and NAT boxes) prevent it.

Gateway nodes announce themselves to other members of the rings in which they participate by subscribing to a multicast group in each of the rings. The group identifiers of these groups are the ringIds of the associated rings. In Figure 12.3 for instance, a node that is a member of both the global ring and *A7*, joins the Scribe groups:

Scribe group *A700...0* in the global ring
Scribe group *0000...0* in ringId *A7*

12.1.4 Routing

Recall that each node knows the ringIds of all rings in which it is a member. We assume that each message carries, in addition to a target key, the ringId of the ring in which the key is stored. Gateways forward messages as follows. If the target ringId of a message equals one of these ringIds, the node simply forwards the message to the corresponding ring. From that point on, the message is routed according to the structured overlay protocol within that target ring.

Otherwise, the node needs to locate a gateway node in the target ring, which is accomplished via a Scribe anycast. If the node is a member of the global ring, it then forwards the message via anycast in the global ring to the group that corresponds to the destination's ringId. The message will be delivered by Scribe to a gateway node for the target ring that is close in the physical network, among all such gateway nodes. This gateway node then forwards the data into the target ring, and routing proceeds as before.

If the sender is not a member of the global ring, then it forwards the message into the global ring via a gateway node by anycasting to the group local Scribe group whose identifier corresponds to the ringId of the global ring. Routing then proceeds as described above.

As an optimization, it is possible for nodes to cache the identities of gateway nodes they have previously obtained. Should the cached information prove stale, a new gateway node can be located via anycast. This optimization drastically reduces the need for anycast messages during routing.

12.1.5 Global Lookup

In the previous discussion, we assumed that messages carry both a key and the ringId of the ring in which the key is stored. In practice, however, applications may need to look up a key without knowledge of where the object is stored. For instance, keys are often derived from the hash of a textual name provided by a human user. In this case, the ring in which the key is stored may be unknown.

The following mechanism is designed to enable the global lookup of keys even when the ring in which it resides is not known to the requester. When a key is inserted into an organizational ring and that key should be visible at globally, a special indirection record is inserted into the global ring that associates the key with the ringIds of the organizational rings where replicas of the key are stored. The ringIds of a key can now be looked up in the global ring. Note that indirection records are the only data that need to be stored in the global ring. To prevent space-filling attacks, only legitimate indirection records are accepted by members of the global ring

12.2 POST Design

ePOST uses the POST messaging system to provide email services. At a high level, POST provides three generic services: *(i)* a shared, secure, durable message store, *(ii)* metadata based on single-writer logs, and *(iii)* event notification. These services can be combined to implement a variety of collaborative applications, such as email, news, instant messaging, shared calendars, and whiteboards.

In a typical pattern of use, users create messages (such as emails in the case of ePOST) that are inserted in encrypted form into the secure store. To send a message to another user or group, the event notification service is used to provide the recipient(s) with the necessary information to locate and decrypt the message. The recipients may then modify their personal, application-specific metadata to incorporate the message into their view, such as a private mail folder in ePOST.

POST assumes the existence of a certificate authority. This authority signs identity certificates binding a user's unique name (e.g., his email address) to his public key. The same authority issues the nodeId certificates required for secure routing in Pastry [108]. Users can access the system from any participating node, but it is assumed that the user trusts her local node, hereafter referred to as the trusted node, with her private key material.

Though participating nodes may suffer from Byzantine failures, POST also assumes that a large majority ($> 75\%$) of nodes in the system behave correctly, and that at least one node from each PAST replica set has not been compromised. If these assumptions are violated, POST's services may not be available, though the durability of stored data is still ensured thanks to Glacier, an archival storage layer that is described in Section 12.4.2. Additionally, POST makes the common assumption that breaking the cryptographic ciphers and signatures is computationally infeasible.

Table 12.1 shows pseudocode detailing the POST API that is presented to applications. The `store` and `fetch` methods comprise the single-copy message store. Similarly, the `readMostRecentEntry`, `readPreviousEntry`, and `appendEntry` methods provide the metadata service, and the `notify` method represents the event notification service.

The most interesting of these APIs is the metadata service, and we describe it in more detail here. Each of the user's logs is given a name unique to the user, denoted below by `LogName`. Applications can scan through a log in reverse order by first calling `readMostRecentEntry`, followed by successive invocations of `readPreviousEntry`. Similarly, applications can write to the log by simply calling `writeLog` with the desired target log's name.

```
// these two methods provide the single-copy message store
Key store(Object)
Object fetch(Key)

// and these methods provide the metadata service
LogEntry readMostRecentEntry(LogName)
LogEntry readPreviousEntry(LogEntry)
void appendEntry(LogName, LogEntry)

// lastly, this method provides the notification service
void notify(User, Message)
```

Table 12.1: POST API

12.2.1 Data Types

POST uses the PAST distributed hash table to store three types of data: *content-hash blocks*, *certificate blocks*, and *public-key blocks*.

Content-Hash Blocks

Content-hash blocks, which store immutable data objects such as email data, are stored using the cryptographic hash of the block's contents as the key. Content-hash blocks can be authenticated by obtaining a single replica and verifying that its contents match the key; because they are immutable, any corruption of the content can be easily detected.

Certificate Blocks

Certificate blocks are signed by the certificate authority and bind a name (e.g. an email address) to a public key. Certificate blocks are stored using the cryptographic hash of the name as the key and are also immutable after creation. Certificate blocks can be authenticated based on their digital signature, since all users are assumed to know the certificate authority's public key.

Public-Key Blocks

Public-key blocks contain timestamps, are signed with a private key, and are stored using a secure hash of the corresponding public key as the key. The signature attached to the block allows for block mutation after creation. First, the nodes storing replicas of the block must verify that the signature on the update matches the already-known public key. To prevent an attacker from trying to roll the block back to an earlier valid state, the storage nodes verify that the timestamps are increasing monotonically. Finally, the object requester must obtain all live replicas, verify their signatures, and discard any with older timestamps.

12.2.2 User Accounts

Each user in POST possesses an account, which is associated with an identity certificate. This certificate is stored as a certificate block, using the secure hash of the user's name as the key. Also associated with each account is a user identity block, which contains a description of the user and the contact address of the user's current trusted node. The identity block is stored as a public-key block, and signed with the user's private key. Finally, each user account has an associated Scribe group used for event notification, with a groupId equal to the cryptographic hash of the user's public key.

The immutable identity certificate, combined with the mutable public-key block, provides a secure means for the certificate authority to bind names to keys, while giving users the ability to subsequently change their personal contact data later without having to interact with the certificate authority.

The Scribe group provides a rendez-vous point for nodes waiting for news from the associated user, or anybody wishing to notify the user that new data is available. For example, users waiting for another user A to come online can subscribe to A's group. Once A is online again, he publishes to his group, informing others of his presence.

12.2.3 Single-Copy Store

While POST stores potentially sensitive user data on nodes throughout the network, the system seeks to provide a level of privacy, integrity and durability comparable to maintaining data on a trusted server. A technique called convergent encryption [176] is used. This allows a message to be disclosed to selected recipients, while ensuring that copies of a given plain-text message inserted by different users or applications map to the same cipher-text, thus ensuring that only a single copy of the message is stored.

To store a message X, POST first computes the cryptographic $\mathit{Hash}(X)$, uses this hash as a key to encrypt X with an efficient symmetric cipher, and then stores the resulting ciphertext with the key

$$\mathit{Hash}\left(\mathit{Encrypt}_{\mathit{Hash}(X)}(X)\right)$$

which is the secure hash of the ciphertext. To decrypt the message, a user must know the hash of the plain-text.

Convergent encryption reduces the storage requirements when multiple copies of the same content are inserted into the store independently. This happens, for example, when a popular document is sent as an email attachment or posted on bulletin boards by many different users.

In certain scenarios, it may be undesirable to use convergent encryption, such as when the plain-text can easily be guessed. In these cases, the POST store can be configured to use conventional symmetric encryption with randomly generated keys.

12.2.4 Event Notification

The notification service is used to alert users and groups of users to certain events, such as the availability of a new email message, a change in the state of a user, or a change in the state of a shared object.

For instance, after a new message was inserted into POST as part of an email or a newsgroup posting, the intended recipient(s) must be alerted to the availability of the message and be provided with the appropriate decryption key. Commonly, this type of notification involves obtaining the contact address from the recipient's identity block. Then, a notification message is sent to the recipient's trusted node, containing the message's decryption key, and is encrypted with the recipient's public key and signed by the sender.

In practice, the notification can be more complicated if the sender and the recipient are not on-line at the same time. To handle this case, the sender delegates the responsibility of delivering the notification message to a set of k random nodes. When a user A wishes to send a notification message to a user B whose trusted node is off-line, A first sends a notification request message to the k nodes numerically closest to a random Pastry key C. This message is encrypted with B's public key and signed by A. The k nodes are then responsible for delivering the notification message (contained within the notification request message) to B. Each of these nodes stores the message and then subscribes to the Scribe group associated with B.

Whenever user B is on-line, his trusted node periodically publishes a message to the Scribe group rooted at the hash of his public key, notifying any subscribers of his presence and current contact address. Upon receipt of this message, the subscribers deliver the notification by sending it to the contact address. As long as not all of the replica nodes fail at the same time, the notification is guaranteed to be delivered. POST relies on Scribe only for timely delivery – if Scribe messages are occasionally lost due to failures, the notification will still be delivered since users periodically publish to the their group.

12.2.5 Metadata

POST provides single-writer logs that allow applications to maintain metadata. Typically, a log encodes a view of a specific user or group of users and refers to stored messages. For instance, a log may represent updates to a user's private email folder, or the history of a public newsgroup. An email or news application would then use such a log consisting of insert, update, and delete records to keep track of the state of the folder or newsgroup.

The log head is stored as a public-key block and contains the location of the most recent log record. Keys for log heads may be stored in the user's identity block, in a log record, or in a message. Each log record is stored as a content-hash block and contains application-specific metadata and the key of the next recent record in the log. Applications can optionally encrypt the contents of log records depending on the intended set of readers.

To allow for more efficient log traversal, POST aggregates clusters of M consecutive log records in a single PAST object. Partially filled clusters are buffered in the log head object, and are added to the log as a separate cluster entry once they are full. This reduces the number of keys associated with log entries by a factor of M and increases the speed of log traversals accordingly.

Other optimizations are used to reduce the overhead of log traversals, including caching of log records at clients and the use of snapshots. POST applications periodically insert snapshots of their metadata into PAST. Thus, log traversals can be terminated at the most recent snapshot.

12.2.6 Garbage Collection

In order to make the PAST DHT practical for use in applications such as ePOST, we found it necessary to introduce a mechanism for removing objects from the DHT.

Disk space is not necessarily a problem, since the rapid growth in hard disk capacity would probably make it possible to store all inserted data ad infinitum. However, the network bandwidth required to repair failed replicas would become unwieldy over time. Such maintenance is necessary to ensure that there always are at least k live replicas of each stored object, and re-replicating each object as necessary.

The obvious solution is to add a `delete` operation to PAST that removes the object associated with the given key. However, a delete method is unsafe, because a single compromised node could use it to delete data at will. Moreover, safe deletion of shared objects requires a secure reference-counting scheme, which is difficult to implement in a system with frequent node failures and the possibility of Byzantine faults.

As an alternative solution, we added leases to objects stored in PAST. Each object inserted into the DHT is given a expiration date by the inserting node. Once the expiration date for a given object has passed, the storage nodes are free to delete the object. Clients must periodically extend the leases on all data they are interested in. The modified PAST API is shown in Table 12.2.

```
void put(Key, Object, Expiration)
Object get(Key)
void refresh(Key, NewExpiration)
```

Table 12.2: Modified PAST API

Adding leases to PAST required other slight modifications. Specifically, the replication protocol must now exchange tuples (*key, expiration*). When a node is told to refresh a key that it already stored with a different lease, it simply extends the expiration date of the stored key if the new lease is longer.

We cannot assume that the clocks on different storage nodes are perfectly synchronized. Therefore, expired objects are not deleted immediately;

instead, they are kept for an additional *grace period* T_G. During this time, the objects are still available for queries, but they are no longer advertised to other nodes during maintenance. Thus, nodes that have already deleted their objects do not attempt to recover them.

12.2.7 POST Security

POST is designed to face a variety of threats, ranging from nodes that simply fail to operate, to attackers trying to read or modify sensitive information. POST must likewise be robust against free riding behavior, including users consuming more resources than they contribute, and to application-specific resource consumption issues, such as the space consumed by spam messages.

Threat Model

Our threat model for POST includes of attacks from both within and outside of POST. Internal attacks can be broken down into two classes: free riding and malicious behavior. Free riding, discussed below, consists of either selfish behavior or simple denial of service. Malicious behavior, however, can consist of nodes attempting to read confidential data, modify existing data, or delete data from the ePOST system.

Data Privacy

While convergent encryption provides the benefit of a single-copy store, it is known to be vulnerable to known-plaintext attacks. An attacker who is able to guess that plaintext of a message can verify its existence in the store, and may be able to determine whether any given node has requested that particular message. This is a particular concern for short messages, messages that are highly structured, or generally any messages with low entropy. To address these concerns, POST uses traditional cryptographic techniques (AES encryption with a random key) to encrypt such messages, and to protect data that is not meant to be shared, such as the logs and other per-user metadata maintained by the system.

Data Integrity

Due to the single-writer property and the content-hash chaining [408] of the logs, it is computationally infeasible for a malicious user or storage node to insert a new log record or to modify an existing log record without the change being detected. This is due to the choice of a collision-resistant secure hash function to chain the log entries and the use of signatures based on public key encryption in the log heads.

To prevent version rollback attacks by malicious storage nodes, public-key blocks contain timestamps. When reading a public-key block (e.g., a log-head) from the store, nodes read all replicas and use the authentic replica with the most recent timestamp. When reading content-hash blocks or certificate blocks, they can use any authentic replica.

Denial of Service

A variety of denial of service (DoS) attacks may be mounted against Peer-to-Peer networks. A common DoS strategy might be to control enough nodes to effectively partition the overlay network, or even to control all of the outgoing routes from a given node. Likewise, DoS attacks may be aimed at controlling all of the replicas of a given document, allowing the attacker to effectively censor any desired document. Pastry's secure routing mechanism provide an effective defense against such DoS attacks, both from within and outside the overlay [108]. When secure routing is used, an attacker would need to control over 25% of the overlay nodes to mount an effective DoS attack.

Another type of DoS attack is space-filling, where a malicious node simply tries to insert as much junk data as possible into the DHT. While this attack is not unique to ePOST, the organizational scoping of rings in ePOST helps to mitigate this attack. Since all nodes in a given ring are in a single administrative domain, space-filling attacks can be detected and the faulty node shut down or punished by the local administrator.

Free Riding

Nodes within the network may try to consume much more remote storage than they provide to the network. Likewise, nodes may wish to fetch objects more often than they serve objects to other nodes. If bandwidth or storage are scarce resources, users will have an incentive to modify their POST software to behave selfishly. Nodes can generally be coerced into behaving correctly when other nodes observe their behavior and, if they determine a node to be a freeloader, will refuse to give it service [448, 135]. Such mechanisms can guarantee that it is rational for nodes to behave correctly.

POST, in its present form, does not yet include any explicit incentives mechanisms [448, 135]. The reason is that within an administrative domain, members generally have external incentives to cooperate. If abuses do occur, they can be localized to an organizational ring, and the offending users can be reprimanded within the organization.

12.3 ePOST Design

Each ePOST user is expected to run a daemon program on his desktop computer that implements ePOST, and contributes some CPU, network bandwidth and disk storage to the system. The daemon also acts as an SMTP and IMAP server, thus allowing the user to utilize conventional email client programs. The daemon is assumed to be trusted by the user and holds the user's private key material. No other participating nodes in the system are assumed to be trusted by the user.

12.3.1 Email Storage

When ePOST receives messages from a client program, it parsers them into MIME components (message body and any attachments) and these are stored as separate objects in POST's secure store. Recall that frequently circulated attachments are stored in the system only once.

The message components are first inserted into POST by the sender's ePOST daemon; then, a notification message is sent to the recipient. Sending a message or attachment to a large number of recipients requires very little additional storage overhead beyond sending to a single recipient, as the data is only inserted once. Additionally, if messages are forwarded or sent by different users, the original message data does not need to be stored again; the message reference is reused.

12.3.2 Email Delivery

The delivery of new email is accomplished using POST's notification service. The sender first constructs a notification message containing basic header information, such as the names of the sender and recipients, a timestamp, and a reference to the body and attachments of the message. The sender then requests the local POST service to deliver this notification to each of the recipients. This message is signed by the sender and encrypted using the receiver's public key in the usual fashion, combining asymmetric public key cryptography with a fast symmetric cipher.

If the recipient of the email is in a different ring than the sender, the recipient has the option of referencing the received email body and attachments in the ring of their originator, or to fetch and insert copies into his own local ring. The latter approach leads to higher availability and greater confidence in message durability, due to the greater replication and the fact that a recipient typically has greater confidence in his own organizational ring. Therefore, ePOST replicates all incoming mail in the recipient's local ring by default.

12.3.3 Email Folders

Each email folder is represented by an encrypted POST log. Each log entry represents a change to the state of the associated folder, such as the addition or deletion of a message. Since the log can only be written by its owner and its contents are encrypted, ePOST preserves or exceeds the level of privacy and integrity provided by conventional email systems with storage on trusted servers. A diagram of the logs used in ePOST is shown in Figure 12.4.

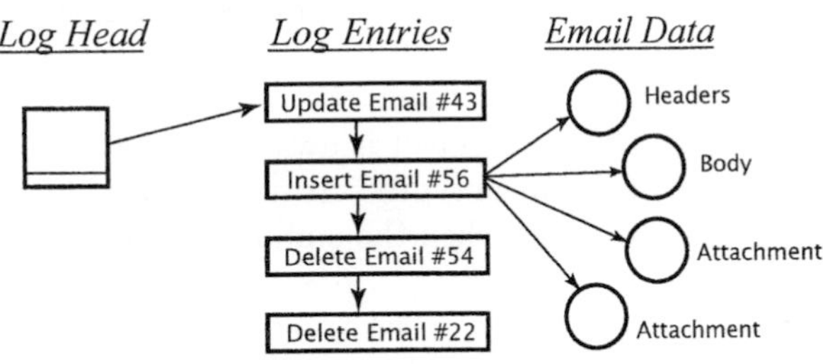

Fig. 12.4: Log structure used in ePOST. Each box or circle represents a separate object in the DHT.

Next, we describe a log record representing an insertion of an email message into a user's folder, such as his inbox. Other types of log records are analogous. An email insertion record contains the content of the message's MIME header, the message's key, and its decryption key, protected by a signature and taken from the sender's original notification message. All of this data is then encrypted with a unique session key, using a low-cost symmetric cipher like AES. As these insertion records need only be legible to the original sender, the session key is encrypted with a master key, also using the cheap symmetric cipher. This symmetric master key is maintained with the same care as the user's private key. This allows the owner of the folder, and none other, to read messages in the inbox and verify their authenticity without performing expensive public key operations. The exact messages are shown in Figure 12.5.

$$
\begin{aligned}
\mathit{EncryptedEmail} &= \mathit{Encrypt}_{\mathit{Hash}(X)}(X) \\
\mathit{MessageHeader} &= (A, B, T, \mathit{Hash}(\mathit{EncryptedEmail}), \mathit{Hash}(X)) \\
\mathit{Notification} &= \mathit{Encrypt}_{K_B}(\mathit{MessageHeader}, \mathit{Sign}_{K_A}(\mathit{MessageHeader}))
\end{aligned}
$$

Fig. 12.5: Messages transmitted sending an email.

12.3.4 Incremental Deployment

To allow an organization to adopt ePOST as its email service, ePOST must be able to interoperate with the existing, server-based email infrastructure. We describe here how ePOST is deployed in a single organization and how it interoperates with conventional email services in the general Internet.

For outgoing mail, if an email recipient is not reachable within ePOST, then the sender's ePOST proxy contacts the recipient's mail server using SMTP. For inbound email, the organization's DNS server provides MX records referring to a set of trusted ePOST nodes within the local organization. These nodes act as incoming SMTP mail gateways, accepting messages, inserting them into POST, and notifying the recipient's node. Suitable headers are generated such that the receiver is aware the message may have been transmitted on the Internet unencrypted. If no identity block can be found for the recipient in the local ring, then the email "bounces" as in server-based systems.

The inbound proxy nodes need to be trusted to the extent that they receive plaintext email messages for local users. Typically, the desktop workstations of an organization's system administrators can be used for this purpose. Administrators of conventional email services own root passwords that allow them to access incoming email anyway. Thus, ePOST provides the same privacy for incoming email from non-POST senders as existing systems, and provides stronger security for email transmitted within ePOST.

12.3.5 Management

If ePOST is to replace existing email systems, there must be a viable management strategy for organizations to adopt when deploying ePOST. The management tasks in ePOST can be broken down into three categories: software distribution, storage, and access. In the paragraphs below, we discuss these tasks in detail and show how they can be minimized in the context of ePOST.

Software

The first management task incurred with ePOST is maintaining the proxy software. This software needs to be kept running and up-to-date as bugs are fixed and features are added. In our deployment, the ePOST proxy is configured as a service that is restarted automatically if it fails. Software upgrades are handled by signing updated code and having users' proxies periodically check and download authorized updates.

To allow administrators to efficiently monitor the ePOST system, we have built a graphical administrative monitoring interface. This application allows administrator to monitor an entire ePOST ring at a glance and to track down any problems. Administrators are automatically alerted to error conditions or unusual behavior.

Storage

In a distributed storage system such as ePOST, a certain level of administration is necessary to monitor the storage pool. For example, administrators need to ensure that space-filling attacks are not taking place and that nodes that are running out of disk space are promptly serviced. Such monitoring can be done using the tool described in the previous section. The administrator is alerted to nodes that are close to their disk space limit, and can then take appropriate actions.

Access Control

Controlling access to ePOST can be broken down into two related tasks: trust and naming. Trust is based on certificates, which users must obtain from their organization to participate in the system. This is no different from current email systems, where each user is required to obtain an account on an email server. For example, in our experimental deployment, we provide a web page where users can sign up and download certificates. In practice, the process may require various forms of authentication before the new certificate is produced.

Naming in ePOST is managed in a manner similar to current systems. Organizations ensure that email addresses are unique and associated with only one public key. This is easy to accomplish, since each user must obtain a certificate from his organization.

ePOST has the potential for requiring substantially lower administrative overhead than conventional email systems, since the self-organizing properties of the underlying Peer-to-Peer substrate can mask the effect of node failures. Additionally, the organic scalability granted to ePOST by the overlay has the potential to significantly reduce the overhead associated with scaling an existing email service to more users.

12.4 Correlated Failures

ePOST relies on *cooperative storage* to store email messages. Each node is required to contribute a small fraction of its local disk space; the system then aggregates this storage and provides the abstraction of a giant single store. As mentioned earlier, this approach is well suited for serverless applications like POST because it is highly scalable - not only in terms of overhead, but also because as the size of the system increases, the storage supply increases also. This allows the system to support organic growth.

Since the system is built out of unreliable components, it must be prepared to handle occasional node failures. Cooperative storage systems like PAST often assume that the node population is highly diverse, i.e., that the nodes are running different operating systems, use different hardware platforms, are located in different countries, etc. Under these conditions, node failures can be approximated as independent and identically distributed. To ensure data durability, it is thus sufficient to store a small number of replicas for each object, and to create new replicas when a node failure is detected.

Unfortunately, most real distributed systems exhibit high diversity only in some aspects, but not in others. For example, the fraction of nodes running Microsoft Windows can be as high as 60% or more in many environments. In such a system, failures are not independent. For example, if the Windows machines share a common vulnerability, a worm that exploits this vulnerability may cause a *large-scale correlated failure* that can affect a majority of the nodes. Moreover, if the worm can obtain administrator privileges on the machines it infects, the failures can even be Byzantine.

The reactive replication strategy in PAST is clearly not sufficient to handle failures of this type. Even if the failure is not Byzantine, there may simply not be enough time to create a sufficient number of additional replicas. As a consequence, early deployments of ePOST sometimes suffered data loss during correlated failures. Since this is not acceptable for critical data like email, the system needed another mechanism to ensure data durability.

12.4.1 Failure Models

If the system must sustain fast-spreading correlated failures such as power outages or Warhol worms [572], a reactive defense that detects and repairs failures as they occur is not enough. Instead, the system must b e *proactive* and prepared for the failure in advance.

An ideal proactive system would foresee which nodes are going to be affected by the next failure and then store the data on the remaining nodes. This method has zero overhead but is infeasible, so practical systems must use an approximation. A common technique, which is used in systems like Phoenix [329], is to use *introspection* to collect information about each node, which is then used to predict correlations between the nodes. The data is then stored on a set of nodes that are expected to fail with low correlation.

Introspective systems are still very storage efficient but crucially depend on the correctness of their failure model. Even small inaccuracies may lead to incorrect placement decisions and thus to data loss in a correlated failure. Moreover, the participants in an introspective system actually have an incentive to report incorrect data, e.g. to reduce their load by making their node

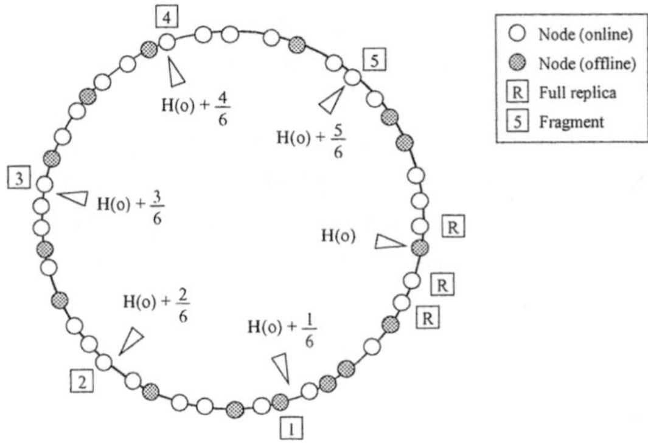

Fig. 12.6: Fragment placement in Glacier.

appear heavily correlated with others. Finally, it is very difficult to identify *all* potential sources of correlation in a realistic system.

12.4.2 Glacier

The durability layer in POST, which is called Glacier, takes a different approach [269]. Instead of relying on a sophisticated failure model, it makes a very simple assumption, namely that the correlated failure does not affect more than a fraction f_{max} of the nodes; all failure scenarios up to that fraction are assumed to be equally likely. In order to tolerate such a wide range of failures, Glacier must sacrifice some capacity in the cooperative store for additional redundancy; thus, it trades abundance for increased reliability.

When a new object is inserted, Glacier applies an *erasure code* to transform it into a large number of *fragments*. Together, the fragments are much larger than the object itself, but a small number of them is sufficient to restore the entire object. For example, Glacier may be configured to create 48 fragments, each of which is 20% the size of the object. This corresponds to a storage overhead of 9.6, but the object can be restored as long as any five fragments survive.

Glacier then attaches to each fragment a so-called *manifest* which, among other things, contains hashes of all the other fragments. This is used to authenticate fragments. Finally, Glacier spreads the fragments across the overlay, calculating the key of fragment i as

$$k_i = K + \frac{i}{n+1}$$

where K is the key of the object and n is the total number of fragments. This ensures that the fragments are easy to find without extra bookkeeping (which may be lost in a failure). Also, if the overlay is large enough, each fragment is stored on a different node, which ensures that fragment losses are not correlated.

For security reasons, Glacier does not allow fragments to be overwritten or deleted remotely. If these operations were permitted, a compromised node could use them to delete its own data on other nodes. However, objects may be associated with a lease, and their storage is reclaimed when the lease expires. Also, Glacier supports a per-object version number to implement mutable objects.

12.4.3 Maintenance in Glacier

Since some fragments are continually lost due to individual node failures and departures, Glacier implements a maintenance mechanism to reconstruct missing fragments. However, because of the high redundancy, Glacier can afford high latencies between the loss of a fragment and its recovery; thus, the maintenance mechanism need not be tightly coupled.

Because of the way fragments are placed in the ring, each Glacier node knows that its peers at a distance $k \cdot \frac{1}{n+1}$ $(k = 1..n)$ in ring space store a set of fragments that is very similar to its own. Thus, each node periodically (say, once every few hours) asks one of its peers for a list of fragments it stores, and compares that list to the fragments in its own local store. If it finds a key for which it does not currently have a fragment, it calculates the positions of all corresponding fragments and checks whether any of them fall into its local key range. If so, it asks its peers for a sufficient number of fragments to restore the object, computes its own fragment, and stores it locally.

Glacier also takes advantage of the fact that nodes often depart the overlay for a certain amount of time (e.g. because of a scheduled downtime) but return afterwards with their store intact. Therefore, Glacier nodes do not immediately take over the ring space of a failed neighbor, but wait for a certain grace period T. If the node returns during that time, it only needs to reconstruct the fragments that were inserted while it was absent; the vast majority of its fragments remains unmodified.

The loosely coupled maintenance mechanism greatly reduces the bandwidth required for fragment maintenance. In the actual deployment which has moderate churn and the configuration mentioned earlier, Glacier uses less bandwidth than PAST, even though it manages over three times more storage.

12.4.4 Recovery After Failures

A large-scale correlated failure has two main effects on a Glacier deployment: First, a large fraction of nodes may lose the fragments they store locally, and second, the overlay may be shattered, and communication with other nodes may become impossible. Both effects may be aggravated by Byzantine failures: Malicious nodes may corrupt their local fragments in order to complicate recovery, and they may mount attacks on the overlay (e.g. an Eclipse attack) to interrupt communication. However, even a malicious node cannot change its certified nodeId and take over a portion of the ring space that is occupied by an unaffected node. Therefore, the fragments on the surviving nodes remain safe as long as their leases do not expire.

While the failure lasts, we cannot assume that the unaffected nodes can make any progress towards recovery, since this would require communication with other nodes. Therefore, these nodes simply 'weather the storm' and do nothing. Eventually, the administrators of the failed nodes will notice the problem and repair their nodes. After that, the maintenance mechanism will gradually recover the lost fragments and thus restore full redundancy. To prevent congestion collapse, the amount of bandwidth each node is allowed to spend on maintenance is limited, so full recovery may take several hours to complete; however, even though the data is not fully durable during that time, it still remains available and can be retrieved on demand.

12.4.5 Object Aggregation

In ePOST, the storage load mainly consists of small objects (email texts and headers). This causes more overhead in Glacier because the number of keys is higher, and thus more storage space and bandwidth is required for per-key metadata such as the fixed-size manifests. To reduce this overhead, ePOST aggregates objects before inserting them into Glacier.

The main challenge in object aggregation is how to do it securely in an environment with large-scale Byzantine failures. Even though there are considerable advantages in performing aggregation on the storage nodes, Glacier cannot allow this because these nodes cannot be trusted. Therefore, each node is required to create and maintain its own aggregates. This includes keeping a mapping from object keys to aggregate keys (which is required to locate objects), extending the leases of aggregates whose objects are still in use, and merging old aggregates whose objects have mostly expired.

The mapping from object keys to aggregates requires special attention because it is crucial during recovery. Without it, the application may be unable to find its objects after a failure without searching Glacier's entire store, which is infeasible. For this reason, the system adds to each aggregate a few pointers to other aggregates, thus forming a directed acyclic graph (DAG). During recovery, an ePOST node traverses its DAG and is thus able to locate all non-expired objects it has inserted. Moreover, the DAG contains a hash tree, which is used to authenticate all aggregates. The only additional requirement for ePOST is to maintain a pointer to the top-level aggregate; this pointer is kept in an object with a well-known key that is directly inserted into Glacier.

12.5 Preliminary Experience

We implemented a version of POST and ePOST on top of FreePastry, an open-source implementation of Pastry, PAST and Scribe, and the POST and ePOST code was released alongside FreePastry 1.4 [233]. Our initial deployment of ePOST began in January of 2004 with very few users. As confidence in the system grew, we expanded our userbase and incorporated new features. Many of our users rely on ePOST as their primary email system, no longer using their conventional accounts. For more information on our deployment, please see `http://www.epostmail.org`.

The current ePOST deployment has two separate ePOST rings: a ring at Rice University limited to members of Rice only, and a ring based on PlanetLab [486], which is open to the public. We currently have approximately 20 registered users in the Rice ring and 73 registered in the PlanetLab ring. We have found the storage and bandwidth requirements to be relatively modest: the average storage requirement on the Rice nodes after one year of use was approximately 500 MB, and the average bandwidth usage was 500 bytes per second per node.

13. Distributed Computing – GRID Computing

Andreas Mauthe (Lancaster University)
Oliver Heckmann (Darmstadt University of Technology)

13.1 Introduction

The idea of GRID computing originated in the scientific community and was initially motivated by processing power and storage intensive applications [213]. The basic objective of GRID computing is to support resource sharing among individuals and institutions (organizational units), or resource entities within a networked infrastructure. Resources that can be shared are, for example, bandwidth, storage, processing capacity, and data [304, 429]. The resources pertain to organizations and institutions across the world; they can belong to a single enterprize or be in an external resource-sharing and service provider relationship. On the GRID, they form distributed, heterogeneous, dynamic *virtual organizations* [221]. The GRID provides a resource abstractions in which the resources are represented by services. Through the strong service-orientation the GRID effectively becomes a networked infrastructure of interoperating services. The driving vision behind this is the idea of "service-oriented science" [215].

The GRID builds on the results of distributed systems research and implements them on a wider scale. Through the proliferation of the Internet and the development of the Web (together with emerging distributed middleware platforms), large-scale distributed applications that span a wide geographical and organizational area becoming possible. This has been taken advantage of within the Peer-to-Peer and the GRID communities more or less at the same time. The GRID has been driven from within the science community, which first saw the potential of such systems and implemented them on a wider scale. Application areas here are distributed supercomputing (e.g., physical process simulations), high-throughput computing (to utilize unused processor cycles), on-demand computing (for short-term demands and load-balancing), data intensive computing (synthesizing information from data that is maintained in geographically distributed repositories), and collaborative computing [225].

It is important to note that the prime objective of GRID computing is to provide access to common, very large pools of different resources that enable innovative applications to utilize them [227]. This is one of the defining differences between Peer-to-Peer (P2P) and GRID computing. Although both

R. Steinmetz and K. Wehrle (Eds.): P2P Systems and Applications, LNCS 3485, pp. 193-206, 2005.

are concerned with the pooling and co-ordinated use of resources, the GRID's objective is to provide a platform for the integration of various applications, whereas initially Peer-to-Peer applications were vertically integrated [217].

Many current GRID implementations are based on the Globus Toolkit^{TM}, an open source toolkit [203, 219]. Within the Globus project, a pragmatic approach has been taken in implementing services needed to support a computational GRID. The Open GRID Services Architecture (OGSA) developed by the Global GRID Forum (GGF) - inspired by the Globus project - develops the GRID idea further and is also concerned with issues that have not been the focus of the Globus project such as architectural and standardization matters. OGSA combines GRID technology with Web services. This has led to a strong service orientation, where services on the GRID are generally autonomous and not subject of centralized control.

Besides Globus and OSGA there is the European driven development around Unicorn. It has especially influenced information GRIDs in the corporate world but is also still very much in the development phase. In this chapter we concentrate on the developments within Globus and GGF. Unfortunately, a comprehensive discussion is not possible within the space of this chapter. It rather provides an overview of the ideas and concepts behind the GRID, but also shows how they have evolved from an infrastructure driven approach towards a service-oriented architecture. This is particularly important since the GRID is still a very active and fast developing area. More information can be found in [225] and on the GGF Web site (www.ggf.org).

In this chapter, the main initiatives and concepts driving GRID developments are introduced. This includes an outline of the architectural concepts behind GRID but also a discussion of the Globus Project and the developments around OGSA. Subsequently, the relationship between Peer-to-Peer and GRID is outlined.

13.2 The GRID Architecture

The GRID idea has evolved over the years and there is no prescribed or standardized GRID architecture. The current understanding of the GRID has been influenced by a number of initiatives and individuals who have been driving the development. Therefore, the GRID architecture presented in the following represents a generally accept view and not a standardized reference framework. It should be regarded as abstraction in which the various GRID tools and services can be located according to their functionality.

A computational GRID is more formally defined as "*a hardware and software infrastructure that provides dependable, consistent, pervasive, and inexpensive access to high-end computational capabilities*" [225]. Different applications can be implemented on top of this infrastructure to utilize the shared resources. If different institutions or individuals participate in such a sharing relationship, they form a *virtual organization* [222]. The concept underlying the GRID facilitates collaboration across institutional boundaries. To achieve this a protocol architecture is proposed and standard components are specified that can be used by the different parties entering into a sharing relationship [227].

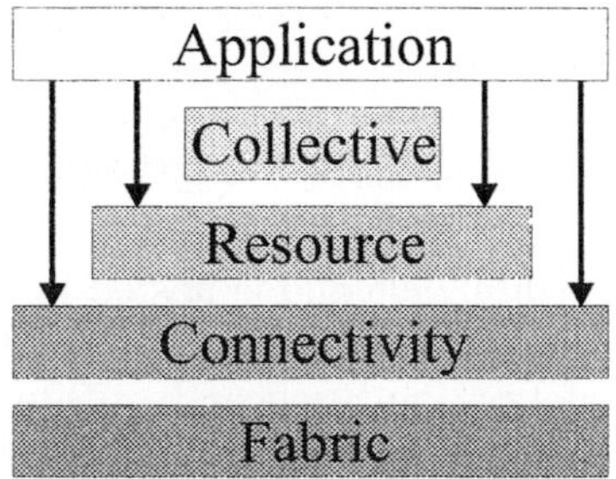

Fig. 13.1: GRID Layered Architecture

The GRID architecture can be described by a layered model where the different components are placed within a layer depending on their functionality and capabilities. An hourglass model (comparable to the Internet), in which a small group of core protocols and components forms the link between the high-level mechanisms and a number of lower level base technologies, has been adopted [67]. The components of the architecture (as depicted in Figure 13.1) are the *Fabric Layer*, the *Connectivity Layer*, the *Resource Layer* and the *Collective Layer* [227]. The applications that reside on top of this infrastructure can use the components of the *Collective*, *Resource* and *Connectivity Layers* directly, depending on their requirements.

The Fabric Layer makes the resources that are provided by the different nodes of the GRID available for common usage, i.e., it provides common access to resources that are shared within a virtual organization. Resources are divided into computing resources, storage, network resources, code storage, and directories [227]. The Fabric Layer implements the resource specific operations and offers a unified interface to the upper layers.

The Connectivity Layer hosts the most important communication and authentication protocols required for GRID specific communication. It enables data exchange between the resources located at the Fabric Layer. The communication protocols employed in this context are predominantly from the TCP/IP protocol suite. Security is provided by a public key infrastructure based on special GRID security protocols [223]. Above the Connectivity Layer, the Resource Layer is responsible for resource management operations such as resource negotiation, resource reservation, resource access and management, QoS control, accounting, etc. The actual resources that are managed, however, are the resources under the control of the Fabric Layer.

The Collective Layer is concerned with the overall co-ordination of different resource groups. It hosts components such as directory services [144], scheduling and brokering services, monitoring and diagnostic services, data replication services, workload management, etc. [227].

Finally, the Application Layer comprises the user applications used to achieve the virtual organization. Applications are utilizing the services offered by the underlying layers. They can directly access these services.

13.3 The Globus Project

The Globus project started in 1996 and is hosted by Argonne National Laboratory's Mathematics and Computer Science Division, the University of Southern California's Information Sciences Institute, and the University of Chicago's Distributed Systems Laboratory. It was one of the first and most visible activities in this area. It is supported by a number of institutional (e.g., National Computational Science Alliance (USA), NASA, Universities of Chicago and Wisconsin) and industry partners (e.g., IBM and Microsoft) [248]. The project is centered on four main activity areas:

1. *Building of large-scale GRID applications* such as distributed supercomputing, smart instruments, desktop supercomputing tele-immersion.
2. Support for planning and *building of large-scale testbeds* for GRID research, as well as for functional GRID systems
3. *Research into GRID related issues* such as resource management, security, information services, fault detection and data management.
4. *Building of software tools* for a variety of platforms (the so-called Globus Toolkit^{TM}), which are, however, considered research prototypes only.

The Globus Toolkit^{TM} supplies the building blocks for a GRID infrastructure, i.e., it provides services and modules required to support GRID applications and programming tools. It is a community-based, open architecture, open source set of services and software libraries [221]. The services are programs that interact with each other to exchange information or co-ordinate the processing of tasks. They can be used independently or together to form a supporting platform for GRID applications.

A Globus service encapsulates a certain functionality and provides an abstraction for resources. For instance, a number of services deal with resource selection, allocation, and management. "Resource", in this context, is a generic term for everything required to process a task. This includes system resources such as CPU, network bandwidth and storage capacity. The *Resource Selection Service* (RSS) provides a generic resource selection framework for all kinds of GRID applications. For a specific case it identifies a suitable set of resources by taking into account application characteristics and system status [392].

An end-to-end management of QoS for different resource types such as bandwidth, CPU, and storage is provided by the *General-Purpose Architecture for Reservation and Allocation* (GARA) system [226][533]. Dynamic feedback is used among resource managers to coordinate resource management decisions [226]. The *Globus Resource Allocation Manager* (GRAM) is part of the lowest level of the resource management architecture. It provides resource allocation, process creation, monitoring, and management services. The GRAM service maps requests expressed in the Resource Specification Language (RSL) into commands to local schedulers and computers [145]. The resource management tools build on existing languages, protocols, and infrastructure. Their capabilities depend on the functionality and capacity of the hosting environments in which they operate, i.e., they can only guarantee a certain level of QoS if this is supported by the underlying networks and operating systems.

A central service within the Globus Toolkit is the *Monitoring and Discovery Service* (MDS-2). This generic service provides a framework for service and data discovery. The MDS-2 service supplies information concerning system configuration and status information to other services. This includes server configuration, location of data replica, network status, etc. Two protocols are used for accessing and exchanging information in this context; namely GRIP - the *GRID Information Protocol* (used to access information about entities) and GRRP - the *GRID Registration Protocol* (used to notify directory services of the availability of certain information) [144].

A number of other services are available within the Globus Toolkit to deal with issues such as:

- security, authentication, integrity and confidentiality (provided by the *GRID Security Service*, GSI);
- the management of data movement and access strategies (provided by *Global Access to Secondary Storage*, GASS);
- data transfer in and replication management (for instance provided by *GridFTP*);
- and the monitoring of the system state (provided by *Heartbeat Monitor*, HBM), cf. [23, 24, 248].

Each Globus service has an API (written in C); in addition Java classes are available for important services. The Globus services have been implemented in a joint effort by the participating project partners. The services support GRID applications that run on existing hardware platforms and hosting environments. Thus, the implementations make extensive use of existing technologies, platforms, languages (e.g. CORBA, Java, MPI Python) and services (such as the LDAP, SLP, DNS, UDDI) whenever deemed appropriate.

13.4 Defining the GRID: The Global GRID Forum Initiative

The *Global GRID Forum* (GGF) subsumes the major activities in the GRID domain. It is a community of users, developers, and vendors that is leading the global standardization effort for GRID computing. GGF promotes the adoption of GRID computing in research and industry by defining GRID specifications and building an international community for the exchange of ideas, experiences, requirements and best practices.

Within GGF the *Open GRID Services Architecture* (OGSA) has been defined. OGSA integrates key GRID technologies (including the Globus Toolkit^{TM}) and combines them with Web services to build an open architecture for GRID services [222]. The goal is to provide a set of well-defined basic interfaces and an architecture that is extensible, vendor neutral and adheres (and in some cases actively contributes) to open standards. The *Open GRID Services Infrastructure* (OGSI) supports the definition of services that compose OGSA by extending WSDL (Web Services Description Language) and XML schema. It builds on the GRID and Web services technologies and defines mechanisms for creating, managing, and exchanging information among GRID services [599]. One of the major issues in this context is how to express the relationship between stateful resources and Web services. The *WS-Resource Framework* has been defined to model stateful resources and to formalize interaction with state [216]. This section introduces OGSA and the basic concepts behind it. Further, some of the current issues in the development of GRID services are discussed. It is important to note, however, that the development within the GRID community and GGF has not stopped. Thus, this provides a snapshot of the current state.

13.4.1 The Open GRID Services Architecture (OGSA)

Within OGSA, everything is regarded as a service - including applications that become Web services. This implies that all components in this environment are virtual objects[1]. OGSA enables the development of virtual infrastructures, which form part of virtual organizations. These virtual organizations can be of different sizes, lifetimes, spanning multiple (physical) organizations and run on heterogeneous infrastructures (i.e., provide a consistent functionality across various platforms and hosting environments) [221].

OGSA defines the mechanisms required for sophisticated distributed systems (including change and lifetime management, and notification). This is done using the Web Services Description Language (WSDL) and associated conventions. The combination of GRID technology and Web services makes

[1] Note, OGSA does not use the term "object" since it is regarded as overused. Instead, it defines services.

best use of the advantages of both technologies. Web services define techniques for describing software components and accessing them. Further, Web service discovery methods allow the identification of relevant service providers within the system regardless of platform or hosting environment-specific features. Web services are open in that they are programming language, programming model, and system software neutral.

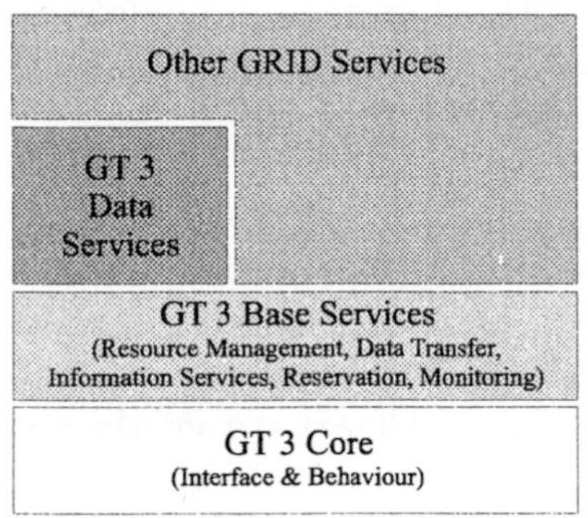

Fig. 13.2: Open GRID Services Infrastructure: GT3

In the context of OGSA, a new version of the Globus toolkit was developed (Globus Toolkit Version 3, GT3). From GT3 onwards the Globus architecture was defined together with OGSA. Currently (i.e. in 2005) GT4 is the most recent version. It is a refined version compared to GT3 where the main concepts are still valid. The Core as shown in Figure 13.2 implements service interfaces and behaviors as specified in the GRID Services Specification [599]. The Core and Base Service Layer are part of the OGSI system framework.

A number of (standard) high-level services that address requirements of eBusiness and eScience applications are being discussed within GGF. Such services include:

- distributed data management services (e.g., for database access, data translation, replica management and location, and transactions);
- workflow services (for coordinating different tasks on multiple Grid resources);
- auditing services (for recording usage data);
- instrumentation and monitoring services (for measuring and reporting system state information); and
- security protocol mapping services (for enabling distributed security protocols to be transparently mapped onto native platform security services).

These services can be implemented and composed in various different ways replacing some of the current Globus toolkit services, for instance, dealing with resource management and data transfer [222].

13.4.2 GRID Services: Building Blocks for the GRID

With the strong service orientation adopted by OGSA the GRID can be regarded as a network of services. Web service mechanisms provide support for describing, discovering, accessing and securing interaction (see chapter 14) for a more detailed discussion on Web services). More formally OGSA defines a GRID service as *a network-enabled entity that represents computational and storage resources, networks, programs, and databases, inter alia.* Within the virtual organization formed by these networked services, clear service definitions *and* a set of protocols are required to invoke these services. Note, the protocols are independent of the actual service definitions and vice versa. They specify a delivery semantic and address issues such as reliability and authentication. A protocol that guarantees that a message is reliably received exactly once can, for instance, be used to achieve reliability, if required. Multiple protocol bindings for a single interface are possible because WDSL is used for the service definition [222]. However, the protocol definition itself is outside the scope of OGSA.

To ensure openness virtual service definitions are used according to which multiple (ideally interworking) implementations can be produced. Thus, a client invoking a service does not have to consider the platform a service instantiation is running on, or have to know anything about the implementation details. The interaction between services happens via well-defined, published service interfaces that are implementation independent. To increase the generality of the service definition, authentication and reliable service invocation are viewed as service protocol binding issues that are external to the core service definition. Though, they have to be addressed within a complete OGSA implementation.

The OGSA services are also concerned with transient service instances within the GRID infrastructure because services are not necessarily static and persistent (i.e., a service can be created and destroyed dynamically). Furthermore, OGSA conventions allow identification of service changes such as service upgrades. The information documenting these changes also states whether the service is backward compatible regarding interface and semantics.

Since GRID services have to run on multiple platforms in a distributed heterogeneous environment, service implementations should, be portable not only in terms of their design, but also as far as code and the hosting environment are concerned. OGSA defines the basic behavior of a service but does not prescribe how a service should be executed. It is the hosting environment, which defines how a GRID service implementation realizes the GRID service semantics [221]. Apart from the traditional OS based implementations, GRID services can also be built on top of new hosting environments such as J2EE, Web-sphere, .NET, JXTA, or Sun ONE. These hosting environments tend to offer better programmability and manageability, they are usually also more flexible and provide a degree of safety.

Despite OGSA not being concerned with implementation details, the definition of baseline characteristics can facilitate the service implementation. Issues that have to be addressed in the context of hosting environments are the mapping of GRID wide names and service handles into programming language specific pointers or references, the dispatch of invocations into actions such as events and procedure calls, protocol processing and data formatting for network transmission, lifetime management, and inter-service authentication.

13.4.3 Stateful Web Services: OGSI and the WS-Resource Framework

As mentioned before, GRID services are Web services conforming to conventions regarding their interfaces and behavior. By using Web services the service paradigm has been firmly adopted for OGSA. However, a major concept lacking in WSDL is *state*.

The Open GRID Services Infrastructure (OGSI) defines the mechanisms for creating, naming, managing the lifetime of instances of services, and exchanging information between GRID services; it forms the basis for OGSA [599]. Further, it is concerned with declaring and inspecting service data state, asynchronous notification of service state change, representing and managing collections of service instances (so-called *ServiceGroups*), and for common handling of service invocation faults [142]. Therefore, WSDL is extended to make it suitable for the definition of these conventions. In particular, these extensions deal with state (i.e., they allow to create and manipulate stateful Web services) and service typed instances. Furthermore, global naming and addressing is an issue addressed by OGSI. GRID Service Handles in conjunction GRID Service References and interface extensions that introduce portTypes are used to address these issues.

Though, OGSI is regarded as too heavy-weight and not fully compatible with the Web services view [142]. To overcome this the *WS-Resource Framework* (WS-RF) [143] is specified that defines the means by which a Web service and stateful resources are composed. WS-RF is primarily concerned with the creation, addressing, inspection, and lifetime management of stateful resources. Its advantage is that it better exploits existing XML and emerging Web service standards (e.g., WS-Addressing). In short, WS-RF defines a Web service resource as a composition of a Web service and a stateful resource described by an XML document associated with the Web service's port type and addressed using WS-Addressing [312].

13.5 GRID and Peer-to-Peer Computing

There is an ongoing argument about GRID and Peer-to-Peer computing, their merits, differences, and commonalities. It is difficult to delineate the two concepts since there is a lot of overlap in their motivation, though they have a different background and take a different approach. According to Foster's three point GRID checklist [214], for example, a GRID is a system that:

1. coordinates resources that are *not* subject to *centralized* control ...
2. ...using standard, open general-purpose protocols and interfaces...
3. ... to deliver non trivial quality of service

From this list especially the first two points apply to many Peer-to-Peer systems as well. Even on a system level the distinction between Peer-to-Peer and GRID is not clear cut. For instance, the PlanetLab initiative originally conceived as testbed for the Peer-to-Peer research community is also used as example of a GRID infrastructure [215].

A comparison of the two areas at a conceptual level is even more difficult since there is first of all no universally accepted definition of Peer-to-Peer. Moreover, the idea of the GRID is also continuously further developed. Originally it was defined as a "hardware and software infrastructure that provides dependable, consistent, pervasive, and inexpensive access to high-end computational capabilities" [225]. Later, the emphasis has shifted towards virtual organizations and the importance of standard protocols in enabling interoperability to build the common infrastructure [214]. Today the focus is on "service-oriented science" and the GRID as infrastructure that enables scientific research by distributed networks of interoperating services [215].

A number of publications are combining both concepts or are describing GRID systems that employ Peer-to-Peer mechanisms [9, 218, 314]. To compare both concepts and assess how much they have in common, it is necessary to characterize Peer-to-Peer in this context in more detail.

In Chapter 2, a Peer-to-Peer system is defined as a self-organizing system of equal, autonomous entities (i.e., peers) that operates preferably without using any central services based on a communication network for the purpose of resource sharing. Here, the emphasis is on the system aspect that allows joint resource utilization. Another characterization stresses that Peer-to-Peer is a class of applications that takes advantage of resources that are available at the edge of the network [217]. This latter definition gives a much more concrete but also restricted view of the nature of Peer-to-Peer computing in that it describes it as "class of application", not systems, components or platform. Therefore, it is important to distinguish between the *Peer-to-Peer paradigm*, which encompasses decentralization, self-organization, and autonomous collaboration between independent entities in a system context, and *Peer-to-Peer applications*, which are mostly vertically integrated applications [217] used for the sharing of specific resources (e.g., file and information sharing [352]). Further, there are also emerging *Peer-to-Peer platforms* that provide an operating system independent middleware layer, which allows sharing of resources in a Peer-to-Peer fashion [404].

13.5.1 Comparing GRID and Peer-to-Peer: Commonalities and Differences

The original motivation behind GRID and Peer-to-Peer applications has been similar; both are concerned with the pooling and organization of distributed resources that are shared between (virtual) communities connected via an ubiquitous network (such as the Internet). The resources and services they provide can be located anywhere in the system and are made transparently available to the users on request. Both also take a similar structural approach by using overlay structures on top of the underlying communication (sub-)system.

However, there are also substantial differences on the application, functional and structural levels. The applications supported through the GRID are mainly scientific applications that are used in a professional context. The number of entities is still rather moderate in size, and the participating institutions are usually known. Current Peer-to-Peer *applications*, in contrast, provide open access for a large, fluctuating number of unknown participants with highly variable behavior. Therefore, Peer-to-Peer has to deal with scalability and failure issues much more than GRID applications. Peer-to-Peer applications are still largely concerned with file and information sharing. In addition, they usually provide access to simple resources (e.g. processing power), whereas the GRID infrastructure provides access to a resource pool (e.g., computing clusters, storage systems, databases, but also scientific instruments, sensors, etc.) [217]. Peer-to-Peer *applications* usually are vertically integrated, i.e. the application itself realizes many of the conceptual and basic functionalities that should be part of and architecture or the infrastructure. An example are overlay structures as part of the application. In contrast, the GRID is essentially a multipurpose infrastructure where the core functionality is provided by a set of services that are part of the architecture. The resources are represented by services that can be used by different applications.

In recent years, a number of Peer-to-Peer middleware platforms have been developed that provide generic Peer-to-Peer support. The functionality they support comprises, for example, naming, discovery, communication, security, and resource aggregation. One example is JXTA [330], an open platform designed for Peer-to-Peer computing. Its goal is to develop basic building blocks and services to enable innovative applications for peer groups. Another, emerging Peer-to-Peer platform is Microsoft's Windows Peer-to-Peer Networking (MSP2P) [119], which provides simple access to networked resources. There is also ongoing research in this area. For instance, in the EU funded project on Market Managed Peer-to-Peer Services (MMAPPS) a middleware platform has been created that incorporates market mechanisms (in particular, accounting, pricing and trust mechanisms) [578]. On top of this platform, a number of applications (i.e., a file sharing application, a medical application, and a WLAN roaming application) have been implemented to show how such a generic platform can be used.

13.5.2 GRID and Peer-to-Peer: Converging Concepts?

The GRID has been successfully in operation within the scientific community for a number of years. However, the potential of the GRID goes beyond scientific applications and can for instance also be applied to the government domain, health-care, industry and the eCommerce sector [62]. Many of the basic concepts and methods could remain unchanged when applied to these new domains. Other issues not within the scope of the current GRID initiative will have to be addressed in the context of these application areas (e.g., commercial accounting and IPR issues). Further, with a more widespread adoption of the GRID, there is a greater need for scalability, dependability and trust mechanisms, fault-tolerance, self-organization, self-configuration, and self-healing functionality. This indicates that mechanisms from the Peer-to-Peer application and platform domain and the Peer-to-Peer paradigm in general could be adopted more widely by the GRID. This would result in a more dynamic, scalable, and robust infrastructure without changing the nature or fundamental concepts. Though, this will only happen in the context of the service-oriented architecture. Thus, the developments between Peer-to-Peer and Web services as described in Chapter 14 and between Peer-to-Peer and GRID are actually running in parallel.

Peer-to-Peer applications are also developing into more complex systems that provide more sophisticated services. A platform approach has been proposed by some vendors and research initiatives to provide more generic support for sophisticated Peer-to-Peer applications. It is expected that developers of Peer-to-Peer systems are going to become increasingly interested in such platforms, standard tools for service description, discovery and access, etc. [217]. Such a Peer-to-Peer infrastructure would then have a lot in common with the GRID infrastructure. However, the goal behind the GRID (i.e., providing access to computational resources encapsulated as services) is not necessarily shared by these middleware platforms. They are built for better and more flexible application support.

Essentially, it is a matter of substantiating the claims represented by the Peer-to-Peer paradigm of providing more flexibility, dynamicity, robustness, dependability and scalability for large scale distributed systems. If this is successful and additional quality of service features (such as performance and efficiency) can also be ensured, Peer-to-Peer mechanisms can become central to the GRID. Peer-to-Peer applications, on the other hand, will have to adopt a more platform-based development to provide sufficient flexibility in a very dynamic environment. It remains to be seen if this means a convergence of the two areas or if they will co-exist, continually influencing each other.

13.6 Summary

The idea for the GRID was conceived within the science community and inspired by the success of the Internet and results produced by distributed systems research. The main target application areas are resource sharing, distributed supercomputing, data intensive computing, and data sharing and collaborative computing. The GRID provides an abstraction for the different resources in form of services.

The architectural view of the GRID can be compared to the Internet hourglass model where a small group of core protocols and components build the link between the high-level mechanisms and a number of lower level base technologies [67]. The various services in this architecture can be located at one of the different layers, namely the Fabric, Connectivity, Resource, and Collective Layer. The Globus Toolkit^{TM} provided the first tools for a GRID infrastructure. These tools exploit the capabilities of the platforms and hosting environments they run on, but do not add any functionality on the system level. Using this pragmatic approach, some remarkable systems have been realized by the Globus project, or with the help of the Globus Toolkit. The OGSA initiative within the Global GRID Forum (conceived within the Globus Project) is developing the original ideas further. It takes a more systematic approach and defines a universal service architecture in which the advantages of GRID technology and Web services are combined. It is strictly service-oriented; i.e. everything is regarded as a service characterized by well-specified platform and protocol independent interfaces. This universal service idea combined with openness and platform independence, allows building very large and functional complex systems. Applying these concepts could provide a way to deal with management issues that have so far restricted the size of distributed systems.

The relationship between Peer-to-Peer and GRID is still a controversial topic. Since GRID is defined as infrastructure formed out of services representing resources, its scope and extent are more well defined than that of Peer-to-Peer. The term Peer-to-Peer is on the one hand, being used for a group of distributed applications (such as the well known file sharing applications); on the other hand it also refers to a paradigm encompassing the concepts of decentralization, self-organization, and resource sharing within a system context [573]. Recently, middleware platforms have been developed that provide generic support for Peer-to-Peer applications, implementing the Peer-to-Peer paradigm in an operating system-independent fashion. The objective of the GRID is to provide an infrastructure that pools and coordinates the use of large sets of distributed resources (i.e., to provide access to computational resources similar to the access to electricity provided by the power grid). The most recent development within the GRID community go towards a strong service orientation. Within GGF the ideas developed in the service-oriented architecture and Web service domain are being adopted. Hence, a convergence between GRID and Peer-to-Peer would actually run in parallel or be predated by a convergence of Peer-to-Peer and Web Services. Though, it has been recognisee that an adoption of Peer-to-Peer principles could be beneficial in terms of scalability, dependability, and robustness. The pooling and sharing of resources is also a common theme in Peer-to-Peer applications. This could be supported by Peer-to-Peer middleware platforms in the future. However, this does not mean global access to computational resources (represented by services) anywhere, anytime. The question of how, indeed if, the two concepts converge is still open.

14. Web Services and Peer-to-Peer

Markus Hillenbrand, Paul Müller (University of Kaiserslautern)

14.1 Introduction

Peer-to-Peer and Web services both address decentralized computing. They can be considered as rather distinct from each other, but a closer look at the Web services technology reveals a great potential for a combination of both Peer-to-Peer and Web services.

The basic idea behind Web services technology is to provide functionality over the Internet that can be accessed using a well-defined interface. This idea of a service-oriented architecture forms the next evolutionary step in application design and development after procedural programming, object orientation, and component-oriented development. During the last twenty years, different middleware approaches and application designs have been introduced to leverage dated technology and provide easy access over open and mostly insecure access networks.

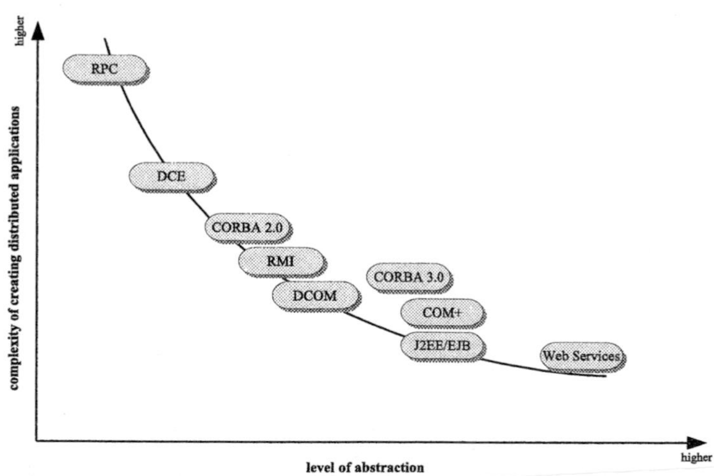

Fig. 14.1: Programming paradigms: abstraction and distribution

The most recognized and well established technologies for creating distributed systems are the Remote Procedure Call (RPC, 1988) from Sun Microsystems, the Distributed Computing Environment (DCE, 1993) from

R. Steinmetz and K. Wehrle (Eds.): P2P Systems and Applications, LNCS 3485, pp. 207-224, 2005.

the Open Software Foundation (OSF), the Common Object Request Broker Architecture (CORBA, 1990s) from the Open Management Group (OMG), the Java Remote Method Invocation (RMI, 1990s) and Java Enterprise Beans (EJB, 1990s) from Sun Microsystems, and the Distributed Component Object Model (DCOM, 1997 and COM+, late 1990) from Microsoft. Each of these technologies introduced a higher level of abstraction for creating distributed applications and reduced the implementation effort necessary to achieve this goal. Figure 14.1 illustrates the relationship between the underlying programming paradigm, the level of abstraction, and the complexity of creating a distributed application.

Distribution aspects have always been an addendum to procedural programming and object-orientation (mostly using some kind of remote procedure call mechanism) and are not intrinsic to the paradigms. Solutions following the component-oriented paradigm provide middleware functionality and software containers that allow for distribution during software development and help managing the resulting software systems. In contrast to this, Web services are based on open, well-defined, and established standards and encompass distribution from within the specifications. In combination with currently evolving additional standards (cf. Chapter 14.2.6) they have a good chance to achieve the goals of a real and secure distributed middleware architecture.

The Web services technology has been initiated by industry and not academia, and more and more large companies are working on Web services technology and apply it in real world applications. Though what is the reason for this development? Unfortunately, there is no commonly used definition for Web services. Instead, several distinct definitions have to be consulted to investigate what Web services are and how to use them. Two major driving forces of the Web services technology – IBM and Microsoft – define Web services as follows:

Definition 14.1.1. *(IBM, 2003) "Web services are self-contained, modular applications that can be described, published, located, and invoked over a network. Web services perform encapsulated business functions, ranging from simple request-reply to full business process interactions. These services can be new applications or just wrapped around existing legacy systems to make them network-enabled. Services can rely on other services to achieve their goals."*

Microsoft favors a similar definition of the Web services technology, but it emphasizes standard Internet protocols:

Definition 14.1.2. *(MSDN, 2001) "A Web service is a programmable application logic accessible using standard Internet protocols, or to put it another way, the implementation of Web-supported standards for transparent machine-to-machine and application-to-application communication."*

The common aspect of definitions 14.1.1 and 14.1.2 is their focus on business and application-to-application communication. A more technical view on Web services is given by the following definition from the World Wide Web Consortium in 2003:

Definition 14.1.3. *(W3C: May, 2003) "A Web service is a software system identified by a URI (Uniform Resource Identifier), whose public interfaces and bindings are defined and described using XML. Its definition can be discovered by other software systems. These systems may then interact with the Web service in a manner prescribed by its definition, using XML based messages conveyed by Internet protocols."*

This definition completely abstracts from the implementation and usage of Web services and is entirely based on XML. During the definition phases of Web services related standards, the W3C has revised this definition several times to make it more specific in terms of technology while trying to keep it as general as possible. As of 2004, the current definition reads as follows:

Definition 14.1.4. *(W3C Feb, 2004) "A Web service is a software system designed to support interoperable machine-to-machine interaction over a network. It has an interface described in a machine-processable format (specifically WSDL). Other systems interact with the Web service in a manner prescribed by its description using SOAP messages, typically conveyed using HTTP with an XML serialization in conjunction with other Web-related standards."*

Compared to definition 14.1.3, not only XML [89] but also WSDL [118, 115] and SOAP [265] are part of the definition. And HTTP [206] is mentioned as the typical transport protocol. This makes the definition of a Web service more precise from a technological view, but also narrows applicability and extensibility.

The relevant standards mentioned in the definitions will be briefly introduced in the next sections. A sample Web service (providing functionality to add an integer or a complex number) will be used to illustrate them.

14.2 Architecture and Important Standards

The Web services technology permits loose coupling and simple integration of software components into applications – irrespective of programming languages and operating systems by using several standards. The basic architecture is shown in figure 14.2.

Three participants interact to perform a task. A *service provider* is responsible for creating and publishing a description of a service interface using WSDL. The provider also contributes the actual implementation of the service on a server responding to requests from clients that adhere to this

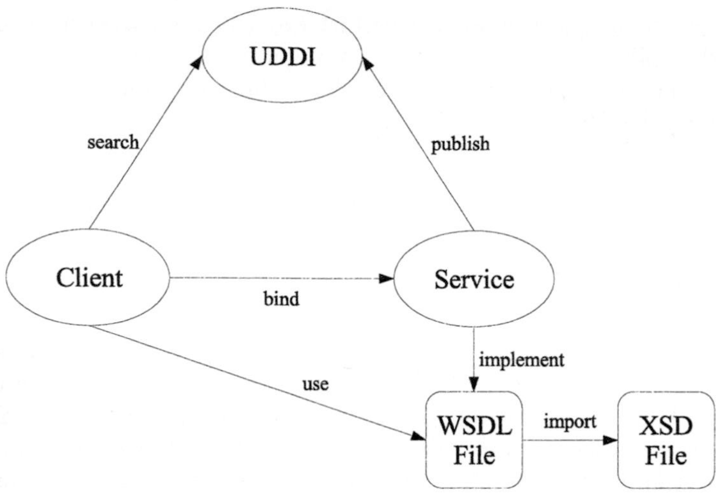

Fig. 14.2: Web services: Overview and Standards

interface description. A *UDDI registry* collects and categorizes interface descriptions and offers them to customers via a browsable directory or a search engine. A *client* can either be a human user or another software component acting on behalf of a user. It discovers a service by asking the UDDI registry and then contacts the actual service using the interface definitions and protocols defined in the associated WSDL document. This WSDL document might refer to external XML Schema (XSD) documents on the Internet where data types for the service are defined (this allows for re-use and compatible data structures).

The basic operational steps to consume a service are *publish*, *find*, and *bind*. A service provider publishes a service using a WSDL service description and the UDDI registry, a service requestor finds this service using the UDDI registry, and the service requestor binds his program to the service endpoint using the protocols defined in the WSDL document (mostly SOAP over HTTP).

The binding process on the client side can be realized using different techniques: stubs, dynamic proxy, or dynamic invocation. The automatic generation of *stubs* at compile time takes a WSDL document and creates a local representation of the remote Web service. This only allows for a tight coupling of client and service. The *dynamic proxy* technique does not create the stubs at compile time but generates a local representation of the remote service at runtime. Only a local interface definition is needed to make the actual call. *Dynamic invocation* on the other hand can be used to create a Web service call completely during runtime – which makes loosely coupled applications possible. In each case the information needed can be retrieved solely from the WSDL document.

The necessary standards and protocols to either publish, find, or bind a Web service will now be explained in greater detail. Exemplification will adhere to the WSDL 1.1 specification because this version is currently widely used and has a large tool support.

14.2.1 XML and XML Schema

XML [89] is the key to platform and programming language neutral data exchange. It provides the mechanisms to create complex data structures as well as it allows for modeling dependencies between data sets. An XML document itself is a plain text file using a given character encoding scheme (e.g. ISO8859-15 or UTF-8). In the following, the necessary parts of the XML specification will be introduced to give a better understanding of the next chapters.

Structure

An XML document adheres to a well defined structure. It is divided into a *header* and a *body* part (cf. Figure 14.3). The header contains useful information for other software systems such as XML parsers. The XML version and character encoding are defined there. The body part of the XML document contains the actual data of the document. This information is contained inside XML elements and uses the "<...>" syntax known from HTML documents. Additionally, these elements can have *attributes* that provide more detailed information. The XML body part can then be seen as a tree consisting of XML elements and attributes attached to the nodes.

XML header

```
<?xml version="1.0" encoding="UTF-8"?>
```

XML body

```
<schema targetNamespace="http://www.icsy.de/books/p2p/types/SimpleMath"
```

XML namespaces

```
    xmlns:xsi="http://www.w3.org/2001/XMLSchema-instance"
    xmlns:tns="http://www.icsy.de/books/p2p/types/SimpleMath"
    xmlns="http://www.w3.org/2001/XMLSchema">
```

XML complex type definition

```
    <complexType name="Complex">
        <sequence>
            <element name="im" type="long"/>
            <element name="re" type="long"/>
        </sequence>
    </complexType>
</schema>
```

Fig. 14.3: XML Schema for the `Complex` data type

XML Namespaces (XMLNS)

XML allows to use any name as an element name. Thus, the vocabulary of XML documents is not fixed. To avoid collisions of such element names, XML namespaces [89] have been introduced in 1999 and were updated in 2004. A namespace can be defined inside an element (usually the root element) and is valid for all child elements ("XML namespaces" in figure 14.3). A namespace is specified using a Uniform Resource Identifier (URI [68]) which itself can either be a Uniform Resource Locator (URL) or a Uniform Resource Name (URN). A URL points to a specific location where more information about the namespace can be found while a URN is just a globally unique name. It is possible to use different namespaces inside an XML document, and the XML document itself can use elements from these namespaces in any suitable order.

XML Schema (XSD)

Together with XML Namespaces, XML Schema [200, 593, 75] is one important building block for creating modular XML documents. Its major goal is to make syntactical restrictions for XML elements, i.e. XML Schemas can be used to assign and define data types. Besides basic data types such as integer, string, date, etc. provided by the standard, it is possible to define new datatypes ("XML complex type definition" in figure 14.3). Using the appropriate XML Schema elements, it is further possible to define new simple (primitive) data types, complex data types (like structures, arrays, etc.) as well as enumerations and choices. It is also possible to define and assign structural patterns restricting the range of values for the data types. Additionally, XML Schemas can be imported into other XML documents, e.g. WSDL documents. This allows for re-use of XML data types and a modular design of XML documents.

14.2.2 WSDL

The Web Services Description Language (WSDL [118, 115]) is an XML based format for describing the interface of a Web service. The WSDL document starts with an XML header and the body is divided into several parts (shown in figure 14.4):

Root Element

The root element of a WSDL document is a `definitions` element and contains a target namespace, the namespaces used throughout the document

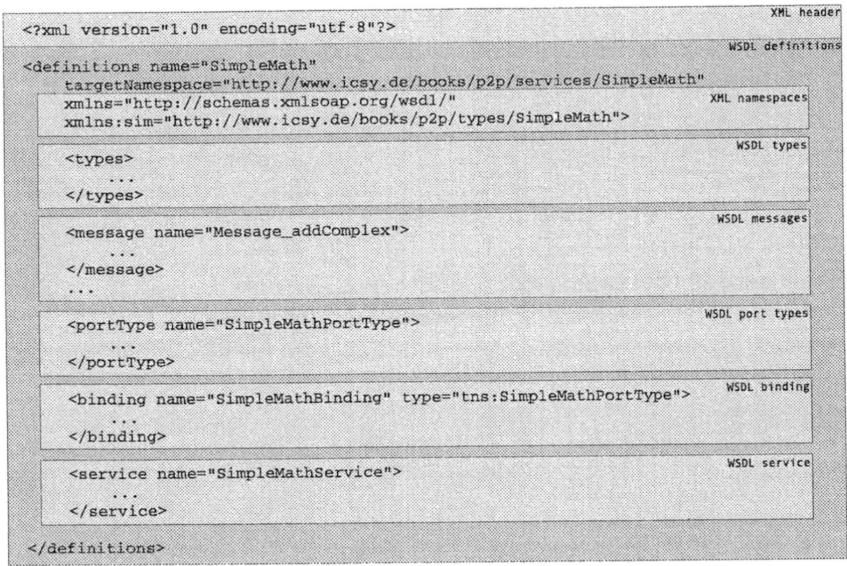

Fig. 14.4: WSDL document and its structure

("XML namespaces" in figure 14.4), and an optional documentation of the Web service.

Types

The data types used by the Web service should be designed using XML Schema. Inside the `types` element it is possible to define data types for the current service or to import data types from remote documents using the XML Schema `import` element. In figure 14.5 the `types` element is used to import the Complex data type defined in figure 14.3. The actual XML Schema file location is specified using the `schemaLocation` attribute and its namespace is specified using the `namespace` attribute accordingly. The `targetNamespace` attribute can be used to map the namespace of the XML Schema document into another namespace.

```
                                                                    WSDL types
<types>
    <xsd:schema targetNamespace="http://www.icsy.de/books/p2p/types/SimpleMath" >
        <xsd:import namespace="http://www.icsy.de/books/p2p/types/SimpleMath"
            schemaLocation="http://localhost:8080/types/SimpleMath.xsd" />
    </xsd:schema>
</types>
```

Fig. 14.5: WSDL types element used to import a XML Schema data type

Messages

Messages are exchanged between the client and the service and represent the data necessary to call a Web service function or to create a response. A `message` element has a name and several parts that make up the message. Every `part` element usually has a type – and this type is either imported or defined in the `types` element. In figure 14.6 four messages are defined. The first (`Message_addComplex`) has two child elements `x` and `y`, and the second message (`Message_addComplexResponse`) contains only one child element `result`. As the name of the message suggests, it is used as a response to the first message. Messages three and four work in the same manner.

```
<message name="Message_addComplex">                                    WSDL messages
      <part name="x" type="sim:Complex"/>
      <part name="y" type="sim:Complex"/>
</message>
<message name="Message_addComplexResponse">
      <part name="result" type="sim:Complex"/>
</message>
<message name="Message_addInt">
      <part name="x" type="xsd:int"/>
      <part name="y" type="xsd:int"/>
</message>
<message name="Message_addIntResponse">
      <part name="result" type="xsd:int"/>
</message>
```

Fig. 14.6: WSDL message element

Port Types

A Web service can have several `porttype` elements[1], each containing a set of operations provided by the Web service. The port types use the messages defined using the `message` elements to create input and output messages for each `operation`. In figure 14.7 the two operations `Message_addComplex` and `Message_addInt` are defined using the messages from figure 14.6 and thus form a request-response operation `addComplex`. With WSDL 1.1 other operation types are possible: one-way (the endpoint behind the operation receives a message), solicit-response (the endpoint receives a message and sends a correlated message), and notification (the endpoint sends a message).

Bindings

The `binding` element assigns a data encoding format and a transport protocol to the Web service operations. It is possible to assign more than one protocol

[1] In the WSDL 2.0 specification the `porttype` element has been renamed to `interface` and extended to support more types of communication.

```
                                                              WSDL port type
<portType name="SimpleMathPortType">
    <operation name="addComplex" parameterOrder="x y">
        <input message="tns:Message_addComplex"/>
        <output message="tns:Message_addComplexResponse"/>
    </operation>
    <operation name="addInt" parameterOrder="x y">
        <input message="tns:Message_addInt"/>
        <output message="tns:Message_addIntResponse"/>
    </operation>
</portType>
```

Fig. 14.7: WSDL port type element

to the same operation. In figure 14.8 both operations are defined to use SOAP over HTTP.

```
                                                              WSDL binding
<binding name="SimpleMathBinding" type="tns:SimpleMathPortType">
    <soap:binding style="rpc" transport="http://schemas.xmlsoap.org/soap/http"/>
    <operation name="addComplex">
        <soap:operation/>
        <input><soap:body use="encoded"
            encodingStyle="http://schemas.xmlsoap.org/soap/encoding/"
            namespace="http://www.icsy.de/services/test/SimpleMath"/></input>
        <output><soap:body use="encoded"
            encodingStyle="http://schemas.xmlsoap.org/soap/encoding/"
            namespace="http://www.icsy.de/services/test/SimpleMath"/></output>
    </operation>
</binding>
```

Fig. 14.8: WSDL binding element

Service

The service element finally defines for each `binding` a `port` as the actual endpoint, i.e. the place in the network where the actual software runs and offers the service[2]. In figure 14.9 the `binding` defined in figure 14.8 is assigned to the SOAP access point provided by the software running on `localhost` on port 8080.

```
                                                              WSDL service
<service name="SimpleMathService">
    <port name="SimpleMathPort" binding="tns:SimpleMathBinding">
        <soap:address location="http://localhost:8080/axis/services/SimpleMathPort" />
    </port>
</service>
```

Fig. 14.9: WSDL service element

[2] In the WSDL 2.0 specification the `port` element has been renamed to `endpoint` in order to clarify the meaning.

14.2.3 SOAP

Designed as an XML-based lightweight protocol, SOAP[3] [265] is responsible for encoding and exchanging data between applications. According to definition 14.1.4 it is used as a communication means between service providers, service requestors, and service brokers. A SOAP message itself can be transported using various transport protocols. Most applications use HTTP (Hypertext Transfer Protocol [206]) as the underlying transport protocol; other protocols are SMTP (Simple Mail Transfer Protocol [357, 433]) or BEEP (Blocks Extensible Exchange Protocol [525]).

A SOAP message acts as a message container that delivers structured and typed data between applications. A SOAP message has three elements:

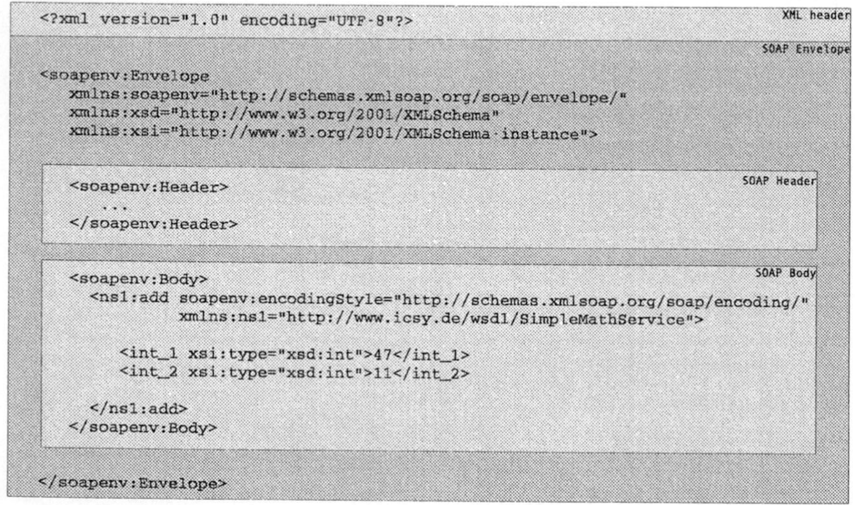

<?xml version="1.0" encoding="UTF-8"?>
XML header
SOAP Envelope
<soapenv:Envelope
xmlns:soapenv="http://schemas.xmlsoap.org/soap/envelope/"
xmlns:xsd="http://www.w3.org/2001/XMLSchema"
xmlns:xsi="http://www.w3.org/2001/XMLSchema-instance">
SOAP Header
<soapenv:Header>
...
</soapenv:Header>
SOAP Body
<soapenv:Body>
<ns1:add soapenv:encodingStyle="http://schemas.xmlsoap.org/soap/encoding/"
xmlns:ns1="http://www.icsy.de/wsdl/SimpleMathService">
<int_1 xsi:type="xsd:int">47</int_1>
<int_2 xsi:type="xsd:int">11</int_2>
</ns1:add>
</soapenv:Body>
</soapenv:Envelope>

Fig. 14.10: The SOAP message structure

The mandatory *envelope* ("SOAP envelope" in figure 14.10) provides a container for the next two elements and is the XML root element where referenced XML namespaces have to be defined.

The optional *header* ("SOAP header" in figure 14.10) can be used to transport additional information to recipients of a SOAP message. A recipient can either be the final destination of the message or any intermediate entity routing the message through a complex distributed Web service application. It can be used for routing information, information about quality of service, billing purpose, etc.

[3] Up to version 1.1 SOAP was an acronym for *Simple Object Access Protocol*. This is no longer the case, SOAP has become a term on its own. One reason for this is that Web services should not be conceived as objects.

The mandatory *body* ("SOAP body" in figure 14.10) finally carries all application specific information for the final recipient. This final recipient must be able to semantically understand the body elements. A fault element inside the body can be used to carry an error message to one of the intermediaries or back to the origin of the message.

An additional standard allows for attachments to be transmitted in MIME encoded form, enabling Web services to process large binary data files.

14.2.4 HTTP

The Hypertext Transfer Protocol (HTTP [206]) is a stateless application-level protocol for exchanging data between two entities. It is primarily used by Web browsers to access Web servers and retrieve HTML pages. Several extensions concerning request methods, header information, and error code have widened the scope of applicability. In the context of Web services it is the most commonly used protocol for exchanging SOAP messages between a client and a Web service.

14.2.5 UDDI

Universal Description, Discovery and Integration (UDDI [454]) can be used to publish or find a specific Web service. UDDI is basically a directory service providing registration and search capabilities for Web services. Such a UDDI registry offers a Web service interface for service providers and service requestors. Based on several meta data information structures and well established categorization formalisms, either of them can store or retrieve Web service information, respectively.

A globally synchronized UDDI registry is currently maintained by IBM, Microsoft, and SAP. It is also possible to establish a private UDDI for closed user groups or applications.

14.2.6 WS-*

In addition to the basic underlying standards and protocols some industry driven standardization efforts are undertaken to retrofit Web services for commercial and secure usage. They are usually referred to as WS-* standards, where * is a placeholder for the purpose of the standard. The following descriptions of the most relevant WS-* standards have been taken from their respective specification; a complete introduction can be found there.

WS-Addressing

The WS-Addressing [86] standard provides transport-neutral mechanisms to address Web services and messages. The specification defines XML elements to identify Web service endpoints and to secure end-to-end endpoint identification in messages. It furthermore enables messaging systems to support message transmission through networks that include processing nodes such as endpoint managers, firewalls, and gateways in a transport-neutral manner.

WS-Federation

WS-Federation [331] defines mechanisms that are used to enable identity, account, attribute, authentication, and authorization federations across different trust realms.

WS-Policy

The Web Services Policy Framework [540] provides a general purpose model and corresponding syntax to describe and communicate the policies of a Web service. It defines a base set of constructs that can be used and extended by other Web services specifications to describe a broad range of service requirements, preferences, and capabilities.

WS-ReliableMessaging

WS-ReliableMessaging [205] describes a protocol that allows messages to be delivered reliably between distributed applications in the presence of software component, system, or network failures. The protocol is described in an independent manner allowing it to be implemented using different network transport technologies.

WS-ResourceFramework

The Web Services Resource Framework [258] defines a family of specifications for accessing stateful resources using Web services. The motivation for these specifications is that while Web service implementations typically do not maintain state information during their interactions, their interfaces must frequently allow for the manipulation of state, that is, data values that persist across and evolve as a result of Web service interactions.

WS-Security

WS-Security [435] describes enhancements to SOAP messaging to provide message integrity and confidentiality. It can be used to accommodate a wide variety of security models and encryption technologies. The specification also provides a general-purpose mechanism for associating security tokens with message content.

WS-Transaction

The WS-Transaction [377] standard describes coordination types – namely Atomic Transaction (AT) and Business Activity (BA) – for building applications that require consistent agreement on the outcome of distributed activities.

14.3 Service Orchestration

As Web services evolve and are deployed on a larger scale, the need for the combination of several Web services in order to create a business process arises. Several languages and specifications can be identified that deal with service orchestration. The most relevant are XML Process Definition Language (XPDL [452]), Business Process Modeling Language (BPML [33]), Web Service Choreography Interface (WSCI [34]), Electronic Business using eXtensible Markup Language (ebXML [455]), and Business Process Execution Language for Web services (BPEL4WS [588]). The latter is currently the most promising candidate for a common standard.

BPEL4WS is based on XML and can be used to combine distributed Web services to a business process. Interaction between Web services can be modeled as well as between the business process and its clients. The clients can thus be detached from the actual business logic and be kept simple.

BPEL4WS is driven by major companies such as IBM and Microsoft and provides a language to implement complex processes by allowing for different actions like calling a Web service, manipulating data, and handling errors. Flow control can be realized using control flow statements like tests, loops, and threads. To the outside, a BPEL4WS business process can be described like a normal Web service and have its own WSDL description – a client does not need to know the internal structure or control flow of the process.

14.4 Comparison of Peer-to-Peer and Web Services

As Peer-to-Peer and Web services are both addressing decentralized computing, it is reasonable to compare the two techniques and show differences that might also be used as incentives for further research and development in this area.

14.4.1 What Can Peer-to-Peer Learn from Web Services?

The Web services standards evolve at a high rate and influence other technologies as well. There are several issues that also concern Peer-to-Peer technology:

XML

All data formats and all data exchange protocols in the Web services area are based on XML. XML Schema is used to define platform and programming language neutral data types, SOAP is used to transfer these data types to the service, and WSDL is used to describe the service itself. New XML standards or enhancements can be integrated into the Web services technology with small effort, as XML security or XML encryption have shown.

Another benefit would be to use XML schema definitions for describing resources, data, services, and peers within a Peer-to-Peer system with meta data. An XML based description of the resources and data shared in a Peer-to-Peer system would be more flexible (with regard different schema files and namespaces) and extensible, because a schema file can be easily extended without having effect on existing software and thus allow for a smooth upgrade or change in meta data description. A more detailed view on schema-based Peer-to-Peer systems is given in chapter 19.

Service Registration

Irrespective of its rather centralized approach, Web services provide an elegant registration mechanism with thorough content description and enhanced search capabilities. Classification schemes can be used to categorize or classify services so that users are able to find them using different search requests.

Security

Web services security is of major importance for Web services to be accepted as building blocks for distributed applications running on the Internet. Several standards have been developed to enable secure communication between Web service entities. These security standards are mostly based on XML and are thus not limited to the Web services world.

Interoperability

One of the design goals of Web services has been to be as open and interoperable as possible. Standardized interfaces (written in WSDL) can be used and accessed by any system capable to process XML documents. There is no artificial language or operating system barrier in a Web services scenario. Together with security standards this accounts for large business processes and applications to be deployed over the Internet using different programming languages and operating systems.

Service orchestration

Web services can be combined to create a business process using Web service orchestration. This allows for re-use and encapsulation. The JXTA SOAP project (`http://soap.jxta.org`) for example brings together Web services and Peer-to-Peer technology by defining a bridge between SOAP and the JXTA protocol. This can be further extended by defining workflows on top of these services. JXTA is explained in more detail in chapter 21.3.1.

14.4.2 What Can Web Services Learn from Peer-to-Peer?

Web services and Peer-to-Peer technologies are used to decentralize computing. However, Web services are based on a client/server architecture. In the following, some aspects of Peer-to-Peer systems will be highlighted that might be applied to the Web services world:

Decentralization

In a Web services scenario, a rather centralized UDDI registry is used to publish and find Web service descriptions. This accounts for a very easy usage but also means that all clients and service providers have to access this single service (or a few central services) and it thus might form a bottleneck and single point of failure. Additionally, the UDDI does not know whether a service is currently available or not. It only delivers stored information to the service requestors. In a Peer-to-Peer system, every node offers its service and distributed search algorithms are used to retrieve information from all nodes. A service currently not available will usually not be found in the system.

Transport Protocols

The success of the World Wide Web and Web services is partly based on the simplicity and scalability of HTTP. Operating in real time and being stateless allows for a tight coordination between client (browser) and server (Web server) – with little overhead. But in systems with a high need for synchronization (like instant messaging) HTTP is inadequate due to its design. This also applies to services that need a lot of time to process a request (large data base operations or complex calculations). HTTP is designed to deliver an answer immediately. Some systems have instead adopted the Simple Mail Transfer Protocol (SMTP) for asynchronous messaging in this case. But there are several other protocols that might prove useful in different usage scenarios. Especially Peer-to-Peer instant messaging protocols are designed to allow for a flexible two-way communication.

Addressing Scheme

Peer-to-Peer systems operate mostly outside the Domain Name Service (DNS) because its nodes might not have a permanent IP address. In order to access the resources of these nodes, a logical and often user-created address is continuously mapped to the current IP address. For Web services this could mean to make them accessible by using different addressing schemes and not only using IP addresses or host names, respectively.

Client/Server Architecture

On the World Wide Web roles like client and server are largely fixed – the Web server is always a server, and a Web browser is always a client. This also applies to Web services running on a Web server. In Peer-to-Peer systems however, these roles are only temporary. A node usually acts as client or server, depending on the current task. This also affects scalability. A strong client/server architecture only scales with the servers, while a Peer-to-Peer infrastructure scales depending on the roles taken by the nodes.

14.4.3 Side-Effects Arising when Joining Web Services and Peer-to-Peer

Compared to either Web services or Peer-to-Peer alone, any combination[4] of the two technologies would theoretically cause side-effects in different areas. The following list is not complete but addresses the most important issues:

[4] Such a combination could be a Peer-to-Peer system using Web service technology or a Web service application scenario adopting Peer-to-Peer techniques.

Bandwidth

Using XML message formats and searching for services using Peer-to-Peer technology in distributed applications will increase the need for bandwidth dramatically compared to a central registry such as UDDI. If there is no central registry, a lot of nodes (peers) of the system have to be queried for their services – this is especially the case when using unstructured Peer-to-Peer systems (cf. Part II).

Security

Security in closed client/server systems can be handled very well. It is easily possible to define access control and access policies. A server can always decide whether to answer a client request or not. If servers are replaced by peers in an open Peer-to-Peer system where all nodes are equal, security cannot be assured as easily anymore. Here new ways for providing similar security have to be found and applied.

Maintenance

The maintenance of distributed systems is a complex task. Security issues, the optimal usage and availability of distributed resources and services, and software deployment become even more complex in a heterogenous combination of Web services and Peer-to-Peer technology.

14.5 Resulting Architectures

Several architectures can be imagined when joining Web services and Peer-to-Peer technologies. One of the most promising can be outlined as follows.

Distributed applications will have two faces: Peer-to-Peer in a closed and rather secure system (i.e. the Intranet or a similar form) and additional Web service access points for external communication on the Internet – as long as security is weak there. It is possible to have the benefits of Peer-to-Peer systems like decentralization, scalability, and availability inside an application, inside a complex system, or inside a company. On the edge to the Internet this is changed to the benefits of Web services like security and standardized WSDL interface descriptions.

This approach could be used to design service brokers (i.e. the entities responsible for finding a service matching a request like in [211]) and search engines (i.e. entities responsible for finding arbitrary information matching a request like in [296]) by using Peer-to-Peer technology internally and offering their results in XML/WSDL.

Further Reading

This chapter about Web services and Peer-to-Peer was only a short introduction into the world of distributed services. A good start for obtaining more knowledge are the following references (in no particular order) [25, 291, 193, 496, 141].

Part V

Self-Organization

15. Characterization of Self-Organization

Hermann De Meer, Christian Koppen (University of Passau)

15.1 Introduction

Self-organization is used in many disciplines to refer to several, related phenomenons. Some of the more prominent phenomenons summarized under the umbrella of self-organization are autonomy, self-maintenance, optimization, adaptivity, rearrangement, reproduction or emergence. An exact match, however, has yet to be accomplished. Even in the context of this book on Peer-to-Peer systems, self-organization is used in various forms to relate to several interesting but distinct properties of Peer-to-Peer networking. Before Peer-to-Peer networks are analyzed in more detail in Chapter 16 for their degree of affinity to self-organization, we juxtapose selected but prominent definitions and criteria of self-organization from all disciplines in this chapter. The purpose of that exercise is to broaden scope and horizon of understanding self-organization in the context of Peer-to-Peer networks. It is hoped such an approach may spearhead new developments and stimulate innovative discussions. Due to the nature of some of the disciplines, the definitions may lack mathematical preciseness and some ambiguities may not be overcome. It is still believed by comparing and relating the existing manifold perspectives and concepts a more objective and thought-provoking discussion in the context of Peer-to-Peer networking can result. This is particularly so as self-organization may offer great potentials and pose high risks by the same token.

The notion of self-organization is not a new one. In fact, its roots may even be traced back to ancient times. It was Aristoteles who stated that "The whole is more than the sum of its parts" [32, 10f-1045a], a simple definition for a phenomenon that nowadays is called *emergence* which is attributed to self-organizing systems. In the 20th century, the pioneer discipline engaging in self-organization was the science of cybernetics, originated as theory of communication and control of regulatory feedback in the 1940s; cyberneticists study the fundamentals of organizational forms of machines and human beings. The name and concept of self-organization as it is understood today emerged in the 1960s, when related principles were detected in different scientific disciplines.

The biologists Varela and Maturana formed the term of *autopoiesis*, a way of organization that every *living* organism seems to exhibit [402, 403]. The chemist Ilya Prigogine observed the formation of order in a special class of chemical system which he then called *dissipative* [495]. The biochemists Eigen and Schuster detected *autocatalytic hypercycles*, a form of chemical

R. Steinmetz and K. Wehrle (Eds.): P2P Systems and Applications, LNCS 3485, pp. 227-246, 2005.

molecules which align with each other and reproduce themselves to build up and maintain a stable structure [551]. The physicist Haken analyzed the *laser* and found that the atoms and molecules organize themselves so that a homogeneous ray of light is generated [271]. The field of *synergetics* resulted as a whole new discipline from this research [272]. These are just some examples, a lot more have appeared in natural, social, economic and information sciences.

Each approach has revealed some basic principles of self-organization, and it is interesting to see how similarities can be identified. Self-organization may appear in different facets or it can be seen as an assembly of several, many or all of the described properties. We first describe the various properties in more detail in Section 15.2, use them to characterize self-organization in Section 15.3 and then apply the results to examples in computer science, emphasizing of what we see as positive impact of self-organization on these example areas, in Section 15.4. Section 15.5 concludes this chapter.

15.2 Basic Definitions

Self-organization is used in many disciplines to refer to several, related phenomenons. Selected but prominent definitions and criteria of self-organization from all disciplines are summarized in this section. The ultimate purpose is to broaden scope and horizon of understanding self-organization in the context of Peer-to-Peer networks. It is hoped such an approach may spearhead new developments and stimulate innovative discussions. Due to the nature of some of the disciplines, some of the definitions of this section may lack mathematical preciseness.

15.2.1 System

> Definition: **System**
>
> *A system is a set of* components *that have* relations *between each other and form a unified whole. A system distinguishes itself from its environment.*

A simple example of a system is a computer network where computers are the components and connections between the computers are the relations. The network can be seen as a single entity (instead of an accumulation of computers) which differs from its environment, e.g., the users of the network.

Another example for a system is a cup of water. It consists of the H_2O-molecules and the intermolecular forces between them. The environment is, strictly speaking, the ceramics of the cup and the rest of the universe. In most cases, it is sufficient to consider only the relevant parts of the environment, such as the cup in this example. The system is not observed as a giant set of single molecules, but as one big entity.

15.2.2 Complexity

The term "complexity" is used to denote diverse concepts coming from domains which exhibit strong differences, like social [57], economic [120] and computer sciences [628]. Even the *theory of complexity* is used to denominate multiple disciplines, including theoretical computer science, systems theory and chaos theory. For example, in theoretical computer science the Landau symbols (e.g., $\mathcal{O}(n), \omega(n), \Theta(n)$) are used to describe the time or space complexity of an algorithm, independently of a certain implementation. The Kolmogorow complexity, the degree of order in a string, is determined by the size of the *shortest* computer program that creates this string. A general definition of complexity is therefore hard to achieve.

Definition: **Complexity**

We use the term complexity to denote the existence of system properties that make it difficult to describe the semantics of a system's overall behavior in an arbitrary language, even if complete information about its components and interactions is known. [58]

We differentiate this meaning from another meaning of the term complexity in the sense of "complicatedness" which describes the number of elements or components of a system [623, Komplexität (orig. in German)].

Complexity as used here is independent of the language that is used for the system description. There are many different perspectives on a system, which lead to different descriptions, although the system remains the same for all descriptions. A cup of water can be described by some *formulae* for the H_2O molecules, the water's volume and temperature. It may as well be described using a large *table* that contains position, size and speed of each molecule. The formulae are a more compact description than the table, but the complexity of the system stays the same for both descriptions.

A system does not need to keep its complexity over time. If it changes so that its behavior can be described more compactly, the complexity of the system is reduced. An example for this are the Bénard convection cells, which are best explained by a small experiment [440]. Consider a closed and completely filled pot of water. It can be easily described because the molecules don't move. Now consider it being heated from the bottom and cooling down from the top. The molecules first move up and then back down because they cool down. More information (the effecting powers) is needed to describe the system – its complexity is increased. If the temperature difference is increased further the water flows suddenly in form of big rolls which are called *convection cells* (Figure 15.1). The water moves up on one side and down on the other side, in a regular movement. The more regular movement can now be easier described by a formula due to a reduced complexity.

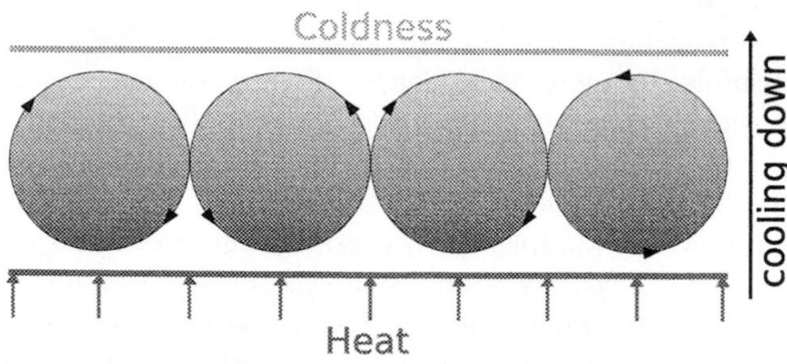

Fig. 15.1: Bénard convection cells.

15.2.3 Feedback

> Definition: **Feedback**
>
> *We use the term "feedback" to describe "the return to the input of a part of the output of a machine, system, or process (as for producing changes in an electronic circuit that improve performance or in an automatic control device that provide self-corrective action)" [409].*

Feedback can lead to effects that do not proportionally depend on the causes [246]. Feedback allows the amplification or attenuation of external influences within a system. An amplification is due to *positive feedback* and an attenuation is due to *negative feedback*.

15.2.4 Emergence

The term "emergence" is used in various disciplines [190] and there is by far no general agreement about its meaning: "First, it is often applied to situations, agent behaviors, that are surprising and not fully understood. Second, it refers to a property of a system that is not contained in any one of its parts. This is the typical usage in the fields of artificial life, dynamical systems, and neural networks for phenomena of self-organization. Third, it concerns behavior resulting from the agent-environment interaction whenever the behavior is not preprogrammed" [488]. The term "emergence" is also used to describe

something *new* or *unknown* – which heavily depends on the current knowledge of the observer [194, p. 4]. We do not pursue further such a view.
We use the following definition of "emergence" for our studies:

> Definition: **Emergence**
>
> *"Emergence refers to unexpected global system properties, not present in any of the individual subsystems, that emerge from component interactions." [104]*

Emergent properties are influenced by, but cannot completely be inferred from, characteristics of the components. Interactions between the components are necessary for emergence [300]. An example for emergence is an ant colony where no central control instance exists that decides about the ants' behavior. Each ant reacts to local stimuli (e.g., in form of chemical substances or contact with other ants) but the combination of ants and their behavior form a working colony which is therefore emergent.
Another example of emergence are deadlocks. When multiple CPUs operate without being affected by each other, there is no reason for a deadlock. But as soon as the CPUs are connected so that they become dependent on each other, deadlocks may occur.

Emergence can often be explained by the *process* of the components' interactions, but not just by the character or count of the components. An important detail is that the emergent structure or property can influence the components retroactively, which is a form of feedback. The rolls in the Bénard system described above are an example for such an emergent structure. Once formed by the water molecules, the (macroscopic) structure of a roll influences the movement of the (microscopic) molecules.

15.2.5 Complex System

> Definition: **Complex system**
>
> *"Complex systems are systems with multiple interacting components whose behavior cannot be simply inferred from the behavior of the components."* [552]

If definitions 15.2.1 and 15.2.2 were combined, a complex system would be a system with a description that needs a lot of information, or in other words, whose behavior cannot be described in a compact manner. "What distinguishes a complex system from a merely complicated one is that in a complex system, some behaviors and patterns emerge as a result of the patterns of relationship between the elements." [623, Emergence]. So *emergence* is a necessary property of complex systems.

15.2.6 Criticality

The term "criticality" is used in many domains but has acquired special importance in the field of thermodynamics. Criticality "is used in connection with phase transitions. When the temperature of the system is precisely equal to the transition temperature, something extraordinary happens. [...] The system becomes critical in the sense that all members of the system influence each other." [323] Since this definition is not general enough to be valid in the context of self-organization, we denote a group of system components an "assembly" and use the following definition:

> Definition: **Criticality**
>
> *"An assembly in which a chain reaction is possible is called critical, and is said to have obtained criticality."[623, Criticality]*

Per Bak identifies a relationship between criticality and order. He uses the term to describe a critical point between order and disorder in complex systems [45]. The degree of order of a complex system can reach from total order to pure disorder. In total order, all relations are structured homogeneously and are stable, no unpredictable behavior can be detected in this case. The water molecules in an ice crystal are an example for this. Due to the minimal amount of energy in the system, every component has a stable position that will not change without external perturbation. In pure disorder, it's much harder to find a rule for the behavior of the components since no persistent stability can be observed. Systems in this state are usually analyzed with stochastic methods. For example, the molecules of water vapor move very fast and collide often, which makes it hard to anticipate their position and movement in future states. States that show little order are also called *subcritical*, those which are largely structured are called *supercritical*.

On the border between these two states lies criticality, which has a big impact on the stability of a system. Under certain circumstances, local perturbations may propagate so that all or most components may eventually get perturbed (if the relations are not static and able to propagate the influence). A chain reaction could easily result so that stability could be lost altogether. Whereas in a disordered system, the influence of a single component is most likely to be absorbed without a big impact on the overall system. Systems that reside in the state of criticality are basically stable, at the same time having the ability to change by keeping perturbations locally [647].

A simple example for a system in a critical state is the well-known Abelian Sandpile Model, first proposed in [47]. In this model, single grains of sand are repeatedly dropped onto a random field of a $n \times n$-grid. If the height of a field exceeds a critical value (e.g., 4), the grains of this field topple down and are equally distributed among the four neighbor fields. Grains that leave the grid are taken out of the system. Figure 15.2 shows a simulation run of the model.

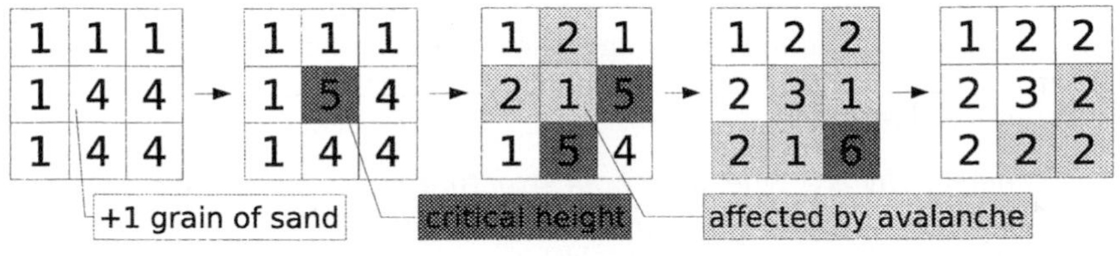

Fig. 15.2: Example for a simulation run of the Abelian Sandpile Model. A single grain of sand causes an avalanche that affects all but the upper left field.

Simulations have shown that this system moves into a critical state, many fields have a height between 1 and 3 – they are stable because another grain of sand will not change the system structure. At the same time, a few fields reside at the critical value of 4 – another grain of sand will cause an avalanche that changes the system's structure [647]. A combination of critical and non-critical field states causes the system to remain stable in most of the cases (because under the assumption of a random distribution of newly dropped sand grains, the probability of hitting a stable field is high), at the same time keeping the possibility for change (at least a few fields can cause a toppling). Bak concludes: "A frozen state cannot evolve. A chaotic state cannot remember the past. That leaves the critical state as the only alternative." [46, p. 6]

Note that some systems (e.g., the Abelian Sandpile Model) have the ability to move themselves into a critical state without external influences. This phenomenon is called *self-organized criticality* [45] and can be observed in most diverse real systems such as earthquakes, stock exchange crashes, traffic jams or sun storms [172].

15.2.7 Hierarchy & Heterarchy

> Definition: **Hierarchy**
>
> *For this context, we define a hierarchy as a rooted tree. "A tree is an undirected simple graph G" satisfying the condition that "any two vertices in G can be connected by a unique simple path. [...] A tree is called a rooted tree if one vertex has been designated the root, in which case the edges have a natural orientation, towards or away from the root."* [623, Rooted Tree]

If a communication system is organized in form of a hierarchy, the communication path between the components is unique, i.e. there is exactly one path between two arbitrary nodes. A level can be assigned to each element, i.e., its distance from the root. This allows us to order the elements partially. Thus, a hierarchy can be seen as an indication of order.

> Definition: **Heterarchy**
>
> *"A heterarchy is a type of network structure that allows a high degree of connectivity. By contrast, in a hierarchy every node is connected to at most one parent node and zero or more child nodes. In a heterarchy, however, a node can be connected to any of its surrounding nodes."*
> [623, Heterarchy]

Compared to a hierarchy, a heterarchy describes a more general type of network; a heterarchy may contain or resemble a tree, but is not limited to it. Although not completely precise, the term *heterarchy* is often used to point out the differences to a hierarchy [609]: since there is no root and all nodes may be arbitrarily cross-linked to each other, no level assignment and thus no order between the nodes can be detected.

If hierarchical and heterarchical organizational forms are applied to communication networks, advantages and disadvantages can be seen. In a hierarchy, there is exactly one single path between two arbitrary nodes A and B. This means that no communication between A and B is possible when one of the nodes on the path between A and B fails; the system would break into two disjoint parts then. A heterarchy can offer a higher fault tolerance because there may be more than one path between A and B. On the other hand, a lot of communication overhead can occur in a heterarchy. This would be the case if *all* nodes were contacted, or if the point of contact was not known in advance. The high number of connections then leads to a lot of communication.

The possibility for a high number of edges in a heterarchy allows for feedback behavior because any node may be able to reach any other node with a small number of hops. In a hierarchy, only neighbor nodes can contact each other so that information usually propagates slower. Thus, a heterarchy can be an indication for feedback.

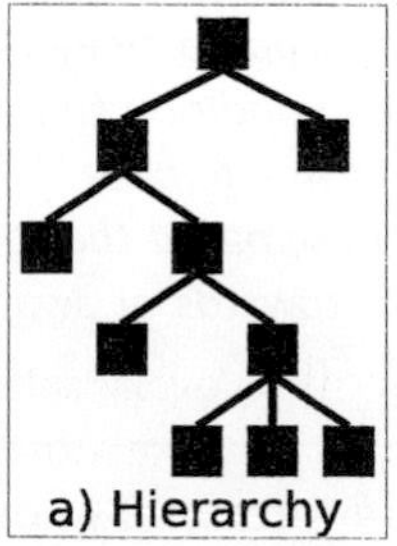

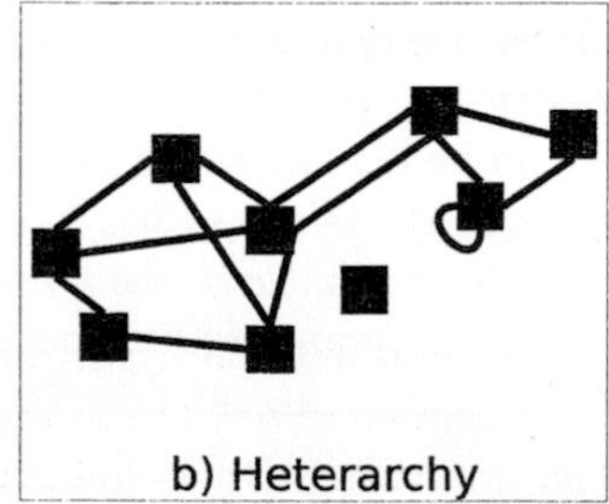

Fig. 15.3: Schematic outline of a) hierarchy and b) heterarchy.

15.2.8 Stigmergy

> Definition: **Stigmergy**
>
> *"Stigmergy defines a paradigm of indirect and asynchronous communication mediated by an environment."* [173, Stigmergy]

It is used mainly in decentralized systems where the individual components of the system communicate with each other by modifying their local environment. An example are ants that can perceive the concentration of pheromones in their environment and adapt their behavior to it. The *source* of the pheromones (usually dropped by other ants) is thereby unimportant. Thus, the environment can mediate triggering ants to behave in a certain way depending on the pheromone concentration. Considering that ants *themselves* are responsible for the pheromone concentration in their environment, stigmergy can be seen as a means to enable self-organization.

15.2.9 Perturbation

> Definition: **Perturbation**
>
> *A perturbation is a disturbance which causes an act of compensation, whereby the disturbance may be experienced in a positive or negative way.* [594, p. 118] (orig. in German)

Perturbations are central to system adaptations mediated by the environment.

15.3 Characteristics of Self-Organization

We now point out some characteristics that can be observed in different systems referred to as self-organizing. A more detailed description about their occurrence in natural, social and information systems is given in [362].

15.3.1 Self-Determined Boundaries

Every system is separated from its environment, so every self-organizing systems is, too. But to enable self-organization, it is important that the border between system and environment is defined *by the system* itself. Otherwise, the environment could shape the system arbitrarily or even completely tear it down. An example for this self-determination is the semi-permeable membrane of a cell. With its help, the cell determines which substances gain access and which are rejected.

15.3.2 Operational Closure & Energetic Openness

To build up its boundaries, a system must be able to operate independently of its environment. That does not mean that the system could survive in complete autarchy – the definition of a system clearly states that there must always exist an environment. A system cannot evolve if it does not obtain some input from its environment such as matter, energy, or information. Thus, a constellation must be found that allows autonomy from the environment on the one hand and interaction with it on the other hand. A system that fulfills these requirements is called *operationally closed* and *energetically open* [402].

15.3.3 Independence of Identity and Structure

Maturana makes a clear distinction between the concept of *organisation* and *structure* of a self-organizing system:

"The term ORGANISATION denotes the relations that must exist between the components of something to recognize it as member of a certain class. The STRUCTURE of something are the components and relations that constitute a certain unity in a concrete manner and realize its organisation." [403, orig. in German] In other words, the structure is a certain instance of components and relations within a system. It may vary (e.g., removal or change of a single component) without the collapse of the system. On the other hand, the organisation is the set of relationships or dependencies that *must essentially* exist for a certain system. With its help, the system can be classified independently of its current structure. In a way, it constitutes the identity of a system, because it does not vary as long as the system exists. To circumvent ambiguities about the term *organisation*, we will denote Maturana's organisation as *identity* from now on.

The distinction between identity and structure allows to explain flexibility and adaptivity, because an influence on a system's structure does not necessarily influence its identity. Thus, the system can be maintained under perturbations. An example for this from software engineering is the principle of information hiding, which postulates that the user should know *what* a certain algorithm does (identity), but not *how* (structure). This allows independence between definition and the current implementation.

15.3.4 Maintenance

To be able to exist over time, a self-organizing system must try to maintain itself. Therefore it needs abilities to repair or recreate defect components. New components do not have to be isomorphic to replaced ones – as long as the identity is sustained the structure may change. The components have to be *viable*, i.e., capable of maintaining identity. Often there are a lot of possibilities for viability so that a form of mutation, one of the basic vehicles for the evolution of a system, can be applied. Another feature of viability (in contrast to isomorphism) is that the system is able to adapt to changes from the environment. If a required input is no longer available the system may change over to use another one and change its structure accordingly.

An example for a self-maintaining entity is a human being – it is permanently recreating its constituting components (the cells). No isomorphic copies are created, though, the appearance of a human being changes over time.

15.3.5 Feedback & Heterarchy

If a system is perturbed, it may have to restructure itself in order to maintain itself. For this reason, the perturbed components must be able to communicate with the rest of the system. A prerequisite for this requirement is the cross-linking of components so that feedback between them becomes possible. This kind of linking allows the components to perform bidirectional communication, amplification or attenuation of external influences, or also recursive application of transformations. All these mechanisms can lead to feedback. Since a heterarchy allows for such cross-linked relations, it is has particular importance for self-organizing systems.

15.3.6 Feedback

Positive feedback can be used to build up viable structures very fast, an example for this is the laser [301]. It consists of a laser medium (e.g., a gas) between two mirrors. If low voltage is imposed the atoms of the laser medium are oscillating in different frequencies so that different colors are produced. The higher the voltage, the more atoms influence their neighbors to oscillate in a viable frequency (which depends on the atoms and the distance of mirrors) – the frequency is amplified through positive feedback.

In this example, not only viable but all kinds of frequencies are produced initially. As the system evolves, the less appropriate ones are sorted out. Randomness plays an important role, because there's no need to know in advance exactly what frequencies are viable.

Negative feedback prevents the system from growing so fast that it would collapse. Even if it is built of viable components only, it can reach a critical size where it might break or cannot react to perturbations fast enough. Therefore, it is necessary to damp positive feedback eventually. In a thermostat the positive feedback of increasing the water flow (and thus the heat) is opposed to the negative feedback of decreasing it. This allows the self-regulatory adaption of temperature independently from the environment.

15.3.7 Criticality

Systems such as the Abelian Sandpile Model (see Section 15.2.6) show that local influences can have global effects: every cell can only influence its 4 neighbor cells. It depends only on the system's state if the addition of another grain of sand triggers a massive toppling, which may reach every cell on the grid. In this case, the reason for the uncertainty of effect is that the system resides in the state of criticality. As described in Section 15.2.6, criticality offers a basic stability as well as the capability for changes. Both properties are essential for evolving systems – instability causes breakdown, inflexibility prevents from growth and adaptivity. Other phenomena which are regarded as being self-organizing, like an evolution [45] or earthquakes [172], are also assumed to reside in a critical state. Therefore, criticality can be seen as an indication for self-organization.

15.3.8 Emergence

It appears that not only the state of criticality but also emergence (see Section 15.2.4) connects local influences and global effects. In systems like ant colonies [174], a set of simple rules in combination with randomness allows the ants to fulfill tasks like building an ant hill or foraging. Although no ant knows the overall environment, the swarm as a whole is able to determine short paths to food sources (a more detailed description is given later in Section 15.4.2). Since the effect depends on the whole system and not only on its parts, it is denoted as *emergent*.

Emergence is often characterized as being unpredictable. Consider the appearance of convection cells in the Bénard system (described in Section 15.2.2). Although the effects of heating and cooling are known as well as the properties of water, the rotational direction of the rolls (clockwise or counter clockwise) cannot be predicted.

15.3.9 Self-Determined Reaction to Perturbations

If a self-organizing system tries to maintain itself, it needs metrics and means to detect and evaluate perturbations. The system can then react, e.g., by adapting the structure to the external influences. Measure and evaluation can be done explicitly, like in a thermostat, but also implicitly. For example, the state of criticality of the Abelian Sandpile Model (see Section 15.2.6) is a way to react to the perturbation of adding grains of sand. The metrics is given by the height of a field, and the evaluation and reaction by the underlying rules for toppling.

The Abelian Sandpile Model also shows that the reaction to such a perturbation is determined autonomously by the system. It is not predictable if the next (randomly located) grain of sand will change the structure of the system or of any part of it. A system can compensate for perturbations on its own, and thus exhibits self-organization.

15.3.10 Reduction of Complexity

Another way that was observed as response to perturbations is the reduction of a system's complexity. An example for this is the Bénard convection (described in Section 15.2.2): if a pot of liquid is heated from the bottom and cooled down from the top, the liquid is shaped in form of *convection rolls*. The behavior of the liquid can then be described by a formula, the behavior of the molecules is determined by a rule. This means that less information is required for their description compared to the state when there was no rule – the complexity is reduced.

Another example is the coupling of multiple independent systems, as described in [293]. The systems described there have symbiotic relations to each other and form a new and stable supersystem which follows rules (whereas the single systems did not). The coupling is irreversible, i.e., once established, the subsystems cannot survive without each other. An instance of this category is the pollination of flowering plants by insects while these get nectar as food.

15.4 Applications in Computer Science

In this section, we describe three examples which show some of the characteristics specified above and their positive effects.

15.4.1 Small-World and Scale-Free Networks

This is a short overview about small-world and scale-free networks with regard to self-organization. For more details we refer to Chapter 6.

Milgram's Experiment

In 1967, the psychologist Stanley Milgram conducted an experiment, often referred to as the small-world experiment [413]. He asked 60 recruits to forward a letter from Kansas to Massachusetts. The participants were only allowed to pass the letter by hand to friends who they thought might be able to reach the destination, no matter if directly or via a "friend of a friend". The perhaps surprising outcome was that the letters reached their target in six steps on average. This lead to the term "small-world".

Small-World Networks

A small-world network is characterized by high sparsity and high clustering. This can be measured by the overall number of edges, which is in $\mathcal{O}(n)$ where n is the number of nodes (in contrast to $\mathcal{O}(n^2)$ for a fully meshed network), and the clustering coefficient which is defined for each node i by:

$$C(i) = \frac{2 \cdot e(i)}{deg(i)(deg(i) - 1)}, \tag{15.1}$$

where $e(i)$ is the number of edges between neighbors of i and $deg(i)$ corresponds to the degree of i [615]. Since $deg(i)$ is the number of neighbors of i, the clustering coefficient describes the relation of actually existing edges between neighbors of i and the maximum number of *possible* edges between them. The more edges actually exist, the higher is the clustering coefficient.

A small-world network can be constructed from an existing regular structured network [615]. In this case, every edge (i, j) is changed to (i, k) with a certain probability p, where k is chosen uniformly at random over all nodes but i and j (with duplicate edges forbidden). The higher p is chosen, the more the network becomes random. Small-world properties are observed somewhere between low and high p [163]. The appropriate value for p is often hard to determine. To cope with these issues, an alternative model was developed.

Scale-Free Networks

The scale-free (SF) model [60] describes networks in a more dynamical way than the small-world model and is mainly based on the two mechanisms:

- Dynamic construction and
- Preferential attachment.

The construction process usually starts with m nodes and no edges. New nodes are added incrementally, and a constant number of edges is attached to them (to stay within $\mathcal{O}(n)$). The probability that an edge from a new node n is connected to a certain node with degree k_i is given by:

$$P(n \rightarrow k_i) = \frac{k_i}{\sum_j k_j}. \tag{15.2}$$

Due to the additivity and homogeneity (on algebraic grounds) of this function, the correlation between the degree of a node and the probability for new nodes to connect to it is linear. This leads to a *scale-free* network, the structure of the system is independent of its current size (Figure 15.4). Scale-free networks show the property that most nodes have a small number of connections while only a few are highly meshed ("hubs"). This relation can be mathematically described by a power law: $P(k) \sim k^{-\gamma}$ (where γ is a system constant). Therefore, these networks are also called *power law networks*. Sometimes they are also denoted *fractal networks*, signifying a correlation to fractals[1]. For power law networks as well as fractals, a part of the system has the same structure as the whole (Figure 15.4). This property, which is called *self-similarity* for fractals, is just another expression for freedom of scale.

Connection to Self-Organization

In addition to Milgram's small-world experiment about social networks [413], other popular networks such as the Internet [325] and the WWW [10], the pattern of viral infections [59], relations between actors or scientists and even computer programs [434] show small-world and scale-free properties. In all cases, the properties appeared as an accidental feature rather than intentionally incorporated – the properties arose in a *self-organized* form.

The incremental building of a scale-free network exposes another correlation to self-organization: every node has only a *local* view on the system and makes a *local* decision about its connections. This results in a *global* scale-free structure, apart from external influences. This structure is a mixed form of hierarchy and heterarchy. It supports scalability, the overhead for connecting to it is constant and the diameter is very small. It is also robust, failure or attack of a random node have little effect on the overall system with high probability due to a high degree of redundancy [18]. However, a targeted attack on hubs can divide the network into disjoint parts (again of the same structure). Randomness is used for the linking between components, which results in flexibility and makes the occurrence of single points of failures (SPoFs) less likely.

[1] A fractal is a geometric object which can be divided into parts, each of which is similar to the original object. [623, Fractal].

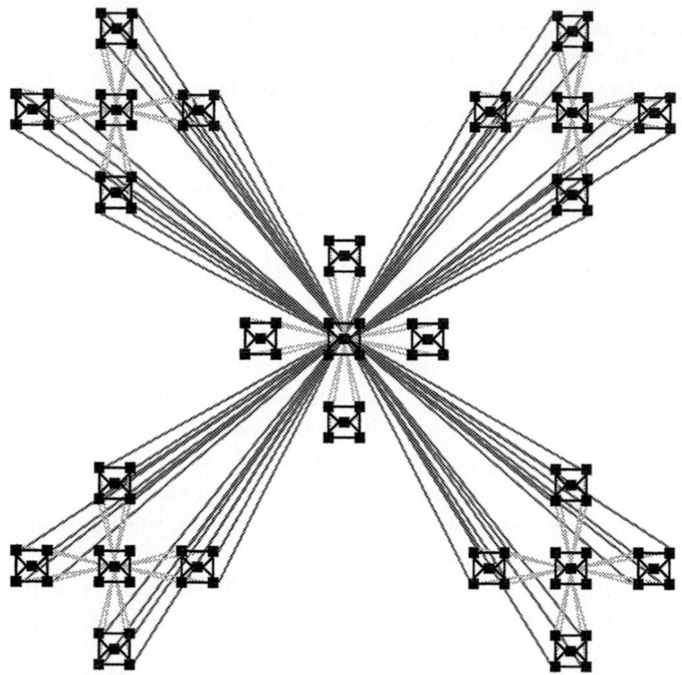

Fig. 15.4: Example for a hierarchical, fractal, scale-free network. Every part of the system has the same structure as the whole.

15.4.2 Swarming

Swarm intelligence is a property that has been investigated in the area of artificial intelligence. Swarm intelligence indicates the ability of single agents to make correct decisions without knowledge of all other members of the swarm and the overall system. A system composed of such agents is coordinated without a dedicated control instance. According to [415], there are five fundamental principles of swarms:

- Proximity – a swarm can make simple calculations about time and space.
- Quality – a swarm can react to indications by the environment.
- Diverse response – activities can be performed in different ways.
- Stability – not every environmental change modifies the swarm.
- Adaptability – a swarm can change its behavior if that seems promising.

These properties have been implemented in many agent-based models. We use the class of *ant algorithms* [87] for our further explanations.

Ant Algorithms

Ant algorithms are used to solve a problem by means of many agents called *ants*. The strategies of these ants have been inferred by watching nature, where real ants use chemical substances ("pheromones") to communicate with each other. Ants spread pheromones while moving around and detecting the trails of their conspecifics. The substance evaporates over time. Ants follow traces with a probability proportional to the strength of the pheromone signals. One application of ant algorithms is the traveling salesman problem (TSP), i.e., finding the shortest cycle through a given number of cities. Ant algorithms are based on a model of foraging behavior of real ants as illustrated in Figure 15.5.

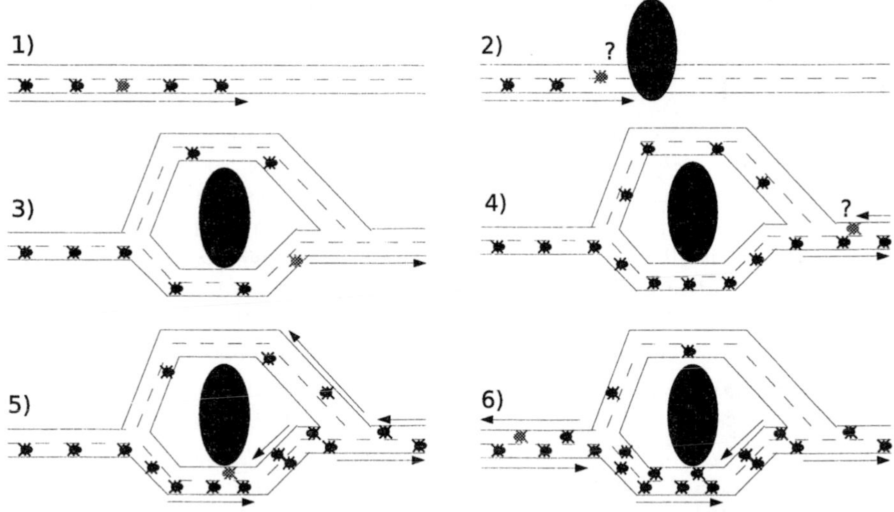

Fig. 15.5: How real ants find the shortest path. 1) Ants move from their nest to a food source. 2) They arrive at a decision point. 3) Some ants choose the upper path, some the lower path. The choice is random. 4) Since ants move approximately at constant speed, the ants which choose the lower, shorter path reach the opposite decision point faster than those which choose the upper, longer, path. 5) Pheromone accumulates at a higher rate on the shorter path, so consequently more and more ants choose this path. 6) The decision of the following ants is influenced by the higher pheromone concentration.

A swarm of ants can find cooperatively an approximative shortest path from their nest to a source of food. This observation has been taken advantage of for finding a solutions to the well-known TSP problem [174].

Connection to Self-Organization

A swarm of artificial as well as real ants exhibits many indications of a self-organizing system. First of all, ants are organized in a form of heterarchy (all ants are equally important), although they don't communicate directly. The ants use stigmergy for communication rather than an explicit communication channel. Spreading of pheromones is a form of positive feedback while the evaporation corresponds to negative feedback. No ant has global knowledge but acts upon very basic, local rules. The use of randomness makes it even simpler. While the collective swarm may find the shortest path (or at least a good approximation of it) based on teamwork, a single ant, following simple rules, could have never completed the task on its own. So the overall collective behavior can be called *emergent* based on interactions the constituent elements that follow simple rules for their behavior.

15.4.3 Cellular Automata

The concept of *cellular automata* can be traced back to the 1940s when John von Neumann investigated self-replicating systems [610]. A cellular automaton can be explained as an accumulation of many deterministic finite automata which all have the same set of rules. It consists of an infinite, n-dimensional grid of homogeneous cells c_i which have a state $s(c_i, t)$ at time t. For each cell c_i, a neighborhood $N(c_i)$ is defined. It can be chosen according to certain metrics, e.g., the two neighbors in each dimension, or the two neighbors and additionally c_i itself. For each combination of states of $N(c_i)$, a rule is defined which determines $s(c_i, t+1)$. The rules are valid for all cells so that the total number of rules is given by the number of cells in the neighborhood to the power of the number of possible states $|N|^{|s|}$.

A very simple example is the *mod* 2-automaton. It is one-dimensional ($n = 1$), has two possible states ($s(c, t) \in \{0, 1\}$) and has only the single rule for all cells y:

$$\forall y : N(y) = (x, y, z) \quad \Rightarrow \quad s(y, t+1) = (x + z) \; mod \; 2. \qquad (15.3)$$

Eq. (15.3) implies that $s(y, t+1)$ is independent of $s(y, t)$. A plot showing the states of this simple automaton over time is illustrated in Figure 15.6.

Unexpectedly, the automaton builds the structure of a well-known fractal, the Sierpinski-triangle. Other automata show similar behavior, but there are differences which lead to the following classification [628]:

- Class 1 (trivial automata): lead to the same state for each cell, independent of the initial state.
- Class 2 (periodic automata): lead to a fixed state for each cell, dependent on the initial state.

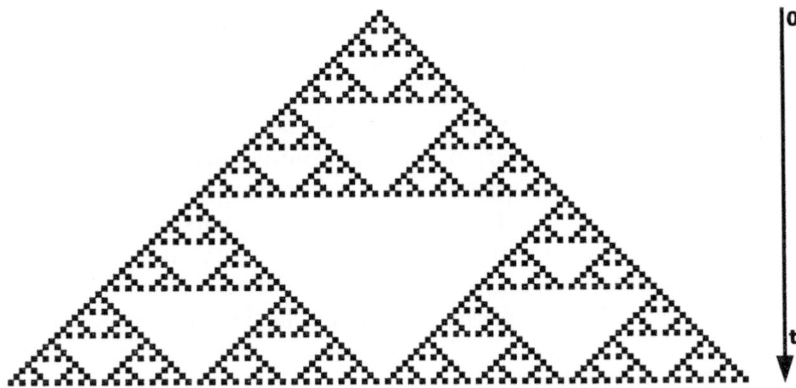

Fig. 15.6: Visualization of the *mod* 2-automaton (time progresses from top to bottom): the Sierpinski-triangle

- Class 3 (chaotic automata): change incessantly without observable structures.
- Class 4: create different, complicated structures that move along the grid over time.

Matthew Cook has shown that class 4 automata can be used for computations and furthermore are Turing-complete [628], which is noteworthy taking the simplicity of the model into account.

Connection to Self-Organization

Animations of cellular automata, showing moving patterns like blinkers or gliders, trigger assumptions about an underlying self-organization. Indeed, several indications can be identified, the iterative and recursive application of simple rules to a local neighborhood may cause an evolution of complex structures. The structures are continuously reproduced. Furthermore, some patterns are self-stabilizing. The current state of a cell is used as input for the modification of future states of the same cell which is a form of feedback. The resulting structures are emergent because no single cell could produce them.

15.5 Conclusions

Self-organization increasingly attracts interest within several areas of computer science. By incorporating self-organization autonomous operation can be fostered. Decentralized control or self-management could be attractive results. Self-organization can be found in many disciplines and a comparative study may therefore reveal stimulating insights. Enabling features of self-organization were identified in this chapter including complexity, feedback, emergence, criticality, heterarchy, stigmergy or perturbation. Characteristics can be used to classify Peer-to-Peer and other systems concerning their degree of affinity to self-organization. Self-organization has widely been praised as being the key for incorporating attractive features into networks and systems. Small-world and scale-free networks are robust as well as efficient, a swarm may subsume a very large number of agents without global control or knowledge, or cellular automata may trigger global structures purely based on locally applied rules. Autonomy, scalability, flexibility or robustness may largely be provided as a result. Other implications of self-organization (for example, an unpredictability of behavior, danger of deadlock creation etc.) may be less attractive.

Most problematic from computer science point of view, however, is the fact that it seems hard to impose control and to exercise management onto those systems for more efficiency, security purpose or general goal orientation. The analysis provided in this chapter aims at providing a first step towards a better understanding of self-organization in general. Further research is needed, however, before more comprehensive and goal-driven control and management will be possible in particular.

16. Self-Organization in Peer-to-Peer Systems

Hermann De Meer, Christian Koppen (University of Passau)

Self-organization is seen as an attractive feature of Peer-to-Peer networks although meaning and significance of this term are far from being clear. In this chapter, principles of self-organization in Peer-to-Peer systems are identified. The potential enabled by incorporating these principles and further potentials of increasing the degree of self-organization are outlined. The Active Virtual Peer (AVP) concept is used as an example for incorporation of an enhanced level of self-organization into Peer-to-Peer systems.

16.1 Introduction

In the year 1999, the first Peer-to-Peer system, Napster [436], began its (short) career in the Internet. The popularity of Peer-to-Peer networks has grown immensely ever since. Nowadays, the traffic load on the Internet appears to be dominated by Peer-to-Peer applications (see Chapter 22 for details). As the downside of the success story scalability and flexibility issues became visible. If well understood and carefully implanted self-organization may provide a useful means to handle these challenges. But since self-organization may resist imposed control if done naively, self-organization can as well be the source of inefficiency. Many Peer-to-Peer systems have been advertised as being self-organizing, although meaning and significance of this claim are far from being clear. There are several classes of Peer-to-Peer systems that exhibit different properties with different degrees of self-organization. Peer-to-Peer systems have to provide services like routing, searching for and accessing of resources. An open question is if and how much can self-organization, with all its illusiveness, emerge as an essential means for improving the quality of the services. Improved service quality, thereby, is to be achieved equally for performance, robustness, security and scalability in an all open world.

Based on the characteristics as outlined in Chapter 15, we describe criteria for self-organization of Peer-to-Peer systems. In Section 16.2.1, these criteria are first introduced and motivated. Following that, the criteria are applied to some of the more popular unstructured and structured Peer-to-Peer systems in Section 16.2.2 and Section 16.2.3, respectively. In each case the overall degree of self-organization incorporated is first identified and then potential enhancements of self-organization are discussed. In Section 16.3 the Active Virtual Peer concept is introduced as an example for a higher degree of self-

R. Steinmetz and K. Wehrle (Eds.): P2P Systems and Applications, LNCS 3485, pp. 247-266, 2005.

organization in Peer-to-Peer systems from certain perspectives. Section 16.4 concludes this chapter.

16.2 Evaluation of Peer-to-Peer Systems

16.2.1 Criteria

The analysis of Peer-to-Peer networks is based on the characteristics of self-organization as introduced in Chapter 15. Since these characteristics still remain somewhat elusive we first provide more specific criteria that can be easier applied for our purpose. The goal is to use simpler criteria for the analysis of the extent to which a Peer-to-Peer system can be characterized as being self-organizing. We divide the criteria into two groups: *basic criteria* and *criteria for autonomy.* A conformity with criteria for autonomy enables a system to adapt autonomously and develop a "life of its own". The criteria to be investigated are the following:

Basic criteria

- **Boundaries:**
  The boundaries of a self-organizing Peer-to-Peer system should be self-determined. In other words, the decision about the affiliation of its components, i.e., the peers, is should be made by the system itself. The boundary of a Peer-to-Peer system can be understood as the point where new, unknown nodes enter the system. Peers which offer new nodes the possibility to join are often called *bootstrap* nodes.
- **Reproduction:**
  A self-organizing Peer-to-Peer system can and does reproduce its structure. This may include addition, removal or change of a peer, its data or its relations or connections to other peers. Reproduction does not necessarily mean the creation of an isomorphic copy but may include mutations.
- **Mutability:**
  A self-organizing Peer-to-Peer system is able to change its structure. The change may concern constitution and number of peers and relations. Possible instances are the change of connections or the formation of clusters.
- **Organization:**
  A self-organizing system is organized in form of a hierarchy, a heterarchy or both. The organization has effects on the system's structure, e.g., whether there are fixed communication paths or single points of failure.
- **Metrics:**
  A self-organizing system is able to detect perturbations triggered from the environment. For Peer-to-Peer systems, the following perturbations are typical:

  - Failure of a peer or connection,
  - Overload or DoS-attacks,
  - Manipulation of data ("fakes").

  In addition, Peer-to-Peer systems often suffer from the problem of "freeriders" – peers which make use of the system without supplying resources. Effects of freeriders are not considered as perturbations because they have their cause *within* the system.
- **Adaptivity:**
  A self-organizing Peer-to-Peer system is able to react to perturbations appropriately. The reaction may include restructuring of peers, authorization of peers to avoid "fakes" and incorporation of redundancy as a further measure of precaution.

Criteria for autonomy

- **Feedback:**
  A self-organizing Peer-to-Peer system is often exposed to positive and negative feedback, whereupon the structure or behavior of the system changes in a balanced way. Feedback includes messages that peers send to each other.
- **Reduction of complexity:**
  A Peer-to-Peer system which is self-organizing develops structures and hides details from the environment to reduce the overall complexity. This may include the forming of clusters or the creation of other entities, e.g., an Active Virtual Peer (AVP) (described in Section 16.3) or a holon which is a *group* of agents that appears as a *single* agent to the outside (the concept of holons is further detailed in [208] and [270]).
- **Randomness:**
  A self-organizing system makes use of randomness as a prerequisite for creativity. This allows the creation of new structures with little effort. An example from another discipline are ant algorithms where ants decide randomly between different paths when they have no sufficient knowledge about their environment (see Section 15.4.2 for details).
- **Self-organized criticality (SOC):**
  A system which is self-organizing drives itself into a state of criticality. Too much order as well as too much disorder are to be avoided by adequate procedures. This should result in an increased degree of flexibility because the system is able to cope with different types of perturbations.
- **Emergence:**
  A self-organizing Peer-to-Peer system shows properties that no single peer has on its own, or properties that may have been unknown at design time. Peers forming a small-world exemplify an emergent structure.

Besides the degree of conformance to these criteria, every system has an **identity** (in the meaning described in Section 15.3.3), or a main purpose, that is an essential characteristic of the system. The identity of a Peer-to-Peer system is (as usual for information systems) imposed from the outside, i.e., from the developers, and does not arise self-determined.

The results of our analysis are presented in Tables 16.1 and 16.2. Explanations are given in Sections 16.2.2 and 16.2.3. We use the following structure for each subsection of Sections 16.2.2 and 16.2.3: the first paragraph gives a very short description of the analyzed Peer-to-Peer system (for details, we refer to other chapters of this book). The second paragraph contains our results concerning the basic criteria identity, boundaries, reproduction, mutability & organization. The third paragraph deals with the basic criteria metrics & adaptivity. The last paragraph illustrates conformance to the criteria for autonomy.

16.2.2 Unstructured Peer-to-Peer Networks

In this subsection, we analyze some of the more popular Peer-to-Peer systems for their ability to self-organize.

	Napster	Gnutella	FastTrack	eDonkey	Freenet
Identity	Filesharing				Anonymity
Boundaries	×	×	○	○	×
Reproduction	×	×	×	×	✓
Mutability	×	×	○	○	×
Organization	×	×	✓	✓	×
Metrics	○	○	○	○	○
Adaptivity	○	×	○	○	✓
Feedback	×	×	×	×	✓
Reduction of complexity	×	✓	×	×	×
Randomness	×	×	×	×	×
SOC	×	×	×	×	×
Emergence	×	✓	×	×	×

Table 16.1: Self-organization in unstructured Peer-to-Peer systems. The symbols show the degree of conformance with the criteria listed in Section 16.2.1.
✓ – full conformance ○ – partial conformance
× – no conformance

Napster

Napster [436] was conceived as a platform to share audio data in the well-known MP3-format.

The server of the system is the only bootstrap node. It admits every peer to enter, so boundary conditions are not actively enforced by the system itself. Of course there could be set external policies for admittance, but these policies are not an integral part of the Peer-to-Peer system. Consequently, one of the essential characteristics of self-organization, namely self-bounding, is not fulfilled. Neither peer structure nor data is actively reproduced; when a peer leaves the system, its data is no longer available if not provided by other peers. Clients cannot take over management tasks from the server and the server does not share files. As a result, mutability is not given as far as the system structure is concerned. The type of organization is a mix of a very flat hierarchy (between the clients and the server) and a heterarchy (among the clients). The heterarchical organization is of advantage – it does not affect the whole system if a single peer fails. Unfortunately, clients direct their search requests to the central server only, which is therefore urgently required for the operation of the system. Thus the server is a single point of failure (SPoF) which ruins the positive effects of the heterarchy.

Metrics can be attained by means of keep-alive-messages (`ping/pong`) that peers exchange among each other; these messages are an appropriate way to detect the failure of a node or connection. If such a message fails to appear, the server can be asked once again for the respective file to be located at another peer. Such a form of adaptivity can be of advantage to the overall system. However, no explicit precaution against or response to overload conditions is taken into account. Similarly no defence against possible DoS attacks or against infiltration by corrupted data is integrated. Thus, the criterion of metrics is not fully satisfied.

Keep-alive-messages are a form of internal communication which is an indication for feedback. But for conformity to criterion "feedback", reactions and structural changes are also necessary. This is not the case in Napster, so feedback is hardly incorporated. No further properties that satisfy the criteria for autonomy are known.

Gnutella

Gnutella [250] was developed to avoid effects of centralization (including limitations of scalability, unused resources on the clients and the server as SPoF). In this section, we refer to version 0.4 of Gnutella, where every peer ("servent") is equal.

Since every servent is equal every servent is a bootstrap node, too. In analogy to Napster, no node is barred from accessing the system, so the boundaries are not determined by the system. Also, no automatic reproduction occurs. A difference to Napster lies in the (strictly) heterarchical organization of the peers. This causes search and signaling being done in form of flooding which has been identified as the main culprit for limitations in scalability [518]. Since the heterarchical organization remains invariant, no restructuring can occur and thus no mutability is given.

Gnutella uses the same mechanism to achieve metrics as in Napster, peers excessively exchange keep-alive-messages. The risk of overloading is notably high due to flooding of messages through the network; there are no provisions against manipulation of data. Concerning adaptivity, Gnutella resembles Napster: a missing `pong` causes the peer which sent the `ping` to terminate related connections. But since the network is flooded with keep-alive messages, adaptivity is even harder to achieve than in Napster.

In analogy to Napster, keep-alive messages are used. But besides the termination of connections no structural changes occur, thus feedback control is not incorporated. An interesting property of a Gnutella network is the connectivity pattern or node degree. Very often the node degrees can be approximated by a power law distribution [517]. Gnutella additionally seems to feature the emergent property of a small-world network. This can be explained by the way the system is used: a few peers have high capabilities (bandwidth and capacity) and provide a lot of files. This is accompanied by many peers primarily connecting to such a privileged servent. Many peers only download something and then disconnect without having offered anything ("freeriders"). This structure is typically formed without external influence and is facilitated by the flexibility of the underlying heterarchy. The traffic is strongly controlled by the servents with high capabilities, which reduces stress on the network resources.
The existence of randomness or an appearance of self-organized criticality cannot be attributed to Gnutella according to the definitions as used throughout this chapter.

FastTrack

FastTrack [202] can be seen as a hybrid of Napster and Gnutella. All peers are equal, but every peer can decide to become a *SuperNode*, which offers services to other peers ("successors") that connect to it. This concept is a structural response to Gnutella's usage profile.

The boundaries of FastTrack can at least be somehow influenced, because the system offers a possibility to limit bandwidth and connection count. When overload is on the raise, a peer can refuse requests (including requests from new nodes that want to enter the network). This feature, however, has to be adjusted manually and is not self-organizing; furthermore it does not allow to reject a request or node based on some characteristics. Thus FastTrack is not fully compliant to the criterion "boundaries". FastTrack clients do not replicate data without user interaction, so no active reproduction occurs. The

SuperNode concept is a form of mutability because it allows differentiation of peers, albeit not automatically. The SuperNode concept allows for a dynamic (but manual) adjustment of the organizational form; besides the underlying heterarchy a (very flat) hierarchy between a SuperNode and its successors can emerge. A drawback of this implementation is that every node is exclusively assigned to one SuperNode (which makes it a local SPoF, a common problem in hierarchies).

FastTrack uses the same mechanisms as Napster to obtain metrics. If a pong-message of a SuperNode is missing its successors connect to a new SuperNode; thus a perturbation may affect the performance of a system but not its basic operation. Such a characteristics can be seen as an indication of a higher level of adaptivity. Another enhanced technique of dealing with overload situations is "swarming": a single peer can download different parts of the same file from various peers simultaneously. The problem of "fakes" is not addressed and could pose a major problem for such a network.

Another newly introduced concept is the "rank" which determines the priority of a peer. The inclusion of this parameter prioritizes the traffic flows. But since it does not change the traffic flows (which would be a change of the structure of the system) this is no form of feedback in the sense of Section 16.2.1. One could argue that the SuperNode concept is an indication for the reduction of complexity; but the change of the peer status must be done manually and is non self-organizing. No further properties were found to conform a criterion of autonomy.

eDonkey

The eDonkey network [185] has strong parallels to FastTrack, but is geared to the transfer of very large files. In addition to swarming, peers can help each other by means of "hording", i.e., swapping received data among each other so that data does not need to be downloaded from (far away) sources. In eDonkey, a peer runs either a client application or a server application or both.

eDonkey conforms to the "boundaries" criterion in analogy to FastTrack: every interested node can connect to a server, while the server may reject requests if it is overloaded. Also in eDonkey, no reproduction is done automatically. Every peer (preferably with high capabilities) can run a server. A server in eDonkey is comparable to the SuperNode concept in FastTrack, thus the same arguments are valid concerning mutability. The organization of peers is quite similar, too; as an enhancement, a client can connect to multiple servers at the same time, which makes the system more robust.

Considerations about metrics go according to the Peer-to-Peer systems analyzed above. The failure of a node does not concern the whole network; if the node ran a server, its clients can connect to another server and continue. Swarming and hording are designed to reduce the traffic load. The use of native UDP-transport could pose a problem due to the lack of congestion, error or flow control. Traffic flows to servers which are offline can continue for a long time, wasting resources. eDonkey is the first Peer-to-Peer system that addresses the problem of "fakes". For this purpose, there are websites which list files with probably incorrect or inconsistent data. This allows the *manual* circumvention of fakes – so no self-organization here.

There are mechanisms to handle priorities and queuing; these have, in analogy to FastTrack, no impact on the structure of the system, but merely reorder the traffic flows. Thus, feedback cannot be detected. Besides, there's no indication for properties that fulfill one of the criteria for autonomy.

Freenet

The identity of the Freenet approach [231] differs from the one of the systems covered so far. Its purpose is to provide an infrastructure for free and anonymous information exchange. The detailed mechanisms are described in [123] and [124].

Like the other approaches, Freenet offers no control for joining or leaving nodes, and thus has no means to decide about its boundaries in a self-determined way. But it provides the reproduction of data: requested information is cached on the nodes between source and target. This results in the movement of data towards its requesters. More than that, it leads to the duplication of popular data while unrequested data is timing out. The data is adapted to user requests. All peers are equal; they are organized in form of a heterarchy which does not allow for mutability of the system structure. In addition, every node only knows a fixed number of neighbors, which leads to inefficiency on the one hand but higher potential for anonymity on the other hand.

The use of metrics, especially the handling of perturbations, is exceptionally interesting in Freenet, as it is hard for perturbations to have an effect on the system at all. A failure of a peer or connection can be tolerated, because its data (at least the popular part of it) is cached on its neighbors. This is also why overload of a node is unlikely to occur: the more peers request data that a certain node holds, the more copies will be made and, thus, later requests will not even reach the original node but be answered by increasingly "closer" nodes. A similar argument applies to the threat of DoS attacks – the intended effect is a temporary high load in the network until an attacker gets swamped by responses. All these properties result from Freenet having the focus on *data*, and not on the peers. An attack or request can not be done to a peer, but to data (which is adapted on demand). The manipulation of data is also hard to achieve because of the multiple encryption techniques and the lack of knowledge about the location of data. As a conclusion, Freenet in fact does offer less *measures* and *reactions* to perturbations but incorporates *preventions* by design.

The adaption of data to user requests is a form of feedback: favored data is "amplified" while unpopular information is deleted. Further conformance to the criteria of autonomy could not be detected.

Note: All mentioned indications of self-organization in Freenet concern the *data* only, and not the structure (which would be necessary for more complete self-organization).

16.2.3 Structured Peer-to-Peer Systems

Structured Peer-to-Peer networks make use of distributed hash tables (DHT) to allow for a more efficient allocation of resources and routing to information.

	Chord	PAST	CAN	NICE
Identity	Allocation	Storage & allocation	Allocation	Distribution
Boundaries	×	×	×	×
Reproduction	○	○	○	○
Mutability	○	○	×	✓
Organization	✓	✓	○	○
Metrics	○	○	○	○
Adaptivity	○	✓	○	○
Feedback	✓	×	×	×
Reduction of complexity	×	×	×	✓
Randomness	×	×	×	×
SOC	×	×	×	×
Emergence	×	×	×	×

Table 16.2: Self-organization in structured Peer-to-Peer systems. The symbols show the degree of conformance with the criteria listed in Section 16.2.1
✓ – full conformance ○ – partial conformance
× – no conformance

Chord

Chord [117], [575] arranges all peers on a ring of size N. Every peer holds a routing table which contains $\log N$ "fingers", i.e., addresses of other peers.

These are not set arbitrarily but in a way to gain small-world characteristics: there are many entries for nearby peers and a few for distant ones. Due to the universality of DHTs, the identity of Chord is not filesharing but allocation of data in a more general way.

In analogy to Gnutella, every peer can serve as a bootstrap node and every unknown node is admitted to the system, so the "boundaries" criterion is not met. Chord does not reproduce peers or connections, but the ring structure is always preserved. Additionally, the redundant storage of data is possible: when a new node enters the system, it obtains the data it is responsible for while its predecessor may keep a copy of (at least a part of) it. In case of the departure of a node, its neighbors redistribute the data among each other. So Chord conforms at least partially the "reproduction" criterion. Since the ring structure is a design principle it is immutable. However, a smart (or maybe dynamic re-) assignment of `ID`s can be used to balance the traffic load so that mutability is partially given. Concerning the organization, arbitrary connections may exist between peers, so peers form a heterarchy. Nevertheless, communication paths are not chosen arbitrarily but structured because every peer has a routing table. This table is different for each peer so that no SPoF exists. This means that every peer is part of *many* hierarchies (i.e., routing tables with distance as order). Taken altogether, Chord implements a sophisticated combination of hierarchy and heterarchy.

Metrics are used as in unstructured Peer-to-Peer systems, the failure of a node can be detected by the absence of keep-alive-messages. If such a failure occurs, the predecessor of the missing node takes over the responsibilities of its successor. This allows a high measure of robustness in conjunction with the application of redundancy. On the other hand, an overload of peers is not unlikely: since data is portioned in disjoint parts, there is only *one* peer for every piece of information. Thus, the nodes which keep popular data are at high risk to be congested. The problem of intentionally faked data or routing tables has not been addressed so far. Taking it all together, Chord offers some mechanisms to support adaptivity.

The peers' routing tables are periodically checked for consistency. This is a form of feedback which is explained as follows. Entry i in the routing table of peer n contains the address of a peer p whose distance to n on the ring is between 2^i and 2^{i+1}. If p fails, n searches for a peer q which is neighbor of p and whose distance to n also is between 2^i and 2^{i+1}. If such a peer q is found, n directs the respective requests to q instead of p. Since this means a change of connections, the system structure is changed (the ring is stabilized). Thus, messages between peers lead to a more stable system structure which preserves consistency and efficiency and conforms to the criterion "feedback". There is no indication for the satisfaction of another criterion for autonomy.

PAST

PAST [476] is an approach for the allocation and archival storage of data. The allocation is managed by Pastry [527], an algorithm based on prefix routing. Each of the b^n peers in a Pastry system is part of n nested clusters and knows $b-1$ peers on each cluster level which resembles a scale-free network. Further details can be found in [526], [528].

Every interested peer gains access to the system, so the boundaries are not exclusively determined by the system. In analogy to Chord, replication is possible; the actual deployment can be adjusted by the replication parameter k on a per-file basis. Since this parameter is an integral part of PAST, at least reproduction of *data* can be identified. The system is immutably structured in form of a $b*$-tree with peers being the leaves. But as in Chord, a dynamic assignment of `IDs` could be used for load-balancing. Another analogy to Chord is the organization. Peers may arbitrarily connect to each other (heterarchy), but communication is forced to traverse along the cluster hierarchy. Additional data structures named `leaf set` and `neighborhood set` allow direct and thus efficient communication to topological or domain specific *nearby* peers. The cluster hierarchy on the other hand offers an upper bound to the number of necessary hops to deliver a message to distant peers. Pulled together, the organization is designed to support for both efficiency and robustness.

Concerning metrics, PAST differs only slightly from aforementioned Peer-to-Peer systems – the number of keep-alive-messages sent to nearby peers is higher than those sent to distant peers. When a failure or overload occurs, redundancy is used to confine effects locally so the global system is safeguarded. The replication parameter, which is crucial to support adaptivity, is adjusted manually only so that self-organization is limited in that respect. PAST offers a dedicated security concept that allows authorization via *smartcards* after a peer has joined. This clearly reduces the danger of fakes (that represent a negative perturbation), but on the other hands restricts strongly the application of the system and number of users.

No property was found to satisfy one of the criteria for autonomy.

CAN

With the approach of content addressable networks (CANs) [504] data is organized in form of D-dimensional vectors; for every dimension a different hash function is used. Requests are routed from a node to both of his neighbors in every dimension, what leads to a complexity of $\mathcal{O}(D \sqrt[D]{N})$ with constant storage cost for each of the N peers.

As in the other cases, no peer willing to enter the system is rejected and thus the boundaries are not exclusively determined by the system itself. First ideas considering reproduction of data (similar to Chord) are described in [505]. Peers are immutably arranged in form of a D-dimensional torus, so mutability in the sense of section 16.2.1 is excluded by design. Peers form a hierarchy because every peer communicates only with its direct neighbors. If failure of a peer p is detected, p's neighbors correct their neighborhood information so that the system stabilizes. Therefore, the occurrence of a SPoF can be excluded in this case.

Peers use keep-alive messages to build up metrics (they check if their neighbors are available). Whenever a failure of a peer p is detected, one of its neighbors takes over p's data range; a proper defined replication scheme could lead to a high degree of adaptivity in this case. It is noticeable that the number of affected nodes in the case of failure is constant, since the failed peer has only influence on its direct neighbors. The problem of "fakes" is not discussed.

Characteristics that conform to the criteria for autonomy could not be identified.

NICE

NICE [449] is a framework for group cooperation such as multicasting. Peers are organized in form of a b-tree (which is kept in balance via merge- and split-mechanisms). A *cluster* is a group of peers on the same level of the b-tree. A cluster has a designated node called *leader* which represents the (exclusive) communication interface between the children and the rest of the system. All leaders of clusters on level i in the b-tree form a new cluster on level $i+1$. NICE can therefore be seen as a hierarchy of leaders with "normal" peers as leaves. A cluster is able to change its leader but the change process may be expensive in terms of management cost.

A joining peer is assigned to the most appropriate cluster (depending on a definable metrics, e.g., the RTT) which means that some characteristics of the new peer are taken into account for the join process. But since these characteristics are only used to decide *where* and not *whether* a new peer is added, the system has few control about its boundaries. One of the main goals of NICE is efficient distribution of data which implies reproduction of data; peers or connections are not reproduced, though. Due to the incorporation of split- and merge-mechanisms, NICE is able to change the system structure which is an indication for mutability. The organization is hybrid because peers within a cluster are fully meshed and can communicate directly which means that (small) heterarchies are encapsulated within the (big) hierarchy of leaders. This hybrid form of organization reveals a possible problem of NICE. Since peers within a cluster can communicate with the rest of the system only via the cluster leader, the leader is a SPoF. An enhancement of NICE, called ZigZag [595], confirms this: the leaders are supported by *vice-leaders* which exclusively care about the distribution of data, while the leaders are responsible for management only.

NICE uses keep-alive ("heartbeat") messages to build up metrics concerning perturbations. The failure or attack of a peer can have system-wide effects if the target of an attack is a leader. But due to highly meshed clusters failures are detected quite fast, the peers then simply elect a new leader. Clusters formations as well as leaders may be changed so that NICE can adapt to perturbations. There are no measures to detect or avoid manipulation of data.

The technique of clustering is an indication for the reduction of complexity. A cluster is constituted of multiple components, but appears as one entity to the outside. Additionally, communication follows clearly defined rules (traversing the *b*-tree). The obedience to rules is another indication for a reduction of complexity (as described in Section 15.3.10). Clustering as incorporated in NICE resembles the concept of "holons" which is further described in [208] and [270].

16.2.4 Summary of Peer-to-Peer Evaluations

None of the analyzed Peer-to-Peer systems can be called fully *self-organized* in terms of the criteria described in Section 16.2.1. In this section some of the advantages and disadvantages of incorporating the principle of self-organization into Peer-to-Peer networks are discussed.

Advantages Gained from Using Self-Organization

The ability of NICE to change the system's structure dynamically allows adaptivity and efficient communication. Gnutella's pure heterarchical design gives enough freedom to cultivate a small-world structure. The DHT approaches combine a "physical" [1] heterarchy with different levels of logical hierarchies; this leads to the situation that no peer is more important than any other, at the same time allowing for efficient communication between arbitrary peers, that is, in $\mathcal{O}(\log n)$ in most approaches. The reproduction of data, especially in Freenet but also in the DHT approaches, increases the robustness of a system significantly. FastTrack can reject new nodes if it is congested, NICE evaluates new peers – first steps to build and control the boundaries of a system. The fake lists developed for eDonkey are at least an attempt to anticipate the manipulation of data.

Disadvantages Implied from Using Self-Organization

None of the investigated Peer-to-Peer networks have the ability to decide completely in a self-determined way about the respective boundaries, which

[1] at least as physical as an overlay network can be

evocates the problem of freeriders and attackers. Even worse, most systems even have no metrics to detect perturbations appropriately, not to mention reactions to perturbations. While Napster and NICE can be taken as examples for the power of hierarchies to assure efficiency, Napster and NICE can also serve as warning examples for the risks of SPoFs that can result from hierarchies. Networks like native Gnutella, on the other hand, may suffer from signaling overhead due to flooding in a (fixed) heterarchical connectivity structure. Most systems have an invariant structure, they are at most able to change the distribution of data.

16.3 Towards More Self-Organization in Peer-to-Peer Overlays

16.3.1 Active Virtual Peers

Self-organization is seen as an attractive feature of Peer-to-Peer networks as it essentially enables running a complex system without exercising stricter form of control and management. We have seen in Chapter 15 how characteristics and criteria can be defined as a basis for an analysis whether Peer-to-Peer systems exhibit crucial properties of self-organization. In fact, most current Peer-to-Peer systems show less resemblance to self-organization as might have been anticipated. A corresponding analysis has been presented in this chapter. Either criteria of self-organization do not apply at all or they apply only if the Peer-to-Peer system at hand had been configured manually. A truly self-organizing Peer-to-Peer system that exhibits important criteria of self-organization and is also operating autonomously is hard to find.

Peer-to-Peer systems are often referred to as being self-organizing where a coherent behavior emerges spontaneously without external coercion or control. Pure Peer-to-Peer architectures, such as early the Gnutella service, however turned out to be non-scalable. As a response, the need to introduce structure and limited control has been recognized, cf. [398]. In order to introduce heterogeneity into unstructured, pure Peer-to-Peer services, various mechanisms have been proposed. The suggestions range from "ultrapeers" and "superpeers", as in Gnutella [563] and Kazaa [558] respectively, to distributed mediation servers and peer caches as in eDonkey2000 [185]. These approaches comprise only partial solutions to a more complex control problem. In particular, variability in service demand or load patterns can only be dealt with in a limited way. The demand for services may form hot spots which may shift within an overlay from one location to another one over time. Peer-to-Peer applications may therefore require a more flexible and dynamic method of control and management [160]. In particular, different control methods should be in place when and where needed, should be flexibly usable in combination with each other, and should be extensible in an evolutionary manner. More generally, it is our goal to introduce and to implement control and structure into Peer-to-Peer applications on demand.

The approach is based on the introduction of the concept of virtual nodes, called Active Virtual Peers (AVP). The proposed approach based on AVPs includes for example a *dynamic* forming and maintaining of Peer-to-Peer overlays or an adaptive routing of signaling and download traffic.

16.3.2 Objectives and Requirements on Control for Peer-to-Peer Overlays

We believe that there exist four areas where the enforcement of control will be beneficiary for such applications.

The first is *access control*. Participants of Peer-to-Peer overlays are typically granted access to all resources offered by the peers. These resources are valuable. Thus, the resource provider, either content provider or network provider, need to identify and regulate the admission to the overlay. In particular for Peer-to-Peer file sharing applications, access control should block off Peer-to-Peer applications or enable controlled content sharing.

The second area is *resource management*. The resources of individual peers have to be treated with care, e.g., low-bandwidth connected peers should not be overloaded with download requests and exploited equally. For Peer-to-Peer file sharing applications, for example, content caching capabilities will improve the performance while reducing the stress imposed on the network.

A third area of interest is *overlay load control*. Overlay load control copes with traffic flows inside the overlay. Its goal is to balance the traffic and load in order to maintain sufficient throughput inside the overlay while also protecting other network services by mapping this load in an optimum way onto the underlying network infrastructure.

Finally, the forth area of command is adaptive *topology control*. Overlay connections may be established or destroyed arbitrarily by the peers since they can join or leave the virtual network at any time. Topology control may enforce redundant connections, thus increasing the reliability of the service. In addition, topology control may force the structure of the virtual network to be more efficient and faster in locating resources when using broadcast protocols.

Having identified the objectives of control for a Peer-to-Peer overlay, it is important to examine how adaptive and un-supervised control mechanisms need to be implemented, without diminishing the virtues of the Peer-to-Peer model or introducing further complexity and overhead to the network. We believe that it is vital to preserve the autonomy of the peers inside a Peer-to-Peer network. Additional control loops, which adapt to the behavior of a Peer-to-Peer overlay, must not interfere with the autonomous nature of any Peer-to-Peer application. To achieve this goal, we suggest implementing control through an additional *support infrastructure*.

16.3.3 An Implementation of the AVP Concept

The main element of the support infrastructure suggested in this section is the Active Virtual Peer (AVP). As its name implies, an AVP is a virtual entity which interacts with other peers inside a Peer-to-Peer network. An AVP is a representative of a community of peers. Its purpose is to enhance, control and make the Peer-to-Peer relation more efficient inside that community. AVPs enable flexibility and adaptivity by the use of self-organization. An AVP consists of various distributed and coordinated components that facilitate different forms of control. By combining these components based on network conditions or administrative policies, we can create AVPs of different functionality.

The AVP performs certain functions, not expected by an ordinary peer. These AVP functions are arranged in horizontal layers as well as in vertical planes, see Figure 16.1. The horizontal layers correspond to the layers on which an AVP imposes control. The vertical separation describes the functional planes of AVPs. These architectural planes have been examined in detail in [160].

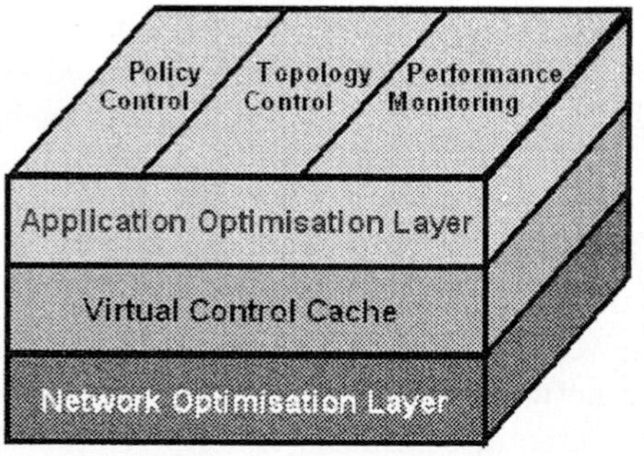

Fig. 16.1: The AVP architectural layers.

The upper horizontal layer of an AVP is called the "Application Optimization Layer (AOL)". It controls and optimizes the Peer-to-Peer relation on the application level. The AOL may apply application-specific routing in conjunction with *access policies*. The routing performed by the AOL is based on metrics such as the state of the peers ("virtual peer state") or the state of the links between peers ("virtual overlay link state") thus changing the peer load and overlay link characteristics such as packet drop rate, throughput, or delay. In addition, the AOL allows for active overlay topology control, which is accomplished in two ways. The Active Virtual Peer may initiate, accept or terminate overlay connections based on access restriction or topology features. Topology characteristics such as the number of overlay

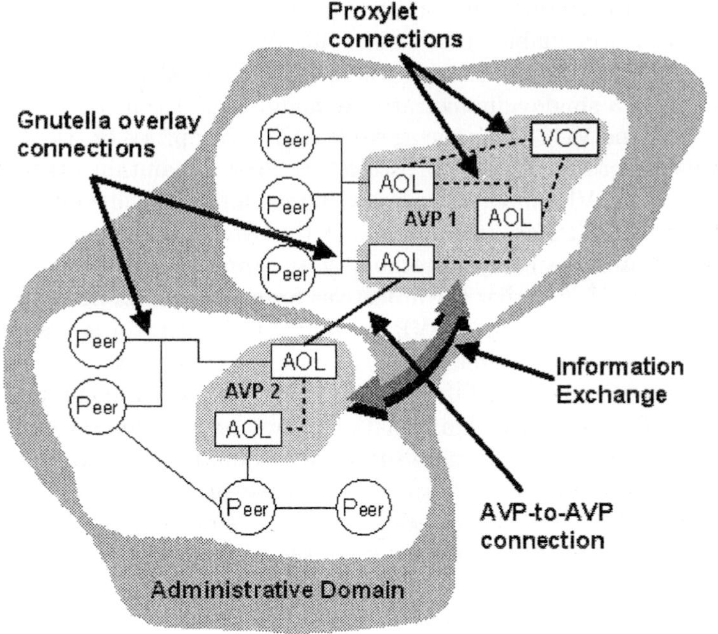

Fig. 16.2: The AVP realm.

connections or characteristic path length can be enforced or may govern the overlay structure. Furthermore, the AOL layer makes also use of the Application Layer Active Networking control mechanisms [242], examined below, for implementing its self-organization features. The AOL can instantiate modules implementing AOL functions whenever and wherever needed. These features enable the AOL to adapt the virtual overlay structure to varying demand, traffic patterns and connectivity requirements by launching new overlay connections and new virtual peers. These self-organization features make the AOL a very flexible architecture.

The middle layer of the AVP is denoted as the "Virtual Control Cache (VCC)". The VCC provides content caching on the application-level similar to conventional proxies. By maintaining often-requested content in close proximity, for instance inside an ISP's domain, large economies in resources and performance gains can be achieved. In addition, the VCC may offer control flow aggregation functions.

The lower layer of AVPs is denoted as the "Network Optimization Layer (NOL)". Its main task is the implementation of dynamic traffic engineering capabilities that map the Peer-to-Peer traffic onto the network layer in an optimized way. The mapping is performed with respect to the performance control capabilities of the applied transport technology. The AVP architecture may apply traffic engineering for standard IP routing protocols [212] as well as for explicit QoS enabled mechanisms like MPLS [630].

Figure 16.2 depicts a scenario where two AVPs, AVP 1 and AVP 2, are located within a single administrative domain. AVP 1 consists of three AOL modules and one VCC component, while AVP 2 comprises of two AOL modules. Multiple ordinary peers, denoted by "Peer", maintain connections to them. The two AVPs maintain overlay connections to each other. The AOL modules of the AVPs are in command of the overlay connections. This way, the AVPs can impose control on the overlay connection.

Having identified earlier the objectives for control of a Peer-to-Peer overlay, it is time to see how the AVP facilitates these control issues. Deployed AVPs create a realm wherein they constantly exchange information. Each AVP consists of multiple AOL and VCC proxylets which communicate and collaborate. The exchange of information allows for coordinated control of the overlay. A realm of AVPs is more suitable to evaluate the conditions inside a particular part of a Peer-to-Peer overlay than a single entity and this knowledge is distributed in order to achieve better results. Again, this capability promotes the flexibility and adaptivity of the AVP approach. Continuing, an AVP imposes control by providing effectors on connection level. The effectors comprise so far the *Router module* and the *Connection Manager module.* The Connection Manager enforces control by manipulating the connections peers maintain with each other. That is a significant difference compared to most Peer-to-Peer applications where the way peers connect to each other is random. By applying connection management, the AVP can enforce different control schemes.

The *Router module* governs the relaying of messages on application-level according to local or federated constraints, e.g., access restriction or virtual peer state information. The *Sensor module* provides state information for the distributed and collaborative control scheme.

The proposed concept relies on Active Virtual Peers as the main building block. The presented AVPs implement means for overlay control with respect to access, routing, topology forming, and application layer resource management. The AVP concept not only allows for a flexible combination of algorithms and techniques but enables operation over an adaptive and self-organizing virtual infrastructure. The significance of the approach is based on the automatic expendability and adaptivity of the whole overlay network as Peer-to-Peer services evolve. From this perspective, AVPs are inherently different to all other Peer-to-Peer systems. While some other Peer-to-Peer systems do comply with criteria of self-organization, a similar autonomy in developing features of self-organization seems unique to AVPs. AVPs adapt to the environment without manual triggers as opposed to other Peer-to-Peer approaches.

16.3.4 Related Work

The concept of AVPs is similar to the "ultrapeers" since both apply a peer hierarchy and reduce signaling traffic. AVPs differ from "ultrapeers", however, because of their overlay load control capability and adaptivity to the underlying network structure. The well-known Kazaa Peer-to-Peer filesharing service [558] applies a concept similar to "ultrapeers". In Kazaa these distinct nodes are denoted as "superpeers".

The OverQoS architecture [580] aims to provide QoS services for overlay networks. Dedicated OverQoS routers are placed at fixed points inside an ISP's (Internet Service Provider) network and connected through overlay links. The aggregation of flows into controlled flows of an overlay enables this architecture to adapt to varying capacities of the IP network and ensure a statistical guarantee to loss rates. This OverQoS approach complements and extends the limited load control provided so far in the AOL proxylet. However, it lacks any adaptivity to the varying network topology as addressed by the AVP.

Resilient overlay networks (RONs) [26] provide considerable control and choice on end hosts and applications on how data can be transmitted, with the aim of improving end-to-end reliability and performance. However, RONs are mostly restricted within single administrative domains.

16.4 Conclusions

Since self-organization in relation to Peer-to-Peer systems seems often to be identified with even more elusive properties such as emergence, criticality or autonomy, it is difficult to define hard criteria for the existence of self-organization and to apply the criteria rigorously. In a very puristic sense, self-organization in Peer-to-Peer systems can yet only be identified in a very limited form. The question, however, remains whether more self-organization would be desirable. And there is good reason to assume that this would indeed be the case.

Internal feedback is an efficient way to keep a system in balance; the same is true for the state of criticality. *b*-trees are an example from computer science that illustrates the benefit of a balanced system: efficient operational modus, controlled management cost and the existence of upper bounds for the traversal. Such balancing operations don't seem to have attracted yet too much attention in the context of Peer-to-Peer networks. Randomness is often used as a means to circumvent complex operations (e.g., in approximations). A flexible structure is the basis for adaptivity and robustness. A dynamical clustering or hierarchy could be basis for a promising approach. Equality of peers counteract the danger of SPoFs and is widely realized in approaches based on DHTs. A self-organizing Peer-to-Peer system should ideally be able to reproduce its structure, and not only its data. The reproduction should occur automatically and not be manually triggered or come from the outside. Viable structures should emerge autonomously. Furthermore, the boundaries of a self-organizing Peer-to-Peer network should be self-determined, a property hardly observed with current Peer-to-Peer systems. Detrimental effects caused by attackers or freeriders should be confined or prevented.

Self-organization reaches beyond the obviously desirable properties like flexibility, adaptivity or robustness. It includes the use of random components that allow the system to create new viable structures. Appearances of emergent properties are entailed that are triggered by interacting components. It extends to the state of criticality that allows for appropriate reaction and restructuring to perturbations. A reduction of complexity for a scalable growth is also often seen as a property of self-organization while maintaining identity. In all cases, control that can be exercised externally is limited to a minimum.

A decentralized self-management comes very close to the ideal of self-organization. In addition, it would be desirable if self-organizing Peer-to-Peer networks could be steered towards a certain overall purposeful goal. Such a steering may take place in accordance to observations made with emergent properties of self-organizing systems. Emergence is relying on simple rules, adapts sensibly to perturbations according to an "implanted" goal and does not develop pathological features under various forms of stress but compensates for stress to a wider extend in a reasonable way. Studying emergence may lead to identifying the simple rules to be implanted into Peer-to-Peer networks such that purposeful behavior may emerge. Pathological behavior in terms of detrimental performance or security should be made autonomously avoidable. If self-organizing systems are seen as systems which "create their own life" purposeful and efficient operation may become a big challenge. Self-organizing Peer-to-Peer systems with the inert property of well-behavedness that can be purposefully "implanted" would be the ideal case. How such an "implant" can be created and inserted is one of the big remaining challenges.

Part VI

Search and Retrieval

17. Peer-to-Peer Search and Scalability

Burkhard Stiller (University of Zürich and ETH Zürich)
Jan Mischke (McKinsey & Company, Inc., Zürich)

17.1 Peer-to-Peer Search and Lookup in Overlay Networks

In large-scale Peer-to-Peer networks without any central server instances, lookup and search , *i.e.*, locating or finding objects by their unique name or a keyword description, respectively, require the collaboration of many nodes. Peers initiate and forward or route queries for objects along overlay links. Other peers who have information on how to locate the searched for objects send their answers via the same or different overlay links back to the initially requesting peer. Finally, the object itself is normally transferred to the requestor by directly using the underlying network protocol, thus, in most cases the Internet Protocol (IP).

The peer initiating a *search request* or *query* is called the *requestor*, a peer holding the requested object the *object owner*. A peer that merely has information on the location of an object, *i.e.*, a link to the object owner, is termed the *indexing node* or *indexer*. The process of receiving and forwarding search requests through the overlay network until it reaches the indexer or owner of the desired object is called *query routing*. Query routing strongly ties the process of searching in the distributed system, defined through a search protocol, to the structure of the underlying overlay network. A controlled communication for search usually involves the explicit design and maintenance of the overlay network.

Figure 17.1 illustrates the relation of Peer-to-Peer applications, search mechanisms, and overlay networks in a systems view. The overlay network builds on top of the network infrastructure that provides end-to-end connectivity between peers. It is usually designed such as to support the Peer-to-Peer search middleware which hides the distributed nature of object lookup and search from the Peer-to-Peer application. While search is a fundamental part of most Peer-to-Peer systems, further middleware functionality is, depending on the application, also required, like distributed accounting, reputation building, or group management. This other functionality can either build on the same overlay network constructed for search, or it can create and use its own, possibly better-suited overlay structure. Examples of such additional, beyond lookup functionality with specific overlay needs include application-level multicast [107] or fault resilient routing like RON (Resilient Overlay Network, [26]). This implies that several overlay structures may coexist in

R. Steinmetz and K. Wehrle (Eds.): P2P Systems and Applications, LNCS 3485, pp. 269-288, 2005.

the same Peer-to-Peer system, each serving a different purpose. Examples of current search overlay networks are given in the following section.

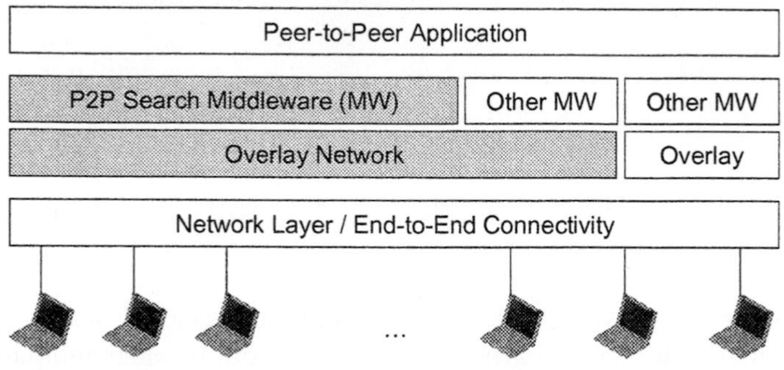

Fig. 17.1: Peer-to-Peer Networks – Systems View and Layering

17.1.1 Problem Statement and Chapter Overview

The move toward large and completely decentralized Peer-to-Peer systems, handling millions of active nodes, imposes huge challenges on distributed search and overlay request routing. Many efforts have been undertaken to design and built middleware that overcomes the hurdles of decentralization, to construct suitable overlay networks, and to design Peer-to-Peer lookup and routing systems. However, a complete and clear structure including the delineation of these particular important and advanced designs is yet missing as well as a formalized comparative evaluation, except on an interesting example-driven basis [536], [52], and [276]. Furthermore, there is no clear statement as to which groups of design will show a viable approach in very large networks. Thus, this chapter and additionally [419] provide answers on how to (1) lay out the problem space for single-identifier lookup in Peer-to-Peer networks, (2) define a formal mathematical framework for scalability, and (3) to develop a highly advanced scheme – termed SHARK – for achieving good scalability in these cases.

17.1.2 Search and Lookup – Functional Options

In much of the literature today, "search" refers to a wide range of operations on values stored in the network. This may encompass uni- or multidimensional search, full-text search, or aggregate operations. In contrast, "lookup" refers to finding the node hosting data for a particular identifier. For this work, the canonical search process has been broken into different phases, where necessary steps and possible short-cuts have been identified. Figure 17.2(a) shows the process from *keywords* over *names* and *addresses* to the *path to target node* hosting the desired resources. Of course, for retrieving a document additional techniques may be applied, such as multiple keyword search or approximate keyword search, however, the full set of information retrieval techniques are limited in this section to Peer-to-Peer search and lookup.

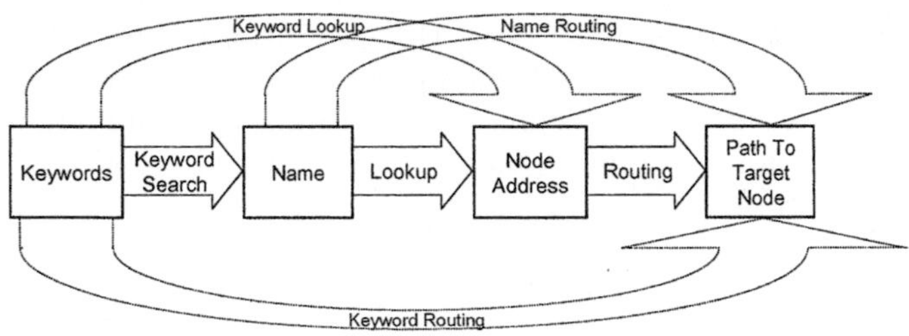

(a) Search in Distributed Systems

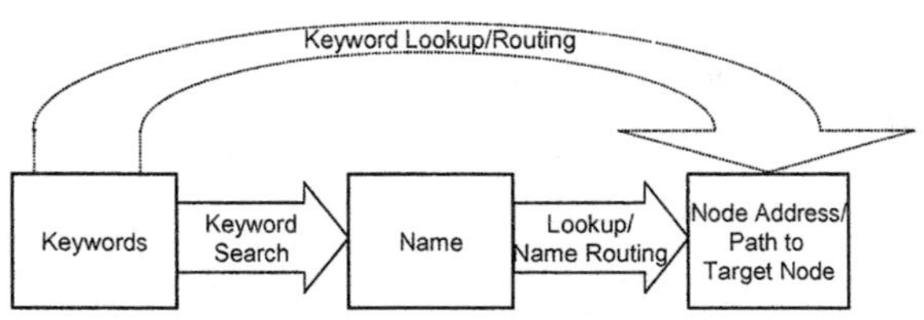

(b) Search in Peer-to-Peer Systems

Fig. 17.2: Search in (a) Distributed and (b) Peer-to-Peer Systems

Usually, a user wants to specify what he is looking for in terms of *keywords*. In the simplest case, keywords are just one or more terms appearing in the desired content or describing the desired resource. More sophisticated approaches apply content/resource meta information based on attribute-value pairs, *e.g.*, the Resource Description Framework (RDF, [462]). *Keyword search* describes the functionality of mapping the resource meta information onto one, or, in the case of multiple matching resources, several unique *names* or identifiers in the network. Examples of such names are the Uniform Resource Locator, URL, or file names in a Unix file system. *Lookup* maps unique names onto *addresses* in the network. Addresses specify the network location of the node hosting the resource with a given name, *e.g.*, the IP address of the host. Finally, *routing* is the process of finding a *path* and moving queries to the *target node.*

Three short-cut mechanisms can help optimize search. *Name routing* combines the (distributed) lookup of the target node address with path identification and query forwarding to that node. *Keyword lookup* returns one or more addresses of nodes hosting resources with given keyword descriptions. Napster is the most prominent example. Finally, *keyword routing* directly routes towards a node hosting specified resources. Keyword routing is sometimes also called *semantic routing* or *content routing.* For the Peer-to-Peer case, the process can be simplified as shown in Figure 17.2(b). Since Peer-to-Peer systems build on overlay networks, routing becomes a trivial task: knowing the target node address, the requestor simply creates a new virtual link to that address. Only few circumstances (like the anonymity requirement in Freenet [122]) lead to a more difficult overlay routing approach, which is an issue separate from search.

17.1.3 Design Space

Based on those initial discussions, the focus for this chapter is drawn on scalable keyword lookup for a single keyword. With the search process defined and disaggregated, it becomes obvious that searching requires a series of mappings, from the keyword space to the name space to the address space to the space of paths to nodes. The fundamental structural options in a distributed environment are the same for each mapping, and a complete classification and in our definition optimum design space is provided in Figure 17.3. The criteria of mutually exclusive and collectively exhaustive branches at each level have directly been built into the classification

A mapping can only be defined through a *computation* or a *table.* A (predefined) computation is difficult to achieve but some attempts have been made, usually involving hashing. More widely adopted are *tables* with (updatable) entries for the desired search items, *e.g.*, a node address for each valid name. Mapping then comes down to finding the desired table entry and looking up the associated value. In a distributed environment, a table can either reside on a *central* entity like a search engine server, or be fully *replicated* on each node, or be *distributed* among the nodes.

Distributed tables are most interesting and challenging in that they require for each mapping to collaboratively find and contact the node that offers the desired information or table entry. Two important aspects distinguish distributed table approaches: the *structure of the table, i.e.* the distribution of table entries to nodes, and the physical or overlay *topology* of the network. The distribution of table entries can happen at random or in a well-designed

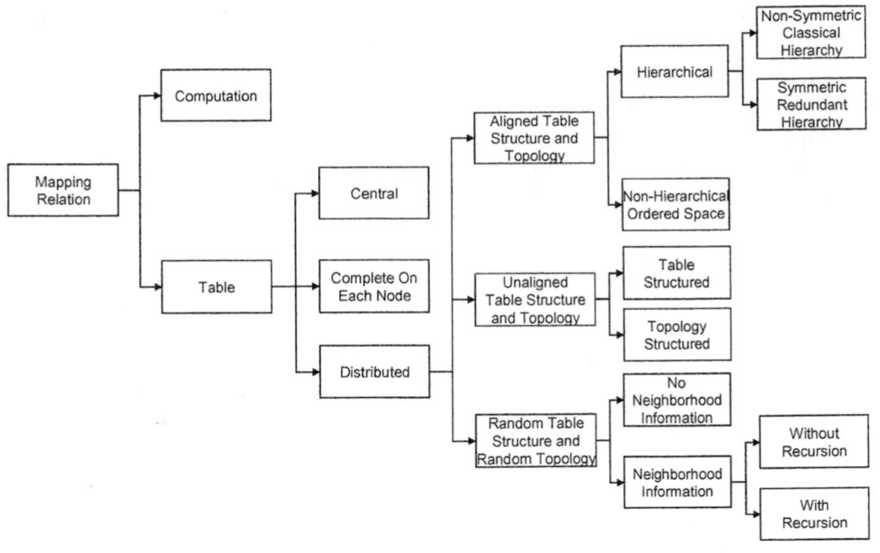

Fig. 17.3: Design Space for Mapping Relations in Distributed Systems

process leading to a clear target table structure; the same applies for the distribution of links and, hence, the topology. Whether the table structure and topology are designed and aligned, or both random or at least one of them designed but not aligned with the other has a substantial implication on search.

In a *random table structure and random topology*, it is natural that each node at least carries information about itself, *i.e.* its address, the names of the objects it hosts, and corresponding keyword descriptions. In addition to information on their own tables, nodes may have knowledge on the table entries of their *neighbors* in an aggregated or non-aggregated form. The knowledge on neighboring table entries will in some cases be restricted to the direct neighbors, but can also involve *recursion*: An arbitrary node A not only learns about the table entries of its neighbors B_i, but also through B_i about B_i 's neighbors C_{ij}, C_{ij} 's neighbors D_{ijk}, and so on. This way, nodes eventually know about most or even all keywords, names, or addresses in the direction of each neighbor in a usually aggregated way.

Rather than keeping explicit knowledge on neighboring table entries, nodes can exploit *implicit knowledge* when the table distribution and topology follow a clear and *aligned structure* that every node knows. The most common approach is certainly the *classical hierarchy*. A root node informs about table areas represented by a number of second-level nodes. The second-level nodes, in turn, delegate to third-level nodes for sub-areas within their own area, and so on, until a request finally reaches the leaf node responsible for the desired entry. Particularly in the quest for scalable Peer-to-Peer search algorithms, "symmetric hierarchies" have been created by adding redundancy. In *symmetric redundant hierarchies*, every node can act as the root or be on any other level of the hierarchy. This can be achieved by replicating root information on table areas on each node as well as second-level information on sub-areas. Symmetric redundant hierarchies show structural similarities to k-ary n-cubes (cf. [535]).

Non-hierarchical structures are also possible and available. In an *ordered space*, the table is split into consecutive areas. Each of the areas is represented on one node. The nodes, in turn, are ordered in the same way, *i.e.* neighboring table areas reside on neighboring nodes. Examples of such spaces are rings or Euclidean spaces, but other forms are possible.

Unaligned table structures and topologies occur when the table is distributed according to a clear structure, but the topology is random, or the topology is designed, but the table structure random, or both table and topology are clearly structured, but in different ways. While the first case is helpful to allow for aggregation of table area information, the second case is advantageous for performance improvements compared to a completely random approach. It appears difficult to gain from the third case.

Designs based on any kind of structured table regardless of the topology are often referred to as *Distributed Hash Tables (DHT)*.

17.1.4 Overlay Topology Requirements

Peer-to-Peer systems of all kinds build on overlay networks. Nodes in Peer-to-Peer networks are required to have physical, link layer and network layer connectivity. For instance, in TCP/IP, every node is connected to the global Internet. It is, however, possible to contact every node via the corresponding network layer protocol in other networks as well, like X.25, or Novell IPX. In fact, it is sufficient to have a transport service that allows every node to send data to every other node. Theoretically, it would, *e.g.*, even be possible to use the Short Message Service (SMS) in GSM (Global System for Mobile Communications) or UMTS (Universal Mobile Telecommunications System) to build an overlay network of mobile nodes, provided appropriate software can be installed on the mobile devices.

The assumption of network layer connectivity allows Peer-to-Peer networks to abstract from the underlying networking infrastructure and its complexities and form an overlay network among themselves, which is discussed elsewhere in this book.

17.1.5 Overlay Topology Parameters

In general, network topologies can be characterized through their degree of symmetry, the network diameter, the bisection width, the average node degree, and the average wire length [313]. The functional and performance requirements determine the desired target characteristics:

- **Symmetry**
  Only symmetric topologies are appropriate for true Peer-to-Peer systems as only in this case all peers are equal from a topology point of view, thus forming the term symmetry with respect to peers' behavior. Consider a non-symmetric topology like the classic tree: It is obvious that the root of the tree has a far more central role than all leaves. At the same time, symmetry assists load-balancing. While, in non-symmetric networks, hot spots with high traffic load (the root in the tree) may exist, the load will balance over available connections in a symmetric network. Examples of symmetric topologies include rings, buses, hyper-cubes, complete meshes, cube-connected circles, or k-ary n-cubes. While symmetry appears to be one of the most basic requirements for a Peer-to-Peer topology, measurements as stated in [535] prove a huge heterogeneity among peer nodes in terms of their uptime, average session duration, bottleneck bandwidth, latency, and the number of services or files offered. Thus, it can make sense to explicitly design asymmetric overlay networks, where some peers adopt a server-like role.
- **Network Diameter (D)**
  The diameter of a network is defined by the number of hops required to connect from one peer to the most remote peer. It strongly influences latency and aggregate bandwidth for communication. In this context, hops in the overlay network have to be counted; actual hops in the underlying networking infrastructure will indirectly be considered through the wire length (cf. below). The average rather than the maximum number of hops between any two nodes in the overlay network is called *characteristic path-length* PL_{Ch} [462].
- **Bisection Width (β)**
  The number of connections from one part of the overlay network to the other part defines its bisection width. Assuming proper load balancing (which can be ensured through symmetry, at least partly), the maximum throughput of the network is proportional to the bisection width (and the average bandwidth of a connection). Even more importantly, there is a direct relation between bisection width and fault tolerance: the bisection width determines the number of links that have to break before the system goes down or, at least, operates only as two partial systems.
- **Node Degree (d)**
  The node degree is defined as the number of overlay links that each peer has to maintain. While a node degree higher than one is desirable for improved

fault tolerance of the network from the perspective of a single peer, the node degree can be a significant inhibitor for scalability: The node degree determines the size of the routing table on each peer with the according impact on memory consumption and processing power.

- **Wire Length** ($\bar{\tau}$)
  The wire length is the average round trip delay of an overlay link, contributing to the latency in the system. The wire length is closely related to mapping an overlay network properly onto a physical network: A low wire length in a Peer-to-Peer overlay network can be achieved by choosing neighbors that are also neighbors or at least physically and topologically close in the underlying network. Closely related to wire length is the notion of stretch: The *stretch* of a path in an overlay network is the ratio of total physical network hops underlying the overlay path that separates two peers to the minimum number of physical network hops between the two when routing is not confined to the overlay network.

17.2 Scalability in Peer-to-Peer Systems

Scalability determines a key metric of distributed systems to describe in which sense this system is able to cope with many occurrences of an event. Thus, the mathematical model and formal definition of scalability is given for the non-Peer-to-Peer world and refined for Peer-to-Peer specifics in order to derive Peer-to-Peer-relevant metrics for scalability and efficiency in all relevant dimensions of scale.

Strict scalability of a system demands that its efficiency asymptotically remain constant as the system grows to large (or infinite) scale [313]. Production systems, for instance, often exhibit significant economies of scale, where efficiency even increases with scale, whereas communication systems tend to demonstrate disadvantages of scale due to the communication overhead involved. Therefore, most Peer-to-Peer systems are unlikely to be strictly scalable. It is thus sensible to introduce a more pragmatic definition and apply it throughout this thesis. *Scalability* is the asymptotic ratio of a system's efficiency to the efficiency of an idealized reference system. Assuming an efficiency of 1 for the reference, this is equal to the asymptotic efficiency behavior of the system. In contrast to scalability, *extensibility* refers to the possibility to grow a system step by step. That means, growing scale can be accommodated for through incremental addition of resources. This avoids the necessity to build a large system right in the beginning, dimensioned to cope with the ultimately expected scale.

It is important to understand that while Peer-to-Peer systems are usually highly extensible – with resources automatically being added along with joining peers – reasonable scalability properties are not ensured. For instance, the Gnutella network can grow simply by new nodes installing the servent and contacting an arbitrary peer in the system, but query traffic can eventually lead to a collapse. In order to quantitatively assess the above measures, it is necessary to define suitable metrics, which determine a standard of measurement that can be applied to a corresponding dimension. This metric quantifies a dimension in that it associates each pair of elements of that dimension with a number or parameter reflecting the distance of these members along that dimension. The metric also defines the unit to measure the distance in.

17.2.1 Definition of Peer-to-Peer Scalability

Before providing a mathematical notation of scalability in a Peer-to-Peer context, this section introduces the notions of resources, efficiency, and scale that the scalability definition directly or indirectly builds upon. *Resources* are the replenishable goods used to perform a certain task or produce a certain product. Replenishable resources of a Peer-to-Peer system are processing power, memory/storage, bandwidth, time/latency. For efficiency and scalability considerations, consumption of these resources has to be separated into productive resource consumption and overhead resource consumption. Productive resource consumption of a Peer-to-Peer system is defined by reference to an idealized, overhead-free system that does not incur any distribution overhead:

- *Processing power*
  Productive is the processing power required on a single processor machine to perform a computation, where the result of the computation should be desired by the service user, otherwise it would be overhead. In Peer-to-Peer, a significant proportion of the processing power might be used for overhead like synchronization and routing in the distributed environment. Processing power is measured in terms of the number of operations on a reference processing unit.
- *Memory/storage*
  Productive is the memory needed for intermediate computation results or content or application storage as demonstrated in a non-distributed environment. In Peer-to-Peer, storage of, *e.g.*, routing tables on a peer node may constitute to the system overhead. Memory/storage is measured in KByte.
- *Bandwidth*
  The bandwidth needed to transmit the desired results of a service, *i.e.*, computation results or content, is productive. There may be communication overhead for discovering other peers, for instance. Bandwidth is measured in KBit per second (Kbit/s).
- *Time/latency*
  Particularly from a service user perspective, time is an important good and waiting times or latency can not only be annoying but also lead to

system malfunctions. Significant latency can result from several hops onto different peer nodes. No latency is productive, all is overhead. Latency is measured in milliseconds (ms).

All resource consumption of a Peer-to-Peer system that is not defined as productive above is considered overhead. More specifically, the overhead comprises all protocols and functionality of the distributed architecture that are necessary to operate the system and to give it certain properties. In a mathematical notation, total resource consumption can be represented by a vector

$$\vec{p}_{tot} = \vec{p}_{prod} + \vec{p}_{OH}; \qquad \vec{p} = \begin{bmatrix} \text{ProcessingPower} \\ \text{Memory} \\ \text{Bandwidth} \\ \text{Latency} \end{bmatrix}$$

including straightforward notations for total (tot), productive (prod), and overhead (OH) resources. Note that resource consumption is a function of scale $\vec{\sigma}$, where the elements of the scale vector denote those different dimensions of scale.

17.2.2 Efficiency and Scale

Efficiency and Scale Efficiency is the ratio of productive resource consumption and total resource consumption. It describes the level of optimization of an approach to perform a task or produce a product with respect to its resource consumption. An efficiency of 1 indicates a perfect approach in that it does not incur any overhead resource consumption. Due to the multi-dimensionality of the resource vector, the ratio of productive to total resource consumption has to be represented as a multiplicative equation:

$$\vec{p}_{prod} = \varepsilon \cdot \vec{p}_{tot}; \qquad \varepsilon = Diag \begin{bmatrix} \text{ProcessingPowerEfficiency} \\ \text{MemoryEfficiency} \\ \text{BandwidthEfficiency} \\ \text{LatencyEfficiency} \end{bmatrix},$$

where Diag() creates a diagonal matrix from a vector, *i.e.*, a matrix with all zeroes except for the diagonal elements. Like the resource consumption, the efficiency heavily depends on the scale $\vec{\sigma}$.

Scale is the size and frequency of tasks or the system performing the tasks along possibly multiple dimensions. In light of the variety of possible dimensions scale can refer to, it is necessary to identify a set of requirements that a proper choice of scale dimensions should fulfill. With an eye to scalability, suitable *scale metrics* have to be mutually exclusive, collectively exhaustive, and relevant:

- *Mutually exclusive:*
  Different dimensions of scale chosen must not overlap. For instance, the number of peers and the number of files per peer are mutually exclusive, whereas the total number of files in the system as a third dimension could be derived from the previous two, resulting in an overlap that is to be avoided.
- *Collectively exhaustive:*
  The set of dimensions chosen has to describe all aspects in terms of size of the system that matter. For instance, the number of peers alone are not sufficient to derive storage requirements for all objects in the system.
- *Relevant:*
  The term "that matter" above already indicates that only those dimensions are to be introduced that are relevant for the specific consideration. For scalability research in particular, in order to be relevant, the selected dimensions have to be (a) *key drivers of efficiency* of the system in consideration: As scalability is defined through the efficiency depending on scale, only scale dimensions that actually have an influence on efficiency are relevant; and (b) *subject to growth*: Only those dimensions that are expected to grow are obviously interesting for scalability. While the number of peers in a system is usually growing, this may, *e.g.*, not be the case in a specific closed-group scenario.

In the sense of the definition of scale above, a task in a Peer-to-Peer system could be, *e.g.*, a file download, a computation, or any combination of these or other simple tasks. The number and the average size of tasks obviously constitute the most high-level scale dimensions for a Peer-to-Peer system. A multiplicative disaggregation automatically ensures that the set of dimensions is mutually exclusive and collectively exhaustive. This yields:

- The size of a task as its productive resource consumption in terms of processing power, memory/storage, and bandwidth.
- The number of tasks that can be disaggregated into the multiplicative components: (a) number of potential peers; (b) average percentage of peer nodes active, *i.e.*, online and responding to Peer-to-Peer messages; (c) average number of objects per peer, *e.g.*, number of services or content files or information items; (d) request frequency, *i.e.*, number of tasks per online peer node, object, and unit of time.

The most important dimensions are the number of peer nodes and the number of objects, as they are set for the fastest growth. While these scale dimensions probably cover most aspects of efficiency, some of the overhead functionality might have additional scale dimensions as key drivers for resource consumption. Even though a detailed evaluation is only possible for a concrete system, one can hypothetically expect a couple of scale dimensions in addition to the ones above. The scale vector can now be defined as

$$\vec{\sigma} = \begin{bmatrix} \text{\#\_peerrs} \\ \text{\%\_online} \\ \text{objects\_per\_peer} \\ \text{task\_frequency} \\ \text{processing\_size\_of\_task} \\ \text{memory\_size\_of\_task} \\ \text{bandwidth\_size\_of\_task} \\ \ldots \end{bmatrix},$$

where these dots symbolize additional scale dimensions that may be required for specific systems.

In summary, mechanisms for managing the (resources of the) Peer-to-Peer network include the Peer-to-Peer overlay network management, driven by the rate of joins to and departures from overlay Peer-to-Peer network, and a QoS control. Mechanisms for offering and retrieving services in a distributed environment address (a) a service description and classification driven by the variety and complexity of services, (b) lookup and search driven by users' total queries per successful query/task, (c) pricing, indexing, and advertising, (d) negotiations and the percentage of negotiated tasks, and (e) contracting driven by the percentage contracts per task. Mechanisms for fulfilling a service cover accounting and charging and invoicing, a.o. driven by the number of clearing or payment authorities. The set of organizational and self-learning mechanisms for peers includes the building and maintenance of peer groups, affected by the diversity of interests of peers, and the reputation of peers, effect by the frequency of reputation updates. Finally, security mechanisms, such as the identification, authentication, authorization, encryption, and decryption, are driven by the percentage of tasks requiring the respective security mechanism.

17.2.3 Scalability Metric and Notation

Building on these notations for scale and efficiency, scalability can now be captured mathematically. Strict scalability, the asymptotically constant efficiency requirement, can be translated into

$$\varepsilon = \varepsilon\left(\vec{\sigma}'\right) \rightarrow const; \vec{\ } \sigma \quad = \infty$$

where ' denotes the matrix/vector transposition. For the non-strict scalability definition, the scalability matrix Σ is defined by

$$\varepsilon_{\text{System}}\left(\vec{\sigma}'\right) = \sum\left(\vec{\sigma}'\right) \cdot \varepsilon_{\text{Reference}}\left(\vec{\sigma}'\right)$$

where the scalability matrix is required to be diagonal. The structure of the matrix is:

$$\sum = \begin{bmatrix} \Sigma_1(\sigma_1, \sigma_2, ...) & 0 & 0 & 0 \\ 0 & \Sigma_2(\sigma_1, \sigma_2, ...) & 0 & 0 \\ 0 & 0 & \Sigma_3(\sigma_1, \sigma_2, ...) & 0 \\ 0 & 0 & 0 & \Sigma_4(\sigma_1, \sigma_2, ...) \end{bmatrix}$$

All elements of the diagonal refer to the corresponding resource in the efficiency matrix, *i.e.*, Σ_1 is the processing-power scalability, Σ_2 is the memory scalability, Σ_3 is the bandwidth scalability, Σ_4 is the latency scalability. Each of these scalability metrics depends on all or a subset of the scale dimensions $\sigma_i, i = 1, 2, ...$

17.3 An Assessment Scheme for Peer-to-Peer Lookup and Search Overlay Network Scalability

The scalability evaluation can be simplified. Rather than by determining the efficiency as a function of scale and then deriving the scalability matrix as defined above, it is possible to investigate scalability by only calculating the overhead for a certain functionality as a function of scale and determining its behavior in a growing system. This allows a straightforward assessment whether or not the overhead grows out of bounds. Furthermore, it does not preclude a more formal determination of percentage efficiency values as described above as a subsequent step.

Usually, a logarithmic increase of overhead resource consumption with scale is regarded as the maximum tolerable. Care is due, though: even a linear increase may be alright if the absolute amount of overhead at maximum expected system size is still low, and, vice versa, even logarithmic or sub-logarithmic increase may be fatal when the starting value is already very close to bearable limits. For illustration, Table 1 gives an idea of expected system sizes and most important resource constraints for different Peer-to-Peer applications.

This section focuses on overhead for lookup and search – for two reasons. First, lookup and search with their complex n-to-n relationship of peers appear most vulnerable to network growth, with the number of nodes that possibly need to get involved growing linearly in n and the number of possible peer relationships even growing with the factorial of n. Second, the assessment scheme may be applied to other schemes and algorithms to allow for an objective comparison.

System	Expected Scale (# Peers)	Resource Constraints
File Sharing Peer-to-Peer Trading	10,000,000	Bandwidth: 56 ... 2,000 Kbit/s Latency: < 7 s
Corporate Backup System	30,000	Storage: 1 ... 10 GB Processing Power: 5% of 1-2 GHz
Peer-to-Peer Special Interest News	1,000	Bandwidth: 56 ... 2,000 Kbit/s Latency: < 7 s
Mobile Collaboration Groupware	50	Bandwidth: 9.6 ... 384 Kbit/s

Table 17.1: Peer-to-Peer System Sizes and Resource Constraints (Illustrative)

17.3.1 Overhead for Lookup and Search

The overhead resource consumption for lookup and search is a function of scale

$$\vec{p}_{OH,\text{search}}\left(\vec{\sigma}'\right) = \vec{p}_{OH}(\text{task\_size}, \text{task\_freq}, \text{queries\_per\_task}, \#\_\text{peers}, \%\_\text{online}, \text{objects\_per\_peer})$$

applying the scale vector defined in Section 17.2.1 and the additional dimension queries_per_task that was identified as being relevant for search task_size stands for bandwidth/memory/processing_size_of_task, respectively.

This expression can be simplified. First of all, task_size is only relevant for productive resource consumption to accomplish tasks, not for overhead. Second, #_peers and %_online will only appear in product form, so it is possible to aggregate. Similarly, it is possible to aggregate the query frequency: query_freq = task_freq · queries_per_task. Finally, search functionality can be separated into query (routing and processing) and overlay network management. The query overhead will be directly proportional to query_freq, while the overlay network management will be independent of it. Abbreviating

$$|o| = \text{objects\_per\_peer}$$

yields

$$\vec{p}_{\text{OH,search}}\left(\vec{\sigma}'\right) = \vec{p}_{\text{query}}\left(n, |o|\right) \cdot \text{query\_freq} + \vec{p}_{\text{OVLmgmt}}\left(n, |o|\right)$$

17.3.2 Dimensions of Lookup and Search Overhead and Quantitative Drivers

Resource consumption comprises the dimensions bandwidth, latency, processing power, and memory/storage. The most crucial scalability dimensions are the ones that refer to the most critical resources. More specifically, the scalability consideration should be focused on the resources that the system runs out of first or that are most expensive. As current utilization of processing power on PCs is usually around 4% [90], and storage is getting cheaper and cheaper, the most critical resources in a Peer-to-Peer system are most likely bandwidth and latency. Bandwidth is particularly scarce as many 'last hop' rather than backbone connections are involved in a Peer-to-Peer network. The following paragraphs will take a closer look at the drivers of bandwidth and latency overhead for queries before giving some intuition on memory and processing power overhead for queries as well as on overlay network management overhead in general.

The *request path-length* PLR is the number of hops that a lookup or search request makes on a Peer-to-Peer overlay network. Depending on the context, it may be a random variable or denote an average.

The *pruning factor* $f_p = PL_R/PL_{CH}$ denotes the average percentage of the characteristic path-length that a request needs to travel before being pruned off. The pruning factor can be calculated from the pruning probability at each hop $p_{p,i}$ (*i.e.*, the probability that the requested object is found at that hop) through

$$fp = \frac{1}{PL_{CH}} \sum_{i=1}^{PL_{CH}} i \cdot \prod_{k=0}^{i-1} (1 - p_p, k); i, k \in \aleph$$

The pruning probability $p_{p,0}$ at node 0, the requesting node, will usually be zero.

The *latency* L for a query is driven by the characteristic path-length PL_{Ch} and the wire length $\bar{\tau}$ as well as the pruning factor f_p:

$$L = PL_R \cdot \bar{\tau} = PL_{Ch} \cdot f_p \cdot \bar{\tau}$$

Routing efficiency ε_{route} is defined as

$$\varepsilon_{\text{route}} = \frac{d - x}{d - 1},$$

where x denotes the number of nodes that a query is forwarded to at any hop. The routing efficiency is defined to be 1 if only one node has to be contacted at each hop and 0 if all d neighbors have to be contacted. In that sense, Gnutella with its flooding approach has a routing efficiency of 0, whereas consistent hashing algorithms like Chord [575] have a routing efficiency of 1.

With the aggregate number of messages sent in the network to resolve a query, m_{agg} and the average size of a query message message_size, the aggregate data transmission B becomes = message_size · $\mathrm{m_a}$. Further analysis yields:

$$B = \text{message\_size} \cdot E\left[\sum_{i=1}^{PL_R} \prod_{k=1}^{i} \left[d - \varepsilon_{\text{route,i}}\,(d-1)\right]\right]$$

, where E[.] yields the expected value in case the request path-length PL_R, the node degree d, and/or the routing efficiency are random variables.

As for the latency, the characteristic path-length and the pruning probability influence the bandwidth overhead (and scalability) in a major way, bearing in mind $PL_R = PL_{Ch} \cdot f$. Furthermore, the routing efficiency plays a significant role. It is also obvious that the packet size should be kept as small as possible. The equation further suggests that the node degree be kept low. However, this applies only if the routing efficiency is smaller than 1. And even then, a lower node degree entails a larger characteristic path-length with its negative influence on aggregate bandwidth. Note that a higher node degree also increases in principle the bandwidth available as it augments the number of links from or to a node. However, these links are only virtual links in the overlay network that all have to be mapped onto one and the same physical access line of a node.

Memory overhead for search is mainly driven by the state information to be kept on each node. In particular, this is the size of the routing table, determined by the node degree d, as well as any other state information like object links to objects on remote nodes. Processing power is mostly consumed for query routing. Hence, the routing table size and thus the node degree should be kept low to keep processing overhead in bounds. The frequency of messages to be routed will automatically be optimized when attempting to reduce the number of aggregate messages m_{agg}.

The overlay network management overhead is too system-specific to be properly addressed in this general section. It comprises all tasks to create and maintain overlay network links and routing tables. In random networks like Gnutella, *e.g.*, it is limited to ping and pong messages only, whereas it becomes more complicated in structured networks like Chord. Typical tasks then include the insertion of new nodes and new object links into the overlay. As for queries, the path-length and the aggregate number of messages for these insertion events have to be evaluated.

17.3.3 The Assessment Scheme

17.2 develops the scheme to assess the scalability of a Peer-to-Peer lookup or a search mechanism. It starts from the most generic or aggregate components or contributors to overhead resource consumption on the left hand side and

Component	Resource	Disaggregation 1	Disaggregation 2	Disagg. 3	Unit	Dependence
p_{query}					n/a	f(n)
	Latency				s	f(n)
			$\bar{\tau}$		s or link layer hops	f(1)
	Latency / Bandwidth		PL_R		hops	f(n)
				PL_{Ch}	hops	f(n)
				f_p	%	f(1)
	Bandwidth				Byte	f(n)
		m_{agg}	(PL_R)		(see PL_R)	(see PL_R)
			ε_{route}		%	f(1)
			d		1	f(n)
		message_size			Byte	f(1)
	Processing Power,	Message frequency	(m_{agg})		(see m_{agg})	(see m_{agg})
	Memory/ Storage	State Information	(d)		(see d)	(see d)
query_freq					s^{-1}	$f(n, \vert o \vert)$
$p_{OVLmgmt}$					n/a	n/a
	Cost of node insertion				n/a	f(n)
	Cost of object insertion				n/a	$f(n, \vert o \vert)$
	other				n/a	n/a

Table 17.2: Scalability Assessment Scheme for Peer-to-Peer Lookup and Search

analyzes the types of resources affected. It then breaks overhead resource consumption down into more specific or granular drivers or metrics on the right hand side in three levels (Disaggregation 1-3), applying the formulae derived throughout this section. For each metric, it shows the respective unit of measurement as well as its expected primary dependence on scale, which in most cases is a function of the number of nodes ($f(n)$) or the number of objects per node ($f(|o|)$). When evaluating the scalability of a lookup or search system, the alternative levels of granularity yield equivalent information and can be chosen at the evaluator's discretion.

17.4 Scalable Search with SHARK

Having outlined the key concepts on search and lookup in overlay networks and having defined the model for a formal Peer-to-Peer scalability approach, a particular scheme termed "SHARK" (Symmetric Hierarchy Adaption for Routing of Keywords) is developed. This novel concept and middleware is scalable and offers a service for search in Peer-to-Peer networks [417, 418] and is discussed in the light of the formal model presented. Rather than flooding a network like Gnutella or imposing numerical IDs on objects like distributed hash tables, it is based on directed routing of keywords in a multidimensional redundant meta-data hierarchy. SHARK autonomously arranges nodes and objects in the network and in semantic clusters. In spite of its rich keyword search capabilities, it achieves a high degree of scalability, outperforming random networks by several orders of magnitude. It can easily be adopted for applications as diverse as file-sharing, Peer-to-Peer trading, or distributed expert and knowledge market places.

A Peer-to-Peer network consists of a set of *nodes* N being connected via a set of *links*. Each neighboring node stores a set of *objects* which constitute to the unique objects in the Peer-to-Peer network. An object is described through *meta-data* M, which determine the essential hierarchical structure for the construction and operation of SHARK. *I.e.*, this example addresses music categorization. The meta-data M^{11} yields the top-level music genre that is further divided into subgenres M^{21}. In a second dimension M^{12}, music is classified by decade of release, then by more granular timing M^{22}. M^0 is the search string, *e.g.*, 'John Patton: Let 'em roll'. In general, applications may choose to add dimensionality just for certain categories, *e.g.*, add an 'instrumentation' dimension to 'rock&roll' in addition to subgenres and timing. Search for objects in SHARK is based on query routing. A *query* is defined through a meta-data description M_q of the desired object(s) and thresholds t_{struct} and t_{rand} for the minimum required similarity of object and query description for the structured and the string expression part of the meta-data description, respectively. SHARK returns a set of *query answers* including is a *similarity metric*. The development of reasonable similarity metrics is orthogonal to and, hence, not focus of this work.

SHARK arranges nodes into a multidimensional *symmetric redundant hierarchy*. The overlay topology exactly matches the structure of the query meta-data such as to exploit the alignment for query routing. Figure 17.4 shows as an example a simplified description of two levels and two dimensions.

Each node is assigned to a *group-of-interest* (GoI) according to the objects it stores and to its prior request behavior. Each GoI represents a leaf in the hierarchy. Let $P^{(1)} = (p^{11}, p^{12})$ denote a position on level one of the hierarchy $P^{(2)} = (p^{11}, p^{12}, p^{21}, p^{22})$, a position on level 2. The values p^{ij} numerically represent the respective meta-data information m^{ij}. Node A in the figure would then be a member of the GoI on a leaf position $P_A = (7, 2, 2, 3)$. In contrast to a classic hierarchy, an symmetric redundant hierarchy adds redundancy so that all peers have symmetric roles in the overlay; *i.e.*, each peer can assume the role of the root of the network or be on any other level.

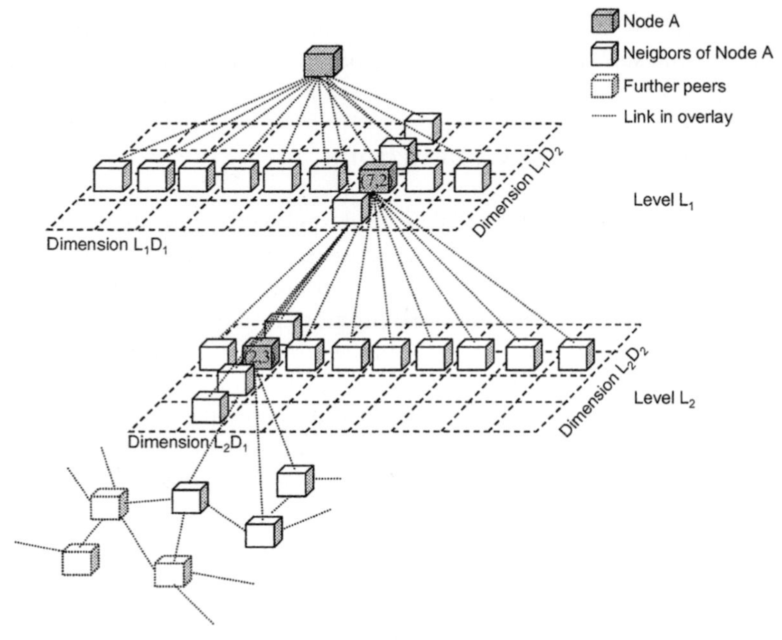

Fig. 17.4: Multi-dimensional Symmetric Redundant Hierarchy in SHARK

This improves fault tolerance and load-balancing as there is no single node acting as a root, and waives the necessity of central infrastructure, hence removing the largest roadblocks for an adoption of hierarchical structures in Peer-to-Peer networks.

SHARK adds redundancy as follows. Each node N_A on a leaf position $P_A^{(2)} = (p_A^{11}, p_A^{12}, p_A^{21}, p_A^{22})$ also assumes partial responsibility for the parent positions $P_A^{(1)} = (p_A^{11}, p_A^{12})$, the parent's parent and so on up to the root (in the two level case, the parent's parent is identical to the root). Hence, each node is virtually replicated on every level of the hierarchy (cf. dark grey nodes in Figure 17.4). The partiality of the responsibility results from two reasons. First, many different peers share the same parent position, thus inherently distributing the load of that position among themselves. Second, a node only maintains links to a subset of the positions on the respective next lower level in the hierarchy. As indicated in the figure, those positions form the relevant level-i-subset for a node N_A that differ from position $P_A^{(i)}$ in only one dimension. We have chosen this approach to limit state information on the nodes as well as the maintenance burden when nodes join or leave the network, thus increasing scalability of the system at the cost of only one additional hop for query routing per level. Within the leaf GoIs, peers maintain links to further neighbors SN_A^R, as indicated in the figure. The overlay network at this stage is, however, unstructured or random. It has been shown that such networks exhibit a power-law distribution of links.

17.5 Summary and Conclusions

This overview on Peer-to-Peer lookup and scalability has shown that efficiency and scalability of these mechanisms can be formalized and may have impacts on existing systems. A heuristic approach to scalability evaluation currently prevails. Therefore, this work provides an analytical yet pragmatic assessment scheme that can help to formalize and standardize scalability investigations of Peer-to-Peer systems. As a newly proposed scheme SHARK has been outlined as a scalable approach of a symmetric hierarchy adaptation, which autonomously arranges nodes and objects in the network and in semantic clusters.

18. Algorithmic Aspects of Overlay Networks

Danny Raz (Technion, Israel Institute of Technology)

18.1 Background and Motivation

This chapter studies basic algorithmic tasks over overlay networks. The main idea is to explore both the communication and the computation needed to perform a task. Unlike many of the work in this area (and other chapters of the book) we mainly consider in this chapter tasks related to information gathering or dissemination, as they can be used as building blocks in many overlay applications.

Overlay networks are logical networks that are created on top of the "real" physical network. Recently, various forms of such overlay networks have been deployed in the Internet. The most popular ones are file sharing Peer-to-Peer (P2P) networks and Content Distribution Networks (CDN). As well explained in other chapters of this book, in a Peer-to-Peer network, users voluntarily contributed their computers to form an overlay network that is then used mainly for file swapping. CDNs are overlay networks that are used to distribute Web context to distribution points of context delivery service providers, aiming at bringing content closer to the end users.

While the specific characterizations of these networks (and other overlay networks) vary, the main features are similar. In overlay networks we are dealing with two layers: a fast underlying network layer, and a much slower application layer. In this application layer, arbitrary complex computations (mostly related to data) are being done. In such an environment it is no longer true that the inter-node computations are fast with respect to the communication delay.

In order to study the algorithmic aspects of such networks one has to consider both the propagation delay through the network, and the computation delay at the overlay nodes. The well known distributed models [37] assume in many cases a global bound on the propagation delay and on the computation delay, in order to bound the overall time complexity, and therefore we need to adopt a different model in our case. The two-layer structure described above is very similar to the situation in an Active Network Node [587], and thus we can adopt the model from [507], based on a similar model for high speed networks [121].

In this model, the underlying networking layer handles packets with minimal delay and thus we assume a fixed constant C units of delay per packet, which includes the propagation delay along the link. In the upper layer, more complex computation is done and thus the time complexity depends on the

R. Steinmetz and K. Wehrle (Eds.): P2P Systems and Applications, LNCS 3485, pp. 289-321, 2005.

exact algorithm and the size of the data. We denote this complexity by $P(k)$, where k is the size of the input to the computation. In this chapter we follow [507] and assume that $P(k) = P \times k$ for some constant P, since we at least need to copy all the data from the fast layer to the computation layer.

Recall that a link in the overlay network is a virtual link and it may be a long path in the underlying network. Figure 18.1 depicts such a network. The big circles represent overlay nodes and the wide dotted lines represent links between nodes in the overlay network. The translation of overlay links to physical links depends on the routing in the underlying (IP) network. For example a packet going from node C to node D may be routed through node E, even though E is not connected to C in the overlay network.

There are two different methods in which overlay networks can handle routing. In the first one, the overlay network takes care of routing, and thus packets are forwarded by the overlay layer to the appropriate virtual neighbor. For example, if node C needs to send a message to node G, it may route it through node B, thus the actual packet may travel more than once over several links of the underlying networks. The second routing method uses the underlying routing, i.e., if node C needs to send a message to node G, it will get its actual address (say IP address) and will send the message directly to this address. The actual performance of the algorithms depends, of course, on the routing methods, and we will carry out the analysis for each of the methods.

Now, under this model, the time complexity (i.e. the time it takes to complete the task) of data collection is no longer just a function of the length of the paths along which the data is collected. In fact, this time complexity also depends on the number of overlay network nodes in which the data is processed, and on the complexity of the processing algorithm itself.

In particular, it is no longer true that the popular solution of collecting data along a spanning tree as described in [37] is optimal. Consider for ex-

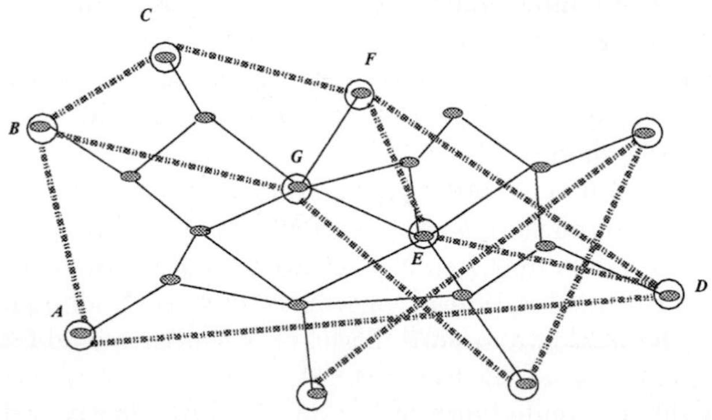

Fig. 18.1: An Example of an Overlay Network.

ample the tree described in Figure 18.2. Since the amount of information passed along each of the nodes on the long path is $O(n)$, the overall time complexity is $\Omega(Pn^2)$. Another naive solution for this problem is to iteratively query each node in the network, however, this solution will require that (for the same tree) n separate messages will arrive to the root, and an overall $\Omega(n^2)$ messages if the overlay network takes care of the routing. The goal is to develop algorithms that will have both a linear time and message complexity.

We start with a simpler problem, where data is collected along a given path in the overlay network. We study different simple algorithms for this case (similar to the one presented in [507] for the active networking case) and analyze their performance in the two overlay routing methods. Then we turn to the algorithm, called *collect-rec* in [507], that uses recursion to collect data. When the algorithm collects data from a path, it partitions the path into two segments, and runs recursively on each segment. The data collected from the second segment is sent to the first node in the path. The complexity analysis of this algorithm shows that the algorithm *time complexity* is $O(nP + nC)$ and the *message complexity* is $O(nlog(n))$ in the first routing method, as in the active networking case. If routing in the overlay network is done using the second method then the algorithm *time complexity* is $O(nP + nd_nC)$ and the *message complexity* can be bounded by $\min O(nd_nlog(n)), O(\bar{d}log(n))$, where d_n is the average distance (in underlying network hops) between overlay neighbors, and $\bar{d}$ is the average distance (in underlying network hops) between any two overlay nodes.

The more general problem is the problem of efficiently collecting data from a general overlay network. We are given a network with a specific node called *root*, where the number of nodes in the overlay network is n, its diameter is D, the number of logical links is m, and each node holds one unit of information. The *root* intends to collect the data from all the nodes in the overlay network. We assume that the network topology is arbitrary and no global routing information is available to the nodes. That is, a node in the overlay network may know the name (or IP address) of its logical neighbors, but no global information about the structure of the overlay network is known. Our aim is to develop an algorithm that solves the problem defined above, with minimal time and message complexity.

The need for such data collection depends on the specific network. For the popular Peer-to-Peer networks, one can think of obtaining a snapshot of the network at a given time, or finding the number of copies of a very popular file. For CDNs, obtaining usage statistics is always a need, and doing so with minimal delay and network overhead is very desirable. As shown before, the naive implementation of collecting data along a given spanning tree may perform badly. One possible approach is to extend Algorithm collect-rec([507]) from a path to a general graph. We explain this method, and generalize the data collection algorithm to an algorithm that collects an arbitrary amount

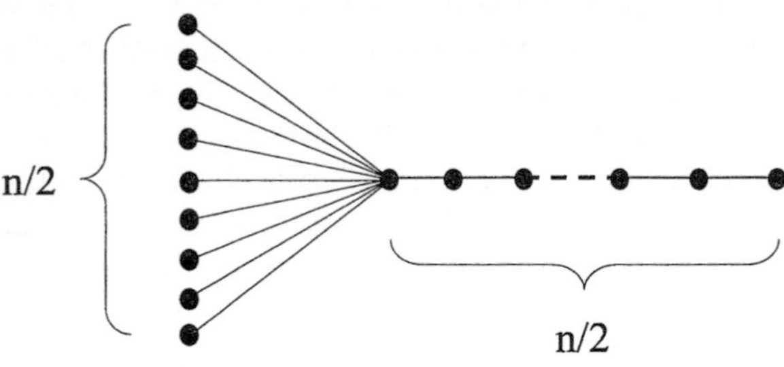

Fig. 18.2: Worst case broom.

of data from any link on a path. This last algorithm is then used as a building block in the more general algorithm that collects data in an almost optimal way from any given spanning tree.

For many overlay applications (such a CDN), assuming that the overlay network maintains a spanning tree is a very natural assumption as some information should be sent (or collected) from all the nodes. For other applications, like a Peer-to-Peer file sharing application, maintaining a global spanning tree may be too expensive since the amount of users that join (or leave) the Peer-to-Peer network each time unit is too big. Nevertheless, in all non-trivial proposals for a structural Peer-to-Peer network, maintaining such a tree requires at most a very small change to the existing infrastructure. If a spanning tree does not exist, one will have to create a spanning tree, and run the algorithm on top of it (assuming the amount of data collected is big enough). In order to create such a tree, one can use the well known algorithm, [37] in which every node that receives a message indicating the creation of the tree, sends this message to all its neighbors. The creation of such a tree in our model will take $O(CD + mP)$ time and $O(m)$ messages. This can be naturally included in the number assigning step of Algorithm collect-rec, resulting in a message complexity of $O(m + nlog(n))$ and a time complexity of $O(mP + nC)$.

The rest of the chapter is organized as follows. We start with the formal definition of the model, then in section 18.3.1 we describe algorithms that collect information from a path in the overlay network. In Section 18.4 we describe a data collecting algorithm that works on a single path but when the amount of data in each node is not fixed. Apart from being an interesting problem by itself, this algorithm presents the basic building block for the more general algorithm, weighted collect on trees, described in Section 18.5. This algorithm collects information from a tree that spans the overlay network. We deal with the creation of such a spanning tree in section 18.6 and with general functions that can be computed from the nodes' data in section 18.7.

Then, in section 18.8 we present a simulation study done to evaluate the performance of these algorithms in an Internet like setting.

18.2 Model Definition

Normally, the nodes of an overlay network are not interior nodes of the underlying IP network. However, in general they may be interior, and recent works such as [503] address "Topologically Aware" overlay networks. Thus, in order to be able to describe the system in a consistent way we assume that all nodes reside inside the network. In such a case, each internal node of an overlay network (see Fig. 18.3) consists of two parts: the *Fast Networking Layer* (FNL), and the *Application Layer* (AL). The FNL is an IP forwarding mechanism that in addition to transmitting the main data traffic, can filter packets destined to the AL from all packets passing through the node and redirect these packets to the AL. The AL provides means for executing the received programs.

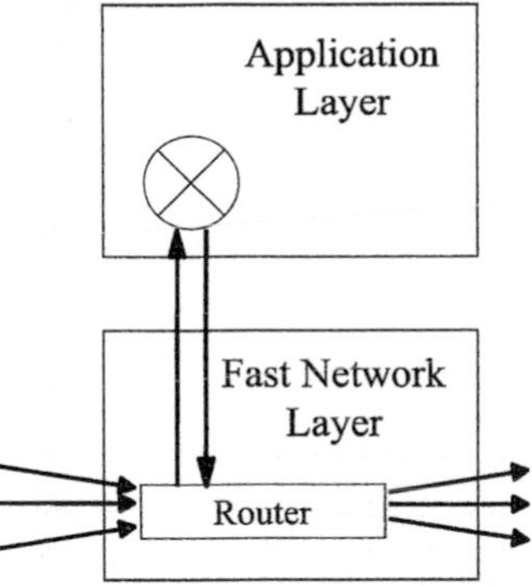

Fig. 18.3: A node structure.

This model is similar to the one introduced in [507] for active networks. It distinguishes between two types of delay: the delay of the message that only passes through the FNL module and the delay of the message that also triggers a computation in the AL. A message that passes only through the FNL suffers a constant delay. We bound this delay by the constant C; note that in practice the propagation time between neighbors (in the overlay network) may vary from 1Ms (in a LAN) to 80Ms (In a WAN). Since in most systems, messages are exchanged using the TCP protocol over links that have enough bandwidth (say more than 144Kbs), the propagation delay of messages is almost constant, which justifies this constant delay assumption.

A message that performs computations in the AL suffers an additional delay of kP time units, where P is a given constant, and k is a measure for the size of the input and output of the local computation. Note, that k is at least linear in the message size, since the message must be copied from the FNL to the AL. Our network in unsynchronized but throughout the chapter we do assume reliability, i.e., messages are never lost.

As explained before, we consider two different methods in which routing is done in the overlay layer. In the first one, the overlay network takes care of routing, and thus packets are forwarded by the overlay layer to the appropriate virtual neighbor. The second routing method uses the underlying routing, i.e., if a node needs to send a message to another overlay node it will get its actual address (say IP address) and will send the message directly to this address. The actual performance of the algorithms depends, of course, on the routing methods, and we will carry out the analysis for each of the methods. We use d_n to denote the average distance (in underlying network hops) between a node and its neighbors, and $\bar{d}$ to denote the average distance (in underlying network hops) between any two nodes in the network. Note that if the overlay network does not use any localization these distances may be equal. However, in many cases (see for example [503]) proximity in the underlying network plays a major part in the creation of the neighboring relation in the overlay network. In such cases d_n may be significantly smaller than $\bar{d}$. In the extreme case where the overlay network is exactly the underlying network, $d_n = 1$ and $\bar{d}$ is the average distance between nodes in the underlying network.

We consider two cost functions. The first one is the *time complexity* that describes the time it takes to accomplish the task. The second cost function we consider is the *message complexity* that counts the number of messages that pass between neighbors in the underlying network during the algorithm execution.

Throughout this chapter we say that a message passes between nodes through the *fast track* if it is not processed by any of the AL's on its way from the source to the destination. Otherwise we say that the message passes through the *slow track*. Note, that a fixed size message that passes through the *fast track* between two nodes of distance n in the overlay network, suffers an average delay of nd_nC time units in the first routing method and an average delay of $\bar{d}C$ in the second routing method. When the same message passes through the *slow track* it suffers an average delay of $nd_nC + nP$ time units, in both methods since the slow track forces the overlay network to send the message from one overlay node to another.

18.3 Gathering Information Along a Path

The problem can be stated as follows. A node v seeks to learn the ids of the nodes along the route (in the overlay network) from itself to another node u. Recall that in our model, v only knows the id of the next hop node along this route.

18.3.1 Basic Algorithms

In a naive implementation (naive), node v queries its next hop node for the id of the second hop node. Then it iteratively queries the nodes along the route until it reaches the one leading to the destination. This method resembles the way the `traceroute` program works, but it does not use the TTL field which is not part of the model. The delay of the naive algorithm is comprised of n activations of an AL level program plus the network delay. The average network delay in the first routing method is $2id_nC$ for $i = 1, 2, \ldots, n-1$ hops, which sums up to $O(n^2)d_nC$ time units. The message complexity in this case is given by $\sum_{i=1}^{n-1} 2id_n = O(n^2)d_n$. Using the second routing method, each message travels on the average $\bar{d}$ underlying network hops, and thus the average delay of the algorithm is $O(n(P + \bar{d}C))$, and the average message complexity is $2n\bar{d}$.

Next we describe two simple algorithms, collect-en-route and report-en-route, (presented in [507]) that improve the above solution to the route exploration problem, and analyze their performance using our model. Following this discussion we turn to more sophisticated solutions that achieve near optimal performances.

collect-en-route

In algorithm collect-en-route the source initiates a single packet that traverses the route and collects the host ids from each node. When the packet arrives at the destination node, it sends the data directly (using only the FNL) back to the source. The packet contains the source node id, the destination node id, and a list of ids it traversed. The source starts the algorithm by sending the message $MSG^*(s, d, \{s\})$ towards the destination, and outputs the list it receives from the destination.

Clearly, the message complexity of this algorithm for a node at distance n is $2d_nn$ in the first routing method, and $d_nn + \bar{d}$ using the second routing method.

The communication delay for this algorithm is $2nd_nC$ and $nd_nC + \bar{d}C$ for the two routing methods since exactly one message traverses the route in each direction. The execution delay at a node at distance i is iP since the message length is increased by one unit each hop. The total delay is given

```
collect-en-route
    for MSG*(s, d, list)
        if i == d
            send Report(list|i) to s
        else
            send MSG*(s, d, list|i) to d
```

Fig. 18.4: collect-en-route for an intermediate node i

by $2nd_nC + \sum_{i=1}^{n} iP = 2nd_nC + \frac{n(n+1)}{2}P$ for the first routing method, and by $nd_nC + \bar{d}C + \sum_{i=1}^{n} iP = nd_nC + \bar{d}C + \frac{n(n+1)}{2}P$ for the second routing method. Note that this algorithm is somewhat more sensitive to packet loss than the previous (and the following) one since no partial information is available at the source before the algorithm terminates. Furthermore, the time-out required to detect a message loss here is significantly larger than with the other algorithms presented here.

report-en-route

In algorithm report-en-route the source sends a request packet downstream the path. When a request packet arrives at a node, it sends the required information back to the source and forwards the request downstream to the next hop. This design minimizes the time of arrival of each part of the route information, while it compromises communication cost. The algorithm uses two message types: a forward going message, MSG^*, that contains the source node id, the destination node id, and a hop counter; and a backward going *Report*. The source starts the algorithm by sending the message $MSG^*(s, d, 0)$, each node increases the hop counter by one, forwards the message towards the destination, and sends a *Report* towards the destination with its id and the hop counter value. The source uses the hop count to order the list of nodes in its output.

```
report-en-route
    for MSG*(s, d, c)
        send Report(id, c + 1) to s
        if i ≠ d
            send MSG*(s, d, c + 1) to d
```

Fig. 18.5: report-en-route for an intermediate node i

The message complexity using the first routing method is clearly $O(d_n n^2)$, and using the second routing method t becomes $O(n(d_n + \bar{d}))$. The communication delay for this algorithm using the first routing method is $2d_n nC$ since exactly one message traverses the route in the forward direction until the destination, and this message is then sent back to the source. If we use the second routing method, the communication delay of the message sent from the destination back to the source is $C\bar{d}$. The execution delay in all the nodes is P since the message length is exactly one unit. The total delay is given then by $n(2Cd_n + P)$ for the first routing method, and $n(Cd_n + P) + C\bar{d}$ for the second routing method.

Algorithm collect-en-route features a linear message complexity with a quadratic delay, while algorithm report-en-route features a linear completion delay with a quadratic message complexity. Combining these two algorithms we can achieve tradeoffs between these two measures. In particular, if both measures are equally important we may want to minimize their sum.

Report-Every-l

An algorithm that enables us to optimize the two measures combined works as follows. First step is to obtain n, the length of the route between the two endpoints. This may be known from previous executions of the algorithm or can be obtained by an algorithm which is linear both in time and message complexity (see next sub-section). Next we send a fixed size message to initiate collect-en-route in n/l segments each of length l. This can be done using a counter that is initialized to l at the beginning of every segment, and decreased by one at every intermediate node. Thus, for the first routing method, the execution of collect-en-route in the segment i starts after at most $(i-1)(Cd_n + P)$ time units, and the overall time complexity is $(n-l)(Cd_n + P) + \sum_{i=1}^{l}(Cd_n + iP) = O(nd_nC + (n + l^2)P)$. The message complexity is $O(nd_n) + \sum_{i=1}^{nd_n/l}(l + il) = O(\frac{n^2}{l}d_n)$. Choosing $l = \sqrt{n}$ results in a linear time complexity while using $O(n\sqrt{n})$ messages. The requirement to balance the two measures (up to a constant factor of P), translates to $l^2 = \frac{n^2}{l}$ which gives $l = n^{2/3}$. For this l value both time and message complexity are $O(n^{4/3})$.

18.3.2 collect-rec

A different approach, however, is needed in order to reduce both the time and message complexity. The following algorithm, collect-rec, achieves an almost linear time and linear message complexity. The main idea is to partition the path between the source and the destination into two segments, to run the algorithm recursively on each segment, and then to send the information about the second segment route from the partition point to the source via the FNL track. In order to do so on the segment (i,j), in each recursive step one needs to find the id of the partition point, k, and to notify this node, k, that it has to both perform the algorithm on the segment (k, j) and report to i. In addition, i has to know that it is collecting data only until this partition point, k, and it should get the rest of the information via the fast track. The partition can be done, naively, in two passes. First we find the segment length. Then sending the segment length and a counter in the slow track allows k to identify itself as the partition node.

The idea behind the algorithm, as described above is very simple. However, the detailed implementation is somewhat complex. A pseudo-code implementation of this algorithm is given below.

```
main(i, d, l)
    if l = 0
        return({val_i})
    send Reach^1_port(i, d, ⌊l/2⌋, ⌈l/2⌉) to d
    L1 ← main(i, d, ⌊l/2⌋)
    L2 ← receive_port()
    return(L1|L2)
```

Fig. 18.6: Function main for some node i.[1]

```
For Reach(s, d, count, l)
    if count > 0
        send Reach(s, d, count − 1, l)
    else
        L ← main(i, d, l)
        send Report(L) to s
```

Fig. 18.7: Reaction of collect-rec for receipt of message Reach()

```
collect(d)
    l ← getlength(s, d)
    L ← main(s, d, l)
    return(L)
```

Fig. 18.8: Algorithm collect-rec for a source node, s.

[1] Subindexing with *port* is to indicate a possible implementation where the port number is used to deliver incoming messages to the correct recursive instantiation.

As explained before, finding the id of the partition point k, and sending the information to this node is the most difficult technical part of the implementation. This is done by sending the Reach() message with a counter that reaches 0 at node k. The id of the node who performed the partition, s, is part of the packet data, and thus once the information regarding the segment is available at node k it can send it directly via the fast track, to s.

The implementation of $getlength(s, d)$, which finds the hop length of the route between s and d, is similar to collect-en-route. The only difference is that the source sends a counter initialized to zero as the third parameter instead of an empty list. Intermediate nodes increase the counter by one instead of concatenating the next hop. Using the first routing method, this requires an average message complexity of $2d_n n$, and time complexity of $(n+1)P+2nCd_n$. If the overlay network uses the second routing method then the average message complexity is $d_n n + \bar{d}$, and the average time complexity is $(n+1)P + C(nd_n + \bar{d})$.

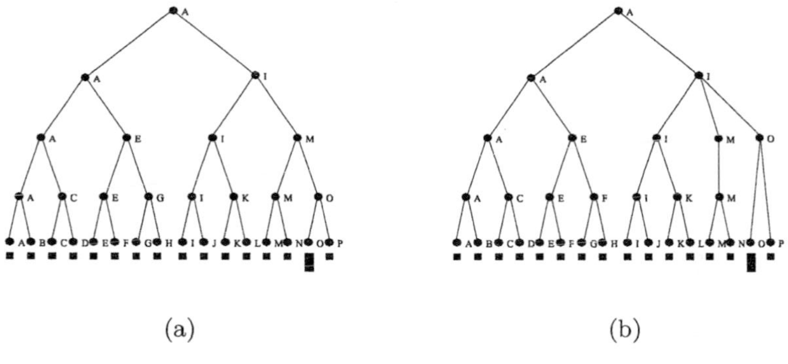

(a) (b)

Fig. 18.9: Example for the logical tree for $n = 16$

In order to analyze the time and message complexity of the algorithm, we need a better understanding of the properties of collect-rec algorithm. Consider the logical tree that is built by collect-rec algorithm (see Figure 18.9.a). This logical tree is built above the logical structure of the overlay network, and it defines the partition of the path into *segments* such that node i is responsible for collecting the information from segment $[i, i + segmentsize_i]$. The tree represents the hierarchy among the segments in the recursive execution of the algorithm. Note, that the same node can appear several times continuously in the logical tree but all the appearances must be on the path from its leaf appearance to the root. The main properties of this logical tree in our case (when each node has one unit of data) are:

1. The number of nodes with height[2] h is bounded by $n/2^h$.
2. At level l, the amount of data that a node sends to its father is smaller than 2^l and greater than or equal to 2^{l-1}. This data is copied at most $log(n) - l$ times during the algorithm run.
3. The distance on the path from a node with height l (a leaf has height 0) to its father in the logical tree is bounded by 2^l.

Using the above properties, one can conclude that the time complexity for a segment of length n is bounded by the time complexity of a segment of length $n/2$ plus a processing time of $n/2$ data units plus sending the Reach() message in the slow track along a (logical) path of length $n/2$, plus sending the data via the fast track back along a path of length $n/2$. All together we get the following recursive formula for the first routing method,

$$TC(n) \leq TC(n/2) + Pn/2 + (P + Cd_n)n/2 + Cd_n n/2,$$

and for the message complexity

$$MC(n) \leq 2MC(n/2) + nd_n.$$

For the second routing method we get the following recursive formulae,

$$TC(n) \leq TC(n/2) + Pn/2 + (P + Cd_n n/2 + C\bar{d}),$$

and for the message complexity

$$MC(n) \leq 2MC(n/2) + d_n n/2 + \bar{d}.$$

By solving these equations and adding the time complexity of $getlength(s, d)$, we can prove the following theorem.

Theorem 18.3.1. *Algorithm collect-rec solves the route detection problem with time complexity of $O(n(P + Cd_n))$, and message complexity of $O(nd_n \log n)$ for the first routing method, and time complexity of $O(n(P + Cd_n) + C\bar{d}\log n)$, and message complexity of $O(n(\bar{d} + d_n + \log n))$ for the second routing method.*

Tables 18.1 and 18.2 summarize the time and message complexity of the algorithms we described for collecting uniform information along a logical path for the two routing methods.

18.4 weighted collect-rec Algorithm

In this section we consider the problem of collecting data along a path where each node has an arbitrary amount of data. If we simply collect the information along the path, the time complexity may be quadratic if all the data is

[2] The height of a leaf in the logical tree is 0, and the height of the root is $\log n$.

algorithm name	time complexity	message complexity
naive	$O(nP + d_n n^2 C)$	$O(d_n n^2)$
collect-en-route	$O(n^2 P + d_n nC)$	$O(d_n n)$
report-en-route	$O(nP + d_n nC)$	$O(d_n n^2)$
report-every-l	$O((n + l^2)P + d_n nC)$	$O(d_n n^2/l)$
collect-rec	$O(nP + d_n nC)$	$O(d_n n \log n)$

Table 18.1: Summary of route exploration algorithms - first routing method.

algorithm name	time complexity	message complexity
naive	$O(nP + \bar{d}nC)$	$O(\bar{d}n)$
collect-en-route	$O(n^2 P + C(d_n n + \bar{d})$	$O(d_n n + \bar{d})$
report-en-route	$O(n(Cd_n + P) + C\bar{d})$	$O(n(d_n + \bar{d}))$
report-every-l	$O((n + l^2)P + C(d_n n + \bar{d})$	$O(d_n n + \bar{d}n/l)$
collect-rec	$O(nP + C(d_n n + \log n\bar{d}))$	$O(d_n n \log n + n\bar{d})$

Table 18.2: Summary of route exploration algorithms - second routing method.

concentrated at the end of the path. collect-rec algorithm is also not optimal for this problem, since when all the data is concentrated in the last node the data is copied $log(n)$ times during its transmission to the first node and thus the *execution complexity* of collect-rec will be $O(nlog(n)P)$. Thus, we developed a new algorithm that improves collect-rec and solves this problem more efficiently.

Our problem can be formally defined as follows: We are given an overlay network with two designated nodes i and j. Node i intends to collect data from all the nodes along the path from itself to j, where the amount of data in each node may vary. Let the length of the path be n and the total amount of data in all the nodes along the path be $\bar{n}$. We assume that no global routing information is available to the node, and thus every node knows only the *ids* of its neighbors. Our goal is to develop an algorithm that solves the described problem while minimizing the *message* and *time complexity*.

18.4.1 Algorithm Description

Our algorithm, called algorithm weighted collect-rec, follows the steps of the collect-rec algorithm. In order to collect the data along the path from node i to node j the algorithm partitions the path into two segments, runs itself on each segment recursively and then sends data from the second segment to i via the Fast Network Layer. However, in our case we cannot assume that the amount of data in each segment is proportional to the segment size since nodes may hold an arbitrary amount of data. Thus we need to adjust the destination of each node's data according to the amount of data that the node sends, and the total amount of data in the system.

Consider the logical tree properties of algorithm collect-rec described in the previous section. Item 2 is not valid for this logical tree if the data is distributed arbitrarily along the path. In the example on Figure 18.9.a node O has 4 units of data while each other node has one unit of data. Since O has extra data, the amount of data processed by node M is not bounded by 2^2. In this case algorithm weighted collect-rec adjusts the logical tree in such a way that O sends its data directly to node I (see Figure 18.9.b). Let $\bar{n}$ be the total amount of data in the tree; we assume for simplicity that $\bar{n} \geq n$ and term the value $\bar{n}/n$ the *amount ratio*. The adjusted tree has the following properties:

1. The number of nodes with height h is bounded by $O(n/2^h)$.
2. If the amount of data that a node sends to its father is greater than $\bar{n}2^l/n$ and smaller than or equal to $\bar{n}2^{l-1}/n$, then the data is copied at most $log(n) - l$ times during the algorithm run.
3. If the amount of data that a node sends to its father is greater than $\bar{n}2^l/n$ and smaller than or equal to $\bar{n}2^{l+1}/n$, then the distance on the path from the node to its father in the logical tree is bounded by $O(2^{log(n)-l})$.

These properties allow the weighted collect-rec algorithm to reach good complexity. weighted collect-rec algorithm uses two parameters to determine the distance of the data transmission. These parameters are the node's position in the basic logical tree, and the amount of data that the nodes in its logical subtree have.

18.4.2 Detailed Algorithm Description

The algorithm consists of three phases. During the first phase the algorithm computes the path parameters, i.e., the path length and the total amount of information along the path, assigns *length level* to each node and defines the destination for each node according to the *basic logical tree*, i.e. a tree that does not consider the amount of data in each node. The purposes of the second phase are to adjust the length of transporting data when required, and to allow each node to know the amount of data it should receive during the last phase and the id of the parent node in the *adjusted logical tree.* In the third phase, all the nodes send their own data and the data they received from other nodes to their parent in the adjusted logical tree. At the end of this phase, the root (the first node in the path) receives all the data, and the algorithm accomplishes its task.

Phase 1

In this phase the algorithm builds the basic logical tree (of collect-rec algorithm) and computes the *amount ratio* which indicates the total amount of data in the path. Later, in the next phase, this information is used to modify the logical tree as needed. Recall that the logical tree defines the partition of the path into *segments* such that node i is responsible for collecting the information from segment $[i, i + segmentsize_i]$. The same idea is deployed in the weighted collect-rec algorithm. The weighted collect-rec algorithm builds a logical tree (see for example Figure 18.9.a), in which links indicate the responsibility of nodes for segments.

At the beginning of the algorithm the *root* sends a message with two counters towards the last node in the path. The counters are the *length* and *total data amount* of the path. The message passes through the Application Layer until it reaches the last node in the path. Each node that is traversed by this message, increments the length and adds its local data amount to the *total data amount.* The last node sends the message to the *root* through the Fast Network Layer.

When the *root* receives the message containing the path parameters, it initiates a recursive partition process. During this process each node i sends partition messages to nodes with numbers $(i + \lfloor segmentsize_i/2^k \rfloor)$, where k changes from 0 to i's *length level*-1. The messages are delivered through the Application Layer. Each such message, destined to node i, contains the address of its sender (i.e., i's parent in the logical tree who is also called i's destination), i's *length level* that describes the length of i's segment, and the *amount ratio.* Partition messages are sent via the Application Layer using a counter in the same way this process is done in algorithm collect-rec. Upon receiving the partition message each node stores all received parameters, it sends a hello message containing its id to its parent in the logical tree, and initiates a partition process on its segment. At the end of this phase, each node knows the ids of its parent and of its children in the basic logical tree. Note, that the *root*'s *length level* is $log(n)$ and the size of its segment is n.

Phase 2

As mentioned above, the goal of the second phase is to compute the *adjusted logical tree.* This includes determining the ids of the parents and children in the new tree, and computing the amount of data that will be collected. This is done by collecting information regarding the amount of data in each segment, and disseminating this information along the hierarchy toward the root. This can be viewed as running algorithm collect-rec when the data collected is the amount of data at each node, and the length of its segment. This information is sufficient in order for each node to determine which of the nodes in its subtree are its children in the adjusted tree, and how much information each one of them sends.

This phase starts with a message *Comput-Adjusted-Tree (n,$\bar{n}$,idList)*, sent by the root using the fast track along the basic logical tree. Upon receiving this message, each node in the tree stores locally the idList that contains the ids of all the logical nodes from the root to it, adds its id to the idList, and forwards the message to the children in its basic logical tree. When a leaf gets this message, it computes the id of its destination according to the idList, and the amount of data it has according to the following rule. If the amount of data is greater than $\bar{n}2^l/n$ and smaller than or equal to $\bar{n}2^{l-1}/n$, then the destination is the $(log(n) - l)$'s element in the idList. It then sends an *AdjustTree(DataList)* message to its parent in the basic logical tree. Upon receiving an AdjustTree(DataList) message from all children, each intermediate node computes the amount of data it should receive, the ids of its children in the adjusted tree, and by adding its own data amount, the amount of data it needs to send up the tree. Using this data and the rule specified above, the node can use the idList it stored to compute the id of its adjusted destination (i.e. its parent in the adjusted tree). It then appends all lists it received from its children, adds its own amount and dest-id, and sends an Adjust() message to its parent in the basic logical tree.

This phase ends when the root gets an Adjust() message from all its children. At this point each node in the tree knows how much information it should get, and the ids of the nodes that will send it information, and also the id of its destination, i.e., its parent in the adjusted logical tree.

Phase 3

In this phase, data is sent along the links of the adjusted logical tree (as described in Figure 18.9). Each node sends data to its destination. The nodes, that receive data from other nodes, must wait until receiving all the data and only then they transmit this received data together with their local data to their *destination*. This is done through the *fast track*. At the end of the phase the *root* receives all the data of the path and the algorithm accomplishes its task.

```
weighted collect-rec-Phase2-3(i)
if received ComputeAdjustTree(n, n̄,idList)
    if(segmentsize_i > 1)
        idList = id | idList
        send ComputeAdjustTree(n, n̄,idList) to Child_L
        send ComputeAdjustTree(n, n̄,idList) to Child_R
    else
        dest = parent
        if (local data amount >0 )
            l= log n + 1 - ⌊log(n/n̄· local data amount)⌋
             dest = idList_l
         DataList = (i,local data amount,dest)
         send AdjustTree(DataList) to perent
         send report(Data) to dest
i=0
while (i < number − of − children)
    if received AdjustTree(DataList)
    i++
    List = List | DataList

dataAmount = processAdjustTree(List)
dataAmount+=local data amount
dest = parent
if (local data amount >0 )
    l= log n + 1 - ⌊log(n/n̄· local data amount)⌋
    dest = idList_l l=⌊log(n̄/n· dataAmount)⌋
DataList = (i,dataAmount,dest) | DataList
send AdjustTree(DataList) to perent
collectedAmount = dataAmount - local data amount
L ← collectData(collectedAmount)
L ← L|(localdata)
send Report(L) to dest
```

Fig. 18.10: Function main (phases 2 and 3) for node i.

18.4.3 Complexity Analysis of weighted collect-rec Algorithm

As explained above, the first and second phases of algorithm weighted collect-rec can be viewed as an execution of algorithm collect-rec, where the data collected is the triple $(i, amount(i), dest(i))$ and not the real data of each node. The only change here is that we added at the beginning of Phase 2 the message *AdjustTree(idList)* which goes down the logical tree. However, since the amount of data in the idList is bounded by the tree hight ($\log n$), the complexity of these phases is the same as the complexity of collect-rec, which can be formally stated as follows.

Lemma 18.4.1. *The time complexity of Phase 1 and Phase 2 is $O(n(P + Cd_n))$, and the message complexity is $O(n(d_n + \log n))$ for the first routing*

```
collectData(n)
    L ← empty
    while( n > 0)
        if received Report(data)
            L ← L|data
            n− = sizeof(data)
    return L
```

Fig. 18.11: Function collectData().

```
processAdjustTree(List)
    amount = 0
    for each entry in List
        if( entry.dest == i) amount+=entry.amount
    return amount
```

Fig. 18.12: Function processAdjustMessage.

method, and time complexity is $O(n(P + Cd_n) + C\bar{d}\log n)$*, and the message complexity is* $O(n(\bar{d} + d_n + \log n))$ *for the second routing method.*

The more difficult part is to analyze the complexity of the third phase in which data is actually sent along the logical links of the adjusted tree. We need to prove the following lemma.

Lemma 18.4.2. *The time complexity of Phase 3 is* $O(n(P + Cd_n))$*, and the message complexity of* $O(n(d_n + \log n))$ *for the first routing method, and time complexity is* $O(n(P + Cd_n) + C\bar{d}\log n)$*, and the message complexity is* $O(n(\bar{d} + d_n + \log n))$ *for the second routing method.*

Proof. When the algorithm collects data all the messages are sent towards the first node in the path, therefore the *communication delay* of phase 3 is $O(Cd_n n)$ using the first routing method and $O(C\bar{d}\log n)$ using the second routing method.

Define the *length level* of a node to be l if its *segment* size is smaller than 2^{l+1} but bigger than or equal to 2^l. A node has an *amount level* l if the amount of data it sends (this includes its own data and the data received from the other nodes during the algorithm execution) is greater than or equal to $(\bar{n}/n)2^l$ and smaller than $(\bar{n}/n)2^{l+1}$. Finally we define the node's *level* to be the maximum between its *length level* and its *amount level.*

According to the algorithm every node sends its data to a node with a higher *level.* The *amount level* of the node determines the *execution delay* in the node. The *execution delay* in the node with *amount level* l_a equals at worst to the amount of data it might process without increasing its *amount level,* hence it equals to $\bar{n}/n(2^{l_a-1})$. There are $log(n)$ possible *amount levels* and processing in the nodes with the same *level* is done simultaneously, hence the *execution delay* of Phase 3 is:

$$\sum_{l=0}^{log(n)} \frac{\bar{n}}{n}(2^l) \leq O(\bar{n}).$$

Therefore the *time complexity* of Phase 3 is $O(n(P+Cd_n))$ for the first routing method, and $O(n(P+Cd_n)+C\bar{d}\log n)$ for the second routing method.

During the data collection phase each node sends one message with data to its destination. The distance (in terms of overlay hops) between the node and its destination is bounded by 2^l where l is the node's *level*. The number of nodes with *level* l is bounded by $n/2^{l-1}$ since there are at most $n/2^l$ nodes with amount level l and at most $n/2^l$ nodes with length level l. Hence, when using the first routing method, the total number of messages passing during the third phase is bounded by

$$\sum_{l=0}^{log(n)} \frac{nd_n}{2^{l-1}}(2^l) \leq O(nlog(n)).$$

If we use the second routing method, the average message complexity is simply $\bar{d}\log n$.

Combining all three phases together we can prove the following theorem.

Theorem 18.4.1. *The time complexity of the algorithm* weighted collect-rec *is $O(n(P+Cd_n))$, and the message complexity is $O(n(d_n+\log n))$ for the first routing method, and the time complexity is $O(n(P+Cd_n)+C\bar{d}\log n)$, and the message complexity is $O(n(\bar{d}+d_n+\log n))$ for the second routing method.*

18.5 Gathering Information from a Tree

In this section we deal with a more general problem where we need to collect information from a general graph, and not from a specific path. First, we assume the existence of a spanning tree rooted at the root, and we want to collect information from all leaves of this tree along the paths to the root. As shown in the introduction to this chapter, the naive solution of collecting data along a spanning tree as described in [37] is not optimal in our model.

One can show that in the first routing method, it is impossible to gather all information with a time complexity lower than $\Omega(DC+nP)$, where D is the diameter of the overlay network. This is true because a message cannot arrive at the most remote element faster than DC time units, and the algorithm must spend at least P time units to copy the message from every element in the network. The message complexity cannot be lower than $\Omega(n)$, since every element in the network must send at least one message, thus the root must process at least n units of data. Moreover, if no global structure such as a spanning tree is available, the message complexity is bounded by $O(m)$,

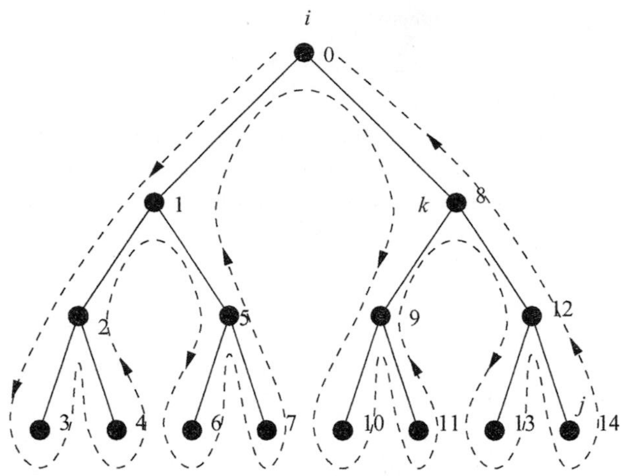

Fig. 18.13: A simple extension of collect-rec.

where m is the number of logical links in the overlay network, since every link in the graph must be tested in order to insure that we cover all nodes.

A first step towards developing algorithms that will have both a linear time and message complexity is to modify collect-rec to work on trees. This can be done (see Figure 18.13) by assigning a number to every node in the tree according to a pre-order visiting starting at the root. We now consider the path that goes from node 1 (the root) to node n, according to this order. Note that node i and node $i+1$ may not be neighbors in the overlay network (for example nodes 11 and 12 in Figure 18.13), and therefore this path is not a simple path. However, the total length of the path in terms of overlay nodes is bounded by $2n$.

Creating such a path requires assigning numbers to the nodes in the tree according to the pre-order visiting order, and allowing nodes in the tree to route messages according to this node number. For this, each node should know its own number, and the number range of each of its subtrees. This can be easily done by a bottom up pass on the tree that collects the sizes of the subtrees, followed by a top down pass on the tree in which every node assigns ranges to each of its subtrees. Since the size of the messages is constant, the time complexity of this process can be bounded by $O(Cd_nD + Pn)$, and the message complexity is $O(n)$.

After this phase we can run Algorithm collect-rec on this path and obtain the message and time complexity of collect-rec. All together we get the following theorem.

Theorem 18.5.1. *One can collect data from any given spanning tree with time complexity of $O(n(P + Cd_n))$, and message complexity of $O(n(d_n +$*

$\log n$)) *for the first routing method, and time complexity of* $O(n(P + Cd_n) + C\bar{d}\log n)$, *and message complexity of* $O(n(\bar{d} + d_n + \log n))$ *for the second routing method.*

However, in practice n might be very big (100,000 nodes or more in a typical Peer-to-Peer network) while the diameter of the network (and thus the height of the spanning tree) is much smaller (typically 10). It is thus both practically important and theoretically interesting to reduce the complexity of the data collecting algorithm in this model.

In the rest of this section we describe an algorithm, called weighted collect on trees, for the general data collection problem. As indicated before, we assume the existence of a spanning tree rooted at the root, and we want to collect information from all leaves of this tree along the paths to the root. Our algorithm follows the ideas presented in the previous section for the weighted collect-rec algorithm. We start with the given spanning tree (as we started with he basic logical tree in algorithm weighted collect-rec, and we modify it by assigning new destinations to some nodes. This is done in a way that data is always sent up the tree towards the root, balancing between the amount of data that a node sends and the length of path along which the data is transported.

In order to do so, we assign what we call a *length level* to each node. These length level values should have the following two properties: The number of the nodes with *length level* l must be greater than or equal to the total number of the nodes with *length level* greater than l, and the distance between a node with *length level* l and the nearest node towards the *root* with *length level* greater than l must be bounded by $O(2^l)$. Finding an appropriate assignment that has the desired properties is not easy. As will be proven later, the following algorithm assigns length level to the nodes of the tree with the desired properties. All leaves have *length level* 0. The *length level* of each internal node is the minimum between the maximum of all the *length levels* in the node's sub-tree plus 1, and the position of the first 1 in the binary representation of the distance of the node from the *root*. Once *length levels* are assigned, each node should send its data to the first node, on the way to the root in the tree, that has a *length level* that is bigger that the node's *length level.*

18.5.1 Detailed Algorithm Description

Phase 1

As explained above, the goals of the first phase are to assign a *length level* to each node, to find the destination of each node, and to compute the number of the adjust messages that each node needs to receive during the second phase.

Definition 18.5.1. *Let $length_{bin}(i)$ be the binary representation of the distance between the* root *and node i.*

Definition 18.5.2. *Let $\eta(i)$ be the position of the least significant bit that equals to* 1 *in $length_{bin}(i)$.*

The algorithm assigns *length level* 0 to all leaves. The *length levels* of all other nodes are defined by the formula $min\{\eta(i), l_m(i) + 1\}$ (where $l_m(i)$ is the maximal *length level* in the sub-tree of i excluding i).

In order to find the distance from each node to the *root*, the *root* disseminates among its children a message with one counter that is equal to 1. Each node that receives such a message stores the value of the counter as the distance to the *root*, increments the counter, and disseminates the message to its children.

Then, the algorithm computes the maximal *length level* in the sub-tree of each node and assigns the *length level* to each node. During this computation each node receives one message from each of its children. This message contains the maximal *length level* in the child sub-tree. Upon receiving this message the node computes both its *length level* and the maximal *length level* in its sub-tree (considering its own level as well), and sends the message with the computed value to its parent. This computation is done bottom up, and it starts in the leaves immediately after receiving the message with the distance to the *root*.

Once a node knows its *length level* it starts searching for its destination. this is done by creating a request that contains the node's *length level* and sending it towards the *root* via the Application Layer. Each node that receives such a request stores the address of the child who sent it. Then, the node forwards the request to its parent iff the node's *length level* is smaller than or equal to the received *length level* and the node did not send a request before with the same *length level*.

If the node's *length level* is bigger than the requested *length level*, it sends a reply with its address and *length level* to the appropriate child. When a node receives a reply, it disseminates the reply to all children who had sent the appropriate requests before, and stores the address from the reply if this is also its own destination.

In order to move on to the last task of the phase, it is important that each node will know that it has received all messages from its subtree. This is done by sending notification messages up the tree. Each leaf sends such a notification immediately after sending its request. Other nodes send their notification when they receive notification from all of their children and finished processing all the received requests. Note, that a node delays the dissemination of replies to its children until it sends a notification towards the *root*. Only after the node notifies its father, it is guaranteed that it knows about all its children who are waiting for the delayed replies.

The last task of the phase is to figure out the number of *length sources* of each node. Recall, that node j is the *length source* of node i if j received i's address as a destination address during the first phase. Denote by $V_l(i)$ the set of the *length sources* of i with the *length level* l. The number of *length sources* equals the sum of $V_l(i)$, for all l smaller than i's *length level*. Next we describe how the algorithm computes $V_l(i)$ for a specific l. Consider the virtual tree that contains all the paths through which the replies with i's address passed. When replies reach their destinations this virtual tree is well-defined, since each node has the addresses of the children that received these messages, and the node will not receive new requests since its children finished sending requests. The root of this sub-tree is i. Note, that two such virtual trees, that are built from the paths passed by the replies with the same *length level*, have no common edges if their roots are distinct. The algorithm then computes the sum of the values of all the virtual tree nodes in a bottom up way, where each node adds the value 1 iff the node's *length level* is l.

Phase 2 and Phase 3

Once the destination of each node is known, the algorithm proceeds exactly as in algorithm weighted collect-rec since the balancing between the amount of data and the *length level* is exactly the same, and sending the data is of course the same.

18.5.2 Complexity Analysis of weighted collect on trees Algorithm

For simplicity, we do not explicitly state the pseudo code that implements the algorithm. The main difference between algorithm weighted collect on trees and algorithm weighted collect-rec is in the first phase and the definition of the *length levels*. Once the logical tree on top of the overlay tree is created, the algorithm and the analysis is very similar to the one in algorithm weighted collect-rec. We begin with two definitions.

Definition 18.5.3. *Let V_l be the group of nodes whose* length level *assigned by the algorithm is l. Denote by n_x the size of V_x.*

Lemma 18.5.1. *The size of V_l is equals to or greater than the sum of sizes of V_i, for all $i > l$, i.e. $n_l \geq \sum_{i=l+1}^{max\ length\ level} n_i$.*

Proof. Consider the group $V_{>l} = \bigcup V_i$ such that $i > (l+1)$. Denote by v_i a node from $V_{>l}$, and by $M(v_i)$ the nearest to v_i node in its sub-tree with *length level* l. Such a node always exists, because under each node with *length level* x there are nodes with all *length levels* less than x. If there are two or more such nodes we can arbitrarily choose one of them.

Consider two distinct nodes v_1, v_2 from $V_{>l}$. There are two cases. The first case is when none of these two nodes is in the sub-tree of the second node. The second case is when one node is in the sub-tree of the second node.

$M(v_i)$ is always in the sub-tree of v_i. Thus, in the first case $M(v_1)$ and $M(v_2)$ are distinct nodes. Consider now the second case. Assume, that v_2 is in the sub-tree of v_1. $M(v_2)$ is in the sub-tree of v_2. Since the *length levels* of the considered nodes is greater than l, both $\eta(v_1)$ and $\eta(v_1)$ are greater than l. Hence, the path from v_2 to v_1 contains at least one node with *length level* equals to l. Henceforth, $M(v_1)$ and $M(v_2)$ are distinct nodes.

In both cases we proved that $M(v_1) \neq M(v_2)$, hence for each v_i there is $M(v_i)$ that is distinct from all other $M(v_j)$ if $v_i \neq v_j$. Thus, $n_l \geq \sum_{i=l+1}^{max\ length\ level} n_i$, and the lemma follows.

Lemma 18.5.2. *The number of the nodes with length level l is bounded by $n/2^l$.*

Proof. In order to prove the lemma it is sufficient to prove the following equation

$$\sum_{i=l}^{max\ length\ level} n_i \leq \frac{n}{2^l} \tag{18.1}$$

since $n_i \geq 0$ for every i.

The proof of Equation 18.1 is obtained using induction on *length level.*

Base case. The *length level* equals to 0. The lemma holds, because the total number of nodes in the tree is n.

Inductive step. Suppose that the lemma holds for all *length levels* less than or equal to l. We prove that the lemma holds also for *length level* $l+1$. Equation 18.1 equals to:

$$n_l + \sum_{i=l+1}^{max\ length\ level} n_i \leq \frac{n}{2^l}. \tag{18.2}$$

According to Lemma 18.5.1 $n_l \geq \sum_{i=l+1}^{max\ length\ level} n_i$. Thus, Equation 18.3 follows from Equation 18.2.

$$2 \sum_{i=l+1}^{max\ length\ level} n_i \leq \frac{n}{2^l}, \sum_{i=l+1}^{max\ length\ level} n_i \leq \frac{n}{2^{l+1}} \tag{18.3}$$

The lemma follows.

Lemma 18.5.3. *The distance from node i with length level l to the nearest node towards the root with a bigger length level is bounded by $2^{(l+1)}$.*

Proof. When the distance from i to the *root* is equal to or smaller than $2^{(l+1)}$ the lemma follows, since the *root* has the highest *length level* among other nodes. Suppose now that the distance to the *root* is greater than $2^{(l+1)}$. There are two cases: the first case is when the first 1 in $length_{bin}(i)$ is placed at position l, and the second case is when the first 1 in $length_{bin}(i)$ is placed at a position greater than l.

Consider the first case. Since the distance from i to the *root* is greater than $2^{(l+1)}$ there is 1 in $length_{bin}(i)$ at position k which is greater than l. Let $\bar{i}$ be the node that lies on the path from i to the *root* and $length_{bin}(\bar{i})$ is the same as $length_{bin}(i)$ except in position l. The $\bar{i}$'s *length level* cannot be smaller than $(l+1)$ because the first 1 in $length_{bin}(\bar{i})$ is at a position greater than l and the maximal *length level* in $\bar{i}$'s sub-tree is at least l since i is in this sub-tree. The distance from i to $\bar{i}$ is 2^l, thus the lemma follows in this case.

Consider the second case. Let k be the position of the first 1 in $length_{bin}(i)$. Let $\bar{i}$ be the node that lies on the path from i to the *root* and the distance between i and $\bar{i}$ is 2^{l+1}. There are two sub-cases, when $k > (l+1)$ and when $k = (l+1)$. When $k > (l+1)$ $length_{bin}(\bar{i})$ has no 1 at positions less than $l+1$. When $k = (l+1)$ $length_{bin}(\bar{i})$ is the same as $length_{bin}(i)$ except in position k. Since the distance from i to the *root* is greater than $2^{(l+1)}$, $length_{bin}(i)$ has 1 at a position greater than k. In the two sub-cases the first 1 in $length_{bin}(\bar{i})$ is in a position greater than l. Since i is in the $\bar{i}$'s sub-tree the maximal *length level* in this sub-tree is at least l. Therefore, $\bar{i}$'s *length level* cannot be smaller than $(l+1)$. The lemma follows.

Before we will prove the next lemma we must note that the maximal *length level* assigned by the algorithm is $log(D)$.

Lemma 18.5.4. *The time complexity of phase 1 is $O(Dd_nC + nP)$ and its message complexity is $O(d_n n \log(D))$.*

Proof. During the first phase the algorithm uses the following types of messages: a message with distance to the root, a message with maximal length level in the sub-tree of each node, a message that notifies the node's father that the node finished sending requests, a message with request for the address of the destination, and a message with reply that contains the destination address. The complexities related to the first three types of the messages are the same. The complexity related to the last two types are also the same. Hence the complexity of the second phase is determined by the complexity related to the messages with distance to the *root* and by the complexity related to the messages with destination address.

Consider the messages with distance to the *root.* Each node receives one such message, thus their *message complexity* is $O(n)$. The messages are disseminated in one direction, hence their *communication delay* is $O(DC)$. In order to evaluate the *execution delay* related to these messages consider a critical path $\{s_0, s_1, ..., s_k\}$, where messages are sent from s_{i+1} to s_i and s_0 is the *root.* The *execution delay* of these messages is equal to the sum of *execution delays* at each node, denoted by t_i:

$$\sum_{i=0}^{k} t_i, \tag{18.4}$$

The node spends a constant time when it sends such a message to each of its children, hence t_i equals to the number of node's children. Since the sum of children in the tree cannot exceed the number of the nodes of the tree, the *execution delay* of the messages with distance to the *root* is bounded by $O(nP)$. The *time complexity* related to the messages with distance to the *root* is $O(DC + nP)$.

Consider now the messages that contain the addresses of the destinations. These messages are always sent in one direction, hence their *communication delay* is $O(DC)$. Since the paths, which messages with the same level but iwhich are sent by the different nodes pass, have no common edges, the *execution delay* is the $\sum_{i=0}^{log(D)} t_i$, where t_i is the *execution delay* of processing messages with level i. t_i consists of the *execution delay* of receiving the message from the node's father and retransmitting the message to the children. According to Lemma 18.5.3 the first component is bounded by 2^{i+1}. The second component is bounded by the number of nodes with *length level* i. According to Lemma 18.5.2 this number is bounded by $n/2^i$. Hence, the *execution delay* is:

$$\sum_{i=0}^{log(D)} 2^{i+1} + \frac{n}{2^i} \leq O(n) \tag{18.5}$$

The *time complexity* of these messages is $O(DC+nP)$. Consider now their *message complexity*. Each node sends one such message to a distance bounded by 2^{i+1}, where i is the node's *length level*, according to Lemma 18.5.3. The number of nodes with *length level* i is bounded by $n/2^i$ according to Lemma 18.5.2. Hence, the *message complexity* of these messages is:

$$\sum_{i=0}^{log(D)} 2^{i+1} \frac{n}{2^i} \leq O(nlog(D)) \tag{18.6}$$

The lemma follows.

As explained, the continuation of the algorithm is very similar to algorithm weighted collect-rec and thus we omit the detailed description and analysis. The overall complexity of the algorithm is stated in the following theorem.

Theorem 18.5.2. *The time complexity of the algorithm* weighted collect on trees *is $O(n(P+Cd_n))$, and the message complexity is $O(n(d_n+\log D))$ for the first routing method, and the time complexity is $O(n(P + Cd_n) + C\bar{d}\log D)$, and the message complexity is $O(n(\bar{d} + d_n + \log n))$ for the second routing method.*

18.6 Gathering Information from General Graphs

In the previous sections we assumed that the overlay network maintains a spanning tree, in which each node knows its parent and its descendants. For many overlay applications (such a CDN) this is a very natural assumption as some information should be sent (or collected) from all the nodes. For other applications, such as Peer-to-Peer file sharing applications, maintaining a global spanning tree may be too expensive since the amount of users that join (or leave) the Peer-to-Peer network each time unit is too big.

Nevertheless, in all non-trivial proposals for a structural Peer-to-Peer network, maintaining such a tree requires at most a very small change to the existing infrastructure. If a spanning tree does not exist, one will have to create a spanning tree, and run our algorithm on top of it (assuming the amount of data collected is big enough). In order to create such a tree, one can use the well known algorithm, [37] in which every node that receives a message indicating the creation of the tree, sends this message to all its neighbors. Each node replies to the first creation message with an "I am your child" message, and to all other messages (i.e. not the first one) with an "already in tree" message. This phase can be combined with the first phase of the algorithms described in the previous section, as they both start with a message being sent from the root down the spanning tree.

The complexity of creating such a tree is independent of the routing method since messages are exchanged only among overlay neighbors. The message complexity is of course $O(d_n m)$, where m is the number of links in the overlay network, and the time complexity is $O(Cd_nD + S_nP)$, where $S_n = \max_{all\ paths\ \pi\ in\ tree} \sum_{n \in \pi} degree(n)$.a

In general the only bound for the value of S_n is $2m$, but in many cases one can build a tree with much better values (see [93] for a discussion on this subject in a different model). If, however, the outdegrees of the overlay network is bounded by $\log n$ and the height of the spanning tree is also logarithmic in the number of nodes, as indeed is the case in most practical scenarios, then the time complexity of creating the tree becomes $O(Cd_nD + P\log n^2)$, and the overall time complexity of gathering information from the entire overlay network without assuming a spanning tree is the same as the one stated in Theorem 18.4.1, namely $O(n(P + Cd_n))$ for the first routing method, and $O(n(P + Cd_n) + C\bar{d}\log D)$ for the second routing method.

18.7 Global Functions

In many cases, exploring the path between two nodes is just an intermediate step towards computing some function along this path. A typical example is bottleneck detection: we want to detect the most congested link along a path. Another typical example is the need to know how many copies of a certain file are available in a Peer-to-Peer file sharing system. In both cases the computation can be done using a single pass on the data (path in the first example, and tree in the second one) using constant size messages.

Bottleneck detection is a special case of a a global sensitive function [121] which we term succinct functions. These functions, e.g., average, min, max, and modulo, can be computed with a single path on the input, in any order, requiring only constant amount of memory. For such functions we can prove the following theorem.

Theorem 18.7.1. *Every succinct function on a path can be computed with time complexity $\Theta(nd_n(P+C))$ and a message complexity of $\Theta(n)$, and these bounds are tight.*

In a similar way, we can define succinct-tree functions as functions from a set of elements $\{X_i\}$ to a single element x, such that if $f(\{x_i\}) = x$ and $f(\{y_i\}) = y$ then $f(\{x_i\} \cup \{y_i\}) = f(\{x\} \cup \{y\})$. Such functions can be computed on a tree using a single bottom up pass with fixed length messages, and thus the following theorem holds.

Theorem 18.7.2. *Every succinct-tree function can be computed on an overlay network with time complexity of $\Theta((Cd_nD + S_nP)$, and message complexity of $\Theta(m)$ ($\Theta(n)$ if a spanning tree is available), and these bounds are tight.*

Note that since we only use messages between neighbors in the overlay network, the same results hold for both routing methods.

18.8 Performance Evaluation

In order to verify the practicality of the algorithms presented in this chapter, we evaluated their performance on large networks that contain thousands of internal nodes. The results were obtained using a specially built simulator that allows us to simulate runs on arbitrary big networks. To make the presentation clear, we only considered the first routing scheme, with $d_n = 1$.

18.8.1 weighted collect-rec Algorithm Performance

In this section we present the results of running the weighted collect-rec algorithm. Figure 18.14 depicts the results of collecting data that is distributed uniformly among all the nodes. The X axis is the path length. In these runs we checked the *time* and *message complexity* of the algorithm for different values of *amount ratio*, from 1 up to 1.8. Remember that the *amount ratio* is the ratio between the amount of the data in all the nodes and the path length. The results show that the message complexity is independent of the amount of transported data. For clarity of the presentation, we plotted in Fig.(18.14.b) the line for the theoretical bound $O(nlog(n))$.

As for time complexity, there is a clear difference in the running time with different *amount ratios*. Note, however, that this difference is not proportional to the difference in the *amount ratio.* This can be explained by the fact that the running time of the first two phases depends only on the path length. The difference in the running time of the algorithm for different *amount rations*, is introduced by the third phase, when the actual data collection is done.

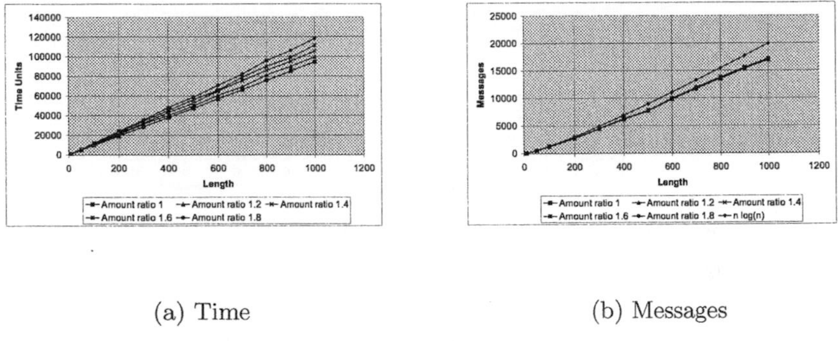

(a) Time (b) Messages

Fig. 18.14: weighted collect-rec performance

Figure 18.15 depicts the results of collecting data from a path where all the data is concentrated in one node. Note, that in this case the node that contains all the data must send the data directly to the *root* during the last phase. In each chart, the X axis describes the distance from the single node that contains data to the *root.* The number of nodes in the path is 100 in charts a and b. Both, the number of messages and the running time increase when data is located further away from the *root.* The initial values show the minimal time and number of messages required to accomplish the first two phases (i.e. the *time complexity* or the *number of messages* when the data is actually located at the *root*). The number of messages increases proportionally to the distance from the node to the *root.* As the node is further away from the *root* the message with the data is transmitted over a greater distance, and the number of messages grows. The growth of the running time looks like a step function. The figures show that the steps appear at values of $n/2^i$. Since the node sends the data directly to the *root* during the last phase, the algorithm must deliver the address of the *root* to this node during the second phase. Considering the path of the address delivering. The message with the address may be processed by other nodes and each time when the maximal *length level* of the nodes that participate in the delivering increases a new step starts. This is because the amount of work done by the node during the second phase is proportional to $n/2^i$. Inside each step (that is better seen for the small values of x) there is a weak increase of the running time. This increase is caused by the growth of the *communication delay* that a message with data suffers when the distance to the *root* increases. The presented results were obtained by running one experiment for each value of x. A larger number of experiments here is useless, since the simulator gives the same results for exactly same starting parameters.

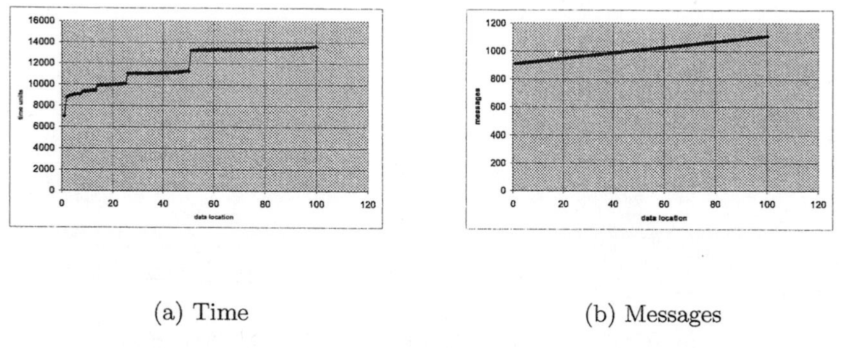

(a) Time (b) Messages

Fig. 18.15: weighted collect-rec performance. All data in one node

Figure 18.16 depicts the results of collecting data from a path where an arbitrary group of nodes contains all the data in the system. The number of nodes in the path is 100 in charts a and b. In each chart the X axis describes the size of the set of the nodes that contains all data. Note that the data is distributed uniformly among all the nodes in the set. The charts show that the running time decreases when the group size grows from $4-5$ up to approximately 20% of n. When the size of the group increases the data processing becomes more parallel and this causes the processing time to decrease. When the size of the group continues to grow, the time required for processing the data in each node increases since there are more data packets. This process balances the effect of the parallel processing and the total time required is the same.

As can be seen from Figure 18.16 (b), the number of messages increases logarithmically with the increasing of the group size. The charts show that as the group grows the average cost (in messages) of adding new nodes decreases. The average value of the standard deviation for the running time is 13% and for the number of messages is 3%. The standard deviation has higher values for the small group and it decreases as the group size increases.

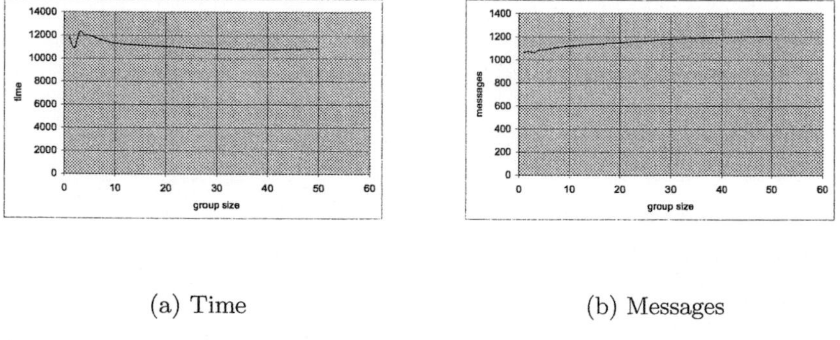

(a) Time (b) Messages

Fig. 18.16: weighted collect-rec performance. All data in a set of nodes

18.8.2 Performance of weighted collect on trees Algorithm

In order to evaluate the weighted collect on trees algorithm we used two network models. The networks created according these models have different topology properties. The first model, denoted by *random tree*, is the network topology where probability that a new node will be linked to an existing node is the same for all existing nodes (also known as $G(n, p)$). However, recent studies indicate that the Internet topology is far from being a random graph [201]. In order to capture spanning trees of such model the described algorithm were also tested on *Barabasi trees.* In this model the probability that a new node will be linked to an existing node with k links is proportional to k [637]. As it will be shown below, the differences in the network models affect the performance of the algorithm. The results of evaluating the performance of weighted collect on trees algorithm is depicted in Figures 18.17. In both charts, the x axis describes the size of the tree. Figure 18.17 (a) shows the results of running the algorithm on *random trees* and Figure 18.17 (b) shows the results of running the algorithm on *Barabasi trees.* The plotted results reflect an average cost taken from 1000 runs per each tree size, and the values of standard deviation do not exceed 4%.

One can observe that both the time and the number messages grow linearly, [3] this agrees with the theoretical analysis. The running time of the algorithm is smaller on *random trees* than on *Barabasi trees.* This is explained by the fact that *Barabasi trees* have a small group of nodes with a larger number of children (in *random trees* the distribution of children among the internal nodes is more uniformly) and these nodes perform a lot of work. The number of messages is greater when the algorithms run on the *random trees.* This can be explained by the fact that the diameter of *Barabasi trees* is less than the diameter of *random trees.*

[3] Note that the time scale is logarithmic.

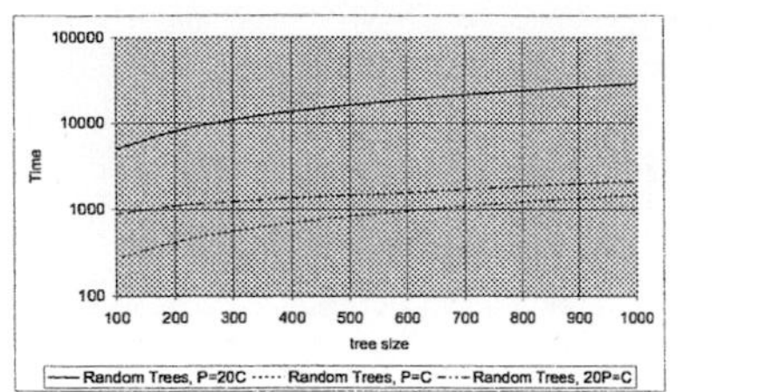

(a) Time for random trees

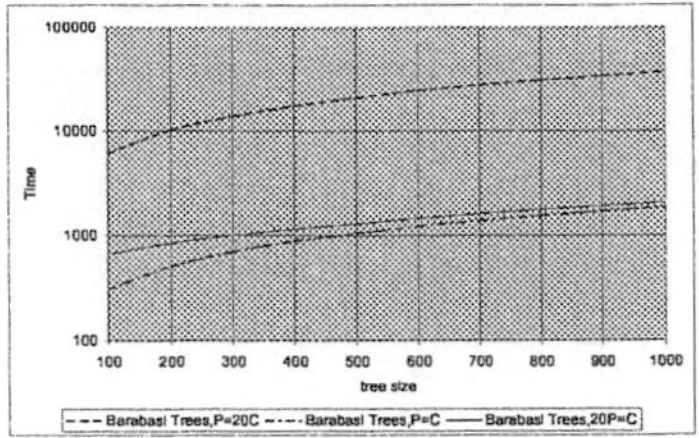

(b) Time for Barabasi trees

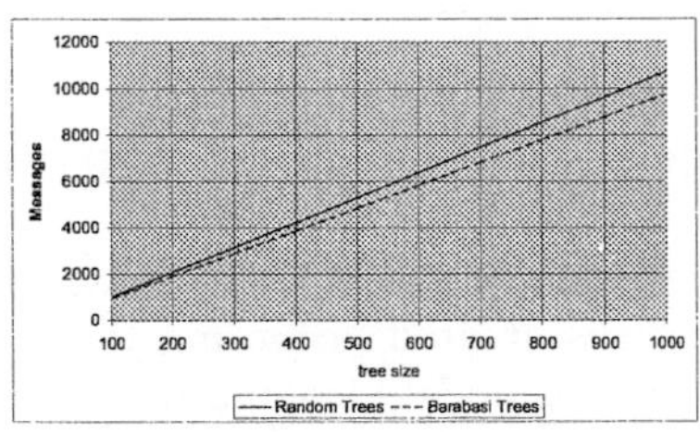

(c) Messages

Fig. 18.17: weighted collect on trees algorithm performance

Note that the actual value of the time complexity depends on the ratio between C and P. In practical scenarios this ratio depends on the network RTT (since C also present the propagation delay), the type of processing, the architecture of the overlay network, and the efficiency of data handling at the nodes. However, in a Peer-to-Peer network, where distant hosts can be neighbors in the overlay layer, this ratio could indeed be small (i.e. ≤ 1), while in local area overlay networks (as in Active Networks prototypes) this ratio could be as big as 20.

When creating the graphs in Figure 18.17, we used $p = c = 1$ to calculate the case $c = p$, $c = 1, p = 20$ to calculate the case $p = 20c$, and $p = 1, c = 20$ to calculate the case $c = 20p$. It is clear then, that the fastest case is when $c = p$. However, as indicated by the graphs the affect of increasing p is much more severe than increasing c. If we look at the Barabasi tree, we see that it takes about 2000 time units to collect information from a 1000 node tree (where $c = 20p$). Assuming $p = 0.1$Ms, we can infer that a 100,000 node graph could be collected in 20 seconds assuming RTT of 2Ms. For more realistic RTTs, and assuming an open TCP connection between peers, one can collect information from 100,000 nodes in less than a minute, using algorithm weighted collect on trees.

19. Schema-Based Peer-to-Peer Systems

Wolfgang Nejdl, Wolf Siberski (L3S and University of Hannover)

19.1 Introduction

When sharing information or resources — the most prominent application of Peer-to-Peer systems — one is immediately faced with the issue of searching. Any application which provides an information collection needs some means to enable users finding relevant information. Therefore, the expressivity of the query language supported by the system is a crucial aspect of Peer-to-Peer networks. Daswani et al. [154] distinguish key-based, keyword-based and schema-based systems.

Key-based systems can retrieve information objects based on a unique hash-key assigned to it. This means that documents for example have to be requested based on their name. This kind of queries is supported by all DHT networks (cf. Chapter 7). Typically, key-based search features are not exposed to end-users, but rather used as basic infrastructure.

Keyword-based systems extend this to the possibility to look for documents based on a list of query terms. This means that users do not have to know the document they are looking for, but can ask for all documents relevant to particular keywords. Non-ranking keyword-based systems find matching resources by executing a string or string pattern matching algorithm, e.g. on the file name. Ranking keyword-based approaches score documents according to their relevance depending on statistics derived from document full text. Chapter 20 describes the latter kind of systems.

Schema-based systems manage and provide query capabilities for structured information. *Structured* means that the information instances adhere to a predefined schema. For example, in a digital archive any document is described using a schema consisting of elements as title, author, subject, etc. In schema-based systems, queries have to be formulated in terms of the schema (e.g. "find all documents with author=Smith"). Nowadays the dominant schema-based systems are relational databases; other important variants are XML and Semantic Web data stores. Schema-based Peer-to-Peer systems are sometimes also called *Peer Data Management Systems* (e.g., in [273]).

Digital archives are an application area where schema-based queries provide significant value. Here, users often need to formulate complex queries, i.e., queries with constraints regarding several criteria, to specify their search. For example, to find recent books about Java programming, one would need to exclude outdated books and to disambiguate between the Java programming language ("find all books where 'Java' occurs in the title, publication

R. Steinmetz and K. Wehrle (Eds.): P2P Systems and Applications, LNCS 3485, pp. 323-336, 2005.

date is less than three years ago, and subject is a subtopic of computer"). Such complex queries are only supported by schema-based systems.

We can observe two converging development lines, one regarding database systems, the other in Peer-to-Peer networks. Databases started as centralized systems, where one server processes queries from all clients. Since then, they have evolved towards a higher degree of distribution, e.g by introducing mediator-based [622] distributed query processing[1]. At the same time Peer-to-Peer systems have developed towards support for more expressive queries [445, 70, 4, 274, 308]. Schema-based Peer-to-Peer systems are the point where these two directions of research meet, as shown in figure 19.1(see also [260]).

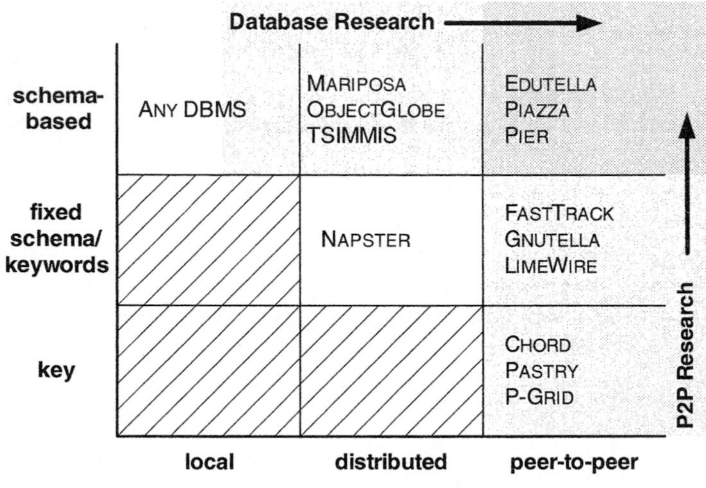

Fig. 19.1: Schema Capabilities and Degree of Distribution

Schema-based Peer-to-Peer systems inherit characteristics of database systems as well as Peer-to-Peer networks:

- *Strict adherence of data to a schema* All data stored at the peers is structured according to a schema. Note that not necessarily all peers share the same schema. For example, a peer storing information about courses, professors and students will use another schema than a digital archive peer storing information about scientific documents. This leads to the requirement of schema mapping in Peer-to-Peer systems (see 19.4)
- *Schema-based query expressions* Query constraints as well as requested information are specified with reference to schema elements. In a heterogeneous network, i.e., where more than one schema is used, queries will be sent to a subset of peers only, depending on the query constraints.

[1] A good overview of distributed database technology is [363].

- *No global knowledge* Maintaining global information such as a schema repository doesn't scale if the network grows, because this information would have to be replicated to all peers, and the update frequency grows with network size. Therefore query processing needs to rely on local information only, and we can't use techniques from distributed databases which require a central mediator.
- *Self-organization and -administration* A Peer-to-Peer network has no administrator who could create indexes, materialized views, etc., as in a central database. All management activities necessary to improve query processing need to be executed in a self-organizing fashion (cf. Chapter 16).

The chapter is structured as follows: Several design dimensions for schema-based Peer-to-Peer systems can be distinguished. These dimensions and possible choices for each dimension are presented in section 19.2. Semantic Web standards allow to represent information in a structured way which is especially suited for sharing. Therefore, they are a perfect basis for a schema-based Peer-to-Peer network. 19.3 exemplifies the connections between design choices by describing an existing Peer-to-Peer system for the Semantic Web. 19.4 includes the advanced topics schema mapping, distributed query plans and top-k query processing.

19.2 Design Dimensions of Schema-Based Peer-to-Peer Systems

Several decisions influence the design of a schema-based Peer-to-Peer system: the choice of the data model and associated query language, how to distribute the data among the peers (data placement), how to connect the peers (topology), and the query routing algorithm all determine search capabilities and performance [154]. This section describes options for each such design dimension along with their consequences for the resulting system.

19.2.1 Data Model and Query Language

The Data model used to store information is tightly connected to the aspect of the query language. Many data models have been proposed for storing structured data and it is out of scope to discuss them in detail. We rather want to mention some basic distinctions with respect to the data model that influence the ability of the system. The most basic way of storing structured data is in terms of a fixed, standardized schema that is used across the whole system. In this view, less complex data models like the one used in key- or keyword-based systems can be considered as special case of a very simple fixed schema. Despite the obvious limitations, fixed schema approaches are often observed in Peer-to-Peer systems because this eliminates the problem of schema interoperability. Interoperability is a problem in systems that allow the user to define and use a local schema. This does not only ask for a suitable integration method, it also leads to maintenance problems, because local schemas can evolve and new schemas can be added to the system when new peers join.

Nevertheless, several schema-based Peer-to-Peer systems which support flexible and/or heterogeneous schemas have been developed in the last years. Nearly all of them have employed common and widespread data models to benefit from well-defined semantics and a lot of experience. The most prevalent are the *relational* (e.g. PIER [308]), the *XML* (e.g. Piazza [273]) and the *Semantic Web* (e.g. Edutella [445], REMINDIN [586]) data model. In these models schemas can be viewed a collection of type definitions which in turn consist of attribute definitions. Taking the relational model as example, table definitions specify types and column definitions the attributes associated with each type.

Usually, one or several default query languages are associated with a data model. For the relational model this is SQL, for XML it is XPath and XQuery (see 19.3.1 for a discussion of query languages for the Semantic Web). To improve query processing efficiency, in schema-based Peer-to-Peer systems often only a subset of the associated query language is supported.

19.2.2 Data Placement

The data placement dimension is about where the data is stored in the network. Two different strategies for data placement in the network can be identified: placement according to ownership and placement according to search strategy.

Placement according to ownership. In a Peer-to-Peer system it seems most natural to store information at the peer which is controlled by the information owner. And this is indeed the typical case. The advantage is that access and modification are under complete control of the owner. For example, if the owner wants to cease publishing of its resources, he can simply disconnect his peer from the network. In the owner-based placement approach the network is only used to increase access to the information.

Placement according to search strategy. The complementary model is the when peers do not only cooperate in the search process, but already in storing the information. Then the network as a whole is like a uniform facility to store and retrieve information. In this case, data is distributed over the peers so that it can be searched for in the most efficient manner, i.e. according to the search strategy implemented in the network. Thus, the owner has less control, but the network becomes more efficient.

Both variants can be further improved in terms of efficiency by the introduction of additional caching and replication strategies. Note that while this improves the network performance, it also reduces the owner's control of information.

19.2.3 Topology and Routing

As with all Peer-to-Peer systems, the choice of topology and corresponding routing algorithms is crucial for schema-based networks. The distinction between unstructured and structured topologies is significant here, too. Hierarchical approaches such as super-peer networks can be of specific use for schema-based networks, and therefore are described separately.

Structured Networks. As shown in Chapter 7, structured networks, especially DHTs allow very efficient access for known keys. Thus, they are a good foundation for the creation of indexes. However, one DHT overlay can't serve for indexing more than one schema element (e.g. one column of a table). To answer queries containing arbitrary constraints one would need to maintain a separate DHT for every attribute. PIER [308] is such a system. It allows for efficient querying, but only for queries based on indexed attributes. For each of them, PIER maintains a DHT overlay network. This works good if network and/or data changes are limited, but at the price of increased maintenance effort otherwise.

Unstructured Networks. In unstructured networks, evaluation of complex queries is much simpler. They are forwarded to relevant peers and fully processed there. Each peer sends back its results, and all result sets are finally merged at the originating peer. A representative such networks is the Piazza system [273].The obvious drawback of such an approach is that some kind of flooding algorithm has to be used to distribute the query within the network. Traditional limitation techniques like time-to-live do only work well if the data is significantly replicated. This is common for file-sharing networks, but does not necessarily apply for information-sharing systems. A better way to reduce query distribution is to let peers apply filters on their connections for each query and send it only in the direction of relevant peers. The relevancy can be determined either based on a content summary provided by each peer [446] or based on the results of previous query evaluations [586].

Introducing short-cuts increases the probability further that a query reaches all relevant peers. Here, all peers continually asses their current connections based on the results of previous queries. If connections didn't yield enough results, they are given up. As replacement, the peer establishes new direct (short-cut) connections to peers relevant for past queries. Over time, this leads to an optimized topology [586]. Interestingly, specific reconnection strategies can lead to the emergence of regular topologies, although not enforced by the network algorithms [542]. This is characteristic for self-organizing systems in other areas (like biology) too, and seems to be a promising middle way between pure structured and pure unstructured networks (cf. Chapter 15).

Super-Peer Networks. Inspired by the mediator work in distributed databases, a special kind of hybrid networks, so-called super-peer networks have gained attention as topology for schema-based Peer-to-Peer networks. The distribution of peer performance characteristics (processing power, bandwidth, availability, etc.) is not distributed uniformly over all peers in a network. Exploiting these different capabilities in a Peer-to-Peer network can lead to an efficient network architecture [635], where a small subset of peers, called super-peers, takes over specific responsibilities for peer aggregation, query routing and possibly mediation. For this purpose, only the super-peers form a Peer-to-Peer network, and all other peers connect directly to the resulting super-peer backbone.

Super-peer-based Peer-to-Peer infrastructures usually exploit a two-phase routing architecture, which routes queries first in the super-peer backbone, and then distributes them to the peers connected to the super-peers. Like database mediators, super-peers only need to know which schema elements each connected peer supports. This is a small amount of information and thus easily indexed and maintained. Another advantage is the ability of super-peers to perform coordinating tasks as creating a distributed query plan for a query (see 19.4.2). The disadvantage of super-peer networks is the need to dedicate explicitly specific nodes to the super-peer role which limits the self-organization capabilities of the network.

When ontologies are used to categorize information, this can be exploited to further optimize peer selection in a super-peer network. Each super-peer becomes responsible for one or several ontology classes. Peers are clustered at these super-peers according to the classes of information they provide. Thus, an efficient structured network approach can be used to forward a query to the right super-peer, which distributes it to all relevant peers [395].

Discussion. Structured and unstructured networks have complementary advantages and disadvantages regarding their use for schema-based networks. The predetermined structure allows for more efficient query distribution in a structured network, because each peer 'knows' the network structure and can forward queries just in the right direction. But this does only work well if query complexity is limited, otherwise too many separate overlay networks have to be created and maintained.

In unstructured networks, peers do not know exactly in which direction to send a query. Therefore, queries have to be spread within the network to increase the probability of hitting the peer(s) having the requested resource, thus decreasing network efficiency. On the other hand, queries can take more or less any form, as long as each peer is able to match its resources against them locally. For support of highly expressive queries, as needed e.g. in ontology-based systems, only unstructured networks are feasible. An exception are some DHT systems which have been extended recently into hybrid networks that also support flooding-based query distribution strategies [106, 393].

Super-peer networks can alleviate the performance issues of pure unstructured topologies, but at the price of introducing two distinct peer classes.

19.3 Case Study: A Peer-to-Peer Network for the Semantic Web

To get an insight of all the issues which have to be solved in a schema-based Peer-to-Peer system it is instructive to take a thorough look at an existing system and the design choices involved in building it. As shown below, the Semantic Web data model is especially suited for sharing of structured data. Therefore a system from that context – Edutella – has been selected as case study.

The aim of the Edutella project [186, 445] is to design and implement a schema-based Peer-to-Peer infrastructure for the Semantic Web. Edutella relies on W3C Semantic Web standards [360, 91] to describe distributed resources, and uses basic Peer-to-Peer primitives provided as part of the JXTA framework ([255], see also 21.3.1).

19.3.1 Semantic Web Data Model and Query Language

In the Semantic Web, an important aspect for its overall design is the exchange of data among computer systems without the need of explicit consumer-producer relationships. The Resource Description Format standard (RDF, [360]) is used to annotate resources on the Web and provide the means by which computer systems can exchange and comprehend data. All resources are identifiable by unique resource identifiers (URIs plus anchor ids). All annotations are represented as statements of the form <subject, property, value>, where subject identifies the resource we want to describe (using a URI), property denotes which attribute we specify, and value the attribute value, expressed as a primitive datatype or an URI referring to another resource. For example, to annotate document `http://site/sample.html` with its author, we could use the statement `<http://site/sample.html` *`dc:creator`* `''Paul Smith''>`.

RDF Schema (RDFS, [91]) is used to define the vocabulary used for describing our resources. RDFS schema definitions include resource classes, properties and property constraints (domain, range, etc.). For example, property *dc:creator* is a property of the standardized Dublin Core metadata schema for document archives [159]. We can use any properties defined in the schemas we use, possibly mix different schemas, and relate different resources to each other, when we want to express interdependencies between these resources, hierarchical relationships, or others.

Another important characteristic of RDF metadata is the ability to use distributed annotations for one and the same resource. In contrast to traditional (non-distributed) database systems, it is not necessary to store all annotations of a resource on one server. One server might collect detailed information about authors, e.g., affiliation and contact information. Other servers which hold document metadata could just reference author URIs defined as part of the author servers data and don't need to repeat that information locally. This ability for distributed allocation of metadata makes RDF very suitable for the construction of distributed repositories.

In the Semantic Web context two types of query languages have been developed, SQL-like and rule-based languages. The former has the advantage that users familiar with SQL very quickly become familiar with the query language. Essentially, they allow the formulation of constraints on the RDF data graph and thus extraction of matching subgraphs.

But, although RDF data are basically graphs, query languages based on simple graph matching and subgraph extraction are not sufficient: they cannot reason about the semantics underlying such data, given in the form of schema languages like RDFS or OWL [407]. Even if we have a query language that takes RDFS into account, this built-in support for exactly one fixed schema language is not sufficient, as it does not allow us to query and combine RDF data expressed in multiple schema languages which is necessary in the case of distributed scenarios where providers can neither be forced to use the same schema nor the same schema language. Therefore, more expressive query formalisms have been investigated, which usually build on rule-like languages [78, 445, 564].

It is therefore required that a query language supports the definition of the semantics of several schema languages. This can appropriately be done with rule languages based on Datalog (or Horn logic in general). In Edutella, the Query Exchange Language (QEL, [451]) provides us with an expressive query exchange language which serves as a common query interchange format, into which local query languages can be translated (quite a common approach in distributed databases). Edutella peers are connected to the network using a wrapper-based architecture, where the wrapper is responsible for translating local query languages into the Edutella common query model.

Edutella peers can be highly heterogeneous in terms of the functionality they offer. In order to handle different query capabilities, Edutella defines several QEL language compliance levels, describing which kind of queries a peer can handle (conjunctive queries, relational algebra, transitive closure, etc.) Obviously, restricting query expressiveness allows for better optimization of query processing, so e.g. for publish/subscribe systems based on such a Peer-to-Peer network, a quite restricted form of queries is sufficient [116]. However, all peers still can use the same internal query representation for all capability levels, thus enabling reuse of existing functionality, e.g., for translation purposes.

19.3.2 Schema-Based Routing Indices

Edutella uses a super-peer topology, where super-peers form the network backbone and take care of routing queries through the network [446]. Only a small percentage of nodes are super-peers, but these are assumed to be highly available nodes with high computing capacity. In the Edutella network they are arranged in the HyperCuP topology [541].

The HyperCuP algorithm is capable of organizing peers into a recursive graph structure from the family of Cayley graphs, out of which the hypercube is the most well-known topology. This topology allows for $\log_2 N$ path length and $\log_2 N$ number of neighbors, where N is the total number of nodes in the network (i.e. the number of super-peers in our case). The algorithm works as follows: All edges are tagged with their dimension in the hypercube. A node invoking a request sends the message to all its neighbors, tagging it with the edge label on which the message was sent. Nodes receiving the message forward it only via edges tagged with higher edge labels (see [541] for details).

The Edutella super-peers employ routing indices, which explicitly acknowledge the semantic heterogeneity of schema-based Peer-to-Peer networks, and therefore include schema information as well as other possible index information. This super-peer backbone is responsible for message routing and integration of metadata. Super-peers in the Edutella network are arranged in the HyperCuP topology discussed in the last section.

Peers connect to the super-peers in a star-like fashion, providing content as well as content metadata. Figure 19.2 shows a very simple example of such a backbone. Alternatives to this topology are possible, as long as they guarantee the spanning tree property for the super-peer backbone, which is required for maintaining our routing indices and distributed query plans [94]. Other topologies are possible for other kinds of indices [137].

Super-Peer/Peer Routing Indices. Edutella super-peers characterize their associated peers using super-peer/peer routing indices. Whenever a new peer connects to a super-peer, it sends a self-description, including some meta-information about available data, during the initial handshake. The super-peer uses this self description to create indices at different granularities which are later on used to select appropriate peers for answering incoming queries. The following indices are always maintained:

- *Schema Index.* A base assumption is that different peers will support different schemas. These schemas are uniquely identified by their respective namespace, therefore the SP/P routing index contains the schema identifier and the peers supporting the respective schema.

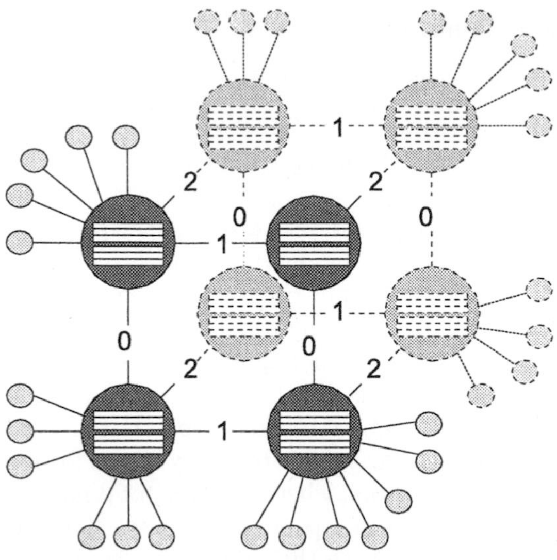

Fig. 19.2: HyperCuP Super-Peer Topology

– *Property/Sets of Properties Index.* This Routing index contains properties or sets thereof thus enabling peers to support only parts of schemas. If a query only refers to the supported property subset, it is forwarded to the corresponding peer.

Additionally super-peers can use even more fine-grained indexes, e.g. a *Property Value Range Index* or even a *Property Value Index* to restrict the set of relevant peers even further, at the price of increased index size.

These SP/P indices are updated when a peer connects to a super-peer, and contain all necessary information about connected peers. Entries are valid only for a certain time, and are deleted when the peer does not renew/update it regularly (e.g., because it leaves the network). Peers notify the super-peer when their content changes in ways that trigger an update of the index.

Super-Peer/Super-Peer Routing Indices. As with peers, queries should not be sent to all super-peers. To achieve this goal super-peer/super-peer routing indices can be used to route among the super-peers. These SP/SP indices are essentially extracts and summaries from the local SP/P indices. They contain the same kind of information as SP/P indices, but refer to the (direct) neighbors of a super-peer. Queries are forwarded to super-peer neighbors based on the SP/SP indices (restricting the basic HyperCuP broadcast), and sent to connected peers based on the SP/P indices.

Update of Edutella SP/SP indices is based on the registration (or update) messages from connected peers. Whenever an SP/P index changes, this change is propagated to (potentially) all super-peers using a (reversed)

HyperCuP broadcast. Whenever an SP/SP index stays the same after the update, propagation stops.

Because one important aspect of Peer-to-Peer networks is their dynamicity, the SP/SP indices are not, in contrast to distributed architectures in the database area (e.g., [88]), replicated versions of a central index, but rather parts of a distributed index similar to routing indices in TCP/IP networks.

When a query arrives at a super-peer, it matches the schema elements occurring in the query against the index information. The query is only forwarded to the peers and along the super-peer connections which use the same schema elements and are therefore able to deliver results. Thus, the indices act as message forwarding filter which ensure that the query is distributed only to relevant peers.

19.4 Advanced Topics

19.4.1 Schema Mapping

Mappings that explicitly specify the semantic relation between information objects in different sources are the basis for the integration of information from different sources. Normally, such mappings are not defined between individual data objects but rather between elements of the schema. Consequently, the nature of the mapping definitions strongly depend on the choice of a schema language. The richer the schema language, the more possibilities exist to clarify the relation between elements in the sources. However, both creation and use of mappings becomes more complex with the increasing expressiveness. There are a number of general properties mappings can have that influence their potential use for information integration:

- Mappings can relate single objects from the different information sources or connect multiple elements that are connected by operators to form complex expressions.
- Mappings can be undirected or directed and only state the relation from the point of view of one of the sources connected.
- Mappings can declaratively describe the relation between elements from different sources or consist of a procedural description of how to convert information from one source into the format of the other
- Declarative mappings can be exact or contain some judgement of how correct the mapping reflects the real relation between the information sources

In the context of Peer-to-Peer information sharing, the use of mappings is currently restricted to rather simple mappings. Most existing systems use simple equality or subsumption statements between schema elements. Approaches that use more complex mappings (in particular conjunctive queries) do not scale to a large number of sources. A prominent example is the Piazza approach [273].

19.4.2 Distributed Query Plans

Currently, data processing in Peer-to-Peer networks works as follows: The Peer-to-Peer network is queried for information satisfying some given conditions, and this query is routed to the peers which can answer it. When the possibly large number of results from distinct data sources is returned to the client peer, further query processing takes place centrally at the client. On the other side, data integration systems such as ObjectGlobe [88] distribute query plans to the distributed hosts as much as possible and thus are able to place operators close to the data sources. To generate the query plans, however, these systems need to know where all data are located.

The naive and straightforward way to combine both approaches is to first use Peer-to-Peer capabilities to find out where data is stored, and then use this information to generate a distributed query plan at the client. This query plan becomes instantiated and executed on different hosts. But this would be not very efficient. Based on the super-peer architecture described in section 19.3.2 the query execution can be optimized by pushing *abstract query plans* through the super-peer-based network, where each super-peer picks and expands those parts of the query plan that can be executed locally [94]. The decision which operations can be executed locally is guided by SP/SP and SP/P indices. This leads to a dynamic *on the fly* distribution and expansion of query plans. Operators are placed next to data sources and thus utilize distributed computing resources more effectively.

The expansion of these abstract query plans can be based on different strategies, related to the quality of clustering in the Peer-to-Peer network. If the data are clustered well with respect to the queries, it is most efficient to push joins in the query as near as possible to the data sources, and then take the union of the results for these joins. If the clustering does not reflect the partitions needed by the query, it is more beneficial to gather the data and do the joins on these data on a central super-peer (see also [349]).

19.4.3 Top-k Query Processing

Meaningful querying for information, whether on the Web or in information systems and databases, often retrieves answers together with an indication of how well the results match the query. Various kinds of metadata available through the Semantic Web offer additional semantic information which may be integrated into the retrieval process. However, this generally comes at the price of large result set sizes that are often unmanageable for the individual user, especially because they are in arbitrary order (at least with respect to the relevance for the user). Since users are usually only interested in a few *most relevant* answers, the goal is to return manageable result sets of answers ranked by their relevance according to the query.

Ranking scores each resource that matches a query using a certain set of criteria and then returns it as part of a ranked list. Additionally, we need to restrict the number of results, to make it easier for the user to use the results, and to minimize traffic in a Peer-to-Peer environment. In databases, this approach is referred to as top-k query processing, where only the k best matching resources are returned to the user.

Top-k ranking in Peer-to-Peer networks has to address two additional challenges [444]:

Mismatch in scoring techniques and input data. Scoring techniques and input data used by the different peers can have a strong impact on getting the correct overall top-scored objects. Since we want to minimize network traffic, but nevertheless integrate the top-scored objects from all different peers (and super-peers) within each super-peer, each super-peer has to decide how to score answers to a given query. In general we want to assume that every peer throughout the network uses the same methods to score documents with respect to a query, though input data to compute these scores may be different.

Using only distributed knowledge. Distributed information and thus different input data to score answers complicates top-k retrieval, because many scoring measures that take global characteristics into account simply cannot be evaluated correctly with limited local knowledge. See section 20.1.2 for a context where some global knowledge (or estimation) is required for correct score calculation.

One algorithm for top-k query evaluation is presented in [54]. It uses the same super-peer architecture as described in section 19.3.2. The algorithm is based on local rankings at each peer, which are aggregated during routing of answers for a given query at the super-peers involved in the query answering process. Each peer computes local rankings for a given query, and returns just the best matches to its super-peer. At the super-peer, the results are merged, using the result scores, and routed back to the query originator. On this way back, each involved super-peer again merges results from local peers and from neighboring super-peers and forwards only the best results, until the aggregated top k results reach the peer that issued the corresponding query. While results are routed through the super-peers, they note in an index the list of peers / super-peers which contributed to the top k results for a query. This information is subsequently used to directly route queries that were answered before only to those peers able to provide top answers. Thus, the distribution of queries can be limited significantly and query processing becomes much more efficient. To cope with network churn, index entries expire after some time, and the query is again sent to all relevant peers. Algorithm details can be found in [54], together with optimality proofs and simulation results.

19.5 Conclusion

Schema-based Peer-to-Peer networks are the next step in the evolution of distributed database query processing. We can see two research directions in this area, infrastructures which view the Peer-to-Peer network as one virtual database, and infrastructures for creating a Peer-to-Peer network of independent, possibly heterogeneous data sources.

To create an efficient distributed, but homogeneous database, structured networks are a suitable foundation, although the issue of multi-dimensional queries has not been solved completely. The paradigmatic example for such a system is PIER. Query processing in such systems is very efficient, at the price of restricted query expressivity. A typical characteristic is that data is not placed on the data owner's peer, but distributed according to the underlying network structure.

On the other hand, for largely heterogeneous networks no pure structured network is suitable as underlying topology, because no global schema exists on which a uniform index could be built. Thus, unstructured networks are the prevalent foundation for such networks. Starting from random graphs, algorithms have emerged which optimize peer connections and thus improve query processing performance. However, these systems do not yet scale to more than thousands of participants. Hybrid topologies (e.g. super-peer networks like Edutella) can improve efficiency further by dedicating peers to the traditional database mediator role.

Schema mapping is still a challenging issue in distributed databases, and therefore it is no wonder that highly scalable solutions do not (yet) exist for the Peer-to-Peer case. However, systems like Piazza have already gone far towards loosely-coupled integration of heterogeneous systems in a Peer-to-Peer network.

The need for more information sharing and information integration on the Web and in other open contexts is growing, and schema-based Peer-to-Peer systems are a promising way to meet these needs. While not yet escaped from research labs, we will probably see practical applications based on such infrastructures soon.

20. Supporting Information Retrieval in Peer-to-Peer Systems

Wolf-Tilo Balke (L3S Research Center and University of Hannover)

This chapter focuses on information retrieval techniques in Peer-to-Peer infrastructures. Peer-to-peer systems are already being used for a vast number of applications in content exchange, but most searching is done by simple keyword lookups. In contrast information retrieval means that not only some more or less matching objects have to be retrieved, but a list of the best matching objects over the entire network given a user's information needs. Since the 1960ies the information retrieval community considers ways to efficiently and effectively query document collections and designs dedicated retrieval systems like e.g. SMART [96]. Usually a query is seen as a (possibly weighted) set of keywords a user specifies to express his/her information need. Documents that contain those (or sufficiently similar) keywords are considered to be relevant to the user's information need as expressed by the query. Thus, for information retrieval in Peer-to-Peer infrastructures the challenge is not only to retrieve documents efficiently, but also to effectively find a set of best matching objects. Usually the degree of effectiveness is measured by a precision-recall analysis, where the precision of a retrieval algorithm is given by the ratio of relevant delivered documents with respect to the size of the delivered result set (i.e. number of correctly retrieved documents divided by the number of all retrieved documents). The recall is given by the ratio of the relevant delivered documents with respect to the all relevant documents in the collections (i.e. number of correctly retrieved documents divided by the number of all relevant documents).

20.1 Content Searching in Peer-to-Peer Applications

Peer-to-peer (P2P) systems are highly distributed computing or service substrates built from thousands or even millions of typically non-dedicated nodes across the Internet that may flexibly join or leave the system at any time. In contrast to centralized system architectures Peer-to-Peer networks try to avoid central services and will usually share local resources like computing power [30] or storage space (e.g. Freenet [124]). They are characterized by a high resilience against failures of single nodes, good scalability by joining resources and a high degree of autonomy for each peer.

R. Steinmetz and K. Wehrle (Eds.): P2P Systems and Applications, LNCS 3485, pp. 337-352, 2005.

20.1.1 Exchanging Media Files by Meta-Data Searches

The first big application of Peer-to-Peer technology was the free exchange of music files (mostly mp3 files, but also a limited amount of videos) over the Internet. As early as 1999 Napster [436] offered a platform to exchange files in a distributed fashion. Peers could offer files for download and directly download files from other peers in the network. The Napster platform was not Peer-to-Peer technology in the strict sense, because Napster still relied on a central server administrating addresses of peers and lists of offered files. The files offered were, however, not moved to the server, but all downloads were directly initiated between two peers. The content searches in the Napster network were made on a restricted amount of meta-data like filename, artist, or song title. Matching this limited meta-data with a user's query keywords content searches thus only decided, if there was a peer offering an adequate file and ordered possible downloads by the expected quality of the download connection.

Since a central index approach could only handle the Napster network's enormous success in terms of scalability by hierarchies of peers and provided a single point of responsibility for the content, from 2000 on the Gnutella [249] network began to build a file exchange platform on a real Peer-to-Peer structure. Content searches were performed by flooding queries from the originating peer to all neighboring nodes within a certain radius (the time to live (TTL) for a query). Also this approach proved not to be scalable beyond a certain point and the Gnutella network spectacularly broke down in August 2000 because of heavy overloads in low bandwidth peers. This breakdown led to the introduction of load-balancing and the construction of schema-based networks (Fast Track, e.g. KaZaA [343] or Morpheus [432]), where a backbone of high bandwidth peers (so-called super-peers) takes a lot of the query routing responsibility. Search in schema-based Peer-to-Peer networks will be discussed in a different chapter of this book.

20.1.2 Problems in Peer-to-Peer Information Retrieval

Previous applications for media exchange dealt mostly with exact or substring matching of simple meta-data descriptions of media files. When it comes to the exchange of (predominantly) textual documents , meta-data is not enough, but fulltext searches have to be supported. Though meta-data can capture some basic traits of a document (e.g. that some text is a 'newspaper article' related to 'sports'), they cannot anticipate and capture all the aspects of a text a user might be interested in. Thus, in information retrieval all terms that can be in some way important for a document should be searchable (i.e. indexed). The second major difference to meta-data-based retrieval is that information retrieval cannot use an exact match retrieval model, but has to rely on ranked retrieval models. These models introduce the notion of a certain degree of match of each document with respect to the query. The higher the degree of match the better the document is expected to satisfy a user's information need. Thus in contrast to simple media file exchanges, where the connection speed was the most interesting factor for choosing a peer for download, information retrieval really has to find the document with best degree of match from any peer within the entire network. A well balanced expected precision and recall of such a content search is thus a major indicator for the effectiveness of the search capabilities.

Very early information retrieval research encountered the necessity to not only take information in each document into account, but also use some background information regarding the entire collection, prominently e.g. the discriminatory power of each keyword within the specific collection. For example considering different news collections, the occurrence of the keyword 'basketball' in a document will have a good discriminatory power in a general news collection, a severely lesser power to discriminate between documents in a sports news collection and virtually no discriminative power within a collection of NBA news. One of the most popular information retrieval measure thus is the well-known TFxIDF type. This measure is a combination of two parts (typically with some normalizations), the term frequency (TF, measures how often a query term is contained in a certain document), and the inverted document frequency (IDF, inverse of how often a query term occurs in documents of the specific collection). Intuitively a document gets more relevant the more often the query term(s) occur in the document and the less often the query terms occur in other documents of the collection (i.e. the more discriminating query terms are with respect to a collection). Though TF can be determined locally by each peer, the IDF measure needs to integrate collection-wide information and cannot be determined locally. A typical instance of the TFxIDF measure (with $s_q(D)$ as the score for query term q in document D and N as the total number of documents in the collection) is e.g. given by:

$$s_q(D) := \frac{TF_q(D)}{max_{t \in D}(TF_t(D))} * \log(\frac{N}{DF_q})$$

Collection-wide information is thus essential to provide proper document scores. In information retrieval research the problem of disseminating collection-wide information was first encountered when retrieval systems moved beyond stand-alone systems over collections like e.g. given by TREC, and had to deal with vast distributed document collections like the WWW. Here due to the random-like distribution of content over the WWW, research on effective retrieval in Web IR applications showed that a complete dissemination with immediate updates is usually unnecessary, even if new documents are included into the collection [607]. The required level of dissemination, however, was found to be dependent on the document allocation throughout the network [606]: random allocation calls for low dissemination, whereas higher dissemination is needed if documents are allocated based on content. In Peer-to-Peer networks such a random-like distribution does usually not hold. In practical applications peers often will not carry a random portion of the entire document collection, but rather a set of documents that represent their individual interests.

Consider e.g. the news servers example from above. In the WWW there are some big centralized news serves like e.g. CNN or the New York Times that deal with all kinds of news, i.e, cover a wide range of topics. Even if news items change, the overall distribution of topics and keywords can be assumed to change only slowly. In contrast in Peer-to-Peer applications peers usually only provide a couple of sets of topically close documents they are interested in. That means that if a peer joins or leaves the network the collection-wide information may considerably change. Thus, a lazy dissemination in settings like the WWW usually has comparable effectiveness as a centralized approach for general queries, but if only parts of the networks containing most promising documents with similar content are queried like in Peer-to-Peer applications, the collection-wide information has to be disseminated and regularly updated. On the other hand this information does not necessarily always need to be completely up-to-date; obviously there is a trade-off between index information that is 'still current enough' given the network volatility and the accuracy of the query results.

Thus, in contrast to previous work in distributed information retrieval, not only the distributed aspect of the retrieval, but also the peers' autonomy and the relatively high network churn are major problems in Peer-to-Peer information retrieval. The problems for information retrieval can be roughly classified into four main categories:

- **Ranked Retrieval Model:** Exact match models will immediately lead to a valid result object once any document has been encountered fulfilling the query predicate. When answering queries in a ranked model a large number of documents have to be compared to find the 'best matching' document or the peers offering them. Moreover, queries often consist of a conjunction of different keywords to express a user's information need, hence the retrieval model has to allow for assessing a document's degree of match for complex queries.
- **Efficient Evaluation Scheme:** An efficient ranked retrieval model does not allow for simply flooding queries until a suitable peer for download is found, because a prohibitive number of peers would have to be addressed. Since the best matching document to a query could be encountered querying the most distant peer, guaranteeing correct retrieval results by flooding queries can only be facilitated by addressing every peer in the network. An efficient evaluation scheme thus needs ways to select most appropriate peers for querying.
- **Reliability Facing Network Churn:** Centralized index structures for the Peer-to-Peer network can provide all necessary information about what documents are available, but this solution does not scale, provides a single

point of failure and needs a high communication overhead for keeping track of content changes in the network (e.g. peers changing their local content by adding or deleting documents or peers joining or leaving the network). Thus distributed index structures that are still reliable even in the face of network churn, have to be used.
- **Integration of Collection-Wide Information:** Queries cannot be answered by the individual peers having only local knowledge, but a peers needs up-to-date collection-wide information for correct scoring. Constantly disseminating this collection-wide information needs a high amount of bandwidth, if the network is rather volatile, with a high number of peers joining or leaving the network. Moreover, quick dissemination is necessary, if peers show a certain locality in their interests and provide document collections for specific topics, instead of a broad variety that resembles the topic distribution of the network.

20.1.3 Related Work in Distributed Information Retrieval

The problem of distributed information retrieval occurred already early in information retrieval literature and was mainly concerned with the merging of results and database content discovery. Together with the emergence of the World Wide Web as a highly distributed information source the research was intensified and the following paragraphs will revisit some important approaches that are also common in today's Peer-to-Peer information retrieval.

Abstracts of Information Sources. To support distributed information retrieval individual collections often have to send abstracts to a central (or distributed) repository. The abstract of a collection is usually simply the set of terms in the collection's inverted index. The most renown technique of efficiently representing these abstracts are Bloom filters [77]. A Bloom filter is data structure in the form of a bit vector compactly representing a set and allowing membership queries. In our case the set represented is the set of terms in a peer's inverted index. The filter computed is created by deriving n different indexes for each term using n different hash functions, each yielding a bit location in the vector. All bits at these positions in the Bloom filter are set to 1. The membership of a query term now can be efficiently determined by hashing the query term using the same n functions and comparing it bitwise with the filter. If there exists a position where a bit is set for the query term, but not in the filter, the query term is definitely not a member of the peer's abstract, which was used for creating the filter. Otherwise, with a certain probability it is member of the peer's abstract (Bloom filters allow for false positives. The probability of false positives is decreasing with growing n). Today Bloom filters are a popular technique for exchanging summaries of a peer's document collection. The PlanetP system for instance uses such

Bloom filters for retrieval and disseminates them throughout the community using gossiping algorithms [140].

Collection Selection. If no central index of all collections' contents is given, choosing 'just the right' collections for querying is a major problem. For the use in distributed environments like the WWW several benefit estimators for collection selection have been proposed. Basically these estimators use aggregated statistics about the individual collections to estimate the expected result quality of each individual collection. Expected qualities can then be used for deciding which collections to select for querying or for determining a querying sequence of the collections. The most popular benefit estimator is the CORI measure [101], which computes the collection score s_i for collection i with respect to a query q as:

$$s_i := \sum_{t \in q} \frac{\alpha + (1-\alpha) * T_{i,t} * I_{i,t}}{|q|}$$

$$\text{with } T_{i,t} := \beta + (1-\beta) * \frac{\log(cdf_{i,t} + 0.5)}{\log(cdf_{i,t}^{max} + 1.0)} \text{ and } I_{i,t} := \frac{\frac{\log(n+0.5)}{cf_t}}{log(n+1.0)}$$

where n is the number of collections, *cdf* the collection document frequency, cdf^{max} the maximum collection document frequency and finally cf_t denotes the collection frequency of query term t, i.e. the number of collections that contain the term. See [101] for appropriate choices of α and β.

Later [100] proposed to use a different formula for computing $T_{i,t}$ subsequently leading to better results:

$$T_{i,t} := \frac{cdf_{i,t}}{cdf_{i,t} + 50 + 150 * \frac{|V_i|}{|V^{avg}|})}$$

where V_i is the term space of the collection i, i.e. the distinct terms in the collection's inverted index. V^{avg} is the average term space of all collections whose inverted index contains term t. However, it is important to notice that statistics like the collection frequency cf_t or the average term space size V^{avg} have to be collected over all peers. That means they are collection-wide information that cannot be determined locally but has to be disseminated globally or estimated. Also the CORI estimators are widely used in Peer-to-Peer information retrieval, because they allow choosing collections with a sufficient quality, while having to exchange only a very limited amount of statistical data.

Metacrawlers. Closely related to the field of collection selection are so-called metacrawlers like e.g. GlOSS [259] (shorthand for Glossary of Server Servers). Metacrawlers have been designed in connection with the text database discovery problem, i.e. the problem of selecting most promising document collections from the WWW with respect to a query. The basic idea is that a metacrawler does not crawl the actual document collection and build a complete index over the documents, but rather collects only metadata about the individual collections like the number of documents in each collection and how many documents for each keyword (above a certain critical threshold number) in a collection are present. Abstracting from the actual information which document contains the keyword, the indexes build by the metacrawler are much smaller than inverted keyword indexes, however, of course due to the aggregation of information also less reliable. For instance the information whether keywords appear conjunctively in any document of the collection is lost. But the resulting index can be handled centrally and the meta-data used for giving probabilities of finding suitable documents in each collection.

In GlOSS the usefulness of a collection for single keyword queries can be characterized by the number of documents that contain the keyword normalized by the total number of documents the collection offers. Building on the assumption that keywords appear independently in documents, the usefulness for multi-keyword queries is given as the product of the normalized numbers for each individual keyword [259]. This basic text database discovery using a central glossary of servers supports boolean retrieval and retrieval in the vector space model (vGlOSS). Experiments on the GlOSS system show that average index sizes can be reduced by about two orders of magnitude and produced a correct estimation (compared to a complete inverted document index) of the most useful collections in over 80% of cases. But still, since the glossary index is a central index, it needs to be updated every time a collection changes and thus does not lend itself easily to information retrieval in Peer-to-Peer infrastructures.

Although the work on distributed information retrieval and metasearch is definitely relevant related research, it addresses only the problem of integrating a small and typically rather static set of underlying retrieval engines and information sources. Such a small federation of systems is of course less challenging than a collaborative search process in highly dynamical Peer-to-Peer systems. We will take a closer look at specific techniques used in Peer-to-Peer infrastructures in the following sections.

20.2 Index Structures for Query Routing in Peer-to-Peer Infrastructures

Since traditional index structures cannot be readily employed in Peer-to-Peer systems, distributed paradigms must be used to find those peers in the network which offer suitable documents. Information retrieval queries then have to be routed directly to those peers. As stated before, given the network churn in typical Peer-to-Peer applications, the overhead of maintaining indexes in the presence of churn is a particularly important aspect.

20.2.1 Distributed Hash Tables for Information Retrieval

The simplest method of querying peer to peer systems is flooding queries iteratively from the querying peer to all adjacent peers until a certain number of hops (the 'time to live' for the query) is reached. While this solution is simple and robust even when peers join and leave the system, it does not scale and will only provide query answers within a limited radius around the querying peer. This can be fundamentally improved if content-based routing is allowed in the network. One of today's main technique for indexing such Peer-to-Peer systems are so-called distributed hash tables (DHTs) (see e.g. [505], [575]) which allow to route queries with certain keys to particular peers containing the desired data without requiring a central index. Typically, an exact match keyword search can be routed to the proper peers in a limited number of hops logarithmic of the network size, and likewise no peer needs to maintain more than a logarithmic amount of routing information. But to provide this functionality, all new content in the network has to be published at the node for the respective key, if new data on a peer arrives or a new peer joins the network. In case a peer leaves the network, the information about its content has to be unpublished. Moreover, if a new document is added to any peer's collection, it will usually contain a large set a of various terms that need to be indexed. Since in DHTs a hashing function decides on what peer the index for each term resides, chances are that a considerable number of peers holding some part of the DHT have to be addressed to fully publish all the information about the new document, see e.g. [237].

Recent research in [393] shows that due to the publishing/unpublishing overhead, distributed hash tables lack efficiency when highly replicated items are requested. In practical settings, they have shown to perform even worse than flooding approaches degrading even further, if stronger network churn is introduced. Therefore, first hybrid Peer-to-Peer infrastructures have been proposed [394] that use DHTs only for less replicated and rare items, where DHTs are efficient, and rely on flooding in the rest of cases. But for the use in practical scenarios, recent investigation of file exchange behavior [113] show that rare items are also rarely queried ('People are looking for hay, not for needles'). Usually, the querying behavior in practical applications follows a Zipf distribution: there is a moderate number of popular items containing many replicas in the network, and a long tail of rarely queried items containing few replicas. Thus, though having a large potential in speed-up by using DHTs in queries for rare items, relying on flooding for the majority of queries does not seem a sensible approach and cannot support information retrieval queries.

Another problem with distributed hash tables is that the retrieval uses exact matches of single keywords, whereas information retrieval queries are usually conjunctions of several keywords. If such a query has to be answered using DHTs the peers offering content for each of the keywords have to be retrieved [347]. The intersection of the individual peer lists then may offer documents also relevant to the conjunctive query. However, there is still no guarantee that a peer in this intersection offers relevant content because the publishing of the peer for each keyword may have been based on different documents. Thus even if a peer offers content for each single keyword, it is not clear whether it offers a single document containing the conjunction of the keyword. Of course, the documents of the respective keyword have to be evaluated with a suitable scoring function to assess their degree of match and thus the ranking of the final result. Obviously, this process is no efficient solution to the information retrieval challenge in Peer-to-Peer infrastructures. Moreover, typical search processes in document collections like browsing navigation or prefetching are complicated by the virtualization of the namespaces by DHTs (see e.g. [347] for a discussion).

20.2.2 Routing Indexes for Information Retrieval

A sophisticated strategy for accurately finding very commonly queried items can be provided using so-called routing indexes . A routing index is a local collection of (key, peer) pairs where the key is either a keyword or a query. The basic notion of a routing index is that in contrast to flooding all neighbors or selecting some randomly, the index points to an interesting peer or in the direction of interesting peers for a query. Peers thus can route a given query along connections that lead to collections of peers relevant for a query. Usually, it is distinguished between links in the default network pointing only in the direction of peers holding interesting collections and real links to some specific peers, forming an overlay and often referred to as shortcuts (since peers in the index do not have to be directly adjacent to the peer keeping the index). A topic-specific clustering of shortcuts represents a semantic overlay that may be completely independent from the underlying physical network.

Routing indexes were first introduced by [137] with the goal to choose best neighbors of a peer to forward a query to until the desired number of results is reached. While this approach only focused on routing, a lot of research soon focused on directly contacting relevant peers using semantic characteristics, like [274] or [444]. Subsequently, routing indexes were extended to different uses in Peer-to-Peer systems like top k retrieval [54]. The maintenance of such a routing index is of only local nature (that means that no publishing/unpublishing overhead like in DHTs is caused), and the recall for the indexed items is usually quite high. Since users in Peer-to-Peer environments are usually interested in popular queries and show a certain consistency in their interests, a routing index in most applications is a good solution.

But the question arises how to construct local indexes in a manner that is both effective in recall and efficient in performance. It is clear that in order to be effective in terms of recall, the local indexes should have a large amount of knowledge of the collections on different peers. On the other hand, having collected a large amount of knowledge calls for constant updates to keep track of changes in the collections. Different routing index policies have been proposed to tackle this trade-off. Generally, it can be distinguished between restricted index sizes and unrestricted index sizes. For restricted index sizes index entries are collected and exchanged, if the maximum index size is reached but new information has been gathered. Getting rid of stale index entries is thus implemented by letting index entries compete with respect to their expected usefulness. One of the most often used strategy here is the LRU-strategy ('least recently used') that assigns higher usefulness to those index entries that have been successfully used in the recent past. The more recent, the more accurate and thus the more useful. However, the optimal size of such restricted indexes is a difficult problem and strongly dependent on the network's actual volatility that is hard to determine locally.

In terms of unrestricted indexes, the peers keeping them locally have to combat network churn in a different way. For structured networks, the work on distributed retrieval in [54] proposes to use a backbone of superpeers for query routing where each superpeer keeps only a strictly locally maintained routing index. Queries are always routed along a minimum spanning tree of the backbone and the individual results are routed back the same way. Each routing index contains the recently asked query terms, all local peers that contributed to the result set of best documents, and the direction in terms of adjacent superpeers, where high quality documents came from. If a superpeer does not have a matching index entry for a query term, it forwards the query in all directions along the backbone and collects accurate information for its index, when the best documents have been determined and the results are routed back. Each index entry is assigned a certain time to live to combat network churn. Experiments show that this kind of index maintenance is especially suitable for Zipfian query frequency distributions like often encountered in Peer-to-Peer scenarios, where it essentially reduces the number of contacted peers and gives a recall comparable to central indexes.

Another approach using unrestricted index sizes are InfoBeacons [131] mainly maintaining a set of local indexes that are loosely coupled to the document sources on the peers. Like in the GlOSS approach [259] the indexes save space by containing only statistics about the documents in the underlying collections. This statistics can then be used to compute the expected usefulness of each known document source. To combat network churn or changes in underlying document collections [131] proposes to apply a 'forgetting factor' that periodically weighs down stale information about a source until it is finally 'forgotten'. In the same way the statistics about a source can be refreshed by evaluating answers to recent queries of that source (a so-called 'experience factor'). By closely investigating the result documents, an InfoBeacon index can not only learn about the query terms, but also about other terms that are contained in some result document.

20.2.3 Locality-Based Routing Indexes

A different approach for routing queries to most interesting document collections is based on the idea of social metaphors. Inspired by information retrieval processes between people in real life, social networks of peers can be used to get queries to the most relevant peers. Experiments about how information is gathered, showed that people in real world settings are quite capable of efficiently constructing chains of acquaintances that will bring them at least close to the desired information, though each person only had very local knowledge of the network (see e.g. [413] or [353]). The resulting so-called 'small worlds' have subsequently been employed to retrieve relevant information with respect to a peer's information need as expressed by the peer's queries.

Using small worlds for retrieval an often made assumption is the principle of interest-based locality. It posits that, if a peer has a particular document that is relevant to a query, it might very probably also have other interesting items that the querying peer is interested in. Building on this principle [571] studied interest-based overlays over Gnutella-style networks and proposes to generate interest-based shortcuts connecting querying peer and content-providing peer. Queries with semantically close information needs can then rely on already established shortcuts. Traces on practical data collections illustrate how peers in the overlay network get very well connected and that the overlay graph shows the highly-clustered characteristics of small world networks with a small minimum distance between any two nodes. The clustering coefficient of a peer is defined to be the fraction of edges that exist between its neighbors over the possible total number of edges. The clustering coefficient is a relevant measure for the degree of the small world characteristic as reflected by the network. Clusters in the shortcut graph can be said to correspond to clusters of interests and peers looking for content within their usual areas of interest, will be successful with high probability by using their shortcuts.

Other work, like e.g. [586], directly relied on social metaphors for routing queries to peers that can be assumed to offer interesting documents. A peer builds an index of shortcuts e.g. by 'remembering' content provider that have offered relevant documents in the past for a query or for queries on semantically similar topics, or by 'overhearing' communications between other peers that are just routed through the peer. Best peers that are likely to offer relevant documents, can then be queried by just following the shortcuts whose topic best matches the query semantics. Randomly sending queries also to some peers from the default network helps to extend the knowledge about relevant peers and is a limited help facing the problems of interest changes and network churn. Experiments show that such shortcut-based approaches can offer a decent recall and dramatically reduce the communication needed for answering queries.

20.3 Supporting Effective Information Retrieval in Peer-to-Peer Systems

20.3.1 Providing Collection-Wide Information

As has been stated, providing collection wide is essential for the retrieval effectiveness. There is a challenging trade-off between reduced network traffic by lazy dissemination however leading to less effective retrieval, and a large network traffic overhead by eager dissemination facilitating very effective retrieval. What is needed is 'just the right' level of dissemination to maintain a 'suitable' retrieval effectiveness. Thus previous approaches to disseminate collection-wide information rely on different techniques.

The PlanetP system [140] does not use collection-wide information like e.g. the inverted document frequency of query terms directly, but circumnavigates the problem by using a so-called inverted peer frequency (IPF). The inverted peer frequency estimates for all query terms, which peers are interesting contributors to a certain query. For each query term t the inverted peer frequency is given by $IPF_t := \log(1 + \frac{N}{N_t})$ where N is the number of peers in the community and N_t is the number of peers that offer documents containing term t. In PlanetP summarizations of the content in the form of Bloom filters are used to decide what content a peer can offer. Since these are eagerly disseminated throughout the network by gossiping algorithms, each peer can locally decide values for N and N_t. The relevance of a peer for answering multi-keyword queries is then simply the sum of the inverted peer frequencies for all query terms. Peers are then queried in the sequence of their IPFs and the best documents are collected until queried peers do no longer improve the quality of the result set. In terms of retrieval effectiveness [140] show that the approach is quite comparable to the use of inverted document frequencies in precision and recall and also the documents retrieved using IPF show an average overlap of about 70% to result sets retrieved using IDF. However, by using gossiping to disseminate Bloom filters the system's scalability is severely limited.

Structured Peer-to-Peer infrastructures allow for a more scalable way of providing collection-wide information than simple gossiping. Based on the notion that in answering a query current collection-wide information is only needed for the query terms, each superpeer can disseminate such information together with a query. [53] shows for a setting of distributed servers hosting collections of newspaper articles that employing an index collecting information like IDFs for certain query terms in parallel to the query routing index can provide sufficiently up-to-date collection-wide information. The basic idea of both indexes is the same: the routing index of a super-peer states what peers are interesting to address for a given query and the CWI index provides collection-wide data for each keyword. The data in the CWI index can change in two ways: like in routing indexes existing entries have only a certain time to live, such that stale entries are periodically removed. On the other hand it can be updated evaluating the answers of the peers that the query was forwarded to. These peers can easily provide the result documents together with local statistics about their individual collections. This statistical information can then be aggregated along the super-peer backbone to give an adequate snapshot of the currently most important document collections for a keyword (e.g. document frequencies and collection sizes can be added up). As stated in [607] the collection-wide informations does usually only change significantly, if new peers join the network with corpora of documents on completely new topics. Since index entries only have a certain time to live, occasionally flooding queries about query terms not in the index (and disseminating only an estimation of the statistics needed), usually refreshes the CWI index sufficiently, while not producing too many incorrect results. Experiments in [53] show that by using an CWI index and disseminating the collection-wide information together with the query, even in the presence of massive popularity shifts the CWI index recovers quickly.

20.3.2 Estimating the Document Overlap

As another important factor for supporting the overall retrieval quality is assessing the novelty of collections as e.g. motivated in [66]. In collection selection approaches usually precomputed statistics about the expected quality of results from a collection is used to minimize the number of collections that have to be accessed. Minimizing the number of collection accesses (and thus the necessary communication) is even more important in Peer-to-Peer settings. Given typical popularity distributions with a high amount of replication of popular items in today's file sharing applications [113], it seems probable that also in document exchange such overlap between the individual peers' repositories will exist. However, accessing promising peers in an information retrieval process that show a high overlap in their collection is not going to improve the result sets. When deriving result sets from distributed sources, like e.g. in [54], the result merging will ignore documents that have occurred before and simply put out requests (and thus probably contact more peers) for more answers until enough distinct documents have been found.

The novelty of a collection a new peer offers always has to be computed with respect to a reference collection, i.e. collections that are already part of the querying peer's local routing index or more general the collection of already returned result documents. [66] defines the novelty of a peer p's collection C_p with respect to a reference collection C_{ref} as:

$$Novelty(C_p) := |C_p| - |C_p \cap C_{ref}|$$

However, since there is usually no information disseminated exactly what documents are given by a certain peer, this information has to be approximated by the information disseminated. Thus, for estimating what is actually in a peer's collection with respect to multi keyword queries the index lists or summaries of the peer have to be investigated. Using Bloom filters as summaries [66] proposes to build a peer p's combined Bloom filter b_p with respect to the query as the bitwise logical AND of its filters for the individual keywords and then estimate the novelty by comparing it to $b_{prev} := \bigcup_{i \in S} b_i$ as the union of those Bloom filters b_i of the set of collections S that have already been investigated previously during the retrieval process. The degree of novelty can then be approximated by counting the locations where peer p's Bloom filter gives set bits that are not already set in the combined filter of previous collections:

$$|\{k | b_p[k] = 1 \wedge b_{prev}[k] = 0\}|$$

Analogously, the overlap between the collections can be estimated by counting the number of bits that are set in both filters. Of course this is only a heuristic measure as the actual documents have been abstracted into summaries. Having the same summary, however, does not imply being the same document, but only being characterized by the same keywords. That means those documents are probably not adding new aspects for the user's information need as expressed in the query. Generally speaking estimating the overlap and preferably querying peers that add new aspects to an answer set is a promising technique for supporting information retrieval in Peer-to-Peer environments and will need further attention.

20.3.3 Prestructuring Collections with Taxonomies of Categories

Retrieval in Peer-to-Peer systems considered two different kinds of paradigms: the meta-data-based queries and the fulltext-based queries. Often it is useful to consider them not as two orthogonally used paradigms, but to integrate them into a single query. A major problem in information retrieval where such an integration is helpful, is for instance the disambiguation of query terms. In Peer-to-Peer systems offering documents that show a certain similarity in terms of their types (like collections of newspaper articles, etc.), the retrieval process can essentially be supported by introducing a common system of categories that classify the documents. Given that categories are usually not entirely independent of each other a taxonomy of the categories can find related categories that are semantically closer than others. A query then can be given using keywords and the category the result documents should be in. The approach given in [53] shows that queries have to be answered in each category separately starting with the category specified in the query. Thus, the query routing index has to contain also category information. If no sufficient number of documents can be retrieved from that category the search has to be extended first to the children of the category and then to its parents. For each category own collection-wide information has to be collected and disseminated, e.g. by building CWI indexes as described above per category.

Following [382] the semantic similarity for different categories c_1 and c_2 can be considered to be determined by the shortest path length as well as the depth of the common subsumer:

$$sim(c_1, c_2) = e^{-\alpha l} \cdot \frac{e^{\beta h} - e^{-\beta h}}{e^{\beta h} + e^{-\beta h}}$$

where l is the shortest path between the topics in the taxonomy tree, h is the depth level of the direct common subsumer, and $\alpha \geq 0$ and $\beta > 0$ are parameters scaling the contribution of shortest path length and depth, respectively. Using optimal parameter ($\alpha = 0.2$ and $\beta = 0.6$) this measure shows a correlation coefficient with human similarity judgements performing nearly at the level of human replication. Experiments in a scenario of federated news collections in [53] show that the retrieval process can be effectively supported, if documents can be classified sufficiently well by a taxonomy of common categories.

20.4 Summary and Conclusion

This chapter has given a brief survey of techniques for information retrieval in Peer-to-Peer infrastructures. In most of today's applications in Peer-to-Peer scenarios simple retrieval models based on exact matching of meta-data are prevalent. Whereas meta-data annotation has to anticipate the use of descriptors in later applications, information retrieval capabilities work on more complex and unbiased information about the documents in each collection offered by a peer. Thus, such capabilities offer much more flexibility in querying and open up a large number of semantically advanced applications.

Generally speaking, information retrieval differs from simple meta-data-based retrieval in that a ranked retrieval model is employed where not only some suitable peer for download needs to be found, but the 'best' documents within the entire network must be located. Moreover and in contrast to Gnutella-style infrastructures, querying has to be performed in a more efficient manner than simple flooding. Generally, only a small number of peers should be selected for querying. In addition, the querying method has to be relatively stable in the face of network churn and since rankings usually rely on collection-wide information, it has to estimated or efficiently disseminated throughout the network.

The basic retrieval problem is heavily related to previous research in distributed information retrieval as is used for querying document collections in the WWW. But the Peer-to-Peer environment still poses different challenges, especially because network churn causes a much more dynamic retrieval environment and centralized index structures cannot be efficiently used. Also, related work in Peer-to-Peer systems, e.g., distributed hash tables can not be readily used either due to the limitations in scalability caused by publishing and unpublishing information in more volatile networks.

Thus, the main problem for Peer-to-Peer information retrieval today is managing the trade-off between the efficient maintenance of local indexes with only limited knowledge about the Peer-to-Peer network's global parameters and the expensive dissemination of dynamically changing global information about the network needed to guarantee a satisfying recall in result sets. Heuristic techniques like estimating the document overlap of collections or integrating taxonomies of document classifications into the retrieval process, have been proved to be helpful and should be further investigated.

21. Hybrid Peer-to-Peer Systems

Vasilios Darlagiannis (Technische Universität Darmstadt)

21.1 Introduction

Peer-to-Peer systems have been receiving considerable attention from the networking research community recently. Several approaches have been proposed as communication schemes in order to supply efficient and scalable inter-peer communication. These schemes are designed on top of the physical networking infrastructure as *overlay networks* taking advantage of the rich flexibility, which is accomplished at low cost. A number of important design approaches has been already presented in previous chapters. Their topologies and operation mechanisms influence greatly the performance of routing and topology maintenance algorithms and hence, the efficiency of the corresponding Peer-to-Peer system.

However, Peer-to-Peer systems are distributed systems with a large number of non-functional requirements such as scalability, dependability (including fault-tolerance, security, integrity, consistency), fairness, etc. These requirements should be met in order to design systems, which are easily deployed on top of the Internet while making use of available resources in an optimal way. Most approaches have been designed to deal with a subset of these requirements. Nevertheless, they have intrinsic limitations fulfilling the complete set of the aforementioned requirements. In most cases, trade-offs in meeting these requirements exist, thus, raising severe constraints.

To elaborate further the aforementioned trade-off issue, we consider the design of a Peer-to-Peer system where fault-tolerance should be supported in the presence of heterogeneous environments (peers may have different physical capabilities and behavioral patterns). In the context of Peer-to-Peer systems where peers represent unreliable components, fault-tolerance is achieved mostly by the employment of redundancy and replication mechanisms. *Pure* DHT-based approaches such as Chord [576] or Pastry [527] suggest a large number of neighbors that usually increases logarithmically with respect to the size of the system. While it has been shown that such approaches provide high fault-tolerance [385][1], they ignore practical limitations raised by peers of low physical capabilities that may not fulfill the continuously increasing requirements as system's size expands. In addition, by ignoring het-

[1] That study assumes a Peer-to-Peer system where both peers' inter-arrival and service (lifespan) time distributions follow the Poisson model. However, as it has been empirically observed in many studies (e.g. cf. [98]) that peer lifespan follows a different distribution.

R. Steinmetz and K. Wehrle (Eds.): P2P Systems and Applications, LNCS 3485, pp. 353-366, 2005.

erogeneity and dealing equally with each peer, the system maintenance cost increases significantly, while the least reliable peers contribute minimally in the fault-tolerance of the system. Further, similar requirement trade-offs (i.e. anonymity versus efficiency, heterogeneity versus load-balance, etc.) appear when pure design approaches are selected.

In this chapter we investigate Peer-to-Peer systems, which follow a hybrid design approach. The word *hybrid* is used in many disciplines such as in biology, in sociology or in linguistics. In general, it is used to characterize *"something derived from heterogeneous sources or composed of incongruous elements"* (Oxford Dictionary). Though initially the term *"hybrid Peer-to-Peer system"* was used in the context of Peer-to-Peer systems to describe approaches that combined both Peer-to-Peer and Client/Server aspects, its usage was broadened to cover further combinations of heterogeneous approaches.

In general, hybrid systems are claimed to be intrinsically better than pure approaches, mostly because of the great heterogeneity observed in deployed systems. They allow for the synergistic combination of two techniques with more strengths and less weaknesses than either technique alone.

In the remaining of this chapter we investigate and define a coarse-grained classification scheme for the observed topologies of the most important, state-of-the-art, hybrid overlay networks, their underlying mechanisms and the algorithms employed to operate on them. Then, we discuss their benefits and drawbacks in a general system-unaware way that does not consider specific Peer-to-Peer systems, where hybrid approaches are compared with non-hybrid approaches.

21.2 Overlay Network Design Dimensions

In order to meet the critical set of the aforementioned (and possibly additional) non-functional requirements for the operation of the Peer-to-Peer overlay networks, a great variety of approaches have been proposed. Analyzing the design mechanisms that characterize the Peer-to-Peer overlay networks, three major design dimensions can be identified to classify the proposed systems (cf. Figure 21.1). An alternative three dimensional approach is presented in [154].

Overlay networks vary in their *structural* design from *tightly structured* networks such as Chord [576] or Pastry [527] to *loosely structured* ones such as Freenet [124] or Gnutella [251]. This design dimension is graphically depicted in the projected axis of the design space in Figure 21.1. Tightly structured (or simply *structured*) overlays continuously maintain their topology, targeting to a "perfect" structure (e.g., a hypercube or a butterfly topology). Structured topologies may require high maintenance cost especially in the presence of high churn rate. Also, they deal uniformly with the shared objects and services provided by the system and they are unaware of their query distribution, a fact that might cause a significant mismatch. Moreover, *Distributed Hash Table* (DHT) based approaches (which is the most common mechanism to build structured overlay networks) cannot support easily range queries[2]. Alternative investigations include several mappings of local data structures to distributed network topologies, such as tries [230] or modifications of traditionally used topologies such as hypercubes [541], butterflies [399] and multi-butterflies [155].

On the other hand, loosely structured (or simply *unstructured*) overlays do not aim to reach a predefined targeted topology, but rather they have a more "random" structure. However, it has been observed that certain connectivity policies (i.e., preferential attachment) may emerge their topology to power-law networks or networks with small-world characteristics. Unstructured topologies are typically inefficient in finding published, rare items and the embedded searching operations are in general considerably costly in terms of network overhead (most approaches use flooding or at best, selective dissemination mechanisms[398]). The observed power-law topology, though it provides a graph with a small diameter[3], it distributes unevenly the communication effort and introduces potential hot spots at these peers with high degree playing the role of a "hub". However, in scenarios where the query distribution is non-uniform (i.e., lognormal, Zipf) unstructured networks may be designed to operate efficiently.

Further, overlay networks may vary on the *dependency* of the peers on each other, as it is shown in the vertical axis of Figure 21.1. Approaches such as Chord or Freenet treat all of the participants equally and they are referred as *pure* or *flat* Peer-to-Peer networks. On the other hand, *hierarchical* approaches such as Napster [436] or eDonkey [185] separate the common overlay related responsibilities and assign the majority (or all) of the tasks to a small subset of (usually) more powerful nodes only (e.g. for resource indexing). These subset of peers is usually named as *"servers"*, *"super-peers"* or *"ultra-peers"*. The fault-tolerance of flat approaches is considerably higher than the hierarchical ones since failures or attacks to any single peer do not have significant consequences. However, such approaches do not deal well with the heterogeneity of the participating peers both in terms of physical capabilities and user behavior. The complexity of flat approaches is usually higher compared to the hierarchical counterparts. On the other hand, hierarchical solutions require a certain infrastructure to operate and may be controlled by third parties easier than the non-hierarchical alternatives. The operational load is unequally balanced among the networked entities and high dependency exists among them.

[2] Range queries are queries searching not for a single item that matches a specific key but rather for a set of items, which are "close" to a description based on e.g. metadata.

[3] Small diameter is a desirable feature for a network topology in order to reduce the maximum number of hops required to reach any destination in the overlay.

Finally, overlay networks can be designed either following *deterministic* or *probabilistic* (e.g., based on Bloom filters [77]) approaches. The selection of the former or the latter approach may improve the accuracy or the efficiency of the Peer-to-Peer systems, respectively. Also, a mixture of these mechanisms may provide improved results. A characteristic example demonstrating both probabilistic and deterministic mechanisms is OceanStore [368]. Deterministic approaches provide repeatedly similarly consistent results (as long as there are no critical intermediate changes in the system) and the provided operations can be well predicted and their cost is upper bounded. On the other hand, probabilistic approaches tolerate some unpredictability on the provided results, aiming to operate at a much lower cost than their deterministic alternatives. Such variation is shown in the horizontal axis of the overlay network design space in Figure 21.1.

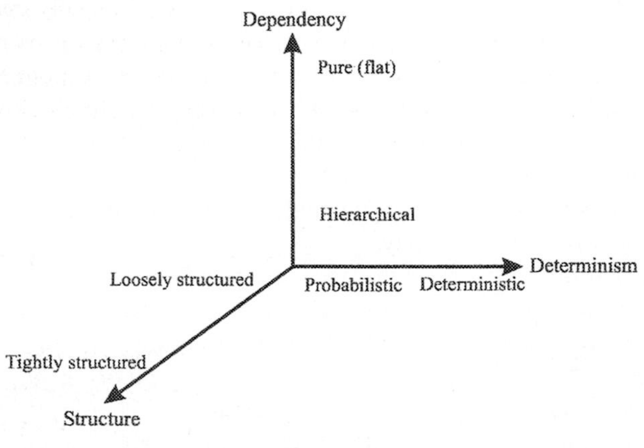

Fig. 21.1: Overlay network design dimensions

In this chapter we focus on systems that lie in the middle of at least one of the axes shown in Figure 21.1, though many of the proposed systems follow hybrid mechanisms in more than one dimensions. By doing so, hybrid designs aim to deal with the limitations of the pure approaches.

21.3 Hybrid Architectures

In this section we focus on Peer-to-Peer systems that mainly follow hybrid approaches in the architectural design of their overlay topologies.

21.3.1 JXTA

JXTA[4] [597] defines a common set of protocols for building Peer-to-Peer applications to address the recurrent problem with existing Peer-to-Peer systems of creating incompatible protocols. The main goal of JXTA is to define a generic Peer-to-Peer network overlay, which may be used to implement a wide variety of Peer-to-Peer applications and services. While JXTA offers the means to developers to design any kind of overlay network that suits to the needs of their applications, JXTA itself develops a hybrid overlay network to orchestrate the deployed applications and services. Peers in the JXTA network are self-organized into *peergroups*. A peergroup represents an ad hoc set of peers that have a common set of interests, and have agreed upon a common set of policies (membership, routing, searching, etc). However, there is a global peergroup as a bootstrap point where all the specialized peergroups can be advertised.

The JXTA specifications define the Resolver Service Protocol as a universal resource binding service. The Resolver Service is used to perform resolution operations found in traditional distributed systems, such as resolving a peer name into an IP address (DNS) or binding an IP socket to a port.

The global JXTA overlay network provides a default resolver service based on *rendezvous* peers. Rendezvous peers are peers that have agreed to index other peer advertisements to facilitate the discovery of resources in a peergroup. A peergroup can have as many rendezvous peers as required to support the size of the peergroup. Rendezvous peers are defined in the scope of peergroups to reduce the communication complexity. Any peer can potentially become a rendezvous peer, unless there are security restrictions.

Rendezvous maintain an index of advertisements published by edge peers via the *Shared Resource Distributed Index (SRDI)* service. Edge peers use SRDI to push advertisement indices to their rendezvous when new advertisements are published. The rendezvous/edge peer hierarchy allows resolver queries to be propagated between rendezvous only, significantly reducing the amount of peers that need to be searched when looking for an advertisement. Such a structure is illustrated in Figure 21.2.

Rendezvous Peers are organized into a loosely-coupled network to reduce the high maintenance cost that occurs in Peer-to-Peer systems with high churn. The JXTA approach separates the cost of a DHT solution into index maintenance, and data access. Project JXTA utilizes a hybrid approach that combines the use of a loosely-consistent DHT with a limited-range rendezvous walker. Rendezvous peers are not required to maintain a consistent view of the distributed hash index leading to the term loosely-consistent DHT. Each rendezvous maintains its own *Rendezvous Peer View* (RPV), which is an ordered list of known rendezvous in the peergroup. Inconsistency among the

[4] The name of JXTA come from the verb *juxtapose*, which means place things side by side to suggest a link together or emphasize the contrast between them.

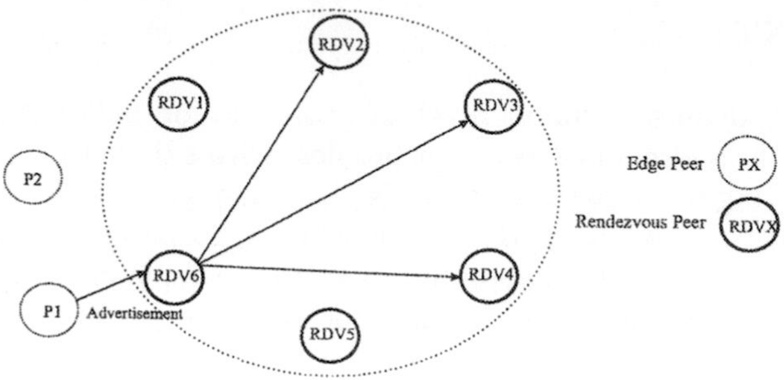

Fig. 21.2: JXTA overlay network

RPVs of different rendezvous peers might occur. A loosely-coupled algorithm is used for converging local RPV. A rumor-based technique is employed to disseminate information about the rendezvous peers. Seeding rendezvous are special rendezvous peers to accelerate the RPV convergence, as all rendezvous should know about all seeding rendezvous of a peergroup.

The hybrid approach of a loosely-consistent DHT combined with a limited range walker to search for advertisements has the advantages of not requiring a strong-consistency DHT maintenance, and is well adapted to ad hoc unstructured Peer-to-Peer networks. However, when very large peergroups are constructed requiring several hundreds of rendezvous the system may suffer considerably from the resulting inconsistency, which becomes a boomerang to the performance of the system.

21.3.2 Brocade

The majority of DHTs assume that most nodes in the system are uniform in resources such as network bandwidth and storage. As a result, messages are often routed across multiple *autonomous systems (AS)* and administrative domains before reaching their destinations.

Brocade is a hybrid overlay network proposal, where a secondary overlay is layered on top of a primary DHT. The secondary overlay exploits knowledge of underlying network characteristics and builds a location-aware layer between "supernodes", which are placed in critical locations in each AS of the Internet. Supernodes are expected to be endpoints with high bandwidth and fast access to the wide-area network and act as landmarks for each network domain. Sent messages across different ASs can be delivered much faster if normal peers are associated with their nearby supernodes that can operate as "shortcuts" to tunnel the messages towards their final destination, thus, greatly improving endpoint-to-endpoint routing distance and reducing network bandwidth usage.

The critical aspects in designing an effective Brocade overlay are the appropriate selection of supernodes and the mappings between supernodes and normal DHT nodes. A straightforward solution is to exploit the hierarchical structure of network domains. Each network gateway may act as a brocade routing landmark for all nodes in its subdomain. An example of this mapping is shown in Figure 21.3. Supernodes are organized in a different DHT (i.e., Tapestry).

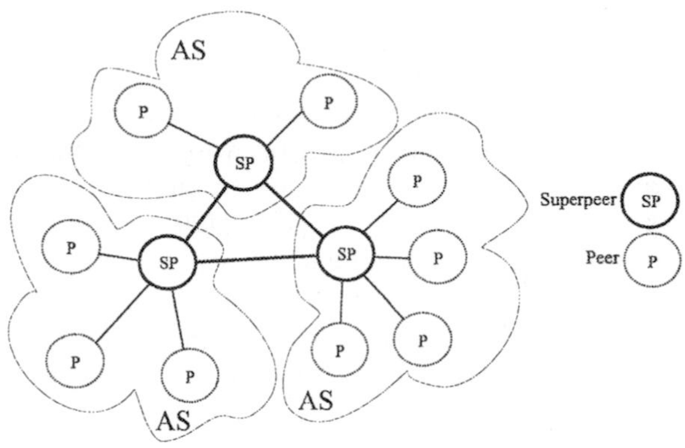

Fig. 21.3: Brocade overlay network

The routing operation works as follows. When a message reaches a supernode, the supernode may do a lookup to determine whether the message is destined for a local node, or whether brocade routing may be useful. In the brocade overlay, each supernode advertises the IDs on this list as IDs of objects it stores. When a supernode tries to route an outgoing message which should be delivered out of the local AS, it uses the supernode DHT to search for destination supernode. By finding the object on the brocade layer, the source supernode forwards the message directly to the destination supernode, which resumes normal overlay routing to the final destination.

Summarizing, Brocade is a hybrid system aiming merely to exploit the underlying network topology to supply more efficient routing services. However, the load balance of the network may be unevenly distributed among the peers. Moreover, superpeers may either act maliciously or become targets of attacks.

21.3.3 SHARK

Pure DHT-based solutions rely on hash functions, which may map advertised items to certain locations in the overlay structure (by assigning hash-generated identifiers both to each item and overlay location). Such mechanisms (while they are very efficient) are limited to single lookup queries of these identifiers. *Range* (or *rich*) search queries based on keywords remain challenging features for such systems. However, usually users prefer to specify what they are looking for in terms of keywords. For instance, a user of a file sharing application could look for a certain genre of music and not for a particular song. Additionally, multiple dimensions of meta-data are also highly desirable, for instance, looking for a document released at a certain period and related with a specific topic.

SHARK (Symmetric Hierarchy Adaption for Routing of Keywords) [421] employs a hybrid DHT solution for rich keyword searching. Its hybrid overlay structure is composed of two parts: a structured one that considers the Group of Interest (GoI) concept of AGILE [420] and several unstructured subnetworks grouping peers with similar interests. Queries are initially being forwarded in the structured part of the network to reach the targeted unstructured subnetwork. Then, they are broadcasted to the set of interesting peers that provide the matched items. SHARK is described in deeper detail in Section 17.4.

21.3.4 Omicron

Omicron (Organized Maintenance, Indexing, Caching and Routing for Overlay Networks) [153] is a Peer-to-Peer overlay network aiming to address issues of heterogeneous, large-scale and dynamic Peer-to-Peer environments. Its hybrid, DHT-based topology makes it highly adaptable to a large range of applications. Omicron deals with a number of conflicting requirements, such as scalability, efficiency, robustness, heterogeneity and load balance.

The rational in Omicron's approach is to reduce the high maintenance cost by having a small, constant number of connections and routing table sizes per peer (at least for the majority of them), while still performing lookup operations at low costs. For this reason the usage of appropriate graph structures (such as de Bruijn graphs) is suggested. However, while the small number of connections reduces the operational cost, it causes robustness problems. To address this issue, clusters of peers are formed with certain requirements on their stability over time. In order to maintain their stability, new joins are directed to the least stable clusters. When the stability of a cluster gets below a certain threshold, a merging operation takes place between the unstable cluster and a neighbor cluster.

Before we present the way de Bruijn graphs are deployed in Omicron, the topology of these graphs and the way the routing algorithm works is described. The upper part of Figure 21.4 shows a $(2,3)$ directed de Bruijn graph denoting a graph with a maximum out-degree of 2, a diameter of 3 and order 8. Each node is represented by k-length (three in this example) strings. Every character of the string can take d different values (two in this example). In the general case each node is represented by a string such as $u_1 u_2 ... u_k$. The connections between the nodes follow a simple left shift operation from node $u_1(u_2...u_k)$ to node $(u_2...u_k)u_x$, where u_x can take one of the possible values of the characters $(0, d-1)$. For example, we can move from node (010) to either node (100) or (101).

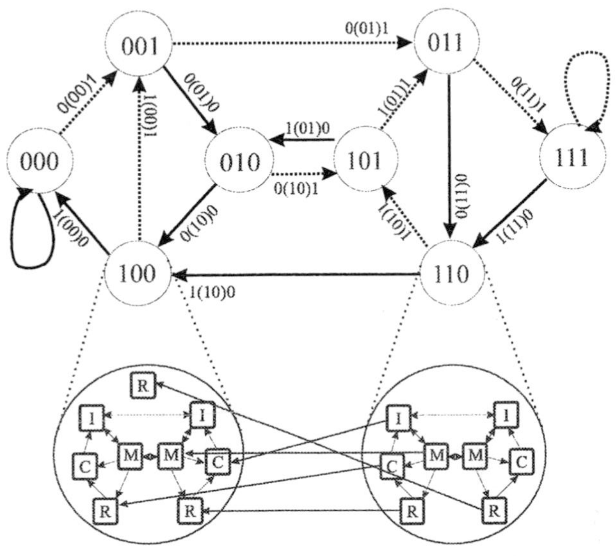

Fig. 21.4: Omicron overlay network

The most attractive feature of de Bruijn digraphs is the constant degree requirement for every node. However, this is also their "Achilles' heel" since robustness is difficult to achieve. As an alternative approach Omicron suggests the construction of clusters of peers and where application of a de Bruijn topology for the inter-cluster communication is proposed. This way the nodes (clusters of peers) of the digraph will be much more stable than single peers.

A dual identification scheme has been introduced for Omicron with a number of advantages. Clusters are assigned a Globally Unique IDentifier (GUID) that is used to route requests over the network. Advertised items are assigned a GUID and are located at the clusters whose GUID matches best. Moreover, peers are assigned their own GUID to trace their actions in the system.

Inter-cluster routing of messages is based on shift operations performed on the cluster GUID to select the neighbor cluster whose GUID matches best to the requested key. The operation is repeated until the final destination is reached.

Going a step further, a role-based scheme is introduced to deal with the heterogeneity of the peer capabilities and user behavior. This scheme fits the contribution of each node to its resource capabilities and aims at the maximization of the cluster efficiency by providing appropriate incentives to peers to take a certain role. The identified roles are based on the core overlay operations:

- **Overlay maintenance.** *Maintainers* perform the most demanding operation since peers are required to maintain complete routing tables, indexing information and cluster organization.
- **Indexing.** *Indexers* are required to handle the indexing responsibilities of the whole cluster in a balanced and co-operative way. Information redundancy is an additional requirement in order to shield the system against the single peer (mis-)behavior. Indexers can provide the final reply to queries when they reach the destination cluster.
- **Routing.** Routing is the most simple operation where *Routers* should forward messages to the neighbor clusters that are closer to the final destination. Combined with the low requirements raised by the de Bruijn digraphs it is a role suitable for any peer, even those that have very low capabilities and an unstable behavior. They participate only in the inter-cluster message forwarding service but they do not have the required information to provide the final reply as Indexers have.
- **Caching.** Although caching is not a basic operation (it is rather considered as advanced operation) it is included in the basic scheme because of the low requirements it poses and the fact that it closes the design gap between the Routers and the other more demanding roles. *Cachers* are expected to perform caching of the indexing information for the most popular items in order to reduce the effort of the Indexers. Studies (i.e. [379]) indicate that there is a Zipf-law distribution of the queries in popular content-related Peer-to-Peer systems.

An illustration of Omicron and a typical intra-cluster structure is pictured in the lower part of Figure 21.4.

It is clear that different requirements are related with each role (apparently, this is the design goal). Peers are "promoted" to adopt roles with higher requirements as they prove their stability and they fulfill the physical capability needs. Incentive mechanisms are present to motivate the promotion procedure.

Finally, an incrementally expandable algorithm has been designed to adapt the exponentially growing de Bruijn graphs to the incrementally expandable Peer-to-Peer systems.

21.4 Hybrid Routing

In this section, we describe hybrid Peer-to-Peer systems that focus on improving the performance of the routing mechanism. The constructed overlay network might also be hybrid, though in general, an additional mechanism such as caching might be required to enable the hybrid routing algorithm.

21.4.1 OceanStore

OceanStore [368] is a Peer-to-Peer storage system built on top of Tapestry [642] to take advantage of its scalable characteristics. However, OceanStore, employs an additional probabilistic mechanism based on attenuated Bloom Filters, resulting to a hybrid solution to improve even further Tapestry's routing performance.

The Bloom Filters algorithm was initially proposed by Bloom in the early '70s [77] to help word processors perform capitalization and/or hyphenation on a document. Bloom filters exploit efficiently the usually present non-uniform distribution of requests, where a small set of items is requested much more often than the rest of the stored items. In general, Bloom filters are capable of answering questions of the type: "Is this item member of that group"? The algorithm uses hash functions, though it requires less space and is faster than a conventional one to one hash-based mapping algorithm. However, it allows errors to happen. While negative replies to the aforementioned question are always correct (the mechanism is capable of replying correctly that an item does not belong to a group), it might provide false positive replies (an item that does not exist in a group might be falsely reported as a member). The probability of false positive replies can be configured with a number of parameters (e.g., increasing the space required for the data structure) and reduced to obey certain predefined bounds.

OceanStore uses attenuated Bloom Filters to provide a fast probabilistic search algorithm, where attenuated Bloom Filters are arrays of such filters. In the context of the OceanStore algorithm, the first Bloom filter (located at position '0') is a record of the objects contained locally on the current node. The ith Bloom filter is the union of all of the Bloom filters for all of the nodes a distance i through any path from the current node. An attenuated Bloom filter is stored for each directed edge in the network. A query is routed along the edge whose filter indicates the presence of the object at the smallest distance.

When the fast probabilistic algorithm fails to provide the requested results, OceanStore activates the Tapestry routing mechanism to forward the request to the final destination. As a result, OceanStore provides replies much faster for the very popular items than is using a Tapestry approach. However, the routing cost is increased for the cases where Bloom Filters provide false replies. Moreover, the dissemination of Bloom Filters may consume considerable bandwidth.

21.4.2 Hybrid PIER

PIER [308] is a distributed query engine built on top of CAN. Similarly to the goal of OceanStore, in order to exploit the advantages of looking for popular items, a hybrid system has been proposed for PIER [394]. Hybrid PIER benefits both from DHTs and popularity-aware mechanisms, which are employed to get an improved overlay network. Hybrid PIER overlay is composed of two components, (i) an UltraPeer-based Gnutella network[5] and (ii), a structured CAN where UltraPeers may only participate. The hybrid search infrastructure utilizes selective publishing techniques that identify and publish only rare items into the DHT (a decision taken by the UltraPeers). The search algorithm uses flooding techniques for locating popular items, and structured (DHT) search techniques for locating rare items.

As long as the distribution of object replicas in the system follow a long tail distribution, such a hybrid system may perform better than a pure DHT alternative. However, the indexing and routing load is not evenly distributed.

21.5 Comparison with Non-hybrid Systems

In this section we compare hybrid solutions with non-hybrid in a general, abstract way, thus avoiding references to specific concrete systems in order to understand better the advantages and the shortcomings of following a hybrid design approach.

On the one hand, hybrid systems have increased complexity since they are combinations of more than one approaches and moreover, merged in a possibly constrained way that reveals the advantages of each sub-component. Hybrid systems naturally follow temporally the non-hybrid approaches that should be first well understood and both their benefits and drawbacks be identified.

On the other hand, hybrid systems may be better designed since their designers learn from the limitations and the mistakes of the pioneered pure approaches. Hybrid solutions show high adaptability to environmental conditions. Usually they are designed considering these conditions and they may reveal certain scenario-aware advantages or avoid related limitations. Performance may be greatly increased and new characteristics may be added to the constrained pure alternatives. Apparently, hybrid approaches may be the only viable way to address the large number of (usually) conflicting requirements raised in large-scale, dynamic and heterogeneous Peer-to-Peer systems.

[5] Based on Gnutella v0.6 protocol.

21.6 Summary and Conclusion

We have examined a large number of important hybrid Peer-to-Peer systems in order to reveal their advantages and the design purpose they serve. Though initially hybrid Peer-to-Peer systems were targeting in merging the Peer-to-Peer and Client/Server paradigms in different services they have been extended to explore a much wider range of combinations. Table 21.1 provides a summary of the main objectives and the key mechanisms to achieve them for each described hybrid systems.

In summary, with respect to the non-functional requirements, all the described systems address the scalability issue with a structured component. JXTA, Brocade and Omicron make heavy use of peers with special characteristics to deal with the heterogeneity of the peers. However, it is only Omicron that addresses heterogeneity in a balanced way where each peer contributes to the common overlay operations. Hybrid PIER and OceanStore take advantage of the popularity distributions for documents to increase their performance and reduce the network overhead. Brocade and Omicron deal in a certain degree with the creation of vicinity-aware overlay construction. Fault-tolerance is mainly achieved through redundancy mechanisms or the assignment of certain responsibilities to stable peers (or combination of both). SHARK and JXTA address the requirement for range queries support.

Hybrid Peer-to-Peer systems are interesting alternatives to pure system designs since they may overcome the limitations of the original approaches. Reality has shown that hybrid systems are usually the ones that are widely deployed and extensively used.

Hybrid Peer-to-Peer systems	Main objectives	Key mechanisms
Omicron	Efficient and stable large scale, heterogeneous, dynamic Peer-to-Peer systems	Clustering, Dynamic role assignment
SHARK	Scalable range queries	Hybrid structural Overlay
JXTA	Low cost overlay management	Role separation
Brocade	Efficient mapping of overlay to underlay network	Location-aware sub-network
OceanStore	Low cost search for popular queries	Bloom Filters based caching
Hybrid PIER	Low cost search for popular items	Hybrid structural overlay

Table 21.1: Objectives of Hybrid Peer-to-Peer systems

What is missing is a more systematic approach that may identify the requirements of the targeted systems, select and appropriately combine the identified components to meet these requirements. There are three main design dimensions to explore in the design of hybrid overlay networks, however, researchers may investigate further options defined in the context of the problem to be solved.

Further Reading

For the interested reader, a number of further citations are provided here to trigger further research areas. A hybrid topology inspired by Peer-to-Peer overlays and applied in mobile ad hoc networks can be found in [364]. A two-tier hierarchical Chord is explored in [238]. Measurement efforts on the KaZaA system can be found in [384]. A hybrid topology that extends Chord to increase the degree of user anonymity can be found in [562]. An early comparison of some pioneering hybrid approaches such as Napster and Pointera is provided in [634]. A hybrid protocol named Borg [641] aims in scalable Application-level Multicast. A generic mechanism for the construction and maintenance of superpeer-based overlay networks is proposed in [428]. A Peer-to-Peer overlay network simulator has been implemented especially to augment the evaluation of a wide range of hybrid designing methods [152]. A hybrid approach on deploying hybrid Content Delivery Networks (CDNs) based on an ad hoc Peer-to-Peer overlay and a centralized infrastructure is described in [633].

Part VII

Peer-to-Peer Traffic and Performance Evaluation

22. ISP Platforms Under a Heavy Peer-to-Peer Workload

Gerhard Haßlinger (T-Systems, Technologiezentrum Darmstadt)

22.1 Introduction

Peer-to-peer (P2P) applications presently contribute the main part of the traffic volume on Internet access platforms in Europe and North America. Distributed file sharing systems first emerged as a widely used application supported by a number of protocols, where the size of most popular networks counts millions of nodes being involved in mutual online data exchange. In addition, large voice over IP networks are using Peer-to-Peer technology and more applications based on a Peer-to-Peer overlay structure are expected to become popular. This has ambivalent consequences on the business models of service and network providers. Peer-to-peer networking is a driving demand of broadband access, motivating many users to subscribe to ADSL access with 1 - 6 Mbit/s line speed as presently offered by Deutsche Telekom and other Internet service providers (ISPs). At the same time Peer-to-Peer overlays also open the market for many additional services as a technology to make them globally present for a small investment in protocol development.

In this context, an efficient transport of data in Peer-to-Peer networks is crucial for the success of Peer-to-Peer applications and is also a main concern of ISPs and especially the network management on the IP layer. Some early versions of Peer-to-Peer protocols were subject to a large messaging overhead. Measurement in the Gnutella network [517] attributed a minimum overhead of 6 kbit/s per connection. In addition, search queries got flooded through the Gnutella network and thus limited its scalability. The current version of Gnutella as well as other popular file sharing networks like eDonkey, BitTorrent or FastTrack have reduced the routing overhead and become scalable with millions of interacting peers. Nevertheless, a significant messaging overhead often remains; see chapter 24 on traffic characteristics and performance evaluation.

The data search and selection of sources for downloading establish routing mechanisms on the application layer, which are usually independent of the routing on the IP network layer. The distribution of data over the Peer-to-Peer network and the (mis-)match of routing strategies on different layers is essential for an efficient bandwidth utilization and data throughput on IP platforms. On the other hand, the diversity and variability of Peer-to-Peer

R. Steinmetz and K. Wehrle (Eds.): P2P Systems and Applications, LNCS 3485, pp. 369-381, 2005.

protocols make it difficult to monitor them or even to control and optimize their performance on the management level of IP platforms.

In this chapter we will have a closer look at the implications of Peer-to-Peer applications on traffic and network management for IP platforms with broadband access. Besides a brief discussion of monitoring and traffic analysis of Peer-to-Peer applications, the main focus is on the efficiency of resource usage and consequences of a dominant Peer-to-Peer workload on the quality of service in IP networks, which support an expanding variety of services.

22.2 Peer-to-Peer Traffic Characteristics

22.2.1 Traffic Mix on IP Platforms

From 1999 Napster has offered a platform for file sharing, which generated a considerable portion of traffic (> 20%) on IP networks in the USA within a few months. Despite the shut-down of Napster due to copyright infringements and persisting problems of illegal content distribution, file sharing traffic has continuously increased until it became the dominant source of traffic [555].

Table 22.1 shows some representative measurement results for the components of the Internet traffic mix in Europe in 2003-2004. Based on the evaluation of TCP ports, more than half of the traffic is attributed to Peer-to-Peer applications. In addition, the Peer-to-Peer traffic portion becomes even larger when observed at application layer [475] e.g. from 50% to almost 80% as reported in [40]. In recent time, most of the FastTrack protocol has been replaced by BitTorrent activity in Deutsche Telekom's and France Telecom's traffic statistics, while eDonkey is still dominant [492].

22.2.2 Daily Traffic Profile

The application mix on IP networks also varies according to the time of day: web browsing (HTTP) oscillates between a peak in heavy traffic hours in the evening and almost no activity for some hours after midnight. Figure 22.1 illustrates the main traffic portions of Peer-to-Peer, web browsing (HTTP) and other applications, which again have been distinguished via TCP standard ports.

Peer-to-peer applications again dominate the traffic volume and at the same time show an overall smoothing effect on traffic profiles as compared with client-server architectures for several reasons:

- Traffic variability over time:
  The daily traffic profiles in broadband access platforms typically show high activity during the day time or in the evening. For Peer-to-Peer traffic, the

Application Mix from TCP Port Measurement	Deutsche Telekom 1st Half 2004	France Telecom 2003	France Telecom Sept. 2004	CacheLogic at an EU Tier-1 Provider in June 2004
eDonkey	60 %	38 %	~ 54.5 %	~ 20 %
FastTrack	6 %	8 %	~ 1 %	~ 10 %
BitTorrent	-	-	~ 3.5 %	~ 16 %
Other Peer-to-Peer	4 %	4 %	~ 1 %	~ 10 %
All Peer-to-Peer	70 %	50 %	~ 60 %	~ 56 %
HTTP	10 %	15 %	-	~ 12 %
Other (non-Peer-to-Peer / unknown)	20 %	35 %	-	~ 32 %

Table 22.1: Port measurement of Peer-to-Peer traffic in Europe

ratio of the peak to the mean rate is usually smaller than 1.5 due to background transfers which often last throughout the night. Web browsing and many other applications have a ratio of 2 or higher. The ongoing Peer-to-Peer data transfers through the night time are initiated by long-lasting background downloads of large video files with sizes often in the Gigabyte range. When peers are connected via ADSL access lines, the throughput of Peer-to-Peer transmission is limited by the upstream speed of the peers. Thus it requires hours or days for a peer to download a file of Gigabyte size at a rate of about 100 kbit/s when peers are staying continuously online.

– Traffic variability over network topology:
The popularity of many Internet servers is often changing dynamically. Traffic sources may spontaneously arise and vanish at different locations in the network topology, where servers are attached. On the contrary, the nodes in large Peer-to-Peer networks are more or less uniformly distributed over the access area. In search phases the Peer-to-Peer protocols often involve supernodes which are similar to servers as traffic sources. Downloads on the other hand run completely distributed among the peer nodes. While spontaneous accesses from many clients to a server can lead to bottlenecks, frequently referenced data is soon replicated and afterwards downloaded from many nodes in a Peer-to-Peer network. Hence, Peer-to-Peer applications lead to a more uniform distribution of traffic sources over the network independent of sudden changes in the popularity of material on the Internet and the locations of originating nodes.

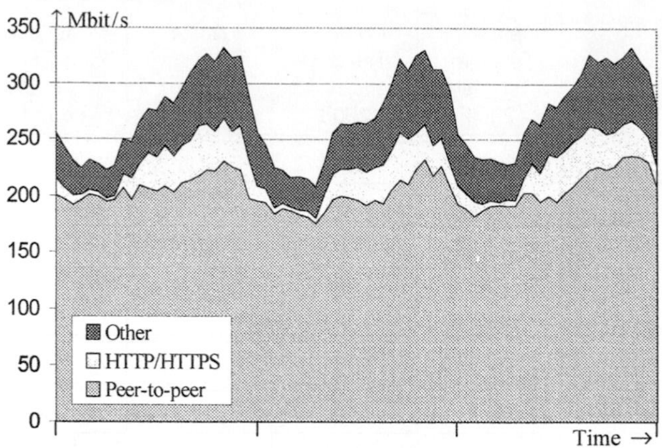

Fig. 22.1: Usual profile of Peer-to-Peer, HTTP and other traffic on Deutsche Telekom's IP platform measured over three days in the 2. half of 2003

– Variability due to different access speeds:
  Most of the Peer-to-Peer source traffic originates from subscribers with a limited access rate especially for uploads. The upload speed is presently in the range of 128 - 512kbit/s even in most broadband access lines. Owing to upload speed limitation and a preference for splitting the transfer of large files into many data chunks, which can be transmitted in parallel TCP connections to and from the peers, the traffic of Peer-to-Peer applications is subdivided into a large number of small flows. Thus the preconditions for the smoothing effect of statistical multiplexing are strengthened due to the increased multiplexing degree for Peer-to-Peer applications. As a consequence, the burstiness of aggregated traffic on network and especially backbone links is significantly reduced.

When the user population and thus the number of parallel sessions is constant and transfer activities in the sessions are independent of each other, then the central limit theorem is applicable to the rate statistics of aggregated traffic being composed of a large number of small and independent flows. Remote access routers at the boundary of IP platforms already aggregate the traffic of hundreds or several thousand users.

As a consequence, the coefficient of variation, i.e. the ratio of the variance to the square of the mean, becomes smaller with a higher level of aggregation and the traffic rate approaches a Gaussian distribution [40, 280]. Simple link dimensioning rules are available for Gaussian traffic with regard to quality of service aspects [278, 281].

22.2.3 Traffic Growth and Prognosis

In recent years, the deployment of broadband access lines for the mass market together with extensive use of file sharing applications pushed the traffic volume [459]. From 2000 to 2003 Deutsche Telekom supplied several million homes with ADSL access and the traffic on the Internet platform increased by a factor of more than 100 over this 3 year period, coming close to the scalability limits of mature carrier-grade routing equipment available on the market. Meanwhile the broadband access penetration is continuously expanding with higher access speeds being offered, while the traffic growth rate is flattening. In general, there are still undoubted requirements for larger bandwidths in telecommunication networks, whereas the future development of Peer-to-Peer traffic is difficult to predict.

Most video files are currently using MPEG compression in order to adapt to limited transmission capacities on account of reduced quality. Television studios presently demand high resolution for their video transmissions in high definition television (HDTV) quality together with coding schemes without loss of information. The corresponding transmission rate amounts to several Gbit/s for a single video stream. Nowadays IP backbone and access speeds would have to be increased about 1000-fold for a widespread transport of video in HDTV quality. Although many people may nowadays be satisfied with low video quality, improving quality for video and further emerging broadband applications will continue to increase demand for even larger bandwidths for at least the next decade.

With regard to Peer-to-Peer applications, the illegitimate use of copyright protected content and the future effect of countermeasures are unknown factors of influence. In addition, legal downloads and video streaming are currently being offered on client-server architectures via Internet under acceptable conditions for the mass market, which may then partially satisfy the requirements of present Peer-to-Peer users. Moreover, scalability and many security aspects including resistance against denial-of-service attacks seem to be handled without much care by current Peer-to-Peer protocols.

On the other hand, the superior efficiency of the Peer-to-Peer principle for fast widespread distribution of large amounts of data is attractive for software distribution, especially when updates are frequently required, e.g., for virus scanning programs. There is a high potential for supporting various upcoming applications by Peer-to-Peer networks including online gaming, radio and TV over IP etc., with some candidates for drivers of future traffic growth among them.

22.2.4 Asymmetrical Versus Symmetrical Access Lines

On the whole, Peer-to-Peer traffic is symmetrical in up- and downstream directions, since an upstream flow from a sources always corresponds to a downstream flow to the destination when no data is lost during transmission. Since many users are at first interested in downloading files, Peer-to-Peer protocols have to take care of a balanced transfer in both directions. Nowadays, protocols in widespread use start to upload data in parallel to a download as soon as the first data chunks of a downloaded file have been received. Moreover, they enforce a give and take policy for each participant such that users with a higher upload volume are preferred when they are requesting downloads.

On the other hand, broadband access lines are usually asymmetrical with smaller upstream rate, e.g., 128 kbit/s versus 1 Mbit/s. Therefore, the upstream capacity in broadband access platforms becomes a bottleneck for Peer-to-Peer applications. In measurement of upstream traffic the Peer-to-Peer portion is very high, since most other transmissions go downstream.

Symmetrical access lines would be more appropriate for Peer-to-Peer data exchange, but if service providers were to replace ADSL lines with symmetrical DSL at comparable speed, then Peer-to-Peer traffic could be expected to increase with the upstream speed. This shows that enforcement of a close relation between up- and download volume of each user is essential to achieve a high throughput of Peer-to-Peer traffic on broadband IP platforms. An adaptation of Peer-to-Peer video streaming to asymmetrical access is studied in [646].

There are other symmetrical broadband applications e.g. video telephony and conferencing, which demand symmetrical access or at least a more balanced ratio of up- to downstream capacity.

22.3 Cross Layer Aspects

22.3.1 Routing on Application and IP Layer

Peer-to-peer networks establish their own routing on the application layer when searching and selecting data sources. They are different from the routing principles on the network layer with consequences for the efficiency and scalability. Earlier versions of the Gnutella network simply forwarded broadcast search requests to all neighbours within a limited distance measured by the hop count, i.e. the number of intermediate nodes. In this way, a large amount of messages were exchanged for each search, which imposed restrictions on the scalability of the Gnutella network [517].

Presently, Peer-to-Peer protocols often introduce hierarchically structured search nodes to reduce the overhead together with functions known from IP routing like hello messages to confirm connectivity to the peers. Nevertheless, a significant messaging overhead can be observed in large Peer-to-Peer networks. The implementation of two independent routing layers causes inefficiency to the extent of the mismatch between different underlying network structures.

22.3.2 Network and Transport Layer Analysis

Monitoring and analysis of Peer-to-Peer traffic is essential for Internet service providers

- to determine the components of the traffic mix, which may indicate shifts and trends in the usage of applications,
- to estimate the overhead in Peer-to-Peer messaging and
- to analyze the Peer-to-Peer network structure and transmission paths to be compared with the routing on the network layer.

The components of traffic can be analyzed by evaluating information in the IP and TCP header, i.e. IP addresses, TCP ports and information about the TCP signaling and connection status. Peer-to-peer protocols are often associated with a standard port or a range of specific ports, which allows them to be recognized on the transport layer. When the search phase relies on a small set of servers then the corresponding requests can be traced by an analysis of IP addresses. The analysis on this layer is supported by sampling mechanisms provided by the router equipment and can be performed at line speed even on backbone links.

However, most widely used Peer-to-Peer protocols can be configured to use any arbitrary TCP port and thus an essential part of Peer-to-Peer traffic cannot be categorized on this layer, which runs over non-standard TCP ports or even standard ports of other applications. Dynamically changing ports are another variant. Recently, the portion of unknown TCP ports is increasing in transport layer statistics, as can be observed e.g. in the Internet2 NetFlow statistics [318].

22.3.3 Application Layer Pattern

To get better insight into Peer-to-Peer traffic components, application level analysis is necessary which also inspects the payload of transmitted packets. Depending on the protocol, patterns can be recognized, which indicate data transmitted in Peer-to-Peer search phases or the initiation of data exchanges. Afterwards they can be traced on the transport layer until the termination of a corresponding TCP connection [285, 160]. Table 22.2 shows examples of patterns observable in current versions of popular file sharing protocols [336].

In general, the analysis on this layer is complex and cannot be performed permanently for the complete traffic on high speed links. Recognition patterns have to be identified for each relevant Peer-to-Peer protocol and, in addition, the analysis has to be updated whenever new protocols or new variants of existing protocols emerge. Although there are approaches for the analysis of several currently used protocols, a complete classification of Peer-to-Peer traffic remains difficult since some protocols have developed techniques to

P2P Protocol	eDonkey2000	FastTrack	BitTorrent
Transport	TCP & UDP	TCP & UDP	TCP
Standard Ports	4661 – 4665	1214	6881 – 6889
Block Sizes	10,240 Byte	65,536 Byte 2,048 Byte	16,384 Byte 32,768 Byte

Characteristic Pattern in Packets	eDonkey: `0xe3`
	eMule: `0xc5`
		TCP:
		`GET /.hash;`
		`GIVE;`
			`GET /announce?info.hash;`
			`GET /torrents/;`
			`GET TrackPak;`
			`0x13 BitTorrent;`
			`0x00000005;`
			`0x0000000d;`
			`0x00004009`

Table 22.2: Characteristic protocol pattern in IP packets and their payload

disguise their purpose also on the application layer. Anonymous Peer-to-Peer actions are addressed in the chapter on security. Nevertheless, several manufacturers of measurement equipment offer tools for monitoring traffic including Peer-to-Peer application layer analysis to some extent.

Besides the analysis of the components of complete data flows, another approach of application layer analysis has been carried out by crawling into Peer-to-Peer protocols [534]. To do this, a node is inserted into a Peer-to-Peer network, which can collect data about the connectivity and structure of the network as well as the status of other nodes.

22.3.4 Distribution of Sources for eDonkey File-Sharing

Peer-to-peer networks have no knowledge of the infrastructure of the underlying IP network structure. Thus, protocols on the application layer can be developed independently of the lower layers. Nevertheless, layered protocols should be coordinated in order to make the transport efficient. One aspect is the length of paths from source to destination in Peer-to-Peer downloads. Figure 22.2 shows an example of source locations, which have been selected for downloading a popular file in the eDonkey network to a destination in Darmstadt, Germany.

On the whole, the sources of the download are partly concentrated in the near of the destination, most of them in Europe, but nevertheless some are spread over the globe and only a minority is located on the IP platform of the same service provider. Thus, most of the traffic for the download originates from a number of remote autonomous systems and is routed as off-net traffic through peering points and the backbone of the IP platform to which the destination is attached.

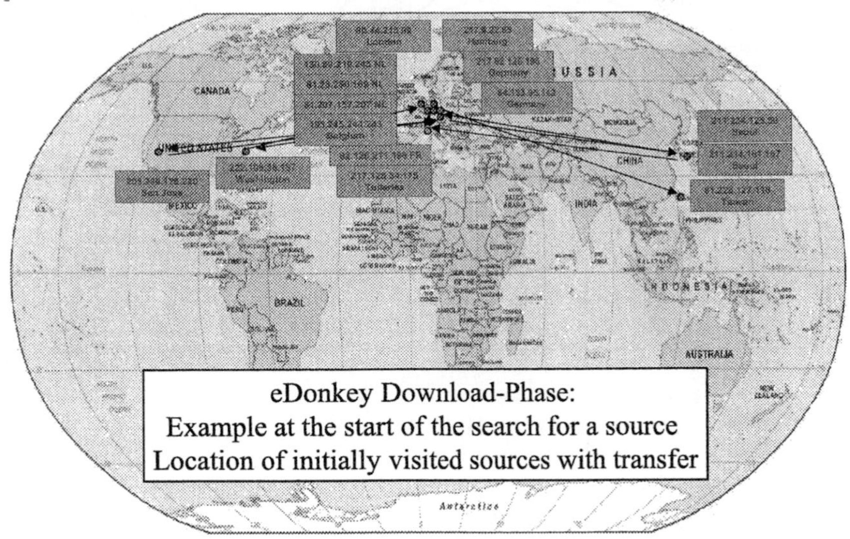

Fig. 22.2: Globally Distributed Sources for Downloading a File with eDonkey

On the other hand, Figure 22.3 illustrates the usual access and backbone structure of broadband access providers. Tree-shaped access areas are attached to the backbone at points of presence (PoPs), where remote access control routers handle the registration and sessions being set up for the users. For large provider networks serving millions of subscribers, it can be expected that a majority of the data of global file sharing systems can already be found to be replicated at some sources on the same ISP platform and often even in the same access area. This especially holds for the most popular and referenced data, since it is observed that the major portion of downloads comes from a small set of very popular files. Thus the source distribution of figure 22.2 indicates unnecessarily long transmission paths increasing the traffic load between autonomous systems and in backbone areas. This leaves potential for more efficient data exchange when a better match of network structures on the application and IP layer could be achieved.

In the considered example, a Linux software file was downloaded. The situation may be different when most audio and video data is transmitted by people in some country in their own language. France Telecom observed that a major part of the file sharing traffic in their Internet platform is locally to France, as can be expected by a differentiation of communities by languages [196].

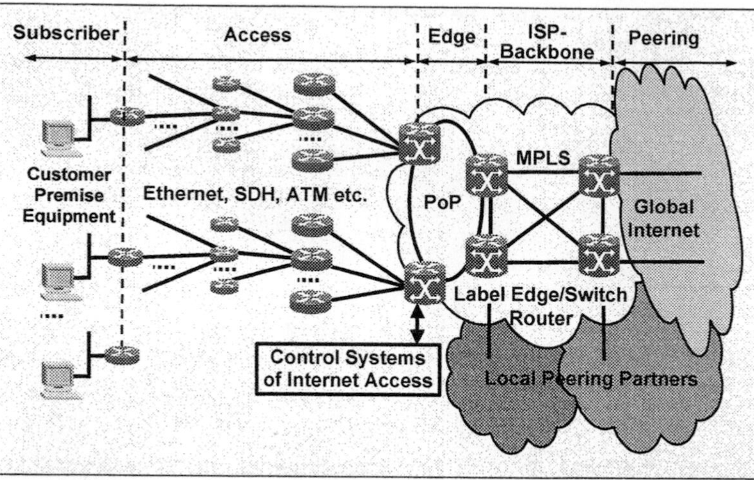

Fig. 22.3: Basic structure of ISP Platforms for Internet Access

22.3.5 Caches for Peer-to-Peer Data

Web caches provide an opportunity to optimize traffic flows. Usual web caches do not apply to Peer-to-Peer traffic and have become inefficient. On the other hand, caches can be set up specially for Peer-to-Peer traffic. Therefore, they act as a proxy node in a Peer-to-Peer network, which stores a large amount of data. A major problem of usual caching is that data in the cache is often expired, while it has already been updated on the corresponding web site. Peer-to-peer file sharing systems are not subject to expired data since data is referenced via unique hash identifiers.

Web caches are not intended to play an active role in Peer-to-Peer networks. They should be transparent and used only to shorten transmission paths to distant nodes, but should not be directly addressed as a source in the Peer-to-Peer network. When a download is requested for some data chunk available in the cache, then the cache can respond instead of a source, which has been selected in the search phase. For transparency reasons, the data should be transferred as if it originated from the selected source with regard to

- the IP addresses,
- the upstream access bandwidth of the source and
- possible changes in the status of the source, e.g. accounting for balanced up- and download volume of Peer-to-Peer network nodes.

However, caches cannot be made completely transparent. A data transfer from the cache will usually have a shorter transmission delay and a cache will not be able to match the available upstream rate of the original source, including time-varying bottlenecks on the transmission path beyond the cache. But at least the online availability and the access speed of the original source should be taken into account. In fact, the upload capacity of the caches will substitute a part of the upload capacity of nodes in the Peer-to-Peer network with consequences for the total data throughput. The efficiency of caches depends on the source selection by the Peer-to-Peer protocol. In principle, unnecessary load on backbone and expensive international links can be avoided.

By this method, caches for Peer-to-Peer traffic have to be adapted to discover data for the most popular protocols in use. They do not reduce the messaging overhead in the search phase. An alternative approach has been taken by eDonkey, where caches of service providers can be directly included as a configuration option of the Peer-to-Peer protocol. An open issue for caching again lies in its partial use for illegal content, which was already a problem before Peer-to-Peer became popular, but is becoming more serious with file sharing.

22.4 Implications for QoS in Multi-service IP Networks

The Internet has developed from data transfer applications to a service integrating platform with steadily increasing variety of service types including file transfer, email, web browsing, voice over IP, Peer-to-Peer data exchange etc. Each service type has its specific quality of service (QoS) demands regarding bandwidth, transmission time, e.g., real time constraints, as well as tolerance for transmission errors and failure situations. Peer-to-peer data exchange is usually of the best effort service type without strict QoS demands. Downloads often run for several hours or days in the background.

Although shorter transfers or even real time transmissions would be desirable for some Peer-to-Peer applications, users are aware that economic tariffs in a mass market impose access bandwidth limitations such that broadband transfers require considerable time even with increasing access speeds.

On the other hand, the impact of Peer-to-Peer traffic on other services has to be taken into account. The present traffic profile in IP networks with a dominant Peer-to-Peer traffic portion of the best effort type suggests that the differentiated services architecture [102, 618, 76] is sufficient as a simple scheme to support QoS by introducing traffic classes to be handled at different priorities.

Since presently less than 20% of the traffic in ISP networks seems to have strict QoS requirements including voice over IP and virtual private networks (VPN), sufficient QoS could be guaranteed for those traffic types by a strict forwarding priority. Even applications like web browsing and email are included in a 20% portion of traffic with the most demanding QoS requirements.

When the network is dimensioned for an essentially larger traffic volume as is generated only by the preferred traffic classes, then they will not suffer from bottlenecks and queueing delay in normal operation. Vice versa, the impact of preferring a small premium traffic class on a much larger portion of Peer-to-Peer traffic is moderate.

The delivery for premium traffic classes can even be assured in some failure situations, e.g. for single link breakdowns, provided that restoration links are available in an appropriate network design. Since overload may occur on those links, the best effort traffic will then often be affected.

Nowadays Peer-to-Peer protocols can cope with temporary disconnections on the application layer and recover transmission from the last current state afterwards. When file transfers via FTP or HTTP protocols are interrupted, an essential part of the transmission is often lost and a complete restart of the transfer may be required. Segmentation and reassembly of large data files into small chunks improves reliability and efficiency of Peer-to-Peer transfers, which is essential for non-assured QoS of best effort transmission.

An obstacle for the application of differentiated services is the difficulty to classify Peer-to-Peer traffic. A treatment with lower priority based on TCP port numbers will increase the tendency to disguise Peer-to-Peer applications by using randomly chosen ports for unknown protocols or by transporting Peer-to-Peer data exchange e.g. over the HTTP port for web browsing. Therefore, the only efficient way to classify traffic seems to be through a declaration and marking of the complete premium type traffic by the users themselves or by the originating servers, combined with a corresponding differentiated tariff scheme. But even then unresolved problems remain for supporting QoS for inter-domain traffic and for QoS-sensitive traffic which is transferred over peering points into a service provider platform.

22.5 Conclusion

Despite of increasing the traffic volume on the Internet, Peer-to-Peer traffic has a smoothing effect on the variability of the traffic rate and the daily profiles on broadband platforms. The geographical distribution of sources becomes more uniform as compared to most other traffic types. Potential for more efficient transport can be seen in unnecessarily long transmission paths due to the source selection in popular file sharing protocols.

These properties partly facilitate the network dimensioning and planning for service providers, but the monitoring, analysis and control of the Peer-to-Peer components and the prediction of their future development remains difficult.

The present traffic mix with a dominant portion of best effort type data exchanges in the background has implications for the quality of service concept, suggesting that differentiated services [1] are sufficient to support QoS-sensitive traffic types. Presently such traffic types generate less traffic volume, even including applications like web browsing. A comprehensive and appropriate classification of service types is still subject to many unresolved issues.

23. Traffic Characteristics and Performance Evaluation of Peer-to-Peer Systems

Kurt Tutschku, Phuoc Tran-Gia (University of Würzburg)

23.1 Introduction

Peer-to-Peer services have become the main source of traffic in the Internet and are even challenging the World Wide Web (WWW) in popularity. Backbone operators and Internet Service Providers (ISP) consistently report Peer-to-Peer-type traffic volumes exceeding 50 % of the total traffic in their networks [42, 337, 372, 556], sometimes even reaching 80 % at nonpeak times [39, 236], see also chapter 22.

Peer-to-Peer services are highly lucrative due to their simple administration, their high scalability, their apparent robustness, and easy deployment. The use of a distributed, self-organizing Peer-to-Peer software might reduce capital and operational expenditures (CAPEX and OPEX) of service operators since fewer entities have to be installed and operated. In a commercial context, high performance Peer-to-Peer means that these services meet tight statistic performance bounds; for *carrier gradeness* this bound is typically 99.999 %, the so called "five nines" concept. Before Peer-to-Peer services or Peer-to-Peer-based algorithms might be released in a production environment, it has to be evaluated whether these Peer-to-Peer-based solutions meet these requirements or not.

This aim of this chapter is to present selected characteristics of Peer-to-Peer traffic and discuss their impact on networks. In addition, the chapter will outline what performance can be expected from Peer-to-Peer-based algorithms and which factors influence Peer-to-Peer performance. First, this chapter discusses in Section 23.2 the relationship of basic Peer-to-Peer functions with performance. Section 23.3 is dedicated to the traffic patterns of popular Peer-to-Peer services. In particular, the characteristics of Gnutella overlays (Section 23.3.1) and of the eDonkey file sharing application in wireline and wireless networks (Section 23.3.2) are investigated. The efficiency of a Chord-like resource mediation algorithm is discussed in Section 23.4. Section 23.5 is devoted to the performance of exchanging resources in a mobile Peer-to-Peer architecture.

R. Steinmetz and K. Wehrle (Eds.): P2P Systems and Applications, LNCS 3485, pp. 383-397, 2005.

23.2 A Concept for Peer-to-Peer Performance

A comprehensive description of the performance of Peer-to-Peer systems is a challenging task. The term "Peer-to-Peer" describes not a single architecture but subsumes a rather huge variety of architectures and applications. A single evaluation metric for Peer-to-Peer services is rather impossible. Peer-to-Peer architectures and Peer-to-Peer algorithms have to be evaluated according to the task they accomplish.

All Peer-to-Peer systems have in common that they are highly distributed application architectures where functional equal entities (*peers*) voluntarily share resources. In order to participate in the resource exchange, Peer-to-Peer systems support two fundamental coordination functions: *a) resource mediation* mechanisms, i. e. functions to search and locate resources or entities, and *b) resource access control* mechanisms, i. e. functions to permit, prioritize, and schedule the access to resources. In addition, since Peer-to-Peer is a networked application architecture, the efficiency and the performance of a Peer-to-Peer system has to be evaluated on the network layer (e. g. by describing the load imposed by a Peer-to-Peer application on the network), as well as on the applications layer (e. g. by considering the time to locate a resource).

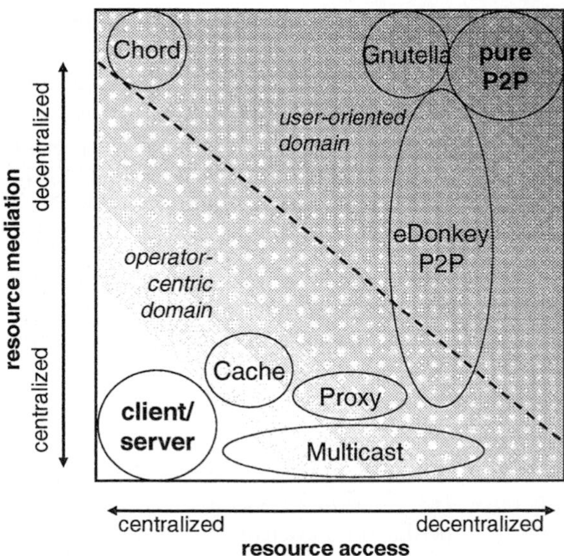

Fig. 23.1: Cartography of Peer-to-Peer applications and content distribution architectures

Figure 23.1 depicts a two-dimensional cartography for comparing Peer-to-Peer systems by their architectural characteristics with other well-established information dissemination mechanisms. The basic Peer-to-Peer control functions *(resource mediation/resource access control)* form the Cartesian space in Figure 23.1. The degree of distribution *(centralization/decentralization)* is used as the range of the axes. The cartography visualizes the architectural options of operators and users for providing information distribution services ("operator-centric" or "user-centric" architectures)[1]. The cartography provides an initial guideline of how to choose the components of a Peer-to-Peer architecture under given application requirements. A specific selection of a Peer-to-Peer-based algorithm will be based on its performance.

The overall performance of Peer-to-Peer services is determined by the combined performance of the two basic control functions. Since the control functions solve different tasks, the algorithms have to be evaluated by separate performance metrics. The *resource mediation functions*, for example, can be evaluated by:

- the needed time to locate a resource (cf. Section 23.4)
- the probability to locate a certain resource
- the amount of communication needed to locate a resource (cf. 23.3.1)

The metrics for *resource access control* are more user-oriented and may comprise:

- the time needed to exchange a resource (cf. Section 23.5)
- the throughput obtained during the exchange of a resource (cf. Section 23.3.2)

The range of the axes of the cartography indicates another constraint for the evaluation of Peer-to-Peer. Decentralization includes scalability, thus the performance of Peer-to-Peer algorithms has to be considered with respect to the *number of entities* participating in the system. Another feature of Peer-to-Peer is the autonomy of the nodes, i. e. the peers may join or leave the system arbitrarily. This leads to the requirements to evaluate Peer-to-Peer algorithms with respect to the *stochastic on-line behavior*, which is summarized under the term "churn", cf. also Section 23.5.

A key reason for the success of Peer-to-Peer systems is their use of application-specific overlays. Peer-to-Peer overlays, however, show a high variability due to the churn behavior of the peers. The *stability of the overlay*, e. g. the life time of overlay connections (cf. Section 23.3.1), and the *consistency of the overlay*, e. g. the probability that an overlay splits, are Peer-to-Peer-specific performance metrics for overlays.

[1] A detailed discussion of Figure 23.1 is provided in [27]

23.3 Traffic Characteristics of Peer-to-Peer-Systems

23.3.1 Gnutella

Gnutella was one of the first successful Peer-to-Peer file sharing applications [335] and sparked largely the wide spread interest in Peer-to-Peer due to its *pure Peer-to-Peer architecture*. The Gnutella service forms an application-specific overlay of Internet accessible hosts running Gnutella-speaking applications like `LimeWire` [388] or `Bearshare` [65]. In Gnutella, the overlay is used for locating files and for finding other peers; the later in order to maintain the integrity of the overlay. The initial version of Gnutella [126] uses a simple flooding protocol combined with a back-tracking mechanisms for locating the resources (files or hosts) in the overlay. While the qualitative evaluation has revealed that Gnutella suffers from scalability problems [518], little is known of quantitative results on the traffic and the dynamics in Gnutella overlays. In particular, time scale and variability of the number of virtual connections have to be characterized [601].

Measurements at an unrestricted Gnutella client have been carried out in March 2002 at the University of Würzburg. The observations (cf. Figure 23.2) reveal that even without sharing files, a Gnutella client is consuming tremendous high amounts of bandwidth for locating resources (files or hosts), reaching up in the order of tens of Mbps.

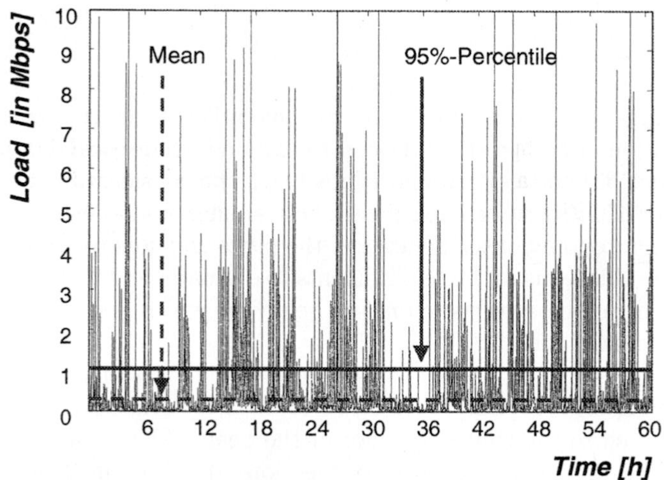

Fig. 23.2: Sum of signaling traffic load

In addition, Figure 23.2 shows that the traffic in Gnutella overlays varies strongly over short timescales. This is mainly due to the use of flooding protocols in Gnutella.

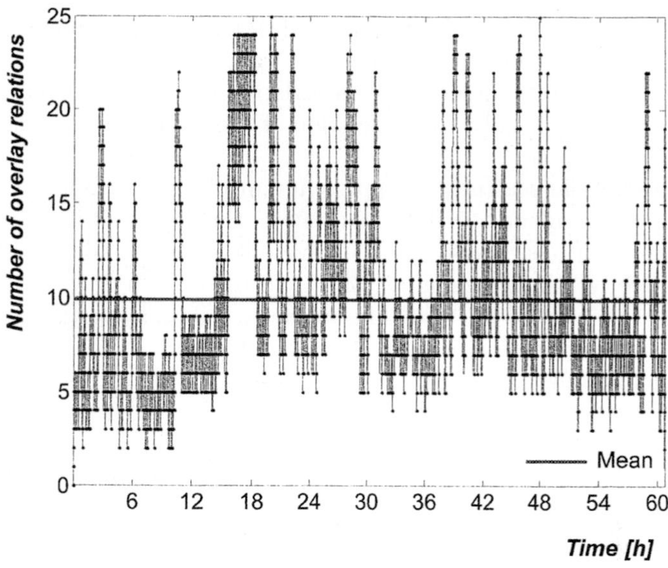

Fig. 23.3: Number of simultaneous overlay relations

In Gnutella, a peer tries to maintain a certain, pre-configured number of overlay connections. Due to the churn behavior of the peer the number of parallel maintained overlay connections can vary significantly, cf. Figure 23.3.

The investigation of the overlay connection holding time in Gnutella showed that the distribution typically has bi-modal characteristic, cf. Figure 23.4.

The modes correspond to a "short" state, where typically host information is transmitted, and to a "stable" mode, where mainly content queries are exchanged. The modes identify the time scales on which a dynamic and adaptive management of Peer-to-Peer overlays and Peer-to-Peer services is of advantage or needed.

23.3.2 eDonkey

The eDonkey Peer-to-Peer filesharing service[2] [410, 589] continues to be one of the most popular file swapping applications in the Internet [616]. The eDonkey system is typically used for exchanging very large files like audio/video CDs or even DVD images, and possesses a hybrid Peer-to-Peer architecture with distinct servers and clients. The eDonkey system makes use of the *multi source download (MSD)* feature, which permits the simultaneous transmis-

[2] This chapter subsumes eDonkey2000 and all its derivatives by the single term eDonkey.

sion of file chunks to a downloading peer. The traffic profile [600] shows that resource mediation traffic (also denoted as "signaling" traffic) and download traffic have significantly different characteristics. Figure 23.5 depicts a scatter plot describing graphically the correlation of the TCP holding time and the size of eDonkey flows.

Each dot in the scatter plot represents an observed eDonkey flow. The brighter dots are identified download flows, the dark dots represent non-download connections. The scatter plot shows that almost all identified download flows are within the same region. In turn, the non-download flows are in an disjunct region of the plot. This graph reveals that download and non-download flows have significantly different characteristics. A Peer-to-Peer traffic model has to distinguish between both types of traffic.

The differences between the types of traffic are underlined in Figure 23.6 and Figure 23.7. The complementary cumulative distribution function (CCDF) of the flow size is depicted in Figure 23.6. Part (a) of Figure 23.6 shows that the download flow size decreases stronger than linear in the log/log plot. That means that the flow sizes don't show a strong "heavy tailed" feature.

An approximation of the observed data with a lognormal distribution achieves a good estimate. The reduced strength of the heavy tail feature is not expected, but can be explained: the download flows are limited due to the segmentation of files into chunks and due to the application of the multiple source download principle. This observation gives evidence that the expected "mice and elephant" phenomenon [479, 73] in eDonkey traffic is not as severe as expected.

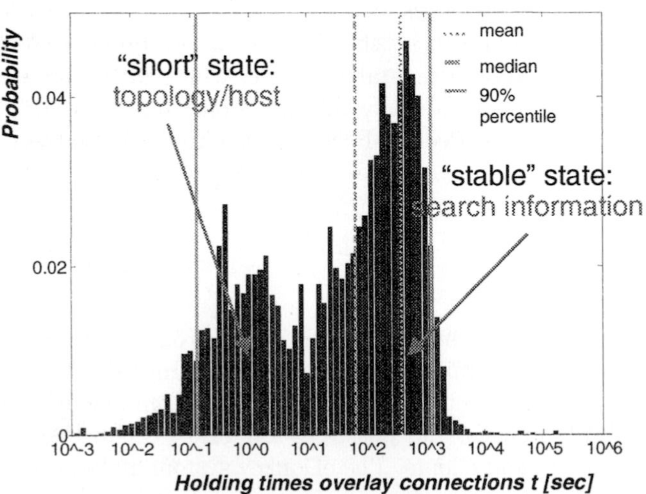

Fig. 23.4: Gnutella overlay connection holding time distribution

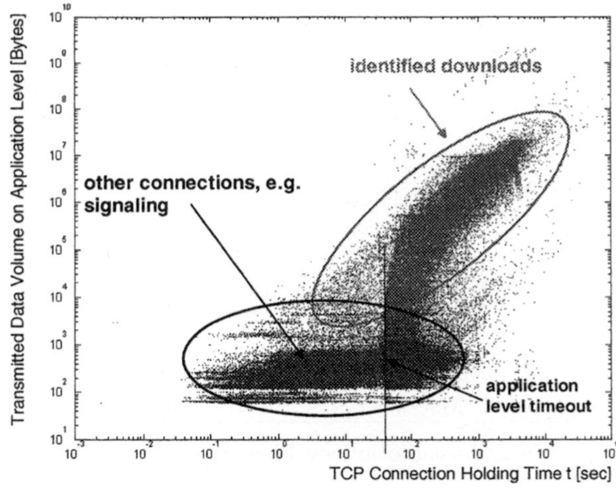

Fig. 23.5: Correlation of eDonkey TCP holding time and flow size

Part (b) of Figure 23.6 depicts the size of non-download flows. The probability that a flow is larger than a given value decreases almost exponentially until a limit (approx. 14 Kbytes). Beyond this limit, the decrease is not regular. This is an expected behavior since non-download flows are typical signaling flows to renew requests.

Figure 23.7 depicts the CCDF of the eDonkey flow holding times on TCP level. The download connection holding time CCDF decrease moderately, cf. Figure 23.7(a), and reminds more of a linear decay in a log/log plot. The CCDF of the holding time of non-download streams, cf. Figure 23.7(b), decreases rapidly as well as un-regularly. This is an expected behavior since non-download connections are short and limited in their sensitivity on TCP flow control.

Mobile Peer-to-Peer Filesharing

The feasibility and throughput of *mobile Peer-to-Peer* file sharing in infrastructure-based GPRS and UMTS mobile networks is examined by measurements in [298]. The measurements have been carried out in networks of two German GPRS network operators and, for the first time, in a UMTS network. The subject of the empirical investigation was the eDonkey application due to its continuing popularity [616] and its hybrid architecture, which give opportunities for network operators to interfere [456].

The measurements demonstrated that mobile Peer-to-Peer is technically feasible for GPRS technology but stability and throughput are unacceptable low if compared to fixed Peer-to-Peer. Particularly, the direct exchange of large parts of files between two mobile peers and multiple source down-

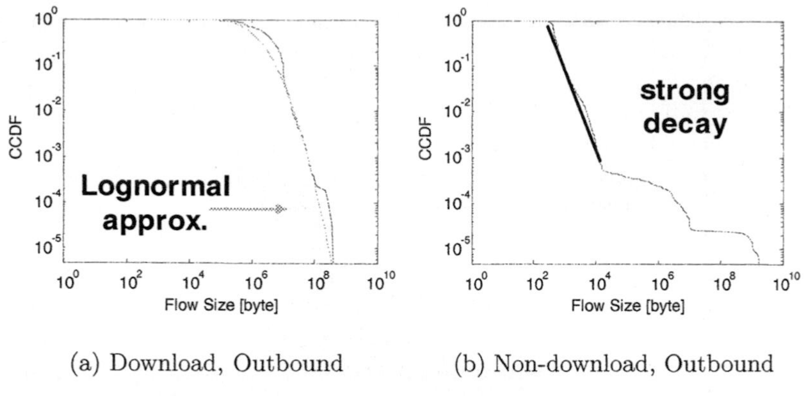

Fig. 23.6: CCDF of the observed eDonkey Flow Size

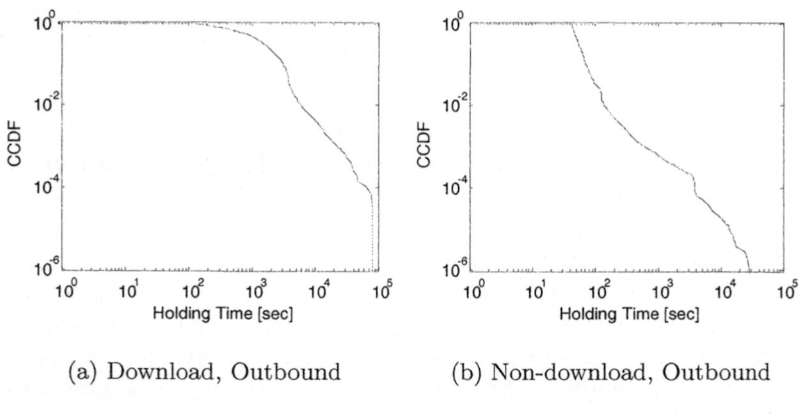

Fig. 23.7: CCDF of the observed eDonkey Flow Holding time

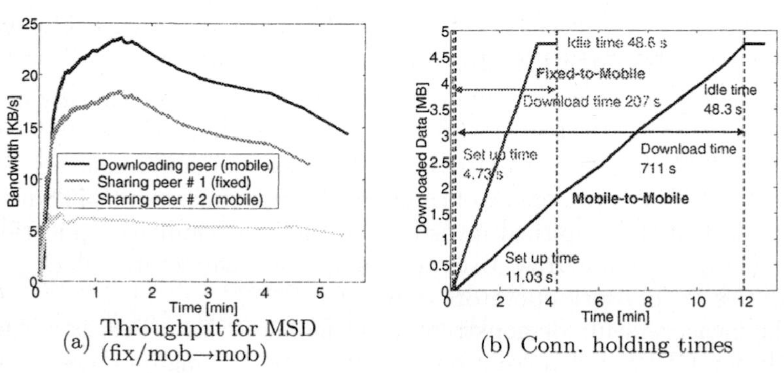

Fig. 23.8: Performance of mobile Peer-to-Peer file sharing in UMTS

load is not practical in GPRS. UMTS technology, in contrast, is more stable and has superior throughput. It extends the capabilities of the GPRS service into sufficient performance for mobile Peer-to-Peer file sharing. Figure 23.8(a) depicts the observed throughput for a multiple source download for a mobile peer downloading from a fixed peer and a mobile peer (abbreviated as fix/mob→mob). The throughput for MSD reaches a sustained level of 25 KBytes/sec. This is a value which even permits the download of larger files.

The number of traversals of the air interface, however, has to be minimized in order to reduce the traffic and the transmission delay. Figure 23.8(b) compares the TCP connection holding times for an eDonkey file part of the same size for a fixed-to-mobile transmission and for a mobile-to-mobile transmission in UMTS. Figure 23.8(a) reveals that the uplink capacity of the providing mobile peer is the bottleneck and that the connection setup time is almost doubled in the mobile-to-mobile transmission. A reduction of the necessary traversal of the air interface can be achieved efficiently by the application of caches, which has also the advantage of overcoming the asymmetric access bandwidths of mobile stations [297].

23.4 Evaluation of a Peer-to-Peer Resource Mediation Mechanism

A distributed and highly scalable approach for Peer-to-Peer resource mediation mechanisms is the concept of *distributed hash tables (DHTs)* [52]. DHT-based Peer-to-Peer algorithms like Chord [575] only need to store the location of $O(\log_2(n))$ other peers where n is the number of peers in the overlay network. They are furthermore able to retrieve information stored in the distributed network using $O(\log_2(n))$ messages to other peers. This statement, however, is very vague. It tells only the order of the magnitude of the search delay and does not provide sufficient details on the actual search time statistics. As a matter of fact the physical link delay, which is highly probabilistic, strongly influences the performance of searches in a Peer-to-Peer overlay network. Thus, the impact of network delay variation on resource mediation times, i. e. search times, in DHT based Peer-to-Peer systems has to be evaluated. The goal is to prove scalability of Chord rings in order to guarantee quality-of-service demands. An analytical model for Chord has to be deduced in order to evaluate the performance in large peer populations [74].

The phase diagram of the search delay is depicted in Figure 23.9. A particular path i is chosen with probability p_i and consists of i network transmissions T_N to forward the query to the closest known finger and one network transmission T_A to send the answer back to the searching peer. By means of the phase diagram, the generating function and the Laplace transform respec-

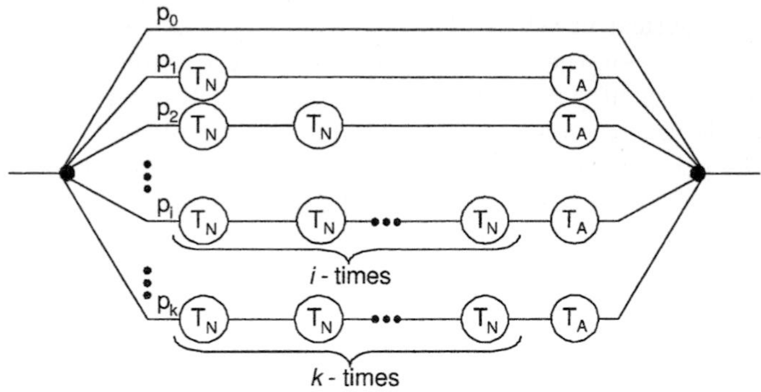

Fig. 23.9: Phase diagram of the search duration T

tively can be derived to cope with the case of discrete-time or continuous-time network transfer delay.

The distribution function of the search delay as seen from a user entering a search query to a peer in the Chord ring is computed. The analysis also gives insight into the quantiles of the search delay.

Figure 23.10, e. g., analyzes different quantiles of the search delay. It can be seen that Chord searches indeed scale logarithmically. One can observe that the search delay bound rapidly increases at smaller values of n, but stays moderate for very large peer populations. The curve is not strictly monotonically increasing as expected since a small decrease can be seen when the population n just exceeds a binary exponential value 2^i. This effect can be explained as follows: once the size of the population crosses the next power of 2, the finger table of each peer grows by one entry. Thus, the mean search duration slightly decreases at this point.

The curve with the 99 %-quantile indicates that 99 percent of search durations lie below that curve. For a peer population of, e. g., $n = 3000$ in 99 percent of all cases the search delay is less then roughly 15 times the average network latency. That is, the curves indicate bounds of the search delay, which can be used for dimensioning purposes. Compared to the mean of the search delay the quantiles of the search delay are on a significantly higher level. Still, the search delay scales in an analogous manner for the search delay quantiles.

Figure 23.11 depicts the 99 %-quantile of the search delay, with the coefficient of variation of T_N as parameter. There are five vertical lines at $n = 512$, 256, 128, 64, and 32 to point out the previously mentioned oscillations at $n = 2^i$. The larger c_{T_N} we choose, i. e. the more variation there is in the network delay, the larger is the 99 %-quantile of the search duration. Therefore, it is more difficult to guarantee Service Level Agreements in networks with larger delay variation. Timeouts, e. g. have to be set to higher values accordingly.

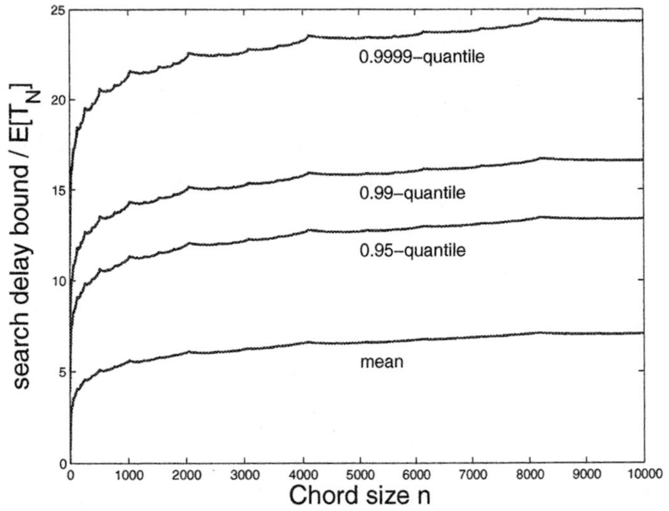

Fig. 23.10: Search delay quantiles

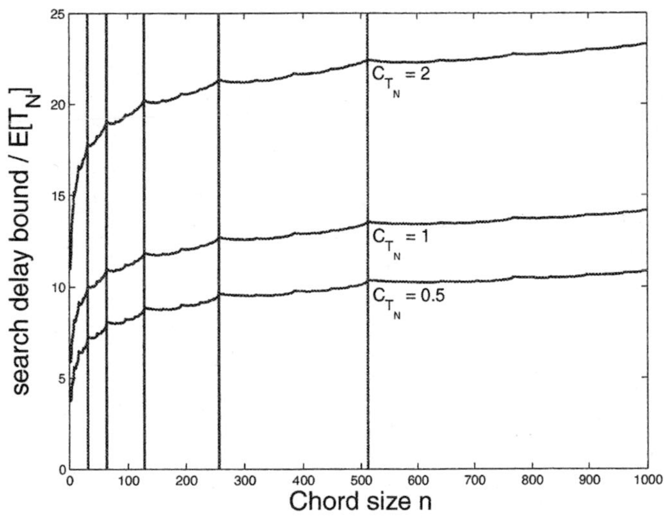

Fig. 23.11: Influence of CoV of T_N on search delay quantile

The numerical results presented above illustrate the dependency of the search duration on the variation of the network transfer delay and analyze the scalability of the Chord-based Peer-to-Peer mediation mechanism. The analysis also gives insight into the quantiles of the search delay, which can be used for system dimensioning purposes. This becomes of particular interest if real-time requirements should be obeyed in case such an algorithms is used to locate users in a Peer-to-Peer VoIP system like Skype [567].

23.5 Evaluation of a Peer-to-Peer Resource Access Mechanism in Mobile Environment

The second key function provided by Peer-to-Peer systems is the group of resource access mechanisms, i. e. algorithms for exchanging files. So far, mainly empirical investigations of their efficiency have been published. A comprehensive measurement-based evaluation of KaZaA [558], for example, is provided in [379] and the empirical performance of the BitTorrent file swapping system [128] is reported in [320, 494]. Two of the few available analytical investigations are presented in [71, 497].

Before deploying resource exchange mechanisms in the wild, it is necessary to validate their capability. In particular, if resources are limited as in mobile networks. Mobile networks differ from wireline networks mainly by the limited capacity of the radio link and the mobility of the users. High overhead for exchanging data is considered to be too expensive in mobile networks and payload traffic should traverse the air interface only once on its way to the requesting peer.

In order to meet these requirements, a hybrid architecture for *mobile Peer-to-Peer file sharing* is proposed in [456] and analyzed in [298]. The suggested architecture, shown in Figure 23.12, is based on the popular eDonkey file sharing network and is enhanced by three specific mobile Peer-to-Peer components: a modified *index server* for mediation, a *cache peer* for storing popular files and a *crawling peer*, which supports mobile peers searching the global community.

The architecture permits the operator to *a)* participate in service creation and service control, *b)* to offer value-added services, while *c)* maintaining the characteristic of direct and efficient Peer-to-Peer interaction between the users, e. g. fast file swapping while minimizing the traffic on the user's uplink.

The impact of the node life time, i. e. the churn behavior, on the download time is depicted in Figure 23.13

Figure 23.13 shows the CCDF for downloading files with average size of 5 MBytes and by applying GPRS as the access technology of mobile peers. Figure 23.13(a) shows the CCDF of the download time for popular files, i. e. the *cache peer* is used (for details see [298]). The mobile peers with the longest churn time of 12 h (red curve in Figure 23.13(a)) have the smallest download times. The more the average churn time decreases in Figure 23.13, i. e. 2 h (green line) and 30 min (blue line), the more the download time increases. Figure 23.13(b) illustrates the CCDF of the download time for unpopular files with respect to the different churn times.

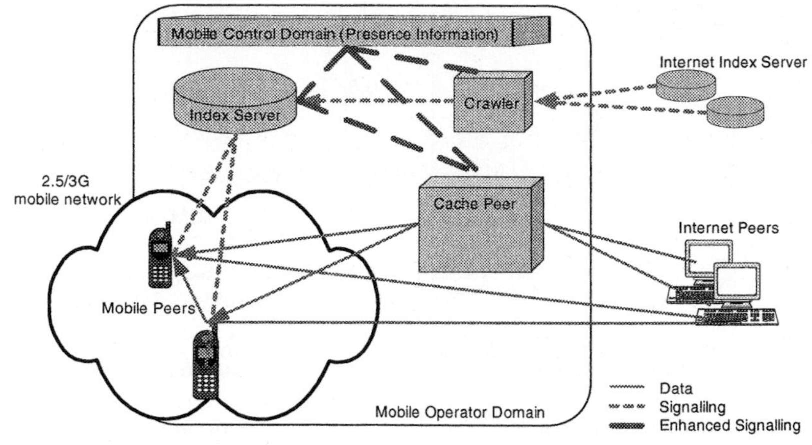

Fig. 23.12: Overview of Mobile Peer-to-Peer Architecture

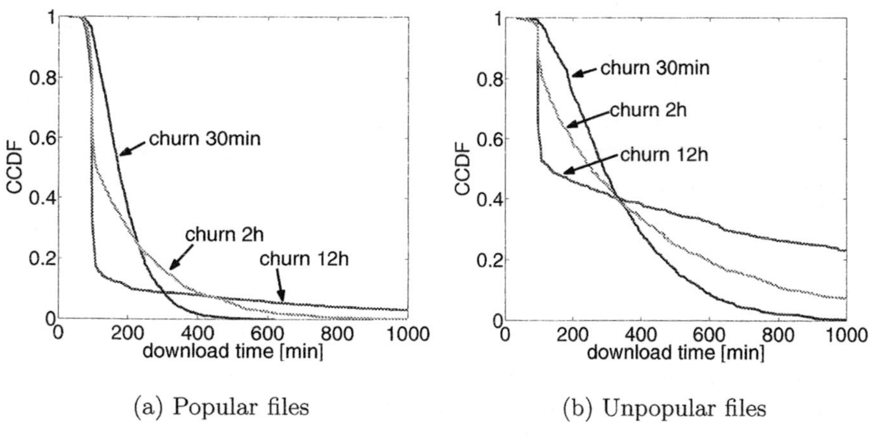

Fig. 23.13: Download time for different churn times

The results shows that churn behavior of the peers has significant impact on the download time of files, however the additional infrastructure entity, the *cache peer*, can reduce this effect.

Figure 23.14 compares the CCDF of the download time for popular and unpopular mp3-files of 8 MBytes. The UMTS subscribers get quite reasonable performance values since the download time exceeds 1 hour only with a small probability. On the other hand, the GPRS subscribers have much higher download times and the shape of the curve is completely different to the CCDF for UMTS. It seems that there exists a minimal required upload/download bandwidth of the peers for a given file size in order to retrieve

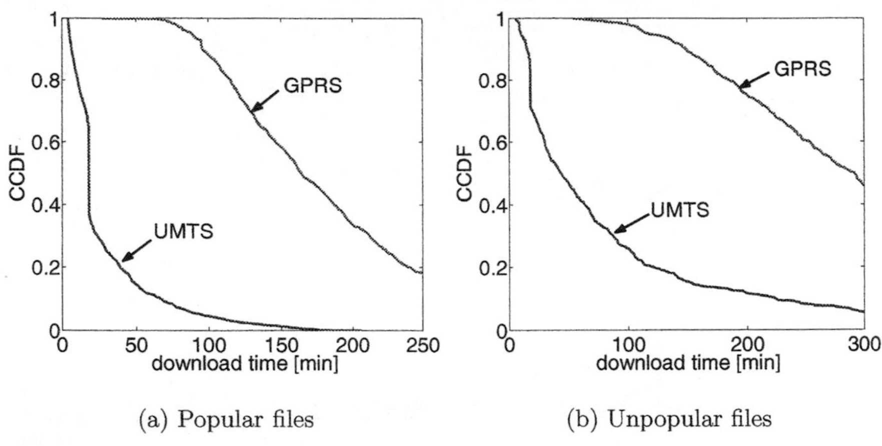

(a) Popular files (b) Unpopular files

Fig. 23.14: Download of mp3-audio files with GPRS and UMTS

a file *efficiently.* The shape of the blue curve in Figure 23.14 is characteristic for the CCDF of the download time in an *efficient* system, while the red one illustrates the behavior for *unefficient* systems. This effect becomes even more obvious for unpopular files which are not cached by the cache peer.

The results of Figure 23.14 show that mobile Peer-to-Peer file sharing is almost impossible with GPRS whereas UMTS is a good candidate for *efficient* Peer-to-Peer file swapping.

23.6 Conclusion

Peer-to-Peer architectures and Peer-to-Peer algorithms have to be evaluated according to the task they accomplish. Peer-to-Peer systems support two functions: *a) resource mediation* mechanisms and *b) resource access control* mechanisms.

The performance of a Chord-based Peer-to-Peer resource mediation mechanisms has been assessed in Section 23.4. It has turned out that the network delay has significant impact on the time to locate a resource and that the algorithm scales even for tight delay bounds, in this way fulfilling carrier grade requirements.

The efficiency of a multiple source download mechanism (resource access mechanisms) has been investigated in Section 23.5. It was shown that the download time depends highly on the type of the air interface as well as on the churn behavior of the peers.

Furthermore, it was shown by measurements that Peer-to-Peer traffic is highly variable and that Peer-to-Peer overlay management has to be performed on two timescales (cf. "short" and "stable" state in and Section 23.3.1). Moreover the measurements have revealed that multiple source download mechanisms do not increase the "mice and elephant" phenomenon (cf. Section 23.3.2) and that these mechanisms can perform efficiently even in mobile environments.

In the case of a mobile environment, measurements and the performance evaluation indicate that an optimal transfer segment size exists, which is dependent on the type of access network and the churn behavior of the peers. The determination of this size is for further research.

Part VIII

Peer-to-Peer in Mobile and Ubiquitous Environments

24. Peer-to-Peer in Mobile Environments

Wolfgang Kellerer (DoCoMo Euro-Labs)
Rüdiger Schollmeier (Munich University of Technology)
Klaus Wehrle (University of Tübingen)

As we have seen in previous chapters, Peer-to-Peer-based applications are not limited to the well-known file sharing applications. Also, the Peer-to-Peer infrastructure is not limited to the hard-wired Internet infrastructure, but is starting to penetrate wireless networks of different characteristics. This chapter discusses the application of Peer-to-Peer based concepts in mobile infrastructure environments – including cellular systems and ad-hoc style networks. Starting with a motivation, application scenarios, and an overview of mobile system characteristics, the main part of this chapter describes challenges and possible solutions for optimizing Peer-to-Peer systems to meet the requirements of mobile scenarios. Both unstructured and structured Peer-to-Peer concepts for mobile scenarios are analyzed and discussed.

24.1 Why Is Peer-to-Peer Technology Interesting for Mobile Users and Mobile Services ?

Peer-to-Peer systems have previously been defined as self-organizing systems supporting to find and use distributed resources, i.e., services (cf. Chapter 2). With the increasing availability of mobile data communications – including Internet access in mobile networks – wired network originated Peer-to-Peer applications become available also to mobile users. They should enjoy the same level of service as they know from fixed line access while being mobile.

Furthermore, the Peer-to-Peer paradigm provides the unique opportunity for service offerings by individual users. For mobile users it is advantageous to be able, e.g., to offer instant services directly instead of uploading them to a centralized server. Moreover, services based on the local proximity of the users can benefit from a Peer-to-Peer style of provisioning without any infrastructure backing. However, for commercial applications there is still a need for some support by special, trusted parties to control service negotiation and to observe the fulfillment of service agreements [569].

However, wireless resources are usually limited and vary in performance and availability, which restricts the use of Peer-to-Peer applications in mobile environments. There are some general features in Peer-to-Peer that already address changes in the conditions of the users communication environment. For example, most Peer-to-Peer solutions can accommodate changes of a

R. Steinmetz and K. Wehrle (Eds.): P2P Systems and Applications, LNCS 3485, pp. 401-417, 2005.

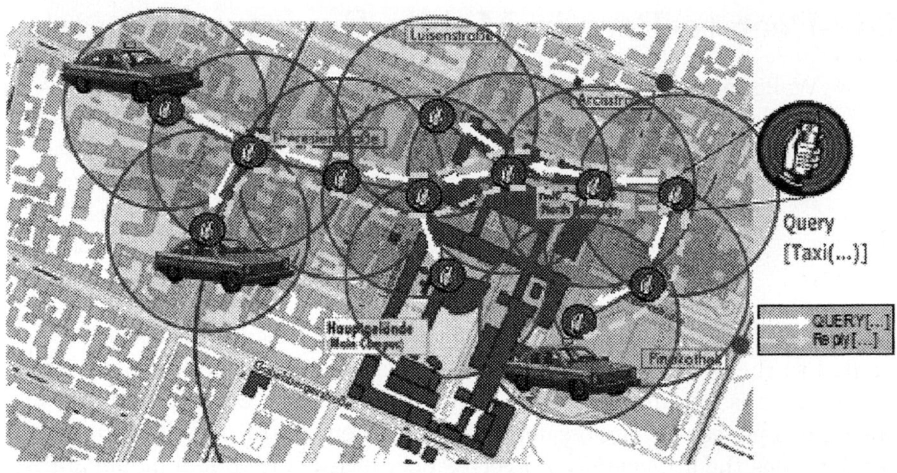

Fig. 24.1: Possible application scenario for location-based services: Locating a taxi.

node's availability caused, e.g., due to failures or joins and leaves of users. Too frequent changes as typical in wireless environments appear as a threat to conventional Peer-to-Peer-systems.

In general, the application of Peer-to-Peer to mobile environments provides a number of opportunities and challenges since, originally, Peer-to-Peer was not designed for mobile environments, which we will outline in what follows. As we will see in the next sections, two scenarios are providing the impetus for the application of Peer-to-Peer concepts in mobile environments.

Besides the well-known file sharing applications based on Peer-to-Peer networks, new wireless applications are also feasible in mobile networks, especially when we consider multi-hop links such as in mobile ad-hoc networks (MANETs). Therefore, we motivate two basic examples in the next two sections, that may be realized with Peer-to-Peer technology on top of an ad-hoc wireless network.

24.1.1 Scenario 1: Taxi Locator

Imagine, for example, a user standing at the side of a road, requires a taxi, but can not see any nearby. The user could now call the central taxi agency and order a taxi, having to state his current position. The agency, which has to track the current location of its taxis, could then direct the nearest one to the user.

If context-based routing was supported by the available MANET, the user could simply send out a request which would be broadcasted in a multihop manner, via a pre-configured number of hops, in its proximity. All participating nodes would forward the request until a taxi receives it, as illustrated in Figure 24.1. The taxi could then reply with an appropriate response message to the requesting node, and finally, pick up the user.

Thus our context-based routing scheme allows the utilization of Location-based Services (LBS) without the need for centralized elements. The underlying MANET limits flooding of the search request to the geographical proximity. Additionally, the creation of all kinds of search requests can be imagined. Possible request categories could thus also include bars, restaurants or closest bus stops.

24.1.2 Scenario 2: University Campus

The second scenario is not that highly dynamic as the first one, but also bases on ad-hoc network technology. On a university campus, today, students and teaching staff are often equipped with wireless technology, like laptops, PDAs, and Smartphones. During courses, seminars, reading groups, or in spare time, they may form groups of collaborating 'peers'. But often, collaboration with networked systems can not be deployed because of missing infrastructure support (e.g., network plugs) or due to restrictive network policies.

A solution to such problems is the formation of spontaneous wireless ad-hoc networks, e.g., based on bluetooth, IEEE 802.11x or both. Students are then able to collaborate, share teaching materials, and many more. After the courses are finished, students then move to the next activity. Thus, the spontaneous groups separate and – after a short and highly dynamic period – form new collaborative groups. These new groups may have a very different purpose.

The formation of spontaneous ad-hoc groups can easily be supported by existing MANET technology. They may also be interconnected by some Internet-connected peers, if two MANETs are within wireless reachability. But the sharing of information, the support for collaboration, and the realization of other services is not directly supported by MANET technology.

We think, that Peer-to-Peer technology has greatly proven to be appropriate for such tasks in the wired Internet. The interesting questions are now:

- Can these Peer-to-Peer-based approaches be used in MANET scenarios, e.g., like the two described here?
- What modifications and adaptations are necessary for such a purpose?

24.2 Introduction to Mobile Communication Systems

Before we take a deeper look into the challenges of Peer-to-Peer communication in mobile environments, we will briefly describe the variety of mobile communication systems and their features [348]. By "mobile communication" we mean systems with at least one hop of the communication path effected by a wireless link. They usually support interactive bi-directional communication. Broadcast systems such as Digital Video Broadcast (DVB) and Digital Audio Broadcast (DAB), or satelite-based systems are not considered in this chapter.

In general, mobile access networks can be divided into two subcategories: cellular networks, and mobile ad hoc networks (MANETs). The latter are realized either with wireless LAN or other short range wireless transmission technology. Table 24.1 summarizes the most important characteristics such as data rate and coverage.

Second generation cellular networks such as the Global System for Mobile Communication (GSM) have been enhanced to offer higher data rates and packet-based communication. For example, by providing up to 50 kbps the General Packet Radio Service (GPRS) in GSM offers much more efficient access to web resources than the 9.6 kbps, data service of GSM itself. With the recent introduction of third generation systems such as UMTS, offering up to 384 kbps, more demanding data services such as audio or video streaming, and the downloading of large media files, are also now possible. The described systems are only a small snapshot of the variety of cellular standards. Integration is expected with the introduction of the fourth generation. Cellular terminals are usually constrained in terms of processing power, storage space and battery power. Though the terminals offer only limited display capabilities, most data formats such as audio, video, image are processed. Connecting a laptop through a mobile phone to a wireless network overcomes end systems limitations, but still leaves data rate restrictions, the general problem of today's commonly available cellular networks such as GSM and GPRS.

System	Data Rate	Coverage	Frequency Range
Cellular Networks			
GSM	9.6 kbps	country-wide	900, 1800,
GSM/GPRS	< 50 kbps	"	1900 MHz
UMTS	< 384 kbps	partially country-wide	2 GHz
Wireless LAN			
IEEE 802.11b	max. 11 Mbps	50-300 m	2.4 GHz
IEEE 802.11a	6-24 Mbps	"	5 GHz
Short Range			
Bluetooth	max. 1 Mbit/s	10 or 100 m	2.4 GHz
IrDA	4 Mbps	line of sight	infrared

Table 24.1: Overview of mobile communication systems

Wireless data networks such as wireless LAN are of increasing importance for wireless access providing data rates of up to tens of Mbps. In contrast to cellular networks, which offer country-wide coverage and a feeling of always being connected, wireless LAN-based access is still restricted to certain isolated locations (hot spots).

Wireless LAN technology, in concert with short range communication, such as Bluetooth, also provides the infrastructure for mobile ad hoc networks. MANETs are self-configuring, multi-hop wireless networks that are not based on any fixed infrastructure such as base stations, hot spots or any central database. A node participating in a MANET acts at the same time as a data source, sink, and router on the network layer. This is very similar to Peer-to-Peer systems in that Peer-to-Peer nodes have the same roles on the application layer (cf. Chapter 2). In multi-hop MANETs, such as illustrated in both example scenarios, nodes in physical proximity are used as relay stations for routing. The main challenge for Peer-to-Peer techniques in MANETs is overcoming the instability of the physical network as connections are changing due to the movement of the nodes. This may lead to long unstable zig-zag routes on the Peer-to-Peer layer.

24.3 Challenges for Peer-to-Peer Techniques in Mobile Networks

Summarizing the observations about mobile communication systems described above, we can set down the following main challenges for Peer-to-Peer techniques in mobile networks: Mobile networks are usually resource-constrained systems limited by low data rates, low processing power, and low storage capacity of mobile terminals. Furthermore, they are characterized by frequent joins and leaves of nodes. This, what we call high churn rate, is resulting from node failures, e.g., when moving out of coverage, exhausted batteries, or from short session times, e.g., due to high online cost. To adapt to the scarce wireless resources, Peer-to-Peer solutions for mobile networks have to employ a more efficient search strategy than current flooding-based concepts. Traffic can also be minimized if Peer-to-Peer networks are aware of the underlying physical topology and long zig-zag routes are thus avoided. This is especially important for multi-hop networks in order to reduce the number of hops for the Peer-to-Peer path and to find the nearest shared resource.

As have been said, we mainly distinguish mobile ad-hoc and cellular networks in mobile environments. Cellular wireless networks are only one-hop wireless networks. Mobile Peer-to-Peer nodes are thus connected to the fixed Internet by a single wireless link. Consequently, we can state that even if the node moves, the physical path to this node does not alter very much. We therefore can regard Peer-to-Peer nodes connected to the Internet via a cellular wireless link as low performance nodes because we have to consider their bandwidth restrictions. Significant changes to the Peer-to-Peer protocol, which take into particular account the mobility of the nodes in cellular wireless systems are therefore not necessary from our point of view.

However, if we want to operate a Peer-to-Peer network on top of a MANET, we certainly do have to take into account the mobility of the nodes. The reason of course is that MANETs are self-configuring, wireless multi-hop networks, within which we have to assume the possibility of the physical path between two nodes changing frequently, due to the movement of the nodes [263]. If the overlay structure was to be established completely independently from the underlying MANET topology, it would result in a significant number of long and unstable zig-zag routes in the MANET layer, as already said. This would lead to high traffic volumes, which might not be sustainable by the MANET [356]. In the following, therefore, we will focus more narrowly on MANETs.

24.3.1 Peer-to-Peer Systems in Mobile Ad-Hoc Networks

Peer-to-Peer and MANET network architectures are very promising concepts. Although they use different layers for operation, we think that the idea to combine both architectures shows a high potential. As described in [547], the architectures have several similarities, but also many differences. To achieve a workable integration of the two architectures, a new inter-layer communication is necessary. Peer-to-Peer protocols are not aware of the underlying MANET and assume a fixed network infrastructure, causing additional and unnecessary network traffic. Thus a simple utilization of ad hoc networks for common Peer-to-Peer applications is not feasible, as we shall now see.

Common Peer-to-Peer applications have optimized algorithms to find information within their overlay network, but for information exchange they generally rely on TCP and assume stable connections. Whenever connections break, Peer-to-Peer nodes assume that their distant communication partners have left the network and switch to other, randomly chosen nodes, which can also provide the requested content, or which offer further connectivity to the network to initiate new search requests.

In MANETs, link breaks are common, as all nodes are in motion. Whenever two adjacent nodes move out of each others' radio range, the link between them breaks. A MANET protocol unaware of the Peer-to-Peer application, tries to re-establish a new route to the same destination, independently from the necessary effort. Instead of trying to create a new route to the same source of information after the network topology changed, other sources could provide the information at less cost. Therefore the MANET nodes have to report route breaks to the upper Peer-to-Peer node which then decides whether the old source is still utilizable, or wether another connection partner is more appropriate.

As common Peer-to-Peer networks operate on top of fixed network infrastructures, Peer-to-Peer nodes mostly do not distinguish between communication partners in close proximity and those more distant. Peer-to-Peer networks use multi-hop connections only for search requests. Subsequent information downloads use direct TCP connections between source and destination. The distance between nodes generally does not affect the stability and error-free operation of connections. Therefore Peer-to-Peer nodes might create connections to distant nodes, even though the information searched for might also be available more close by.

The distances between communication partners in MANETs are quantified by the number of intermediate hops. It is the most important parameter for route lifetimes [263]. Numerous unnecessarily lengthened routes induce additional routing overhead, delay data packet transmissions and as a result, greatly reduce overall network performance. Therefore, the client application must classify incoming search replies according to the hop distances to their respective destinations. As a consequence, a combined Peer-to-Peer-MANET approach must be well aware, on the one hand, of the underlying network infrastructure, and on the other hand, of the overlaying application.

This situation introduces specific requirements on flexibility and resilience of Peer-to-Peer systems in ad-hoc networks. Another difference between wired and wireless networks is that global connectivity cannot be presumed in mobile ad-hoc networks. Even if the network splits up in several parts the Peer-to-Peer system still have to be operational to enable communication between nodes.

Limited resources of mobile devices – such as computational power, memory, energy, and bandwidth – complicate the situation even more. Consequently, mobile Peer-to-Peer-systems have to use these scarce resources efficiently. Avoiding unnecessary transmissions may be thought of as an example. In regions with a high density of nodes low bandwidth must be expected because of the shared medium. Because of the long distances between nodes a low signal quality has to be expected in regions with a low density of nodes. Therefore, ad-hoc networks have an obviously lower bandwidth while the self-organization of the network causes a noticeably higher overhead.

24.4 Solutions for Peer-to-Peer in Mobile and Wireless Networks

In the following, we will present and discuss approaches to enable the use of Peer-to-Peer applications in a mobile environment [286]. As seen in the previous parts of this book, Peer-to-Peer technology can roughly be divided into two basic approaches: structured and unstructured Peer-to-Peer systems (see Chapter 2). Therefore, we will discuss the use of both paradigms separately in Sections 24.4.1 and 24.4.2 though there may be some overlapping similarities between both.

24.4.1 Solutions Based on Unstructured Peer-to-Peer Networks

If we want to employ Peer-to-Peer networks in MANETs as mentioned in Section 24.3, we have to take into account, in contrast to cellular wireless networks, that the topology of the underlying physical network frequently changes. Due to the assumed node movements (sensor networks are not regarded in this context), the links between the nodes frequently change leading to frequent path breaks [263]. Therefore it is necessary to align the virtual to the physical topology to avoid zig-zag routes as described in [550].

Summarizing, we can state that although pure Peer-to-Peer networks and MANETs employ similar networking approaches, their combination by simply establishing a Peer-to-Peer network upon a MANET, without providing any interaction between them will most probably show low performance [356]. Thus, only recently have some approaches been developed to provide content-based routing, caching, or Peer-to-Peer networking in mobile ad hoc networks, which take into consideration the physical topology.

7DS [387], for example, employs local broadcast messages to provide an infrastructure for web browsing without a direct connection to the Internet. Therefore, every node acts as a mobile cache, which is continually renewed if a direct connection is available.

Besides providing Internet content in MANETs, ORION [356] is, next to the Mobile Peer-to-Peer protocol (MPP) [548, 264], a system, which aims to provide Peer-to-Peer services in a MANET indexMPP. ORION provides a general purpose distributed lookup service and an enhanced file transmission scheme to enable file sharing in MANETs. In contrast to MPP, ORION, to a certain extent, separates the Peer-to-Peer network from the physical network. In order to describe the methods used and the properties exploited for Peer-to-Peer in MANETs, we will first describe some of the details of the Mobile Peer-to-Peer protocol.

The Mobile Peer-to-Peer protocol adapts the overlay structure to the physical MANET structure via a cross-layer communication channel between the physical network layer and the virtual Peer-to-Peer layer [547]. This integrated approach significantly reduces the messaging overhead and increases the search success rate compared with approaches using a separated treatment of the overlay and the physical networks. Further, MPP allows the introduction of a variety of new services, since it provides the possibility of context based-routing and location-based services, instead of simple address routing as is provided by current MANET routing algorithms. Thus new services like the search for a taxi or a cash dispenser in your proximity can be

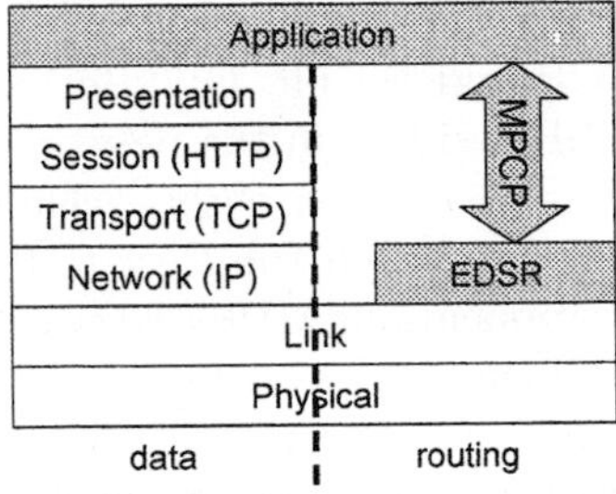

Fig. 24.2: Layered structure of MPP

realized without the necessity for further location-sensitive sensors and central instances. Further applications of such a combined approach have been described previously.

To minimize the effort to create a new protocol and to benefit from former developments, the MPP protocol stack reuses existing network protocols as much as possible. For node-to-node communication, the protocol utilizes an enhanced version of the Dynamic Source Routing (DSR) protocol [326] . For the transportation of user data it uses HTTP over TCP, as illustrated by Fig. 24.2. Thus the Enhanced Dynamic Source Routing (EDSR) requires only a new application layer protocol and minor changes within the DSR protocol. To connect the application layer protocol (MPP) with the physical network layer protocol (EDSR), the Mobile Peer Control protocol (MPCP) is used.

Since MANETs already provide routing algorithms which enable the localization of network participants by their IP addresses, an additional Peer-to-Peer implementation of this functionality is unnecessary and even degrades the performance. Consequently, EDSR is designed to perform the necessary routing tasks on the network layer and supplements the application layer protocol (MPP). This approach provides valuable advantages compared with a separate treatment of both networks:

- The MANET controls the organization of the network. Thus changes in the topology of the mobile network are taken into account automatically by the Peer-to-Peer network.
- The network layer is responsible for routing and the application controls the data exchange.
- The integration of both networks avoids redundant information requests.
- The inter-layer communication of the protocol optimizes performance, since the overlay network can be optimally adjusted to the physical network.
- The application layer protocol MPP simplifies the implementation of new services.

The separation of data exchange and routing tasks allows the reuse of existing protocols like TCP and HTTP. Only for routing tasks must MPP directly interact with EDSR residing in the network layer (cf. Fig. 24.2).

MPP allows distant peers to transparently exchange data. Therefore MPP is responsible for file transfers within the Peer-to-Peer network and resides in the Peer-to-Peer client application. MPP utilizes HTTP for data exchange since it is simple to implement and well tested. The HTTP content range header is able to resume file transfers in case of network errors due to link breaks. EDSR is mostly based on the DSR protocol, but additionally specifies new request and reply types to provide the means for finding peers by criteria other than the IP address. EDSR thus extends DSR and therefore EDSR nodes can be an integral part of DSR networks.

MPCP is the inter-layer communication channel between the application and the network layer. Thus MPCP links the EDSR Protocol in the network layer with the Peer-to-Peer application in the application layer. Using MPCP, the application can register itself in the EDSR layer to initialize search requests and to process incoming search requests from other nodes. It communicates to the corresponding protocol all incoming and outgoing requests and responses, exept the file exchange itself.

On startup, the Peer-to-Peer application on the mobile device announces itself to the EDSR layer via MPCP. If a user initializes a data search, MPCP forwards the request to EDSR which transforms it into a search request (SREQ). Similar to DSR route requests (RREQ), EDSR floods SREQs through the MANET. EDSR nodes receiving the request, forward it to the registered Peer-to-Peer application via MPCP. Thus the Peer-to-Peer application can determine whether locally shared data satisfies the request's criteria. If the request matches the description of a file shared by the node, the application initializes an EDSR file reply. This reply is sent back to the source node and contains all necessary information for the file transfer. Similar to DSR route replies (RREP), a file reply (FREP) includes the complete path between source and destination.

To compare the performance of a protocol adapted to the underlying physical network, like MPP, with a protocol which establishes its overlay still completely independently of the physical layer, we use an analytical approach. First, we have to evaluate the number of reachable nodes in a MANET environment.

If we assume x_0 neighbors on a per node average and a radio reach of R_0, we can compute the node density as:

$$nodedensity = \frac{x_0}{R_0^2 \Pi} \tag{24.1}$$

If we further assume a uniform distribution of the nodes in the plane, the cumulative distribution of the distance between two nodes is given by:

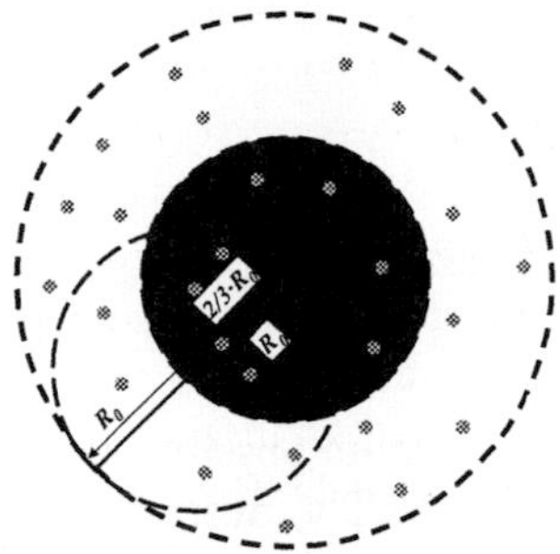

Fig. 24.3: Multihop reach of an average ad hoc node

$$F(r) = \frac{r^2 \Pi}{R_0^2 \Pi} = \left(\frac{r}{R_0}\right)^2 \tag{24.2}$$

which results in an increasing probability of occurrence for an increasing distance between two ad hoc nodes. The pdf of this function can now be computed by taking the derivate of $F(r)$:

$$f(r) = \frac{2r}{R_0^2} \tag{24.3}$$

This simply reflects the fact that the differential surface increases linearly with an increasing radius r. Accordingly, this also means that the probability of occurrence of nodes within the distance r also increases linearly. Thus the average distance between two nodes can be computed by:

$$\bar{d} = \int_0^{R_0} \frac{2r}{R_0^2} \cdot r dr = \frac{2}{3} R_0 \tag{24.4}$$

This means, as illustrated by Figure 24.3, that the multihop reach of an average node only increases by $\frac{2}{3}R_0$ instead of R_0. Thus the number of reachable nodes via h physical links can be computed by:

$$\Delta N_{phys} = \begin{cases} R_0^2 \Pi \cdot \frac{x_0}{R_0^2 \Pi} = x_0, \; h = 1 \\ \left(\left(1 + (h-1) \cdot \frac{2}{3}\right)^2 - \left(1 + (h-2) \cdot \frac{2}{3}\right)^2\right) R_0^2 \Pi \cdot \frac{x_0}{R_0^2 \Pi} \\ = \frac{8}{9} h x_0, \; h > 1 \end{cases} \tag{24.5}$$

If we now assume that a node in a Peer-to-Peer network does not adapt its overlay network to the underlying physical network, then it must establish its connections randomly. From equation 24.5 we can already observe that the further away a node is, in terms of physical hops, the higher the probability is that it connects to it. If we assume random selection, we can compute the probability in detail by:

$$p_{con}(h) = \frac{\Delta N_{phys}}{\left(R_0 + (h_{\max} - 1) \cdot \frac{2}{3} R_0\right)^2 \Pi \cdot \frac{x}{R_0 \Pi}} = \begin{cases} \frac{1}{\left(1+\frac{2}{3}(h_{\max}-1)\right)^2}, & h = 1 \\ \frac{8h}{9\left(1+\frac{2}{3}(h_{\max}-1)\right)^2}, & h > 1 \end{cases} \tag{24.6}$$

where h_{max} defines the maximum possible number of physical hops, which is commonly limited to six [263]. The average path length of a not-adapted overlay network in a physical network can thus be computed by:

$$\begin{aligned} l &= 1 \cdot \left(1 + \tfrac{2}{3}(h_{\max} - 1)\right)^{-2} + \sum_{h=2}^{h_{\max}} \tfrac{8}{9} h^2 \left(1 + \tfrac{2}{3}(h_{\max} - 1)\right)^{-2} \\ &= \left(\tfrac{8}{9}\left(\tfrac{h_{\max}(h_{\max}+1)(2h_{\max}+1)}{6} - 1\right) + 1\right)\left(1 + \tfrac{2}{3}(h_{\max} - 1)\right)^{-2} \end{aligned} \tag{24.7}$$

Thus if we assume, for example, a maximum of six hops in the overlay network, we can compute the average path length in a not-adapted overlay network to 4.31 physical hops. This means that every message is transmitted in the network 4.31 times more often, than in an adapted overlay network like in MPP. In MPP, every overlay message is transmitted only once via one physical link, as a result of the cross-layer communication channel between the physical and the application layers. Further reduction of signaling traffic can thus be achieved because no additional keep-alive messages are necessary.

24.4.2 Solutions Based on Structured Peer-to-Peer Networks

Due to characteristics like flexibility, scalability, and resilience, structured Peer-to-Peer systems became a common approach for building decentralized self-organizing networks of any size. In particular, Distributed Hash Tables (DHT) have been proven as the primary design choice, as already discussed in Chapter 2 and Part III[1]. On the other hand, ad-hoc networks gain greater importance due to the increasing occurrence of scenarios without a centralized infrastructure. Whenever there is need for a scalable data management without any infrastructure, the combination of ad-hoc network- and DHT-technology seems to be an obvious solution [286]. The question, whether this is a fruitful combination, will be discussed in the following.

In general, DHTs have been developed for the infrastructural Internet, and therefore, some basic assumptions can not be directly applied for the use in ad-hoc networks. In the following, we will show the main differences

[1] Therefore, in the following, we will focus on DHTs as the state-of-the-art technique in structured Peer-to-Peer systems and will use both terms interchangeably.

between these network technologies, discuss resulting problems, give solutions for dedicated problems, and will show scenarios in which ad-hoc networks and DHT-protocols may be combined.

Challenges

As shown in Part III, numerous DHT approaches with versatile characteristics determined by the subjacent topological structure (routing geometry) exist. This structure induces different characteristics regarding flexibility and resilience. A high flexibility in the choice of neighboring nodes enables optimizations with respect to the underlaying network topology. A resilient DHT structure can still operate without the need for evoking expensive recovery-algorithms – even if many nodes fail at the same time. These issues are essential for the DHT to react flexibly on topological changes of the underlying network.

Flexibility in the Choice of Neighboring Nodes

According to [266], the flexibility of a DHT is the "*algorithmic freedom left after the basic routing geometry has been chosen*". For a Peer-to-Peer system this freedom is essential to build an efficient overlay-network. DHT structures with a high degree of flexibility are capable of adapting the routing to the frequent changes in an ad-hoc network. Two respective approaches have been proposed in [266].

Proximity node selection (PNS) describes the selection of nodes as optimal routing-table entries. A node can build its routing table with respect to several criteria, e.g., hop-count, delay, bandwidth, battery life, remaining capacity, or transmission power. As a result, short paths and stable underlay-connections improve overlay routing. This pre-selection of neighboring peers can be integrated into existing DHT protocols if the DHT structure is flexible enough. As shown in [266], PNS can easily be achieved in ring-based DHTs such as Chord. The strict rules for building the routing table make an efficient PNS impossible for tree-, butterfly-, or hypercube- based DHTs. With node movement in mind, the PNS procedure has to be repeated from time to time to achieve continuous improvements.

Proximity route selection (PRS) can be used to find optimal routes when using a pre-existing routing table. During the routing process a node can decide to which known node the request will be routed to. This decision is made upon the same criteria which are used for PNS. Less latency and a higher network stability can be achieved when routing to weak nodes, which are likely to fail, is omitted. Depending on the geometric structure used by a DHT, the routing protocol is able to adapt its routing behavior. According to [266], hypercube based DHTs are very well suited to use PRS because of varying, equidistant paths between two distant nodes (all are shortest). On the other hand, tree and butterfly based DHT protocols are not capable of using PRS because there is only one path existing in the DHT structure that allows a decrease in the distance between the two nodes. For this reason the routing algorithm does not allow any variations. Ring-based DHT-protocols have to make a tradeoff between an increased hop-count in the overlay and an eventually shorter or more stable path in the underlay.

In wireless networks the inherent broadcasting of packets to neighbors can be used to improve the peers overlay routing, e.g., like "shortcuts" in the overlay network. Routing to these surrounding peers causes just one hop in the underlying network which makes it very efficient. Keeping the connections to these nodes causes only small amounts of locally restricted network traffic.

If the ad-hoc network protocol is able to analyze packets, a message can be intercepted by a node which takes part at the routing process in the underlay network. This node may redirect the request to a node which is closer to the destination based on stored information on surrounding peers. The decision whether intercepting a message or not must be taken in respect to the progress that would be achieved in the overlay structure compared to the distance on the alternative route. If connection speed is not an issue, even nodes not directly involved in the routing may intercept a message. The route can be changed, and a route change message has to be sent to the node responsible for processing the routing request. If no route change message is received within a specified period of time, the routing progress will be continued. However, this procedure will decrease network traffic at the cost of increased latency. Route interception and active routing of non-involved peers can be used to achieve more redundancy, leading to a more stable network in case of node failures.

Resilient Networks

DHTs are considered to be very resistant against node failures. Backup and recovery mechanisms, that use distributed redundant information, ensure that no information is lost if a node suddenly fails. Depending on the subjacent DHT topology, the DHT experiences a reduced routing performance until the recovery has finished. [266] shows that especially tree and butterfly based topologies are vulnerable to node failures. Due to the high flexibility of ring based topologies, these DHTs are still operable in case of massive node failures.

When DHT protocols are used in an ad-hoc environment, resilience has to be considered as a very important issue. The resilience of a DHT determines how much time may pass before expensive recovery mechanisms have to be evoked. As the quality of connections in ad-hoc networks is highly dependent of the environment of the nodes, some nodes may be temporarily inaccessible or poorly accessible because of node movement. If the recovery process is started too early, an avoidable overhead is caused if the node becomes accessible again. If the topological structure allows the DHT protocol to delay recovery mechanisms without losing routing capability these costly recovery measures can be avoided. This approach has a positive effect on the maintenance costs of a DHT. In a worst case scenario, a node which is partly available and unavailable over a longer period of time can stress the whole network because of numerous join and leave procedures. This scenario can easily be provoked by node movement along the network perimeter. Resilience is therefore an important factor when DHTs are used in combination with ad-hoc networks. Resilient DHT structures are capable of compensating node failures and are able to use recovery mechanisms more accurately.

Member Selection Based upon Node Characteristics

To avoid problems with heterogenous nodes in ad-hoc networks it is important to judge the suitability of nodes by means of measurable criteria. The duration of the connection to the network, energy, link quality, or node mobility are indicators for the reliability of a node. If the decision whether a node may join the network or not, is based upon these parameters, a higher stability can be achieved due to a network consisting of reliable nodes. If free-riding is not a problem or if measures can be taken against free-riders, nodes rejected because of their low reliability could still use the DHT without being involved in the routing process. That way all nodes can benefit from the DHT without imposing weakness.

The indicators described above can also be used to predict node failures due to low energy or weak connections. Nodes which are likely to fail soon can inform their neighboring nodes in the DHT about their likely failure. Costly recovery mechanisms can be avoided, which leads to a lower overhead caused by sudden node failures.

Splitting and Merging DHTs

A separation of the network into multiple parts may be caused by the failure of one single node. For the nodes connected to a smaller part of the separated network the separation is equal to the failure of the majority of all nodes. This can hardly happen in infrastructural networks. Thus, a higher degree of redundancy is necessary to keep a DHT operational. By distributing a nodes' information to n neighbors the probability of a fatal DHT failure can be kept below $1/2^n$ if the network splits up in two equal parts.

Common DHT approaches are built upon the fact that only one instance of a DHT – accessible for every node in a global network – exists. When DHTs are used in an ad-hoc network this assumption leads to a serious problem: If two independent DHTs (parts of a separated DHT or completely independent DHTs) encounter, suited methods – to either merge those structure or to enable communication between them – have to be found.

Merging two DHTs imposes a vast amount of network traffic. Many key-value pairs have to be redistributed and new neighborhood connections must be established. This stress may often be unacceptable, especially if the connection between the DHTs is weak or short-lived. A method to merge large DHT structures has to be designed in respect to the limitations (low bandwidth, high latency, etc.) of an ad-hoc network, to avoid network overload. Criteria like the stability of inter-DHT connections must be judged to avoid a merge of two DHTs which is likely to split up again. However, if the merging of DHTs is omitted – and structured communication between DHTs is chosen as an alternative – continuously separating a DHT will create many small DHTs and causes an enormous communication overhead. In both cases the simultaneous coexistence of DHTs requires an unambiguous DHT-identification.

Improving the Teamwork Between Ad-Hoc Network and DHT
The characteristics of the underlying ad-hoc network protocol has great effect on the performance of the overlay as the DHT induces a constant flow of control and query messages. An optimized interaction between ad-hoc network and DHT is essential to create an efficient combination. Two aspects of the teamwork between over and underlay will be discussed exemplarily in the following section.

Reactive routing algorithms as AODV maintain their routing tables as they process routing requests. Old routes (to other nodes) become invalid after a certain period of time. If the time between keep-alive-messages, which are sent by the DHT-nodes is shorter than the time that may pass before an AODV-route becomes invalid, constant route finding requests can be avoided. The steadily used routes never become invalid and efficient underlay routing on overlay connections is possible.

On the other hand, proactive routing algorithms [483] are suited better for the use of PNS. PNS opens many connections to different nodes to examine the connection characteristics of many potentially optimal neighbors. The best nodes will be chosen as routing table entries. High initial delay and the additional overhead caused by the route requests of an reactive ad-hoc protocol interdict the use of PNS in reactive ad-hoc networks. These examples show that an arbitrary combination of ad-hoc network protocols and DHT protocols can result in inefficient solutions.

24.5 Summary

In this chapter, we have investigated the opportunities and challenges of the application of Peer-to-Peer concepts to mobile environments. A discussion of mobile network characteristics shows that mobile ad-hoc networks impose most severe problems in terms of low data rate, limited terminal capabilities, and high churn rate to conventional Peer-to-Peer systems. Therefore, they are in the focus of this chapter.

Although there is an inherent similarity of ad-hoc networks and Peer-to-Peer systems a powerful combination of both technologies cannot be created without a careful investigation of the resulting problems. Common Peer-to-Peer systems must be modified in many ways to enable their use in ad-hoc networks. Due to the nature of ad-hoc networks the choice of a specific Peer-to-Peer approach has to be considered carefully.

Structured and unstructured Peer-to-Peer-concepts have been discussed for their suitability to run on ad-hoc networks. As of their robustness and reactive behavior, unstructured Peer-to-Peer concepts seem the natural choice for ad-hoc networks. The application of cross-layer interworking of application layer and routing layer protocol, as described here, improves the performance of unstructured Peer-to-Peer systems over ad-hoc networks significantly. This is shown with an example protocol and in an analytical investigation.

Regarding the practical use of structured Peer-to-Peer concepts (DHT structures) in ad-hoc networks further investigation on split and merge algorithms for multiple DHTs are necessary. Furthermore, the impact of node movements on the DHT structure will be interesting topics of future research. The question what degree of redundancy is needed to provide a stable service – while operating in a highly dynamic network – has to be answered if real-life applicability is the final goal.

As applications operating on DHTs gain greater importance in the infrastructural Internet, efficient porting to wireless scenarios might also be needed soon. DHT structures suited for the use in ad-hoc networks could provide a generic interface which enables their usage without profound modifications. Applications like the ones presented in Part IV might be usable in ad-hoc scenarios if efficient Peer-to-Peer solutions can be provided for the challenges discussed in this chapter.

25. Spontaneous Collaboration in Mobile Peer-to-Peer Networks

Andreas Heinemann, Max Mühlhäuser
(Darmstadt University of Technology)

25.1 Introduction and Motivation

The field of *mobile* Peer-to-Peer networks (MP2P) has various forms and currently there exists no coherent view on what is understood by it. The term *mobile* emphasizes that nodes/peers in the network are mobile, and therefore need to be equipped with some kind of wireless communication technology. Examples of nodes include pedestrians with mobile devices [284] or vehicles with wireless communication capabilities [632]. Since all mobile Peer-to-Peer networks construct an overlay over an existing wireless network, implementations range from MP2P over mobile ad hoc networks (MANETs) [156] to MP2P over cellular based networks [299, 298].

This chapter looks into a specific class of application for mobile Peer-to-Peer networks. Here the Peer-to-Peer network is formed by humans carrying mobile devices, like PDAs or mobile phones, with ad hoc communication capabilities. All presented applications exploit the physical presence of a user to support digital or real-life collaboration among them. The integration of wireless communication technologies like Bluetooth or IEEE 802.11b WiFi into mobile devices makes this kind of mobile Peer-to-Peer networks feasible.

As stated by Dave Winer, *"The P in P2P is People"* [624]; most of the Peer-to-Peer systems rely on the users' will to contribute. This could be observed in the success of first generation file-sharing applications like Napster [438] or Gnutella [252].

The key issue of user contribution prevails even more in mobile Peer-to-Peer networks, where in general anonymous users form the network with their personal devices. Resources on the device are typically limited. Especially battery power can be a problem. A user risks draining his battery by contributing its resources to other users. The device may also become unavailable for personal tasks, like accessing the calender or making phone calls. However user contribution may be stimulated by the usefulness of an application.

Currently, we see the emergence of several mobile Peer-to-Peer applications, both as commercial products and in research, as described in Section 25.2. As stated above, all these applications make use of the physical presence

R. Steinmetz and K. Wehrle (Eds.): P2P Systems and Applications, LNCS 3485, pp. 419-433, 2005.

of a user to support collaboration among participating parties. This leads us to our hypothesis:

> Often, people in close proximity share a common goal or have a related motivation. Some of them may have valuable information relevant but unknown to others.

The common goal for these mobile Peer-to-Peer applications is to make this information available to other interested parties. Through this, we see new forms of spontaneous collaboration that can be distinguished in *active* and *passive* collaboration (cf. Section 25.1.2).

25.1.1 Mobile Peer-to-Peer Networks and Mobile Ad Hoc Networks

A thorough comparison of (infrastructure-based) Peer-to-Peer and mobile ad hoc networks (MANETs) has been carried out in [82]. The fundamental commonalities between the two are:

- *Decentralized architectures.* Neither network type relies on a central component (a centralized server).
- *Transient connectivity.* In both kinds of networks, nodes connect and disconnect unpredictably. In addition, MANET nodes are mobile and they move in and out of the communication range (which may appear to other nodes as a disconnection).
- *Heterogeneity of resources.* A mobile ad hoc network may be formed by different mobile devices, such as a laptop, mobile phone, or PDA. These devices typically differ in battery life, CPU power, and storage capacity. Likewise, computers that run the same Peer-to-Peer application typically vary in their specification.
- *Sharing of resources.* In both network types, a user actively shares her resources (battery power, CPU power, storage capacity, network connection) with others and the network exploits these resources to provide its services.
- *Identity management.* Both networks have to address the identification of any entity (e.g., nodes, peers, users, and content). This may also include privacy protection, in order to allow users to act anonymously within the network or application.
- *Routing and message forwarding.* Although MANETs handle routing on the network layer and Peer-to-Peer networks handle it typically on the application layer, routing remains a critical issue for both kinds of network.

On the other hand, there exist the following differences:

- *Network size.* Whereas MANETs are generally concerned with networks of a few hundred nodes, modern Peer-to-Peer networks can span much larger networks

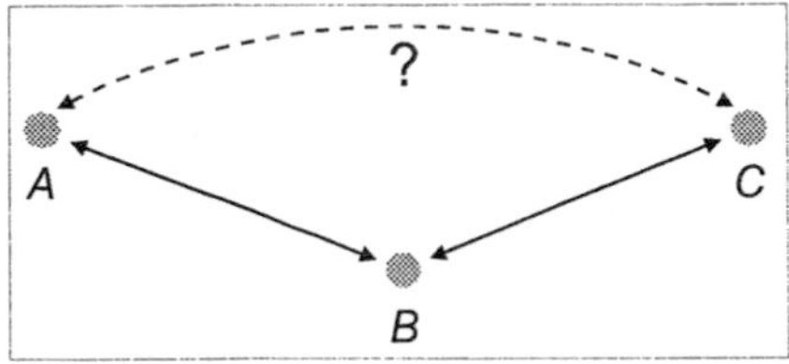

Fig. 25.1: Multi-hop communication.

- *Focus in the ISO/OSI Model.* Research and development of mobile ad hoc networks particularly focuses on the network layer. Several multi-hop routing algorithms have been proposed (see [484, 327]). Conversely, research in Peer-to-Peer networks addresses more the construction of overlay networks in the application layer.

As stated in the introduction, this chapter focuses on *mobile* Peer-to-Peer networks and applications. In many ways, mobile Peer-to-Peer networks are similar to MANETs, since they are also formed by individuals carrying a mobile device. Hence, the networks are of a similar size. However, there are certain important differences between the traditional MANETs and the mobile Peer-to-Peer networks we consider here. MANETs have been investigated in the context of military networks, emergency response, and sensor networks. These networks have several key characteristics in common, namely that *all nodes* in the network are strongly related to each other, trust each other, and share a goal they want to accomplish.

Mobile Peer-to-Peer networks, as we consider them, are formed between *anonymous groups of individuals.* This poses several additional challenges to the network. Consider the situation in Figure 25.1 with A, B, and C as mobile nodes, that is, individuals equipped with mobile devices. A is in communication range of B but not in range of C, who, on the other hand, is in communication range of B. If A wants to communicate with C, all traffic has to be routed via B. Bearing in mind that A, B, and C, a priori, do not know each other, two questions arise:

- What is the incentive for node B to route messages between A and C? Why should node B be willing to donate part of her battery power to enable communication between A and C ?
- Why should node A and C trust and rely on node B for their communication? Node B could easily eavesdrop, manipulate, or just reject messages.

Without an incentive scheme and extra security mechanism built in, the standard multi-hop communication schemes of MANETs appear to fall short of providing for communications in mobile Peer-to-Peer networks.

The alternative to the multi-hop MANETs are the so-called one-hop networks. In these networks, information is not forwarded over several hops;

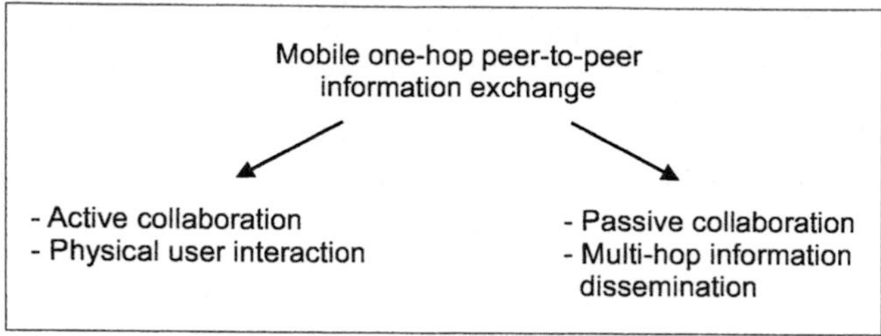

Fig. 25.2: Design space of mobile one-hop Peer-to-Peer communication

instead all communications always happen between two directly connected nodes, both of which have a *direct incentive* to participate in this communication.

We define mobile Peer-to-Peer networks to be such one-hop communication networks, where the individual nodes participate only when they have a direct interest in participating. This avoids the problems of incentives for traditional MANETs in standard situations. These one-hop networks will be the focus for the rest of this chapter. Note that limiting the communications to a single hop on *the network layer* does not limit multi-hop information propagation on *the application layer*, as we demonstrate in Section 25.4.1.

25.1.2 One-Hop Peer-to-Peer Design Space

Starting from the one-hop communication approach, the Peer-to-Peer design space for applications is divided into two general areas, as shown in Figure 25.2:

- **Active collaboration** focuses on the physical proximity of users. In addition to the exchange of digital information with users nearby, this allows using the device as a *link* to the user itself. Via non-intrusive user notification, this could lead to real world collaboration, such as a conversation. *Tap* and *tickle*, two form of digital gestures from the Socialight project (see Section 25.2.4), are a good example for non-intrusive user notification.
- **Passive collaboration** aims to collect and pass any kind of information to users in the vicinity without user interaction. Shark [553] and AdPASS [577] are the most prominent examples for this kind of application scenarios. Passive collaboration leads to on-the-fly information dissemination. In other terms, it is a form of digital *word-of-mouth* communication.

Applications that include both forms of collaboration are also possible.

The second important aspect in the design space is the relation among the users participating in the system. Questions to be answered are:

- Is the number of users known/fixed or unknown/open?
- Are the users identifiable or do they work with pseudonyms or even act totally anonymous?

Answers to these questions have impact on the usage and suitability of the mobile Peer-to-Peer building blocks we present in Section 25.3.

25.1.3 Chapter Overview

The rest of this chapter is organized as follows. Section 25.2 presents emerging applications for mobile Peer-to-Peer networks, namely in the following domains: enterprise knowledge management, spontaneous recommendation passing, conference collaboration, spontaneous encounter with friends and foafs[1], and spontaneous advertisement passing. Common building blocks for mobile Peer-to-Peer networks and applications are derived from these examples in Section 25.3. Following this analysis, the *iClouds* project is presented in Section 25.4. iClouds provides an architecture that includes building blocks for easier mobile Peer-to-Peer application development. This chapter concludes with Section 25.5.

25.2 Application Domains and Examples

This following list of applications is not meant to be exhaustive. Earlier work include the 7DS system [471, 472] and similar ideas can be found in more recent work [158, 256]. Nonetheless the examples present a variety of interesting and useful applications and are sufficient for the identification and extraction of common functionality.

25.2.1 Shark

Shark [553] supports management, synchronization and exchange of knowledge in mobile user groups. The system distinguishes three components: the *Shark Mobile Station*, the *Shark Central Station* and the *Shark Local Station.*

The mobile station runs on a mobile phone and is able to exchange knowledge with a nearby central station, local station or another mobile station. Bluetooth is used for ad hoc communication. The knowledge is stored using TopicMaps [319]. The central station manages the complete knowledge base.

[1] foaf = friend of a friend

Local stations store and manage only location relevant knowledge. This allows for simple location based services. Each local station synchronizes its knowledge with the central station.

One possible application for Shark is enterprise knowledge management. Here, each mobile staff member is equipped with a mobile station. Local stations are installed at subsidiaries. A customer (with his own mobile station) is able to learn about all kinds of information about the enterprise, e.g., product descriptions, price lists or white papers, while talking to a mobile staff member or visiting a subsidiary or shop.

25.2.2 MobiTip

The MobiTip [529] system allows its users to express their opinions on anything of interest in the environment. Opinions are aggregated and presented to the users as tips or recommendations. Opinions are entered in free text form on the user's device (a mobile phone) and shared in a Peer-to-Peer manner on-the-fly with users nearby using Bluetooth.

A typical example is a shopping mall, where MobiTip users share their personal views on certain shops or product offers.

The core MobiTip system can be extended by so-called *connection hotspots*. A connection hotspot is placed at a selected location, e.g., the entrance of a shopping mall, to collect tips and pass them to future visitors. This idea is similar to the time-shifted communication in the Socialight system based on *Sticky Shadows* (see Section 25.2.4).

25.2.3 SpotMe

A quite advanced collaboration system and tool for conferences, symposia, and corporate meetings is called SpotMe [561]. With a special purpose handheld device (with similar size to a mobile phone), each user can exchange information with other users in a Peer-to-Peer manner. Communication to a local server via base stations is also possible.

A user's device is personalized during the conference registration process. This step includes taking a photo of the attendee. The photo with other contact information is stored on the device and in a central database. Users can query this database during the event. Thus, they learn who is actually on site. The *radar* function allows a user to scan all other attendees in a range of 30 meters. With this information, a user can look for a conversational partner or simply identify the people sitting nearby at lunch. A user can specify special interest in another user. The device will then give a notice when this other user is nearby. This may help to start a conversation.

Several other functions require the communication with the local server, e.g., *last minute agenda update*, *news dissemination* and *questionnaires.*

SpotMe includes some basic post event services. The collected data and contact information is made available for every participant online on the web and sent as e-mail.

25.2.4 Socialight

Socialight [332], a mobile social networking platform that uses mobile phones, supports spontaneous encounter and interaction with friends and friends of friends. Using the current or past location of friends, Socialight enables real-time and time-shifted communication.

Location of users is determined by infrastructure based technology (GPS and Cell-ID), or ad hoc by signal recognition of Bluetooth devices nearby. Users have to register on a central platform before using Socialight. The platform also stores information about the social network of users.

Peer-to-peer communication among users may happen via *Tap & Tickle* or *Sticky Shadows.* Tap & Tickle are two digital gestures that allow users to exchange information by vibration of their devices. Pressing a button on a user's phone will make his friend's phone vibrate once (Tap) or rhythmically (Tickle). This is meant as a non-intrusive way to communicate with nearby friends.

With Sticky Shadows, users can attach digital information to a certain location. This digital information is recognized by friends when they pass the same location at a different time. Examples include restaurant reviews for friends, sales or shopping recommendations, and educational purposes, where teachers set Sticky Shadows for students.

25.2.5 AdPASS

AdPASS [577] is a system to spread digital advertisements (ads) among interested users. Each user specifies his interests in a profile that is stored on the mobile device. The communication scheme resembles the way information is spread by word of mouth between human beings, e.g., when recommending something to someone else.

As an incentive for users to take part in the system, AdPASS provides an anonymous bonus point model that rewards a user who carries an advertisement on the way down from the vendor to a potential customer.

AdPASS has three kinds of participants:

- A *merchant* disseminates digital advertisements within its vicinity. For example, there are several fixed nodes located in a merchant's shop. These *information sprinklers*, which are stationary transmitter units, are described

in [288]. Customer devices learn about advertisements while their owners are browsing the shop.
- A *customer* carries a mobile device (PDA). This device collects advertisements and transports or passes the ads to other interested customers. Ideally, some of them come to the shop and buy the advertised good.
- A *mediator* keeps track of the users' accumulated bonus points. It works similar to a central database that both the merchant and the customer can access (e.g. via the Internet). Thus, it guarantees reachability to the customers In addition, the mediator acts as an "anonymizer" to guarantee customers' anonymity.

Figure 25.3 illustrates the different communication steps. The participants interact as follows:

1. Customer A visits a merchant. While being in the shop, his device learns about several advertisements and filters them against his personal profile. The advertisements are stored on the user's device. In the example, customer A learns about a DVD advertisement.
2. Customer A (after leaving the shop) encounters another potential customer B (on the street for instance), who is interested in the ad. B stores the ad and then later passes it on to another interested user C.
3. C itself is taken with the ad, goes to the shop and buys the advertised good. C also passes information to the merchant about how he has learned about the ad – in our example, via A and B.
4. The merchant informs the mediator which customers should be rewarded bonus points.
5. Assuming that there is a Internet connection available, A, B, and C can download their bonus points from the mediator's server onto their devices. This can happen for example during a PC-to-device synchronization operation.

A detailed description about AdPASS, including how the bonus point system works and how user anonymity is provided, is given in [577].

25.3 Building Blocks for Mobile Peer-to-Peer Networks

Analyzing the example applications in Section 25.2 identifies a number of common functionalities among them. These building blocks for mobile Peer-to-Peer applications are described as services in this section.

Presence Awareness Service
Provides the application with information about which other nodes or users are currently active and in communication range. This service typically also provides some kind of neighbourhood information.

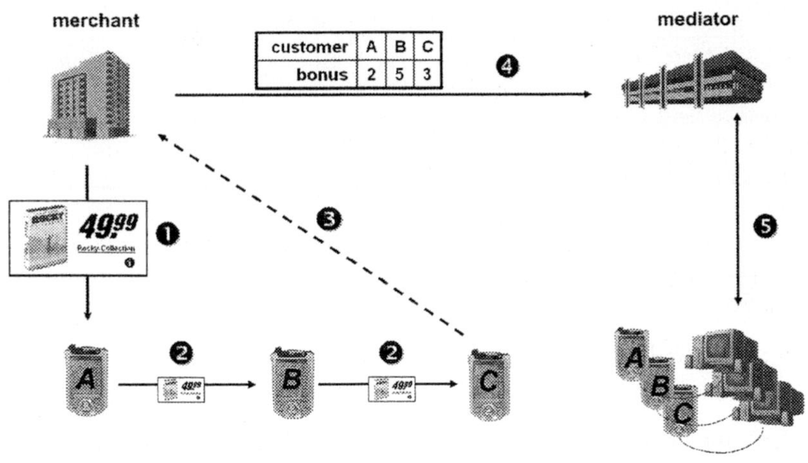

Fig. 25.3: Communication steps

Message Exchange Service
A service that allows sending messages to and receiving messages from peers in the neighbourhood.

Information Filtering Service
Since in mobile Peer-to-Peer applications there is also the danger of SPAM, there should be a way to filter out information that might not be relevant to the user. This functionality is provided by an information filtering service.

Information Distribution Service
The information distribution service offers three functional choices. A peer can give information it receives straight away to other peers. The user may also review a received piece of information and decide on a per item basis whether to share it with other peers. Finally, the information may not be shared at all.

Security Service
To support data or communication integrity, the security service offers sign and encrypt operation on information items. This may involve public/private-key cryptographic operations, based on some PKI or other trusted sources.

Identity Management Service
The system design has to specify how a user appears in the system. Users can act anonymously, under a pseudonym or with assigned identities. The identity management service supports this design criteria.

	Project				
Service	Shark	MobiTip	SpotMe	Socialight	AdPASS
Presence Awareness	✓	✓	✓	✓	✓
Message Exchange	✓	✓	✓	✓	✓
Info. Filtering	✓	✓	✓	✓	✓
Info. Distribution	✓	✓			✓
Security					✓
Identity Management	✓	✓	✓	✓	✓
Incentive Schemes					✓
Reputation					
User Notification			✓	✓	

Table 25.1: Common mobile Peer-to-Peer service integration

Service for Incentive Schemes
As stated in the introduction, user contribution is an important issue in mobile Peer-to-Peer applications. Contribution can be stimulated by introducing some kind of incentive schemes for individual users. These schemes may vary from application to application, but may rely on common basic service functionality, e.g., accounting, to implement a certain incentive scheme.

Reputation Service
This service allows individual users to build a reputation within an application. Other users might value received information based on the reputation of the user who sends out information. This may especially be needed for systems with anonymous users. Currently, none of the presented projects in Section 25.2 use a reputation service. Nonetheless, this is an important service for future mobile Peer-to-Peer applications.

User Notification Service
This service instantly notifies the user of incoming information that may require some sort of instant reaction. For example, a real-life conversation with a discussion partner can only happen while the partner is nearby.

Table 25.1 summarizes the common services and their conceptual usage in the presented sample applications.

The next section presents the iClouds project. The project goal is to design a sound and coherent architecture for mobile Peer-to-Peer applications. This architecture integrates the identified set of common building blocks/services for mobile Peer-to-Peer application.

25.4 The iClouds Project

Within the scope of mobile Peer-to-Peer networks, the iClouds Project [289, 287] investigates several kinds of collaboration among mobile users. Based on the one-hop communication paradigm, the iClouds architecture separates common mobile Peer-to-Peer application requirements as services. Making use of these services, the architecture facilitate easy and rapid application development in this emerging area. We will describe the architecture in Section 25.4.3.

iClouds devices are small mobile devices, such as a PDA or mobile phone, with ad hoc communication support (Bluetooth or 802.11b WiFi). There is no need for any central servers in the iClouds architecture; instead, each device is completely independent. A special kind of iClouds devices are *information sprinklers*. An information sprinkler is mounted at a dedicated location to support simple location based services. Local station (Shark), base station (SpotMe) and connection hotspot (MobiTip) reflect similar concepts.

The diameter of the iClouds communication horizon (see Figures 25.4(a) and 25.4(b)) should not exceed a few hundred meter. iClouds users are given the opportunity for spontaneous collaboration. When two iClouds users "see" each other, they should be within a short walking distance from each other (a couple of minutes at maximum).

Following the assumption form the introduction (cf. Section 25.1.1), we specifically exclude multi-hop communication on the network layer. All communications happen directly between the concerned parties. On the application layer, iClouds supports indirect multi-hop information dissemination,as described below.

25.4.1 Multi-hop Information Dissemination

Information in iClouds can pass through several nodes, as shown in Figure 25.5 and Figure 25.6, assuming certain conditions are met. We call the first scenario *information passing*. Information can only pass between A and B or between B and C, since A and C are not in communication range. Their communication horizons overlap, but the devices themselves do not fall into the other's communication horizon. In this situation, information can pass from A to B and on from B to C if and only if it passes from A to B, and it would get to C if B and C were in communication range and have interest in the same information provided by A.

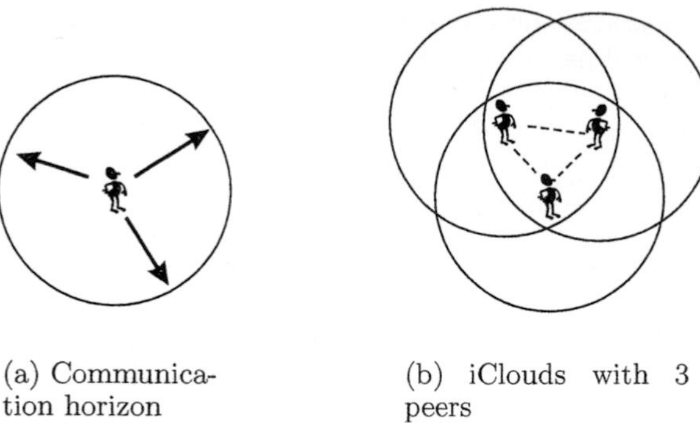

(a) Communication horizon

(b) iClouds with 3 peers

Fig. 25.4: Information clouds

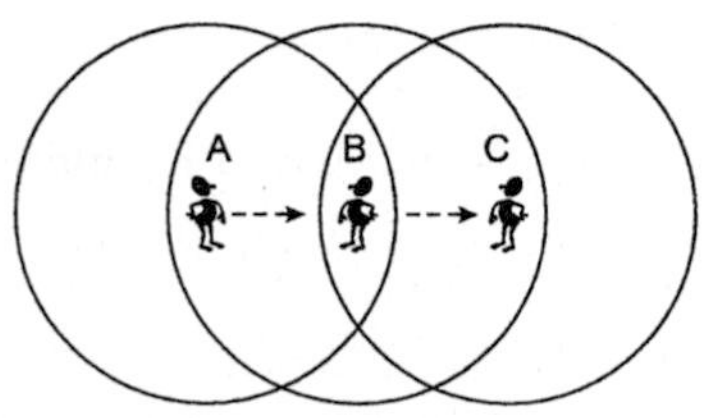

Fig. 25.5: Information passing in iClouds

The second scenario in which information is transported with iClouds involves physical movement of nodes, as shown in Figure 25.6. This is called *information moving*. In Figure 25.6, B gets some information from A. B later meets C, who is interested in the same information and B passes it to C. Again, a prerequisite for the information to get from B to C is that B and C share interest in the same information.

25.4.2 Data Structures and Communication Semantics

The two most important data objects found on the iClouds device are two information lists (*iLists* for short):

- *iHave*-list (information have list or information goods):
  The iHave-list holds all the information the user wants to contribute to other users.
- *iWish*-list (information wish list or information needs):
  In the iWish-list, the user specifies what kind of information he is interested in.

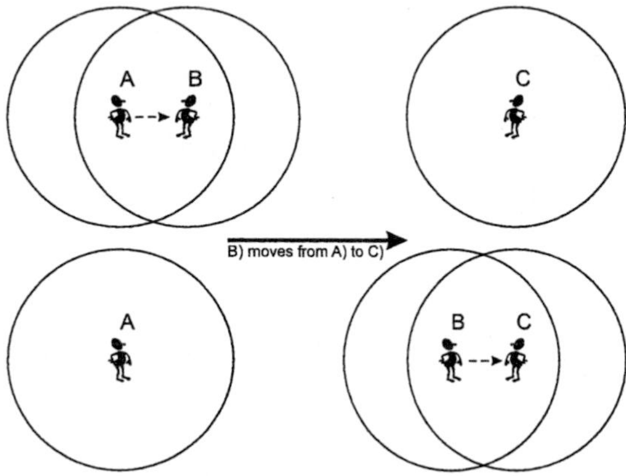

Fig. 25.6: (Physical) Information moving in iClouds

	pull (from Bob)	push (to Bob)
iHave-list	Standard search	Advertise
iWish-list	Active service inquiry	Active search

Table 25.2: Information flow semantics (from Alice's point of view)

Each iClouds device periodically scans its vicinity to see if known nodes are still active and in communication range and also to see if any new nodes have appeared. Information about active nodes is stored in a neighbourhood data structure.

By exchanging iLists, the iClouds devices align their information goods and needs. Items on the iWish-lists are matched against items on the iHave-lists. On a match, information items move from one iHave-list to the other.

For example, consider two iClouds users, Alice and Bob, who meet on the street. When their iClouds devices discover each other, they will exchange their iHave-lists and match them locally against their iWish-lists. If an item on Bob's iHave-list matches an item on Alice's iWish-list, her iClouds device will transfer that item onto her iHave-list.

There are two main communication methods for transferring the iLists. Peers can either *pull* the iLists from other peers or they can *push* their own iLists to peers they meet. Either of these two operations is applicable to both lists, which gives four distinct possibilities of communication. Table 25.2 summarizes these possibilities, along with their real-world equivalents.

In each of the four cases shown in Table 25.2, the matching operation is always performed on the peer who receives the list (Alice's peer in pull and Bob's peer in push). A key strength of iClouds is that each of the four possible combinations corresponds to an interaction in the real world:

- *Standard search.*
  This is the most natural communication pattern. Alice asks for the information stored on Bob's device and performs a match against her information needs (specified in her iWish-list) on her device.
- *Advertise.*
  This is a more direct approach. Alice gives her information goods straight to Bob and it's up to Bob to match this against the things he is interested in. As an example, consider an iClouds information sprinkler mounted on shopping mall doorways pushing advertisements onto customer devices when they enter the building. This is implemented in the AdPASS system (cf. Section 25.2.5).
- *Active service inquiry.*
  This is best suited for shopping clerks. They learn at a very early stage what their customers are interested in. An example of this query could be: "*Can I help you, please tell me what are you looking for?*".
  In general, especially for privacy reasons and user acceptance, we believe it is a good design choice to leave the iWish-list on the iClouds device. Hence, this model of communication would likely be extremely rare in the real world.
- *Active search.*
  With active search, we model the natural "*I'm looking for X. Can you help me?*". This is similar to the standard search mechanism, except that the user is actively searching for a particular item, whereas in the standard search, the user is more passive.

25.4.3 Architecture

Figure 25.7 shows the architecture that is proposed and used in iClouds. There is a general distinction between a communication layer and a service layer. The communication layer provides simple one-hop message exchange between peers in communication range. A neighbourhood data structure keeps track of active peers in the vicinity.

The common services are located on the next layer. Each service can use functionality provided by other services or by the communication layer below. Note that the service layer is extensible for new services that might be needed by future applications.

The applications reside on the topmost. To fulfil its purpose, an application has access to both the service and the communication layer.

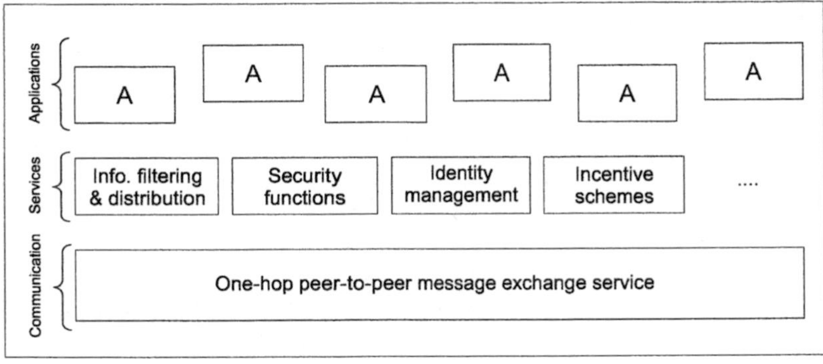

Fig. 25.7: iClouds architecture

25.5 Conclusion

This chapter points out that there are several similarities in mobile Peer-to-Peer applications. The analysis of emerging applications in this area identifies a set of common services that serve as basic building blocks.

The iClouds architecture aims to provide a framework for mobile Peer-to-Peer application developers who do not want to re-invent common functionality over and over again. The architecture is implemented in Java as a lightweight set of classes and runs on Java2 Micro Edition compliant mobile devices with 802.11b WiFi communication support.

26. Epidemic Data Dissemination for Mobile Peer-to-Peer Lookup Services

Christoph Lindemann, Oliver P. Waldhorst (University of Dortmund)

26.1 Motivation and Background

Building efficient lookup services for the Internet constitutes an active area of research. Recent issues concentrate on building Internet-scale distributed hash tables as building block of Peer-to-Peer systems, see e.g., [505], [575]. Castro et al. proposed the VIA protocol, which enables location of application data across multiple service discovery domains, using a self-organizing hierarchy [111]. Recently, Sun and Garcia-Molina introduced a partial lookup service, exploiting the fact that for many applications it is sufficient to resolve a key to a subset of all matching values [581]. The paper discusses various design alternatives for a partial lookup service in the Internet. However, none of these papers consider distributed lookup services for mobile ad-hoc networks.

In MANET, lookup services can be implemented using either unstructured or structured Peer-to-Peer networks as described in Chapters 24.4.1 and 24.4.2, respectively. However, such approaches put some requirements on the MANET environment: (1) The MANET must provide a high degree of connectivity, such that a given node can contact each other node at any time with high probability. (2) The nodes in the MANET must exhibit low mobility in order to minimize the required number of updates of routing tables and other structures. Typically, both structured and unstructured approaches will perform poorly in scenarios with low connectivity and high mobility. This chapter descibes an approach for building a Peer-to-Peer lookup service that can cope with intermittent connectivity and high mobility. The approach builds upon the observation by Grossglauser and Tse, that mobility does not necessarily hinder communication in MANET, but may support cost-effective information exchange by epidemic dissemination [262].

As a first approach to epidemic information dissemination in mobile environments, Papadopouli and Schulzrinne introduced Seven Degrees of Separation (7DS), a system for mobile Internet access based on Web document dissemination between mobile users [470]. To locate a Web document, a 7DS node broadcasts a query message to all mobile nodes currently located inside its radio coverage. Recipients of the query send response messages containing file descriptors of matching Web documents stored in their local file caches. Subsequently, such documents can be downloaded with HTTP by the inquiring mobile node. Downloaded Web documents may be distributed to other

R. Steinmetz and K. Wehrle (Eds.): P2P Systems and Applications, LNCS 3485, pp. 435-455, 2005.

nodes that move into radio coverage, implementing an epidemic dissemination of information.

Using a related approach, Goel, Singh, Xu and Li proposed broadcasting segments of shared files using redundant tornado encoding [253]. Their approach enables nodes to restore a file, if a sufficient number of different segments have been received from one or more sources. In [351], Khelil, Becker, Tian, and Rothermel presented an analytical model for a simple epidemic information diffusion algorithm inspired by the SPIN-1 protocol [290]. Both systems implement a push model for information dissemination. That is, shared data is advertised or even actively broadcasted without a node requesting it. Hanna, Levine, and Mamatha proposed a fault-tolerant distributed information retrieval system for Peer-to-Peer document sharing in mobile ad hoc networks [275]. Their approach distributes the index of a new document to a random set of nodes when the document is added to the system. The complete index of a document, i.e., all keywords matching it, constitutes the smallest unit of disseminated information. Recently, Small and Haas proposed an epidemic approach for collecting information in a hybrid network consisting of mobile nodes and fixed infostations [568]. Their architecture, denoted as Shared Wireless Infostation Model (SWIM), actively transfers information among wireless nodes on each contact, until information is unloaded to one of the infostations.

All approaches [470], [253], [351], [275], and [568] are tailored to specific applications like file-sharing and collecting information. Recall that global lookup operations are a building block of many distributed applications. Thus, such applications require a general-purpose lookup service. In the remainder of this chapter, we present a general-purpose distributed lookup service for mobile applications that uses epidemic information dissemination.

26.2 Passive Distributed Indexing

26.2.1 Overview

In this section, we describe the concept of a lookup service denoted Passive Distributed Indexing (PDI, [389]), that supports resolution of application-specific keys to application-specific values. As building block, PDI stores index entries in index caches maintained by each mobile device. Index entries are propagated by epidemic dissemination, i.e., they are exchanged between devices that get in direct contact, similar to the spread of an infections disease. By exploiting node mobility, such contacts occur randomly between arbitrary devices. Using the information disseminated in this way, PDI can resolve most queries locally without sending messages outside the radio coverage of the inquiring node.

By local resolution of queries, PDI effectively reduces network traffic for the resolution of keys to values for applications possessing a sufficiently high degree of temporal locality in their query streams. Thus, deployment of PDI is attractive for various mobile applications. For example, since queries in a Peer-to-Peer (P2P) file sharing system follow a Zipf-like distribution [570], [355], PDI can implement a distributed search algorithm for such application, that can be complemented by an effective transport protocol for subsequent transfers of located files, e.g., [189]. Moreover, since it has been shown that user queries for Internet search engines possess high temporal locality [631], PDI can support searching in Web-based information portals or even the World Wide Web without connection to an Internet search engine. Further mobile applications effectively supported by PDI include instant messaging (IM) and mobile city guides. In an IM application a lookup service resolves user identifier to the terminal the user is currently logged on and the current presence state of a user, e.g., available, busy, or away. In a city guide a user queries for names and locations of places of interest, e.g., sights, hotels, or restaurants. Both mobile applications are likely to exhibit high locality in the query behavior, too.

In the remainder of this chapter, we consider a MANET consisting of several mobile nodes, e.g. mobile users equipped with notebooks or PDAs and wireless network interfaces as illustrated in Figure 26.1. All mobile nodes collaborate in a shared application that uses a distributed lookup service. Radio coverage is small compared to the area covered by all nodes, e.g., less than 5% of the covered area. Subsequently, we assume IEEE 802.11x in the ad hoc mode as underlying radio technology [315]. However, we would like to point out that that the approaches described in this chapter could be employed on any radio technology that enables broadcast transmissions inside a nodeÂs radio coverage.

26.2.2 Basic Concept

PDI implements a general-purpose lookup service for mobile applications. In general, PDI stores index entries in the form of pairs (k, v). Keys k and values v are both defined by the mobile application. For example, in case of a file sharing application, keys are given by keywords derived from the file name or associated meta-data. Values are given by references to files in form of URIs. Opposed to Distributed Hash Table systems like [505], [575], PDI does neither limit the number of keys matching a value nor the number of values matched by a key. However, some mechanisms implemented in PDI require that a value is unique in the system. That is, it is only added to the system by a single node. This can be easily achieved by extending the application specific value v by a unique node identifier for a node n. For example, the node identifier i_n may be derived from the node's IP address or the MAC address of the radio interface. For ease of exposition, we will abbreviate the unique value given by (v, i_n) pairs just by v.

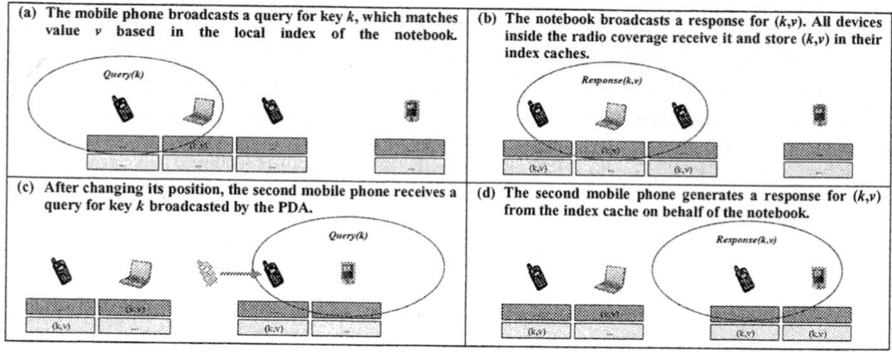

Fig. 26.1: Illustration of epidemic information dissemination with PDI

A node n may contribute index entries of the form (k, v) to the system by inserting them in a local index. In Figure 26.1, the local index is drawn as the first box below each mobile device. We refer to such an index entry as *supplied.* The node n is called the *origin node* of an index entry. For example, the notebook shown in Figure 26.1 is the origin node of the index entry (k, v). A key k matches a value v, if (k, v) is currently supplied to the PDI system. Each node in the system may issue queries in order to resolve a key k to all matching values v_i (see Figure 26.1a). A node issuing a query is denoted as *inquiring node.*

Query messages are sent to the IP limited broadcast address 255.255.255.255 and a well-defined port, using the User Datagram Protocol UDP. Using the IEEE 801.11 ad hoc mode, all nodes located inside the radio coverage of the inquiring node receive a query message. Each of these nodes may generate a response message. A response message contains the key from the query and all matching values from either the local index or a second data structure called index cache. To enable epidemic data dissemination, PDI response messages are sent to the IP limited broadcast address 255.255.255.255 and a well-defined port, too. Thus, all mobile nodes within the radio coverage of the responding node will overhear the message (Figure 26.1b). Not only the inquiring node but also all other mobile nodes that receive a response message extract all index entries and store them in the index cache (see Figure 26.1b). In Figure 26.1, index caches are drawn as the second box below mobile devices. Index entries from the index cache are used to resolve queries locally, if the origin nodes of matching values reside outside the radio coverage of the inquiring node (see Figures 26.1c and 26.1d). Obviously, the index cache size is limited to a maximum number of entries adjusted to the capabilities of the mobile device. The replacement policy least-recently-used (LRU) is employed if a mobile device runs out of index cache space. By generating responses from index caches, information is disseminated to all other nodes that are in direct contact, similar to the spread of an infectious disease. By exploiting node mobility, index entries are disseminated within the network without costly global communication. However, information is only transferred when actively requested by a node. In fact, PDI builds and maintains an index distributed among mobile node of the MANET in a passive way.

26.2.3 Selective Forwarding for Extending Radio Coverage

Recall that all PDI messages are send to the limited broadcast address and received by all nodes located inside the radio coverage of the sender. Depending on the transmission range of the wireless network interfaces, this may considerably limit the number of nodes that receive a message. PDI includes a flooding mechanism that controls forwarding based on the content of a message. The mechanism is illustrated in Figure 26.2. Query messages are flooded with a TTL with value TTL_{query}, which is specified by the inquiring node. For detecting duplicate messages, each massage is tagged with a unique source ID and a sequence number as described above. We will show in Section 26.4 that $TTL_{query} \leq 2$ yields a sufficient performance in most scenarios. Thus, PDI communication remains localized despite of the flooding mechanism.

Similarly to query messages, response messages are forwarded with time-to-live TTL_{query}. Recall that the payload of query messages consists of a few keys. Thus, query messages are small and may be flooded without significantly increasing network load (see Figure 26.2a and 26.2b). In contrast, response messages can contain numerous values that may each have a considerable size, depending on the application using PDI. Therefore, flooding of complete response messages will significantly increase network load, even if the scope of flooding is limited to two hops. For the cost-efficient flooding of response messages, PDI incorporates a concept called selective forwarding. That is each node that receives a response message will search the index cache for each index entry contained in the message (see Figure 26.2d). If an entry is found, the node itself has already sent a response for this query with high probability (e.g., as shown in Figure 26.2c). Therefore, forwarding this index entry constitutes redundant information. Using selective forwarding, each relay node removes all index entries found in its local index cache from the response message, before the message is forwarded (see Figure 26.2e).

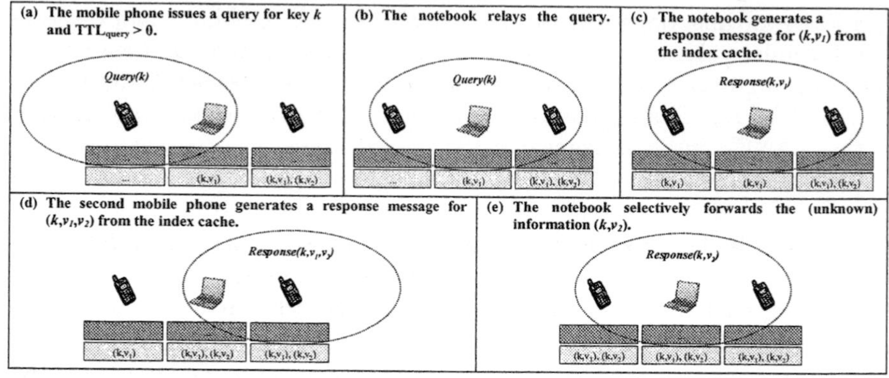

Fig. 26.2: Message forwarding in PDI

26.3 Consistency Issues

26.3.1 Configurable Value Timeouts for Dealing with Weak Connectivity and Node Failures

The basic concept of PDI as described in Sections 26.2.2 and 26.2.3 does not take into account intermittent connectivity and spontaneous departures of nodes; circumstances under which all information previously supplied by a node expire. Examples of these cases include node failure or nodes leaving the area covered by the system. In such cases, an implicit invalidation mechanism can achieve cache coherency. Timeouts constitute a common concept to implement implicit invalidation in several distributed applications, as they can assure cache consistency without the need to contact the source of the cached information. PDI defines the concept of value timeouts to approximate the most recent information about the state of an index entry at the origin node. Value timeouts limit the time any index entry (k, v) with a given value v will be stored in an index cache. By receiving a response from the origin node of (k, v), the corresponding value timeout will be reset. Let $age\left((k, v)\right)$ be the time elapsed since (k, v) has been extracted from a response message generated by its origin node. We define the age a_v of value v as $a_v = min_k\left(age\left((k, v)\right)\right)$, i.e., the time elapsed since the most recent response message of this kind was received. If at a node holds $a_v > T$ for the given timeout value T, all pairs (k, v) are removed from its index cache. PDI implements only one timeout per value v rather than an individual timeout for each index entry (k, v). This is motivated by the observation that in most applications modification of an index entry (k, v) for a given v indicates a substantial change of the value. Subsequently, all other index entries (k', v) are likely to be influenced. For example, in a file sharing system a pair $(keyword_i, URI)$ is removed when the file specified by URI is withdrawn from the system. Thus, all other pairs $(keyword_j, URI)$ also become stale. Note that depending on the application the concept of value timeouts can be easily extended to incorporate individual timeout durations T_v for each value v. Such duration may be included in a response message generated by the origin node. For ease of exposition, we assume in the remainder of this paper a global timeout value T for all values in the system.

To determine the current age of a value, an age field is included in the response message for each value. This age field is set to zero in each response from the origin node. When receiving a response message, a node n extracts the age of each value and calculates the supply time s_v. That is the time of generating a response for this value by the origin node. Assume that the response message contains age a_v, then s_v is determined by $s_v = c_n - a_v$, where c_n denotes the local time of node n. s_v is stored in the index cache together with v. Note that v might already be present in the index cache with supply time s'_v. The copy the index cache might result from a more recent response by the origin node, i.e., $s_v < s'_v$. Thus, in order to relate the age of a value to the most current response from the origin node, the supply time is updated only if $s_v > s'_v$. When a node generates a response for a cached index entry (k, v), it sets the age field for each value v to $a_v = c_n - s_v$. Note that only time differences are transmitted in PDI messages, eliminating the need for synchronizing clocks of all participating devices.

26.3.2 Lazy Invalidation Caches for Dealing with Data Modification at the Origin Node

Additional to the scenarios described above, a node produces stale index entries by modifying information. That is the case when an index entry is removed from the local index. One way to handle such modification of information is to wait until the timeouts of the values in the stale index entries elapse. Depending on the application and the timeout duration T, this straightforward solution may cause severe inconsistency, especially if T is large. A more effective way to handle information modification in distributed applications constitutes the explicit invalidation by control messages. Examples of explicit invalidation schemes include the invalidation of cached memory blocks in distributed shared memory (DSM) systems, or the invalidation of documents in web caches. To achieve consistency, the origin node of an item sends invalidation messages to exactly those nodes that are caching this item. In DSM systems, the origin node of a shared page sends invalidation messages to all nodes sharing this page. In web caching systems, the origin server of a web document sends invalidation messages to each web cache that holds a copy of the document. Note that both mechanisms require that the origin node knows of all copies of an item and is connected to all sharers. Unfortunately, in a mobile environment consisting of nodes with limited resources, connectivity

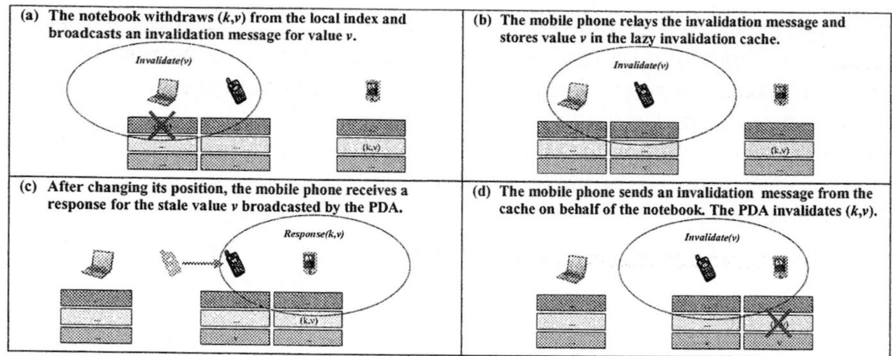

Fig. 26.3: Epidemic dissemination of invalidation messages using lazy invalidation caches

of nodes cannot be guaranteed nor directories for all cached copies of a shared item can be maintained. To address these constraints in mobile systems, PDI defines the concept of lazy invalidation caches implementing explicit invalidation of values by epidemic dissemination of invalidation messages. As basic idea of PDIÂs explicit invalidation mechanism, a node removes all index entries (k, v) from the index cache when it receives an invalidation message for value v. Flooding with a TTL with value TTL_{inv} is a straightforward way to propagate invalidation messages. Unfortunately, in mobile systems even a multi-hop connection between two nodes frequently does not exist. Subsequently, stale index entries remain in the index caches of nodes that are not reached by the invalidation message. Note that these index entries will be redistributed in the system due to the epidemic dissemination. We have shown that even repeated flooding of invalidation messages does not significantly reduce the number of hits for stale index entries [389].

This observation is consistent with [162], which reports that deleted database items ÂresurrectÂ in a replicated database environment due to epidemic data dissemination. In [162], a solution is proposed that uses a special message to testify the deletion of an item, denoted as death certificate. Death certificates are actively disseminated along with ordinary data and deleted after a certain time. In contrast, we propose a more or less passive (or ÂlazyÂ) approach for the epidemic dissemination of invalidation messages, which is illustrated in Figure 26.3. For the initial propagation of an invalidation message by the origin node, we rely on flooding as described above (Figure 26.3a). Each node maintains a data structure called lazy invalidation cache, which is drawn as a third box below the mobile devices in Figure 26.3. When a node receives an invalidation message for a value v it does not only relay it, but stores v in the invalidation cache (Figure 26.3b). Note that an entry for v is stored in the invalidation cache, regardless if the node stores any index entry (k, v) for v in the index cache. Thus, every node will contribute to the propagation of invalidation messages, so that distribution of information and invalidation messages is separated. To enable the epidemic dissemination of the invalidation message, a node scans the invalidation cache for all values contained in an overheard response message (Figure 26.3c). If a value v is found, the node will generate an invalidation message, because the hit in the invalidation cache indicates that the index cache of a nearby node contains a stale entry (Figure 26.3d). The invalidation message is not flooded through the entire network, but only with a certain scope TTL_{inv} similar to forwarding query and response messages as described in Section 26.2.3. A node that receives a cached invalidation message for value v will store v in the invalidation cache, and remove all index entries (k, v) from the index cache. Additionally, the node checks whether it has recently received hits for v in response to an own query, which must also be invalidated and may not be passed to the application running on top of PDI.

As the index cache size, the invalidation cache size is limited to a fixed number of values and LRU replacement is employed. We have shown in [389] that setting the invalidation cache size to a fraction below 20% of the index cache size achieves a sufficient reduction of false hits assuming a reasonable rate of data modification. Note that LRU replacement does neither guarantee that an invalidation cache entry is kept until all stale index entries are invalidated, nor that it is removed after a certain time, inhibiting a node indefinitely from restoring a value it has invalidated once. Increasing the invalidation cache size solves the first problem, though, doing so amplifies the second problem. To avoid this tradeoff, maintaining the supply time of invalidation messages similar to the supply time of values as described by Section 26.3.1 yields an efficient mechanism to decide whether a result for a value is more recent than an invalidation message.

26.4 Performance Studies

26.4.1 Simulation Environment

To evaluate the performance of the PDI and the proposed consistency mechanisms, we conduct simulation experiments using the network simulator ns-2 [198]. We developed an ns-2 application implementing the basic concepts of PDI, selective forwarding, value timeouts, and lazy invalidation caches as described in Sections 26.2 and 26.3. An instance of the PDI application is attached to each simulated mobile node, using the UDP/IP protocol stack and a MAC layer according to the IEEE 802.11 standard for wireless communication. Recall that PDI can be configured by the four parameters shown in Table 26.2. As goal of our simulation studies, we will show that PDI can be configured to the demands of different applications by adjusting these parameters. Therefore, we have to define detailed models of the system in which PDI is deployed.

The performance of PDI is affected by several characteristics of the mobile environment. We separate these characteristics into system characteristics and application characteristics. System characteristics describe the mobile environment. These characteristics include the density of mobile nodes as well as their arrivals and departures, the transmission range of the wireless communication interfaces, and the mobility model, describing the movement of the mobile nodes. Application characteristics are specific to the mobile application using PDI. These characteristics include the number of values supplied by each mobile node, the matching between keys and values, the distribution of keys in the queries as, the distribution of pause times between two successive queries by the same mobile node, and the validity of a value.

For modeling system characteristics, we assume that N mobile users equipped with mobile devices participate in a mobile application. Assuming the two-ray ground reflection model, we configure the transmission power of the wireless interface to provide a radio-coverage with a radius R. We assume that the mobile nodes move in an area of size A according to the random waypoint (RWP) mobility model [92], which is commonly used to mimic the movement of pedestrians. According to this mobility model, each node starts at a location chosen uniformly at random inside the simulation area and moves to another randomly chosen location. The speed of the node is chosen uniformly from $(0, v_{max}]$, where the maximum speed v_{max} may be different in different experiments. When a node reaches its destination, it rests for a period T_{hold}, before it continues its movement to the next randomly chosen destination at randomly chosen speed. Note that the assumption of movement at pedestrian speed might constitute a conservative assumption for disseminating information by exploiting mobility.

In the remainder of this paper, we will use a workload model inspired by a Peer-to-Peer file sharing application. To capture the characteristics of this application, we assume that the application defines a set of keys $\mathcal{K}$ with cardinality $K = |\mathcal{K}|$. We associate each key with its popularity rank, i.e., $\mathcal{K} = 1, \ldots, K$, where key 1 is the most frequently requested key. Additionally, the application defines a set of values $\mathcal{K}$ with cardinality $V = |\mathcal{V}|$. We use an arbitrary numbering of values, i.e., $\mathcal{V} = 1, \ldots, V$. The values are equally distributed among the mobiles nodes, i.e., each node contributes the same number of values. To determine the matching between keys and values we define a selection function. The selection function $w_{select}(k)$ denotes the probability that a key k matches a given value v for $k = 1, \ldots, K$ and $v = 1, \ldots, V$. Note that the selection function is independent of v. Following [634], the selection function can be well represented by an exponential distribution with mean $1/\alpha$:

$$w_{select}(k) = \alpha e^{-\alpha k}$$

To determine which keys are used in queries, we define a query function with probability density function (pdf) $w_{query}(k)$ that denotes the probability that a query is for a given key k. As shown in [570], [355], query popularity in Peer-to-Peer file sharing systems follows a Zipf-like distribution, i.e., the query function for $k = 1, \ldots, K$ is given by:

$$w_{query}(k) \sim k^{-\beta}$$

To determine the timestamps of queries issued by the mobile users, we define a pause function $w_{pause}(t)$ that denotes the probability that a node pauses for the time t between two successive queries, $0 \leq t \leq \infty$. We assume that pause times are exponentially distributed with mean $1/\lambda$, i.e., the pause function is given by:

$$w_{pause}(t) = \lambda e^{-\lambda t}$$

Up to this point, the model of system and application characteristics is still not suitable for evaluating the consistency mechanisms presented in Section 26.3, since it does not incorporate node departures and data modifications. To take node departures into account, we assume that the time t between two successive arrivals or departures, respectively, follows an exponential distribution with pdf $w_{arrival}(t)$, $0 \leq t \leq \infty$. We adjust the arrival and departure rates such that approximately dN for $0 \leq d \leq 1$ nodes will arrive or depart during the considered simulation time T, respectively. Thus, we define $\mu = dN/T$ and assume that he arrival function for $0 \leq t \leq \infty$ is given by a is given by an exponential distribution with mean $1/\mu$:

$$w_{arrival}(t) = \mu e^{-\mu t}$$

Then, the number of arrivals or departures in simulation time T is Poisson distributed with a parameter given by $\mu T = dN$ (i.e., it has mean dN), matching our assumption. Arriving nodes enter the system with empty index and invalidation caches and contribute values that are not used by any node that is already in the system. Departing nodes do not send invalidation messages for supplied data, i.e., all index entries supplied by a departing node expire.

To consider value modifications, we assume that each value expires exactly once during a simulation of length T. Thus, we define an expiration function with pdf $w_{expire}(t)$ that denotes the probability that a value expires after a time t, $0 \leq t \leq T$, as continuous uniform distribution:

$$w_{expire}(t) = \frac{1}{T}$$

If not stated otherwise, all parameters defining system and application characteristics are chosen as shown in Table 26.1. The default settings of the PDI protocol parameters are shown in Table 26.2.

We choose performance measures to evaluate the recall and the coherence of the results delivered by PDI. Recall is measured by the hit rate HR, i.e., $HR = H_F/K_F$ for H_F denoting the number of up-to-date hits and K_F

Parameter	Value
Total simulation time T	7200 s
Simulation area A	1000 m × 1000 m
Number of devices N	64 or 80
Maximum speed v_{max}	1.5 m/s
Rest Period T_{hold}	50 s
Transmission range R	115 m
Number of keys K	512
Number of values V	16
Parameter of selection function α	1/100
Parameter of query function β	0.9
Parameter of pause function λ	1/120
Fraction of arriving / departing nodes d	0.3

Table 26.1: Default values for simulation parameters

the total number of all up-to-date matching values currently in the system. Coherence is measured by the stale hit rate SHR, i.e., $SHR = H_S/(H_S + H_F)$, where H_S denotes the number of stale hits returned on a query. Note that stale hit rate is related to the information retrieval measure *precision* by $precision = 1 - SHR$.

In all experiments, we conduct transient simulations starting with initially empty caches. For each run, the total simulation time is set to 2 hours. To avoid inaccuracy due to initial warm-ups, we reset all statistic counters after a warm-up period of 10 min. simulation time. Furthermore, we initialize positions and speed of all nodes according to the steady state distribution determined by the random waypoint mobility model [85] to avoid initial tran-

PDI Protocol Parameter	Default Value
Index cache size	2048 entries
Selective forwarding TTL	4 hops
Value timeout	1000 s
Invalidation cache size	128 entries

Table 26.2: Default values for PDI configuration parameters

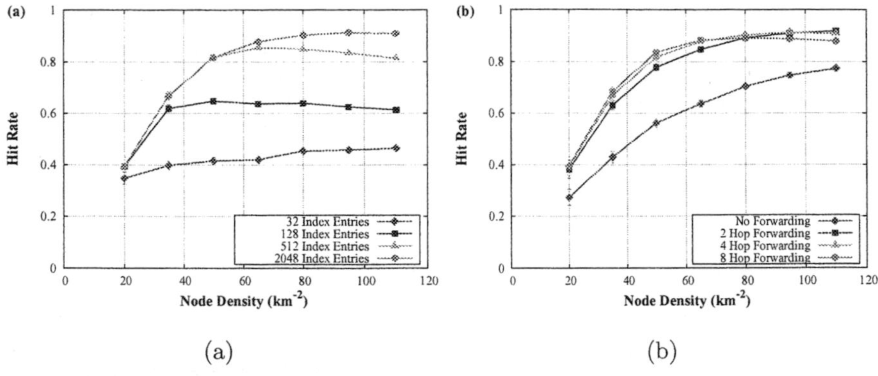

(a) (b)

Fig. 26.4: Recall vs. system size for (a) different index cache sizes and (b) different numbers of forwarding hops

sients. For each point in all performance curves, we performed 100 independent simulation runs and calculated corresponding performance measures at the end of the simulation. In all curves 99% confidence intervals determined by independent replicates are included.

26.4.2 Sensitivity to System Characteristics

To evaluate the performance of PDI with respect to the system characteristics, we do not consider consistency aspects in our first experiments. That is, we do not model value expiration, assuming that all values are valid during a simulation run. Furthermore, we do not consider node arrivals and departures, assuming that the community of PDI users is static during the simulation time. The impact of consistency issues is evaluated in Section 26.4.4.

In a first experiment, we investigate the sensitivity of PDI to the node density, i.e., the number of mobile nodes moving in the simulation area and participating in the application that uses PDI. The results of this performance study are shown in Figure 26.4. Figure 26.4 (a) plots the hit rate as a function of node density for different sizes of the index cache. We find that for a small number of nodes, the size of the local index caches has only a limited impact on the performance of PDI. In these scenarios, a low node density limits the epidemic information dissemination due to a lack of contacts between the nodes. For an increasing node density, we observe three different effects. First, an increasing number of contacts between the nodes significantly foster epidemic information dissemination for sufficient large index caches (i.e., 128 index cache entries or more). Second, connectivity increases with node density. Thus, selective forwarding increases hit rate even for small index caches (i.e., 32 index entries). Third, the hit rate for large caches decreases

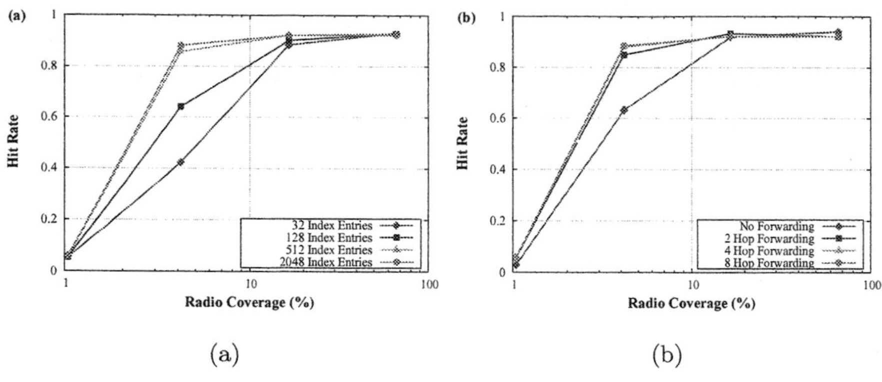

Fig. 26.5: Recall vs. radio coverage for (a) different index cache sizes and (b) different numbers of forwarding hops

when the node density passes a certain number of nodes. To understand this effect, recall that the overall number of values in the system increases with node density because each node contributes additional values to the lookup service. Furthermore, the keys in queries are selected according to a Zipf-like selection function. Due to the heavy tailed nature of this function, responses to a large number of queries must be cached in order to achieve high hit rates. Thus, the hit rate decreases even for large caches when the number of index entries for popular queries exceeds cache capacity and the epidemic dissemination of data decreases. We conclude from Figure 26.4 (a) that epidemic data dissemination requires a sufficient node density. To gain most benefit of the variety of values contributed to the lookup service by a large number of nodes, sufficient index cache size should be provided. In properly configured systems with a reasonable node density, PDI achieves hit rates up to 0.9.

Similar to the impact of index cache size, the impact of message forwarding is limited in systems with a low node density, as shown in Figure 26.4 (b). Forwarding messages for more than four hops yields only marginal improvements in the hit rate due to limited connectivity. However, for an increasing node density, the hit rate grows faster in systems with message forwarding enabled than in non-forwarding systems, as increasing connectivity favors selective forwarding. In environments with about 64 nodes, configuring the system for packet forwarding can improve hit rate by almost 30%. Nevertheless, non-forwarding systems benefit from growing node density as it fosters epidemic information dissemination. Thus, the benefit of selective forwarding with $TTL_{query} \geq 4$ hops becomes negligible, if the number of mobile nodes becomes larger than 64. In these scenarios, forwarding messages over multiple hops will decrease the variety of information stored in the index caches, because forwarded results replace other results in a high number of caches. Thus, fewer different results are returned from the caches for succes-

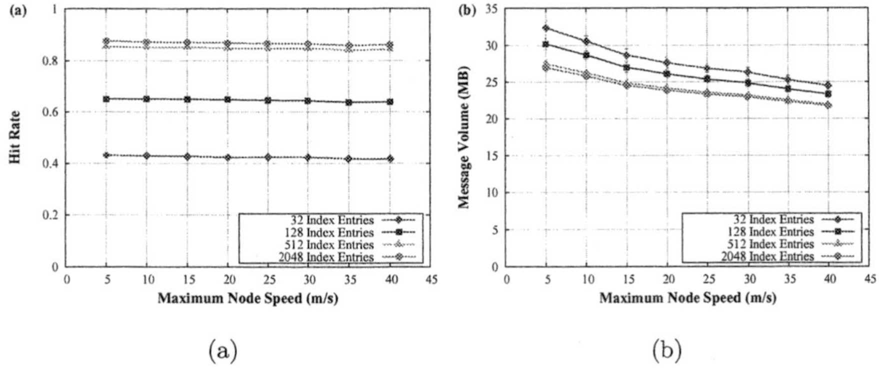

(a) (b)

Fig. 26.6: (a) Recall vs. mobility for different index cache sizes and (b) message volume vs. mobility for different numbers of forwarding hops

sive queries. We conclude from Figure 26.4 (b) that message forwarding is beneficial in system environments showing a medium node density, while in systems with high node density message forwarding should be disabled.

In a second experiment, we investigate the sensitivity of PDI to the transmission range of the wireless communication interfaces used by the mobile nodes. The results of this study are shown in Figure 26.5. Figure 26.5 (a) shows hit rate as a function of transmission range for different cache sizes. For a transmission range below 100 meters, i.e., a radio coverage of about 1% of the simulation area, PDI does not gain sufficient hit rates despite index cache size. Here, in most cases broadcasted query messages are received only by a small number of nodes. Consistent with the results shown Figure 26.4 (b), given a reasonable size of the index cache and a transmission range of 115 meters (i.e., a radio coverage of about 4% of the considered area) PDI achieves sufficiently high hit rate for Peer-to-Peer search queries. For larger transmission ranges, most queries will reach the origin nodes of index entries (k, v) for a query v. Thus, PDI does not benefit from caching index entries. We conclude from Figure 26.5 (a) that for short-range communication devices the number of participating devices must be high to enable the effective employment of PDI, whereas for long-range communication, the system does not significantly benefit from PDI.

Figure 26.5 (b) shows hit rate as a function of transmission range for different values of TTL_{query}. We find that message forwarding has no impact in systems with small transmission ranges, while system with medium transmission ranges heavily benefit from forwarding. As another interesting result, we find that for high transmission ranges PDI with message forwarding disabled gains best performance. Here, unnecessary forwarding of PDI messages will result in a substantial number of collisions of wireless transmissions, as confirmed by the examination of ns-2 trace files. These collisions reduce the number of response messages that reach the enquiring node. We conclude from Figure 26.5 (b) that in environments with medium wireless transmission ranges, message forwarding should be enabled to benefit from PDI. If transmission range is high, message forwarding should be disabled to avoid congestion of the wireless medium.

As final system parameter, we investigate the sensitivity of PDI to node mobility in Figure 26.6. Figure 26.6 (a) plots the hit rate as a function of maximum node speed. Increasing device velocity from pedestrian speed to the speed of cars in an urban environment, we find that hit rate is almost independent of node speed for the considered application scenario. Recall that according to the pause function a node sends queries in an average interval of 120s, while the holding time defined by the random waypoint mobility model is 50s. That is, with high probability the node will change position between two successive queries, so that epidemic information dissemination is large despite of node mobility. Nevertheless, PDI benefits from increasing mobility in terms of total volume of transmitted PDI messages as shown in Figure 26.6 (b). As increasing mobility fosters epidemic information dissemination to some extend, message volume is reduced up to 25% depending on node mobility. As information is more equally distributed across the simulation area for high mobility scenarios, most queries can be resolved locally, i.e., from nearby nodes. Results from more distant nodes will be suppressed by the selective forwarding mechanism, resulting in substantial savings in message volume. We conclude from Figure 26.6 that PDI performs well for a reasonable degree of mobility, while high mobility increases the benefit of selective forwarding.

In an experiment not shown here, we employ the Reference Point Group Mobility Model (RPGM) [303], which organizes nodes into groups that move together across the simulation area. [303] argues that group mobility is more realistic than individual mobility in mobile scenarios. Obviously, group mobility reduces epidemic information dissemination, since nodes primarily get in touch with members of their own group. The experiments show that PDI performance is reduced by at most 10% for scenarios with few nodes (and few groups, respectively). However, when the number of nodes exceeds 80, simulation results converge against the results for the RWP mobility model, since contacts among groups frequently occur. We conclude from these experiments that PDI performs well even for more realistic mobility models if a reasonable node density is provided.

26.4.3 Sensitivity to Application Characteristics

To evaluate the performance of PDI with respect to the characteristics of the application runing on top of it, again, we do not consider consistency issues originating from node departures and data modifications. As first application

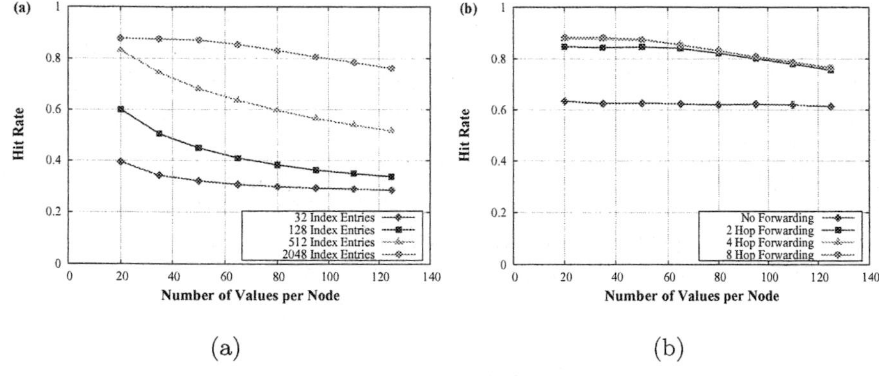

(a) (b)

Fig. 26.7: Recall vs. shared data for (a) different index cache sizes and (b) different numbers of forwarding hops

characteristics, we consider the overall data volume managed by PDI. Note that data volume depends on the number of values supplied by each node, which may be very different for different mobile applications. For example, for a Peer-to-Peer file sharing application, we assume that the number of values is up to 100, where each node in an instant messaging application only contributes a single value. For searching a Web portal or even the entire WWW, the overall number of values might be considerable larger, but does not depend on the number of nodes. To capture the characteristics of these different applications, we perform a sensitivity study with respect to the data volume managed by PDI.

Figure 26.7 plot hit rate as a function of the number of values contributed by each node. We investigate in Figure 26.7 (a) that the hit rate of PDI decreases with a growing number of values for all considered index cache sizes. Furthermore we observe that PDI is most sensitive to the number of values for medium index cache sizes (i.e., 128 and 512 index cache entries). As observed in Figure 26.4 (a), index caches of these sizes cannot provide high hit rates for an increasing amount of data, whereas a large cache can handle the data easily. Recall that the performance of small caches shows low sensitivity to the data provided to the system, as the hit rate is primarily determined by selective forwarding. To illustrate the impact of selective forwarding at larger index cache sizes, we investigate the performance of different forwarding options for an index cache size of 2048 index entries and an increasing number of contributed values in Figure 26.7 (b). We find that setting $TTL_{query} = 2$ improves hit rate by 40%, while setting $TTL_{query} \geq 4$ improves hit rate by less than 5% compared to $TTL_{query} = 2$. We conclude from Figure 26.7 that large index caches should be provided and selective forwarding enabled to handle large numbers of values.

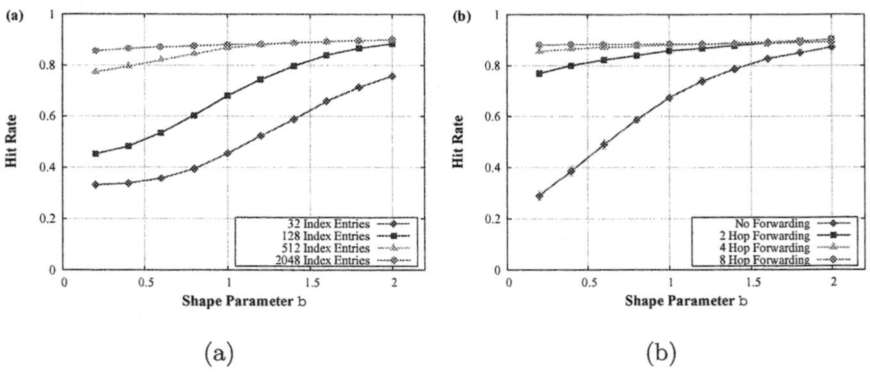

Fig. 26.8: Recall vs. locality for (a) different forwarding options and (b) different numbers of forwarding hops

In an experiment not shown here, we found that PDI is almost insensitive to the shape parameter of the matching function α, which determines the distribution of the number of values matched by a key. As all caching-based mechanisms, PDI performance depends on locality in the query stream. Recall that the selection function is given by a Zipf like distribution with shape parameter *beta*. If $0 < \beta \leq 0.5$, the locality in the query stream is low, whereas $\beta > 1$ indicates high locality. Hit rate as a function of the shape parameter β is shown in Figure 26.8 for different index cache sizes and forwarding options, respectively. Figure 26.8 (a) reveals that PDI is extremely sensitive to locality in the query stream for small sizes of the index cache (i.e., 32 and 128 index cache entries). For large cache sizes (i.e., 512 and 2048 entries), PDI can achieve a hit rate of more than 0.75 despite of the locality. Figure 26.8 (b) shows that PDI is most sensitive to query locality if no selective forwarding is enabled. With $TTL_{query} \geq 2$, however, PDI can effectively combine results from several index caches and effectively cope with low locality. We conclude from Figure 26.8 that sufficient index cache size should be provided and 2 hop forwarding enabled if the application using PDI provides low locality.

26.4.4 Impact of Consistency Mechanisms

In the final simulation experiments, we investigate the coherence of index caches maintained by PDI with and without the invalidation mechanisms presented in Section 26.3. These performance curves are shown in Figures 26.9 and 26.10. Figure 26.9 (a) plots hit rates as a function of node density for different sizes of the index cache. Comparing Figure 26.9 (a) with Figure 26.4 reveals that the hit rate is reduced due to cache space occupied by stale index entries. Stale hit rates as a function of node density is plotted

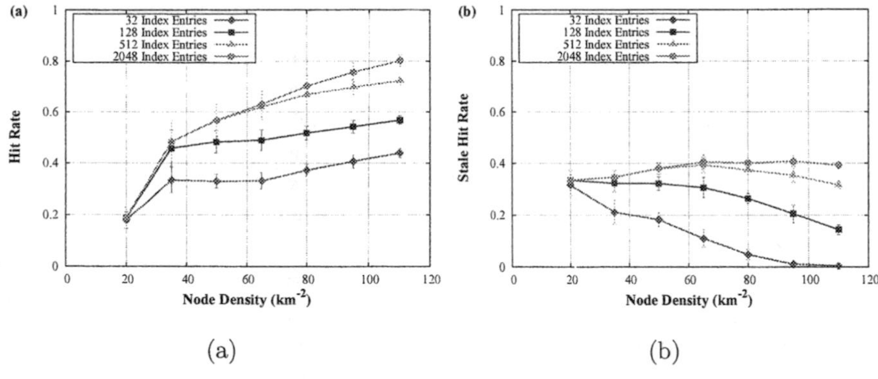

(a) (b)

Fig. 26.9: (a) Recall and (b) coherency vs. system size without invalidation

in Figure 26.9 (b). We find that without invalidation the stale hit rate may reach 0.4. For smaller index cache sizes, the stale hit rate decreases with node density. Jointly considering Figures 26.9 (a) and (b) reveals that for an increasing node density the stale hit rate drops rapidly at the point when the growth of the hit rate slows down. Looking closer at the index caches in these scenarios, we find that the content of the caches is highly variable. Thus, stale index entries are removed early from the caches. We conclude from Figure 26.9 (b) that large caches yield a high amount of stale hits if no invalidation mechanism is used. In contrary, small index caches naturally reduce stale hits, while they fail to provide high hit rates as shown in Figure 26.9 (a). This evidently illustrates the need for invalidation mechanisms in order to achieve both high hit rates and low stale hit rates.

In a last experiment, we investigate the performance of an integrated approach combining both value timeouts and lazy invalidation caches to take into account both weak connectivity and information modification. In further experiments presented in [389], we found that suitable configuration of value-timeouts reduces the stale hit rate due to intermittent connectivity and node failure by 75%. Furthermore, lazy invalidation caches of moderate size reduce stale results due to data modification by more than 50%. Thus, we fix the duration of the value timeout to 1000s and the invalidation cache size to 128 entries, since these parameters achieved best performance for the considered scenario [389]. Figure 26.10 (a) plots the hit rate versus node density. We find that hit rate is reduced mostly for small systems due to invalidations of up-to-date index entries by value timeouts. This leads to a decrease of at most 20%. The performance of index cache sizes of both 512 and 2048 is equal because a large cache cannot benefit from long-term correlations between requests due to the short timeout. For growing number of nodes, the hit rate converges towards results without an invalidation mechanism as shown in Figure 26.9 (a).

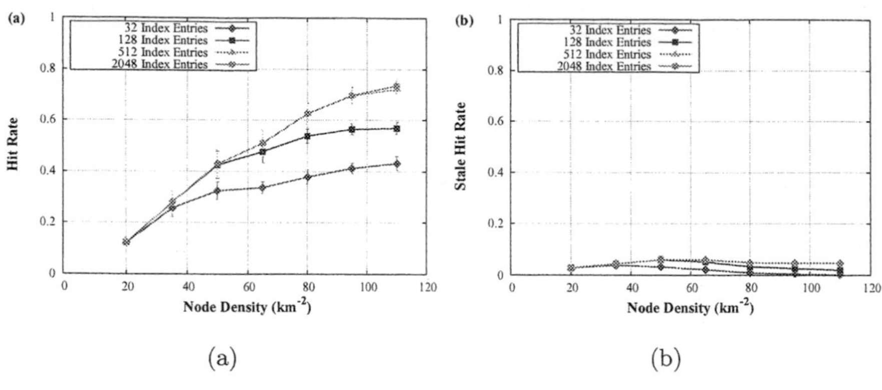

(a) (b)

Fig. 26.10: (a) Recall and (b) coherency vs. system size for hybrid invalidation

As settlement for the reduction of hit rate, the stale hit rate is significantly reduced compared to a system without invalidation. As shown in Figure 26.10 (b), the stale hit rate is below 5% for all considered index cache sizes. We conclude from Figure 26.10 that the integrated approach comprising of the introduced implicit and explicit invalidation mechanisms can effectively handle both spontaneous node departures and modification of information. In fact, for large index caches, the stale hit rate can be reduced by more than 85%. That is, more than 95% of the results delivered by PDI are up-to-date.

26.5 Summary

In this chapter, we described a distributed lookup service for mobile applications denoted Passive Distributed Indexing (PDI). As key concept, PDI employs epidemic dissemination of (key, value) pairs among mobile devices. To foster information dissemination for devices with limited radio transmission range, PDI incorporates a bandwidth-efficient message relaying mechanism denoted selective forwarding. To provide coherent results in environments with frequently changing data, PDI incorporates implicit invalidation by configurable value timeouts and explicit invalidation by lazy invalidation caches.

In an extensive simulation study, we illustrated the recall and the result coherence achieved by PDI for different system and workload characteristics. We found that with the suitable configuration of index cache size and selective forwarding PDI can achieve hit rates of more than 90% despite of system and application characteristics. Considering result coherence, we found that a combination of both invalidation mechanisms provides more than 95% up-to-date results. All presented simulation results are based on a workload model inspired by a Peer-to-Peer file sharing application. However, we have shown that PDI can cope with different application characteristics using appropriate configurations. Thus, PDI can be employed for a large set of mobile applications that possess a sufficiently high degree of temporal locality in the request stream, including Web-portal and Web search without connection to the search server, instant messaging applications, and mobile city guides.

In recent work, we have developed a general-purpose analytical performance model for epidemic information dissemination in mobile and hoc networks [390]. Currently, we are employing this modeling framework to optimize PDI protocol parameters for selected mobile applications. Based on the results, we are adopting PDI for developing software prototypes of a mobile file sharing system, a mobile instant messaging application, and disconnected Web search.

27. Peer-to-Peer and Ubiquitous Computing

Jussi Kangasharju (Darmstadt University of Technology)

27.1 Introduction to Ubiquitous Computing

Ubiquitous computing was introduced by Marc Weiser in the early 1990s [619]. In Weiser's vision, computers would become ubiquitous, that is, they would be present in every facet of human life. This vision has sometimes also been called the vision of the disappearing computer, since, as Weiser said, once computers become so commonplace that they are everywhere, they become such a natural part of the environment that we no longer notice them. Hence, it can be said that once computers are everywhere, they are, in fact, nowhere.

This vision is a logical consequence in the evolution of computer systems. In the early days of mainframe computers, several users shared a single computer's resources. In the current PC-era, one user typically uses a single computer. With the advent of new devices, such as PDAs and cell phones, we can already see that in the future a single user is likely to interact with several computers. However, today's world is still far from the vision of Marc Weiser, where computers are a natural part of the environment and interaction with them happens seamlessly.

The early days of ubiquitous computing were mainly focused along two axes. On the one hand, researchers were building new kinds of interaction devices, to explore how a person would live in a ubiquitous world. One of the most famous examples is the ParcTab [613] system which consists of palm-sized mobile computers that can communicate wirelessly through infrared transceivers to workstation-based applications. Since then, there have been many other projects around similar devices [602, 381, 598]. Such devices serve as prototypes for experimenting in building larger scale ubiquitous computing environments and serve as basis for determining the requirements such environments pose on the interaction devices.

Another important focus area has been location, or positioning systems. Many ubiquitous applications require that they be able to locate the user and adapt their behavior as a function of the movements of the user. An overview of different location systems can be found in [295]. Indoor location systems have been based on magnetism, ultrasound [12, 114], infrared [15] or radio waves (RF) [44, 467] as the transmission medium. Each of the systems has its strengths and weaknesses in terms of accuracy, range, and deployment cost, and none of them can yet be considered as "the best solution for all situations". It is likely, that future ubiquitous computing architectures will need to deal with several positioning systems concurrently.

R. Steinmetz and K. Wehrle (Eds.): P2P Systems and Applications, LNCS 3485, pp. 457-469, 2005.

Recent developments in ubiquitous computing are more concerned with defining and implementing architectures for formalizing and crystallizing the vision of ubiquitous computing. These architectures also have the role of tying together all the individual devices, services, and users. Some examples of such architectures are Sahara [499], Mundo [277] and Oxygen [465]. These architectures focus on the interactions between the different devices in the ubiquitous environment, with a particular emphasis on the communication needs and requirements of such environments. Indeed, these architectures highlight the need for efficient communication infrastructures, mechanisms, and protocols for building ubiquitous computing architectures.

In this chapter, we will focus on the communication needs of ubiquitous computing architectures. As we will see, ubiquitous computing architectures exhibit many properties similar to Peer-to-Peer systems. However, in contrast to the traditional, "PCs on the Internet"-like Peer-to-Peer systems, ubiquitous Peer-to-Peer systems have several additional challenges emerging from the nature of ubiquitous computing architectures. The goal of this chapter is to present an overview of the challenges and discuss current approaches for solving the communication problems in ubiquitous computing architectures.

The rest of this chapter is organized as follows. In Section 27.2 we discuss the characteristics of ubiquitous computing applications. In Section 27.3 we present the main features of communication architectures in ubiquitous applications. Section 27.4 looks into middleware in ubiquitous environments and discusses the requirements for such middleware. Section 27.5 compares the properties of Peer-to-Peer systems and ubiquitous computing applications and discusses the use of Peer-to-Peer middleware for ubiquitous computing. Finally, Section 27.6 presents the research challenges in Peer-to-Peer ubiquitous computing.

27.2 Characteristics of Ubiquitous Computing Applications

Ubiquitous computing applications have very different characteristics from traditional stand-alone computer applications, or Internet applications. In the ubiquitous computing world, we may have a very large number of devices involved in any interaction, typically in an ad hoc fashion. This is in stark contrast to the traditional computing world, where data is typically placed in certain well-known places and interactions are more structured. In this section, we will look at some of the main characteristics of ubiquitous computing applications, paying special attention to the characteristics which separate them from the "traditional" applications.

Table 27.1 presents a summary of the different characteristics we will discuss in this section.

Characteristics	Typical properties
Information	Small units, rapidly changing
Network	Wireless, ad hoc
Collaboration	Small devices, grouping, communities
Sharing	Limited devices, shared resources
Context	Behave "smartly", use context

Table 27.1: Summary of Characteristics of Ubiquitous Applications

27.2.1 Information

Information in ubiquitous applications plays quite a different role than in traditional applications. In the latter case, the user is often either a source or a consumer of information, and this governs the use and properties of the information transmitted in the applications.

In contrast, the information in ubiquitous applications is more often than not information sent from one small device to another; the information delivered to a human user plays a relatively small role in this world. Information in ubiquitous applications is also typically in small units and it may change rapidly. One good example which illustrates this are all manners of sensors which are a common building block of ubiquitous applications. For example, a motion sensor is constantly sending information about whether or not it detects movement. The actual amount of information is very small (i.e., is movement detected or not) and the state may change rapidly and asynchronously.

Ubiquitous applications must therefore be able to handle several flows of (possibly) rapidly changing information coming from a multitude of sources.

27.2.2 Network

Communication networks in ubiquitous computing applications also exhibit several characteristics which reflect these new applications. Often, the communications happen over ad hoc connections which are formed as the different ubiquitous devices come into communication range of each other. This implies that the network topology is highly dynamic and can change unpredictably.

Furthermore, since wired networks are typically not feasible for use in ubiquitous applications, owing to their distributed and dynamic nature, we must resort to wireless communication networks. Unfortunately, wireless network links are far more unreliable than wired links, and the data rates which can be achieved are considerably lower.

All of the above factors require us to rethink the communication abstractions in ubiquitous computing applications. We will revisit this issue in Section 27.3.

27.2.3 Collaboration

Because ubiquitous devices are typically small and have only very limited capabilities, they must collaborate in order to deliver useful services. This collaboration not only includes simple communications between devices, but extends to actual cooperation and active sharing of resources and information.

To achieve this collaboration, we need to resort to techniques such as grouping or communities which can be formed in an ad hoc manner. Such groups can be formed by, for example, the devices carried by a person, or all the devices in a given room. The devices within a group share a context and normally need to be aware of each other and each other's capabilities and needs.

27.2.4 Sharing Resources

Again, the limited resource of ubiquitous devices compel us to have them share their resources, in order to enable them to offer more sophisticated services. We consider the term "resources" in the broadest sense and include in it, not only computing power and storage capability, but also information contained in a device, as well as any additional devices attached to it.

27.2.5 Context Information

Since ubiquitous applications and devices can be used in many different circumstances, they need to be aware of the context in which they are being used. One good example of context information is the current location of a device, which may determine its behavior (e.g., when outside, a mobile phone might ring loud, whereas in a meeting it would set itself to vibration mode). Other context information are current environment conditions (light, temperature, etc.) or higher level information, such as the stored preferences of the current user [166].

27.3 Communications in Ubiquitous Computing Architectures

In this section, we will discuss the communication needs of ubiquitous computing architectures. In particular, we will present the publish/subscribe-communication paradigm as an attractive option for ubiquitous applications.

As we discussed in Section 27.2, the communication needs of ubiquitous computing applications differ greatly from those of traditional applications. Because of the highly autonomous nature of these new applications and their highly dynamic behavior, a centralized approach to managing connections (e.g., a fixed server handling all the devices in one room) is not possible. This leads us to investigate self-organizing communication paradigms.

Self-organizing communication models are very attractive for ubiquitous applications, since they allow us to handle the dynamics of the applications in a scalable and robust manner. One promising communication paradigm for ubiquitous computing is publish/subscribe communication [195, 103]. In the Publish/Subscribe interaction scheme, subscribers have the ability to express their interest in an event, or a pattern of events, and are subsequently notified of any such event, generated by a publisher, which matches their registered interest. The event is then asynchronously propagated to all subscribers that registered interest in it. The strength of this event-based interaction style lies in the full decoupling in time, space and synchronization between publishers and subscribers.

One major advantage of a publish/subscribe communication model is that it allows us to hide much of the communication handling from the application. Because ubiquitous environments may present many challenges for the communication layer (poor links, dropped connections, many errors, etc.) it is highly advantageous to be able to incorporate all communication code in a middleware layer. This frees the application programmer from having to worry about possible error conditions and it also allows the middleware to select the best possible communication means at any given time, without this having to be programmed into the application.

27.4 Ubiquitous Computing Middleware

The key glue which holds ubiquitous computing applications together is a middleware layer. This middleware provides the application with an interface for communicating with the "rest of the world", but it also protects the application from the environment (especially in terms of communication problems and issues).

However, because of the characteristics of ubiquitous applications, this middleware must take into account many different factors, and it must fulfill several requirements. In the rest of this section we will discuss these requirements in more detail.

27.4.1 Support for Heterogeneous Devices

The world of ubiquitous computing is highly heterogeneous; no longer is there a single dominant device type, such as a desktop computer. Instead, we have many different kinds of devices, small sensors, personal devices, traditional computers, large wall displays, etc. All these different devices have very different characteristics and these must be accounted for in a middleware. One example are the communication capabilities of the devices, i.e., what kinds of capabilities does the device possess and what does it "cost" to use them.

27.4.2 Resource Constraints

Many ubiquitous devices are very resource-constrained. Consider, for example, a simple temperature sensor which normally would include only the sensor, a simple processor with a minimal amount of memory, and means for communicating with other devices. Because of these constraints, a middleware must have a small memory footprint so that it can be embedded in as many devices as possible. Even though the cost of memory is decreasing, it will not be feasible to equip thousands and millions of ubiquitous devices with enough memory and processing power to run conventional middleware.

A consequence of the requirement of a small memory footprint is the modularity of the middleware. If we build the middleware around a small, minimal kernel, with additional services which can be plugged in and unplugged on-demand, we satisfy the requirements of a small memory footprint (since unnecessary services can be unloaded) and we have a flexible system which can adapt to rapidly changing conditions.

27.4.3 Mobility Support

Ubiquitous applications and devices are highly mobile, hence the middleware must be able to handle this. We can distinguish two kinds of mobility which require connections to be handed off during the communication.

On the one hand, we have horizontal handoffs (or handovers), which are currently commonly used in mobile phone networks. In a mobile phone network, a horizontal handoff occurs when the phone moves from the coverage of one base station to another. During this move, the base stations must transfer the communication resources to the new base station and the mobile phone must then switch to this base station. In the ubiquitous computing world, we do not necessarily have base stations, but can define a horizontal handoff in an analogous manner. A horizontal handoff occurs when the device must change its communication partners, but it continues to use the same technology (e.g., BlueTooth or WLAN) for the communication.

On the other hand, we have vertical handoffs which occur when the device must change communication technology in order to maintain the connection. For example, a device in a WLAN hotspot which moves out of the reach of the access point must switch to, e.g., UMTS, to remain connected.

Although horizontal handoffs are currently much more common, vertical handoffs are likely to become more common with the proliferation of WLAN networks. Some horizontal handoffs (especially in mobile phone networks) can already be handled with current technology, but other types of handoffs, especially vertical handoffs, usually result in broken connections.

Ubiquitous middleware must therefore have efficient support for both kinds of handoffs, across a wide range of different networking technologies.

27.4.4 Networking Support

Networks and communication links between devices in ubiquitous computing form spontaneously and in an ad hoc manner, without any necessary planning in advance. This type of spontaneous networking implies that nearby devices need to be found as they come in range, and communication links must be formed on demand. This sets requirements for the middleware, implying that it must handle these situations efficiently.

Another particular characteristic of ubiquitous networks is that devices may disconnect and be unavailable for long periods of time. In other words, "disconnected" is a normal state, not an exception as in traditional fixed networks. The middleware must support long disconnects without having the applications have to deal with them. In practice, this may seem to the application as if the network was performing extremely slowly, but when the network connection is resumed, the application should be able to continue as if nothing had happened.

Ubiquitous networks are typically based on radio communications (e.g., BlueTooth, GSM, UMTS, WLAN, etc.). Radio links are, by their nature, broadcast media and are therefore also well suited for (local) multicast communications. Unfortunately, BlueTooth for example, goes to great lengths to make it impossible for the application to use multicast, since BlueTooth makes all links point-to-point. Such behavior should be discouraged in a ubiquitous middleware, since the multicast (and broadcast) capabilities of the underlying radio medium come "for free".

27.4.5 Performance Issues

Ubiquitous computing environments present many challenges for building high-performance systems. Many of these challenges stem from the nature of ubiquitous devices, which was discussed in Section 27.2. Because of the different nature of the applications, we must emphasize different factors when looking at the performance of ubiquitous middleware and applications.

Naturally, the more "traditional" performance metrics, such as processor speed, network bandwidth, etc., are also important in ubiquitous computing, but in addition to those, there are several other factors to consider.

For example, ubiquitous applications typically run over wireless networks. Although the bandwidth of wireless networks is increasing, it is doing so at a much slower rate than the bandwidth of wired networks or CPU speeds. This implies that wireless bandwidth should be treated, to some degree, as a "rare commodity", and middleware and protocols should be designed to take this explicitly into account. In other words, applications should not assume that data can be transferred easily from one node to another on demand; instead, applications should be prepared to work with slow connections and even the occasional disconnect.

Furthermore, ubiquitous devices are often very constrained in terms of processing power and memory. This puts a limit on the amount of processing that can be done locally, and further implies that any heavy computation might best be done on a networked server (keeping in mind the constraints of the slower network, as mentioned above). The same applies for the on-board storage of the device. Although CPU power and memory capacity are increasing at a rapid pace, it may not be feasible to equip every single device with a fast CPU and a large amount of memory for reasons of cost and power-efficiency.

Power-efficiency is the third major difference between traditional and ubiquitous applications. Many ubiquitous devices run on batteries and every action they perform consumes the on-board batteries. Like wireless network bandwidth, battery capacities are also growing very slowly (compared to other components) and are likely to be the primary limitation for ubiquitous devices and applications in the near future. Battery life is possibly the most crucial of the performance aspects, since when the battery runs out, the device can no longer function at all.

A high-performing ubiquitous application is therefore not necessarily one which performs its tasks in the shortest time, but one which can take into account the above three factors and be the most efficient in those terms. This may include designing protocols which, for example, avoid periodic maintenance messages (which consume battery power, since they require using the network device and can jam networks), and instead are able to tolerate network partitions and occasional inconsistencies (and thus prolong battery life).

27.5 Peer-to-Peer and Ubiquitous Computing

Peer-to-peer networks and systems are based on the principles of self-organization, resource sharing, and independent devices collaborating to form a larger system. These basic characteristics match well with the typical characteristics of ubiquitous applications, where the conditions are similar. Therefore, it is natural to consider Peer-to-Peer technologies as a building block of ubiquitous computing architectures and applications.

Peer-to-peer networks are typically based on (highly) autonomous peers collaborating to provide the different services. The peers provide the resources for the network and for other peers to use, but individual peers remain independent in their actions. Individual peers are free to go offline and come online as they please. These properties are the cornerstone of Peer-to-Peer organization principle and are one of the main strengths of Peer-to-Peer networks.

In fact, if we look at Peer-to-Peer systems and networks from this organizational point of view, we can abstract their inherent capabilities and properties and apply these same principles and properties to other kinds of systems. By drawing the parallels between Peer-to-Peer organization and the organization of entities in other systems (ubiquitous computing architectures in our case), we can observe the similarities and exploit the power of Peer-to-Peer systems in other fields.

Peer-to-peer principle is an attractive choice for organizing ubiquitous computing systems for several reasons. As we look at ubiquitous computing architectures, we can immediately see many common points with the Peer-to-Peer organization principle. In ubiquitous computing architectures, there are many completely autonomous devices (e.g., sensors, user devices, etc.) scattered in the environment. Each of these devices has some functionality which is important to other devices, i.e., each device provides some resources for all other devices, services, and applications. A device may rely on the information provided by another device in order to complete its function. Furthermore, the mobility of the devices and the limited range of communication implies that, from the point of view of a single device, other devices appear to have highly intermittent connectivity. In some cases, devices may also disconnect in order to conserve battery life.

From the above comparison, we can see a possible mapping of the Peer-to-Peer principle to ubiquitous computing architectures. At first sight, this mapping appears quite straight-forward, due to the large similarities between the two systems.

The main area of application for the Peer-to-Peer organization principle in ubiquitous computing lies in building communication architectures for ubiquitous computing. As mentioned earlier, the key focus in ubiquitous computing lies in efficient communication architectures which allow the different devices to offer their services to other entities in the environment. Such communication architectures exhibit many Peer-to-Peer-like properties and can benefit from the same principles as traditional Peer-to-Peer systems in the Internet. However, ubiquitous computing has a host of special requirements, which stem from the nature of the applications and devices, as we have presented above. This implies, that the traditional Peer-to-Peer solutions may not be applicable in ubiquitous computing.

Before Peer-to-Peer solutions can be applied to ubiquitous computing, we need to evaluate their suitability. As our discussion above shows, there are many similarities between Peer-to-Peer systems and ubiquitous computing architectures which suggest the possibility to leverage Peer-to-Peer technologies in ubiquitous computing. However, many of the constraints and special requirements of ubiquitous computing make traditional Peer-to-Peer solutions unsuitable for ubiquitous computing. Peer-to-peer systems are based on overlay networks, which require significant effort just to maintain the overlay structure. For ubiquitous devices, such effort implies large battery consumption, just to be able to send messages to other devices. Traditional Peer-to-Peer solutions implicitly assume that the peers are PCs connected to the Internet with high-bandwidth links (where even a 56 kbps modem link would be called high-bandwidth for a ubiquitous sensor with only a few bits per second infrared communication means!). Traditional Peer-to-Peer solutions need to be adapted to handle the high dynamics and unpredictability of ubiquitous computing.

Abstracting the communication components into a middleware layer is especially important for ubiquitous computing. Even in the traditional Internet, code for communication has to handle several different kinds of failures (DNS failures, connection failures, etc.). In ubiquitous computing, the number of possible failures is much higher (see Section 27.4) and we cannot assume application programmers to be able to handle all possible errors. Indeed, this would be the same as assuming that the application programmer would be aware of all possible situations in which her application would be used. Clearly this is not feasible. A middleware layer is responsible for hiding the communication problems from the application and provides support for the application programmer.

Peer-to-peer middleware for ubiquitous computing is still a topic of ongoing research. The requirements for such a middleware are known, as outlined in Section 27.4, but there are still many open challenges. As a conclusion, we can say that Peer-to-Peer technologies and principles are a promising building block for ubiquitous computing middleware.

27.6 Research Challenges in Ubiquitous Peer-to-Peer Computing

In this section, we will outline the major research challenges in the area of ubiquitous Peer-to-Peer infrastructures. Each of the topics mentioned below has several interesting research problems, which need to be solved before ubiquitous infrastructures can become a commodity. Some of these problems have been studied in the more traditional computing world, but whether existing solutions are applicable to ubiquitous computing (due to the special requirements) remains an open question.

27.6.1 Heterogeneous Devices

The heterogeneity of devices and networks in the ubiquitous computing world is a big challenge. Applications and communication protocols must adapt themselves to a variety of platforms and conditions. This includes running on low-power devices with slow connections, as well as high-power servers with gigabit networks. In addition, networks in the ubiquitous computing world are typically wireless and therefore highly unpredictable, both in terms of available bandwidth, as well as the availability of a network connection in the first place.

27.6.2 Efficient Algorithms

Because of the constrained nature of ubiquitous devices, we need efficient algorithms for the organization of, and communication in, these networks.

On the one hand, the algorithms must be efficient in terms of the algorithmic performance; for example, a search algorithm must find the desired object or service in a short time. This aspect of efficiency can in some cases be directly adopted from the algorithms in the traditional systems, but may need to be adapted to the specifics of the ubiquitous application.

On the other hand, considering the constrained resources of ubiquitous devices, the algorithms must be efficient in how they use the available resources. This includes taking into account things such as signaling overhead, and possibly leveraging compression technologies for cases where we can trade off CPU and battery power for better bandwidth utilization.

27.6.3 Security and Privacy

In a world where a multitude of devices are scattered around and are observing their environment, security and privacy issues are of paramount importance. Security allows us to authenticate the devices with which we communicate (and vice versa!) and is an important building block for establishing trust. The world of ubiquitous computing is moving in a direction where more and more of our everyday activities are taking place in the digital world and therefore it is vital that we (as human users) are able to trust the devices and architectures handling our affairs.

Likewise, in a world with many devices observing us, privacy issues have an important role to play. These issues include the technical problems of handling and preserving user privacy, through the use of technologies such as anonymous (or pseudonymous) communications and transactions. Another aspect of privacy concerns the non-technical issues, such as user acceptance, and more generally, the expectations of the society as a whole with regard to what level of privacy can be expected in widespread adoption of ubiquitous computing architectures.

27.6.4 Scalable Architectures

Due to the large number of devices in ubiquitous infrastructures (millions, even billions in a global infrastructure), the underlying architecture must be very scalable to handle them. This ties in with the efficient algorithms, but also goes a step beyond, by extending the notion of efficiency to the global level. The architectures must be designed in such a way as to allow the efficient algorithms to work and enable a seamless interaction between any components that need to communicate.

27.6.5 Next Generation Peer-to-Peer Middleware

Probably the most important challenge in the research on ubiquitous infrastructures is the development of a next generation middleware for ubiquitous applications. As we discussed in Section 27.4, the requirements of such a Peer-to-Peer middleware are already laid down, but a lot of work is still needed to turn those requirements into an efficient and scalable infrastructure.

Peer-to-peer technologies are an attractive building block, since they, by their nature, support autonomous self-organization, intermittent ad hoc networks, and exploitation of resources of the edge devices.

27.7 Summary

In this chapter we have discussed ubiquitous computing architectures and how Peer-to-Peer technologies can be applied to them. We have outlined typical characteristics of ubiquitous applications and analyzed their needs, especially in terms of communication. Efficient communication architectures are a key component in building middleware ubiquitous computing architectures. Middleware is an important building block for ubiquitous computing architectures and asynchronous communication means, such as publish/subscribe provide an interesting basis for communication architectures in ubiquitous computing.

The Peer-to-Peer organization principle can also apply to ubiquitous computing. In the Peer-to-Peer principle, peers act autonomously, but collaborate with other peers to provide services. In a similar vein, ubiquitous computing devices act autonomously, but depend on each other in their actions. Peer-to-peer middleware is an interesting possibility for solving the communication problems in ubiquitous computing and providing an asynchronous communication abstraction to the applications. We finished the chapter by providing an overview of open research problems in the area of ubiquitous Peer-to-Peer infrastructures.

Part IX

Business Applications and Markets

28. Business Applications and Revenue Models

Thomas Hummel (Accenture Technologie Labs)
Steffen Muhle, Detlef Schoder (University of Cologne)

28.1 Introduction

With the maturation of its technology, Peer-to-Peer applications have come increasingly into the focus of business. The promise to do business in a faster, more cost-effective and flexible way has lead to the rise of various start-ups as well as the engagement of established market players. They have created a broad variety of Peer-to-Peer business applications and services that have come to the market. However, there has to be a viable revenue model behind these business applications and services to lead them to economic success. In other words, applications should not only be highly successful in terms of adoption rates, like Instant Messaging, but also in terms of revenue generation. This chapter contains a discussion of revenue models for Peer-to-Peer business applications.

It is certainly questionable whether there is a need for Peer-to-Peer revenue models at all. Peer-to-Peer applications often focus on the principle of reciprocity, i.e., they realize barter structures like the early version of Napster did. But this idea does not always hold, e.g., Peer-to-Peer applications, like Instant Messaging, are provided as an infrastructure. Although indirect revenues from ad space and cross-selling efforts are possible (a driving force behind the free availability of AIM is to strengthen the online community), direct revenue models are still of interest. For example, when digital file exchanges deal with the property rights of third parties and want to reimburse these third parties plus recover their operating costs, a viable business model is required.

Throughout this chapter, potential direct revenue models for Peer-to-Peer applications and the issues they face will be presented. An abstract view will be given that represents a generic Peer-to-Peer interaction and that allows the evaluation of the potential for revenue generation for the parties involved. Specifically, there will be a discussion of the following points:

1. Who are the parties that participate in a Peer-to-Peer interaction, direct and indirect, in other words, who are the players that need to be part of a revenue model so that they can recover their costs?
2. What are the open issues that Peer-to-Peer revenue models have to resolve?

R. Steinmetz and K. Wehrle (Eds.): P2P Systems and Applications, LNCS 3485, pp. 473-489, 2005.

3. How can these parties potentially recover their cost and earn a margin of profit?

The notion of a service and application style will be introduced, different revenue models will be revealed and their relevant properties will be identified. The abstract view of Peer-to-Peer interaction will be the reference in the analysis of the application/service styles. The discussion at the end of the chapter suggests ways of dealing with the shortcomings from which current revenue models suffer.

28.2 Definitions

28.2.1 Peer-to-Peer Applications and Service Styles

From the user perspective Peer-to-Peer business applications can be classified into four different categories:

- **Instant Messaging**: applications and services for the direct exchange of messages between two or more interacting parties (humans and/or machines).
- **Digital Content Sharing**: applications and services for the exchange of digital content. Compared to simple messages, the generation of digital content is more costly and complex. Furthermore, additional functionality like digital rights management is often connected with the content.
- **Grid Computing**: applications and services that allow customers to send computing tasks to a peer that temporally hosts a server application, which manages the distribution, analysis, integrity checks and security of the data sets to other computers that can offer some processing capacity.
- **Collaboration**: applications and services to work or play in ad hoc groups that do not necessarily include organizational hierarchies. Unlike Instant Messaging, Collaboration applications support working groups particularly with regard to their coordination and cooperation.

All business applications can be provided in an application or a service style. In this chapter, Peer-to-Peer *application style* is defined as the use of software that is either provided as a packaged solution (such as Lotus Instant Messaging, Groove, etc.) or through a set of common definitions and methodologies, i. e. programming models like J2EE and .NET, protocol definitions like Gnutella and the like. The user buys the software and runs it on his own, i.e., no third party is involved. A Peer-to-Peer *service style* is a service provided to third parties which is based on a Peer-to-Peer interaction model. The software is not bought, but its functionality is leased by the user. Therefore a Peer-to-Peer application provided in a service style is not a once-bought-used-forever model.

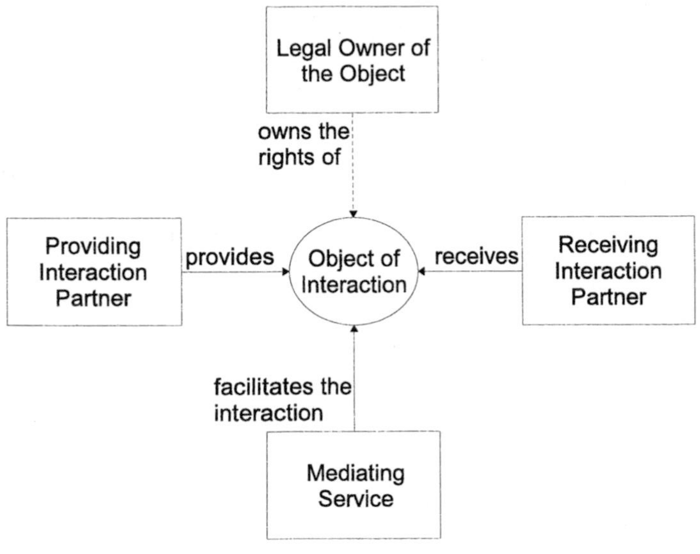

Fig. 28.1: Referential View of Peer-to-Peer Interactions.

28.2.2 A Referential View of Peer-to-Peer Interaction Styles

Looking at the broad variety of different application/service styles that fit the concept of Peer-to-Peer, it is likely that there is no one-size-fits-all revenue model for all these styles. Differentiated considerations are needed which should be guided by a common pattern. In this chapter an abstract reference view of the different Peer-to-Peer interaction styles shall be given, which can then be mapped to different application/ service styles.

At the center of the reference view (Figure 28.1) is the object of interaction. Depending on the relevant application/service style, the object can be a message, a file, a data stream, a transaction, or a data object. Different roles can perform operations on this object, which is provided from a providing interaction partner to a receiving interaction partner. The rights to the object are the property of its legal owner. A mediating service facilitates the interactions involving the object. The following overview outlines this view.

To facilitate the reading of this chapter, the elements of this abstract reference view will be referred to as the Object, Provider, Receiver, Mediator and Owner throughout the remainder of this text. It is important to note that this view refers to roles not to participants. As a matter of fact, a participant can play several roles at the same time. For example, the role of the Provider can be taken by the same participant as the role of the Owner. In specific situations some of the roles can be omitted altogether, e.g., in the case where no Mediator is required to match the Receiver and Provider. Provider and

Receiver can reverse their roles throughout an interaction sequence, i.e., the Receiver can become the Provider in a following interaction step and vice versa.

28.2.3 Business Models and Revenue Models

The terms "business model" and "revenue model" are often used interchangeably. However, for clarification distinctions should be made. A *business model* is the totality of processes and arrangements that define a company's approach to commercial markets in order to sell services and/or goods and generate profits. In contrast, a *revenue model* is part of a business model. It includes all arrangements that permit the participants in business interactions to charge fees that are covered by one or several other participants in order to cover costs and add a margin to create profits.[626]

Revenues can be generated in a direct or indirect way. In the direct way, the receipts come directly from the customer. When an indirect revenue model is adopted, the actual product will be provided for free. The gain is received from a third party who is in one way or another interested in the diffusion of the product. These two categories of possible revenue models can be reassigned (adapted from Laudon and Traver [378]):

- **Indirect revenue models** can be advertisements, affiliate models, or a bundling. When the advertising model is adopted, the third party wants to communicate a sales message that is visible during the usage. It should be considered that the message is influenced by the reputation of the advertising media. In the case of the affiliate model, the vendor receives revenue for passing customers to an affiliate partner, who sells the products or services. For every purchase, the vendor receives a commission. The bundling model is similar onto the affiliate model. The revenue is generated by products or services that are connected to the free offering. Even though the basic service is free, the customer has to pay for the additional offering.
- **Direct revenue models** are sales, transaction fees, and subscriptions. In the sales model the customer pays directly for the object. Two forms have to be distinguished. In the first one, licenses for the Peer-to-Peer business application itself are sold. This model corresponds with the application style. The second form is to use the application as an infrastructure to sell goods or services. If the transaction fee model is used, the company will be assigned the role of the mediating service. It provides a service that facilitates a transaction between the Provider and the Receiver. The Mediator earns a fee for every transaction between them. Unlike the transaction fee model, in the subscription model the fee is paid independently of the actual usage. It is rather paid periodically, e. g. every month or year.

Peer-to-Peer application styles and Peer-to-Peer service styles are not mutually exclusive, e.g., a vendor might sell licenses for the use of specific software and add some specific professional services for which he charges service fees. A Peer-to-Peer software vendor needs to come up with a licensing model, whereas a service provider has to develop an approach for the billing of the service. There are several prerequisites that a viable revenue model needs to fulfil. As an absolute minimum, two important features are required:

- **Differentiated Charging**: A viable revenue model needs to be capable of covering costs and earning a margin of profit. However, in order to be efficient a revenue model needs to provide a differentiated pricing structure, i. e. the capability to charge according to criteria that are tied to the patterns of usage.
- **Allocation Effectiveness**: The capability of a revenue model to create a revenue stream to the appropriate Receiver, i.e., to the party that has incurred the cost, is called allocation effectiveness.

28.3 Revenue Models for Peer-to-Peer Business Application/Service Styles

In the following, the interaction style will be mapped to the reference view. Thus, potential revenue models and issues in the application style setting as well as in the service style setting can be examined.

28.3.1 Instant Messaging

Instant Messaging (IM) refers to applications that enable two participants to exchange information in real time. Typically this is done through typed text messages, but various Instant Messaging applications have extended the functionality to include voice messaging. Although the capability to exchange files has practically become a standard feature in most messaging applications, it will not be discussed here but in the following section on Digital Content Sharing.

Applying the reference view introduced above, the Object is a message and the Owner is identical with the Provider, i.e., the sender of the message. The software usually provides some specific functionalities, like a "buddy list", which provides presence services, i.e., a list of currently logged-on and thus reachable interaction partners. This service, that often includes various other functionalities like finding people based on their profile, does not have to be central. Actually, three primarily different topologies exist which influence possible revenue models for instant messengers. The first one is not really Peer-to-Peer from the technical point of view: In this topology the buddy list service as well as the actual messaging service is provided by a server. However, the communication takes place between two autonomous peers. In the more decentralized design the buddy list is managed by a server but the communication is self-governed by the communication partners. In both cases the Provider of the service acts in the role of the Mediator. As long as the central software is used within the boundaries of a corporate network, the service infrastructure Provider is the internal IT department (or the outsourced equivalent). Once the software is used across organizations, connectivity between the users is required and this can either be an ISP or a Provider of an IM service. If the pure Peer-to-Peer topology is adopted both (the message exchange and the buddy list service) are organized by peers, so that no server is involved. One example for the latter is Skype.

The revenue model for an application style is rather straightforward and can be built around license fees as well as around optional professional services (integration support etc.). There are various models for license fees (e.g., base fee and yearly maintenance fee, upgrade fees, etc.). The vendor faces the challenge of opting for the best one to generate sufficient revenues – always assuming that the application provides enough value to attract buyers and that it generates sufficient revenues to offset costs plus provide a margin of profit.

The situation becomes significantly more complicated when IM is delivered as a service style. Currently the most popular IM services on the Internet are AIM, ICQ, MSN, and Yahoo!. Today these services are available for free. It is sufficient to download and install a client application and attach it to the network of the respective IM service provider. Highly successful services like AIM claim to have 200 million users [411]. Although these figures refer to the number of accounts rather than the real users, Instant Messaging has unquestionably been a huge success in terms of adoption rates. It is clear that a substantial infrastructure is needed to provide the users a stable and convenient service, and obviously there is cost associated with that. Providing the service for free is a viable revenue model only if an indirect one is adopted (one of the main reasons for AOL to provide AIM is to attract users to its ISP service).

An undifferentiated subscription fee for using the service is the simplest possibility. However it is not a very efficient one because it can hardly account for differentiated charging. Heavy users and occasional users would not be discriminated and in the end the difficulty is to strike a pricing scheme that satisfies the occasional as well as the heavy users. Various modifications to this approach could be suggested like a fee per log on, a fee per log on and day, or a fee for the time during which a user periodically connects the mediation server. A periodical connection is necessary for the user to keep his buddy list up-to-date and to notify the server that he is still online. It is clearly more interesting to take a transaction fee and bill for the actual usage, but that is anything but simple. Where IM services are really built as Peer-to-Peer applications (e.g., ICQ [414]), the communication between two participants is direct – i.e., there is no application server which connects them for the message exchange. The only possibility for a third person to find out about a message transfer is by monitoring the network providers' hubs (on the network level). This makes charging per usage quite difficult – a billing system would need to be able to get hold of, count and attribute network packets to specific users. If the architecture of the services is realised in pure Peer-to-Peer style, which is totally without a mediation service, even the realization of a pay per time model is problematic. However, where IM services are built in a client-server model (like MSN [414]) this problem is minor, because the application server has control over the conversations and because it can log the usage.

New problems arise with the emergence of interactive agents. Although these agents have not found a wide diffusion yet, they can provide additional services for the user of Instant Messaging. To put it simply, interactive agents are pieces of software accessible through the IM infrastructure as if they were real users. Advanced agents such as Active Buddy even provide interaction with a rather sophisticated natural language dialogue [130]. Such interactive agents enable the execution of transactions over the Instant Messaging infrastructure in a way which is very convenient for the user [439]. These agents deliver for example important news or act as a text based service hotline, which can help to solve customer problems. It is possible that they will play a role in the currently emerging web services. IM services today have only weak possibilities to deal with interactive agents on their networks. Even if they succeed in detecting them (which is already only possible if an interactive agent does not behave in the similar way as a real IM client), they face the challenge of understanding what exactly the conversation is all about. The trouble is that a charging approach that builds on the amount of information exchanged is not a good fit with these agents. Human-human interaction is often chatty - a human-application interaction which aims at performing a transaction should be expected to be fairly brief. As long as the IM service provider has no means of differentiating between a transaction and a conversation, it has no means of performing any type of differentiated billing either. Appropriate charging is only possible if the IM infrastructure service provider owns the interactive agent or has at least an alliance with the Provider of the agent. Microsoft has good reasons to weave its MSN Messenger deeply into the .NET services infrastructure and build it on a client-server model. It remains to be said that three popular IM services go into the market of the application style IM or have already failed in doing so: MSN already bundles the MSN client with Windows XP and sells an application named "Live Communications Server", whereas AOL announced that it would stop developing "AIM Enterprise" in order to cooperate with IMlogic. Yahoo! dropped its messenger because instead of buying the business version, the free version was being used by companies, as Yahoo! stated [345].

Judging from the criteria that have been defined for viable business models above, the application style allows for a differentiated charging through various licensing models and fulfils the criteria of allocation effectiveness (as long as the software is not illegally copied). However, when it comes to a service style, revenue models for Instant Messaging face quite significant challenges with respect to a differentiated charging structure. Allocation effectiveness is not a problem for centralized and hybrid Peer-to-Peer architectures since IM clients need to log on to the service provider's network. However, this becomes a problem in pure Peer-to-Peer architectures. In this case it is rather difficult to trace the communication between users in order to bring it to account.

28.3.2 Digital Content Sharing

File sharing has become infamous through the quick rise and fall of Napster. Although Napster collapsed with its first model, its place has been taken over by others such as KaZaa, Morpheus, Grokster, and eDonkey. The music industry is amidst a ferocious fight against the free exchange of music by submitting empty music files or files that contain only part of a song plus some affixed commercial content. Beside these technical weapons, the music industry threatens users and service providers with lawsuits. By means of rigorous penalties the users should be discouraged from sharing illegal media files. For example, the RIAA made a settlement with four students in the USA who ran a service for searching MP3 files in their college network. The students pay penalties of between $ 12,000 and $ 17,000 each [83]. In Germany, a trainee settled to the amount of EUR 8,000 [478].

Whatever the fate of the various file sharing applications and the communities behind them will be in the end, they have shaken up the value chain of the music industry and they might well lead to changes in business models [310]. Although such digital media exchanges have become the best-known examples, they should not be mistaken for the only possible instantiation of this application/service style. Two points are important here:

1. The exchange of entertainment media files is only one specific type of content exchange. Any other digital content can also be exchanged, e.g., design documents, training documents, reports etc. Thus, Digital Content Sharing can be used as a decentralized form of knowledge management. If an adequate index service exists, the documents containing the knowledge of the network participants can be accessed without forcing them to save these documents on a central server.
2. The definition needs to be broader than just file sharing. It should include streaming content as well since this type of content can also be recorded and exchanged in a Peer-to-Peer manner (such an extension to include streaming content clearly leads to specific challenges in the technological

implementation, but it does not change the considerations for revenue models).

In terms of the reference view introduced above, the roles of the Provider and Receiver are obvious. But the most important point is that the Owner is not necessarily the Provider or Receiver – he can be a third party. Depending on the specific implementation of the file exchange, there can be a Mediator providing a central catalogue of contents available as well as providing additional services, even though that is not a necessity for digital content exchanges. Napster, for example, was essentially a Mediator; it ran a central directory to which the client's software connected in order to match the Sender with the Receiver. In this case, only the exchange of the files as such was performed in a Peer-to-Peer manner. Peer-to-Peer Digital Content Sharing applications that are built on the Gnutella protocol do not need a Mediator. They work on a pure Peer-to-Peer model even for matching Sender and Receiver [396].

As an application style, software of Digital Content Sharing can be implemented in corporate networks, e.g., for the facilitation of knowledge exchange between employees. Peer-to-Peer collaboration tools also typically provide such Peer-to-Peer file exchange functionalities. Again, the vendor of such software can adopt various license models and provide consulting services for implementation, training, and operations to create additional revenues. The application style is not limited to the borders of a single corporation. Various Digital Content Sharing communities can be connected across several organizations in a more or less ad hoc manner. Furthermore, a mediating service Provider could act in such intercorporate Peer-to-Peer exchanges by providing catalogue services for the content supplied by different organizations as well as other value added services. This can be the software vendor, the participating organizations, or a third party. It brings us to a service style type of Digital Content Sharing. If the Provider is also the Owner, then the revenue model is fairly straightforward and the Provider can charge a fee for the transfer of the object.

Things become significantly more complicated if Digital Content Sharing applications are operated in a service style and if the Owner is not identical with the Provider. The most prominent case is Napster, which made its market entry as a free service and allegedly intended to create a revenue stream from advertisements. In principle, other revenue models would also have been possible, like membership fees for subscriptions, log in fees, or even a match making fee. However, given the legally precarious situation of the whole approach, such revenue models would have been debatable anyway. Today there exists no serious Peer-to-Peer service for distributing legal content. Whatever the real business idea of the makers of Napster and the look-alikes is, the real problem is that the legal owner of the rights of the exchanged files is not a participant in the transactions and hence he can not cover his costs. BMG, EMI, Sony, Universal Music and Warner Music never participated in the original Napster transactions, and the BMG Napster did not do more than stop the illegal activity. For digital content exchanges that embrace a Mediator approach, one could think of implementing a billing step into the content exchange, where any or both of the participants are required to pay fees for exchanging content and those could then be paid to the Owner. If, for the moment, it is assumed that this would be technically feasible, then the Mediator adopts the role of an aggregating middleman for the content which can be conveniently searched and compiled.

But it is questionable whether anybody other than the Owner should be involved as a Provider. Why should the content first be bought from an Owner and then be sold to another Receiver when at the same time the Owner needs to be part of that transaction again and he needs to be properly reimbursed? Even though this distribution model could lead to technical advantages, its economical benefits are not clear. It would be easier for the Receiver to buy the content directly from the Provider. One might argue, however, that the intermediary function can add additional value: Today's digital content exchanges integrate usually the recordings from different music groups which would not be the case with separate download sites. But that is hardly convincing – the music industry could run a joint catalogue service without major problems since the artists are regularly bound through exclusive contracts. Finally, there is the question of control. Digital content exchanges perform an unbundling of content and provide a possibility for free reassembly through the user: Rather than buying a complete album, consumers can buy selected titles only and create their own specific albums to their tastes. The music industry and artists alike have good reasons to be reluctant to agree on the unbundling and recompilation of the content. It is rather difficult to determine an appropriate price for popular as opposed to less popular titles. Apart from that, a full CD can be sold for a higher price than, e.g., the three popular titles only [125, 604]. Anyhow, it seems that the music industry cannot surrender the market demand for digital content. Several distribution services have started up recently, e.g., the Apple iTunes store. But nearly all of the serious upcoming Providers are based on a client-server architecture because more control over the distribution process is guaranteed. In short: taking an additional party into the transaction simply because he or she happens to have the digital content at hand does not add any clear economic value. It is more reasonable if the Provider once again becomes identical with the Owner, in other words, the record companies sell the content themselves or with the help of a few centralized licensed sellers. Then it is likely to look more like iTunes, which follows a client-server-based approach rather than a Peer-to-Peer exchange.

Finally all these considerations will only hold for Peer-to-Peer exchanges if a *billing scheme* can be built into the digital content exchange and if the fees can be allocated accordingly. If no Mediator is involved, e.g., if a digital content exchange is built on the decentralized Gnutella protocol, the enforcement of a payment will be very difficult to achieve since interactions are not centrally managed in the first place. Furthermore, there is always the possibility to copy and forward the contents once a Receiver has them. A billing scheme, even a well-built one, is not a content protection scheme, and even if contents are bought legally once, they can be illegally copied infinite times thereafter. Consequently, any (legal) revenue model will need to provide for the *protection of digital rights.* In addition, it will need to *enforce the payments* to the appropriate legal owner. As simple as this may sound, there are difficult technical challenges to solve, and the question of whether digital content can be protected at all is still open [267]. The failure of the SDMI initiative is quite an instructive example. The music industry asked the Multimedia Telecom Italia Lab to create an encryptable and thus a safe digital music format. The lab agreed and promised the amount of $ 25,000 to those who managed to break the code. When the group of people that had managed to break the code wanted to publish their accepted paper, the music industry filed for a court injunction and the paper was banned from publication. Prof. Edward Felten from the University of Princeton put the paper on the Internet, where it can still be downloaded [136]. Another problem with digital rights protection systems is that the Providers always have to make tradeoffs between the security of such systems and the usability. If the protection system is too restrictive, then it can deter potential customers from buying the media file. Whether the music industry will win the fight against digital content exchanges is an open question. In the end, it might be wiser for the music industry to adopt a new business model instead. Rather than trying to crush the online exchange communities, the music industry could try to develop them and own the communities [310]. This way, through word of mouth advertising, marketing affects can be achieved. This applies especially to smaller labels and independent artists.

If these considerations are put in the context of the criteria for viable revenue models introduced above, it can be stated that there is currently no viable revenue model for Peer-to-Peer digital content exchanges in service style and it is likely that there will never be one. The point is that it is very difficult – if not impossible – to enforce allocation effectiveness when Me is in the game. Digital content exchanges, where the Owner is identical with the Provider, face comparable issues if the Provider does not sell the Object itself but if he only sells limited rights to its usage. As soon as digital content is provided to a Receiver, it is vulnerable to copying and handing over to third parties. Differentiated charging, on the other hand, is easier to achieve since digital content exchanges could be priced individually. The real issue to resolve for digital content exchanges is its protection at such a level that the customers are restrained from infringing the copyright. If protection needs to be given up, new approaches will have to be found for the business models.

One example is the approach of Marillion, a group that has a long history of releasing records the traditional way. It has built up a faithful community of fans over the years. When Marillion's contract with their record label expired, they decided not to renew it. Instead they promoted the new record using the Internet. The band members wrote to their fan base and asked if they would be willing to pay for the CD in advance in order to finance the making of the record. The response was overwhelming. Some fans even offered to pay for two CDs "if that would help them". When the production was finished, the CD was offered through the band's web site – not for download, but for ordinary purchase through a secure web link. It remains to be said, however, that there are other examples of such approaches that failed, e.g., Stephen King's experiment with an online book. A recent remarkable approach without protection is addressed by the Potato System [493]. This system tries to induce the users to license the media files by offering them the possibility of earning a commission. When a user registers a media file and hands this file to a friend he gets a commission if his friend buys a license as well. So the users are motivated to license and to recommend the file. But whether this model will work is questionable. Due to the absence of copyright protection, the Owner has no chance to enforce his rights. It is likely that this will be the main obstacle for music labels participating in this model.

28.3.3 Grid Computing

Grid Computing refers to the coordinated utilization of distributed computing resources [544]. Of all Peer-to-Peer applications, Grid Computing is the one that least fits the definition of Peer-to-Peer computing in its contemporary realizations that are suitable for industrial use. Their computational model is regularly client-server-based rather than decentralized. None of today's models work without a special server that manages the distribution, analysis, integrity checks and security of the data sets. Peer-to-Peer in this case refers to the idea of having complex problems broken down into parts that are solved more or less independently by peers and that are then put together to one solution. In doing so peers act autonomously to a large extend. They can choose, if and when they are willing to provide their computing power. Examples for applications that use this computing model are SETI@Home [28] and MoneyBee [426]. However, if the vision of Grid Computing in its pure understanding should become true, peers should not only be able to provide computing power, but to demand the resources available in the network.

The point of Grid Computing is more about the work getting done by peers than about the organization of the work [178]. Grid Computing has not been very commonly used so far. Early applications in this area have focused on the aggregation of computer processing cycles to solve complex mathematical problems. Future applications can be expected in various areas, such as Biological and Chemical Engineering, Economics and Financial Modelling. It is interesting to see that IBM's patent on distributed computing technologies was ranked as one of the five top patents to watch by the MIT technology review in 2001 [583].

If Grid Computing is mapped to the reference view, the Provider(s) can be interpreted as the one(s) providing available computing power and the Receiver as the one using this computing power to solve complex problems. The providing interaction partner can as well be seen as the one who provides the task to be processed. In this chapter, the focus lies on the computing power because of the interest in its payment. The Mediator is the central server application, which manages the distribution, analysis, integrity checks, and security of the data sets.

Dougherty et al. have distinguished four different revenue models for Grid Computing: the enterprise software sale, the public Internet exchange, an application service provider (ASP) and a B2B exchange model, though the ASP and B2B models "have not yet developed and may never develop" [178, p. 114]. The enterprise software sale model is identical with the view of an application style, i.e., the revenue model is about selling distributed computing software for installation behind the firewall or "enterprise grid". The rationale is to provide more control over the contributing resources which will lead to higher availability and better security. Apart from that, the LAN/WAN capacities typically allow the transport of much larger data sets. A revenue model is typically straightforward and consists of license fees and professional services for implementation.

The public Internet exchange or "mixed grid" approach is of the service style. The idea is to provide access to vast computing power on a worldwide scale. An example is Moneybee where Grid Computing is used to predict stock prices and exchange rates. Participants download and install a free screen saver that uses the idle PC resources when the screen saver is on in order to perform complex operations that are downloaded from a Moneybee server. Thereafter results are uploaded to the Moneybee server [426].

With respect to revenue models, Grid Computing is a quite different situation than the other Peer-to-Peer interaction styles. As far as the Mediator is concerned, there is a need to distinguish whether the service manages the Grid Computing tasks on behalf of a third party or whether the mediating service is identical with the Receiver. If the work is done on behalf of a third party (which corresponds to the ASP model in [178]), the cost for the mediating service plus a margin will need to be charged. If the mediating service is provided by the Receiver, then the business utilization of the grid computation results will have to cover the cost. In both cases, the issue is how to determine the computing cost per Provider and how to compensate the Providers. Mediators currently ask users to donate their excess resources. In exchange, they offer a portion of these resources to non-profit organizations, or else they provide "sweepstakes entries" for prizes. The Providers at Moneybee contribute their resources free of charge. Their incentive is to get part of the results (forecasts for stock prices and exchange rates) that the system generates. It may certainly be that many other Grid Computing tasks are taken on by Providers in a similar way for free (e.g., when they are bundled with attractive add-ons like the lively graphics of a screen saver hosting the client application as SETI@home does). What, however, if the Providers want to be reimbursed monetarily for offering their excess resources? From the technical point of view, it is not very difficult to employ a pay-per-use model where the client application records resource usage and provides the data to the mediating service which then reimburses based on usage. The real problem is that the price paid for the resource supply is likely to be rather low and (micro-) payments will need to be organized in a very efficient way, if the transaction is not to use up all the benefit. It is doubtful whether financial incentives will be capable of attracting a sufficient number of Providers – at the end of the day a non monetary incentive seems to be the better idea.

In summary, even though Grid Computing probably has the most straightforward revenue model of the core Peer-to-Peer applications, it still faces the challenge of creating enough business to generate sufficient micro payments to attract a sufficient subscriber base. Judging from the criteria for revenue models, there are no problems regarding the allocation effectiveness or efficiency. The questions is whether Grid Computing will create sufficient business value to earn its own living, once Providers want to charge for the use of their resources.

28.3.4 Collaboration

Collaboration supporting Groupware applications have been around for about fifteen years with differential success in providing functions beyond email and workflow. Typically groupware functionality includes some of the functions of email, chat, bulletin boards, calendaring/scheduling, file sharing (push and pull models), and search. Today it is available in different facets of existing client-server tools. Peer-to-Peer concepts can add some flexibility that client-server-based groupware lacks today, such as facilitated personalized categorization of data and information, and the creation of ad hoc working groups across organizations [560]. In the following, Groupware applications that are used in the business context, will be considered. In this context the workgroups are composed of defined and authenticated members. For that reason, generally no problems arise in respect of copyright protection. The files are not shared blindly, but are given to the other group members to enable cooperation.

Like Instant Messaging and Digital Context Sharing, Groupware applications can be built according to three major topology types: Within the first, communication is handled by a server. Thus Peer-to-Peer in its pure conception is not achieved. If the second topology is adopted, the communication will take place between the clients, but a server gives additional services. Within the third, no server is involved at all. According to the reference view, the Mediator can be the server which facilitates the communication or which offers additional services, depending on the topology type. The Provider and Receiver are the communication partners of the workgroup, whereas the Object is the message or document that is exchanged between them. As described, the Provider generally is the legal owner of the Object or is at least authorised to hand it on to the Receiver.

The method of selling groupware as an application style is unlikely to change with new architectures underlying the software. Various licensing models as introduced in Section 28.3.1 can be used. A special opportunity arises from the complexity of groupware applications via the aggregation of different functions and their high integration in daily work. It can be assumed that a comparatively high demand for professional services exists.

If groupware applications are hosted and brought to the users in the form of a service style, the above considerations for the core applications of Instant Messaging and Digital Content Sharing can be carried forward. A transaction-based billing can only be arranged if a central instance that can observe the usage of the service is used. In the case where the communication is held by a server, a transaction-based fee can be accounted for by the amount of transferred data or the usage time. Otherwise, only the usage of the services provided by the server can be brought into account, e.g., the catalogue service for members and files, memory to store files of temporary offline peers, or security services such as logging. Whether it is possible to adopt the service style in the case of a completely decentralized architecture is questionable. In this case, the considerations of Instant Messaging apply. It should be added that the Provider of a Peer-to-Peer collaboration service style should consider whether he wants to bill for every user or for a complete group. It is inherent in collaboration that the work between two members can also benefit the other group members. So it seems adequate to leave the choice of accounting method to the customer.

With respect to the criteria for revenue models the danger is that allocation effectiveness cannot be ensured. If the infrastructure employs a real Peer-to-Peer model, the revenue model will face efficiency challenges. It is the bundling of various services (such as IM and File Sharing and other, potentially non-Peer-to-Peer services) that makes groupware interesting. Revenue models for groupware service styles can then be built around various other criteria. The Peer-to-Peer functionality is only one of them.

28.4 Discussion

Summarizing the considerations, it can be concluded that revenue models for Peer-to-Peer application styles are not different from revenue models for traditional application styles. Revenue models for Peer-to-Peer service styles face important challenges, especially in the areas of Instant Messaging and Collaboration (where differentiated charging is difficult to achieve) as well as in digital content exchanges (where allocation effectiveness is difficult to achieve). Because Instant Messaging and Collaboration Providers only make infrastructure available and because digital content exchange affects copyrights belonging to third parties, these three applications require an accounting centre. However such a centre is difficult to build into Peer-to-Peer architecture. That is not the problem with adopting revenue models for Grid Computing, which least faces issues of the core Peer-to-Peer applications. The transaction only takes place between Provider and Receiver, so that a central instance has not to be paid. But still, the overhead of administering (micro-)payments is likely to diminish the attractiveness of these revenue models.

The open question is what kind of strategies the different parties (Mediators, Owners, etc.) could employ to increase their revenue. Until now, the focus has been on direct revenue models for specific Peer-to-Peer interactions, in order to understand what kind of issues charging and payment mechanisms they will face. The focus on a revenue model for just one specific interaction, as initially considered, is a rather tight restriction. As a matter of fact, real world examples of Peer-to-Peer applications follow more a bundling approach. Examples of service models are AIM as a means of fostering the AOL online community and the close integration of MSN in the .NET infrastructure. The benefits of bundling digital information goods as well as price discrimination are well known [49, 50, 604] and the various Peer-to-Peer areas could very well take advantage of this approach.

Instant Messaging services could be bundled with services which use the existing infrastructure and which extends the basic services. One possibility is to provide additional services through interactive agents. IM services would then give access to agents that provide various services. These services can be rather rudimentary, like information services (access to news, stock quotes, and the like) or advanced, like a secure access to bank accounts, hosted personal calendars etc. This does not mean that the IM service provider controls the bank accounts or calendars. It is sufficient that it provides a ubiquitous infrastructure that conveniently integrates with applications of those providing the services in the first place (e.g., banks). These services will become even more valuable if they are combined with contextual information. For Example, mobile users could be given instant information based on their current location through an interactive agent. These services fall under the label "Location Based Services". IM service providers would need to cooperate with the companies offering these services to set up the required applications and infrastructure as well as to provide convenient yellow pages so that the IM access can be found easily by anybody using the IM services. There are interesting opportunities for price discrimination as well. Another possibility for bundling is shown by Skype. The Luxembourgian company offers a fully decentralized Peer-to-Peer Instant Messenger providing a VoIP infrastructure that allows making telephone calls between peers for free. The beta-version of Skype was made public at the end of August 2003. Due to the easy installation process, the easy-to-use user interface and the good sound quality, Skype could – as it stated – adopt 10 million users in the first year, with more than 600,000 users having logged on on average [199]. So, it was successful in adopting a huge user community. This community gives Skype a user base to establish a revenue model based on a costly service called SkypeOut. The latter started at the end of July 2004 allowing users to make prepaid calls in conventional telecommunication networks. It is conceivable that Skype could use its VoIP infrastructure for further services, e.g., for a radio program or for music distribution. For both IM bundling revenue models, the very basic and rudimentary IM services could still be free (not the least since even a small fee can put communities that have grown accustomed to free-of-charge using at the risk of breaking apart). Additional services could be charged on a pay-per-use basis. Premium services for secure access (e.g., for connections to bank agents) could have a base subscription fee.

When it comes to *Digital Content Sharing*, it is currently unclear how the battle between file exchanging and the music (or other, e.g., film) industry will finally turn out. But as described above, it might be a better strategy to try owning the communities. Clearly, owning a community would hardly be possible if the participants of that community were required to pay for something that they could get for free somewhere else. Once again, the way to make such communities work would be to bundle the digital content with other information goods that are not easily available through illegal content exchanges. Examples would be reductions for concert tickets, fan articles that could be ordered exclusively through the community, chat services with the artists, competitions where authentic belongings from the artists can be won.

Bundling is not really a remedy for *Grid Computing* revenue models. If the transfer of the (micro-) payments generates too much overhead, then revenue in the sense of a pecuniary compensation might not be the way to go. However, providing information goods as a reimbursement could be feasible. For example, the screen saver running the distributed computing task might not just be made of lively graphics but it might provide an information channel, such as Moneybee does (even though Moneybee is not Peer-to-Peer) [426]. These information channels can report parts of the grid-wide computed results news independent of the computing task. At the end of the day, that approach brings the revenue model back to barter-like structures.

Services for supporting *Collaboration* have possibilities for bundling similar to IM. Basic services like document handover and communication can be provided for free. Additional services, which fall back on central components, can be charged per use. These central components can be especially catalogue, buffering and security services. These services are not required for smaller workgroups and Collaboration tasks, but they might become essential with rising requirements.

29. Peer-to-Peer Market Management

Jan Gerke, David Hausheer (ETH Zurich)

This chapter focuses on the *economic* aspects of Peer-to-Peer networks. In particular, it describes the most important requirements and presents a basic architecture for a *market-managed* Peer-to-Peer system supporting commercial applications going beyond pure file sharing. In general Peer-to-Peer systems can be used to share *any* kind of resource, including but not limited to, computing power, storage space, network capacity, files, and any combination thereof, *e.g.*, online games or multimedia streams. In the following, the term *service* will be used to refer to the individual provision of goods or resources by peers. The main goal is a completely decentralized and generic marketplace for efficient trading of such services among peers.

It has been observed in Peer-to-Peer file sharing applications, that in the absence of appropriate economic and social mechanisms, Peer-to-Peer systems can suffer from the behavior of selfish peers, which do not cooperate [11]. This is also known as the *free-rider problem.* As peers are autonomous entities, they need to be given the right *incentives* for offering services to other peers and to behave correctly. Without any central regulator, this is clearly a non-trivial problem to be solved. Any approach has to consider both economic and technical aspects in an integrated manner. This chapter tries to investigate how a technically viable *and* incentive-compatible Peer-to-Peer system can be built. Two case studies are presented which show how particular parts of this given problem can be solved.

The remainder of this chapter is organized as follows. Section 29.1 derives key requirements for a market-managed Peer-to-Peer system based on the main problems identified. Section 29.2 describes the architecture of such a system and outlines its core elements and mechanisms. Section 29.3 then presents two specific approaches towards a Peer-to-Peer market. First, a Peer-to-Peer middleware is presented which enables the architecture and focusses on service negotiation and management aspects. Second, Peer-to-Peer double auctions are described, which make it possible to extend the system with a completely decentralized pricing mechanism. Finally, Section 29.4 concludes this chapter.

29.1 Requirements

A set of key requirements need to be met in order to support real-world applications by the design of a market-oriented Peer-to-Peer architecture. The

R. Steinmetz and K. Wehrle (Eds.): P2P Systems and Applications, LNCS 3485, pp. 491-507, 2005.

main goal is to support market mechanisms, while maintaining the technical benefits of Peer-to-Peer networks. The core functional and non-functional requirements for such an architecture are derived from the various problems currently observed in many Peer-to-Peer systems.

29.1.1 Main Problems

Peer-to-Peer systems are based on the idea that peers offer services to other peers. Ideally and in the absence of a monetary payment system, each peer should contribute as much as it uses from other peers. However, as peers are autonomous entities acting in a rational way, it is unlikely that such cooperation is going to happen without appropriate incentives for peers to share their resources. In fact, it was shown in [11] that 70% of Gnutella users share no files at all. Thus, many users in Gnutella compete for the resources offered by only a few peers, which leads to a major degradation of the overall system performance.

Some Peer-to-Peer systems use specific accounting or reputation mechanisms to deal with this problem, such as BitTorrent's tit-for-tat mechanism [128], eMule's credit system [589], or KaZaA's peer points [558]. However, most of these mechanisms are purely file sharing-oriented and can thus hardly be used for other types of services. Moreover, due to weak security measures these mechanisms can usually not be applied to commercial purposes.

Another major problem faced in Peer-to-Peer networks, is the fact that individual peers are usually unreliable, i.e. they may be faulty or even act maliciously. Peers may often join and leave the system, lose messages or stored data, or deliberately misuse or harm the system. Replication can help to increase data availability and reliability, however, without appropriate synchronisation techniques replicated data may quickly become inconsistent. In a commercial environment this problem becomes even more essential. A peer may increase its own benefit by acting maliciously against potential competitors, *e.g.*, by not forwarding other peers' service offers. It is hardly feasible to use accounting mechanisms or payments as an incentive to fulfill such basic tasks, as it may be difficult to check whether a particular task has been performed correctly or not. Also, the necessary accounting effort may quickly exceed the effort for the actual task.

As a consequence of decentralisation and the potentially large size of a Peer-to-Peer network, the efficient and scalable design of appropriate search mechanisms and other distributed tasks is another difficult problem. Existing Peer-to-Peer overlay infrastructures such as Pastry or Chord (cf. Chapter 8) allow for efficient request routing, but have limited support against malicious peers or insecure networks. In fact, many Peer-to-Peer mechanisms currently do not consider malicious behavior at all.

29.1.2 Functional Requirements

The following three main functional goals form the basis for a completely decentralized and generic Peer-to-Peer marketplace:

Service Support
The targeted Peer-to-Peer system needs to support completely different services, including purely resource-based services such as processing power, storage, or transportation, as well as higher level services such as content or software applications going beyond pure file sharing. Also, combinations of existing services offered by different peers need to be supported, to create new, value-added services. The service usage model described in Section 29.2.2 illustrates how such combinations of distributed services may look like.

Market-Based Management
The most important goal is the creation of a marketplace for trading different services, managed by true market mechanisms which provide appropriate incentives. On the one hand, the traditional way for this is by introducing a currency that can be used in exchange for the services being provided. On the other hand, barter trade is a suitable alternative which has to be supported, too. Barter is a simple form of trade where services are directly exchanged against other services, *e.g.*, a peer may only download a file if it also provides one. The market model described in Section 29.2.1 further details market-related aspects of the Peer-to-Peer architecture.

Decentralization
Today, many Internet-based marketplaces such as eBay [183] are based on centralized infrastructures. However, a true Peer-to-Peer-based system must use only Peer-to-Peer mechanisms which must be able to function without any central components. Only this type of approach offers the full advantage of the Peer-to-Peer concept and ensures that no central point of failure exists.

29.1.3 Non-functional Requirements

Apart from the key functional goals, a market-based Peer-to-Peer system is subject to the following non-functional requirements:

Efficiency

The adopted core mechanisms should lead to an economically efficient allocation and use of the services being traded among the market participants. Economic efficiency is reached when the services are allocated in a way which maximizes the overall social benefit of all participants. Additionally, as far as the technical design of the mechanisms is concerned, an efficient use of technical resources like network capacity, memory space, and processing power has to be achieved. In a distributed system, network resources (i.e. communication bandwidth) determine clearly the main bottleneck. Thus, size and number of exchanged messages have to be minimized.

Scalability

With respect to the technical performance, a solution should be capable to operate under any load, i.e. any number of market participants or services being offered. A system is scalable if the performance does not decrease as the load increases. A centralized system does not scale well under these circumstances, because the load on it increases as more participants make use of it. Therefore, a central system can quickly become overloaded, especially if no centralized load-balancing concepts are applied. In contrast, Peer-to-Peer systems benefit from the characteristic that the load caused by a participating peer can be compensated by those additional resources provided by that peer. Emerging Peer-to-Peer overlay infrastructures (cf. Chapter 21) benefit from this advantage and provide, in addition, scalable and efficient routing mechanisms which can be used for object replication and load-balancing purposes.

Reliability

It is important that a system designed for real-world applications is available continuously and performs correctly and securely even in the case of individual failures. Centralized systems are highly vulnerable against total failures or Denial-of-Service attacks which can basically make a system unusable. Peer-to-Peer systems are by design more robust against such failures or attacks. But at the same time they can suffer from the fact that those peers are autonomous entities, which may not behave as intended by the designer of the mechanism as mentioned earlier. A solution has to minimize the impact and prevent or discourage such behavior.

Accountability

Making the services being traded among the peers *accountable*, is another inevitable requirement for a market-managed Peer-to-Peer system. An accounting or payment mechanism is required which provides the notion of a common currency that can represent the value of the individual services. This may be a scalar value, which can be aggregated over time and thus represents the current credit of a peer. Peer-to-Peer accounting systems are discussed in detail in Chapter 32. One of the main challenges of an accounting system is clearly to bind the accounting information to a real identity, thus making re-entries of peers under a new identity costly and therefore unattractive. Karma [608], PPay [636] or PeerMint [283] are potential systems that may be used for this purpose. A similar mechanism is needed to keep track of a trader's reputation, considering its behavior in the past, such as cheating, freeriding, or running malicious attacks. There are trust mechanisms like EigenTrust [334] which are able to aggregate such information in an efficient way. The trust metric is needed to be able to exclude misbehaving peers from the system.

Further desirable properties, such as privacy or anonymity, exist, which may contradict accountability, as it is difficult to guarantee accountability and anonymity at the same time. It depends on the dedicated target applications, if a system has to comply with them.

29.2 Architecture

The previous section introduced the concept of service markets based on Peer-to-Peer networks. It also stated the main requirements that a system has to fulfill to enable such a market. This section describes the architecture of such a system (cf. [240]). The architecture primarily consists of three models. The market model describes the roles of service providers and service consumers in the market. The service usage model describes the different ways of using services. The peer model describes the architecture of a single peer. It is extended through the description of key mechanisms which have to be implemented on every peer, in order to enable the Peer-to-Peer-based service market.

29.2.1 Market Model

The classical market is a place where sellers and buyers meet to exchange goods against payment, *e.g.*, money. While in old times this market corresponded to a closed physical location, nowadays the term is used in a much broader sense, *e.g.*, to describe a national or even the global market.

The goods traded in the market described here are services (cf. Chapter 14). Thus, the sellers and buyers are *service providers* and *service consumers*. However, participants in the market are not restricted to either provide or consume a service. Rather, they can take on any of these *roles* at any point of time. This means, that they can provide a service to a second participant and later use a service from a third participant or vice versa. They can even do both at the same time, as shown in Figure 29.1.

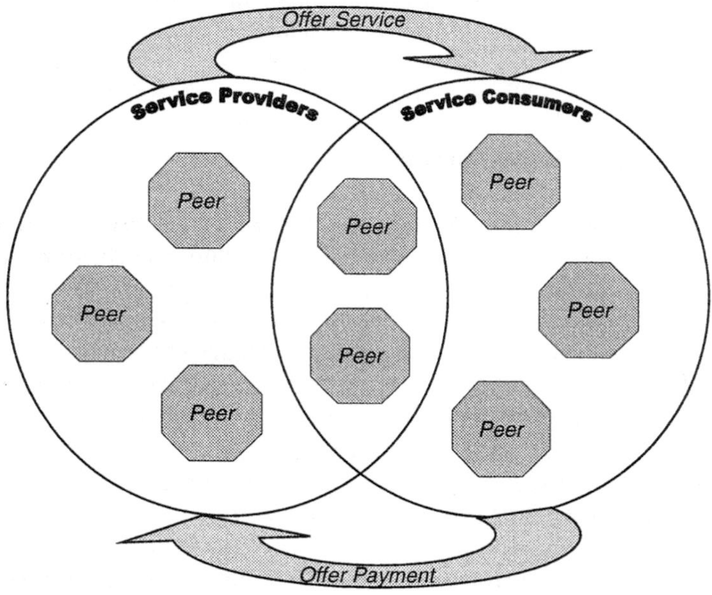

Fig. 29.1: The Market Model

The participants of the service market are peers of an underlying Peer-to-Peer network, so the market covers the complete Peer-to-Peer network. When properly implemented, such a Peer-to-Peer-based market offers low barriers to entry to potential service providers as they do not have to spend a lot of money on marketing first. Rather, Peer-to-Peer search mechanisms allow consumers to easily find any service offering, not just the most visible ones.

As any market, this market shall lead to an equilibrium of supply and demand. Especially, the competition between service providers shall lead to the deployment of new services as well as low prices for existing services. In order to achieve this, the market must give incentives for not overcharging a service and for providing a proper Quality of Service (QoS). On the one hand, the long-term development of the market provides some incentives by itself. If the price of a service is considered to be too high noone will use it and the provider will be forced to lower the price of the service. Similarly, consumers are not likely to use the services of a provider who previously provided them a low QoS. However, the basic market forces are not enough if prices are to be created dynamically in accordance to the current market situation. Neither do they prevent a provider from providing low QoS if the user base is large enough. Thus, additional incentives have to be provided to stimulate a proper behavior in the market. *E.g.*, auction mechanisms (cf. Section 29.3.2) allow to create prices for services dynamically on short notice. Reputation mechanisms allow users to judge the quality of service providers and the services they offer, while Service Level Agreements (SLAs) allow to specify the QoS and terms of service usage in a legally enforceable way.

29.2.2 Service Usage Model

The term *service* is defined as functionality which is offered by one peer to other peers, and which can be accessed through input and output interfaces. Services are described through service descriptions, which describe each service's functionality and interfaces, but also its non-functional characteristics such as terms of usage, *e.g.*, prices and methods of payment. *Services instances* can be used by applications, which are programs running on peers which are not provided as services themselves and offer user interfaces. In addition, service instances can be used by other service instances. As mentioned earlier, examples of services include the provision of basic resources like computing power and storage space, as well as higher-level functionality, *e.g.*, the provision of weather forecasts or booking services.

The service usage model shown in Figure 29.2 shows the various uses of services. The most straightforward case is a peer providing a service instance to another peer, where it is used by an application. Such a case is depicted in Figure 29.2 between Peer 2 and Peer 4. Naturally, applications can use several services at the same time, as is done by the application running on Peer 2. Similarily, the same service can be provided to several users at the same time (Peer 4 providing instances of the same service to Peer 2 and Peer 3). Finally, services can also be used by other services. In Figure 29.2 a service running on Peer 3 which is being provided to Peer 1 is using a local service as well as a service provided by Peer 4. The details of this *service composition* are hidden from the application running on Peer 1 which only sees the single service it uses.

29.2.3 Peer Model

Having laid the foundation for a Peer-to-Peer system through its market and service usage models, it is now essential to derive the internal structure of a peer. To ensure a sufficient degree of modularity of the architecture, a layered structure is used for the peer model. The lowest layer are the resources that are locally available at a certain peer node. On top of this layer services are executed which can draw on local resources, such as storage space, computing power or content. They can also access remote resources through other ser-

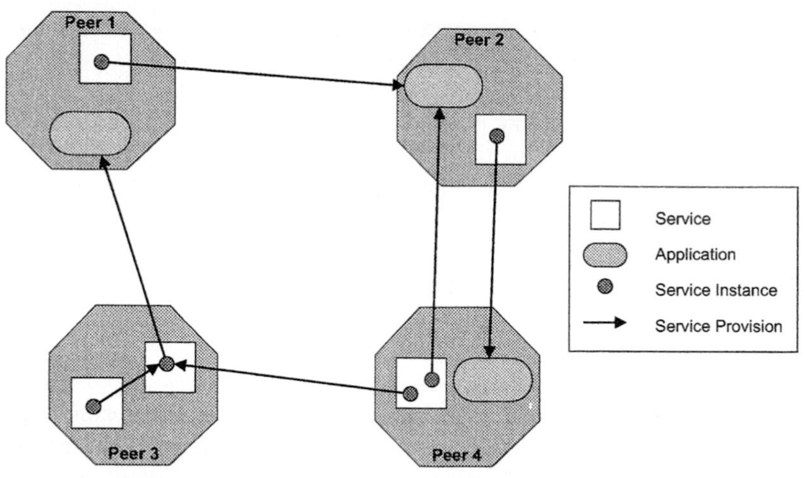

Fig. 29.2: The Service Usage Model

vices. Finally, in parallel to the services layer, core functionality is required to uphold the Peer-to-Peer network and facilitate the smooth operation and interaction of services. Figure 29.3 illustrates the abstract architecture of each peer participating in the market.

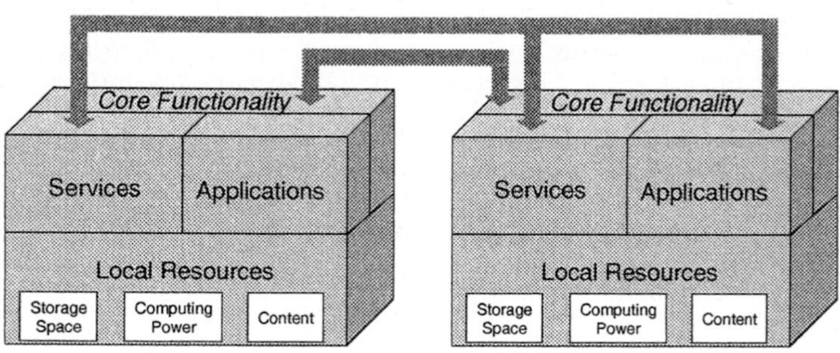

Fig. 29.3: The Peer Model

The core functionality layer on each peer node provides the functionality needed to uphold the peer network services. It is in charge of some basic local functionality like local resource management as well as distributed functionality and protocols like service discovery or reputation. In particular, it includes all functionality needed to enable pricing, metering, and charging and, hence, to support market management of the system. The core functionality layer on each peer accesses and cooperates with the corresponding layers on remote peers but does not access remote or local services.

29.2.4 Key Elements and Mechanisms

The models presented above determine the general structure of a service-oriented market based on a Peer-to-Peer network. Still, the core functionality within each peer, which is responsible for enabling the complete architecture, must be defined in detail and its mechanisms must be identified. The core functionality must handle the management and interaction of services. Therefore, typical business processes for the management and interaction of businesses in a common market provide a reasonable structure for the definition of the core functionality's mechanisms. Table 29.1 describes this structure. Business processes on the left hand side are translated into necessary core functionality mechanisms on the right hand side. While these mechanisms alone are not able to carry out the corresponding business processes in a completely autonomous manner, they are important tools supporting users and user agents. Section 29.3.1 describes how the identified mechanisms work together within a Peer-to-Peer middleware, in order to enable the architecture.

Business Processes	Required Core Functionality Mechanisms
Strategy development	Offline task of the service provider
Product management	
Human resource management	
Budgeting and controlling	Resource management and QoS control
Marketing and selling	Service description, discovery, pricing and negotiation
Contracting	Service level agreements
Order fulfillment	Service execution, accounting, charging
Business development	Service composition uses existing core functionality
External security mechanisms	Security mechanisms included

Table 29.1: Mapping business processes to core functionality

While strategy development, product management, and human resource management are without any doubt highly important processes for any business, they mainly occur in the offline world, in a Peer-to-Peer services environment as well as in a client-server one. It is the service provider's task to think of a successful strategy, draft accurate business plans, employ, train, and retain the right people and develop services accordingly. Hence, the architecture does not need to take these processes into consideration.

Budgeting and controlling, the optimum allocation of resources and the controlling thereof can be translated into local resource management and QoS control.

Marketing, guiding a customer towards a product, is mapped onto service description and discovery, certainly one of the most important mechanisms within the core functionality. Sales, selling the product, then corresponds to service negotiation.

In the normal business world the creation of contracts would be the task of a legal department. In the core functionality the contracts are represented as electronic Service Level Agreements (SLAs), which can be negotiated by the core functionality itself, by applications acting as user agents, or by human users themselves.

After a contract has been finalised, the provider needs to fulfill it, including the capturing of all accounting and charging information for the invoicing and payment steps.

Business development, the cutting of major deals and cooperations to augment the business, corresponds to service composition, the cooperation of several services to deliver a joint result as described in the service usage model. However, this task is not part of the core functionality, but merely uses important parts of it, *e.g.*, service discovery, service negotiation and SLAs.

Finally, while offline businesses can leave security tasks to a high degree to governmental authorities (police, courts), security aspects are crucial for a Peer-to-Peer services architecture, *e.g.*, identification, authentication, authorization, encryption/decryption mechanisms.

29.3 Case Studies

The last two sections introduced the concept of a Peer-to-Peer based service market and a system architecture to enable such a market. Still, this has merely given an overview over the whole topic. Therefore, the purpose of this section is to give a more detailed view on two sub topics to serve as examples of the involved complexity and problems. First, the design of a Peer-to-Peer middleware is introduced. Its purpose is to implement the key mechanisms described in the previous sections, thus enabling the architecture, which in turn enables the service market. This middleware has been developed and implemented within the EU-funded MMAPPS project [591] where it has been successfully used as a basis for various Peer-to-Peer-applications. Second, one key mechanism, namely pricing, is presented in even more detail. Its specific implementation uses the overlay network Pastry to enable auctions for services in a completely decentralized manner.

29.3.1 Peer-to-Peer Middleware

Different implementations of core functionality described in Section 29.2.3 can exist on different platforms and access the local resources through platform dependent interfaces. However, all implementations follow a common standard of protocols to communicate with each other and offer a uniform interface to applications in the form of APIs (Application Programmers Interfaces). Thus, platform dependent details are hidden from the application and its programmers. Together, the core functionalities of all peers act as a middleware (cf. [69]), which makes it possible to treat the collection of all peers as a single service-oriented Peer-to-Peer network.

Only the API of the local core functionality implementation is visible to a service or application developer and thus the distributed nature of the middleware is hidden from him. Therefore, in this section the single implementation of the core functionality is also referred to as 'middleware'. A modular approach has been chosen for designing this middleware. This approach has the following benefits:

- Details are hidden from modules which are not concerned by them.
- Implementors don't have to consider the complexity of the complete middleware but only the less complex single modules.
- It facilitates maintenance, especially plugging in new modules.

The Peer-to-Peer middleware consists of six modules as shown in Figure 29.4. These modules belong to three different groups. The central group are the Service Support modules, namely the Service Negotiation and Service Management module. These modules are responsible for managing service related information, i.e., service descriptions and SLAs, and for controlling service execution. In order to enable the effects of market forces, additional functionality is provided by Market Management modules, namely Pricing to determine the price of services in the market, and Accounting and Charging (A&C) to collect information about service usage and calculate charges based on this information. Finally, the Enabling modules provide basic functionalities needed to enable the Peer-to-Peer network and offer support to the other modules. The Search module is used to search and find services in the Peer-to-Peer network, and the Security module provides encryption and identity management to all other modules, especially access control to the Service Negotiation module.

In Figure 29.4 each arrow represents a data flow. Dotted arrows denote remote interfaces, i.e., a module of one peer communicating with a module of the same type on another peer. When a new service is deployed, it sends its

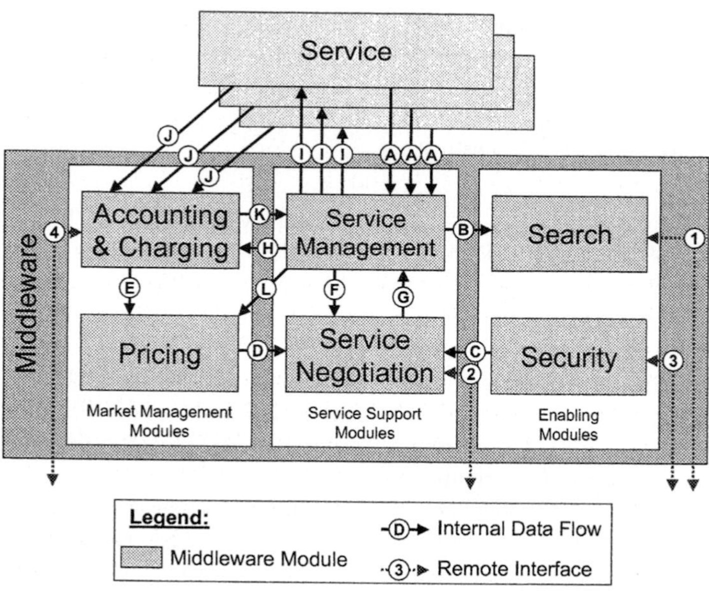

Fig. 29.4: The Middleware Design

description to the local Service Management module via *interface A*. From there the service description is forwarded to the Search module via *interface B*. Thus, whenever a remote peer searches a service via the remote *interface 1*, the Search module can compare the requirements stated in the received service description to the service descriptions it has stored. If this comparison leads to a match, the remote peer can decide to negotiate the terms of service usage via the remote *interface 2*. In this case, the Service Negotiation module will first let the Security module check the remote peer's access rights. The results of this check are returned via *interface C*. In order to perform this check, *i.e.*, to authenticate the remote peer, the Security module may contact other peers via the remote *interface 3*. The Pricing module calculates an appropriate price for the service requested and sends it to the Negotiation module via *interface D*. In order to do so, it can retrieve information about past peer behavior from the A&C module via *interface E*. Furthermore, it can be configured by the Service Management module via *interface L*, *e.g.*, to support a new service or to adapt to a change in the service market. In order to make such decisions, the Service Management module can also retrieve information about the past from the A&C module via *interface K*. If a service negotiation is successful, the negotiation module uses *interface G* to send the final SLA to the Service Management module to start the service delivery.

After informing the A&C module about the forthcoming service delivery via *interface I*, the Service Management module instantiates, configures and starts a new service instance through *interface I*. During the service delivery, the service instance reports its status by sending events to the A&C module via *interface J*. The A&C module compares these events against the SLA and informs the Service Management module via *interface K* when necessary, *e.g.*, in the case of an SLA breach or when the service instance has finished. The Service Management module controls the service delivery via *interface I*, *e.g.*, stops it in the case of an SLA breach. For special purposes the A&C module can contact remote A&C modules, *e.g.*, to receive an immediate payment through tokens (cf. Chapter 32).

The middleware design has been described in more detail in [239] and [241]. A prototype has been implemented within the MMAPPS project [591] based on the JXTA framework [255]. The prototype serves as a proof of concept, showing the middleware enables the architecture presented in Section 29.2. It specifically fulfills the functional requirements of service support and market-based management, as well as the non-functional requirements of efficiency and accounting (cf. Section 29.1). The other requirements of decentralisation, scalability and reliability depend on the underlying Peer-to-Peer framework, JXTA. The middleware does not impede these requirements, since it does not introduce centralized entities nor unscalable protocols into the Peer-to-Peer environment.

29.3.2 PeerMart: Peer-to-Peer Auctions

Online auctions like eBay [183] are becoming increasingly popular marketplaces for trading any kind of services over the Internet. Auction-based markets benefit from the flexibility to adjust prices dynamically and enable to achieve efficient supply allocations (for an overview on auctions cf. [234]). However, those markets usually rely on a central component, i.e. the auctioneer which collects price offers of all participants and performs matches.

PeerMart, which is the second case study presented in this chapter, combines the advantages of an economically efficient auction mechanism with the scalability and robustness of Peer-to-Peer networks. It is shown, how PeerMart implements a variant of the Double Auction (DA) on top of a Peer-to-Peer overlay network, as an efficient pricing mechanism for Peer-to-Peer services. Other than in a single-sided auction, like the English Auction or the Dutch Auction, in the Double Auction both providers and consumers can offer prices. The basic idea of PeerMart is to distribute the broker load of an otherwise centralized auctioneer onto clusters of peers, each being responsible for brokering a certain number of services. PeerMart differs from existing work, such as [165] and [460], since it applies a structured rather than a random Peer-to-Peer overlay network, which enables deterministic location of brokers and is more efficient and scalable. It resolves the chicken and egg problem between providing incentives for services and being itself dependent on peers' functionality by introducing redundancy. Under the assumption, that a certain amount of peers behave correctly, PeerMart is thus able to provide a high reliability even in the presence of malicious or unreliable peers. Key design aspects of PeerMart are presented briefly in the following.

Basic Design

The basic pricing mechanism in PeerMart works as follows: Providers and consumers which are interested in trading a particular service, have to contact a responsible broker from which they can request the current price. Brokers (realized by clusters of peers) answer such requests with two prices:

- the current bid price, i.e. the current highest buy price offered by a consumer
- the current ask price, i.e. the current lowest sell price offered by a provider

Based on this information, consumers and providers can then send their own price offers (bids or asks) to the brokers. Continuously, brokers run the following matching strategy:

- Upon every price offer received from a peer, there is no match if the offer is lower (higher) than the current ask price (bid price). However, the offer may be stored in a table for later use.
- Otherwise, if there is a match, the offer will be forwarded to the peer that made the highest bid (lowest ask). The resulting price for the service is set to the mean price between the two matching price offers.

To implement this mechanism in a decentralized manner, PeerMart uses Pastry [527], a structured Peer-to-Peer overlay infrastructure. The overlay is applied for peers joining and leaving the system, and to find other peers (brokers) in the network. Every peer is given a unique 128-bit node identifier (nodeId), which can be calculated from a peer's IP address or public key using a secure hash function. In PeerMart it is assumed that every peer has a public/private key pair, which is also used to sign and verify messages. Furthermore, it is assumed that each service has a unique service identifier (serviceId). For content services this can be achieved, *e.g.*, by calculating the hash value of the content data. The serviceId needs to have at least the same length as the nodeId, to be able to map the services onto the address space of the underlying network. The only varying service parameter considered at this stage is the price.

A set of n peers (called broker set) which are numerically closest to the serviceId are responsible to act as brokers for that service. Each peer in a broker set keeps an auction table for the service to store $m/2$ highest bids and

$m/2$ lowest offers (m can be adjusted depending on the service popularity). As it is assumed that multiple services are available, multiple broker sets will exist concurrently, each being responsible for a dedicated service. A broker set corresponds to a leaf set in Pastry. It consists of $n/2$ numerically closest larger nodeIds and $n/2$ numerically closest smaller nodeIds for a particular serviceId.

When a new service is offered for the first time, the corresponding root node (the node numerically closest to the serviceId) has to notify the other peers in its leaf set about the new service. If the root node fails to do that (*e.g.*, because it is a malicious node), the following fallback method can be applied. Recursively, peers on the path to the serviceId can be contacted, until the next closest node in the leaf set is found. This peer then takes over the responsibility of the root node and notifies the other peers. Furthermore, every peer keeps a list of nodeIds of other peers which are in the same broker set for a particular service. This list is updated regularly based on changes in the leaf set which are notified to a PeerMart instance by its local Pastry node.

An example for the double auction mechanism in PeerMart is given in Figure 29.5. Two providers (P1, P2) and a consumer (C1) are interested in trading a particular service (serviceId x). Pastry routes their requests to the corresponding root node which returns the list of peers in the broker set. If the root node fails to return the broker set, the same fallback method as described above can be applied. Broker peers can now be contacted directly to get the current bid or ask price and to notify new price offers. Apart from the price, every offer contains a sequence number and a valid time and is signed with the peer's private key. The valid time cannot be larger than a maximum time t. For every peer only the newest offer is kept. After an offer becomes invalid it will be removed from the table.

Concurrently, other broker sets exist which are responsible for other services. Note that a peer can act as a provider, a consumer, and as a broker for several services at the same time. Note also, that only the first request (to identify the broker set for a particular service) is routed through the overlay network. All subsequent messages (namely price offers) are sent directly over the underlying IP network.

Broker Set Synchronization

As a countermeasure against faulty or malicious peers, initial price requests and subsequent price offers are always sent to f randomly selected broker peers in parallel ($1 <= f <= n$). f is a design parameter that has to be set very carefully with respect to the ratio of malicious peers, desired reliability, and message overhead, for which there is always a trade-off. Broker peers receiving an offer either reject it or store it in their tables according to the strategy described above. Every broker peer forwards pairs of locally

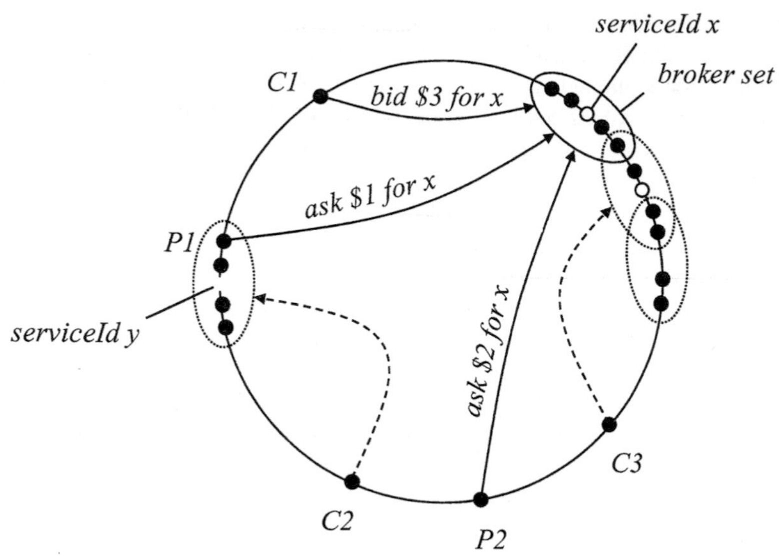

Fig. 29.5: Double Auction in PeerMart.

matching offers to all other peers in the broker set. Based on the signature of an offer, brokers can verify its validity. In addition to the offers matching locally, a broker also forwards the current highest bid and lowest ask, if it has not already been sent earlier. Thus, only potential candidates for a match are synchronized among peers in a broker set. Based on the offers received from other brokers the current bid price (ask price) can be determined and a globally valid matching can be performed by every broker. Asks and bids matching globally are finally forwarded to the corresponding peers by those broker peers which initially received them.

In this redundant approach message loss is implicitly considered. When a message is lost accidentally between two brokers, it appears as if one of the brokers would act maliciously. However, so far timing issues have not been dealt with, and it was assumed that all messages are sent without any delay. In PeerMart a slotted time is used for every individual auction to tackle the problem of message delays. Time slots have a fixed duration which has to be longer than the maximum expected round trip time between any two peers. Every time slot has a sequence number starting at zero when a service is traded for the first time. Price offers from providers (consumers) are collected continuously. At the end of every even time slot, the potential candidates for a match are forwarded to the other brokers and arrive there during an odd time slot. Candidates arriving during even time slots are either delayed or dropped, depending on the sequence number. At the end of every odd time slot, the final matches are performed and notified to the corresponding peers. Since after this synchronization process all broker peers have the same information needed to match offers, no matching conflict can occur. In the rare case that more than one peers quoted exactly the same price within the same time slot, a broker peer gives priority to the one that came in first. After synchronization, the price offer which was prioritized by most brokers is selected.

A prototype of PeerMart has been implemented and is available as open source software for testing purposes [481]. More details about the implementation and results obtained from various experiments can be found in [282]. These results show that PeerMart provides a reliable, attack-resistant Peer-to-Peer pricing mechanism at a low overhead of messages and necessary storage space and scales well for any number of peers trading services. The mechanism is completely decentralized and suitable for trading any types of services. Hence, it fulfills all the requirements stated in Section 29.1.

29.4 Conclusion and Outlook

In this chapter, the economic and technical aspects of a market-managed Peer-to-Peer system were described in detail. A comprehensive list of requirements for such a system was given, and a generic architecture was outlined containing key components and mechanisms of a Peer-to-Peer-based marketplace. Finally, two case studies were presented, giving a more detailed view on two individual aspects of the overall approach. The first case study described modules of a Peer-to-Peer middleware which is centered around core service negotiation and management functionality. The second case study presented the design of an auction-based pricing mechanisms based on a Peer-to-Peer overlay network. Both studies covered specific parts of the proposed architecture.

Further important aspects exist and have been discussed in this chapter, such as accounting and reputation, which have not been covered in detail. Accounting is described separately in the next chapter.

30. A Peer-to-Peer Framework for Electronic Markets

Michael Conrad, Jochen Dinger, Hannes Hartenstein, Marcus Schöller, Martina Zitterbart (ITM, University of Karlsruhe (TH))
Daniel Rolli (IWM, University of Karlsruhe (TH))

30.1 Markets as Peer-to-Peer Systems

Markets — in their ideal form — naturally represent Peer-to-Peer (P2P) systems: market participants can be both client *and* server when exchanging offers, general messages, or goods. They can directly address each other, and interact in a decentralized and autonomous fashion. Most market implementations in history, however, were far from this ideal form.

As the construction and application of electronic markets began with the emerging Internet, the prevailing paradigm for network communication was client-server. To find a coherent implementation, market designers at that time fell back on this most self-evident network topology. The design of electronic marketplaces is still influenced by proven traditional implementations. Stock exchanges, for example, that were among the driving forces for electronic markets are one such archetype. They classically fulfill the role of an intermediary by reducing the number of communication links between participants and providing a common contact point for aggregated market information. So, by acting as client-server systems they reduce transaction costs significantly.

And still, at their very core, some non-electronic stock exchanges show — and always have shown — the Peer-to-Peer paradigm, as on the physical trading floor traders (peers) interact directly when exchanging stocks. They exhibit this trade paradigm that, in the course of the development of centralized market software systems, has been losing ground.

With the liberalization of markets, the formerly 'dependent' market participants are now regaining autonomy in their market decisions. Harmonization of markets unifies different groups of participants and thereby increases the number of those that can interact with each other. This constitutes the main theme of this chapter: when a market *per se* is a Peer-to-Peer system and participants regain autonomy, how can we design an appropriate architecture for electronic markets that comprehensively implements the Peer-to-Peer paradigm? While investigating this question, we particularly focus on the support of spontaneity and interoperability by means of self-organization in liberalized and harmonized markets.

R. Steinmetz and K. Wehrle (Eds.): P2P Systems and Applications, LNCS 3485, pp. 509-525, 2005.

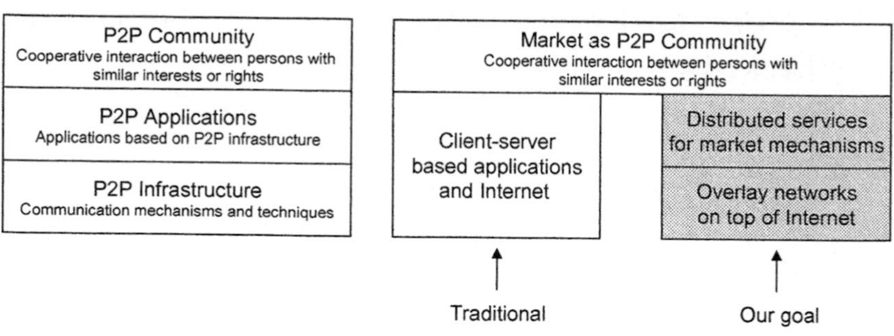

Fig. 30.1: The Peer-to-Peer paradigm at various levels of a system: the traditional architectures as well as our view for electronic markets.

To systematically analyze Peer-to-Peer systems, the Peer-to-Peer paradigm can be seen at three different levels, according to [545]: community, application, and infrastructure. As mentioned above, a market can be regarded as a Peer-to-Peer community at the top level. The remaining challenge is whether, and if so, how the application and infrastructure levels can be developed in compliance with the Peer-to-Peer paradigm. After presenting our approach, we also discuss its benefits and drawbacks.

30.1.1 Service and Distribution Basics

We propose a Peer-to-Peer architecture for electronic markets where all three levels are based on the Peer-to-Peer paradigm (Figure 30.1). A market participant is a peer not only by taking part in the marketplace and its mechanisms, but also by contributing to these mechanisms. For example, peer nodes may provide storage for storing intentions (statements of offers) and processing power for discovery requests. To design such an integrated Peer-to-Peer concept for electronic markets, the structure of the marketplace and the market mechanisms is translated into a distributed service-oriented approach.

Service orientation seems to be a suitable approach because of the clear functional separation. The functional separation facilitates extensions of market mechanisms and reusing existing ones. In our view services can be provided by a single peer or by a set of peers as outlined in Section 30.2.2. For different applications the common services can be reused with additional services building on them. In the following, we call these common services 'basic services'. The ones tailored to our market application are called 'application services'.

As basic services we have identified:

- document service that acts as repository for intentions
- authentication service to authenticate users and intentions
- protocol service that records the various steps of transactions

Examples of application services are:

- optimization service that determines the best offer (according to some specified criteria) out of a set of intentions
- legal mediator that checks whether a potential contract adheres to the legal policies of the market participant.

The various basic and application services (application level) have to be matched with appropriate overlay network techniques (infrastructure level) for providing the required 'quality of service'. Quality of service requirements in this context can be characterized, for example, by robustness of a service, search efficiency or accuracy, and depend on the corresponding service.

It is thus not only the fact that on the community level a market represents a Peer-to-Peer system that commends a Peer-to-Peer-implementation of the application and infrastructure level. For us, the rationale is as follows: a perfect market would offer total information to every participant and would show no communication or exchange delays, i.e. no transaction costs. However, it is quite obvious that any centralized system will impose a lack of scalability and flexibility, barriers to the market, e.g., via transaction costs and a single point of failure. Compared to centralized systems, Peer-to-Peer provides substantial advantages with the main general benefit of scalability. The seamless integration of nodes to the network enables, firstly, the adequate increase of storage or computation power, secondly, the addition of new market mechanisms on the application level, and thirdly, the integration of whole market segments in the course of harmonization. It also allows for the combination of already existing but idly distributed resources to cooperate in a Peer-to-Peer system, thereby immensely reducing the investment costs compared to setting up new resources. A distributed and self-organizing system can also reduce market barriers and transaction costs, as well as encourage spontaneity with respect to market participation. In addition, such an integrated Peer-to-Peer design can improve robustness.

Clearly, the benefits are matched against various challenges of a distributed design. First of all, there is the question of how to find intentions and services. Therefore one needs search methods as well as standardized ways to express intentions. Thus, ontologies come into play. Secondly, secure and reliable operation of market transactions has to be ensured without a centralized trusted third party.

30.1.2 SESAM Project Structure

The proposed architecture has been developed within the framework of the SESAM project of the priority research program 'Internet Economy' funded by the German Ministry of Education and Research (BMBF). The complete project covers three scenarios: multi-utility markets, virtual power plants, and wearable services. The latter two scenarios are of central interest regarding the Peer-to-Peer paradigm. In the virtual power plant scenario, we assume that many small devices producing electricity are deployed at locations such as houses, small companies, and public buildings. The owners of these power plants want to maximize their profit by selling the energy to the bidder with the highest offer. The purchaser on the other hand wants to buy energy as cheap as possible. From this starting point many interesting questions arise: How does a purchaser find the cheapest offer? Can the purchaser and seller enter the contract without personal adhesion? How are mini power plants controlled to maximize profit? What to do if a mini power plant breaks down? How is accounting accomplished?

These questions lead to several subprojects:

Electronic Contracting – Business processes are subject to legal rules. In order to achieve transparency and seamlessness with high spontaneity in the markets, the harmonization of the law must be promoted and signing of contracts must be automated in the network.

Spontaneity, Transparency and Incentives. – The considered scenarios require smooth and comprehensible interaction of various connected components and services. Transparency and incentives for the actors involved are preconditions for the functioning of such self-organizing markets.

Optimization, Control and Business Models – Due to their inherent decentralized nature and dynamics, self-organizing and spontaneous markets require specially adapted business models as well as completely new decentralized optimization and control mechanisms.

Robustness and Security – One important requirement for the commercial success of the applications is the security and robustness of all participating components and processes against active and passive breakdowns and attacks of 'normal' activity.

The results of the virtual power plant scenario get carried onto the field of so-called wearable services. New markets could emerge through communication among small devices like PDAs, mobile phones, and sensors in clothes or worn directly on the body.

To build an integrated Peer-to-Peer system for electronic markets as outlined above, an architecture is needed that brings together service orientation and overlay networks. In particular, the provision of standardized interfaces to a pool of overlay networking techniques is needed. In this chapter we will describe our service-oriented Peer-to-Peer architecture (Section 30.2) and discuss various architectural considerations concerning security/dependability issues (Section 30.3).

30.2 A Service-Oriented Peer-to-Peer Architecture

As mentioned in the previous section, markets and market mechanisms should be modeled using services, where a service represents a functional unit, and in which services can be loosely coupled through service composition. Examples are a document service for storing intentions or an optimization service that analyzes various offers and determines an optimal one. A service-oriented approach helps to easily create new applications based on already available services, thus, reuse, extensibility, and spontaneity are facilitated.

Since we argued that services should be distributed, in order to efficiently use idle resources (e.g., to reduce transaction costs or market barriers), a service will not in general reside on a single server but will be supported by peers of an overlay network. Therefore, we introduce the notion of a *ServiceNet* as an overlay network that provides a specific service. Clearly, service discovery is a required first service to locate other services or, entry points to services. Services themselves will be operated by collaboration between peer nodes as it is the case for the document service.

The document service represents a decentralized document pool where participants can insert and search for documents. In our scenarios this service is used, e.g., for offering electricity. This service provides three basic functions: *insert*, *search* and, *revoke*. The *search* functions can be parameterized using a query language. This language allows expressing a keyword-based search. Revoking documents would be the same as deleting them in the event that we could guarantee the deletion. E.g., in unstructured Peer-to-Peer networks where the document locations are 'unknown' the deletion can not be guaranteed. With this document service, organized as a ServiceNet, each participant provides some resources for storage of documents and for processing of queries or *revoke* operations.

When a set of intentions matching a query is found, the market participant (or his agent) might submit this set to an optimization service. This service estimates the best offer out of the given set based on the energy consumption profile of the participant and prices implied in the offers. Here, the user can benefit from a distributed service discovery mechanism (to find an appropriate optimization service) but also from the Peer-to-Peer approach in case the optimization is shared by various peers.

The document and optimization service were selected to serve as representative examples. Other services could focus on contracting and matching. But even with the two examples mentioned above, it can be seen that ServiceNets for various services will require different forms of Peer-to-Peer network organization. For example, the paper [52] outlines that keyword-based queries are not trivially carried out by a Distributed Hash Table (DHT) based Peer-to-Peer network. Therefore, we need an architecture where service instances on each peer easily can be attached to a specific Peer-to-Peer networking approach, i.e., we need an 'overlay API' such as the one for DHT-based methods [148].

Following the above reasoning, we will now first make a quick digression to traditional service-oriented architecture. Then, we will discuss the concept of a ServiceNet in more detail and outline the peer node architecture that brings together service orientation and overlay networks.

30.2.1 Service Orientation

Service-oriented architectures (SOA) utilize services as basic elements to realize applications [473]. Services are characterized by:

- Service Description. This description includes, in particular, the functionality that is provided by a service. All functionality of a service is provided through interfaces. A well-known interface description language is necessary for such interface descriptions.
- Autonomy. Services are autonomous entities that can be considered a black-boxes, i.e., the concrete implementation cannot be seen from the outside and only the interfaces are visible.

Services that are composed together to an application or system are loosely coupled. Thus, a service can be exchanged without influencing the system itself. The only requirement is that the functionality and interfaces are the same. This is in contrast to distributed object oriented approaches, like CORBA [133], that lead to tight coupling.

Furthermore, traditional service-oriented architectures follow the Publish-Find-Bind paradigm. Services are published by the service provider in a service registry. Service consumers can search in the registry for services and, finally bind a service from a provider.

Web Services are an option to implement a service-oriented architecture. Therefore they propose three main specifications following the Publish-Find-Bind paradigm.

- SOAP [265] is a protocol for exchanging structured information based on XML. It is independent from the underlying transport protocol. So-called bindings are employed to use SOAP over a specific transport protocol.
- WSDL, the Web Services Description Language [115] is used to define interfaces. It is also based on XML and makes it possible to describe a service as a so-called endpoint.
- UDDI, the Universal Description Discovery and Integration [454] defines an interface for a service registry. In such a registry, developers can publish and

find services during the design of an application. Applications themselves can use the registry to find services with suitable interfaces at runtime.

These specifications supplement each other, but can also be used on their own. Furthermore, those specifications can be used to realize platform-independent applications, which do not rely upon specific programming languages. Web Services implementations exist for all major platforms and programming languages.

As identified in Section 30.1, reuse and extensibility in content and mechanism are essential. Service-oriented architectures take these two key points into account. New applications can be rapidly created out of existing services by combining them. New services can easily be deployed and adopted because of the well defined interfaces. Furthermore, the loose coupling is similar to typical Peer-to-Peer systems where peers are loosely coupled. Web Services can be used as building blocks of our architecture because of their clearly defined interface language and message format.

However, these service-oriented architectures emerged from the client-server approach and therefore do not take Peer-to-Peer mechanisms and self-organization into account. For example, UDDI defines interfaces for a service registry and is therefore not centralized, but current implementations are centralized and do not benefit from the Peer-to-Peer approach. In addition, content-based addressing as a key principle of Peer-to-Peer network organization is not taken into account. Current service-oriented architectures focus on addressing systems without considering the content.

30.2.2 ServiceNets

When services are offered through the collaboration of multiple participants, a ServiceNet is created. Peer-to-Peer file sharing and the document service mentioned before are examples of such ServiceNets. From a functional point of view, how many functions a ServiceNet offers is independent of the number of peers forming the ServiceNet. But the non-functional aspects, such as robustness and available content, might differ drastically with respect to the degree of distribution. These non-functional issues, which can be seen as quality or guarantees, also characterize a service, and might provide ServiceNets with the competitive edge over a centralized approach as indicated in Section 1.

A ServiceNet can be used from participating peers as well as from 'external peers' that do not participate in the ServiceNet. Mobile devices could, for example, be such service consumers where active participation within a ServiceNet is perhaps not reasonable because of very temporary availability.

Each ServiceNet uses an underlying Peer-to-Peer network that provides self-organizing mechanisms for network organization. Hence, there is a one-to-one mapping between a ServiceNet and a Peer-to-Peer network. For example,

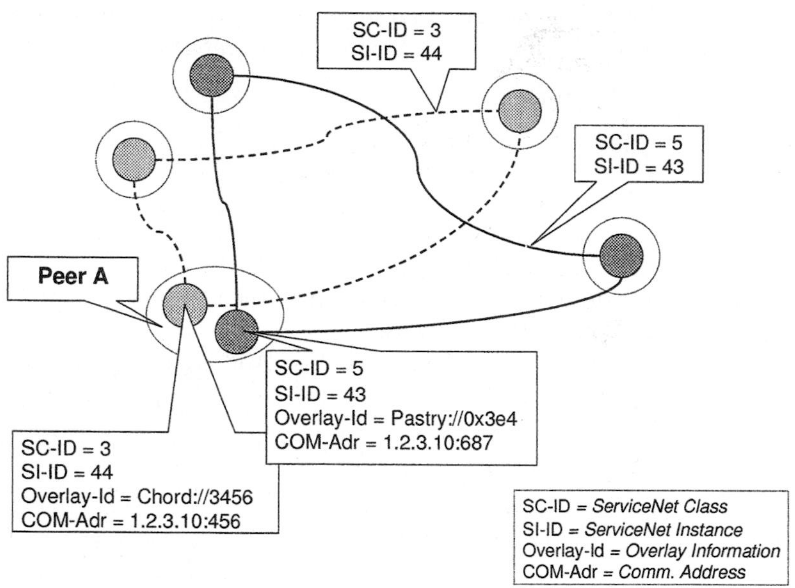

Fig. 30.2: ServiceNet example

an identity management service, which offers functions that are all based on a unique key, could use a DHT-based Peer-to-Peer network. On the other hand, the document service implements a keyword search for which a DHT-based Peer-to-Peer network may not be suitable. For a document service, an unstructured Peer-to-Peer network, like GIA [113], might be more suitable.

Using one Peer-to-Peer network for one ServiceNet has the advantage that the characteristics of the Peer-to-Peer network can be better considered. Clearly, to assist the process of service creation, a 'catalogue' is needed so that one can find the suitable Peer-to-Peer network for a specific service and ServiceNet, respectively, based on the required functionality or constraints. For example, service developers and providers must characterize their service by answering questions such as 'Is there a unique key for data elements?' etc. Afterwards they should get a recommendation for a Peer-to-Peer network their service should use. Papers like [346] provide an aid in building such a catalogue. Currently we are developing a model that gives us a basis for describing the characteristics and behavior of Peer-to-Peer networks. This model will then be used for simulation and evaluation.

A peer in a ServiceNet (Figure 30.2) is characterized by:

- *ServiceNet Class.* A ServiceNet Class (SC) is a unique identifier for the type of service which the ServiceNet offers. Thereby all peers of a ServiceNet offer the same kind of interface and functionality. A document service is one kind of service class.

- *ServiceNet Instance.* A ServiceNet Instance (SI) is a unique identifier of an instantiated ServiceNet Class. If there are two Document Services for example, they are both instantiated from the same Class, but the instances are independent of each other. E.g., if a ServiceNet uses Chord [575] as the underlying Peer-to-Peer network, one ServiceNet instance also corresponds to one Chord ring.
- *Overlay Information.* All 'overlay-specific information' can be summarized herein, such as Peer-to-Peer organization form and so on. A simple example could appear as follows: Chord://3456. Here the first part identifies the Peer-to-Peer network form and the second part the identifier that the node has in a specific Peer-to-Peer network.
- *Communication Address.* The Communication Address corresponds to the one that a peer uses in the communication network. A communication network could be an IP network or a Bluetooth network, for example.
- *Meta Information.* Meta-Information summarizes all additional information about a ServiceNet. This could be class-depended information or instance-depended information. An example: 'This ServiceNet was founded by UKA'.

Because there can be various ServiceNets, service discovery is needed. Service discovery offers publishing and searching functions. Therefore it has the same function as the service registry in service-oriented architectures. If we think of extensibility regarding mechanisms, service discovery is especially necessary for finding and publishing new services. In contrast to a lot of existing service registries, our service discovery is decentralized, i.e., the discovery itself is provided by a ServiceNet.

30.2.3 Peer Architecture

In this section we will outline our peer architecture which integrates the principles mentioned above. This platform offers a basis for current and future services for electronic markets. The architecture of a peer is depicted in Figure 30.3. This architecture can be divided into the following parts:

- *Communication Layer.* This layer provides an abstraction from a concrete communication network like networks based on IPv6. This layer gives the layer above the possibility to send and receive messages.
- *Overlay Layer.* The overlay layer makes various overlay techniques available. Chord and Pastry would be examples for DHT-based Peer-to-Peer networks and GIA could be an example for an unstructured network. This layer knows the appropriate algorithms and is responsible for initializing procedures. For example, when a peer wants to join a ServiceNet, this layer handles the initializing procedure like building a 'finger table' [575].
- *SOAP-Processor.* The SOAP-Processor translates programming language objects into corresponding SOAP messages. These messages will be ex-

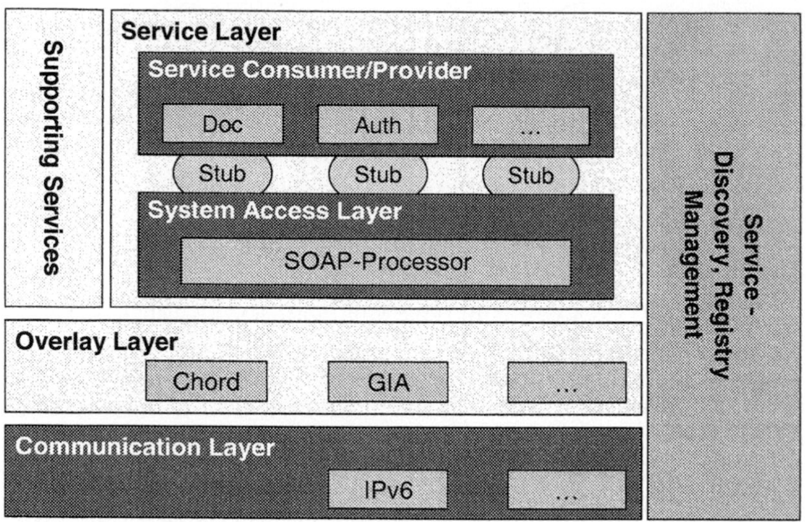

Fig. 30.3: Peer Architecture

changed between peers. These messages are used because of their independence from specific transport protocols that are used in the communication layer, and programming languages that are used for implementing the services.

- *Service Consumer/Provider.* This part summarizes all service consumers and providers. The connection between the underlying SOAP-Processor is handled through stubs that can be generated out of the WSDL description of a service. In this part all existing and future services will appear.
- *Service Management.* The Service Management includes all functions that are necessary to find, publish and bind services. Therefore, the Service Management makes use of the ServiceNet called service discovery, which was mentioned in the previous section. If a service is bound, the management has to inform the overlay layer so that a proper initialization can take place.
- *Supporting Services.* These are additional services that support the service developer by simplifying recurring tasks. For example, supporting services can support the handling of transactions. This would involve session handling and possibly calling roll-back functions, and compensations handlers, etc. In such cases, existing specifications like WS-AtomicTransaction [377] can be used.

30.3 Security, Robustness, and Privacy Challenges

Challenges with respect to security, robustness, and privacy can again be expressed in terms of community, application, and/or infrastructure requirements. Needs of the higher layers can be translated into infrastructure requirements while lower layer characteristics influence the security, robustness and privacy of the whole system. Conflicts between ease-of-use, security, robustness and market requirements have to be resolved: our project demands an open system that encourages potential users to participate in the electronic market. On the other hand, it is also a requirement that we are able to conclude a legally binding contract. Therefore, contracts have to be traceable, such that they can be retraced by a judge.

Moreover, natural persons and companies alike want to control the disclosure of information. There are differences between the US approach to privacy regarding personally identifiable information and the EU approach to data protection. According to [209], the US law is driven by 'the right to be alone' and the European law by the 'right of informational self-determination'. Hence in the US the main concern is to protect personal information against unauthorized usage. Besides that, (natural) persons in Europe have the right to determine what happens with their personally identifiable information. For example, they can cause that their email address is deleted within 30 days. These issues have to be considered in the system design.

Thus, security, robustness, and privacy can all be considered as cross-layer issues and the proper placements of respective functionalities on the various layers as well as their appropriate interactions are a key to success. In the following we first present a threat analysis in a top-down fashion. Afterwards we list technical challenges that arise primarily from following the Peer-to-Peer paradigm on the 'infrastructure' and 'application' layers. We then present three of these issues — persistent signatures, privacy aware data handling, and trust models — in greater detail.

30.3.1 Attack Classification/Threat Analysis

Following the classification of [458] we can differentiate between profitable attacks and 'merely' malicious ones. Profitable attacks take direct advantage of the attack, e.g., a participant can try to modify the search algorithms such that his offers always are found and hence the offers of competitors are not available. Malicious attacks intend only to destroy something and do not directly profit from that.

We can further classify attacks according to their target in: market place, market participants, and market objects. The aim of attacking the market place is to influence the system as a whole. These attacks range from denial-of-service attacks that cause a system breakdown to 'free riding' [366], which normally does not bring the system down but influences it negatively. The attack against a market participant tries to prevent or influence a single participant or group from trading without aiming to influence the whole market. For example, a company can try to prevent a competitor from trading in order to sell more of its own products. The attack against market objects arises especially in Peer-to-Peer systems because there is not necessarily a dependency between market participant and object. A market object can be any good or item related to trading in the market place, e.g., an electricity offer.

In addition, we can distinguish between threats of external and internal origin. External threats result from someone that is not participating in the system, whereas internal threats result from participants. Internal attackers can make use of their knowledge of topologies and protocols to influence the system. Solutions for external threats are not our focus. Furthermore when we can deal with internal threats in an open system, we can inherently deal with external threats. However, the distinction can be used to clarify the new challenges.

To protect ourselves against internal attackers, we must evaluate the mechanisms of the involved Peer-to-Peer networks. Attacks can be directed at the routing and searching mechanisms, but also at the storing and replication mechanisms. The analysis gets more complex since most modifications of one mechanism have a direct impact on one or more of the others. In Section 30.2 we noted that we are using various Peer-to-Peer networks. This means that we must evaluate them all regarding security threats, but to do this efficiently we discuss common requirements that we have for a secure and robust system in Section 30.3.2. Based on these requirements, we will outline some generic solutions that can be applied to various Peer-to-Peer networks and systems in Section 30.3.3.

30.3.2 Peer-to-Peer-Related Challenges

Besides traditional issues like end-to-end security and service robustness, new challenges arise from using a Peer-to-Peer network:

Partial encryption. In contrast to traditional networks where routing and data is always clearly separated in header and payload, Peer-to-Peer systems sometimes mix those up. For example, performing a search in GIA [113] means that every involved node has to search in its local store of objects. If we could assume that all nodes store only their own objects, then there would not be a problem. But if we think about replication, then object encryption and integrity become problematic. If we encrypt the whole object like the payload in typical network protocols, nodes will not be able to search for these objects. Hence, we have to encrypt the object in such a way that essential information is accessible for routing and searching.

Persistent signatures. In some Peer-to-Peer systems replication mechanisms ensure that data is replicated to several places for safety reasons. If we use communication channel encryption, we can ensure that the data has not been exchanged between two parties. However, we can not guarantee the originator of the data, if the data was replicated on an intermediate peer. Therefore, we have to ensure that the signatures created by the originator are not lost on intermediate peers.

Privacy-aware data handling. Regarding privacy two main challenges arise. Through the replication mechanism, data and personally identifiable information may be distributed over the network. In contrast to the primary goal of the replication mechanism, the goal of privacy is to minimize the number of stored data objects that include personal information. Furthermore, the user (in Germany) has the right [97] to modify, block or delete personal information about him or herself. Such obligations are difficult to guarantee in a Peer-to-Peer system.

Topology robustness. Another issue that arises is fault-tolerant routing. As mentioned before, most Peer-to-Peer systems provide fault-tolerant routing for safety, but we also have to ensure that no malicious node can influence the routing table of nodes in such a way that some nodes can not be accessed, objects can not be found, or the whole market breaks down. Therefore, the routing and stabilizing algorithms of the involved Peer-to-Peer networks have to be reviewed. The algorithms should offer multiple or by-pass routes and they have to be stable against denial-of-service attacks.

Incentives. Besides the reachability attack mentioned above, an attacker can try to benefit from the network by 'free riding', i.e., using the resources of others but not contributing his or her own. To avoid such attacks incentives and fairness control measurements are necessary.

Trust models. In traditional systems there is always a central trustable entity. All system participants trust this entity and therefore it can be used for authentication issues. Certainly, this is not always a single system, but the authentication and trust problem is solved by centralizing it. Examples of such architectures are PKI and Kerberos. Also some Peer-to-Peer systems (e.g., PAST [526]) are based on some external trusted entities. As a result of this authentication problem, encryption and integrity become more difficult in Peer-to-Peer systems. Although it is easy to verify the integrity, without be able to verify the authentication this integrity check is useless. For designing appropriate distributed authentication mechanisms, threats like whitewashing [204] and the Sybil Attack [177] also have to be kept in mind.

Multiple signatures. Many trust models use cryptography to secure their trust information. Most often integrity of the trust information is guaranteed by attaching a signature. The requirement for such multiple signatures arises in some distributed trust models. Typical centralized models usually attach a single signature for each item of trust information. In distributed trust

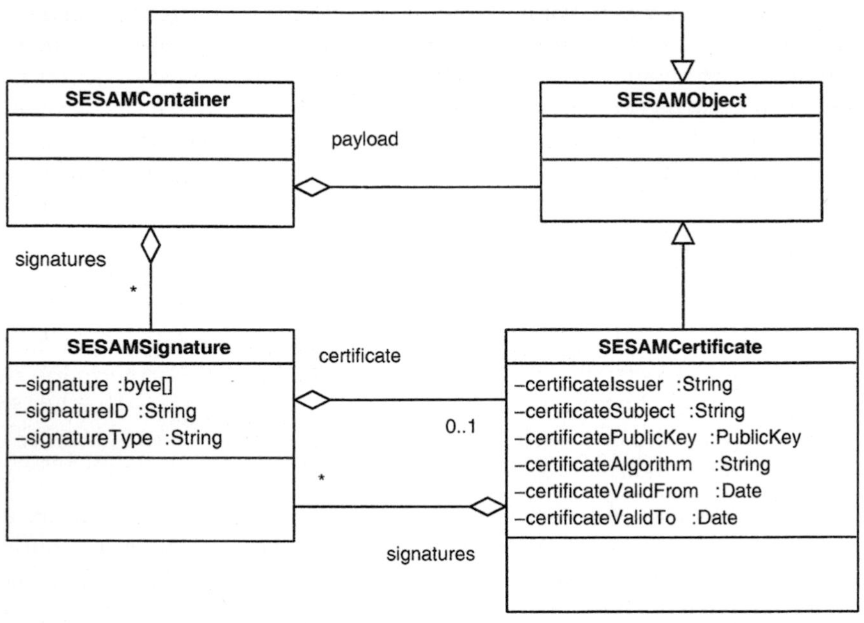

Fig. 30.4: The SESAM Data Model

models multiple issuers may sign the trust data as is done in PGP. Besides that, alternative trust models, like reputation or recommendation systems, require multiple signatures attached to a single item of trust information.

30.3.3 Selected Issues

Having analyzed the robustness and security requirements for our framework we now focus on persistent signatures, privacy-aware data handling and trust models.

Persistent Multiple Signatures

As described in Section 30.3.2, a mechanism to provide persistent signatures on data objects is required. We designed our data model based on the concepts of S/MIME [500] and PGP [645]. As shown in Figure 30.4, the signatures and certificates are an integral part of the data objects. This implies that any component which distributes or stores the objects will automatically serialize the object together with its signatures and certificates. Thus, the signatures are persistently coupled to the object they sign.

The root class of the data model is SESAMContainer, which consists of two attributes: payload and signatures. The payload is always a subclass of SESAMObject. Every SESAMObject can carry a list of SESAMSignatures, where every list element contains a single signature. The SESAMSignature class defines a set of common attributes and the attribute certificate referencing the related certificate. The class SESAMCertificate includes the public key, which was used to create the signature, and attributes containing information about issuer, subject and validity of the certificate.

The content (payload) of a data object can be integrity-protected with one or more independent signatures of different peers. To be able to remove one or more of these signatures without invalidating other signatures of this object, every two signatures must be independent of each other. Therefore, no previously existing signature will be included in the generation of a new signature. This proceeding can be useful if the validity period of the data object should be longer than the validity period of a signature and the corresponding certificate.

Trust Models

Using the data structure introduced in the last section (Figure 30.4) we can ensure the integrity of data objects. To enable applications for a distributed marketplace where electronic contracting is supported, authenticity of a peer's identity is a major issue.

While the integrity of data objects is provided by signatures, peer identity will be provided by digital certificates. Each signature contains an attribute which links a certificate to the public key used. This attribute itself must included in the generation of the signature, otherwise an attacker is able to change the used certificate. A certificate itself contains one or more signatures. This mechanism is suitable for building any trust model from simple certificate lists up to more complex certificate trees such as in reputation systems.

The diversity of applications in a Peer-to-Peer marketplace requires for different trust models to verify identities. Therefore, we develop trust model plugins which implement various trust models. First, we implement common trust models such as Certificate Authority based (X.509 [629]) or distributed models (PGP [645]). Later, plugins to support reputation and recommendation systems are added. All plugins are used by the trust component which offers a common interface for checking identities. The certificate and the chosen trust model are the input parameters of the verification method of the trust component.

Privacy-Aware Data Handling

Implicit routing in Peer-to-Peer networks can be used to guarantee anonymity as outlined in [169, 17, 124, 168]. Anonymity is a good way to establish privacy, because without personally identifiable information there are no privacy issues regarding personal information. But some market scenarios, like concluding an electricity contract require personal information for the delivery and accounting. Thus complete anonymization is no solution for that scenario. Anonymization as mentioned above 'only' anonymizes on the communication level, but on the higher level personal information can still be exchanged. For example, let's assume the communication between a browser and web server is not traceable, but the user enters his name on a registration form. Then the communication itself is anonymous, but not the transaction as a whole on the application layer.

Therefore we have to integrate mechanisms for correctly handling personally identifiable information. The project 'Platform for Privacy Preferences (P3P)' [620] is an approach by the World Wide Web Consortium (W3C) that facilitates for website operators the expression of their privacy policy. This standard can be used to inform users, but not to enforce the correct handling of data. The goal of the Enterprise Privacy Authorization Language (EPAL) [35] is to 'provide the ability to encode an enterprise's privacy-related data-handling policies and practices'. Thus policies can be easily exchanged between different applications and also be automatically enforced. In [427] an approach of identifier-based encryption (IBE) is presented to control the disclosure of personal information. This approach goes beyond EPAL by involving a third party in the process of information disclosure.

Through our modular approach, we can integrate the Peer-to-Peer networks mentioned above that guarantee anonymity in order to offer anonymity mechanisms to service developers. For scenarios where this is insufficient, our next step is to integrate the principles from EPAL and further approaches like IBE.

30.4 Summary

In this chapter we have argued that markets should be viewed as Peer-to-Peer systems on the community, application and infrastructure levels to achieve scalability, spontaneity and reliability in liberalized and harmonized electronic markets. While many proposals favor a tight connection of an application to a specific overlay network, the challenge we address is that of bringing together service orientation (as the Peer-to-Peer paradigm on the application level) with various overlay network techniques (as Peer-to-Peer networks on the infrastructure level). We presented our concept of 'ServiceNets' and the peer node architecture. We argued that there exist many benefits of such a distributed approach to electronic markets. However, securing this approach is a difficult task. We presented the basic security challenges as well as some ideas to tackle them. The proposed framework is a first step to enable Peer-to-Peer markets: future work will have to come up with a catalogue of criteria for deciding which overlay network organization to use for which service, a good Peer-to-Peer network API, and a complete security framework. Thus, an easily deployable framework can be created that makes market participation more spontaneous and less costly.

Part X

Advanced Issues

31. Security-Related Issues in Peer-to-Peer Networks

Luka Divac-Krnic, Ralf Ackermann
(Darmstadt University of Technology)

31.1 Introduction

The main characteristic of great autonomy of peers in Peer-to-Peer networks and the resulting "openness" of such networks makes them vulnerable to diverse attacks on their integrity and security. The possibility and the feasibility of obstruction of a Peer-to-Peer network as a whole, or forthright attacks on a single peer depend largely on a usage scenario of a Peer-to-Peer network. This aspect conditions the possibilities of attacks one has to either take care of or ignore.

When deciding what kind of threats to treat, one has to consider the tradeoff between the performance one wishes a particular Peer-to-Peer network to reach and the level of security one wants to achieve. Due to the different topologies Peer-to-Peer networks have, they face different kinds of threats which one has to consider.

The security concerns can be divided between at least two layers: breaches of security on the application layer and those on the networking layer. We will discuss security issues in the following two subchapters based on this differentiation.

31.2 Security Concerns on the Application Layer

In the following we specify the breaches of security that may take place on the application layer of a Peer-to-Peer network. This presupposes a direct act by a (malicious) user upon a Peer-to-Peer network through the application interface which enables direct user-to-network interaction. This can happen without a substantial effort by the user. Furthermore, we introduce the notion of a malicious node", meaning a node in the Peer-to-Peer network (and a user behind it) that uses the network improperly, whether deliberately or not.

Malicious nodes on the application layer may give incorrect responses to requests. They might report falsely about their bandwidth capacity in order, e.g., to not have much traffic routed over their own node or they might (in the case of file sharing) freeride in the network [11].

R. Steinmetz and K. Wehrle (Eds.): P2P Systems and Applications, LNCS 3485, pp. 529-545, 2005.

These problems are usually met with incentives, where peers are rewarded for good behavior and penalized for bad. Virtual money for file exchanges was introduced by the now defunct Mojo Nation project [425]. Credits are given to peers in eMule [589] as a reward for files being uploaded and used as an entitlement for raising one's priority in the upload queue of another peer-client.

Following are security issues that arise from different applications of Peer-to-Peer networks.

31.2.1 File Sharing Applications

In a completely decentralized and open Peer-to-Peer network, it is relatively easy to disseminate spurious files that do not contain what their names or metadata suggest, but instead random content or binary data. Thus users get annoyed by contents that they were not looking for, and wasted their resources to download them or cache them temporarily. These files can be arbitrary files tagged with names that imply content that is usually searched for in a particular network.

As stated in [463] some individuals are hired and paid by IFPI (International Federation of the Phonographic Industry) [316] to fill the file-sharing networks with files with legitimate titles, but containing silence or random noise. This process is called "network poisoning" and such files are referred to as "junk" or "rogue" files. The aim was to make networks so disreputable, that casual users would give up downloading files.

The reason for these actions is of course the copyright issues. Guidelines for what kinds of files may or may not be placed in the network can be easily set for a small group of users, e.g., inside of a company, but it is nearly impossible to enforce them in an open network that spans multiple domains.

Furthermore, those downloading files from unknown peers exposes themselves to infection with viruses. "Mandragora" was a virus made by Spanish virus-developers back in 2000 [371]. It was merely 8 kB and was exploiting the possibility of blanking the file extensions in Windows computers. The virus would scan the searches of a Gnutella client, intercepting one and reporting itself as a successful hit. When downloaded by another peer not noticing a very small file and not realizing that it was executable, it just installed itself on the new computer. This virus was not meant to do any damage, but only to expose the weaknesses of the Gnutella file sharing network.

31.2.2 Data Backup Service

One of the primary tasks in any kind of company environment is to efficiently and reliably ensure data management and backup through automated periodic copies. The traditional backup approach in companies is to use a backup server to maintain backup copies of data across the whole company. Consequently backup servers are high-end, powerful, and expensive data storage devices. Considering the large expenses for administration of these and the usually low hard-disk utilization of individual workstations, a Peer-to-Peer-based backup solution would save some of the backup budget of a company. Several designs like [63], [386] or [134] deal with this topic.

There are basically two kinds of security issues here. One is the existence of sensitive data of certain peers that should not be visible to other peers in a network. This is a unique characteristic of a Peer-to-Peer backup system; a client-server solution with a backup server would not have to deal with such issues. A possible solution is to encrypt all the backups with a secret key which only the owner-peer knows, but in the event of crash the passwords written on it would also be lost. Taking into account the additional complexity for users of such system, the sensitive data should instead be backed up individually by users themselves using some traditional techniques like burning data on digital media carriers such as CDs.

The other security issue affects the performance of a Peer-to-Peer backup solution. Considering the variable availability of single workstations, a backup would have to be saved on more than one workstation to ensure its availability with a high probability in case of a crash. If there are, e.g., four backup copies of each file, the peer-workstations taking part in Peer-to-Peer backup would have to have a utilization of their hard disks of approximately 20 percent in order to have the remaining 80 percent used by the backup application. Disregarding this constraint, the system might not have enough resources for smooth functioning and data might be lost.

This possibility can be regarded as a "violation of an agreement" between peers rather than an intentional attack on the system's resources. If hard disk capacities continue to grow, then this specific problem will be mitigated. However, this solution is more applicable for backup of text-based files than for large multimedia content, because of the unique restriction of Peer-to-Peer backup described above.

31.2.3 File Storage Service

The file storage service provides the storage of files on more than one location in a Peer-to-Peer network by using a uniquely defined e.g. alphanumeric character sequence for each file, called "handle". Contrary to file-sharing mechanisms where users are looking for specific content, the searches in the file storage system can be accomplished only with help of these specific handles which are mapped to a unique peer or a file in the network. Any peer in the network can locate a file by using it, and the peer with writing rights can update these files as well. In order to get a handle to find a file, a peer has to obtain it through some other communication path than the Peer-to-Peer network itself, like an e-mail exchange, an external website, or even through out-of-band communication.

A file storage application may be used to enable an anonymous and decentralized publication of contents (chapter 31.4.4). The security concern here is the enforcement of an access control among peers in regard to read/write rights on files. An access control list may be associated with each handle provided that all peers behave well. Once malicious peers participate in the network, the files would have to be encrypted with secret keys (chapter 31.4.3) and provided only to a smaller set of peers that are proven legitimate. In anonymizing solutions (chapter 31.4.4) attacks could be directed at making the files unavailable to legitimate peers by deleting them altogether.

31.3 Security Concerns on the Networking Layer

As Peer-to-Peer systems distribute resources and responsibilities into the network, they also distribute security weaknesses allowing malicious peers to take advantage of the vulnerabilities of the system. Malicious peers in a Peer-to-Peer system are those which do not follow correctly the protocol which peers use to administer themselves in a Peer-to-Peer network. They seek to misguide other peers by providing them with false information about the state of the network.

These attacks are mostly relevant in structured Peer-to-Peer networks that use distributed hash table (DHT) lookup. The reason is their structure's vulnerability to false information about the routing in the network: the nodes are mutually dependent on the correctness of each other's routing tables.

31.3.1 Invalid Lookup

A malicious node may forward lookups to an invalid node, a non-existing node or an existing but random node. Incorrect lookups would result in a waste of bandwidth, time, and efficiency of a lookup until the TTL (time-to-live) runs to zero and the requestor ceases to retransmit its queries. Deriving node identifiers by a cryptographic hash of its IP address and a port, like in Chord [576], can make it easy to tell if the correct node is approached since these are needed to contact the node. By deriving node identities from public keys of participants, a longer-term solution may be reached [565]. This solution has performance disadvantages due to the cost of signatures, but provides validity of the origin of a message.

31.3.2 Invalid Routing Update

Nodes in a distributed hash table (DHT) lookup system build their routing tables by consulting other nodes. A malicious node here may corrupt the routing tables of others by sending invalid updates. In this case not only could malicious nodes direct queries to invalid nodes, but well-behaving nodes might give wrong routing information as well, due to invalid routing updates of their own. A more sophisticated attack would be to provide nodes that actually contradict general criteria of routing (high latency, low bandwidth). CAN [504] uses measurements of RTT (round-trip-time) to favor lower latency paths in routing updates. This method may be used for choosing nodes with high latency path as well.

Pastry [527] makes these invalid routing tables easier to detect by forcing entries to have a correct prefix. This way malicious nodes can not produce totally random routing tables without being easily detected. Another way of ensuring that a given node in an update table is authentic, is for every node to ascertain that this node is actually reachable [565]. This method would however cause enormous costs in bandwidth and delay.

31.3.3 Partition

When a node contacts another node in order to join a Peer-to-Peer network, it might falsely join a parallel malicious network which aims to observe the particular behavior of some nodes or contents of a network by running the same protocols as the legitimate one [565]. By providing even the look up capability into the original network and having a node connecting both of these networks or having some original data from the legitimate one, this coalition of malicious nodes could manage to "camouflage" itself and its true intent. A new node might feel itself well off in the network, whereas it is actually subject to observation of its actions which are supposed to be kept private.

The use of public keys, though expensive, can establish some stronger identity than mere IP-addresses, which are subject to frequent changes. If a node has successfully joined a legitimate network in the past, it possesses certain knowledge about the network and possibly nodes that successfully answered its queries. It can indirectly check the routing tables of other nodes, by performing random queries to gain knowledge about possible different views of the network than its own.

31.3.4 Sybil Attack

The Sybil Attack is a name for a node or any other single entity on a network presenting multiple identities to other nodes. Thus other nodes might believe in having an interaction with some distinct nodes whereas in fact there is only one entity they are addressing. This would mean that given particularly huge resources (bandwidth, disk space, computing power) some "deceiving" peer could gain control of a large part of a Peer-to-Peer network, thus undermining its redundancy [177], which is one of its basic properties. However, considering a Peer-to-Peer network to be made up of nodes at the "edges of a network" [28], one could assume rather moderate resources at the disposition of each peer. In a network of several hundred thousand nodes, such a peer could presumably cause rather little damage.

In order to prevent the generation of multiple identities in a Peer-to-Peer network, computational puzzles, like in HashCash [41], might be used. This is an old solution for defense from DoS (denial-of-service) attacks. Before joining the network a peer has to solve some computational problem, thus is forced to use his CPU-cycles needing more time to join than usual. But in the case of an attacker with huge resources, it would at best slow down the process of generation of false identities and the process of these "virtual" nodes joining the network. In structured Peer-to-Peer networks like Chord, CFS, and Pastry where the network determines different tasks that certain peers have to do, hashing of IP addresses is performed partly to establish some kind of identity of individual peers. This would surely complicate and prolong the process of a Sybil Attack.

The most "intrusive" method of binding an identity directly to a node would be, of course, to provide a distinctive identification for each computing unit that is taking part in a network. The commercial platform EMBASSY [292] provides cryptographic keys embedded inside of every hardware device. Of course a user has to implicitly trust that these devices have an embedded key (and not an arbitrary one) and the users actually use these as they are supposed to. The concept of Pretty Good Privacy (PGP) [644] web-of-trust may vouch for established identities for other "newcomers" in the network, but may also be misused by the malicious node to subvert the chain of trust. As a last resort for keeping all the possible weaknesses of the aforementioned solutions somewhat under control, one can rely on certification authorities and similar trusted agencies.

As stated in [171] "one can have, some claim, as many electronic personas as one has time and energy to create". Primarily this energy can be a decisive constraining factor for success in such an attempt.

31.3.5 Consideration of Implications of Topology

Structured networks like nodes in a Chord [575] ring impose an additional burden on the available bandwidth of nodes. A considerable communication overload occurs, which makes nodes vulnerable in ways they would not be in a fully decentralized network like Gnutella [250].

Each instance of join and leave a structured network causes a DHT to rebalance its keys and the data among the nodes which generates a considerable traffic load and degrades the performance of the system [565]. In a Gnutella network this kind of overload is feasible with a sudden increase of search messages which will flood the network, as its search-protocol does not scale, so this condition would be considered standard. In DHT systems this excess data transfer and control traffic would render the whole network inefficient and impair the secure functioning of the system.

In a classic denial-of-service attack (DoS) where an attacker generates arbitrary packets and overloads a targeted node, it would seem as if the targeted node failed in a normal way. As every node in a DHT is responsible for certain data, some of it would be unavailable for a certain period of time. The possible damage here or in a decentralized Peer-to-Peer network will however seem much smaller than in centralized Peer-to-Peer networks like the former Napster or a hybrid Peer-to-Peer network with super-peers. By having the servers attacked with a DoS, whole portions of the network would be "knocked out" for a certain time.

In order not to become too suspicious to many other nodes at once and to make its own malicious behavior more difficult to detect, a node may behave well with some part of the peers in a network and follow the protocol correctly. In a DHT system those peers would be the immediate ones in the vicinity of the malicious node's identifier space [565]. Good behavior with these peers guarantees, at least, longer connectivity to the whole Peer-to-Peer network, as these peers would keep the malicious node in their routing tables. Legitimate reports of bad nodes would not be distinguishable from false accusations of the good ones. Public keys and digital signatures here would help gain some assurance in the legitimacy of the reports by having all peers sign their responses.

In conclusion, a structured topology of nodes provides considerable improvement in performance of the network as well as sensitivity to abrupt changes in the protocol behavior due to the possible impact of malicious nodes.

31.4 Security Concepts for Selected Systems

In following sections we will introduce some solutions which deal with security in the Peer-to-Peer area in quite different ways. The first two address security in a "traditional" manner. This means ensuring that basic "building blocks" of security are met, such as having a protected privacy of communication and maintaining the integrity of messages. The other solutions aim at using the characteristics of a Peer-to-Peer network for ensuring the anonymity of users behind the network rather than a secure data flow among nodes.

The single most technologically advanced solution is "Groove", which is discussed in the next section. A system called "SixFour" is subsequently described, which is an example of a most rudimentary solution for ensuring confidentiality of an electronic data exchange. Finally, we will introduce "Freenet" and other anonymizing solutions.

31.4.1 Groove

"Groove", of Groove Networks Inc. [261], is a Peer-to-Peer groupware tool. It concentrates on providing extensive support for the collaboration of participants on a group-project. It offers so-called "workspaces" for aggregation of documents, messages, and application-specific data which are shared confidentially and unaltered among group-members. Groove especially serves the purpose of synchronizing documents and incremental parts of documents in a secure way.

It does not need any administration and acts like an ad hoc virtual VPN (virtual private network). Bootstrapping the whole constitution of a group is accomplished by one participant inviting others to join the group. It orients around already mentioned "workspaces", where all the messages and documents related to any collaboration activities are saved.

The documents in these workspaces or even parts of these documents, like incremental changes during some processing, are synchronized among all peers. One is able to work offline and upon reconnecting, the system will automatically synchronize the changes. This means that all changes will be transmitted with help of so-called "delta messages" to all Groove-peers taking part in a shared space.

Groove offers, besides the permanent secured connection, different applications on its platform as well, like permanent chat sessions, notepads, a calendar, and a file archive. Besides offering an infrastructure for communication, it is a commercial product oriented towards the needs of users collaborating on a project and offers different add-on components of its software such as Enterprise Management Servers, which can take some of the decentralized tasks and administer them centrally.

All shared space data is encrypted on the hard disks as well, where it is only readable and editable by its owner. This security configuration is always on: it cannot be switched off by an administrator or accidentally by a random peer. Groove provides authentication, data privacy, and data integrity.

Groove has chosen Component Object Model (COM) as its component integration model. COM is Microsoft's framework for developing and supporting program component objects. The Groove Development Kit (GDK) is free for further development. For the distribution or selling of software developed with the GDK one needs an additional licence from Groove Networks Inc.

Groove uses the following basic encryption technologies:

- Symmetric Key Encryption: the standard encryption algorithms are AES and DES.
- Public Key Technology: the standard encryption algorithm is RSA-1; used for securely sending symmetric encryption keys over the network and for signing documents.
- Hashing: the standard encryption algorithm is SHA-1; it is used for password management (password hashed into a secret key), integrity protection (storing a hash of data along with data), and signatures (hashing data to be signed).
- Message Authentication Code (MAC): the standard encryption algorithm is Keyed-Hash Message Authentication Code (HMAC); it is used for signatures for data integrity; a key is used in the MAC computation when communication participants share a secret key.

Authentication

Groove's security model is based on an authentication mechanism that binds a user's identity to specific actions within a Groove environment. Generally, Groove depends on relationships that are rooted in a real-world collaboration because the very forming of a working space begins with an invitation (via e-mail, a telephone call, or face-to-face contact) to a user to join a specific group of people, whose relationships are represented through membership in a workspace.

Before being invited to a workspace, a user must configure his Groove software on his local device by creating his own account, including attributes describing him as a user. This account is stored as an encrypted XML-object. An account may contain more than one identity, e.g., one for personal and one for professional use. Each of these identities will possess sets of keys for communication with users in different workspaces.

Groove offers several ways for members of a workspace to authenticate others members of the same workspace. One of them is fingerprinting of the users' public keys with SHA-1. This method includes an out-of-band contact between the members of a workspace to confirm that the fingerprint is correct. Groove can also use its own PKI where a so-called Management Server would act as a CA (certification authority) for its own domain.

Besides authentication of persons, Groove performs data authentication as well. This is accomplished by using public key signature technology to "mark" the communication between peers and thus map actions in the workspaces to digital identities. Instant messages are signed with 2048-bit RSA keys and incremental changes in workspaces are signed with 1536-bit ESIGN keys.

A login into a Groove network may proceed either by a password or by a smart card. Both these logins are protected locally on the hard-disk with different keys: User Key and Master Key. User's password is processed through a PBKDF2 algorithm (Password-Based Key Derivation Function 2, RFC 2828) that has additional parameters to hamper guessing attacks. There are two master keys: the first protects the user's other cryptographic keys (like workspace keys) and the second protects non-cryptographic user data (like tool and contact data).

A user is obtaining relevant data from two databases when participating in Groove. The account database contains personal contact information for each identity (name, phone number, e-mail, public parts of RSA or ElGammal keys) and private keys associated with the identities held by the account.

Workspace Security

The beginning of a collaboration of peers in a workspace is accomplished by one peer inviting another to join the workspace he just set up. As stated above Groove depends on real-world relationships, so an invitation will be directed at someone personally well known. An invitee who does not yet have Groove software may be invited by an e-mail which will contain a URL of where to download it, public keys of the inviting peer, and cryptographic protocol settings for the workspace the invitee shall join. After receiving this e-mail, the invitee should phone the peer inviting and authenticate each other by checking their fingerprints.

After confirmation by the inviting peer, all other members in the workspace will get to know about the invitee as a new member by a so-called "add member delta" message and the invitee will receive the workspace with shared keys used by other peers. From then on the invitee's identity will appear on each of the other user's workspaces and by trusting the inviting peer they might begin working with their new member. The "add member delta" message contains data about the new member (ESIGN public key, Diffie-Hellman public key, and other information) and makes the old members aware of a new member joining them.

There is always someone who has to actually make a first step and kick-start a project on which others will collaborate: Groove uses for this purpose a hierarchy of roles and access controls. The three basic roles are: manager, participant, and guest (with declining access rights). The initiator of a new workspace automatically gets the role of manager and can therefore assign roles to others and invite or even un-invite peers to or from the workspace.

The roles themselves map to certain permissions related to actions in the workspace and actions with tools in the workspace.

By uninviting a peer from a workspace, which only the manager of the workspace may do, a "rekey delta message" is sent to all peers in the workspace except to the uninvitee, which contains the new workspace group key encrypted in each member's pair-wise key. The uninvited peer gets a delta message informing him he is uninvited and removes all the data from his workspace.

Communication over Relay Servers

With "relay services" users may exchange changes in workspace with a time gap between the two actions. When a user goes offline the relay service will "notice" it, save the changes, and pass them to a partner peer of the same workspace that may be offline when this peer gets online again.

Groove software randomly chooses a relay server from a list it contains and registers a new account that a user previously set up. From now on, the software uses only this relay server and sends, along with its contact information, also the URL of its relay server in order for other Groove peers to acquire the full communication path. More precisely, an actual relay-to-workspace communication is taking place with a secret key established between them, whereas due to end-to-end encryption the relay service can not access data inside delta or instant messages but only the header information needed to locate another peer.

Furthermore, relay servers can enclose the messages in an HTTP - compatible format and use ports 80 or 443 (mostly configured open) to circumvent the firewalls that may separate two peers collaborating over Groove. This capability may well arouse suspicion with managers of the company or network administrators of a company's LAN who may not approve of arbitrary data being exchanged across the company's boundaries.

Conclusion

Without relay servers Groove's ad hoc synchronization of data made offline would not work. This centralized feature plays an important role in an effective collaboration in Groove, so the Peer-to-Peer paradigm of fully autonomous entities is constrained here. Such a server is still a single point of failure and a potential target for a DoS attack. Furthermore, at the deepest level of integration, any platform that wishes to integrate and further develop Groove will have to support the Component Object Model (COM).

31.4.2 SixFour (6/4) Peer-to-Peer

The SixFour Peer-to-Peer system [566] obtained its name from the date of the Tiananmen Square protests in Beijing in 1989. The developers intended this system for potential users who live in oppressive countries with limited access to free press. The basics of the system enable a peer to establish an encrypted connection to a trusted peer outside of his country and then have this peer further forward any other requests into the Internet. The aim is to enable peers to get data confidentially from the Internet thus evading censorship.

A peer wanting to connect to the SixFour network would already have to know the address of the trusted peer and his RSA public key. The authenticity of the key would have to be checked at the website of the SixFour developers, hacktivismo.com. For this purpose the peers would have to know the appropriate signature of Hacktivismo [268].

The trusted peer simply has to forward the requests of peers that "hang" on them so they can access any TCP- or UDP-based service on the Internet, provided the trusted peer itself has access to these services, too. One of the important criteria for becoming a trusted peer is to provide a permanent IP-connection (permanent IPv4 address). The most reasonable entities to become trusted peers (according to the idea of developers) seem to be, e.g., human rights organizations or NGOs promoting democratic values.

The routing inside of the SixFour network is anonymous if it occurs over more than 3 nodes. That is, every peer in the routing protocol knows only the RoutingID, the source, and the target of the packet. The routing topology of the SixFour network is like Gnutella's, in that every peer is connected with several others and floods his own requests or routes other requests at random to his neighbors. Duplicate requests are rejected according to their RoutingID. The node-to-node encryption is a classical SSL over port 443 and the end-to-end encryption is RSA-based.

The shortcomings of this system are primarily the question of the establishment of the relationship between a peer inside a "censored" part of the Internet and a trusted peer "outside". How does a potential peer inside a "censored" part of the Internet come to know which IP-address is an address of a trusted peer, through which he could make requests and not be afraid of possible reprimand from the "censor"? It seems that only some kind of out-of-band information gathering would help.

Furthermore, it is not clear how these trusted peers could be protected from possible attacks from entities that would have an interest in disrupting the SixFour network (like those very countries whose censorship SixFour tries to break). The possible attackers on trusted peers presumably have the same or even better know-how than the developers of any free software on the market and possibly strong financial backing as well. An additional criterion before accepting entities acting as trusted peers could be a display of security measures that these peers employ locally and set requirements for.

Otherwise one would never know which trusted peer could be compromised, thus compromising the whole network.

Before becoming a serious application with wide acceptance, SixFour would have to establish a wider community of users and proof of a longer stable functioning (without security flaws and compromise of peers). It offers the basic functionality of confidential data exchange and anonymity in the network, but it does not tackle at all the question of key distribution. Although at the beginning of a possible future enhancement, SixFour is a fresh example of what Peer-to-Peer-systems are good for beyond simple file-sharing.

31.4.3 Freenet

Freenet [124] is a Peer-to-Peer system that enables publication, retrieval and replication of data whose authors and readers remain anonymous: a node can not know whether the node to which a file is forwarded is the actual requestor or itself a mere "forwarder" of the file. From another point of view a node can not know whether the node, from which it is obtaining a file is the actual originator or merely a forwarder of the file. Trust and adequate search of the network are still open issues in this system.

The cornerstones of the architecture of this system are the knowledge of the nodes of the immediate neighbors (routing tables are not exchanged between nodes), association of files with hash-keys, and distributed storage of files (the owners of a hard drive do not know implicitly what is stored on their site). The emphasis of the system lies heavily on the protection of privacy of users; in this case the disconnection of an association of a file with its originator or submitter and a possible user (reader) of the same file. The primary purpose of the network as a whole is censorship-resistant storage.

The files are replicated in the parts of network where they are most frequently requested and deleted in those parts of the network where they are seldom requested. Freenet acts like a distributed file system with location independence and transparent replication.

Security Architecture

Every Freenet peer runs a node that provides some storage space for the network. When adding a file, a user assigns a globally unique identifier (GUID) to that file. This GUID will be sent when retrieving a file as well. The GUID is calculated using the SHA-1 hash and made up of 2 keys: the content-hash key (CHK) and the signed-subspace key (SSK). CHKs are hashed contents of the files using the SHA-1. SSK is used to make up a specific namespace that anyone (who has the keys) can read, but only its owner can write to. A peer first generates an arbitrary public-private key and chooses a text description of the subspace. One then calculates the SSK by hashing both the public part of the key and the descriptive string, concatenating them, and hashing them again.

In order to retrieve the file, one needs the public key and the descriptive string (to recreate the SSK). To add to, or update the file, one would need the private part of the key to be able to compute the valid signature, which the nodes storing the file would check and accept, or reject if false. The SSK key can be used to store an indirect file containing a pointer to a CHK: a file is stored under its CHK, which is in turn stored as an indirect file under the SSK. Given the SSK the original file is retrieved in 2 steps, and the origin of the file is obscured a step further.

One of the most distinctive characteristics of Freenet is that management of the node and the management of the storage of the same node is somewhat disjointed. If a node gets a query, it first checks it own store. The peculiarity here is that the semantics of the content of the store itself is not comprehensible to humans. The comparison between the request and the possible file in the storage has to be computed.

If the request is not satisfied, the node forwards the request to the node with the closest key to the one requested. This information will be gathered at one specific node through time by having many requests running through it. When the request is successful, each node which passed the request now passes the file back and creates an entry in its routing table binding the data holder with the requested key. On the way back the nodes might cache the file at their stores. This way subsequent searches find the requested file faster.

For requesting and inserting a file, Freenet offers the possibility of adding a mix-style "pre-routing" of messages [124]. This way the messages would be encrypted by a succession of public keys which establish a route that this message will follow. When the message reaches the end-point of this pre-routing path it is injected into the Freenet network and thus the true originator of the message is "obliterated".

Inserting a file works similar to requests. A user assigns a GUID and sends an insert message first to his own node with a new key and a TTL value. The insert might fail because the same file is already in the network (CHK collision) or there is a different file with the same description (SSK collision). The checking for a same possible file refers to a lookup whether the key already exists; if not, the node searches for the numerically closest key and forwards the insert message to the corresponding node. If the TTL expires without collision the final node sends the message that the insert may be performed. On the way to the final node, the file is cached by every intermediary node, the data is verified against the GUID and a routing entry is made pointing to the final node as the data holder.

The makers of Freenet recommend encrypting all data before inserting them into the network. Since the network does not perceive this encryption since it only forwards already encrypted bits, the inserters have to distribute the secret keys as well as the corresponding GUIDs directly to the end users. This is performed through some out-of-band means such as personal communication. The same method is used when adding a new node to Freenet: a user wishing to join sends his new public key and a physical address to a node whose physical address he already knows.

In order not to let only one node decide what key to assign to a joining node (and allow a sort of unilateral access to certain data) a chain of hashes of the seeds of each node and XOR'ed results with other seeds down the path and hashes thereof (called "commitments") is produced to provide the means for every node to check if other nodes revealed their seeds truthfully. The key for a joining node is assigned as the XOR of all the seeds.

A still open issue is search adequacy of the Freenet network for relevant keys. There is still no effective way to route searches, leaving the dissemination of keys solely to out-of-band means. One possible solution is to build public subspaces for indirect keyword files. When inserting files, one could insert several indirect files corresponding to search keywords for the original file, so an indirect file would have pointers to more than one file (more than one hashed key as content).

The management of storage determines how long a file will be kept by the popularity of the file, measured by the frequency of the requests per file. Files that are seldom requested are deleted when a new file has to be inserted. Even when a file is deleted at one node, another one may still have a copy of it. The node that already deleted it, will still have an entry in its routing table pointing to the original data holder, as the routing tables entries are much smaller than data and will be kept longer.

31.4.4 Further Peer-to-Peer Anonymizing Solutions

Following are several more solutions that have as a priority the anonymization of a connection, transaction, data stream, or communication between two peers in a network. These systems do not protect specific data from access by an unauthorized peer or intrusions into peer-machines. They try to make facets of communication between two peers invisible or not back-traceable by a supposed eavesdropper. Usually the high connectivity of nodes in a Peer-to-Peer network is used to obscure the path an arbitrary message has taken.

Tarzan

Tarzan [229] determines sequences of mix-style relays randomly chosen from a pool of volunteer peers in the network. The relays are all equal peers which can be originators or relays of traffic, since they can not know whether they are the first hop in a path. The two ends of a communication session inside the Tarzan network are a node running an application and another node running a NAT that forwards the traffic to an end destination. Tarzan performs a nested encryption per hop and encapsulates it in a UDP packet. These encryptions are performed in the sequence of the nodes that will be passed through, so the biggest share of encryptions is situated at the node seeking anonymity. The method is similar to Onion routing [582] with the difference that the nodes are chosen randomly and dynamically instead of using a fixed set. In order to choose the relays, Tarzan uses the Chord lookup algorithm (relays are in a Chord ring) with a random lookup key. When that key's successor is found, it responds with its IP address and public key. Tarzan claims thus to provide anonymity in cases of malicious Tarzan participants, inquisitive servers on the Internet, and observers with some limited capability to see traffic on some links.

Publius

Publius [611] claims to be a censorship-resistant web publishing system. The motivation for this system is the possible, presumably unfair legal attacks from powerful corporate entities or similar litigious organizations which try to prevent publishing of "unpleasant" details about them or practices related to them.

A system-wide list of available static servers is assumed. The content is encrypted by the publisher and spread over some of the web servers. The publisher takes the key, K, that is used to encrypt the file and splits it into n shares, such that any k of them can reproduce the original K, but k-1 give no hints how to reproduce the key. Each server receives the encrypted content and one of the shares. At this point, the server has no idea what it is hosting; it is simply a store of random-looking data. To browse content, a retriever must get the encrypted content from some server and k of the shares.

The publishing process produces a special URL that is used to recover the data and the shares and that is cryptographically tied to the URL so that any modification to the content or the URL results in the retriever being unable to find the information, or a failed verification. Only publishers can update or delete their Publius content. The Peer-to-Peer character of this system is limited because of static IP addresses and the static set of servers. However, the content is in fact distributed and the servers which host the content are autonomous.

Onion Routing

Onion Routing [582] is a system for anonymous Internet connections based on mix-networks. A user creates a layered data structure called an "onion" that specifies the encryption algorithms and keys to be used as data is transported to the target node. As data passes through each router on the way to the final target, one layer of encryption is removed according to a directive found on the outer layer of the "onion". So the onion gets "peeled off" a layer every time it passes through a router. The final target of the "onion" gets only plain text (data).

Crowds

Users in this system [508] submit their requests through a "crowd" - a group of Web surfers running the Crowds software. Crowds users forward HTTP requests to another randomly selected member of their crowd. A path is configured as the request crosses the network and each Crowds member encrypts the request for the next member on the path, so the path is not predetermined before it is submitted to the network. Thus an end server or the forwarding Crowds member cannot know where a request really originated. By using the symmetric ciphers Crowds claims to perform better than mix-based solutions. A drawback of Crowds is that each peer on the path of the data to the intended destination can "see" the plain text.

31.5 Conclusion

The large amount of security vulnerabilities in Peer-to-Peer networks surely needs a considerable monitoring by all peers that are interested in the unobstructed working of the network. As already stated, there is always a tradeoff in Peer-to-Peer networks between security and performance issues.

Peer-to-Peer networks are supposed to be open to every peer that wishes to voluntarily provide his resources and in return consume the resources of others. Authenticating every one of them and signing all their messages would create a new overload which could bring the performance of a network nearly to a standstill. In accordance with its open character a Peer-to-Peer networks' primary concerns are not "classic" security measures, but the smooth functioning of a protocol that binds the peers in a network. This is what security concerns in Peer-to-Peer networks should focus on.

Though Groove orients itself toward one specific use of its network, it seems to be an up-to-date solution for classic security management. The use of relay servers diminishes somewhat a "real" Peer-to-Peer character, but the standard security features work just as well without them.

The anonymization tools constitute an "instrument" that the abundance of autonomous nodes with an adequate innovative communication protocol may establish. However they may always be a focus of social debate whether providing such means to keep the identity of wrongdoers unknown is justified. As always, all man-made tools, including Peer-to-Peer-networks, may or may not be used in a legitimate way.

32. Accounting in Peer-to-Peer-Systems

Nicolas C. Liebau, Vasilios Darlagiannis, Oliver Heckmann
(Darmstadt University of Technology)
Andreas Mauthe (Lancaster University)

32.1 The Purpose of Accounting

Today's Peer-to-Peer (P2P) systems seem to work fine for file sharing applications. Though, is that true for all kinds of applications or is it just true for file sharing of copyright protected content? In the latter case, clear incentives for sharing exist - users download copyright protected media content for free. Even here free riding is a widespread behavior [11]. Therefore, many file sharing systems introduced incentive systems, like the eMule credit system [192] or BitTorrent [320]. Obviously, for legally used Peer-to-Peer file sharing applications giving incentives to users for sharing their resources in a fair manner is an important feature.

Another important feature of Peer-to-Peer systems is fair resource allocation. In fact, some people define the free rider problem as part of the resource allocation problem [167]. However, we distinguish between incentives and resource allocation. The goal of resource allocation is to allocate the available resources in a fair manner among the system's entities such that bottlenecks are avoided. Resource allocation is an important feature for applications where quality of service is critical.

We can imagine the Peer-to-Peer paradigm being used for business applications where users sell and offer services. Here, it is an important feature that users can prove they delivered a service or paid for a service received. This requires trustworthy bookkeeping.

All three of these features - incentives, resource allocation, and business support - have a common requirement. Information is needed about the actions in the Peer-to-Peer system as well as evaluation of this information. Peer-to-Peer systems cannot easily provide this kind of information because it is completely distributed. The lack of information leads to the free rider problem because users feel completely anonymous. Furthermore, this missing information makes it difficult to do resource allocation. And without knowing who bought/sold a service, business applications are impossible. The missing functionality is obviously accountability. Accountability in information systems is defined as the process of tracing information system activities to a responsible source [443]. If we can introduce accountability into Peer-to-Peer systems, we can solve the problem of missing information and with it add the aforementioned features to Peer-to-Peer systems.

R. Steinmetz and K. Wehrle (Eds.): P2P Systems and Applications, LNCS 3485, pp. 547-566, 2005.

32.2 Why Is Not Accounting in Peer-to-Peer Straight Forward?

Looking at Client/Server systems, accounting was never seen as a major issue because it is intuitively easy. It was not even a real research topic (see e.g. RADIUS [509]). To do accounting in Client/Server systems the server simply logs every access activity of the client. The server can do so because all communication is done either between client and server or between two clients over the server. Two clients never communicate directly.

In Peer-to-Peer we have exactly the opposite situation. There is no server but almost exclusively direct Peer-to-Peer communication. There is no unit in the network that could log all the communication within the system. All that can be done in Peer-to-Peer is limited to local observations. A peer logs itself the communication in which it is involved. Accordingly, there is no straightforward solution for gaining system-wide knowledge about the activities in the system using this locally gathered information.

Furthermore, the problem is very complex because the collected information must be stored and used in a trustworthy manner. Otherwise the accounting system will not be reliable. For example KaZaA's participation level [342] is an accounting system with a trustworthiness problem. The system stores locally at the peer information about the peer's contribution to the system in form of uploads. This information is evaluated and determines the maximum download speed for the peer itself. Obviously, there is a strong incentive to manually increase the participation level in order to cheat. And cheating is easy, especially since *KaZaA Lite* (also known as *K++*), which does not include the download limiter, is freely available [344].

This real life example leads directly to the next issue with accounting in completely distributed autonomous systems: If there are defined rules of behavior then there must also be a way to enforce them. In the case of KaZaA the participation rule cannot be enforced because cheating cannot be detected. Accordingly users get benefits only from using the KaZaA Lite client application instead of using the original KaZaA client application.

Consequently, three aspects make accounting in Peer-to-Peer difficult: The required information is distributed throughout the whole system, the information must be stored and used in a trustworthy manner, and behavior rules for incentive systems or resource allocation must be enforceable.

Finally, a fourth aspect should not be forgotten: An accounting system for Peer-to-Peer should use the scarce resources of the system (e.g. bandwidth) economically.

32.3 The Solution Space – A Classification of Peer-to-Peer Accounting Schemes

This section outlines the different design parameters for building an accounting system that meets the described requirements. The problem can be structured into two main parts: *Information collection* covers the options how and in which form information is collected. *Information storage* concerns the options of where the collected information can be stored.

32.3.1 Information Collection

In Peer-to-Peer systems there are only a few options where accounting information could be collected. Assuming real Peer-to-Peer connections (without a third peer in the middle as a "trusted party"), the information can only be collected at the service provider peer, at the service receiver peer, or at both peers. This collection process usually consists of a metering process and an evaluation process. The metering process measures the used bandwidth (the amount of data received/sent), time (the duration of the service), or collects some service specific signals like "file complete". The evaluation process interprets this information to generate accounting events. These events determine when an accounting record is created.

Accounting records contain the accounting information and can take several forms.

Plain Numbers

The simplest form is plain numbers. For every peer there exists an account balance stored somewhere in the Peer-to-Peer systems. For example, for each MByte uploaded the peer's account balance is increased by one. Plain numbers can be changed very easily, therefore, this kind of accounting record is especially vulnerable to fraud. Nevertheless, this form of information consumes very little space and bandwidth when it is transferred between peers.

Receipts

Receipts are documents of fixed form that can contain all kinds of accounting information, e.g. transaction partners, transaction object, metering information, and an evaluation of it. This evaluation could be the information how this receipt modifies the peer's account balance. This part of information would be similar to plain numbers. In comparison with plain numbers, the additional information of a receipt adds some trustworthiness to the accounting information, because more information is available, which could help to detect fraud.

Signed Receipts

Signed receipts are normal receipts with a signature to add integrity to the information contained in the receipt. This is a very important step to achieve trustworthiness of information. Additionally, a signature authenticates a receipt. Working with signed receipts requires that every peer owns a private/public key pair. Such a key pair can e.g. be issued by a central authority or peers could create the key pair themselves and using Public Key Infrastructure (PKI) the keys would be certified. E.g. JXTA [412] uses self signed certificates. This approach has the disadvantage that these keys are not persistently associated with a peer. A peer can easily create a new key pair if it wants to revoke its identification. This problem can be elaborated for example by using a Web of Trust as implemented by PGP [543] or the cryptoID-project of JXTA [139]. A central authority implementing a PKI does not have this disadvantage, though its usage seems contrary to the Peer-to-Peer paradigm. Nevertheless, the responsibilities of a central authority within the Peer-to-Peer system could be reduced to issuing certificates with keys and approving the validity of keys. The services offered in the system would continue to be delivered in a Peer-to-Peer manner.

Receipts are normally signed by the author of the contained information. Indeed, receipts could also be signed by the transaction partner to include an agreement about the information in the receipt. This can also be accomplished by bilaterally signing a receipt. However, one should bear in mind that each signature increases the size of the receipt. And size matters for the efficiency of the accounting system in terms of created overhead. Depending on the cryptography mechanism used, the size of the signature could be large. For example, today's RSA signatures are typically chosen to be not smaller than 1024 bit.

Tokens

In the context of this chapter the term *token* is used for any kind of issued document. An issuer issues a specific number of these documents (tokens). Thus, the number of tokens available in a Peer-to-Peer system can be limited. This results in a specific characteristic that is otherwise hard to achieve - through issuing a limited number of tokens they become a scarce resource. Accordingly, tokens can represent other scarce resources. However, they are not that easy to handle like normal receipts, because two major problems must be addressed: *Forgery* and *Double Spending*, both of which have to be avoided. With respect to double spending a token must be clearly identifiable. Thus, a they must contain a unique identification. Also, there must be a mechanism built into an accounting system to check for double spending. To avoid forgery it must be ensured that only the issuing authority can create a token and therefore, a token must be signed by the issuing authority with its private key.

There are several options for the token issuing authority in an accounting system. For example, in digital cash systems a central bank issues the tokens (e.g. [546]). This option ensures trustworthiness and control; however, this does not conform to the Peer-to-Peer paradigm. In [636] a micropayment scheme for Peer-to-Peer systems is presented that relieves the central bank many of its responsibilities. The second option is that each peer issues its own tokens. Here tokens are very similar to signed receipts. It is also difficult to control the number of tokens issued by every peer. Therefore, determining the economic value of a peer's token is difficult, too. The third option is a compromise between the first and second option. It is issuing tokens by a subgroup of peers and controlling the subgroup's actions in order to control the total number of tokens in the system. In the second part of this chapter an accounting system using this approach is presented.

Token-based accounting systems can further be distinguished by the usage of the tokens. Tokens can either be used as kind of micropayment system or as receipt, i.e. a token represents exactly a specific part of a provided/consumed service (e.g. 1 MByte data transfer). Tokens become receipts by adding accounting information to the token. Here, a token can represent all kinds of transactions or parts of transactions.

Proof of Work

Proof of Work (PoW) is another micropayment concept where a user has to show that he performed some computationally difficult problem to be eligible to receive a service [167]. Nevertheless, PoW cannot be redeemed by the receiver for something of value to him. Therefore, they can be used to avoid denial of service attacks or flooding attacks. Further, they do not present an economic measure [167]. Also, to create a PoW, CPU cycles that are a limited and that might be traded in the Peer-to-Peer system (and will then represent a scarce resource themselves) are needed. Therefore, PoW in general can be regarded as improper for accounting systems.

32.3.2 Information Storage

In whichever form accounting data is collected, it must be stored at some place in the network, a so called account. The account location is an important design parameter because it strongly influences the traffic overhead of an accounting system. For every transaction, one or more accounting records accumulate and must be transferred to the account. Also, the location influences how easy it is for a peer to manipulate accounting records and defraud the system. There are three basic alternatives for the account location: accounts can be located locally at the peer that collects the data, at a central server, or remotely at a peer other than the collecting peer. Centrally held accounts obviously are contrary to the Peer-to-Peer paradigm. For every transaction communication with the central entity would be necessary to transfer the record. Therefore, this solution is out of the question. The advantages and disadvantages of the two other alternatives shall now be elaborated.

Local Accounts

Storing accounting records at the place where they accrue has the obvious advantage of reduced traffic, because the records do not need to be sent to the account holder. However, using local accounts poses an important trust problem. Using plain numbers or self-signed receipts to store information enables users to easily change the contained information in order to defraud the accounting system. The appearance of KaZaA Lite as competitor to KaZaA is an example to this behavior [344]. Therefore, receipts should be signed either by the transaction partner or a third party. Alternatively, tokens should be used. Accordingly, accounting records need to be transferred between the transaction partners. Therefore, in terms of bandwidth usage, storing accounting records locally is only advantageous in comparison to other storage location, if the transaction partner needs to get the records for some reason. For example, both transaction partners have to agree about the contained accounting information. Further advantages are that users have immediate control over the collected accounting records. No redundancy need be built into the system, because a peer's accounting records are not needed when it is offline. Also, users are themselves responsible for doing a data backup.

Remote Accounts

The alternative location for storing accounting records is third peers. Using third peers, hence separating account holders from account owners, clearly makes it more difficult for any one peer to fraudulently manipulate accounting records. Accordingly, depending on the Peer-to-Peer application's requirements, special mechanism to ensure information integrity such as signing might not be needed.

However, using remote accounts requires the exchange of more administrative messages between peers. This stems from the need for redundancy. Because the account holder is not always available, several account holders per peer, each holding a replication of the account, are required. All replications of an account need to be kept consistent. Therefore, mechanisms to detect potential inconsistencies as well as mechanisms for determining the actual account status in a situation of disagreement are required. For example, a Byzantine quorum might be used for the latter case.

32.4 Proposed Accounting Schemes

In this section the presented structure of Peer-to-Peer accounting systems is used to classify the known accounting systems. However, most of the related work was not designed as accounting systems but as economic frameworks. Economic frameworks contain an accounting mechanism and use it to introduce economic based incentives into the Peer-to-Peer system. That is, users have to "pay" accounting units to receive a service and gain accounting units if they provide a service. Accordingly, these systems are concerned with the economic value of an accounting unit. Therefore, they either include mechanisms to regulate the amount of accounting units in the Peer-to-Peer system or try to give users guidelines to assess the economic value of an accounting unit.

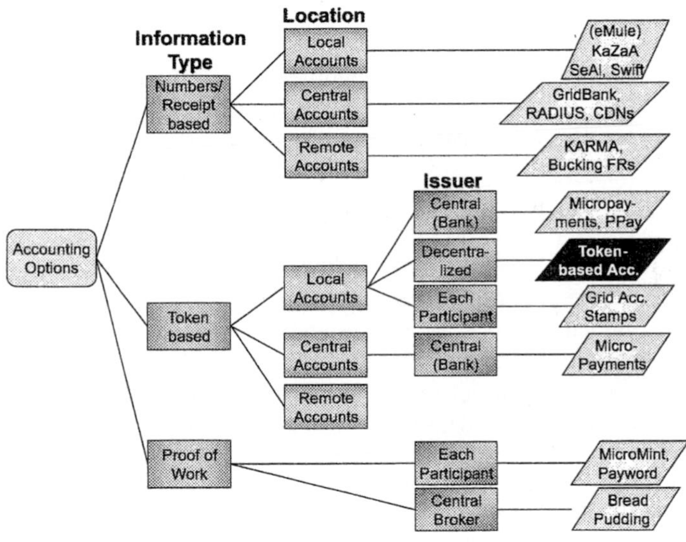

Fig. 32.1: Classification of the Related Work

32.4.1 Plain Numbers-Based Systems

Currently the two most widely used Peer-to-Peer accounting mechanisms are KaZaA's participation level [342] and eMule's credit system [192]. Both systems account for the amount of data uploaded and downloaded and store the collected information locally. KaZaA's system uses the ratio of uploads to downloads (measured in amount of data transferred) to calculate a peer's actual maximal allowed download speed. The higher this ratio is the higher is the maximal allowed download speed. This is a typical incentive mechanism for file sharing systems. However, KaZaA's system is easy to cheat because the accounting information is stored locally. In fact in the KaZaA clone KaZaA Lite [344] the participation level is removed. In contrast, eMule's credit system is used to determine a requestor's position in the provider's download queue. The position is determined by the amount of data the requestor uploaded to the provider. This system has the obvious advantage, that it cannot be cheated. The provider keeps his accounting records that only influence his own behavior. The disadvantage is that this system only accounts for local observations. A peer could have upload to the system much more than it downloaded. However, if it downloads from a peer to which it did not upload before, it will get a bad position in the provider's download queue.

Another system that uses local accounts to store plain numbers as accounting information is Swift [584]. In contrast to the both systems mentioned before, it is not used in practice yet. Swift basically is a behavior model for Peer-to-Peer file sharing to support fair large scale distribution of files in which downloads are fast. Each peer maintains a credit for every other peer it is connected to. A peer will only upload to a peer with a positive credit balance. Because the accounting data only affects the local peer behavior, peers have no incentive to falsify the collected information.

A system taking into account a peer's actions in the overall system is Karma [603]. Karma stores for every peer in the system a value that represents Its balance of uploads against downloads. This balance is stored at remote peers. These remote peers are called a peer's bank set. The bank set consists of multiple peers, for redundancy reasons. The balance of a peer must not be lost. Accordingly, a bank set is rather large - a suggested size is 64 peers. For every transaction the bank sets of the provider and receiver peer communicate to adjust the peers' balance according to the transaction value. Further, Karma includes the concept of an epoch. At the beginning of each epoch every peer's balance is adjusted accordingly in order to avoid inflation.

In [14] another system using remote accounts is presented. So called accountants store a peer's balance. Like in Karma the accountants are third peers. To ensure that the balance is not lost a set of accountants is required for each peer. With every transaction the balance of the two transaction partners is updated to the new value. A non-mediated and a mediated settlement protocol are presented.

There are other systems known to do accounting using numbers. However these systems are not compliant with the Peer-to-Peer paradigm. These systems use a central server to do the accounting. Examples are the accounting mechanism in RADIUS [509], accounting mechanisms in content distribution networks [95], and the accounting mechanism for GRID called Gridbank [61].

32.4.2 Receipt-Based Systems

SeAl [453] is a Peer-to-Peer accounting system that uses locally stored receipts. SeAl is working based on favors. For every transaction a receipt is created and stored locally at the receiver and provider. As a result of the transaction, the receiver owes the provider a favor. A favor can be paid back by the receiver by providing a service to the provider. Also the provider can use a favor by redirecting service requests of other peers to the receiver. Furthermore, peers can publish Blacklist Reports about peers behaving against the system's rules. For each service request a score is calculated (using paid back favors and Blacklist Reports) that influences the request's position in the provider's request queue. Accordingly, not all accounting data is stored locally. However, for Blacklist Reports there exist no accounts for storage.

32.4.3 Token-Based Systems

One class of token based accounting systems are micropayment systems that use tokens as a micro currency. For payment these tokens are transferred between users. (Micropayment systems just modify centrally hold bank accounts on request belong to the plain numbers-based systems.) All micropayment systems use a central broker or bank. Thus, they are not appropriate for Peer-to-Peer systems. A micropayments system tailored to Peer-to-Peer systems is presented in [636]. It relieves the broker of some task and these tasks are facilitated by the peers of the system. As a result the broker can even go off-line for short time periods and the system can still continue to operate.

Mojo Nation [441] was one of the earliest Peer-to-Peer systems to use a payment protocol. Users had to use a virtual currency called Mojos to obtain a service from another peer. Mojo Nation still required a centralized trusted third party to issue the Mojos and to resolve double-spending issues.

A system using stamps for peers' "evidence of participation" is presented in [431]. Every peer issues personalized stamps and trades these with other peers. If peer A requests a service from peer B, peer A has to pay a specific amount of peer B's stamps back to B. There is no limit how many stamps a peer issues. However, if a peer issues too many stamps in comparison to its offered services the stamps will devalue. Thus, the peer will have difficulty obtaining other stamps, as rational nodes will not wish to purchase its stamps. This way the stamps protocol combines a virtual currency and reputation.

32.4.4 Proof of Work-Based Systems

In [520] two micropayment systems based on Proof of Works are presented. In both systems each participant issues his own secrets. As mentioned before, using such systems poses the problem for users to determine the economic value of another user's virtual currency. In order to overcome the need to identify the exchange rate of two users' virtual currency in [321] Proof of Work-based systems are extended to work with a central broker that issues secrets centrally. This way only one virtual currency exists in the system. However, there is no way known to construct such a system according to the Peer-to-Peer paradigm.

32.5 Token-Based Accounting Scheme

Within the scope of the EU Project "Market Management of Peer-to-Peer Services" (MMAPPS) we were in need for a highly flexible and trustworthy accounting scheme for Peer-to-Peer systems. In response to that need we developed the here presented token-based accounting scheme.

32.5.1 Prerequisites

The token-based accounting system assumes that users can clearly be identified through a permanent id, (e.g. through a private/public key pair proven through a certificate issued from a certification authority). Depending on the application scenario, alternative approaches like [139] are also applicable. Apart from the certification authority it is intended to avoid any central element.

Further, we assume the use of a reputation mechanism in the Peer-to-Peer system. This system is used to publish fraudulent behavior that technical mechanisms cannot detect. The reputation mechanism assigns a reputation value to each peer that represents the trustworthiness of the peer. A possible solution is presented e.g. in [333].

32.5.2 Overview

The primary goal of the proposed system is to collect accounting data and to enable system-wide coordination of resource service usage based on the collected information. To enable the usage of receipts for coordination in a distributed system, the receipts must have the basic characteristic of the resources and services they represent, i.e. they must be scarce. Therefore, the receipts must be issued. Accordingly, every user has a limited amount of receipts it can use in transactions. Thus, in the presented approach tokens are used rather as issued receipts than as a virtual currency. As a result, the tokens must not have the characteristics of micropayments, namely anonymity and untraceability [112]. Therefore, tokens have a clear owner that is contained in the token. This enables local tokens storage. Otherwise (if anonymity should be maintained) untraceable tokens have to be stored at trusted remote accounts to control double spending.

Each peer holds an account with a specific amount of tokens clearly issued to it. A peer spends a token by sending it to its transaction partner in order to receive a service. Accordingly, when a peer provides a service it collects foreign tokens from other peers. Peers cannot spend foreign tokens. Using the token aggregation process, peers exchange the collected foreign tokens against new ones. To achieve trustworthiness new tokens are signed with the systems shared private key using threshold cryptography [164]. Thus, a token must be signed by a quorum of peers to become valid. The token structure ensures protection against forgery, double spending and stealing. The three basic protocols of the token-based accounting system are *Token Aggregation*, *Check for Double Spending*, and *Payment*.

32.5.3 Token Structure

Figure 32.2 shows the information contained in a token. A new unused token contains the first five information fields starting from the right hand of the figure. The issuing date and time in milliseconds together with the serial number and the owner id serve as unique identification of a token. This is required to enable the detection of double spending. Further, this way double spending can be traced to the owner. During the creation of a batch of new tokens the serial number is randomly selected for every token. Thereby, guessing which tokens exist in the system becomes hard. The account id is used to allocate a token clearly to a specific application. Cross application usage and trade of tokens are possible. The account id field is optional. The fifth field contains the signature of the information contained in the first four fields, signed with the system's private key. This prevents forgery.

Since a token is basically a receipt, it contains further information about the transaction for which a token is used. The service consumer is the token owner.

Before the owner sends the token to the service provider, it also adds the service provider's id to the token as well as information about the transaction (such as transaction object, date and information about the quality of the service provisioning). The owner finally signs the complete token using its private key. Subsequently, the contained information cannot be changed by the service provider. The required information in a token is the information needed for unique identification, i.e. the system signature, the service provider

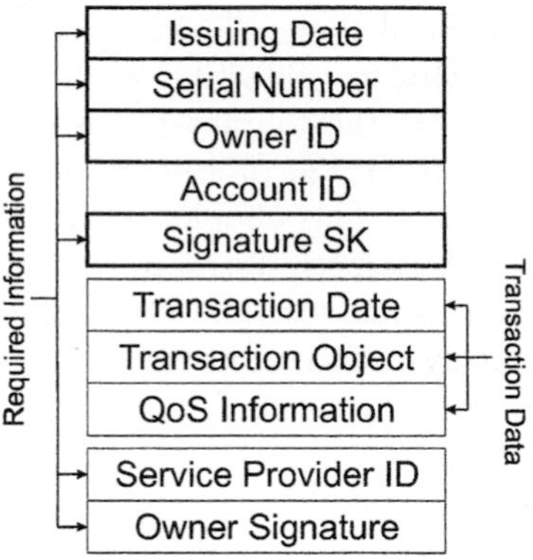

Fig. 32.2: Token Structure

as well as the service provider's signature. This prevents tokens from being stolen. Because unused tokens contain the owner, only the owner can spend them. Used tokens are signed and contain the receiver of the token. Only the receiver is allowed to exchange tokens against new, own tokens. A token has no intrinsic value; it rather presents an accounting event. The value of a token is determined in the token aggregation process.

32.5.4 Token Aggregation

The Token Aggregation process is used to exchange foreign tokens a peer collected for new tokens issued to that peer. The eight-step Token Aggregation procedure is shown in Figure 32.3 (a).

First the *exchanging peer* EP locates a *trusted peer* TP (1). Trusted peers are eligible to exchange tokens and possess one part of the system's private key [164]. EP sends its N collected foreign tokens $(Fn_1, ..., Fn_N)$ to TP (2). TP checks the foreign tokens for their validity. Only tokens signed by the owner and spent only once are valid for exchange.

Using the aggregation function $M = A(Fn_1, ..., Fn_N)$ TP calculates the amount M of new tokens EP must receive in return for the foreign tokens. The aggregation function is public and can take any form. TP now creates M new, unsigned tokens $(Un_1, ..., Un_M)$ (3).

To sign the new tokens with the system's private key using threshold cryptography [164] TP now locates further trusted peers (4). EP is not allowed to choose the quorum of trusted peers itself. This alleviates the problem of potential collaboration and fraud. The number of required trusted peers to sign a token is determined by the used secret sharing scheme. The system's trustworthiness increases proportional with the size of the quorum of trusted peers.

TP sends the new tokens to this quorum of trusted peers (5). Each peer of the quorum signs now the tokens with its part of the system's private key (6). The resulting partial tokens $(Pn_1, ..., Pn_M)$ are transmitted back to EP (7). Finally, EP combines the partial tokens to new complete tokens $(Tn_1, ..., Tn_M)$ (8).

It is important to mention that the aggregation function adds an additional degree of freedom to the system. With an appropriate aggregation function specific economic systems can be implemented.

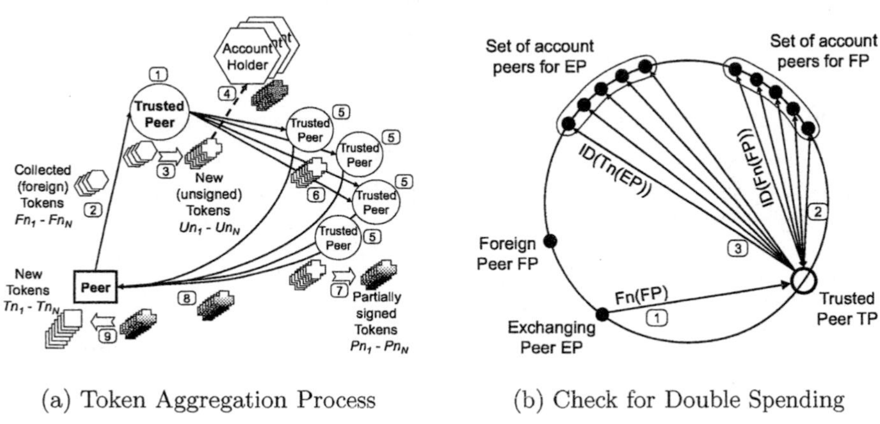

(a) Token Aggregation Process (b) Check for Double Spending

Fig. 32.3: Token Operations

32.5.5 Check for Double Spending

To check for double spending a token must be clearly identifiable. To facilitate the check in an efficient manner, for every peer (the account owners) there is a set of account holding peers, i.e. the *account holder set*. The account holder peers are organized in a DHT manner, such as Pastry [527] (see Figure 32.3 (b)). Account holders hold a list of tokens currently issued to the account owner. The list is filled with the required information during token aggregation. After new tokens have been created (Figure 32.3 (a), step 3), TP sends a list of these new tokens to the exchanging peers account holders (Figure 32.3 (b), step 3).

During the token validity check of the token aggregation process, TP will ask the account holders responsible for a token, if the token is valid (Figure 32.3 (b), step 2). The account holders will remove the token from the list. Accordingly, if the token is not in the list, it is an invalid token. TP will discard such a token and the Peer-to-Peer system's reputation mechanism will be informed about the incident.

In order to avoid message manipulation, every message sent to the account holders must be signed with the senders private key. To keep the list between the account holders consistent, all account holders for one specific account exchange the list whenever the set of account holders changes. This takes place only when peers of that set join or depart from the system. Consistency checks are only necessary, if the sender does not receive all confirmation messages.

32.5.6 Transactions

During transactions the token-based accounting system accounts for resource usage, service usage, or a combination of both. Service usage is valued differently than resource usage. A service for example detects water marks in pictures. Since special software is needed to provide such a service, it is valued higher than the sum of the used resources. A token can contain information about the used resources and value information of the service itself. The information is added to a token before it is sent to the service provider. By this means information contained in a token can be used as basis for an external payment mechanism.

Standard Transaction

The standard transaction process is shown in Figure 32.4 (a). After a service has been requested by the service consumer C, the service provider P informs C about the terms and conditions of the service, including the number of tokens it expects in return for the service. If C accepts the terms and conditions, the service provisioning phase begins.

During this phase tokens can be transmitted before, after, or during the service provisioning. For example a token can be transmitted after 1 MB transferred or after 1 minute service received. Before a token is transmitted, C fills in the required accounting information. C has no incentive to falsify this information, because it influences only the token exchange of P. Then C signs the token with its own private key and sends it to P. P checks the signature of the received token using C's public key, which can be contained in the token as owner id or transmitted with the service request. Thus, it can be verified, that the token sender is also the token owner.

P can choose not to continue to provide the service, if the contained accounting data was incorrect. As a result of each transaction C's own token balance decreases and P's foreign token balance increases.

Transaction partners could try to gain tokens by not paying tokens after receiving a service or by not delivering the service after receiving tokens. In order to avoid that transactions can be split into several parts. Then C sends a signed token to P after P delivered a part of the service; e.g. C sends a tokens after each MByte received data of a 5 MByte file transfer. A further approach that eliminates the incentive for transaction partners to cheat on the other partner is now presented.

Trustable Transaction

In a scenario where tokens are used as virtual currency, a more trustworthy settlement process might be required. Here, the transaction party that delivers last has an incentive to cheat the other party. It still receives the full benefit but does not have to deliver its part of the deal. Therefore, we have designed and implemented a trustable payment procedure that eliminates the incentive to cheat for the transaction partners. In addition, double spending of tokens is not only detectable, but becomes impossible. Figure 32.4 (b) shows the procedure. After a service request is received, P notifies C about the conditions and terms of the transaction, including the required amount of tokens. C answers with the token ids of the tokens it intends to spend for the transaction. Now P contacts the account holders responsible for C ($AH(C)$) and checks if the tokens are valid. $AH(C)$ mark in the token list these tokens as "*planned to spend*". Using the same tokens in another transaction becomes impossible. If all tokens are valid, P informs C that the transaction phase can begin. C starts the transaction by sending an unsigned token to P. C loses the token. However, since it is not signed by C, P cannot exchange it against own tokens. P has no incentive not to provide the service. Therefore, P now provides the agreed service. Because C already lost the token, it has no intention keeping the token for itself. C will sign the token and send it to P. If C should fail to send the signed token, P can present the unsigned token to $AH(C)$. The possession of the token proves that the transaction had started and the token will be removed from the list and is finally lost for C. The aforementioned reputation system provides further incentives against such malicious behavior. On the other hand, if both peers are consenting to cancel the transaction, C does not lose its tokens. P informs $AH(C)$ in order to remove the "*planned to spend*"-mark in the token list.

32.5.7 Trust & Security Considerations

It is crucial for the use of an accounting mechanism that the information it provides is correct. Therefore, the token-based system has been designed to provide a high degree of trust for distributed systems.

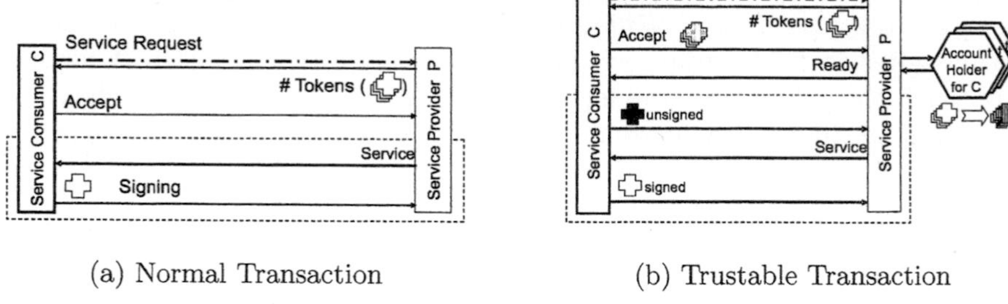

(a) Normal Transaction (b) Trustable Transaction

Fig. 32.4: Transaction Procedures

Robbery

Tokens were designed to eliminate robbery. Tokens contain the owner id that cannot be changed without detection through the system signature. Spent tokens contain the token receiver secured through the owner's signature.

Forgery

The system signature on each token ensures that the basic token data cannot be changed and that no peer can create tokens itself. Thus, the system signature prevents forgery and is crucial for the trustworthiness of the system. Accordingly, fraudulent collaboration of trusted peers must be avoided.

This can be achieved if in a quorum of trusted peers there is at least one trustworthy peer. The probability of a quorum consisting of at least one good peer can be determined using the hypergeometric distribution. The resulting probability p defines the trust level of the system according to:

$$p(T,t,p_g) = \frac{\binom{T\cdot(1-p_g)}{t}}{\binom{T}{t}}, \text{ where } \begin{array}{ll} T & \text{number of trusted peers} \\ t & \text{quorum size} \\ p_g & \text{percentage of good peers} \end{array}$$

Figure 32.5 shows the required quorum size for specific trust levels. For example to achieve a trust level of 99.9% with 50% bad trusted peers in the system a quorum size of ten is required. However, because the trusted peers are selected using the aforementioned reputation system the percentage of bad trusted peers can be assumed to be much lower than 50%. Moreover, because the trusted peers are not aware which other peers belong to a quorum, having only bad peers in a quorum does not mean that this results in fraud. The chosen (bad) trusted peers must also collaborate. Thus, the quorum peers must know which other peers have been chosen for the quorum. Thus, the archived trust level is higher.

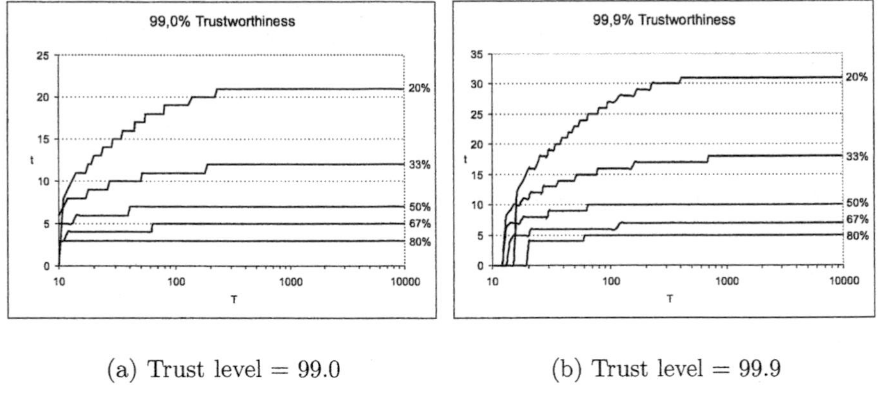

(a) Trust level = 99.0 (b) Trust level = 99.9

Fig. 32.5: Required quorum size for trust levels by percentage of good peers

Furthermore, peers can only become trusted and receive a part of the shared system private key, if their reputation is above a specific threshold value. Accordingly, the proportion of bad peers among the trusted peers can be assumed less than the proportion of bad peers in the whole system. The actual trust threshold value depends on the used reputation system.

Additionally, threshold cryptography provides different proactive mechanisms to secure the key from being compromised. The key parts will be updated periodically using proactive secret sharing [498]. This makes the old key parts obsolete without changing the actual key. The system's public key remains the same. Further, a new system key will be created periodically using the decentralized method presented in [81]. This is enforced by tokens being valid only for a specific period of time. Therefore, the unique token id contains the creation date and time. Outdated tokens can be exchanged for new tokens using the Token Aggregation process. If the system's private key is kept secret the system can be considered secure.

Double Spending

The verification for double spending relies on the data hold at the account holders. Thus, users might try to corrupt their token list at the account holders. This is avoided by not allowing peers to send any queries or enquiries to the account list. Rule breaches are reported to the reputation system. Further, the token list at the account holders is a positive list. If a peer plans to double spend a token, it has to avoid that the token is marked in the list as planned-to-spend and later removed from it during token aggregation; though in both actions the peer is not involved.

Malicious peers trying to remove tokens from the token list of another peer must guess token ids of existing tokens. That is very hard because the creation date and time in milliseconds and the random serial number have to be guessed correctly. Therefore, this kind of messages is obvious malicious behavior and will be reported to the reputation system.

In Peer-to-Peer systems (even if using a DHT) it cannot be guaranteed that a remote account at the account holders is never lost. In such a case the account owning peer would not be eligible to receive services anymore. Since in the token-based system the tokens are stored locally, users can secure themselves against loss by making a backup of their tokens. The loss of an account at the account holders will just influence the ability to check for double spending. Since a peer can not notice if its remote account is lost, it must assume that double spending would still be detected. Hence, it will be discouraged to cheat.

32.5.8 Performance Analysis

We have implemented the token-based accounting system based on JXTA 2.2.1 [412]. Measurements of message sizes were used to simulate the accounting scheme with the simulator presented in [152].

To study the performance of the token-based accounting system two use cases have to be distinguished - costs for maintenance and costs for transactions.

Maintenance

Maintenance costs arise from keeping the remote accounts consistent and from the requirement to keep the systems private key secret. This involves calculating key updates at one quorum of trusted peers and distributing new key parts afterwards to the rest of the trusted peers. Table 32.1 summarizes the complexity of the maintenance actions, where k denotes the size of the bank-sets and a (t, T) secret sharing scheme is used, where T denotes the number of trusted peers in the system.

Account Consistency		System Key Related Operations	
Node Arrival	O(k)	Key Update Calculations	O(t)
Node Departure	O(k)	Key Update Distribution	O(t)

Table 32.1: Account Holder Set & System Key Maintenance Complexity

Transactions

For the analysis we assume a conservative ratio of 67% good peers in the system. Further, we set a trust level of 0,1% which results in a quorum size t of 6 trusted peers. Furthermore, we set the account holder set size k to 4. We model a file sharing scenario, where for 1 MB download 1 token is required and the average file size s is 5 MB. Users exchange tokens in different batch sizes b. The trustable transaction procedure is used. If n transactions are carried out the average number of accounting messages M sent in such a scenario results in:

$$M(n,k,t,b) = n(2s + 2k) + \frac{ns}{b}(1 + 2k\frac{b}{s} + 2k + 2t)$$

For 100 transactions exchanging 500 tokens with a batch size of 20 results in 3125 messages. Simulating this scenario the token-based accounting system creates an additional overhead of less than 1% (for the mentioned example it is less than 3,5 MB overhead for file transfers of 500 MB). Figure 32.6 (a) shows the generated traffic for different batch sizes and up to one million transactions. As it can be expected, the overall traffic generated by the token-based accounting system is reduced as the batch size increases. However, the effect levels off after a batch size of 20. Figure 32.6 (b) shows the influence of increased quorum size. The effect is not strong. Even with a very high trust level (t=18) the system still generates not more than 1% of overhead. The effect of size of account holder set for the generated traffic is very small and therefore the graph is omitted here.

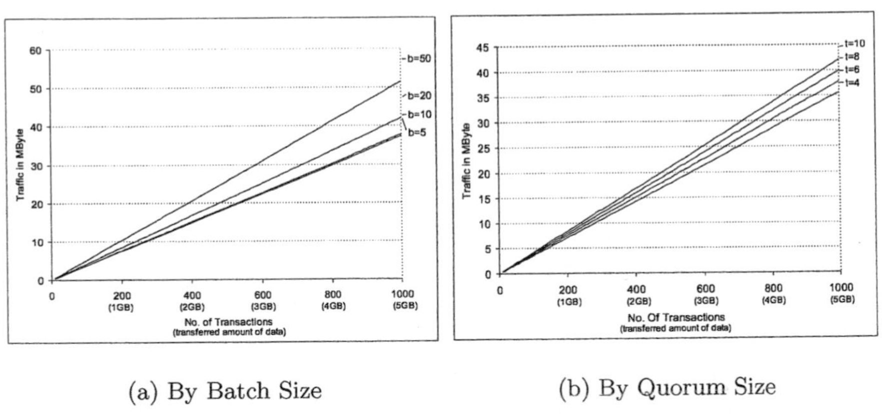

(a) By Batch Size

(b) By Quorum Size

Fig. 32.6: By Token-Accounting Scheme Generated Traffic

32.5.9 Summary & Conclusions

One of the biggest challenges for a wider deployment of Peer-to-Peer systems is to retrieve, collect and use information about the resource utilization within the system. It is crucial that the information is secure and reliable while the core features of Peer-to-Peer are still maintained.

The presented token-based accounting scheme is flexible and trustworthy. Its basic purpose is to collect accounting information of transactions. This information can be used to coordinate the behavior of the system's entities to achieve a higher system performance. Further, the collected information can be used as basis for pricing and price finding processes. Moreover, this builds the foundation for the development of a market within Peer-to-Peer systems. Further, the collected accounting information could be the basis for a payment system to support commercial applications.

Since the responsibility of creating tokens is delegated to a randomly selected quorum of peers, fraudulent behavior is prevented. Only if all peers in the quorum would be malicious, tokens can be forged. Also, a trustable payment mechanism is available that does not require to involve a third party. Thus, this approach is especially scalable.

The token-based accounting scheme is very flexible through the introduction of the aggregation function. Here the exchange ratio of used tokens against new tokens can be defined by the usage policy. Thus, different economic models can be implemented.

The further steps are detection of the need for a system key update or system key creation procedure. Also the economic behavior of the system with respect to inflation and deflation will be evaluated using simulations.

33. The PlanetLab Platform

Timothy Roscoe (Intel Research, Berkeley)

PlanetLab is an extensively used, global, community-maintained platform for researchers to develop, deploy, and evaluate widely-distributed applications such as Peer-to-Peer systems. Because of PlanetLab's shared nature, and its unusual design goal of continuous replacement of components by the research community, it can also be viewed somewhat as a Peer-to-Peer system (and an ongoing research project) itself. This chapter describes PlanetLab's goals and origins, and discusses in detail the design principles that have governed its development and growth so far. It also discusses some of the methodological issues in performing research using a platform like PlanetLab – what can be learned from experimentation on PlanetLab, and what research claims can be validated by the system.

This overview of PlanetLab's architecture and development is necessarily brief. More details can be found in a series of documents called PlanetLab Design Notes, or PDNs, which are available on the PlanetLab web site at `http://www.planet-lab.org/`.

33.1 Introduction and History

The PlanetLab platform for distributed applications arose in March 2002 from the intersection of several trends in computing research.

First of these was a sense of frustration among the networking research community that the Internet and its protocols had become "ossified": so much infrastructure, commerce, and communication by now depended on the Internet that experimenting with radically new approaches at scale was impossible. At the same time, routing protocols like BGP had become so embedded in the network infrastructure that changing them even in an incremental manner became a delicate issue which most Internet Service Providers have shied away from.

The corresponding effect on networking research was a reluctance to explore radically different approaches on the one hand, and an reluctance to build real networks and systems on the other, with researchers relying instead predominantly on analytical results, simulations from programs like `ns2` [592], or network emulation using platforms like EmuLab [621].

This issue was captured succinctly in a report commissioned by the U.S. National Academy of Sciences entitled `''Looking Over the Fence at Networks''` [442]. The report also suggested a potential way out of the im-

R. Steinmetz and K. Wehrle (Eds.): P2P Systems and Applications, LNCS 3485, pp. 567-581, 2005.

passe: networking research could use the concept of an *overlay* to deploy, and attract users to, a new network architecture without needing to explicitly change the underlying Internet. This naturally led to discussion of how researchers could deploy overlay networks at sufficient scale to gain both experience and real users.

The second trend was rather more optimistic: the emergence of Peer-to-Peer systems both as a major research agenda, and at the same time the source of a significant proportion of traffic on the Internet. Early 2002 saw the end of the "Internet boom", and there was a feeling that client-server applications over the wide-area was now a mature and well-understood area, and Peer-to-Peer systems provided a new direction in research.

However, this sense of excitement with a rich new research agenda encountered similar problems to the classical networking community: how to try out and validate ideas with such systems at scale. As with networking, ideas such as structured overlay networks were investigated mostly by simulation; in the rare cases that a real deployment took place, it involved a very small number of distributed hosts. For example, the original Chord paper [575] reported experience deploying the system on only 10 sites.

Thirdly, a variety of related technologies had matured at approximately the same time. These ranged from techniques for managing systems composed of computers and networking elements, in the fields of cluster-based computing and data center provisioning, to operating system virtualization techniques and resource control mechanisms. It was felt that these mechanisms could form the basis of an approach to moving research agendas in networking and distributed systems out of the current impasse.

This was the context in which David Culler (of U.C. Berkeley) and Larry Peterson (of Princeton University), incorporating an earlier idea from Tom Anderson (of the University of Washington), met in early 2002 to discuss building a community-maintained, shared, distributed platform for deploying and evaluating wide-area services such as Peer-to-Peer systems. An informal workshop was convened at Intel Research in Berkeley in March of 2002, with enthusiastic attendence from systems researchers at U.S. universities, to discuss the scheme.

The result of this meeting was a vision of a collection of machines spread around the globe, contributed by participating institutions who provide local server hardware, bandwidth, power, and cooling, in return for a share in the worldwide platform.

A position paper outlining the PlanetLab vision followed [485], and Intel Research provided initial seed funding for the project. This consisted of donating the first 100 machines, shipped to about 40 universities worldwide, and providing operational support for the platform until 2004, when responsibility for maintaining PlanetLab shifted to the PlanetLab Consortium, based at Princeton University in New Jersey.

From the beginning, the target application area for PlanetLab has been *planetary-scale systems*, Peer-to-Peer applications prime among these. Planetary-scale applications are characterized as involving computation spread geographically across a wide area, for some subset of the following reasons:

- **Removing latency:** to serve a large, dispersed user population and still provide fast end-to-end response time, computation must be moved towards users to reduce the round-trip time for messages between users and the service. One obvious example of such services are content distribution networks (CDNs) like Akamai, who are in the business of moving content closer to a worldwide user population.
- **Spanning domain boundaries:** the service executes in many geographical locations so as to have a presence in many physical areas, legal jurisdictions, financial domains, etc. Examples of this kind of requirement include censorship-resistant systems like FreeNet [124], and federated archival storage systems like that envisioned by Oceanstore [368], which is intended to survive the physical destruction or financial dissolution of any participating service provider.
- **Multiple vantage points:** the application needs to process and correlate data in real time from many physical locations. For example, network mapping and measurement applications were among the first services deployed on PlanetLab and continue to be major users of the platform. PlanetLab has also been used to deploy distributed crawlers of Peer-to-Peer networks like Gnutella.

PlanetLab was enthusiastically taken up as a research vehicle, and has rapidly become a canonical part of how large-scale networked systems research is performed. At time of writing, PlanetLab consists of over 500 machines worldwide at more than 250 sites, with a significant presence in North America, Europe, China, Russia, Brazil, India, and elsewhere.

33.2 Architectural Principles

While supporting Peer-to-Peer systems, and wide-area distributed systems in general, is the main goal of PlanetLab, the community model by which sites donate local resources in return for a fraction of the global testbed means that PlanetLab itself can also be considered a Peer-to-Peer system. Indeed, from the outset PlanetLab has aimed at the twin goals of *decentralized operation* (reducing or removing entirely any centralized management facility) and *decentralized development* (encouraging the community to contribute the software infrastructure required by the platform).

Taken together, these requirements are somewhat novel for a large-scale distributed system, even a Peer-to-Peer system. It means that PlanetLab has to be designed not so much as a single artefact, but as a continuously evolving social *process*.

This is complicated by the tension between two usage models for PlanetLab. The first is as a testbed for experiments: a system is implemented and then deployed on PlanetLab for the purpose of obtaining measurement results for a paper. The second is as a platform to support long-running services in the wide area: several applications such as CoDeeN [468] and OpenDHT [340] have been running continously on PlanetLab and attracting real users for over a year, at time of writing.

To cope with these tensions, the PlanetLab team adopted a number of design principles to follow as the platform evolved [486]. Some of these only became clear during the course of the initial PlanetLab deployment, but others were identified at the original March 2002 workshop, including the three main principles of *application-centric interfaces*, *distributed virtualization*, and *unbundled management*.

33.2.1 Application-Centric Interfaces

A central concern in the design of any platform for supporting applications is the *execution environment*: what set of APIs must applications be written to? The prior experience of some of the PlanetLab design team (who had been involved in attempts to standardise interfaces for "active networks") led to a strong desire to keep application interfaces as conventional as possible.

There were several motivations for this. One was encouraging uptake: experience had shown that an unconventional API was less likely to be adopted by developers. But there was a more practical, short-term issue: a strong desire to get something working as fast as possible, since PlanetLab had an eager user community well before the first node came online.

Linux was chosen from the outset as the initial execution environment. The choice greatly facilitated development, since applications could be debugged on laboratory machines or clusters before deployment. A Linux execution environment was also easy to deploy - the first version of PlanetLab was indeed based on an unmodified Linux distribution.

As PlanetLab has evolved, new functionality has been added to the environment. For example, users were provided early on with a virtualized Linux machine to themselves, rather than explicitly sharing a physical machine, for a greater degree of isolation between projects. As a second example, it was long recognized that access to raw networking sockets was desirable for implementing new transport protocols, performing network measurements, etc.

In both these cases, functionality has been provided by modifying the kernel *underneath* the interface to the execution environment (the Linux application binary interface or ABI in this case), without changing the interface in any fundamental way. In the case of raw sockets, a user obtains such a socket in the conventional Linux manner, but the precise behaviour of the socket depends on privilege granted to that user's project by the organization administering that PlanetLab node.

Not all PlanetLab functionality can be presented through the operating system interface. For example, the ability to change the resource allocation for a project has no clear representation or analogue on a Linux machine. Consequently, an *orthogonal* interface to the PlanetLab-specific software running on a machine provides this access without polluting the operating system ABI. This interface to the "node manager" (discussed below) is not required by conventional users, but is essential for implementing what PlanetLab calls "infrastructure services": services which perform useful functions as part of the normal running of PlanetLab (for example, resource location and brokering).

Longer term, the principle of keeping the execution environment as conventional as possible will remain, though Linux will cease to be the only option. By replacing the Linux kernel with a virtual machine monitor such as Xen [179], different operating system execution environments can be employed depending on user needs. Keeping the interface to the node manager orthogonal to the execution environment allows each to evolve, and diversify, separately.

33.2.2 Distributed Virtualization

The key abstraction in PlanetLab is the *slice*: a distributed collection of virtual machines, in which an application or service executes. A PlanetLab virtual machine is often referred to as a *sliver*, and forms a resource container [56] for the application on a particular physical node.

PlanetLab faced a difficult choice as to the node virtualization mechanism – the node software that presents a virtual machine abstraction to slices. Like most of PlanetLab, this has evolved over time and is expected to change further in the future. The key requirements are those of any operating system: multiplexing the node resources, resource isolation (ensuring that one sliver does not gain unfair use of resources allocated to another on the same machine), security (ensuring that one sliver cannot gain unauthorized access to the state of another sliver), and abstraction (presenting the execution environment discussed in the previous section).

Initially, PlanetLab slivers were simple accounts on an unmodified Linux system. Each participating PlanetLab institution was allocated the same 10 user ids on every PlanetLab node. These simple Unix accounts were rapidly replaced by virtual Linux kernels using the "VServer" patch [391], which provides an illusion of multiple Linux machines over a single underlying, modified kernel. In time (and after some experimentation with different approaches), the static allocation of 10 slices was replaced by a fully dynamic system where slivers are created on demand on the nodes selected by the slice owner.

In addition to the VServer modifications, the PlanetLab Linux kernel has undergone a series of other modifications over time. Throughout, however, the strategy has been to prefer externally supported (and so relatively "standard") code to custom-written modules and patches, so as to reduce the burden of support and development. At the same time, modifications made by the PlanetLab support team (some minor changes to the VServer patch for example), have where possible been fed back to the original developers. The resource isolation mechanism was provided for some time using a version of the SILK (Scout paths In the Linux Kernel) [64] module, which has now been replaced by the more widely used Linux Class-based Kernel Resource Management (CKRM) extensions.

Modifications to the Linux kernel were by no means the only virtualization option on the table at PlanetLab's inception. Full-scale virtual machine technologies like VMware are attractive because they provide the ability to run multiple unmodified operating systems, including custom kernels. However, full virtualization does not currently provide the scalability required: it is not unusual for around 100 slices to be active on a PlanetLab node, in particular shortly before a major conference deadline.

Another promising direction was *isolation kernels* [350]. Isolation kernels are very small hypervisors, making verification of isolation and security properties much easier. Rather than fully virtualizing the whole ia32 processor architecture and PC hardware, systems like Denali and Xen [179] perform *paravirtualization*: they present a virtual hardware abstraction which is close to the underlying architecture but much more efficient to virtualize.

Paravirtualization solutions were not mature in early 2002, but Xen has become widely used since, making PlanetLab's transition to a Xen-based node architecture increasingly attractive. While this allows several different execution environments, as discussed above, it would not entail changes to the PlanetLab node manager interface.

PlanetLab encounted unexpected complexity in virtualizing the network on a node. Since PlanetLab nodes exist on the public network and their resources are donated by participating institutions, they typically have a single globally-routable IP address each. Consequently, services running in slices must share the space of available port numbers for listening sockets, just like any set of processes on a single machine. However, PlanetLab's target applications include network measurement infrastructures and routing overlays, making access to raw sockets from many slices in a safe, efficient, and controlled manner an important requirement for PlanetLab.

Even simple port contention can be a challenge. More than one Peer-to-Peer-based replacement for the Domain Name Service has been deployed on PlanetLab, and for compatibility with DNS all of them want to listen on UDP port 53. A user-supplied DNS multiplexer, running in a slice, provided a solution to this dilemma.

33.2.3 Unbundled Management

A final design principle that characterizes PlanetLab as a platform is *unbundled management.* Like any large, decentralized, federated system, PlanetLab faces significant management challenges. In addition to the two roles for PlanetLab mentioned above (supporting short-term experiments and long-running services), PlanetLab is also a research project in its own right, indeed, it is a research project that is being pursued by a number of the participating institutions simultaneously.

For PlanetLab to succeed as a community-built artifact and true Peer-to-Peer system, therefore, it is important that the research community is able to contribute functionality to the platform in the form of long-running *infrastructure services* that perform essential management functions (resource discovering, slice creation, etc.), *and* that different approaches to implementing these services can be tried out "for real" by different groups simultaneously. We call this principle *unbundled management*: management of the platform is as much as possible carried out by multiple, competing services contributed by users.

As a side effect, this principle has also enabled PlanetLab to become operational extremely quickly, albeit with a centralized management infrastructure. Since the intention has always been that all of PlanetLab's management functionality will be replaced by the community, this freed up the initial implementors to rapidly deploy a simple, provisional management architecture, as long as it was all replaceable in time.

The long-term goal, however, is for PlanetLab to evolve into a fully decentralized Peer-to-Peer system itself, with little or no need for the centralized "PLC" (or "PlanetLab Central") database currently used to manage the physical nodes themselves (installing the system software), slices, and user accounts.

What kinds of system design decisions does the principle of unbundled management lead to? The most immediate implication is that interfaces to system information must be as low-level as possible, while remaining sharable: multiple management subsystems on a node (themselves likely structured as Peer-to-Peer systems) must be able to use the same interface instances. Interfaces for querying PlanetLab management state are typically based on a standard format [524] which supplies tuples with a minimum of preprocessing.

A consequence of exporting management interfaces at as low a level of abstraction as possible is that the concepts that such interfaces deal with on a node are purely local to the node. Any distributed abstractions, including slices themselves, require some external service to implement them.

The decision has so far been reasonably successful: discovery services like SWORD [461] and monitoring services like CoMon [474] are now widely used by PlanetLab users, despite not being maintained by the core PlanetLab support team.

A more complex example is that of resource allocation. While the PlanetLab consortium has laid out a "framework" for resource allocation [490], this largely focuses on the representation of resources on nodes in the form of *tickets*, which represent promises of future resources, and *leases*, which represent resources currently bound to a sliver. Details of how tickets may be exchanged, and how the set of resources required by a slice are to be assembled, are again left for 3rd-party services to define and implement. The intention is to foster a number of different resource allocation schemes coexisting alongside each other; as well as the initial one (PLC), at least two others have been built: the Emulab portal [617] and SHARP [235].

33.3 PlanetLab Methodology

While some small-scale wide-area distributed testbeds existed previously, PlanetLab is the first such platform which is widely available to researchers in many countries with broad coverage over the globe. It has had, and continues to have, a significant influence in how much work in distributed and Peer-to-Peer systems is carried out: it is now possible to deploy many more large systems and evaluate them alongside each other "for real" on the Internet.

However, there has yet to appear consensus within the research community about what results obtained on PlanetLab actually mean, or how to use PlanetLab to derive valid experimental results. This section reviews the current state of thinking about how best to use broad-coverage testbeds in general, and PlanetLab in particular.

33.3.1 Using PlanetLab

We start by briefly describing what is, at time of writing, the way most researchers and students use PlanetLab: creating and controlling slices through the PlanetLab Central (PLC) web interface, or a command line tool which talks to PLC. Other interfaces exist, for example slices can be created via the Emulab portal [617].

Users log into PLC and create a slice, giving it a name, for example `ucb_p2ps`. The first half of the name identifies the creating institution, while the second is an arbitrary name for the slice. Having done this, users then add nodes from anywhere on PlanetLab to the slice. Having added a node, say `planet1.berkeley.intel-research.net`, to the slice, the user can log into the machine via secure shell with a command like:

```
$ ssh ucb_p2ps@planet1.berkeley.intel-research.net
```

What the user sees when logging in looks like a networked Linux machine. She can install programs, run code, `su` to root, create new user accounts, run programs like `tcpdump`, etc.

This lack of restriction on what users can do in slices leads to great flexibility in the code that can run, as well as providing a familiar programming environment (PlanetLab applications are usually compiled on users' desktop machines and then deployed on PlanetLab).

That said, there are significant differences between the runtime environment of a program running on a PlanetLab node and one running on a workstation or server in a lab: network conditions are very different, and the machine is always being shared with other projects. This has led to some debate about the kinds of experimental results that PlanetLab can provide, and the kinds of claims about system designs that can legitimately be made based on such results.

33.3.2 Reproducibility

Can PlanetLab be used to obtain reproducible results?

Naturally, the answer to this question depends a lot on what "reproducible" means. PlanetLab has never been intended as a testbed suitable for quantitatively reproducible experiments, in the sense that `ns2`, EmuLab, or ModelNet is. A number of factors contribute to the basic unpredictability of results obtained on the Internet, and PlanetLab in particular.

As numerous measurement studies have shown, observed conditions on the Internet can change quite radically over a wide variety of timescales. Furthermore, contention for resources (CPU, network bandwidth, disk activity) on PlanetLab itself varies considerably: despite the increasing provision of resource isolation on the platform, it will always be possible for one slice to "notice" the load imposed by others. Consequently, experiments on PlanetLab where, for example, different design choices for a Peer-to-Peer system are compared by running each choice consecutively for an hour or a day and measuring the performance of each, are unlikely to convince peer reviewers in the research community.

However, it is still possible to make valid comparisons between the performance of different systems running over PlanetLab. Running services over a long period of time with extensive measurement can provide clear evidence of what options or algorithms can make a real difference to performance, a methodology used by a number of projects (for example, the CoDeeN content distribution network). In many cases, this approach works best in conjunction with simulations, which we discuss below.

Another, complementary approach to providing some reproducibility of results on PlanetLab has to date not been explored in detail, but presents an interesting area of research in its own right. If conditions both on Planet-

Lab and the Internet in general can be measured continuously (for example, by some kind of "weather service"), it may be possible for the state of the environment at the time of a particular experiment to be sufficiently *characterized* that the results obtained can be rigorously compared with those of other experiments which are found, after the fact, to have been conducted under the same conditions.

There is, however, a different sense in which PlanetLab provides for reproducibility: the functionality of systems can be verified, and indeed used, by peer research groups. This has, of course, always been the case for small-scale (in terms of deployment) systems like compilers and operating systems, but the availability of PlanetLab now means that large-scale distributed systems built by research groups can also be taken up and used by other teams. Of course, this tends to impose a different standard to that by which such systems have traditionally been evaluated, a topic we return to below.

33.3.3 Representivity

Alongside the issue of how, and in what sense, experimental results from PlanetLab are reproducible is the question of the extent to which they are *representative* of reality. Like the issue of reproducibility, this has a number of aspects.

PlanetLab nodes are situated in a wide variety of places, including commercial colocation centers, industrial labs with commercial ISP connections, universities with dual-homed connections to academic and commercial networks, and DSL lines and cable modems. Consequently, PlanetLab machines provide an excellent set of vantage points from which to observe the Internet as a whole. PlanetSeer [640] is an example of a service leveraging this: observation of user traffic to the CoDeeN proxy network from all over the Internet is used to detect, triangulate, and diagnose Internet routing anomalies.

At the same time, however, the actual locations of PlanetLab nodes themselves is heavily skewed. Almost all nodes have much more bandwidth than a typical domestic U.S. or E.U. broadband connections, and the overwhelming majority are connected to lightly loaded academic networks with very different traffic characteristics to the commercial Internet. Banerjee, Griffin, and Pias [55] were to the first to point this out in print, and analyze the situation in some detail, but the immediate practical implication is that measurements of Internet paths *between PlanetLab nodes* are not likely to be representative of the Internet as a whole.

It is suggested in [55] that PlanetLab node locations might be chosen in the future so as to converge PlanetLab's network coverage to be representative of the Internet. However, resource constraints make this unlikely: PlanetLab is primarily maintained by sites, which are usually universities, hosting machines locally in exchange for access to the global platform.

This kind of representative coverage is important for empirical measurements of the Internet as it currently is experienced by ordinary users. The issue is very different if we consider PlanetLab as a way of testing out services for a future Internet or, more radically, a testbed for network architectures (including Peer-to-Peer services) which may supplant or replace the Internet. It is also worth remembering that many applications may not be targeted at networks like the Internet. Enterprise IP networks, for example, are often architected very differently to an ISP.

Networking aside, it is important to remember that PlanetLab nodes are shared between many projects, and this is a rather different deployment scenario to commercial services, which at time of writing typically are hosted on dedicated servers. In this respect, Peer-to-Peer applications to be deployed on domestic machines (which are presumably used for other applications as well) are closer to PlanetLab's situation.

A comprehensive study of PlanetLab's availability has yet to be undertaken, but it is clear that PlanetLab is significantly less stable at the node level than a well-run commercial hosting service. This is both a challenge and an opportunity: it is much harder to rely on any single PlanetLab node being available, but plenty of services have been deployed that demonstrate an impressively high degree of reliability despite fluctuations in the underlying platform.

Ultimately, a researcher has to be clear about the resemblence or otherwise between PlanetLab as a deployment environment and the motivating application environment for his or her research.

33.3.4 Quantitative Results

It is important to realize the value that PlanetLab brings to a Peer-to-Peer systems project, and avoid the trap of naively transferring experimental methodologies based on repeatable simulations and idealized models to an inappropriate environment. PlanetLab's significance is that, perhaps for the first time, researchers have access to the experience of having to cope with everything that a real systems environment can throw at any design.

PlanetLab can be used to *validate* simulation results. Modulo the representivity caveats above, if a system does not behave on PlanetLab as it does in simulation, there is likely to be some aspect of the real environment not captured by the simulator. If the disparity is large, this casts doubt on the validity of the simulation results. Conversely, if the measured behaviour of a system on PlanetLab matches closely the simulation results, this provides a supporting argument for simulation-based claims about how the system scales beyond what can be tested directly on PlanetLab.

In this way, PlanetLab can be valuable in designing simulators, since it provides an excellent source of phenomena, situations, and conditions that a simulation might need to take into account. Furthermore, long-term deployment of a service on PlanetLab can be used to quantitatively measure the effect of algorithmic or implementation changes in a way not possible with simulation or emulation environments. Finally, PlanetLab deployment may be used to characterize and model workloads to drive simulation design.

33.3.5 Qualitative Experience

The drawbacks and challenges mentioned in the sections above illustrate, to some extent, the tensions involved in any form of computer systems research, including Peer-to-Peer systems. On the one hand, there is the scientific aspect: experimental results should be reproducible by the experimenter, independently verifiable by the scientific community, and an accurate portrayal of nature. On the other hand is the engineering aspect: systems research is about creating new kinds of computer systems, and understanding not simply how they work, but understanding how to build them in the first place.

Ultimately, perhaps PlanetLab's greatest value is that it provides an opportunity to learn from the real world, demonstrate the *qualitative* feasibility of a system, attract real users, and provide a longer-term deployment platform for genuinely useful services.

There are great challenges in building robust Peer-to-Peer systems that can operate even at the scale of PlanetLab (about 500 nodes), when exposed to the full reality of the Internet. Nodes fail, and the resources available to a PlanetLab sliver (CPU, network bandwidth, etc.) can vary suddenly and dramatically over even quite small timescales. The network itself is not homogeneous even in connectivity: some pairs nodes on PlanetLab can never directly communicate over IP, even though they both have excellent connectivity to a variety of other PlanetLab nodes. Many assumptions implicitly made by laboratory-based evaluations are violated by PlanetLab: packets are seen to be duplicated, nodes are not fail-stop, etc. Almost all researchers who have deployed a service on PlanetLab report their first experience of seeing their code, which tested fine in the lab, fail for some unknown reason when run on PlanetLab.

Despite this, a remarkable number of highly robust services have been created and deployed on PlanetLab. Furthermore, it's likely that many of the insights gained by the researchers who have built and maintained these applications could not have been produced with a large-scale deployment.

33.4 Effects on the Internet

As numerous studies have shown, Peer-to-Peer applications such as BitTorrent, Gnutella, Kazaa, etc. have had a profound effect on the traffic mix observed on the Internet at large. However, it has been hard to capture the implications of such systems for the future design of the Internet itself, since by their very nature these applications, and the effects they have on the network, are not tracked in any detail.

The experience of running applications on PlanetLab – even though such deployments are at a much smaller scale than a successful Peer-to-Peer filesharing application, for example – has led to a number of insights about how Peer-to-Peer applications interact differently with the Internet. Three features of Peer-to-Peer applications lead to this difference in behaviour.

33.4.1 Many-to-Many Connections

Peer-to-Peer services are, for the most part, *many-to-many* applications: a particular node running a component of a Peer-to-Peer service can be expected to contact a large number of peer nodes in a small amount of time, in contrast to clients in a traditional client-server application.

The many-to-many communication patterns of PlanetLab nodes running many Peer-to-Peer systems simultaneously has caused problematic interactions with IP routers, particularly low-end hardware which implements a "caching model" of network forwarding. Such routers have a hardware engine which can forward packets at line speed, using a cache of flows (based on packet 5-tuples). Flows which "miss" in the cache are handled by the route processor (typically a small embedded 32-bit RISC processor). PlanetLab overlay applications have been seen to generate new source-destination pairs at a sufficient rate to overwhelm the processor on such routers, causing the router to reboot (losing network connectivity in the process).

The Internet architecture, of course, strongly enshrines the idea that any node should be able to address a packet to any other node, at any time. What has happened in this case is that router vendors have optimized their hardware for a "common case" (the Web, email, and other TCP-based applications) which does not include the communication patterns of Peer-to-Peer systems. If Peer-to-Peer systems continue to grow as a proportion of Internet traffic, this common-case assumption will become increasingly untenable.

33.4.2 Many Alternative Routes

A component of a Peer-to-Peer system running on a single node (a sliver, to use the PlanetLab terminology) often has a large number of alternative nodes to contact in order to fulfil some particular function. For example, a filesharing system typically has many replicas of desired data scattered across the network, and a routing overlay typically has many, roughly equivalent, intermediate nodes that it can route traffic through (indeed, many DHT implementations by design keep multiple node addresses for each entry in their routing table). In contrast, a traditional web client (for instance) typically has few or no alternative addresses to contact in the event of a failure to contact the server.

This opens up a new design space for node-to-node communication protocols. For example, if one is interested in minimizing message latency in the presence of failures, as in DHTs like Bamboo [510], it pays to have very aggressive timeouts on the hop-by-hop exchanges by which messages are routed through the DHT. Even if a node is simply being a little slow, it's probably worthwhile to reroute the message around the node and along an alternate path, as long as this does not unduly increase network congestion.

Such fine-grained control over, and rapid reaction to, message timeouts is not possible with TCP as it is implemented in a mainstream operating system kernel. Furthermore, TCP's policy of reliable, in-order delivery of messages is not appropriate for many, if not most, high-performance Peer-to-Peer systems. Consequently, almost all the Peer-to-Peer applications deployed on PlanetLab today use UDP-based, TCP-friendly custom transport protocols rather than vanilla, kernel-based TCP. This is in stark contrast to traditional Internet applications, which are mostly TCP-based.

33.4.3 Overlays and Traffic Correlation

While only a few Peer-to-Peer applications claim to provide overlay networks to their users, in effect some kind of overlay network is at the heart of every Peer-to-Peer system. This leads to a *correlation* of traffic between nodes that is qualitatively different from traditional point-to-point TCP connections. For example, a flow traversing several overlay hops appears to the underlying IP network as a series of highly correlated point-to-point connections, whose path may bear no resemblance to the IP routing tables in operation at the time. Peer-to-Peer systems whose implicit overlay networks exhibit multicast behaviour further complicate this issue.

Some researchers are beginning to study the effects of such overlays on underlying ISP-based networks, for example [350]. While such work is currently at an early stage, it does appear that the traffic characterists of Peer-to-Peer overlays do not interact with typical ISPs traffic engineering policies in the way that traditional applications do.

33.5 Long-Term Goals

As was its intention, PlanetLab continues to evolve as a platform for deploying broad-coverage Peer-to-Peer services. As the platform grows, there is a trend towards the decentralization of control: the functionality unique to PlanetLab

Central (PLC) is expected to decrease, though PLC itself will most likely remain as one resource broker among many.

Beyond merely supporting distributed and Peer-to-Peer applications, however, recall that an explicit motivation for PlanetLab was to break the impasse facing Internet researchers, in not being to able introduce architectural changes in the Internet. Overlay networks using the underlying Internet were suggested as a way out of the problem.

Recently, the term *network virtualization* [559] has been coined to describe the use of overlays above a network like the Internet to provide Internet-like functionality themselves. By providing the ability to run multiple virtual networks with real users, the argument goes, alternatives to the Internet can be explored at scale without replacing the current infrastructure.

There are two broad schools of thought as to where this might lead. One says that by experimenting with alternative network architectures, the networking community in the broadest sense (researchers, carriers, governments, etc.) can select a new network architecture with properties preferable to the Internet, and then continue to use network virtualization as a way to incrementally deploy it.

The other, slightly more radical, school of thought is that network virtualization *is* the next architecture, in other words, future networked applications will operate in the main by setting up per-application virtual Peer-to-Peer networks, which then connect with other applications at many points.

In any case, investigating issues such as these requires the ability firstly to place computation at many points in the world (for routing and forwarding calculations), and secondly to acquire network paths between such points whose resources are guaranteed in some way, possibly probabilistically. PlanetLab provides the former, existing commercial ISPs' virtual private network (VPN) services or optical switched wavelength paths could provide the latter. A combination of the two holds real possibilities for implementing the successor to the Internet.

Bibliography

[1] K. Aberer, V. Kalogeraki, and M. E. Koubarakis, "Databases, information systems and peer-to-peer computing", In *Proc. 1. Internat. DBISP2P workshop*, Berlin, Germany, 2004, Springer LNCS 2944.

[2] K. Aberer, "Scalable Data Access in P2P Systems Using Unbalanced Search Trees", In *4th Workshop on Distributed Data and Structures (WDAS'2002)*, Carleton Scientific, 2002.

[3] K. Aberer, P. Cudré-Mauroux, A. Datta, Z. Despotovic, M. Hauswirth, M. Punceva, and R. Schmidt, "P-Grid: A Self-organizing Structured P2P System", *ACM SIGMOD Record*, 32(3), 2003.

[4] K. Aberer, P. Cudré-Mauroux, and M. Hauswirth, "A Framework for Semantic Gossiping", *SIGMOD Record*, 31(4), 2002.

[5] K. Aberer, A. Datta, and M. Hauswirth, "Efficient, self-contained handling of identity in Peer-to-Peer systems", *IEEE Transactions on Knowledge and Data Engineering*, 16(7), 2004.

[6] K. Aberer, A. Datta, and M. Hauswirth, "Multifaceted Simultaneous Load Balancing in DHT-based P2P systems: A new game with old balls and bins", In *Self-* Properties in Complex Information Systems*, "Hot Topics" serices, Lecture Notes in Computer Science, LNCS 3460, Springer, 2005.

[7] K. Aberer, A. Datta, M. Hauswirth, and R. Schmidt, "Indexing data-oriented overlay networks", In *31st International Conference on Very Large Databases (VLDB)*, Morgan Kaufmann, 2005.

[8] K. Aberer and M. Hauswirth, "Overview on Peer-to-Peer Information Systems", In *WDAS*, Carleton Scientific, 2002.

[9] T. Ackermann, R. Gold, C. Mascolo, and W. Emmerich, "Incentives in Peer-to-Peer and Grid Networking", Research Note 02/24, UCL-CS, 2002.

[10] L. A. Adamic, "The Small World Web", In *Proceedings of ECDL'99*, pp. 443–452, Springer, 1999.

[11] E. Adar and B. A. Huberman, "Free Riding on Gnutella", First Monday, volume 5, number 10, http://www.firstmonday.dk/issues/issue5_10/adar/, Oktober 2000.

[12] M. Addlesee, R. Curwen, S. Hodges, J. Newman, P. Steggles, A. Ward, and A. Hopper, "Implementing a Sentient Computing System", *Computer*, 34(8):50–56, 2001.

[13] A. Adya, W. J. Bolosky, M. Castro, G. Cermak, R. Chaiken, and J. R. Douceur, "FARSITE: Federated, Available, and Reliable Storage for an Incompletely Trusted Environment", http://research.microsoft.com/sn/Farsite/OSDI2002.pdf, 2002.

[14] A. Agrawal, D. J. Brown, A. Ojha, and S. Savage, "Bucking Free-Riders: Distributed Accounting and Settlement in Peer-to-Peer Networks", UCSD Tech Report CS2003-0751, UCSD, 2003.

[15] E. Aitenbichler and M. Mühlhäuser, "An IR Local Positioning System for Smart Items and Devices", In *Proceedings of the 23rd IEEE International Conference on Distributed Computing Systems Workshops (IWSAWC03)*, pp. 334–339, 2003.

[16] R. Akavipat, L.-S. Wu, and F. Menczer, "Small World Peer Networks in Distributed Web Search", In S. I. Feldman, M. Uretsky, M. Najork, and C. E. Wills, editors, *Proceedings of the 13th international conference on World Wide Web - Alternate Track Papers & Posters, WWW 2004, New York, NY, USA, May 17-20, 2004*, pp. 396–397, ACM, 2004.

[17] J. Al-Muhtadi, R. Campbell, A. Kapadia, M. Mickunas, and S. Yi, "Routing Through the Mist: Privacy Preserving Communication in Ubiquitous Computing Environments", , University of Illinois at Urbana-Champaign, CS, 2002.

[18] R. Albert, H. Jeong, and A. Barabasi, "Error and attack tolerance of complex networks", *Nature*, 406:378 – 382, 2000.

[19] R. Albert and A.-L. Barabási, "Statistical Mechanics of Complex Networks", *Reviews of Modern Physics*, 74:47–97, 2002.

[20] R. Albert, A.-L. Barabsi, and H. Jeong, "Scale-free characteristics of random networks: The topology of the world wide web", *Physica Review A*, 281:69–77, 2000.

[21] R. Albert, H. Jeong, and A.-L. Barabsi, "Error and Attack Tolerance of Complex Networks", *Nature*, 406:378–381, July 2000.

[22] H. J. Albert-László Barabási, Réka Albert, "Mean-Field Theory for Scale-Free Random Networks", *Physica A*, 272:173–187, 1999.

[23] B. Allcock, J. Bester, J. Bresnahan, A. Chervenak, I. Foster, K. Kesselman, S. Meder, V. Nefedova, D. Quesnel, and S. Teuck, "Data Management and Transfer in High-Performance Computational GRID Environments", *Parallel Computing*, 2001.

[24] W. Allcock, I. Foster, S. Tueck, A. Chervenak, and K. Kesselman, "Protocols and Services for Distributed Data-Intensive Science", In *Proc. of ACAT 2000*, ACAT, 2000.

[25] G. Alonso, F. Casati, H. Kuno, and V. Machiraju, *Web Services – Concepts, Architectures and Applications*, Springer Verlag, 2004.

[26] D. G. Andersen, H. Balakrishnan, M. F. Kaashoek, and R. Morris, "Resilient Overlay Networks", In *Proc. 18th ACM Symposium on Operating Systems Principles*, Banff, Canada, October 2001.

[27] F.-U. Andersen, H. de Meer, I. Dedinski, C. Kappler, A. Mäder, J. Oberender, and K. Tutschku, "An Architecture Concept for Mobile P2P File Sharing Services", In *Workshop at Informatik 2004 - Algorithms and Protocols for Efficient Peer-to-Peer Applications*, Ulm, 2004.

[28] D. Anderson, *SETI@home*, chapter 5, pp. 67–76, O'Reilly, Sebastopol, 2001.

[29] D. Anderson, J. Cobb, E. Korpela, M. Lebofsky, and D. Werthimer, "SETI@home: An Experminent in Public-Resource Computing", *Communications of the ACM*, 45(11):56–61, 2002.

[30] S. Androutsellis-Theotokis and D. Spinellis, "A Survey of Peer-to-Peer Content Distribution Technologies", In *ACM Computing Surveys*, Vol. 36(4), 2004.

[31] D. Angluin, J. Aspnes, J. Chen, Y. Wu, and Y. Yin, "Fast Construction of Overlay Networks", In *17th ACM Symposium on Parallelism in Algorithms and Architectures*, ACM, 2005.

[32] Aristotle, "Metaphysica", In W. Jaeger, editor, *Metaphysica*, Oxford University Press, 1957.

[33] A. Arkin, "Business Process Modeling Language", 2002, http://www.bpmi.org/bpml-spec.htm.

[34] A. Arkin, S. Askary, S. Fordin, W. Jekeli, K. Kawaguchi, D. Orchard, S. P. Riemer, S. Struble, P. Takacsi-Nagy, I. Trickovic, and S. Zimek, "Web Service Choreography Interface (WSCI) 1.0", 2002, http://www.w3.org/TR/wsci/.

[35] P. Ashley, S. Hada, G. Karjoth, C. Powers, and M. Schunter, "Enterprise Privacy Authorization Language (EPAL 1.2)", 2003.

[36] J. Aspnes and G. Shah, "Skip graphs", In *Fourteenth Annual ACM-SIAM Symposium on Discrete Algorithms*, ACM, 2003.

[37] H. Attiya and J. Welch, *Distributed Computing: Fundamentals, Simulations, and Advanced Topics*, McGraw-Hill Publishing Company, UK, 1998.

[38] Audiogalaxy, "Audiogalaxy Homepage", http://www.audiogalaxy.com/, 2004.

[39] N. Azzouna and F. Guillemin, "Analysis of ADSL traffic on an IP backbone link", In *GLOBECOM 2003*, San Francisco, California, 2003.

[40] N. Azzouna and F. Guillemin, "Experimental analysis of the impact of peer-to-peer applications on traffic in commercial IP networks", *European transactions on Telecommunications: Special issue on P2P networking and P2P services, ETT*, 15/6:511 – 522, 2004.

[41] A. Back, "Hash cash - a denial of service counter-measure", , 2002.

[42] A. Backbone, "Internet2 Netflow, Weekly Reports, Week of 20020218, 20020923, 20030505", http://netflow.internet2.edu/weekly, 2003.

[43] P. Backx, T. Wauters, B. Dhoedt, and P. Demester, "A Comparison of Peer-to-Peer Architectures", In *Eurescom Summit 2002*, 2002.

[44] P. Bahl and v Padmanabhan, "RADAR: An In-Building RF-Based User Location and Tracking System", In *Proc. IEEE Infocom 2000, IEEE CS Press, Los Alamitos, Calif.*, pp. 775–784, 2000.

[45] P. Bak, *How Nature Works: the science of self-organized criticality*, Springer-Verlag, New York, 1996.

[46] P. Bak and M. Paczuski, "Mass Extinctions vs. Uniformitarianism in Biological Evolution", *Physics of Biological Systems*, 1996, http://arxiv.org/pdf/cond-mat/9602012.

[47] P. Bak, C. Tang, and K. Wiesenfeld, "Self-Organized Criticality", *Physical Review A*, 38:364–374, 1988.

[48] M. Baker, R. Buyya, and D. Laforenza, "Grids and Grid Technologies for Wide-Area Distributed Computing", *International Journal on Software: Practice & Experience (SPE)*, 32(15):1437–1466, 2002.

[49] Y. Bakos and E. Brynjolfsson, "Bundling Information Goods: Pricing, Profits and Efficiency", *Management Science*, 45(12):1613–1630, 1999.

[50] Y. Bakos and E. Brynjolfsson, "Bundling and Competition on the Internet: Aggregation Strategies for Information Goods", *Marketing Science*, 19(1):63–82, 2000.

[51] H. E. Bal, K. P. Löhr, and A. Reinefeld, editors, *Proceedings of the Second IEEE/ACM International Symposium on Cluster Computing and the Grid*, Washington, DC, 2002.

[52] H. Balakrishnan, M. F. Kaashoek, D. Karger, R. Morris, and I. Stoica, "Looking up Data in P2P Systems", *Communications of the ACM*, 46(2), 2003.

[53] W.-T. Balke, W. Nejdl, W. Siberski, and U. Thaden, "DL meets P2P - Distributed Document Retrieval based on Classification and Content", In *European Conference on Digital Libraries (ECDL)*, Vienna, Austria, 2005.

[54] W.-T. Balke, W. Nejdl, W. Siberski, and U. Thaden, "Progressive Distributed Top-k Retrieval in Peer-to-Peer Networks", In *IEEE International Conference on Data Engineering (ICDE)*, pp. 174–185, Tokyo, Japan, 2005, IEEE Computer Society.

[55] S. Banerjee, T. G. Griffin, and M. Pias, "The Interdomain Connectivity of PlanetLab Nodes", In *Proceedings of the Passive and Active Measurement Workshop (PAM)*, 2004.

[56] G. Banga, P. Druschel, and J. C. Mogul, "Resource Containers: A New Facility for Resource Management in Server Systems", In *Operating Systems Design and Implementation*, pp. 45–58, 1999.

[57] Y. Bar-Yam, "Complexity rising: From human beings to human civilization, a complexity profile", , NECSI, 1997.

[58] Y. Bar-Yam, *Dynamics of Complex Systems*, Westview Press, 1997.

[59] A. Barabási, Z. Dezsö, E. Ravasz, S.-H. Yook, and Z. Oltvai, "Scale-free and hierarchical structures in complex networks", *Sitges Proceedings on Complex Networks 2004*, 2002.

[60] A.-L. Barabási and R. Albert, "Emergence of Scaling in Random Networks", *Science*, 286:509–512, October 1999.

[61] A. Barmouta and R. Buyya, "GridBank: A Grid Accounting Services Architecture (GASA) for Distributed Systems Sharing and Integration", In *17th Annual International Parallel & Distributed Processing Symposium (IPDPS 2003) Workshop on Internet Computing and E-Commerce*, Nice, France, April 22-26 2003.

[62] T. Barth and M. Grauer, *GRID Computing – Ansätze für verteiltes virtuelles Prototyping*, Springer- Verlag Berlin, Heidelberg, 2002.

[63] C. Batten, K. Barr, A. Saraf, and S. Trepetin, "pStore: A Secure Peer-to-Peer Backup System", Technical Memo MIT-LCS-TM-632, Massachusetts Institute of Technology Laboratory for Computer Science, 2002.

[64] A. Bavier, M. Bowman, B. Chun, D. Culler, S. Karlin, L. Peterson, T. Roscoe, and M. Wawrzoniak, "Operating Systems Support for Planetary-Scale Network Services", In *Proceedings of the 1st Symposium on Networked Systems Design and Implementation (NSDI'04), San Francisco, CA, USA*, 2004.

[65] BearShare, "Version 2.6.0", , Free Peers Inc, 2002.

[66] M. Bender, S. Michel, P. Triantafillou, G. Weikum, and C. Zimmer, "Improving Collection Selection with Overlap-Awareness", In *International ACM Conference on Research and Development in Information Retrieval (SIGIR)*, Salvador, Brazil, 2005.

[67] W. Benger, I. Foster, J. Novonty, E. Seidel, J. Shalf, W. Smith, and P. Walker, "Numerical Relativity in a Distributed Environment", In *Proceedings of the 9th SIAM Conference on Parallel Processing for Scientific Computing*, 1999.

[68] T. Berners-Lee, R. Fielding, and L. Masinter, "RFC 2396: Uniform Resource Identifiers (URI): Generic Syntax", IETF, 1998.

[69] P. A. Bernstein, "Middleware: A Model for Distributed Systems Services", *Communications of the ACM*, 39(2):86–98, 1996.

[70] P. A. Bernstein, F. Giunchiglia, A. Kementsietsidis, J. Mylopoulos, L. Serafini, and I. Zaihrayeu, "Data Management for Peer-to-Peer Computing: A Vision", In *Proceedings of the Fifth International Workshop on the Web and Databases*, Madison, Wisconsin, 2002.

[71] A. Bharambe, C. Herley, and V. Padmanabhan, "Analyzing and Improving BitTorrent Performance", Microsoft Research Technical Report MSR-TR-2005-03, 2005.

[72] A. R. Bharambe, M. Agrawal, and S. Seshan, "Mercury: Supporting scalable multi-attribute range queries", *SIGCOMM Comput. Commun. Rev.*, 34(4), 2004.

[73] S. Bhattacharyya, C. Diot, J. Jetcheva, and N. Taft, "Pop-Level and Access-Link-Level Traffic Dynamics in a Tier-1 POP", In *1nd Internet Measurement Workshop, San Francisco, USA*, 2001.

[74] A. Binzenhöfer and P. Tran-Gia, "Delay analysis of a chord-based peer-to-peer file-sharing system", In *ATNAC 2004*, Sydney, 2004.

[75] P. V. Biron and A. Malhotra, "XML Schema Part 2: Datatypes Second Edition", W3C, 2004, http://www.w3c.org/TR/xmlschema-2.

[76] R. Bless, K. Nichols, and K. Wehrle, "A Lower Effort Per-Domain Behavior (PDB) for Differentiated Services", RFC 3662, December 2003.

[77] B. H. Bloom, "Space/time trade-offs in hash coding with allowable errors", *Communications of the ACM*, 13(7):422–426, 1970.

[78] H. Boley, S. Tabet, and G. Wagner, "Design Rationale of RuleML: A Markup Language for Semantic Web Rules", In *Proceedings of the International Semantic Web Working Symposium (SWWS01)*, Stanford, CA, USA, 2001.

[79] B. Bollobás and O. Riordan, "The Diameter of a Scale-Free Random Graph", *Combinatorica*, 24:5–34, 2004.

[80] B. Bollobás and O. M. Riordan, "Mathematical results on scale-free random graphs", In S. Bornholdt and H. G. Schuster, editors, *Handbook of Graphs and Networks - From the Genome to the Internet*, Wiley-VCH, 2003.

[81] D. Boneh and M. Franklin, "Efficient Generation of Shared RSA keys", *Journal of the ACM (JACM)*, 48(4):702–722, July 2001.

[82] J. Borg, "A Comparative Study of Ad Hoc & Peer to Peer Networks", M.S. Thesis, University College London, Faculty of Engineering, Department of Electronic & Electrical Engineering, 2003.

[83] J. Borland, "Campus file swappers to pay RIAA", http://news.com.com/Campus+file+swappers+to+pay+RIAA/2100-1027_3-999332.html, 2003.

[84] S. Bornholdt and H. G. Schuster, editors, *Handbook of Graphs and Networks - From the Genome to the Internet*, Wiley-VCH, first edition, 2003.

[85] J. Y. Boudec, "Understanding the Simulation of Mobility Models with Palm Calculus", IC/2004/53,, EPF Lausanne, 2004.

[86] D. Box and F. Curbera, "Web Services Addressing (WS-Addressing)", W3C, 2004, http://www.w3.org/Submission/ws-addressing/.

[87] N. Boysen, "Ameisenalgorithmen", , Universität Hamburg, Institut für Industriebetriebslehre und Organisation, 2004.

[88] R. Braumandl, M. Keidl, A. Kemper, D. Kossmann, A. Kreutz, S. Seltzsam, and K. Stocker, "ObjectGlobe: Ubiquitous query processing on the Internet", *VLDB J.*, 10(1):48–71, 2001.

[89] T. Bray, J. Paoli, C. M. Sperberg-McQueen, E. Maler, F. Yergeau, and J. Cowan, "Extensible Markup Language (XML) 1.1", W3C, 2004, http://www.w3.org/TR/xml11/.

[90] E. Brewer, "Lessons from Giant-Scale Services", *IEEE Internet Computing*, 4(5):46–55, July/August 2001.

[91] D. Brickley and R. V. Guha, "RDF Vocabulary Description Language 1.0: RDF Schema", W3C, 2004, http://www.w3.org/TR/rdf-schema.

[92] J. Broch, D. Maltz, D. Johnson, Y. C. Hu, and J. Jetcheva, "A Performance Comparison of Multi-Hop Wireless Ad Hoc Network Routing Protocols", In *Proc. 4th ACM Mobicom*, pp. 85–97, Dallas, TX, 1998.

[93] E. Brosh and Y. Shavitt, "Approximation and Heuristic Algorithms for Minimum-Delay Application Layer Multicast Trees", In *IEEE INFOCOM 2004*, Hong Kong, April 2004.

[94] I. Brunkhorst, H. Dhraief, A. Kemper, W. Nejdl, and C. Wiesner, "Distributed Queries and Query Optimization in Schema-Based P2P-Systems", In *Proceedings of the First International Workshop on Databases, Information Systems, and Peer-to-Peer Computing (DBISP2P)*, Berlin, Germany, 2003, Springer.

[95] R. Brussee, H. Eertink, W. Huijsen, B. Hulsebosch, M. Rougoor, W. Teeuw, M. Wibbels, and H. Zandbelt, "Content Distribution Networks - State of the Art", TI/RS/2001/027, Telematica Instituut, June 2001.

[96] C. Buckley, A. Singhal, M. Mitra, and G. Salton, "New retrieval approaches using SMART", In *International Text REtrieval Conference (TREC-4)*, 1995.

[97] Bundesrepublik Deutschland, "Bundesdatenschutzgesetz (BDSG)", Bundesgesetzblatt I 2003 S.66, 2003.

[98] F. E. Bustamante and Y. Qiao, "Friendships that last: Peer lifespan and its role in P2P protocols", In *Proceedings of the International Workshop on Web Content Caching and Distribution*, 2003.

[99] J. Byers, J. Considine, and M. Mitzenmacher, "Simple Load Balancing for DHTs", In *Proceedings of 2nd International Workshop on Peer-to-Peer Systems (IPTPS '03)*, Berkeley, USA, 2003, IEEE.

[100] J. Callan, "Distributed Information retrieval", In *Advances in information Retrieval*, Kluwer Academic Publishers, 2000.

[101] J. Callan, Z. Lu, and W. B. Croft, "Searching Distributed Collections with Inference Networks", In *International ACM Conference on Research and Development in Information Retrieval (SIGIR)*, Seattle, WA, USA, 1995.

[102] B. Carpenter and K. Nichols, "Different services in the Internet", In *Proceedings of the IEEE (2002)*, pp. 1479–1494, 2002.

[103] A. Carzaniga, *Architectures for an Event Notification Service Scalable to Wide-area Networks*, Ph.D. Thesis, Politecnico di Milano, Milano, Italy, 1998.

[104] J. L. Casti, "Complexity", *Encyclopaedia Britannica*, 2005.

[105] M. Castro, "Practical Byzantine Fault Tolerance", http://www.lcs.mit.edu/publications/pubs/pdf/MIT-LCS-TR-817.pdf, 2001.

[106] M. Castro, M. Costa, and A. Rowstron, "Debunking some myths about structured and unstructured overlays", In *Proceedings of the 2nd Symposium on Networked Systems Design and Implementation*, Boston, MA, USA, 2005.

[107] M. Castro, M. Jones, A. Kermarrec, A. Rowstron, M. Theimer, H. Wang, and A. Wolman, "An Evaluation of Scalable Application-level Multicast Built Using Peer-to-peer Overlays", In *INFOCOM 2003*, San Francisco, CA, U.S.A., April 2003.

[108] M. Castro, P. Druschel, A. Ganesh, A. Rowstron, and D. S. Wallach, "Security for structured peer-to-peer overlay networks", In *Proceedings of the 5th USENIX Symposium on Operating Systems Design and Implementation (OSDI '02)*, Boston, Massachusetts, 2002.

[109] M. Castro, P. Druschel, A.-M. Kermarrec, and A. Rowstron, "SCRIBE: A large-scale and decentralised application-level multicast infrastructure", *IEEE Journal on Selected Areas in Communications*, 20(8), 2002.

[110] M. Castro, M. B. Jones, A.-M. Kermarrec, A. Rowstron, M. Theimer, H. Wang, and A. Wolman, "An evaluation of scalable application-level multicast built using peer-to-peer overlays", In *IEEE Twenty-Second Annual Joint Conference of the IEEE Computer and Communications Societies (INFOCOM 2003)*, 2, pp. 1510–1520, IEEE, 2003.

[111] P. Castro, B. Greenstein, R. Muntz, C. Biskidiuan, R. Kermani, and M. Papadopouli, "Locating Application Data across Service Discovery Domains", In *Proc. 7th ACM Mobicom*, pp. 28–42, Rome, Italy, 2001.

[112] D. Chaum, A. Fiat, and M. Naor, "Untraceable electronic cash", In *CRYPTO '88*, volume 403 of LNCS, pp. 319–327, Springer Verlag, 1990.

[113] Y. Chawathe, S. Ratnasamy, L. Breslau, N. Lanham, and S. Shenker, "Making Gnutella-like P2P Systems Scalable", In *SIGCOMM '03: Proceedings of the 2003 conference on Applications, technologies, architectures, and protocols for computer communications*, pp. 407–418, New York, NY, USA, 2003, ACM Press.

[114] A. Chen, R. R. Muntz, S. Yuen, I. Locher, S. I. Park, and M. B. Srivastava, "A Support Infrastructure for the Smart Kindergarten", *Pervasive Computing*, pp. 49–57, 2002.

[115] R. Chinnici, M. Gudgin, J.-J. Moreau, J. Schlimmer, and S. Weerawarana, "Web Services Description Language (WSDL) Version 2.0 Part 1: Core Language", W3C, 2004, http://www.w3.org/TR/wsdl20.

[116] P.-A. Chirita, S. Idreos, M. Koubarakis, and W. Nejdl, "Publish/Subscribe for RDF-based P2P Networks", In *Proceedings of the 1st European Semantic Web Symposium*, Heraklion, Crete, 2004.

[117] Chord, http://www.pdos.lcs.mit.edu/chord/, Poject Homepage.

[118] E. Christensen, F. Curbera, G. Meredith, and S. Weerawarana, "Web Services Description Language (WSDL) 1.1", W3C, 2001, http://www.w3.org/TR/wsdl.

[119] E. Chtcherbina, B. Freisleben, and T. Friese, "Peer-to-Peer Computing: Microsoft P2P versus Sun JXTA", *JavaSPEKTRUM*, 5, 2004.

[120] Y. Chun-Xia, Z. Tao, Z. Pei-Ling, L. Jun, and T. Zi-Nan, "Evolvement Complexity in an Artificial Stock Market", *Chinese Physics Letters*, 22(4):1014–1017, 2005.

[121] I. Cidon, I. Gopal, and S. Kutten, "New Models and Algorithms for Future Networks", *IEEE Transactions on Information Theory*, 41(3):769 – 780, May 1995.

[122] I. Clarke, "Freenet's Next Generation Routing Protocol", http://freenet.sourceforge.net/index.php?page=ngrouting, 2003.

[123] I. Clarke, S. G. Miller, T. W. Hong, O. Sandberg, and B. Wiley, "Protecting Free Expression Online with Freenet", *IEEE Internet Computing*, 6(1):40–49, 2002.

[124] I. Clarke, O. Sandberg, B. Wiley, and T. W. Hong, "Freenet: A Distributed Anonymous Information Storage and Retrieval System", In *ICSI Workshop on Design Issues in Anonymity and Unobservability*, 2000.

[125] M. Clement and G. Nerjes, *Bedeutung von Peer-to-Peer Technologien für die Distribution von Medienprodukten im Internet*, p. 71ff, Springer, 2002.

[126] Clip2, "The Gnutella Protocol Specification v0.4 (Document Revision 1.2)", http://www.clip2.com/GnutellaProtocol04.pdf, 2001.

[127] B. Cohen, "Incentives to Build Robustness in BitTorrent", http://bitconjurer.org/BitTorrent/bittorrentecon.pdf, 2004.

[128] B. Cohen, "Incentives Build Robustness in BitTorrent", In *Workshop on Economics of Peer-to-Peer Systems*, Berkeley, CA, USA, 2003.

[129] R. Cohen, K. Erez, D. ben Avraham, and S. Havlin, "Resilience of the Internet to Random Breakdown", *Physical Review Letters*, 85(21), November 2000.

[130] Conversagent, http://www.conversagent.com, 2004.

[131] B. F. Cooper, "Guiding Queries to Information Sources with InfoBeacons", In *ACM/IFIP/USENIX International Middleware Conference*, Toronto, Canada, 2004.

[132] C. Cooper and A. Friezer, "A General Model of Web Graphs", *Random Structures & Algorithms*, 22(3):311–335, 2003.

[133] CORBA, "Common Object Request Broker Architecture", http://www.corba.org/, 1997.

[134] L. P. Cox, C. D. Murray, and B. D. Noble, "Pastiche: Making backup cheap and easy", In *Fifth USENIX Symposium on Operating Systems Design and Implementation*, pp. 285–298, New York, NY, USA, 2002, ACM Press.

[135] L. P. Cox and B. D. Noble, "Samsara: Honor Among Thieves in Peer-to-Peer Storage", In *Proceedings of the Nineteenth ACM Symposium on Operating Systems Principles (SOSP'03)*, Bolton Landing, NY, 2003.

[136] S. A. Craver, M. Wu, B. Liu, et al., "Reading Between the Lines: Lessons from the SDMI Challenge", http://www.cs.princeton.edu/sip/sdmi/index.html, 2001.

[137] A. Crespo and H. Garcia-Molina, "Routing Indices For Peer-to-Peer Systems", In *International Conference on Distributed*, Vienna, Austria, 2002, IEEE Computer Society.

[138] J. Crowcroft and I. Pratt, "Peer to Peer: Peering into the Future", In *Proceedings of the IFIP-TC6 Networks 2002 Conference*, pp. 1–19, 2002.

[139] Crypto-ID Project, http://crypto-id.jxta.org, 12 2004.

[140] F. Cuenca-Acuna, C. Peery, R. Martin, and T. Nguyen, "PlanetP: Using Gossiping to Build Content Addressable Peer-to-Peer Information Sharing Communities", In *International IEEE International Symposium on High Performance Distributed Computing (HPDC-12)*, 2003.

[141] F. Curbera, M. Duftler, R. Khalaf, W. Nagy, N. Mukhi, and S. Weerawarana, "Unraveling the Web Services Web: An Introduction to SOAP, WSDL, and UDDI", *IEEE Internet Computing*, March/April 2002:86–93, 2002.

[142] K. Czajkowski, D. Ferguson, I. Foster, J. Frey, S. Graham, T. Maquire, and S. Tuecke, "From Open GRID Services Infrastructure to WS-Resource Framework: Refactoring & Evolution", http://www-fp.globus.org/wsrf/, 2004.

[143] K. Czajkowski, D. Ferguson, I. Foster, J. Frey, S. Graham, I. Sedukhin, D. Snelling, S. Tuecke, and W. Vambenepe, "TWS-Resource Framework", http://www-fp.globus.org/wsrf/, 2004.

[144] K. Czajkowski, S. Fitzgerald, I. Foster, and K. Kesselman, "GRID Information Services for Distributed Resource Sharing", In *Proc. of 10th IEEE Symposium on High Performance Distributed Computing*, IEEE Computer Society, 2001.

[145] K. Czajkowski, I. Foster, N. Karonis, C. Kesselman, S. Martin, W. Smith, and S. Tuecke, "A Resource Management Architecture for Metacomputing Systems", In *Proc. of IPPS/SPDP '98 Workshop on Job Scheduling Strategies for Parallel Processing*, Springer-Verlag, 1998.

[146] F. Dabek, E. Brunskill, M. F. Kaashoek, D. Karger, R. Morris, and I. Stoica, "Building Peer-to-Peer Systems with Chord - A Distributed Lookup Service", In *Proceedings of the 8th Workshop on Hot Topics in Operating Systems*, pp. 81–86, 2001.

[147] F. Dabek, M. F. Kasshoek, D. Karger, R. Morris, and I. Stoica, "Wide-area cooparative storage with CFS", In *Proceedings of the 18th ACM Symposium on Operating Systems Principles*, pp. 202–215, 2001.

[148] F. Dabek, B. Zhao, P. Druschel, J. Kubiatowicz, and I. Stoica, "Towards a Common API for Structured Peer-to-Peer Overlays", In *2nd International Workshop on Peer-to-Peer Systems (IPTPS '03)*, Springer, 2003.

[149] Dagstuhl, "Seminar 04111: "Peer-to-Peer Systems", http://www.dagstuhl.de/04111/, 2004.

[150] Y. K. Dalal and R. M. Metcalfe, "Reverse path forwarding of broadcast packets", *Communications of the ACM*, 21(12):1040–1048, 1978.

[151] H. Damker, *Sicherheitsaspekte von P2P-Anwendungen in Unternehmen*, Springer, Berlin, 2002.

[152] V. Darlagiannis, A. Mauth, N. Liebau, and R. Steinmetz, "An Adaptable, Role-based Simulator for P2P Networks", In *Proceedings of International Conference on Modelling, Simulation and Visualization Methods (MSV'04)*, pp. 52 – 59, Las Vegas, Nevada, USA, 2004.

[153] V. Darlagiannis, A. Mauthe, and R. Steinmetz, "Overlay Design Mechanisms for Heterogeneous, Large Scale, Dynamic P2P Systems", *Journal of Networks and System Management*, 12(3):371–395,, 2004.

[154] N. Daswani, H. Garcia-Molina, and B. Yang, "Open Problems in Data-sharing Peer-to-Peer Systems", In *Proceedings of the 9th International Conference on Database Theory*, Springer, 2003.

[155] M. Datar, "Butterflies and Peer-to-Peer Networks", In *Proceedings of ESA 2002 (LNCS)*, 2002.

[156] A. Datta, "MobiGrid: P2P Overlay and MANET Rendezvous - a Data Management Perspective", In *CAiSE 2003 Doctoral Symposium*, 2003.

[157] A. Datta, M. Hauswirth, R. John, R. Schmidt, and K. Aberer, "Range queries in trie-structured overlays", IC/2004/111, Ecole Polytechnique Fédérale de Lausanne, 2004.

[158] A. Datta, S. Quarteroni, and K. Aberer, "Autonomous Gossiping: A Self-Organizing Epidemic Algorithm for Selective Information Dissemination in Wireless Mobile Ad-Hoc Networks", *Lecture Notes in Computer Science*, 3226:126–143, 2004.

[159] DCMI Usage Board, "DCMI Metadata Terms", 2005, http://dublincore.org/documents/dcmi-terms/.

[160] H. de Meer, K. Tutschku, and P. Tran-Gia, "Dynamic Operation in Peer-to-Peer Overlay Networks", *Praxis der Informationsverarbeitung und Kommunikation (PIK) – Special Issues on Peer-to-Peer Systems*, 26(2):65–73, 2003.

[161] S. E. Deering and D. R. Cheriton, "Multicast routing in datagram internetworks and extended LANs", *ACM Transactions on Computer Systems (TOCS)*, 8(2):85–110, 1990.

[162] A. Demers, D. Greene, C. Hauser, W. Irish, J. Larson, S. Shenker, H. Sturgis, D. Swinehart, and D. Terry, "Epidemic Algorithms for Replicated Database Maintenance", In *Proc. 6th Symp. on Princliples of Distributed Computing (PODC 1987)*, pp. 1–12, Vancover, Canada, 1987.

[163] O. Densmore, "An Exploration of Power-Law Networks", , Sun Microsystems Laboratories, 2001.

[164] Y. Desmedt and Y. Frankel, "Threshold cryptosystems", In *CRYPTO '89*, volume 435 of LNCS, pp. 307–315, Springer-Verlag, 1989.

[165] Z. Despotovic, J.-C. Usunier, and K. Aberer, "Towards Peer-To-Peer Double Auctioning", In *37th Hawaii International Conference on System Sciences*, Waikoloa, HI, USA, 2004.

[166] A. K. Dey, *Providing Architectural Support for Building Context-Aware Applications*, Ph.D. Thesis, Georgia Institute of Technology, 2000.

[167] R. Dingledine, M. J. Freedman, and D. Molnar, *Peer-To-Peer: Harnessing the Power of Disruptive Technologies*, chapter Accountability, pp. 217 – 340, O'Reilly & Associates, 1st edition, March 2001.

[168] R. Dingledine, M. J. Freedman, and D. Molnar, "The Free Haven Project - Distributed Anonymous Storage Service", , Massachusetts Institute of Technology, 2000.

[169] R. Dingledine, N. Mathewson, and P. Syverson, "Tor: The Second-Generation Onion Router", In *Proceedings of the 13th USENIX Security Symposium*, ACM, 2004.

[170] C. Diot, B. N. Levine, B. Lyles, H. Kassem, and D. Balensiefen, "Deployment issues for the IP multicast service and architecture", *IEEE Network*, 14(1):78–88, 2000.

[171] J. S. Donath, "Identity and Deception in the Virtual Community", In *In Kollock, P. and Smith, M. (Eds.) Communities in Cyberspace: Perspectives on New Forms of Social Organization. Berkeley*, University of California Press, 1997.

[172] D. Dooling, "1,000 Shares of Magnetar at 12-1/2! Quakes on pulsars follow the same power law as the stock market, traffic jam", *Science @ NASA*, 1999, http://science.msfc.nasa.gov/newhome/headlines/ast08dec99_1.htm.

[173] M. Dorigo, G. D. Caro, and T. Stuetzle, "Ant Algorithms", *Special Issue on Future Generation Computer Systems (FGCS)*, 16(8), 2000.

[174] M. Dorigo and L. M. Gambardella, "Ant Colony System: A Cooperative Learning Approach to the Traveling Salesman Problem", *IEEE Transactions on Evolutionary Computation*, 1(1):53–66, 1997.

[175] S. Dorogovtsev, J. Mendes, and A. Samukhin, "Structure of Growing Networks with Preferential Linking", *Physical Review Letters*, 85, 2000.

[176] J. Douceur, A. Adya, W. Bolosky, D. Simon, and M. Theimer, "Reclaiming Space from Duplicate Files in a Serverless Distributed File System", In *Proceedings of the International Conference on Distributed Computing Systems (ICDCS'02)*, Vienna, Austria, 2002.

[177] J. Douceur, "The Sybil Attack", In *1st International Workshop on Peer-to-Peer Systems (IPTPS '02)*, Springer, 2002.

[178] D. Dougherty, L. Gonze, K. Truelove, and S. Clay, *Distributed Computation*, p. 101ff, O'Reilly, 2001.

[179] B. Dragovic, K. Fraser, S. Hand, T. Harris, A. Ho, I. Pratt, A. Warfield, P. Barham, and R. Neugebauer, "Xen and the Art of Virtualization", In *Proceedings of the ACM Symposium on Operating Systems Principles*, 2003.

[180] E. Drinea, M. Enachescu, and M. Mitzenmacher, "Variations on Random Graph Models for the Web", , Harvard University, Department of Computer Science, 2001.

[181] P. Druschel, F. Kaashoek, and A. Rowstron, "Peer-to-Peer Systems", In *Proceedings of the First International Workshop, IPTPS 2002*, Cambridge, MA, USA, 2002, Springer, Revised Papers.

[182] P. Druschel and A. Rowstron, "Scalable, Distributed Object Location and Routing for Large-Scale Peer-to-Peer Systems", In *Proceedings of IFIP/ACM International Conference on Distributed Systems Platforms (Middleware)*, pp. 329–350, Heidelberg, 2001.

[183] eBay Inc, "The eBay Homepage", http://www.ebay.com/, 2004.

[184] Edonkey, "Edonkey Client and Protocol Description", http://silicon-verl.de/home/flo/software/donkey/, 2003.

[185] eDonkey2000, http://www.edonkey2000.com, 2003.

[186] Edutella, "The Edutella Project", http://edutella.jxta.org/, 2005.

[187] J. Edwards, *Peer-to-Peer Programming on Groove*, Addison-Wesley, Indianapolis, 2002.

[188] Efarm-Project, "ed2k Protocol Documentation Client - Serveur Version 3.0", http://www.efarm-project.net/data/docs/Protocol_V3_1_EN.pdf, 2003.

[189] S. ElRakabawy, A. Klemm, and C. Lindemann, "TCP with Adaptive Pacing for Multihop Wireless Networks", In *Proc. ACM International Symposium on Mobile Ad Hoc Networking and Computing (MobiHoc 2005)*, Urbana-Champaign, IL, 2005.

[190] Emergence, "Complexity and Organization", http://www.emergence.org/.

[191] eMule, "eMule Project Team Homepage", http://www.emule-project.net, 2002.

[192] eMule's Credit System, http://www.emule-project.net/home/perl/help.cgi?l=1&rm=show_topic&topic_id=134, December 2004.

[193] M. Endrei, J. Ang, A. Arsanjani, S. Chua, P. Comte, P. Krogdahl, M. Luo, and T. Newling, *Patterns: Service-Oriented Architecture and Web Services*, IBM Redbook, 2004.

[194] H. Esser, *Die Konstruktion der Gesellschaft*, volume 2, Campus Verlag GmbH, Frankfurt/Main, 1. edition, 2000.

[195] P. Eugster, P. Felber, R. Guerraoui, and A.-M. Kermarrec, "The Many Faces of Publish/Subscribe", *ACM Computing Surveys*, 35(2):114–131, 2003.

[196] Eurescom study P1553, "P2P-ISP The impact of peer-to-peer networking on network operators and Internet service providers", www.eurescom.de/public/projects/P1500-series/P1553, 2005.

[197] Fachgespräch, "Qualität in Peer-to-Peer-Systemen", http://www.kom.e-technik.tu-darmstadt.de/ws-p2p/, 2003.

[198] K. Fall and K. Varadhan, *The ns-2 Manual*, The VINT Project, UC Berkeley, LBL, and Xerox PARC, 2003.

[199] J. Fallows, "Internet Calling, Skype Is Living Up to the Hype", *The New York Times*, 2004, September 5, 2004.

[200] D. Fallside and P. Walmsley, "XML Schema Part 0: Primer Second Edition", W3C, 2004, http://www.w3c.org/TR/xmlschema-0.

[201] M. Faloutsos, P. Faloutsos, and C. Faloutsos, "On Power-law Relationships of the Internet Topology", In *SIGCOMM*, pp. 251–262, 1999.

[202] FastTrack, http://en.wikipedia.org/wiki/FastTrack.

[203] G. Fedak, C. Germain, V. Neri, and F. Cappello, "XtremWeb: A Generic Global Computing System", In *Proceedings of Workshop on Global Computing on Personal Devices*, IEEE Computer Society Press, USA, 2001.

[204] M. Feldman, C. Papadimitriou, J. Chuang, and I. Stoica, "Free-riding and whitewashing in peer-to-peer systems", In *PINS '04: Proceedings of the ACM SIGCOMM workshop on Practice and theory of incentives in networked systems*, pp. 228–236, ACM Press, 2004.

[205] C. Ferris and D. Langworthy, "Web Services Reliable Messaging Protocol (WS-ReliableMessaging)", IBM, 2005, http://www.ibm.com/developerworks/library/specification/ws-rm/.

[206] R. Fielding, J. Gettys, J. Mogul, H. Frystyk, L. Masinter, P. Leach, and T. Berners-Lee, "RFC 2616: Hypertext Transfer Protocol – HTTP/1.1", IETF, 1999, http://www.ietf.org/rfc/rfc2616.txt.

[207] FIPS, "Secure Hash Standard", FIPS PUB 180-1, Federal Information Processing Standards Publication, 1995.

[208] K. Fischer, "Holonic multiagent systems – theory and applications", In P. Barahona and J. J. Alferes, editors, *EPIA*, pp. 34–48, Springer-Verlag, 1999.

[209] S. Fischer-Hübner, *IT-Security and Privacy - Design and Use of Privacy-Enhancing Security Mechanisms*, volume 1958, Springer, Lecture Notes in Computer Science edition, 2001.

[210] G. Foest and R. Paffrath, "Peer-to-Peer (P2P) and Beyond", *DFN Mitteilungen*, 3(58), 2002.

[211] F. Forster and H. de Meer, "Discovery of Web Services with a P2P Network", In *Proceedings of International Conference on Computational Science*, pp. 90–97, 2004.

[212] B. Fortz and M. Thorup, "Internet traffic engineering by optimising OSPF weights", In *Proceeding of IEEE INFOCOM 2002*, pp. 519–528, 2000.

[213] I. Foster, "The Grid: A New Infrastructure for 21st Century Science", *Physics Today*, 55(2), 2002.

[214] I. Foster, "What is the GRID? A Three Point Checklist", *GRID today, Dailly News and Information for the Global GRID Community*, 1(6), 2002.

[215] I. Foster, "Service-Oriented Science", *Science*, 308(5723):814–817, 2005.

[216] I. Foster, J. Frey, S. Graham, S. Tuecke, K. Czajkowski, D. Ferguson, F. Leymann, M. Nally, I. Sedukhin, D. Snelling, W. Vambenepe, and S. Weerawarana, "Modelling Stateful Resources with Web Services", http://www-106.ibm.com/developerworks/library/ws-resource/ws-modelingresources.pdf, 2004.

[217] I. Foster and A. Iamnitchi, "On Death, Taxes, and the Convergence of Peer-to-Peer and Grid Computing", In *2nd International Workshop on Peer-to-Peer Systems (IPTPS '03)*, 2003.

[218] I. Foster and A. Iamnitchi, *A Peer-to-Peer Approach to Resource Location in the Grid Environments*, Kluwer Publishing, 2003.

[219] I. Foster and C. Kesselman, *GLOBUS2002project: A Toolkit-Based Grid Architecture'*, Morgan Kaufmann Publishers, 1999.

[220] I. Foster and C. Kesselman, *The Grid: Blueprint for a New Computing Infrastructure*, Morgan Kaufmann, San Francisco, 2nd edition, 2004.

[221] I. Foster, C. Kesselman, J. Nick, and S. Tuecke, "Grid Services for Distributed System Integration", *IEEE Computer*, 36, 2002.

[222] I. Foster, C. Kesselman, J. Nick, and S. Tuecke, "The Physiology of the GRID", GLOBUS2002project Technical Report, Globus Alliance, 2002.

[223] I. Foster, C. Kesselman, G. Tsudik, and S. Tuecke, "A Security Architecture for Computational Grids", In *Proceedings of ACM Conference on Computers and Security*, 1998.

[224] I. Foster, C. Kesselman, and S. Tuecke, "The Anatomy of the Grid", http://www.globus.org/research/papers/anatomy.pdf, 2002.

[225] I. Foster and C. Kessleman, *Computational GRIDS*, Morgan Kaufmann, San Francisco, 2nd edition, 2004.

[226] I. Foster, A. Roy, and V. Sander, "A Quality of Service Architecture that Combines Resource Reservation and Application Adaptation", In *Proceedings of the 8th International Workshop on Quality of Service*, Springer, 2000.

[227] I. Foster, C. Kesselmann, and S. Tuecke, *Die Anatomie des Grid*, p. 119ff, Springer, 2002.

[228] P. Francis, "Yoid: Extending the Internet Multicast Architecture", , ICSI Center for Internet Research, 2000.

[229] M. J. Freedman and R. Morris, "Tarzan: A Peer-to-Peer Anonymizing Network Layer", In *Proceedings of the 9th ACM Conference on Computer and Communications Security (CCS 2002)*, Washington, D.C., 2002.

[230] M. J. Freedman and R. Vingralek, "Efficient Peer-to-Peer Lookup Based on a Distributed Trie", In *Proceedings of the 1st International Workshop on Peer-to-Peer Systems (IPTPS02)*, Cambridge, MA, 2002.

[231] Freenet, http://freenetproject.org/.

[232] Freenet, "Freenet Homepage", http://freenetproject.org/cgi-bin/twiki/view/Main/WebHome, 2001.

[233] FreePastry, http://freepastry.rice.edu.

[234] D. Friedman, "The Double Auction Market Institution: A Survey", In D. Friedman and J. Rust, editors, *The Double Auction Market: Institutions, Theories, and Evidence*, pp. 3–25, Addison-Wesley, 1993.

[235] Y. Fu, J. Chase, B. Chun, S. Schwab, and A. Vahdat, "SHARP: an architecture for secure resource peering", In *SOSP '03: Proceedings of the nineteenth ACM symposium on Operating systems principles*, pp. 133–148, New York, NY, USA, 2003, ACM Press.

[236] J. E. Gabeiras, "Panel Presentation on "Issues in Peer-to-Peer Networking" at COST279 Mid-Seminar", 2004.

[237] P. Ganesan, Q. Sun, and H. Garcia-Molina, "Adlib: a Self-Tuning Index for Dynamic P2P systems", In *IEEE International Conference on Data Engineering (ICDE)*, Tokyo, Japan, 2005.

[238] L. Garces-Erce, E. Biersack, P. Felber, K. W. Ross, and G. Urvoy-Keller, "Hierarchical Peer-to-Peer Systems", In *Proceedings of Euro-Par*, 2003.

[239] J. Gerke, "Specification and Implementation of the Peer-to-Peer Middleware (Final)", Deliverable D10 of the MMAPPS Project, ETH Zurich, TIK, 2004.

[240] J. Gerke, D. Hausheer, J. Mischke, and B. Stiller, "An Architecture for a Service Oriented Peer-to-Peer System (SOPPS)", *Praxis der Informationsverarbeitung und Kommunikation (PIK)*, 26(2), 2003.

[241] J. Gerke and B. Stiller, "A Service-Oriented Peer-to-Peer Middleware", In *14. Fachtagung Kommunikation in Verteilten Systemen 2005 (KiVS 05)*, LNCS, Kaiserslautern, Germany, 2005, Springer.

[242] A. Ghosh, M. Fry, and J. Crowcroft, "An architecture for application layer routing", *Active Networks, LNCS*, 1942:71–86, 2000.

[243] Gift, "Gift Homepage", http://gift.sourceforge.net/, 2003.

[244] GI/ITG Workshop, "Peer-to-Peer Systems and Applications", http://ps-group.org/events/p2p-ws05/, 2005.

[245] E. Gilbert, "Random Graphs", *Annals of Mathematical Statistics*, 30:1141–1144, 1959.

[246] M. Gleich, *Die zehn Gesetze der Netze*, chapter 4, pp. 60–123, Hoffmann & Campe, 2002.

[247] Global Grid Forum, http://www.gridforum.org/, 2004.

[248] GLOBUS, "The GLOBUS2002 Project", http://www.GLOBUS2002project.org, 2002.

[249] Gnutella, "http://gnutella.wego.com", 2000.

[250] Gnutella, http://www.gnutella.com, 2003.

[251] Gnutella 2, http://www.gnutella2.com.

[252] Gnutella Network, http://en.wikipedia.org/wiki/Gnutella (seen 04/2005), 2000.

[253] S. Goel, M. Singh, D. Xu, and B. Li, "Efficient Peer-to-Peer Data Dissemination in Mobile Ad-Hoc Networks", In *Proc. Int. Wortshop on Ad Hoc Networking (IWAHN 2002)*, Vancover, Canada, 1987.

[254] A. Goldberg and P. Yianilos, "Towards an archival intermemory", In *Proccedings of the IEEE International Forum on Research and Technology Advances in Digital Libraries*, pp. 147–156, Santa Barbara, 1998.

[255] L. Gong, "Project JXTA: A Technology Overview", , Sun Microsystems, Palo Alto, CA, USA, 2001.

[256] D. Görgen, H. Frey, and C. Hutter, "Information Dissemination Based on the En-Passent Communication Pattern", In *Kommunikation in Verteilten Systemen (KiVS 2005)*, pp. 129–141, 2005.

[257] R. L. Graham, D. E. Knuth, and O. Patashnik, *Concrete Mathematics*, Reading, Massachusetts, second edition, 1994.

[258] S. Graham, "Web Services Resource Framework", IBM, 2003, http://www-106.ibm.com/developerworks/webservices/library/ws-resource.

[259] L. Gravano, H. Garcia-Molina, and A. Tomasic, "GlOSS: Text-Source Discovery over the Internet", In *ACM Transactions on Database Systems (TODS)*, Vol. 24(2), 1999.

[260] S. Gribble, A. Y. Halevy, Z. G. Ives, M. Rodrig, and D. Suciu, "What Can Databases Do for Peer-to-Peer", In *Proceedings of the Fourth International Workshop on the Web and Databases*, Santa Barbara, CA, USA, 2001.

[261] Groove Networks, http://www.groove.net, 2004.

[262] M. Grossglauser and D. Tse, "Mobility Increases the Capacity of Ad-hoc Wireless Networks", *IEEE/ACM Trans. on Networking*, 10:477–486,, 2002.

[263] I. Gruber and H. Li, "Path Expiration Times in Mobile Ad Hoc Networks", In *European Personal Mobile Communications Conference (EPMCC'03)*, 2003.

[264] I. Gruber, R. Schollmeier, and W. Kellerer, "Performance Evaluation of the Mobile Peer-to-Peer Protocol", In *Fourth International Workshop on Global and Peer-to-Peer Computing (GP2PC'2004)*, 2004.

[265] M. Gudgin, M. Hadley, N. Mendelsohn, J.-J. Moreau, and H. F. Nielsen, "SOAP Version 1.2 Part 1: Messaging Framework", W3C, 2003, http://www.w3.org/TR/soap12/.

[266] K. Gummadi, S. Gribble, S. Ratnasamy, S. Shenker, and I. Stoica, "The Impact of DHT Routing Geometry on Resilience and Proximity", In *Proceedings of ACM Sigcomm 2003*, ACM Press, 2003.

[267] S. Haber, B. Horn, J. Pato, T. Sander, and R. E. Tarjan, *If Piracy Is the Problem, Is DRM the Answer?*, p. 224ff, Springer, 2003.

[268] Hacktivismo, http://www.hacktivismo.com, 2005.

[269] A. Haeberlen, A. Mislove, and P. Druschel, "Glacier: Highly durable, decentralized storage despite massive correlated failures", In *Proceedings of the 2nd Symposium on Networked Systems Design and Implementation (NSDI'05)*, Boston, Massachusetts, 2005.

[270] C. Hahn, B. Fley, and M. Schillo, "Strategic Adaptation in Self-organizing Multiagent Systems", In *Proceedings of the Fourth International Workshop on Modelling Artificial Societies and Hybrid Organizations (MASHO'03)*, 2003.

[271] H. Haken, "Synergetik: Vergangenheit, Gegenwart, Zukunft", In K. Mainzer, editor, *Komplexe Systeme und Nichtlineare Dynamik in Natur und Gesellschaft*, chapter 2, pp. 30–45, Springer Verlag, Berlin, 1999.

[272] H. Haken and A. Wunderlin, *Synergetik: eine Einführung; Nichtgleichgewichts-Phasenübergänge und Selbstorganisation in Physik, Chemie und Biologie*, Springer, Berlin, 3. edition edition, 1990.

[273] A. Y. Halevy, Z. G. Ives, J. Madhavan, P. Mork, D. Suciu, and I. Tatarinov, "The Piazza Peer Data Management System.", *IEEE Trans. Knowl. Data Eng.*, 16(7):787–798, 2004.

[274] A. Y. Halevy, Z. G. Ives, P. Mork, and I. Tatarinov, "Piazza: Data Management Infrastructure for Semantic Web Applications", In *Proceedings of the Twelfth International World Wide Web Conference*, Budapest, Hungary, 2003, ACM.

[275] K. Hanna, B. Levine, and R. Manmatha, "Mobile Distributed Information Retrieval for Highly Partitioned Networks", In *Proc. 11th IEEE Int. Conf. on Network Protocols*, pp. 38–47, Atlanta, GA, 2003.

[276] F. Harrell, Y. Hu, G. Wang, and H. Xia, "Survey of Locating & Routing in Peer-to-Peer Systems", http://www.cs.ucsd.edu/classes/fa01/cse221/projects/, August 2002.

[277] A. Hartl, E. Aitenbichler, G. Austaller, A. Heinemann, T. Limberger, E. Braun, and M. Mühlhäuser, "Engineering Multimedia-Aware Personalized Ubiquitous Services", In *Proceedings of IEEE Multimedia Software Engineering*, Newport Beach, CA, 2002.

[278] F. Hartleb and G. Haßlinger, "Comparison of link dimensioning methods for TCP/IP networks", In *Proc. IEEE Globecom*, pp. 2240–2247, 2001.

[279] N. J. Harvey, M. B. Jones, S. Saroiu, M. Theimer, and A. Wolman, "SkipNet: A Scalable Overlay Network with Practical Locality Properties", In *In proceedings of the 4th USENIX Symposium on Internet Technologies and System (USITS '03)*, 2003.

[280] G. Haßlinger, "Quality-of-service analysis for statistical multiplexing with Gaussian and autoregressive input modeling", 2001.

[281] G. Haßlinger, "Implications of traffic characteristics on quality of service in broadband multi service networks", In *Proc. 30th EUROMICRO Conf., Multimedia and Telecommunications*, pp. 196–204, Rennes, France, 2004.

[282] D. Hausheer and B. Stiller, "Decentralized Auction-based Pricing with PeerMart", In *9th IFIP/IEEE International Symposium on Integrated Network Management (IM 2005)*, Nice, France, 2005.

[283] D. Hausheer and B. Stiller, "PeerMint: Decentralized and Secure Accounting for Peer-to-Peer Applications", In *2005 IFIP Networking Conference*, University of Waterloo, Waterloo Ontario Canada, 2005.

[284] A. Hayes and D. Wilson, "Peer-to-Peer Information Sharing in a Mobile Ad Hoc Environment", In *Sixth IEEE Workshop on Mobile Computing Systems and Applications (WMCSA'04)*, pp. 154–162, 2005.

[285] O. Heckmann, A. Bock, A. Mauthe, and R. Steinmetz, "The eDonkey File-Sharing Network", http://www.kom.e-technik.tu-darmstadt.de/publications/abstracts/HBMS04-1.html, 2004.

[286] T. Heer, H. Niedermayer, L. Petrak, S. Rieche, and K. Wehrle, "On the Use of Structured P2P Indexing Mechanisms in Mobile Ad-Hoc Scenarios", In *Workshop on Algorithms and Protocols for Efficient Peer-to-Peer Applications, INFORMATIK 2004, Vol. 2*, LNCS-LNI Vol. 51, GI, 2004.

[287] A. Heinemann, "The iClouds Homepage", http://www.iclouds.tk.informtik.tu-darmstadt.de, 2003.

[288] A. Heinemann, J. Kangasharju, F. Lyardet, and M. Mühlhäuser, "Ad Hoc Collaboration and Information Services Using Information Clouds", In T. Braun, N. Golmie, and J. Schiller, editors, *Proceedings of the 3rd Workshop on Applications and Services in Wireless Networks, (ASWN 2003)*, pp. 233–242, Bern, Switzerland, 2003, Institute of Computer Science and Applied Mathematics, University of Bern.

[289] A. Heinemann, J. Kangasharju, F. Lyardet, and M. Mühlhäuser, "iClouds - Peer-to-Peer Information Sharing in Mobile Environments", In H. Kosch, L. Böszörményi, and H. Hellwagner, editors, *Proceedings of the 9th International Euro-Par Conference, (Euro-Par 2003)*, Lecture Notes in Computer Science, pp. 1038–1045, Klagenfurt, Austria, 2003, Springer.

[290] W. Heinzelman, J. Kulik, and H. Balakrishnan, "Adaptive Protocols for Information Dissemination in Wireless Sensor Networks", In *Proc. 5th ACM Mobicom*, pp. 174–185, Seattle, WA, 1999.

[291] M. Hendricks, B. Galbraith, and R. Irani, *Professional Java Web Services*, Wrox Press Ltd., 2002.

[292] Hewlett-Packard Company&WaveSystem Corporation, "The EMBASSY E-Commerce System", http://www.wave.com/technology/embassy.html, 2004.

[293] F. Heylighen, "(Meta)Systems as Constraints on Variation - A Classification and Natural History of Metasystem Transitions", *World Futures: the Journal of General Evolution*, 45:59–85, 1995.

[294] F. Heylighen, "Self-organization", *Principia Cybernetica*, 1997.

[295] J. Hightower and G. Borriello, "Location Systems for Ubiquitous Computing", *Computer, Issue on Location Aware Computing*, 34(8):57–66, 2001.

[296] M. Hillenbrand, J. Götze, and P. Müller, "Voice over IP - Considerations for a Next Generation Architecture", In *Proceedings of Euromicro 2005*, IEEE, 2005.

[297] T. Hoßfeld, K. Tutschku, F. U. Andersen, H. de Meer, and J. Oberender, "Simulative Performance Evaluation of a Mobile Peer-to-Peer File-Sharing System", In *Next Generation Internet Networks NGI2005*, Rome, Italy, 2005, IEEE.

[298] T. Hofeld, K. Tutschku, and F.-U. Andersen, "Mapping of File-Sharing onto Mobile Environments: Enhancement by UMTS", In *Mobile Peer-to-Peer Computing MP2P, in conjunction with the 3rd IEEE International Conference on Pervasive Computing and Communications (PerCom'05)*, pp. 43–54, Kauai Island, Hawaii, 2005, IEEE Computer Society.

[299] T. Hofeld, K. Tutschku, and F.-U. Andersen, "Mapping of File-Sharing onto Mobile Environments: Feasibility and Performance of eDonkey with GPRS", In *Wireless Communications and Networking Conference, 2004. WCNC. 2005 IEEE*, IEEE Computer Society, 2005.

[300] W. Hofkirchner, "Information und Selbstorganisation – Zwei Seiten einer Medaille", In N. Fenzl, W. Hofkirchner, and G. Stockinger, editors, *Information und Selbstorganisation. Annäherungen an eine vereinheitlichte Theorie der Information.*, pp. 69–99, StudienVerlag, Innsbruck, 1998.

[301] H. Honermann, *Selbstorganisation in psychotherapeutischen Veränderungsprozessen*, Ph.D. Thesis, Otto-Friedrich Universität Bamberg, Bamberg, 2002, http://elib.uni-bamberg.de/volltexte/2002/6.html.

[302] T. Hong, "Performance", In A. Oram, editor, *Peer-to-Peer: Harnessing the Power of Disruptive Technologies*, O'Reilly, March 2001.

[303] X. Hong, M. Gerla, G. Pei, and C. Chiang, "A Group Mobility Model for Ad Hoc Wireless Networks", In *Proc. ACM Int. Workshop on Modeling, Analysis and Simulation of Wireless and Mobile Systems (MSWiM 99)*, pp. 53–60, Seattle, WA, 1999.

[304] W. Hoschek, J. Jaen-Martinez, A. Samar, H. Stockinger, and K. Stockinger, "Data Management in an International Data Grid Project", In *Proceedings of the 1st IEEE/ACM International Workshop on Grid Computing*, Springer-Verlag London, UK, 2000.

[305] Y. hua Chu, A. Ganjam, T. E. Ng, S. G. Rao, K. Sripanidkulchai, J. Zhan, and H. Zhang, "Early Experience with an Internet Broadcast System Based on Overlay Multicast", In *USENIX Annual Technical Conference*, USENIX, 2004.

[306] Y. hua Chu, S. G. Rao, S. Seshan, and H. Zhang, "Enabling Conferencing Applications on the Internet using an Overlay Multicast Architecture", In *Proceedings of ACM SIGCOMM*, ACM, 2001.

[307] Y. hua Chu, S. G. Rao, and H. Zhang, "A Case for End System Multicast", In *Proceedings of ACM SIGCOMM*, Santa Clara, CA, 2000.

[308] R. Huebsch, J. M. Hellerstein, N. Lanham, B. T. Loo, S. Shenker, and I. Stoica, "Querying the Internet with PIER", In *Proceedings of 29th International Conference on Very Large Data Bases*, Morgan Kaufmann, 2003.

[309] K. Y. Hui, J. C. Lui, and D. K. Yau, "Small-World Overlay P2P Networks", In *Proceedings of the IEEE International Workshop on Quality of Service (IWQoS), 2004*, Montreal, Canada, 2004.

[310] J. Hummel and U. Lechner, "The Community Model of Content Management - A case study of the music industry", *JMM*, 3(1):4ff, 2001.

[311] T. Hummel, *Instant Messaging - Nutzenpotenziale und Herausforderungen*, pp. 59–70, Springer, 2002.

[312] M. Humphrey, "State and Events for Web Services: A comparison of five WS-Resource Framework and WS-Notification Implementations", In *Proceedings of 14th IEEE International Symposium on High Performance Distributed Computing (HPDC-14)*, IEEE Computer Society Press, 2005.

[313] K. Hwang, *Advanced Computer Architecture*, McGraw-Hill Series in Computer Science, Singapore, 1993.

[314] A. Iamnitchi, I. Foster, and D. Nurmi, "A Peer-to-Peer Approach to Resource Discovery in Grid Environments", Report TR-2002-06, University of Chicago, 2002.

[315] IEEE CoputerSocietyLANMANStradards Committee, *Wireless LAN Medium Access Control (MAC) and Physical Layer (PHY) Specifications*, IEEE Strandard 802.11-1997, New York, NY, 1997.

[316] IFPI, "IFPI - International Federation of the Phonographic Industry", http://www.ifpi.org, 2005.

[317] iMesh, "iMesh homepage", www.imesh.com, 2004.

[318] Internet2, "netflow statistics, weekly reports", http://netflow.internet2.edu, 2001–2004.

[319] ISO/IEC, "13250: Topic Maps", 1999.

[320] M. Izal, G. Urvoy-Keller, E. W. Biersack, P. A. Felber, A. A. Hamra, and L. Garces-Erice, "Dissecting BitTorrent: Five Months in a Torrent's Lifetime", In *Proceedings of Passive and Active Measurements (PAM)*, 2004.

[321] M. Jakobsson and A. Juels, *Communications and Multimedia Security*, chapter Proofs of Work and Bread Pudding Protocols, pp. 258–272, Kluwer Academic Publishers, 1999.

[322] J. Jannotti, D. K. Gifford, K. L. Johnson, M. F. Kaashoek, and J. James W. O'Toole, "Overcast: Reliable Multicasting with an Overlay Network", In *Proceedings of 4th Symposium on Operating System Design & Implementation (OSDI 2000)*, USENIX, 2000.

[323] H. J. Jensen, *Self-Organized Criticality*, volume 10, Cambridge University Press, Cambridge, Cambridge Lecture Notes in Physics edition, 1998.

[324] H. Jeong, B. Tombor, R. Albert, Z. Oltvai, and A.-L. Barabási, "The Large-Scale Organization of Metabolic Networks", *Nature*, 407:651, 2000.

[325] H. Jeong, Z. Neda, and A. Barabasi, "Measuring preferential attachment in evolving networks", *Europhysics Letters*, 61(4):567–572, 2003, http://www.nd.edu/~etworks/PDF/Preferential-Feb2003.pdf.

[326] D. Johnson and D. Maltz, "Dynamic Source Routing in Ad Hoc Wireless Networks", *Mobile Computing (Kluwer Academic Publishers)*, 1996.

[327] D. B. Johnson, D. A. Maltz, and J. Broch, *DSR: The Dynamic Source Routing Protocol for Multi-Hop Wireless Ad Hoc Networks*, chapter 5, pp. 139–172, Addison-Wesley, 2001.

[328] M. A. Jovanovic, F. S. Annexstein, and K. A. Berman, "Scalability Issues in Large Peer to Peer Networks - A Case Study of Gnutella", Technical Report, Univ. of Cincinati, 2001.

[329] F. Junqueira, R. Bhagwan, A. Hevia, K. Marzullo, and G. M. Voelker, "Surviving Internet Catastrophes", In *Proc. 2005 Usenix Annual Technical Conference*, 2005.

[330] JXTA, "v2.0 Protocol Specifications", http://www.jxta.org, 2004.

[331] C. Kaler and A. Nadalin, "Web Services Federation Language (WS-Federation)", IBM, 2003, http://www.ibm.com/developerworks/library/ws-fed/.

[332] Kamida IncNew York, "The Socialight Homepage", http://socialight.net (seen 04/2005), 2005.

[333] S. Kamvar, M. Schlosser, and H. Garcia-Molina, "EigenRep: Reputation Management in P2P Networks", In *Proceedings of the 12th International World Wide Web Conference*, 2003.

[334] S. D. Kamvar, M. T. Schlosser, and H. Garcia-Molina, "The EigenTrust Algorithm for Reputation Management in P2P Networks", In *Twelfth International World Wide Web Conference (WWW)*, Budapest, Hungary, 2003.

[335] G. Kan, *Peer-to-Peer – Harnessing the Power of Disruptive Technologies*, chapter Chapter 8: Gnutella, O'Reilly, 2001.

[336] T. Karagiannis, A. Broido, N. Brownlee, and M. Faloutsos, "Filesharing in the Internet: A Characterization of P2P Traffic in the Backbone", Technical Report, 2003.

[337] T. Karagiannis, A. Broido, N. Brownlee, and kc Claffy, "Is P2P dying or just hiding?", In *In Proceeding of IEEE Globecom 2004*, Dallas, 2004.

[338] D. Karger and M. Ruhl, "Simple Efficient Load Balancing Algorithms for Peer-to-Peer Systems", In *Proceedings of 4th International Workshop on Peer-to-Peer Systems (IPTPS '04)*, San Diego, USA, 2004.

[339] F. Karinthy, "Láncszemek", In *Minden másképpen van*, pp. 85–90, 1929.

[340] B. Karp, S. Ratnasamy, S. Rhea, and S. Shenker, "Spurring Adoption of DHTs with OpenHash, a Public DHT Service", In *Proceedings of the 3rd International Workshop on Peer-to-Peer Systems (IPTPS 2004)*, Lecture Notes in Computer Science Hot Topics Series, Springer-Verlag, 2004.

[341] K. Katrinis, G. Parissidis, B. Brynjlfsson, O. Helgason, G. Hjlmtsson, and B. Plattner, "Multi-Source Multimedia Conferencing over Single-source Multicast", In *Proceedings of 2nd ACM International Workshop on Multimedia Interactive Protocols and Systems (MIPS 2004)*, ACM Press, 2004.

[342] KaZaA, "Accounting", http://www.kazaa.com/us/help/glossary/ participation_ratio.htm.

[343] Kazaa, "Kazaa Homepage", http://www.kazaa.com/us/index.htm, 2003.

[344] KaZaA Lite, http://k-litetk.com.

[345] G. Keizer, "AOL Drops AIM Enterprise", http://www.informationweek.com/showArticle.jhtml?articleID=22101095, 2004.

[346] M. Kelaskar, V. Matossian, P. Mehra, D. Paul, and M. Parashar, "A study of discovery mechanisms for peer-to-peer applications", In *Proc. 2nd IEEE/ACM CCGRID*, ACM Press, 2002.

[347] P. Keleher, B. Bhattacharjee, and B. Silaghi, "Are Virtualized Overly Networks Too Much of a Good Thing?", In *International Workshop on Peer-to-Peer Systems (IPTPS)*, Cambridge, MA, USA, 2002.

[348] W. Kellerer, C. Bettstetter, C. Schwingenschlögl, P. Sties, K. E. Steinberg, and H. J. Vögel, "(Auto)Mobile Communication in a Heterogeneous and Converged World", *IEEE Personal Communications Magazine*, 8(6):41–47, 2001.

[349] A. Kemper and C. Wiesner, "Hyperqueries: Dynamic Distributed Query Processing on the Internet", In *Proceedings of 27th International Conference on Very Large Data Bases*, pp. 551–560, Rome, Italy, 2001.

[350] R. Keralapura, N. Taft, C. N. Chuah, and G. Iannaconne, "Can ISPs Take the Heat from Overlay Networks?", In *Proceedings of the 3rd Workshop on Hot Topics in Networks (HotNets-III)*, San Diego, 2004.

[351] A. Khelil, C. Becker, J. Tian, and K. Rothermels, "An Epidemic Model for Information Diffusion in MANETs", In *Proc. 5th ACM Int. Workshop on Modeling, Analysis and Simulation of Wireless and Mobile Systems (MSWiM 2002)*, pp. 54–60, Atlanta, GA, 2002.

[352] F. Kileng, "Peer-to-Peer File Sharing Technologies: Napster, Gnutella and Beyond", Technical Report 18/ 2001, Telenor, 2002.

[353] J. M. Kleinberg, "Navigation in a Small World", *Nature*, 406:845, 2000.

[354] J. M. Kleinberg, "The Small-World Phenomenon: an Algorithmic Perspective", In *Proceedings of the 32nd Annual ACM Symposium on Theory of Computing*, 2000.

[355] A. Klemm, C. Lindemann, M. Vernon, and O. Waldhorst, "Characterizing the Query Behavior in Peer-to-Peer File Sharing Systems", In *Proc. ACM Internet Measurement Conference (IMC 2004)*, pp. 55–67, Taormina, Italy, 2004.

[356] A. Klemm, C. Lindemann, and O. Waldhorst, "A Special-Purpose Peer-to-Peer File Sharing System for Mobile Ad Hoc Networks", In *Proc. IEEE Semiannual Vehicular Technology Conference (VTC2003-Fall)*, Orlando, FL, 2003.

[357] J. Klensin, "RFC 2821: Simple Mail Transfer Protocol", IETF, 2001, http://www.ietf.org/rfc/rfc2821.txt.

[358] A. Klimkin, "eDonkey Protocol v0.3", http://search.cpan.org/src/KLIMKIN/P2P-pDonkey-0.01/doc/eDonkey-protocol, 2003.

[359] T. Klingberg and R. Manfredi, "Gnutella 0.6 RFC", 2002.

[360] G. Klyne and J. J. Carroll, "Resource Description Framework (RDF): Concepts and Abstract Syntax", W3C, 2004, http://www.w3.org/TR/rdf-concepts/.

[361] Kontiki, http://kontiki.com/, 2004.

[362] C. Koppen, "Selbstorganisierende Systeme", M.S. Thesis, University of Passau, Faculty of Mathematics and Computer Science, 2005.

[363] D. Kossmann, "The state of the art in distributed query processing", *ACM Comput. Surv.*, 32(4):422–469, 2000.

[364] H. Koubaa and Z. Wang, "A Hybrid Content Location Approach between Structured and Unstructured Topology", In *Proceedings of the Third Annual Mediterranean Ad Hoc Networking Workshop*, 2004.

[365] B. Krishnamurthy and J. Rexford, *Web Protocols and Practice: HTTP/1.1, Networking Protocols, Caching, and Traffic Measurement*, Addison-Wesley Professional, 2001.

[366] R. Krishnan, M. D. Smith, Z. Tang, and R. Telang, "The impact of free-riding on peer-to-peer networks", In *System Sciences, 2004. Proceedings of the 37th Annual Hawaii International Conference on*, pp. 199–208, IEEE, 2004.

[367] J. Kubiatowicz, D. Bindel, Y. Chen, S. Czerwinski, P. Eaton, D. Geels, R. Gummadi, S. Rhea, H. Weatherspoon, W. Weimer, C. Welles, and B. Zhao, "Oceanstore: An Architecture for Global-Scale Persistent Storage", In *9th International Conference on Architectural Support for Programming Languages and Operating Systems*, 2000.

[368] J. Kubiatowicz, D. Bindel, Y. Chen, S. Czerwinski, P. Eaton, D. Geels, R. Gummadi, S. Rhea, H. Weatherspoon, C. Wells, and B. Zhao, "OceanStore: an Architecture for Global-scale Persistent Storage", In *Proceedings of the 9th International Conference on Architectural Support for Programming Languages and Operating Systems*, pp. 190–201, ACM Press, 2000.

[369] R. Kumar, P. R. S. Rajagopalan, D. Sivakumar, A. Tomkins, and E. Upfal, "Stochastic Models for the Web Graph", In *Proceedings of the 41st IEEE Symposium on Foundations of Computer Science*, November 2000.

[370] M. Kwon and S. Fahmy, "Topology-aware overlay networks for group communication", In *Proceedings of the 12th international workshop on Network and operating systems support for digital audio and video*, pp. 127–136, ACM Press, 2002.

[371] La red de Gnutella, "afectada por el virus 'Mandragora', que consume ancho de banda", 2001, http://www.ciberpais.elpais.es/d/20010308/cibersoc/soc2.htm.

[372] S. A. Lab, "IP Monitoring Project (IPMON) Home Page", http://ipmon.sprintlabs.com/ipmon.php/.

[373] K. Lakshminarayanan, I. Stoica, and K. Wehrle, "Support for service composition in i3", In *MULTIMEDIA '04: Proceedings of the 12th annual ACM international conference on Multimedia*, pp. 108–111, New York, NY, USA, 2004, ACM Press.

[374] O. Landsiedel, K. Lehmann, and K. Wehrle, "T-DHT: Topology-Based Distributed Hash Tables", In *Proceedings of Fifth International IEEE Conference on Peer-to-Peer-Computing*, IEEE, September 2005.

[375] O. Landsiedel, H. Niedermayer, and K. Wehrle, "An Infrastructure for Anonymous Internet Services", In *Proceedings of International Workshop on Innovations In Web Infrastructure (IWI 2005), 14th International World Wide Web Conference - WWW2005*, May 2005.

[376] A. Langley, *Freenet*, pp. 123–132, O'Reilly, Sebastopol, 2001.

[377] D. Langworthy, "Web Services Transactions specifications", IBM, 2004, http://www.ibm.com/developerworks/library/ws-transpec.

[378] K. C. Laudon and C. G. Traver, *E-commerce: business, technology, society*, p. 63ff, Addison Wesley, 2004.

[379] N. Leibowitz, M. Ripeanu, and A. Wierzbicki, "Deconstructing the KaZaa Network", In *3rd IEEE Workshop on Internet Applications (WIAPP'03)*, 2003.

[380] B. Leuf, *Peer-to-Peer. Collaboration and Sharing over the Internet*, Addison-Wesley, Boston, 2002.

[381] S. F. Li, M. Spiteri, J. Bates, and A. Hopper, "Capturing and Indexing Computer-based Activities with Virtual Network Computing", In *Proceedings of ACM Symposium on Applied Computing*, Como, Italy, 2000.

[382] Y. Li, Z. Bandar, and D. McLean, "An Approach for Measuring Semantic Similarity between Words Using Multiple Information Sources", In *IEEE Transactions on Knowledge and Data Engineering (TKDE)*, Vol. 15(4), 2003.

[383] Z. Li and P. Mohapatra, "QRON: QoS-Aware Routing in Overlay Networks", *IEEE Selected Areas in Communications*, 22(1):29–40, 2004.

[384] J. Liang, R. Kumar, and K. Ross, "Understanding KaZaA", 2004.

[385] D. Liben-Nowell, H. Balakrishnan, and D. Karger, "Observations on the Dynamic Evolution of Peer-to-Peer Networks", In *Proceedings of the 1st International Workshop on Peer-to-Peer Systems (IPTPS02)*, 2002.

[386] M. Lillibridge, S. Elnikety, A. Birrell, M. Burrows, and M. Isard, "A Cooperative Internet Backup Scheme", In *USENIX 2003 Annual Technical Conference*, pp. 29–42, 2003, HP System Research Center, Palo Alto, USA.

[387] S. Lim, W. Lee, G. Cao, and C. R. Das, "A Novel Caching Scheme for Internet based Mobile Ad Hoc Networks", In *International Conference on Compouter Communication Networks (ICCCN'2003)*, 2003.

[388] LimeWire, "Version 2.4", , Lime Wire LCC, 2002.

[389] C. Lindemann and O. Waldhorst, "Consistency Mechanisms for a Distributed Lookup Service supporting Mobile Applications", In *Proc. 3rd Int. ACM Workshop on Data Engineering for Wireless and Mobile Access (MobiDE 2003)*, pp. 61–68, San Diego, CA, 2003.

[390] C. Lindemann and O. Waldhorst, "Modeling Epidemic Information Dissemination on Mobile Devices with Finite Buffers", In *Proc. ACM. Int. Conf. on Measurement & Modeling of Computer Systems (ACM SIGMETRICS 2005)*, Banff, Canada, June 2005.

[391] Linux VServer Project, http://linux-vserver.org, 2004.

[392] C. Liu, L. Yang, I. Foster, and D. Angulo, "Design and Evalutation of a Resource Selection Framework for GRID Applications", GLOBUS2002project Technical Report, Globus Aliance, 2002.

[393] B. Loo, J. Hellerstein, R. Huebsch, S. Shenker, and I. Stoica, "Enhancing P2P File-Sharing with an Internet-Scale Query Processor", In *International Conference on Very Large Databases (VLDB)*, Toronto, Canada, 2004.

[394] B. T. Loo, R. Huebsch, I. Stoica, and J. M. Hellerstein, "The Case for a Hybrid P2P Search Infrastructure", In *Proceedings of the 4th International Workshop on Peer-to-Peer Systems (IPTPS04)*, 2004.

[395] A. Löser, W. Nejdl, M. Wolpers, and W. Siberski, "Information Integration in Schema-Based Peer-To-Peer Networks", In *Proceedings of the 15th Conference On Advanced Information Systems Engineering (CAISE 03)*, Klagenfurt/Velden, Austria, 2003, Springer.

[396] S. M. Lui and S. H. Kwok, "Interoperability of Peer-To-Peer File Sharing Protocols", *ACM SIGecom Exchanges*, 3(3):25ff, 2002.

[397] Q. Lv, P. Cao, E. Cohen, K. Li, and S. Shenker, "Search and Replication in Unstructured Peer-to-Peer Networks", In *Proceedings of the 16th ACM International Conference on Supercomputing*, pp. 84–95, ACM, 2002.

[398] Q. Lv, S. Ratnasamy, and S. Shenker, "Can Heterogeneity Make Gnutella Scalable?", In *Proceedings of the 1st International Workshop on Peer-to-Peer Systems (IPTPS02)*, 2002.

[399] D. Malkhi, M. Naor, and D. Ratajczak, "Viceroy: A Scalable and Dynamic Emulation of the Butterfly", In *PODC '02: Proceedings of the twenty-first annual symposium on Principles of distributed computing*, pp. 183–192, ACM Press, 2002.

[400] G. Manku, M. Bawa, and P. Raghavan, "Symphony: Distributed Hashing in a Small World", In *Proceedings of the 4th USENIX Symposium on Internet Technologies and Systems (USITS 2003)*, 2003.

[401] L. Mathy, N. Blundell, V. Roca, and A. El-Sayed, "Impact of Simple Cheating in Application-Level Multicast", In *Proceedings of IEEE Infocom*, IEEE, 2004.

[402] H. R. Maturana and F. J. Varela, *Autopoiesis and Cognition: The Realization of the Living*, D. Reidel, Dordrecht, Holland, 1980.

[403] H. R. Maturana and F. J. Varela, *Der Baum der Erkenntnis*, Scherz, München, 1987.

[404] A. Mauthe and D. Hutchison, "Peer-to-Peer Computing: Systems, Concepts and Characteristics", In *Praxis in der Informationsverarbeitung & Kommunikation (PIK)*, K. G. Sauer Verlag, 2003.

[405] P. Maymounkov and D. Mazieres, "Kademlia: A Peer-to-Peer Information System Based on the XOR Metric", In *International Workshop on Peer-to-Peer Systems (IPTPS'02)*, 2002.

[406] McAfee Rumor, http://www.mcafeeasap.com/intl/en/content/ viruss-can_asap/rumor.asp, 2004.

[407] D. L. McGuiness and F. van Harmelen, "OWL Web Ontology Language Overview", http://www.w3.org/TR/owl-features/, 2004.

[408] R. Merkle, "A digital signature based on a conventional encryption function", In *Proceedings of Advances in Cryptology (CRYPTO'87)*, 1987.

[409] Merriam-Webster, "The Dictionary", http://www.m-w.com/.

[410] MetaSearch Inc., "edonkey2000 Homepage", http://www.edonkey2000.com, 2003.

[411] C. Metz, "IM Everywhere", *PC Magazine*, 22(20):128ff, 2003.

[412] S. Microsystems, "Project JXTA", http://www.jxta.org, 12 2004.

[413] S. Milgram, "The Small World Problem", *Psychology Today*, 1(1):60–67, May 1967.

[414] M. Miller, *Discovering P2P*, p. 213ff, Sybex Press, San Francisco, 2001.

[415] M. M. Millonas, "Swarms, phase transitions, and collective intelligence", In C. G. Langton, editor, *Artificial Life III*, Addison Wesley Longman, 1994.

[416] D. S. Milojicic, V. Kalogeraki, R. Lukose, K. Nagaraja, and J. Pruyne, "Peer-to-Peer Computing", http://www.hpl.hp.com/techreports/2002/HPL-2002-57.pdf, 2002.

[417] J. Mischke and B. Stiller, "Rich and Scalable Peer-to-Peer Search with SHARK", In *5th Int'l Workshop on Active Middleware Services (AMS 2003), in association with IEEE High Performance and Distributed Computing Symposium (HPDC-12) and Global Grid Forum (GGF-8)*, Seattle, WA, U.S.A., June 2003.

[418] J. Mischke and B. Stiller, "An Efficient Protocol Specification, Implementation, and Evaluation for a Highly Scalable Peer-to-Peer Search Infrastructure", In *9th IEEE/IFIP Network Operations and Management Symposium (NOMS'04)*, Seoul, Korea, April 2004.

[419] J. Mischke and B. Stiller, "A Methodology for the Design of Distributed Search in P2P Middleware", *IEEE Networks*, 18(1), January/February 2004.

[420] J. Mischke and B. Stiller, "Peer-to-Peer Overlay Network Management Through AGILE", In *IFIP/IEEE International Symposium on Integrated Network Management (IM)*, Kluwer Academic Publishers, 2003.

[421] J. Mischke and B. Stiller, "Rich and Scalable Peer-to-Peer Search with SHARK", In *5th International Workshop on Active Middleware Services (AMS 2003)*, 2003.

[422] M. Mitzenmacher, "A Brief History of Generative Models for Power Law and Lognormal Distributions", http://www.eecs.harvard.edu/~michaelm/postscripts/tempim1.ps, 2005.

[423] mlDonkey, "mlDonkey Homepage", http://mldonkey.org, 2003.

[424] A. Moffat and A. Turpin, *Compression and Coding Algorithms*, Kluwer Academic Publishers, New York, 2002.

[425] Mojo Nation, http://www.mojonation.net/, 2000.

[426] Moneybee, http://www.moneybee.net, 2004.

[427] M. C. Mont, K. Harrison, and M. Sadler, "The HP time vault service: exploiting IBE for timed release of confidential information", In *WWW '03: Proceedings of the twelfth international conference on World Wide Web*, pp. 160–169, ACM Press, 2003.

[428] A. Montresor, "A Robust Protocol for Building Superpeer Overlay Topologies", In *In Proceedings of the 4th IEEE International Conference on Peer-to-Peer Computing*, 2004.

[429] R. Moor, C. Baru, R. Marciano, A. Rajasekar, and M. Wan, *Data-Intensive Computing*, Morgan Kaufmann Publishers, 1999.

[430] T. Moreton, I. Pratt, and T. Harris, "Storage, Mutability and Naming in Pasta", http://www.cl.cam.ac.uk/users/tlh20/papers/mph-pasta.pdf, 2002.

[431] T. Moreton and A. Twigg, "Trading in Trust, Tokens, and Stamps", In *Proceedings of the Workshop on the Economics of Peer-to-Peer Systems*, Berkeley, California, June 2003.

[432] Morpheus, "http://www.morpheus.com", 2001.

[433] H. M. Mountain, J. Kopecky, S. Williams, G. Daniels, and N. Mendelsohn, "SOAP Version 1.2 Email Binding", W3C, 2002, http://www.w3.org/TR/soap12-email.

[434] A. P. Moura, Y.-C. Lai, and A. E. Motter, "Signatures of small-world and scale-free properties in large computer programs", *Phys. Rev. E 68, 017102 (2003)*, 2003, http://arxiv.org/PS_cache/cond-mat/pdf/0306/0306609.pdf.

[435] A. Nadalin, C. Kaler, P. Halam-Baker, and R. Monzillo, "Web Services Security", 2004, http://docs.oasis-open.org/wss/2004/01/oasis-200401-wss-soap-message-security-1.0.pdf.

[436] Napster, "http://www.napster.com", 1999.

[437] Napster, "Napster Messages", http://opennap.sourceforge.net/napster.txt, 2000.

[438] Napster Network, http://en.wikipedia.org/wiki/Napster, 1999.

[439] R. Naraine, "Can AOL make money from IM?", www.atnewyork.com, 2002.

[440] A. Narasimhan, "Rayleigh-Benard Convection: Physics of a Widespread Phenomenon", *Resonance: Journal of Science Education*, 4(6):82–90, 1999.

[441] P. M. Nation, "Peer-driven Content Distribution Technology", http://www.mojonation.net/, February 2000.

[442] National Academy of SciencesComputer Science and Telecommunications Board, *Looking Over the Fence at Networks: A Neighbor's View of Networking Research*, National Academies Press, Washington, D.C., 2001.

[443] National Security Telecommunications and Information Systems Security Committee (NSTISSC), *National Information Systems Security (INFOSEC) Glossary*, Number NSTISSI No. 4009, January 1999.

[444] W. Nejdl, W. Siberski, U. Thaden, and W. T. Balke, "Top-k Query Evaluation for Schema-Based Peer-to-Peer Networks", In *International Semantic Web Conference (ISWC)*, Hiroshima, Japan, 2004.

[445] W. Nejdl, B. Wolf, C. Qu, S. Decker, M. Sintek, A. Naeve, M. Nilsson, M. Palmér, and T. Risch, "EDUTELLA: a P2P Networking Infrastructure based on RDF", In *Proceedings of the 11th International World Wide Web*, Hawaii, USA, 2002, ACM.

[446] W. Nejdl, M. Wolpers, W. Siberski, C. Schmitz, M. Schlosser, I. Brunkhorst, and A. Löser, "Super-Peer-Based Routing and Clustering Strategies for RDF-Based Peer-to-Peer Networks", In *Proceedings of the Twelfth International World Wide Web Conference*, Budapest, Hungary, 2003, ACM.

[447] Next Page Inc, http://www.nextpage.com/pdfs/collateral/wp/nxt4_build_wp090903lo.pdf, 2004.

[448] T.-W. Ngan, D. S. Wallach, and P. Druschel, "Enforcing Fair Sharing of Peer-to-Peer Resources", In *Proceedings of the 2nd International Workshop on Peer-to-PeerSystems (IPTPS03)*, Berkeley, CA, 2003.

[449] NICE, http://www.cs.umd.edu/projects/nice/.

[450] H. Niedermayer, S. Rieche, K. Wehrle, and G. Carle, "On the Distribution of Nodes in Distributed Hash Tables", In *Proceedings of Workshop Peer-to-Peer-Systems and -Applications, KiVS 2005*, Kaiserslautern, Germany, 2005.

[451] M. Nilsson and W. Siberski, "RDF Query Exchange Language (QEL)", http://edutella.jxta.org/spec/qel.html, 2004.

[452] R. Norin, "Workflow Process Definition Interface – XML Process Definition Language", http://www.wfmc.org/standards/docs/TC-1025_10_xpdl_102502.pdf, 2002.

[453] N. Ntarmos and P. Triantafillou, "SeAl: Managing Accesses and Data in Peer-to-Peer Sharing Networks", In *Proceedings of the Fourth IEEE International Conference on Peer-to-Peer Computing*, 2004.

[454] OASIS, "Universal Description, Discovery and Integration (UDDI)", 2004, http://www.oasis-open.org/committees/uddi-spec.

[455] OASIS and UN/CEFACT, "Electronic Business using XML (ebXML)", http://www.ebxml.org.

[456] J. Oberender, F. U. Andersen, H. de Meer, I. Dedinski, T. Hoßfeld, C. Kappler, A. Mäder, and K. Tutschku, "Enabling Mobile Peer-to-Peer Networking", In *Mobile and Wireless Systems, LNCS 3427*, Dagstuhl, Germany, 2005.

[457] F. Oberholzer and K. Strumpf, "The Effect of File Sharing on Record Sales - An Empirical Analysis", http://www.unc.edu/~cigar/papers/FileSharing_March2004.pdf, 2004.

[458] P. Obreiter, B. König-Ries, and M. Klein, "Stimulating Cooperative Behavior of Autonomous Devices - An Analysis of Requirements and Existing Approaches", 2003-1, Faculty of Informatics, University of Karlsruhe, 2003.

[459] A. Odlyzko, "Internet traffic growth: Sources and implications", *Proc. SPIE*, 5247:1–15, 2003.

[460] E. Ogston and S. Vassiliadis, "A Peer-to-Peer Agent Auction", In *First International Joint Conference on Autonomous Agents and Multi-Agent Systems (AAMAS)*, Bologna, Italy, 2002.

[461] D. Oppenheimer, J. Albrecht, D. A. Patterson, and A. Vahdat, "Distributed resource discovery on PlanetLab with SWORD", In *Proceedings of the First Workshop on Real, Large Distributed Systems (WORLDS '04)*, 2004.

[462] A. Oram, *Peer-to-Peer: Harnessing the Power of Disruptive Technologies*, O'Reilly & Associates, Inc., Sebastopol, CA, USA, 2001.

[463] A. Orlowski, "I poisoned P2P networks for the RIAA – whistleblower", 2003.

[464] P. E. os and A. Rényi, "On Random Graphs I.", *Publicationes Mathematicae Debrecen*, 5:17–61, 1959.

[465] Oxygen, "Oxygen Project Web Site", http://oxygen.lcs.mit.edu.

[466] P2P-Radio, http://p2p-radio.sourceforge.net/, 2004.

[467] K. Pahlavan, X. Li, and J.-P. Mäkelä, "Indoor Geolocation Science and Technology", *IEEE Communications*, pp. 112–118, 2002.

[468] V. Pai, L. Wang, K. Park, R. Pang, and L. Peterson, "The dark side of the Web: An open proxy's view", In *Proceedings of the 2nd Workshop on Hot Topics in Networks (HotNets-II)*, 2003.

[469] P. R. Pandurangan and E. Upfal, "Building low-diameter P2P Networks", In *Proceedings of the 42nd annual IEEE Symposium on the Foundations of Computer Science*, pp. 1–8, 2001.

[470] M. Papadopouli and H. Schulzrinne, "Effects of Power Conservation, Wireless Coverage and Cooperation on Data Dissemination among Mobile Devices", In *Proc. 2nd ACM MobiHoc 2001*, pp. 117–127, Long Beach, NY, 2001.

[471] M. Papadopouli and H. Schulzrinne, "Seven Degrees of Separation in Mobile Ad Hoc Networks", In *Proceedings of the IEEE Conference on Global Communications (GLOBECOM)*, pp. 1707–1711, San Francisco, USA, 2000, IEEE Computer Society.

[472] M. Papadopouli and H. Schulzrinne, "Design and Implementation of a Peer-to-Peer Data Dissemination and Prefetching Tool for Mobile Users", 2001.

[473] M. P. Papazoglou and D. Georgakopoulos, "Service-oriented computing", *Commun. ACM*, 46(10):24–28, 2003.

[474] K. Park and V. Pai, "CoMon: A Monitoring Infrastructure for PlanetLab", http://comon.cs.princeton.edu/, 2005.

[475] A. Parker, "The true picture of peer-to-peer file sharing", www.cachelogic.com/research/index.php.

[476] PAST, http://research.microsoft.com/~antr/PAST/.

[477] R. Pastor-Satorras, E. Smith, and R. Solé, "Evolving Protein Interaction Networks Through Gene Duplication", *Journal of Theoretical Biology*, 222(2):199–210, 2003.

[478] F. Patalong, "Deutscher KaZaA-Nutzer muss 8000 Euro zahlen", http://www.spiegel.de/netzwelt/politik/0,1518,303298,00.html, 2004.

[479] V. Paxson and S. Floyd, "The failure of the Poisson assumption", *IEEE/ACM Trans. on Networking*, pp. 226–244, 1995.

[480] PeerCast, http://www.peercast.org/, 2004.

[481] PeerMart, "A Decentralized Auction-based P2P Market", http://www.peermart.net/, 2004.

[482] D. Pendarakis, S. Shi, D. Verma, and M. Waldvogel, "ALMI: An Application Level Multicast Infrastructure", In *Proceedings of 3rd Usenix Symposium on Internet Technologies & Systems (USITS)*, USENIX, 2001.

[483] C. E. Perkins, *Ad Hoc Networking*, Addison-Wesley, 2000.

[484] C. E. Perkins and E. M. Royer, "Ad-hoc On-Demand Distance Vector Routing", In *Proceedings of the 2nd IEEE Workshop on Mobile Computing Systems and Applications*, pp. 90–100, New Orleans, USA, 1999, IEEE Computer Society.

[485] L. Peterson, D. Culler, T. Anderson, and T. Roscoe, "A Blueprint for Introducing Disruptive Technology into the Internet", In *Proceedings of the 1st Workshop on Hot Topics in Networks (HotNets-I)*, 2002.

[486] L. Peterson and T. Roscoe, "The Design Principles of PlanetLab", PDN–04–021, PlanetLab Consortium, 2004.

[487] L. Petrak, S. Rieche, and K. Wehrle, "Dienstgüte in strukturierten hierarchischen Overlay Netzwerken.", In *Proceedings of Workshop Peer-to-Peer-Systems and -Applications, KiVS 2005*, pp. 197–200, Kaiserslautern, Germany, 2005.

[488] R. Pfeifer and C. Scheier, *Embodied Cognitive Science*, chapter 4, p. 137, MIT Press, 1999, http://beat.doebe.li/bibliothek/w00505.html.

[489] Planet DESCENT, http://www.planetdescent.com/, 2004.

[490] PlanetLab Consortium, "Dynamic Slice Creation", PDN–02–005, 2002.

[491] C. G. Plaxton, R. Rajaraman, and A. W. Richa, "Accessing Nearby Copies of Replicated Objects in a Distributed Environment", In *9th Annual ACM Symposium on Parallel Algorithms and Architectures*, ACM, 1997.

[492] L. Plissonneau, J. Costeux, and P. Brown, "Analysis of Peer-to-Peer traffic on ADSL", In *PAM2005: Passive & active measurement workshop*, Boston, 2005.

[493] Potatosystem, http://www.potatosystem.com, 2004.

[494] J. A. Pouwelse, P. Garbacki, D. H. Epema, and H. J. Sips, "The Bittorrent P2P File-sharing System: Measurements and Analysis", In *Proceedings of the 54th International Workshop on Peer-to-Peer Systems (IPTPS'05)*, Ithaca, USA, 2005.

[495] I. Prigogine, "Time, structure and fluctuations", In T. Frängsmyr and S. Forsé;n, editors, *Nobel Lectures in Chemistry 1971–1980*, Singapore, 1977, World Scientific Publishing Company.

[496] G. V. Putte, J. Jana, M. Keen, S. Kondepudi, R. Mascarenhas, S. Ogirala, D. Rudrof, K. Sullivan, and P. Swithinbank, *Using Web Services for Business Integration*, IBM Redbook, 2004.

[497] D. Qiu and R. Srikant, "Modeling and Performance Analysis of BitTorrent-Like Peer-to-Peer Networks", In *Proceedings of the ACM SIGCOMM 2004*, Portland, USA, 2004.

[498] T. Rabin, "A simplified approach to threshold and proactive RSA", In *Proceedings of Crypto*, 1988.

[499] B. Raman, S. Agarwal, Y. Chen, M. Caesar, W. Cui, P. Johansson, K. Lai, T. Lavian, S. Machiraju, Z. M. Mao, G. Porter, T. Roscoe, M. Seshadri, J. Shih, K. Sklower, L. Subramanian, T. Suzuki, S. Zhuang, A. D. Joseph, R. H. Katz, and I. Stoica, "The SAHARA Model for Service Composition Across Multiple Providers", In *Proceedings of Pervasive Computing*, Zurich, Switzerland, 2002.

[500] B. Ramsdell, "Secure/Multipurpose Internet Mail Extensions (S/MIME) Version 3.1 Message Specification", IETF, RFC 3851 (Proposed Standard), 2004.

[501] A. Rao, K. Lakshminarayanan, S. Surana, R. Karp, and I. Stoica, "Load Balancing in Structured P2P Systems", In *Proceedings of 2nd International Workshop on Peer-to-Peer Systems (IPTPS '03)*, Berkeley, USA, 2003.

[502] S. Ratnasamy, M. Handley, R. Karp, and S. Shenker, "Topologically-Aware Overlay Construction and Server Selection", In *Proceedings of IEEE Infocom 2002*, IEEE, 2002.

[503] S. Ratnasamy, M. Handley, R. Karp, and S. Shenker, "Topologically-aware overlay construction and server selection", In *Proceedings of IEEE INFOCOM'02*, 6 2002.

[504] S. Ratnasamy, *A Scalable Content-Addressable Network*, Ph.D. Thesis, University of California, Berkeley, 2002, http://berkeley.intel-research.net/sylvia/thesis.pdf.

[505] S. Ratnasamy, P. Francis, M. Handley, R. M. Karp, and S. Shenker, "A Scalable Content-Addressable Network", In *SIGCOMM*, pp. 161–172, ACM Press, 2001.

[506] S. Ratnasamy, M. Handley, R. Karp, and S. Shenker, "Application-level Multicast using Content-Addressable Networks", In *Proceedings of 3rd International Workshop on Networked Group Communication (NGC)*, Springer Verlag, 2001.

[507] D. Raz and Y. Shavitt, "New Models and Algorithms for Programmable Networks", *Computer Networks*, 38(3):311–326, February 2002.

[508] M. K. Reiter and A. D. Rubin, "Crowds: anonymity for Web transactions", In *ACM Transactions on Information and System Security*, pp. 66–92, 1998.

[509] RFC 2866, "RADIUS Accounting", http://www.freeradius.org/rfc/rfc2866.html, 2000.

[510] S. Rhea, D. Geels, T. Roscoe, and J. Kubiatowicz, "Handling Churn in a DHT", In *Proceedings of the 2004 USENIX Technical Conference, Boston, MA, USA*, 2004.

[511] S. Rhea, B. Godfrey, B. Karp, J. Kubiatowicz, S. Ratnasamy, S. Shenker, I. Stoica, and H. Yu., "OpenDHT: A Public DHT Service and Its Uses.", In *Proceedings of ACM SIGCOMM*, August 2005.

[512] S. Rieche, L. Petrak, and K. Wehrle, "Comparison of Load Balancing Algorithms for Structured Peer-to-Peer Systems", In *Workshop on Algorithms and Protocols for Efficient Peer-to-Peer Applications, INFORMATIK 2004, Vol. 2*, LNCS-LNI Vol. 51, GI, 2004.

[513] S. Rieche, L. Petrak, and K. Wehrle, "A Thermal-Dissipation-based Approach for Balancing Data Load in Distributed Hash Tables", In *Proceedings of IEEE Conference on Local Computer Networks. (LCN 2004)*, Tampa, USA, 2004.

[514] S. Rieche, K. Wehrle, O. Landsiedel, S. Goetz, and L. Petrak, "Reliability of Data in Structured Peer-to-Peer Systems", In *Proceedings of HOT-P2P '04: Hot Topics in Peer-to-Peer Computing*, Volendam, Netherlands, 2004.

[515] M. Ripeanu, "Peer-to-Peer Architecture Case Study: Gnutella Network", In *Proceedings of IEEE 1st International Conference on Peer-to-Peer Computing*, 2001.

[516] M. Ripeanu and I. Foster, "Mapping the Gnutella Network: Macroscopic Properties of Large-Scale Peer-to-Peer Systems", In *1st International Workshop on Peer-to-Peer Systems (IPTPS)*, LNCS 2429, Springer, 2002.

[517] M. Ripeanu, I. Foster, and A. Iamnitchi, "Mapping the Gnutella Network: Properties of Large-Scale Peer-to-Peer Systems and Implications for System Design", *IEEE Internet Computing Journal*, 6(1), 2002.

[518] J. Ritter, "Why Gnutella Can't Scale. No, Really.", 2001, http://www.darkridge.com/~jpr5/doc/gnutella.html.

[519] R. Rivest, "The MD5 Message-Digest Algorithm", RFC 1321, 1992.

[520] R. L. Rivest and A. Shamir, "PayWord and MicroMint: Two Simple Micropayment Schemes", In *Security Protocols Workshop*, pp. 69–87, 1996.

[521] T. G. Robertazzi, "Ten Reasons to Use Divisible Load Theory", *IEEE Computer Society: Computer magazine*, 36(5):63–68, 2003.

[522] C. Rohrs, "The PING/PONG Scheme", http://rfc-gnutella.sourceforge.net/Proposals/PING-PONG, 2002.

[523] C. Rohrs, "QUERY Routing for the Gnutella Network", http://rfc-gnutella.sourceforge.net/Proposals/QRP/QUERY_routing.htm, 2002.

[524] T. Roscoe, L. Peterson, S. Karlin, and M. Wawrzoniak, "A Simple Common Sensor Interface for PlanetLab", PDN–03–010, PlanetLab Consortium, 2003.

[525] M. Rose, "RFC 3080: The Blocks Extensible Exchange Protocol Core", IETF, 2001, http://www.ietf.org/rfc/rfc3080.txt.

[526] A. Rowstron and P. Druschel, "PAST: A large-scale, persistent peer-to-peer storage utility", In *HotOS VIII*, Schoss Elmau, Germany, 2001.

[527] A. Rowstron and P. Druschel, "Pastry: Scalable, Distributed Object Location and Routing for Large-Scale Peer-to-Peer Systems", In *IFIP/ACM International Conference on Distributed Systems Platforms (Middleware)*, pp. 329–350, Heidelberg, Germany, November 2001, Springer.

[528] A. Rowstron and P. Druschel, "Storage management and caching in PAST, a large-scale, persistent peer-to-peer storage utility", In *18th ACM SOSP'01*, Lake Louise, Alberta, Canada, 2001.

[529] S. Rudström, M. Svensson, R. Cöster, and K. Höök, "MobiTip: Using Bluetooth as a Mediator of Social Context", In *UbiComp 2004: Ubiquitous Computing: 6th International Conference, Adjunct Proceedings (demo)*, 2004.

[530] D. Salomon, *Data Compression. The Complete Reference.*, Springer, New York, 1997.

[531] J. Saltzer, D. Reed, and D. Clark, "End-to-end arguments in system design", *ACM Transactions on Computer Systems (TOCS)*, 2(4):195–206, 1984.

[532] K. Samant and S. Bhattacharyya, "Topology, Search, and Fault Tolerance in Unstructured P2P Networks", In *Proceedings of the 37th Hawaii International Conference on System Sience (HICCS'04)*, IEEE Computer Society, 2004.

[533] V. Sander, W. Adamson, I. Foster, and A. Roy, "End-to-End Provision of Policy Information for Network QoS", In *Proc. of 10 IEEE Symposium on High Performance Distributed Computing*, IEEE Computer Society, 2001.

[534] S. Saroiu, K. Gummadi, and S. Gribble, "A Measurement Study of Peer-to-Peer File Sharing Systems", In *Proceedings of Multimedia Computing and Networks (MMCN'02)*, San Jose, CA, USA, January 2002.

[535] S. Saroiu, P. Gummadi, and S. Gribble, "Exploring the Design Space of Distributed and Peer-to-Peer Systems: Comparing the Web, TRIAD, and Chord/CFS", In *1st International Workshop on Peer-to-Peer Systems (IPTPS '02)*, Cambridge, MA, U.S.A., March 2002.

[536] S. Saroiu, P. Gummadi, and S. Gribble, "A Measurement Study of Peer-to-peer File Sharing Systems", UW-CSE-01-06-02, Department of Computer Science & Engineering, University of Washington, Seattle, WA, U.S.A., 2002.

[537] N. Sarshar, V. Roychowdury, and P. O. Boykin, "Percolation-based Search on unstructured Peer-To-Peer Networks", In *2nd International Workshop on Peer-to-Peer Systems (IPTPS)*, LNCS 2735, Springer, 2003.

[538] S. Savage, T. Anderson, A. Aggarwal, D. Becker, N. Cardwell, A. Collins, E. Hoffman, J. Snell, A. Vahdat, G. Voelker, and J. Zahorjan, "Detour: a Case for Informed Internet Routing and Transport", *IEEE Micro*, 19(1):50–59, 1999.

[539] S. Savage, A. Collins, E. Hoffman, J. Snell, and T. E. Anderson, "The End-to-End Effects of Internet Path Selection", In *Proceedings of ACM SIGCOMM*, ACM Press, 1999.

[540] J. Schlimmer, "Web Services Policy Framework", IBM, 2004, ftp://www6.software.ibm.com/software/developer/library/ws-policy.pdf.

[541] M. Schlosser, M. Sintek, S. Decker, and W. Nejdl, "HyperCuP — Hypercubes, Ontologies and Efficient Search on P2P Networks", In *Proceedings on the International Workshop on Agents and Peer-to-Peer-Systems*, Bologna, Italy, 2002, Springer.

[542] C. Schmitz, "Self-organization of a small world by topic", In *Proceedings of the 1st International Workshop on Peer-to-Peer Knowledge Management*, Boston, MA, USA, 2004.

[543] B. Schneier, *Applied Cryptography*, John Wiley & Sons, 2nd edition, 1996.

[544] D. Schoder and K. Fischbach, *Peer-to-Peer Anwendungsbereiche und Herausforderungen*, pp. 3–21, Springer, Berlin, 2002.

[545] D. Schoder and K. Fischbach, "Peer-to-Peer-Netzwerke für das Ressourcenmanagement", *Wirtschaftsinformatik*, 45(3):313–323, 2003.

[546] B. Schoenmakers, "Basic Security of the ecashTM Payment System", In B. Preneel and V. Rijmen, editors, *Course on Computer Security and Industrial Cryptography*, volume 1528 of *Lecture Notes in Computer Science*, chapter State of the Art in Applied Cryptography, Berlin, Leuven, Belgium, June 3-6 1998.

[547] R. Schollmeier, I. Gruber, and M. Finkenzeller, "Routing in Mobile Ad Hoc and Peer-to-Peer Networks. A Comparison", In *Networking 2002. International Workshop on Peer-to-Peer Computing*, 2002.

[548] R. Schollmeier, I. Gruber, and F. Niethammer, "Protocol for Peer-to-Peer Networking in Mobile Environments", In *International Conference on Computer Communications (ICCCN03)*, 2003.

[549] R. Schollmeier and F. Hermann, "Topology-Analysis of Pure Peer-to-Peer Networks", In *Fachtagung Kommunikation in Verteilten Systemen (KiVS 2003)*, 2003.

[550] R. Schollmeier and G. Kunzmann, "GnuViz - Mapping the Gnutella Networks to its Geographical Locations", *Praxis der Informationsverarbeitung und Kommunikation (PIK)*, 26(2):74–79, 2003.

[551] P. Schuster, "Catalytic hypercycle", In A. Scott, editor, *Encyclopedia of Nonlinear Science*, New York, 2004, Taylor and Francis.

[552] F. Schweitzer, "Coordination of Decisions in Spatial Multi-Agent Systems", In *International Workshop on Socio- and Econo-Physics*, 2003.

[553] T. Schwotzer and K. Geihs, "Shark - a System for Management, Synchronization and Exchange of Knowledge in Mobile User Groups.", *Journal of Universal Computer Science*, 8(6):644–651,, 2002.

[554] SCVI, http://www.scvi.net/, 2004.

[555] S. Sen and J. Wang, "Analyzing peer-to-peer traffic across large networks", In *Proceedings of ACM SIGCOMM Internet measurement workshop*, Marseille, France, 2002.

[556] S. Sen and J. Wang, "Analyzing Peer-to-Peer Traffic Across Large networks", *ACM/IEEE Transactions on Networking*, 12(2), 2004.

[557] Seti, "Homepage of the Seti@Home Project", http://setiathome.ssl.berkeley.edu, 2004.

[558] Sharman Networks Inc., "Kazaa Media Desktop", http://www.kazaa.com/, 2001.

[559] S. Shenker, L. Peterson, and J. Turner, "Overcoming the Internet Impasse through Virtualization", In *Proceedings of the 3rd ACM conference on Hot Topics in Network (HotNets-III)*, 2004.

[560] C. Shirky, *P2P Groupware*, p. 145ff, O'Reilly, 2001.

[561] Shockfish SA Switzerland, "The SpotMe Homepage", http://www.spotme.ch/, 2005.

[562] A. Singh and L. Liu, "A Hybrid Topology Architecture for P2P Systems", In *Proceedings of the 13th International Conference on Computer Communications and Networks*, 2004.

[563] A. Singla and C. Rohrs, "Ultrapeers; another step towards Gnutella scalability", , Gnutella developer forum, 2002.

[564] M. Sintek and S. Decker, "TRIPLE — A Query, Inference, and Transformation Language for the Semantic Web", In *Proceedings of the 1st International Semantic Web Conference*, Springer, 2002.

[565] E. Sit and R. Morris, "Security Considerations for Peer-to-Peer Distributed Hash Tables", In *IPTPS 2002*, 2002.

[566] SixFour Manual, 2003, http://www.brain-pro.de/Seiten/six/readmeintro.html.

[567] Skype, "Skype Homepage", http://www.skype.com/, 2004.

[568] T. Small and Z. Haas, "The Shared Wireless Infostation Model - A New Ad Hoc Networking Paradigm (or Where there is a Whale, there is a Way)", In *Proc. 4th ACM MobiHoc 2003*, pp. 233–244, Annapolis, MD, 2003.

[569] M. Solarski, L. Strick, K. Motonaga, C. Noda, and W. Kellerer, "Flexible Middleware Support for Future Mobile Services and Their Context-Aware Adaptation", In V. W. Finn Arve Aagesen, Chutiporn Anutariya, editor, *IFIP International Conference, INTELLCOMM 2004, Bangkok, Thailand, November 23-26, 2004, Springer LNCS 3283*, pp. 281–292, Springer-Verlag GmbH, 2004.

[570] K. Sripanidkulchai, "The Popularity of Gnutella Queries and its Implications on Scalability", In *Proc. O'Reilly Peer-to-Peer and Web Services Conf*, 2001.

[571] K. Sripanidkulchai, B. Maggs, and H. Zhang, "Efficient Content Location Using Interest-Based Locality in Peer-to-Peer Systems", In *Annual Joint Conference of the IEEE Computer and Communications Societies (INFOCOM)*, San Francisco, CA, USA, 2003.

[572] S. Staniford, V. Paxson, and N. Weaver, "How to Own the Internet in Your Spare Time", In *Proceedings of the 11th USENIX Security Symposium*, San Francisco, CA, 2002.

[573] R. Steinmetz and K. Wehrle, "Peer-to-Peer-Networking & -Computing", *Informatik-Spektrum*, 27(1):51–54, 2004, Springer, Heidelberg (in german).

[574] I. Stoica, D. Adkins, S. Zhuang, S. Shenker, and S. Surana, "Internet Indirection Infrastructure", In *Proceedings of ACM SIGCOMM*, August 2002.

[575] I. Stoica, R. Morris, D. Karger, F. Kaashoek, and H. Balakrishnan, "Chord: A Scalable Peer-To-Peer Lookup Service for Internet Applications", In *Proceedings of the 2001 ACM Sigcomm Conference*, pp. 149–160, ACM Press, 2001.

[576] I. Stoica, R. Morris, D. Liben-Nowell, D. Karger, M. F. Kaashoek, F. Dabek, and H. Balakrishnan, "Chord: A scalable Peer-to-Peer Lookup Service for Internet Applications", *IEEE Transactions on Networking*, 11(1):17–32, 2003.

[577] T. Straub and A. Heinemann, "An Anonymous Bonus Point System For Mobile Commerce Based On Word-Of-Mouth Recommendation", In L. M. Liebrock, editor, *Applied Computing 2004. Proceedings of the 2004 ACM Symposium on Applied Computing*, pp. 766–773, New York, NY, USA, 2004, ACM Press.

[578] B. Strulo, "Middleware to Motivate Co-operation in Peer-to-Peer Systems (A Project Discussion)", *P2P Journal*, 2004.

[579] M. Stump, "Peer-to-Peer Tracking Can Save Cash: Ellacoya", http://www.ellacoya.com/news/pdf/10_07_02_mcn.pdf, 2002.

[580] L. Subramanian, I. Stoica, H. Balakrishnan, and R. Katz, "OverQoS: Offering Internet QoS Using Overlays", In *Proc. of 1st HotNets Workshop*, 2002.

[581] Q. Sun and H. Garcia-Molina, "Partial Lookup Services", In *Proc. 23rd Int. Conf. On Distributed Computing Systems (ICDCS 2003)*, pp. 58–67, Providence, Rhode Island, 2003.

[582] P. F. Syverson, D. M. Goldschlag, and M. G. Reed, "Anonymous Connections and Onion Routing", In *IEEE Symposium on Security and Privacy*, pp. 44–54, Oakland, California, 1997.

[583] D. Talbot, "Distributed Computing, subsection in 5 Patents to Watch", *MIT Technology Review*, 104(4):42, 2001.

[584] K. Tamilman, V. Pai, and A. Mohr, "SWIFT: A System With Incentives For Trading", In *Proceedings of Second Workshop of Economics in Peer-to-Peer Systems*, 2004.

[585] A. Tarlano, W. Kellerer, R. Schollmeier, and J. Eberspächer, "Compression Scheme Negotiation", 2004.

[586] C. Tempich, S. Staab, and A. Wranik, "REMINDIN': Semantic Query Routing in Peer-to-Peer Networks Based on Social Metaphors", In *Proceedings of the Thirteenth International conference on the World Wide Web*, New York, NY, USA, 2004, ACM.

[587] D. L. Tennenhouse, J. M. Smith, W. D. Sincoskie, D. J. Wetherall, and G. J. Minden, "A Survey of Active Network Research", *IEEE Communications Magazine*, 35(1):80–86, January 1997.

[588] S. Thatte, "Business Process Execution Language for Web Services Version 1.1", 2003, ftp://www6.software.ibm.com/software/developer/library/ws-bpel.pdf.

[589] The eMule Project, "The eMule Homepage", http://www.emule-project.net/, 2004.

[590] The Globus Alliance, http://www.globus.org/, 2004.

[591] The MMAPPS Consortium, "Market Management of Peer to Peer Services", http://www.mmapps.org/, 2004.

[592] The Network Simulator – ns-2, http://www.isi.edu/nsnam/ns/.

[593] H. S. Thompson, D. Beech, M. Maloney, and N. Mendelsohn, "XML Schema Part 1: Structures Second Edition", W3C, 2004, http://www.w3c.org/TR/xmlschema-1.

[594] R. Todesco, "Hyperkommunikation", In M. Böhler and B. Suter, editors, *Hyperfiction*, pp. 113–124, Stroemfeld Verlag, 1999.

[595] D. A. Tran, K. A. Hua, and T. Do, "ZIGZAG: An Efficient Peer-to-Peer Scheme for Media Streaming", In *Proceedings IEEE INFOCOM*, IEEE Press, 2003.

[596] J. Travers and S. Milgram, "An Experimental Study of the Small-World Problem", *Sociometry*, 32, 1969.

[597] B. Traversat, A. Arora, M. Abdelaziz, M. Duigou, C. Haywood, J.-C. Hugly, E. Pouyoul, and B. Yeager, "Project JXTA 2.0 Super-Peer Virtual Network", http://www.jxta.org/project/www/docs/ JXTA2.0protocols1.pdf, 2003.

[598] T. Truman, T. Pering, R. Doering, and R. Brodersen, "The InfoPad Multimedia Terminal: A Portable Device for Wireless Information Access", *IEEE Transactions on Computers*, 47(10), 1998.

[599] S. Tuecke, K. Czajkowski, I. Foster, J. Frey, S. Graham, C. Kesselman, T. Maquire, T. Sandholm, D. Snelling, and P. Vanderbilt, "Open GRID Services Infrastructre (OGSI) Version 1.0", GWD-R, Global Grid Forum, 2003.

[600] K. Tutschku, "A Measurement-based Traffic Profile of the eDonkey File-sharing Service", In *Proceedings of the 5th Passive and Active Measurement Workshop (PAM2004)*, pp. 12–21, Antibes Juan-les-Pins, France, 2004, Springer Verlag.

[601] K. Tutschku and H. de Meer, "A measurement study on signaling on Gnutella overlay networks", In *Fachtagung-Kommunikation in Verteilten Systemen (KiVS) 2003*, pp. 295–306, Leipzig, Germany, 2003, Springer Verlag.

[602] E. Tuulari and A. Ylisaukko-oja, "SoapBox: A Platform for Ubiquitous Computing Research and Applications", In *Proceedings of Pervasive Computing*, Zurich, Switzerland, 2002.

[603] E. G. S. V. Vishnumurthy, S. Chandrakumar, "KARMA : A Secure Economic Framework for Peer-to-Peer Resource Sharing", In *Proceedings of the Workshop on the Economics of Peer-to-Peer Systems*, Berkeley, California, June 2003.

[604] H. R. Varian, "Pricing Information Goods", http://www.sims.berkeley.edu/~hal/Papers/price-info-goods.pdf, 1995.

[605] A. Vazequez, A. Flammini, A. Maritan, and A. Vespignani, "Modelling of Protein Interaction Networks", *ComplexUs*, 1, 2003.

[606] C. Viles and J. French, "Dissemination of Collection Wide Information in a Distributed Information Retrieval System", In *International ACM Conference on Research and Development in Information Retrieval (SIGIR)*, Seattle, WA, USA, 1995.

[607] C. Viles and J. French, "On the Update of Term Weights in Dynamic Information Retrieval Systems", In *International Conference on Information and Knowledge Management (CIKM)*, Baltimore, MD, USA, 1995.

[608] V. Vishnumurthy, S. Chandrakumar, and E. G. Sirer, "KARMA: A Secure Economic Framework for Peer-to-Peer Resource", In *Workshop on Economics of Peer-to-Peer Systems*, Berkeley, CA, USA, 2003.

[609] E. von Goldammer, "Heterarchie und Hierarchie - Zwei komplementäre Beschreibungskategorien", *Vordenker - Webforum für Innovatives in Wissenschaft, Wirtschaft und Kultur*, 2003, http://www.vordenker.de/heterarchy/a_heterarchie.pdf.

[610] J. von Neumann, *Theory of Self-Reproducing Automata*, University of Illinois Press, Urbana, 1966.

[611] M. Waldman, A. D. Rubin, and L. F. Crannor, "Publius: A robust, tamper-evident, censorship-resistant web publishing system", In *Proceedings of 9th USENIX Security Symposium*, pp. 59–72, 2000.

[612] D. W. Wall, *Mechanisms for Broadcast and Selective Broadcast*, Ph.D. Thesis, Stanford University, 1980.

[613] R. Want, B. Schilit, A. Norman, R. Gold, D. Goldberg, K. Petersen, J. Ellis, and M. Weiser, "An Overview of the Parctab Ubiquitous Computing Environment", *IEEE Personal Communications*, 2(6):28–43, 1995.

[614] S. Wasserman and K. Faust, *Social Network Analysis: Methods and Applications*, Cambridge University Press, first, reprinted edition, 1999.

[615] D. J. Watts and S. H. Strogatz, "Collective dynamics of 'small-world' networks", *Nature*, 393(6684):440–442, 1998.

[616] G. Wearden, "eDonkey Pulls Ahead in Europe P2P Race", http://business2-cnet.com.com/2100-1025_3-5091230.html, 2003.

[617] K. Webb, M. Hibler, R. Ricci, A. Clements, and J. Lepreau, "Implementing the Emulab-PlanetLab Portal: Experience and Lessons Learned", In *Proceedings of the 1st Usenix Workshop on Real, Large Distributed Systems (WORLDS)*, 2004.

[618] K. Wehrle, "IP-QoS: Scalable and Flexible Quality-of-Service with Differentiated Services.", In *The Industrial Information Technology Handbook*, pp. 1–17, 2005.

[619] M. Weiser, "The Computer for the 21st Century", *Scientific American*, 265:66–75, 1991.

[620] R. Wenning, "The Platform for Privacy Preferences 1.1 (P3P1.1) Specification", http://www.w3.org/P3P/1.1/, 2005.

[621] B. White, J. Lepreau, L. Stoller, R. Ricci, S. Guruprasad, M. Newbold, M. Hibler, C. Barb, and A. Joglekar, "An Integrated Experimental Environment for Distributed Systems and Networks", In *Proceedings of the Fifth Symposium on Operating Systems Design and Implementation*, pp. 255–270, Boston, MA, 2002.

[622] G. Wiederhold, "Mediators in the Architecture of Future Information Systems", *IEEE Computer*, 25(3):38–49, 1992.

[623] Wikipedia-Community, "Wikipedia – The Free Encyclopedia", http://en.wikipedia.org/wiki/Main_Page, 2001.

[624] D. Winer, "P2P is Bigger", http://davenet.scripting.com/2000/09/13/p2pIsBigger/ (seen 04/2005), 2000.

[625] WinMX, "WinMX Homepage", http://www.winmx.com/, 2004.

[626] B. W. Wirtz, *Electronic Business*, p. 210ff, Gabler, 2001.

[627] R. Wojciechowski and C. Weinhardt, *Web Services und Peer-to-Peer-Netzwerke*, Springer, 2002.

[628] S. Wolfram, *A New Kind of Science*, Wolfram Media, Inc., 1. edition, 2002, http://www.wolframscience.com/nksonline.

[629] X.509, *Information technology - Open Systems Interconnection - The Directory: Public-key and attribute certificate frameworks*, International Telecommunication Union – Telecommunication Standardization Sector (ITU-T) / International Organisation for Standardization, 2003.

[630] X. Xiao, A. Hannah, B. Bailey, S. Carter, and L. M. Ni, "Traffic engineering with MPLS in the Internet", *IEEE Network Magazine*, 14(1):28–33, 2000.

[631] Y. Xie and D. O'Hallaron, "Locality in Search Engine Queries and Its Implications for Caching", In *Proc. IEEE INFOCOM 2002*, pp. 1238–1247, New York, NY, 2002.

[632] B. Xu, A. Ouksel, and O. Wolfson, "Opportunistic Resource Exchange in Inter-Vehicle Ad-Hoc Networks", In *2004 IEEE International Conference on Mobile Data Management (MDM'04)*, pp. 4–12, IEEE Computer Society, 2004.

[633] D. Xu, H.-K. Chai, C. Rosenberg, and S. Kulkarni, "Analysis of a Hybrid Architecture for Cost-Effective Streaming Media Distribution", In *In Proceedings of SPIE/ACM Conference on Multimedia Computing and Networking (MMCN 2003)*, 2003.

[634] B. Yang and H. Garcia-Molina, "Comparing Hybrid Peer-to-Peer Systems", In *Proceedings of Very Large Databases (VLDB)*, 2001.

[635] B. Yang and H. Garcia-Molina, "Improving Search in Peer-to-Peer Networks", In *Proceedings of the 22nd International Conference on Distributed Computing Systems (ICDCS02)*, Vienna, Austria, 2002.

[636] B. Yang and H. Garcia-Molina, "PPay: Micropayments for Peer-to-Peer Systems", In *Proceedings of the 10th ACM Conference on Computer and Communications Security (CCS)*, Washington, DC, USA, October 2003.

[637] S.-H. Yook, H. Jeong, and A.-L. Barabasi, "Modeling the Internet's large-scale topology", *Prooceedings of the National Academy of Sciences of the United State of America*, 99(21), October 2002.

[638] B. Zhang, S. Jamin, and L. Zhang, "Host multicast: A framework for delivering multicast to end users", In *Proceedings of IEEE Infocom*, IEEE, 2002.

[639] H. Zhang, A. Goel, and R. Govindan, "Using the Small-World Model to Improve Freenet Performance", In *Proceedings of the 21st IEEE Infocom 2002*, 2002.

[640] M. Zhang, C. Zhang, V. Pai, L. Peterson, and R. Wang, "PlanetSeer: Internet Path Failure Monitoring and Characterization in Wide-Area Services", In *Proceedings of the Sixth Symposium on Operating Systems Design and Implementation*, 2004.

[641] R. Zhang and Y. C. Hu, "Borg: a hybrid protocol for scalable application-level multicast in peer-to-peer networks", In *Proceedings of the 13th International Workshop on Network and Operating System Support for Digital Audio and Video*, pp. 172–179, 2003.

[642] B. Y. Zhao, L. Huang, J. Stribling, S. C. Rhea, A. D. Joseph, and J. Kubiatowicz, "Tapestry: A Resilient Global-scale Overlay for Service Deployment", *IEEE Journal on Selected Areas in Communications*, 22(1):41–53, 2004.

[643] Y. Zhu, B. Li, and J. Guo, "Multicast with Network Coding in Application-Layer Overlay Networks", *IEEE Selected Areas in Communications*, 22(1):107–120, 2004.

[644] P. R. Zimmermann, *The official PGP user's guide*, The MIT Press, Cambridge, MA, USA, 1995.

[645] P. R. Zimmermann, *PGP Source Code and Internals*, MIT Press, 2005.

[646] M. Zink and A. Mauthe, "P2P streaming using multiple description coded video", In *Proc. 30th EUROMICRO Conf., Multimedia and Telecommunications*, pp. 240–247, Rennes, France, 2004.

[647] D. N. Znamenski, *A mathematical analysis of models with self-orgnized criticality; sandpiles and evolution*, Ph.D. Thesis, Thomas Stieltjes Institute for Mathematics, Amsterdam, 2003, http://euridice.tue.nl/~dznamens/Math/Disser.pdf.

Index

Lecture Notes in Computer Science

For information about Vols. 1–3628

please contact your bookseller or Springer

Vol. 3728: V. Paliouras, J. Vounckx, D. Verkest (Eds.), Integrated Circuit and System Design. XV, 753 pages. 2005.

Vol. 3726: L.T. Yang, O.F. Rana, B. Di Martino, J. Dongarra (Eds.), High Performance Computing and Communcations. XXVI, 1116 pages. 2005.

Vol. 3725: D. Borrione, W. Paul (Eds.), Correct Hardware Design and Verification Methods. XII, 412 pages. 2005.

Vol. 3718: V.G. Ganzha, E.W. Mayr, E.V. Vorozhtsov (Eds.), Computer Algebra in Scientific Computing. XII, 502 pages. 2005.

Vol. 3717: B. Gramlich (Ed.), Frontiers of Combining Systems. X, 321 pages. 2005. (Subseries LNAI).

Vol. 3715: E. Dawson, S. Vaudenay (Eds.), Progress in Cryptology – Mycrypt 2005. XI, 329 pages. 2005.

Vol. 3714: H. Obbink, K. Pohl (Eds.), Software Product Lines. XIII, 235 pages. 2005.

Vol. 3713: L. Briand, C. Williams (Eds.), Model Driven Engineering Languages and Systems. XV, 722 pages. 2005.

Vol. 3712: R. Reussner, J. Mayer, J.A. Stafford, S. Overhage, S. Becker, P.J. Schroeder (Eds.), Quality of Software Architectures and Software Quality. XIII, 289 pages. 2005.

Vol. 3711: F. Kishino, Y. Kitamura, H. Kato, N. Nagata (Eds.), Entertainment Computing - ICEC 2005. XXIV, 540 pages. 2005.

Vol. 3710: M. Barni, I. Cox, T. Kalker, H.J. Kim (Eds.), Digital Watermarking. XII, 485 pages. 2005.

Vol. 3708: J. Blanc-Talon, W. Philips, D. Popescu, P. Scheunders (Eds.), Advanced Concepts for Intelligent Vision Systems. XXII, 725 pages. 2005.

Vol. 3706: H. Fuks, S. Lukosch, A.C. Salgado (Eds.), Groupware: Design, Implementation, and Use. XII, 378 pages. 2005.

Vol. 3703: F. Fages, S. Soliman (Eds.), Principles and Practice of Semantic Web Reasoning. VIII, 163 pages. 2005.

Vol. 3702: B. Beckert (Ed.), Automated Reasoning with Analytic Tableaux and Related Methods. XIII, 343 pages. 2005. (Subseries LNAI).

Vol. 3699: C.S. Calude, M.J. Dinneen, G. Păun, M. J. Pérez-Jiménez, G. Rozenberg (Eds.), Unconventional Computation. XI, 267 pages. 2005.

Vol. 3698: U. Furbach (Ed.), KI 2005: Advances in Artificial Intelligence. XIII, 409 pages. 2005. (Subseries LNAI).

Vol. 3697: W. Duch, J. Kacprzyk, E. Oja, S. Zadrożny (Eds.), Artificial Neural Networks: Formal Models and Their Applications – ICANN 2005, Part II. XXXII, 1045 pages. 2005.

Vol. 3696: W. Duch, J. Kacprzyk, E. Oja, S. Zadrożny (Eds.), Artificial Neural Networks: Biological Inspirations – ICANN 2005, Part I. XXXI, 703 pages. 2005.

Vol. 3695: M.R. Berthold, R. Glen, K. Diederichs, O. Kohlbacher, I. Fischer (Eds.), Computational Life Sciences. XI, 277 pages. 2005. (Subseries LNBI).

Vol. 3694: M. Malek, E. Nett, N. Suri (Eds.), Service Availability. VIII, 213 pages. 2005.

Vol. 3693: A.G. Cohn, D.M. Mark (Eds.), Spatial Information Theory. XII, 493 pages. 2005.

Vol. 3692: R. Casadio, G. Myers (Eds.), Algorithms in Bioinformatic. X, 436 pages. 2005. (Subseries LNBI).

Vol. 3691: A. Gagalowicz, W. Philips (Eds.), Computer Analysis of Images and Patterns. XIX, 865 pages. 2005.

Vol. 3690: M. Pěchouček, P. Petta, L.Z. Varga (Eds.), Multi-Agent Systems and Applications IV. XVII, 667 pages. 2005. (Subseries LNAI).

Vol. 3687: S. Singh, M. Singh, C. Apte, P. Perner (Eds.), Pattern Recognition and Image Analysis, Part II. XXV, 809 pages. 2005.

Vol. 3686: S. Singh, M. Singh, C. Apte, P. Perner (Eds.), Pattern Recognition and Data Mining, Part I. XXVI, 689 pages. 2005.

Vol. 3685: V. Gorodetsky, I. Kotenko, V. Skormin (Eds.), Computer Network Security. XIV, 480 pages. 2005.

Vol. 3684: R. Khosla, R.J. Howlett, L.C. Jain (Eds.), Knowledge-Based Intelligent Information and Engineering Systems, Part IV. LXXIX, 933 pages. 2005. (Subseries LNAI).

Vol. 3683: R. Khosla, R.J. Howlett, L.C. Jain (Eds.), Knowledge-Based Intelligent Information and Engineering Systems, Part III. LXXX, 1397 pages. 2005. (Subseries LNAI).

Vol. 3682: R. Khosla, R.J. Howlett, L.C. Jain (Eds.), Knowledge-Based Intelligent Information and Engineering Systems, Part II. LXXIX, 1371 pages. 2005. (Subseries LNAI).

Vol. 3681: R. Khosla, R.J. Howlett, L.C. Jain (Eds.), Knowledge-Based Intelligent Information and Engineering Systems, Part I. LXXX, 1319 pages. 2005. (Subseries LNAI).

Vol. 3679: S.d.C. di Vimercati, P. Syverson, D. Gollmann (Eds.), Computer Security – ESORICS 2005. XI, 509 pages. 2005.

Vol. 3678: A. McLysaght, D.H. Huson (Eds.), Comparative Genomics. VIII, 167 pages. 2005. (Subseries LNBI).

Vol. 3677: J. Dittmann, S. Katzenbeisser, A. Uhl (Eds.), Communications and Multimedia Security. XIII, 360 pages. 2005.

Vol. 3676: R. Glück, M. Lowry (Eds.), Generative Programming and Component Engineering. XI, 448 pages. 2005.

Vol. 3675: Y. Luo (Ed.), Cooperative Design, Visualization, and Engineering. XI, 264 pages. 2005.

Vol. 3674: W. Jonker, M. Petković (Eds.), Secure Data Management. X, 241 pages. 2005.

Vol. 3673: S. Bandini, S. Manzoni (Eds.), AI*IA 2005: Advances in Artificial Intelligence. XIV, 614 pages. 2005. (Subseries LNAI).

Vol. 3672: C. Hankin, I. Siveroni (Eds.), Static Analysis. X, 369 pages. 2005.

Vol. 3671: S. Bressan, S. Ceri, E. Hunt, Z.G. Ives, Z. Bellahsène, M. Rys, R. Unland (Eds.), Database and XML Technologies. X, 239 pages. 2005.

Vol. 3670: M. Bravetti, L. Kloul, G. Zavattaro (Eds.), Formal Techniques for Computer Systems and Business Processes. XIII, 349 pages. 2005.

Vol. 3669: G.S. Brodal, S. Leonardi (Eds.), Algorithms – ESA 2005. XVIII, 901 pages. 2005.

Vol. 3668: M. Gabbrielli, G. Gupta (Eds.), Logic Programming. XIV, 454 pages. 2005.

Vol. 3666: B.D. Martino, D. Kranzlmüller, J. Dongarra (Eds.), Recent Advances in Parallel Virtual Machine and Message Passing Interface. XVII, 546 pages. 2005.

Vol. 3665: K. S. Candan, A. Celentano (Eds.), Advances in Multimedia Information Systems. X, 221 pages. 2005.

Vol. 3664: C. Türker, M. Agosti, H.-J. Schek (Eds.), Peer-to-Peer, Grid, and Service-Orientation in Digital Library Architectures. X, 261 pages. 2005.

Vol. 3663: W.G. Kropatsch, R. Sablatnig, A. Hanbury (Eds.), Pattern Recognition. XIV, 512 pages. 2005.

Vol. 3662: C. Baral, G. Greco, N. Leone, G. Terracina (Eds.), Logic Programming and Nonmonotonic Reasoning. XIII, 454 pages. 2005. (Subseries LNAI).

Vol. 3661: T. Panayiotopoulos, J. Gratch, R. Aylett, D. Ballin, P. Olivier, T. Rist (Eds.), Intelligent Virtual Agents. XIII, 506 pages. 2005. (Subseries LNAI).

Vol. 3660: M. Beigl, S. Intille, J. Rekimoto, H. Tokuda (Eds.), UbiComp 2005: Ubiquitous Computing. XVII, 394 pages. 2005.

Vol. 3659: J.R. Rao, B. Sunar (Eds.), Cryptographic Hardware and Embedded Systems – CHES 2005. XIV, 458 pages. 2005.

Vol. 3658: V. Matoušek, P. Mautner, T. Pavelka (Eds.), Text, Speech and Dialogue. XV, 460 pages. 2005. (Subseries LNAI).

Vol. 3657: F.S. de Boer, M.M. Bonsangue, S. Graf, W.-P. de Roever (Eds.), Formal Methods for Components and Objects. VIII, 325 pages. 2005.

Vol. 3656: M. Kamel, A. Campilho (Eds.), Image Analysis and Recognition. XXIV, 1279 pages. 2005.

Vol. 3655: A. Aldini, R. Gorrieri, F. Martinelli (Eds.), Foundations of Security Analysis and Design III. VII, 273 pages. 2005.

Vol. 3654: S. Jajodia, D. Wijesekera (Eds.), Data and Applications Security XIX. X, 353 pages. 2005.

Vol. 3653: M. Abadi, L. de Alfaro (Eds.), CONCUR 2005 – Concurrency Theory. XIV, 578 pages. 2005.

Vol. 3652: A. Rauber, S. Christodoulakis, A M. Tjoa (Eds.), Research and Advanced Technology for Digital Libraries. XVIII, 545 pages. 2005.

Vol. 3651: R. Dale, K.-F. Wong, J. Su, O.Y. Kwong (Eds.), Natural Language Processing – IJCNLP 2005. XXI, 1031 pages. 2005.

Vol. 3650: J. Zhou, J. Lopez, R.H. Deng, F. Bao (Eds.), Information Security. XII, 516 pages. 2005.

Vol. 3649: W.M. P. van der Aalst, B. Benatallah, F. Casati, F. Curbera (Eds.), Business Process Management. XII, 472 pages. 2005.

Vol. 3648: J.C. Cunha, P.D. Medeiros (Eds.), Euro-Par 2005 Parallel Processing. XXXVI, 1299 pages. 2005.

Vol. 3646: A. F. Famili, J.N. Kok, J.M. Peña, A. Siebes, A. Feelders (Eds.), Advances in Intelligent Data Analysis VI. XIV, 522 pages. 2005.

Vol. 3645: D.-S. Huang, X.-P. Zhang, G.-B. Huang (Eds.), Advances in Intelligent Computing, Part II. XIII, 1010 pages. 2005.

Vol. 3644: D.-S. Huang, X.-P. Zhang, G.-B. Huang (Eds.), Advances in Intelligent Computing, Part I. XXVII, 1101 pages. 2005.

Vol. 3643: R. Moreno Díaz, F. Pichler, A. Quesada Arencibia (Eds.), Computer Aided Systems Theory – EUROCAST 2005. XIV, 629 pages. 2005.

Vol. 3642: D. Ślezak, J. Yao, J.F. Peters, W. Ziarko, X. Hu (Eds.), Rough Sets, Fuzzy Sets, Data Mining, and Granular Computing, Part II. XXIII, 738 pages. 2005. (Subseries LNAI).

Vol. 3641: D. Ślezak, G. Wang, M. Szczuka, I. Düntsch, Y. Yao (Eds.), Rough Sets, Fuzzy Sets, Data Mining, and Granular Computing, Part I. XXIV, 742 pages. 2005. (Subseries LNAI).

Vol. 3639: P. Godefroid (Ed.), Model Checking Software. XI, 289 pages. 2005.

Vol. 3638: A. Butz, B. Fisher, A. Krüger, P. Olivier (Eds.), Smart Graphics. XI, 269 pages. 2005.

Vol. 3637: J. M. Moreno, J. Madrenas, J. Cosp (Eds.), Evolvable Systems: From Biology to Hardware. XI, 227 pages. 2005.

Vol. 3636: M.J. Blesa, C. Blum, A. Roli, M. Sampels (Eds.), Hybrid Metaheuristics. XII, 155 pages. 2005.

Vol. 3634: L. Ong (Ed.), Computer Science Logic. XI, 567 pages. 2005.

Vol. 3633: C. Bauzer Medeiros, M. Egenhofer, E. Bertino (Eds.), Advances in Spatial and Temporal Databases. XIII, 433 pages. 2005.

Vol. 3632: R. Nieuwenhuis (Ed.), Automated Deduction – CADE-20. XIII, 459 pages. 2005. (Subseries LNAI).

Vol. 3631: J. Eder, H.-M. Haav, A. Kalja, J. Penjam (Eds.), Advances in Databases and Information Systems. XIII, 393 pages. 2005.

Vol. 3630: M.S. Capcarrere, A.A. Freitas, P.J. Bentley, C.G. Johnson, J. Timmis (Eds.), Advances in Artificial Life. XIX, 949 pages. 2005. (Subseries LNAI).

Vol. 3629: J.L. Fiadeiro, N. Harman, M. Roggenbach, J. Rutten (Eds.), Algebra and Coalgebra in Computer Science. XI, 457 pages. 2005.